AI-Assisted Special Education for Students With Exceptional Needs

Ashish Kumar
Bennett University, India

Anand Nayyar
Duy Tan University, Vietnam

Rohit Kumar Sachan
Bennett University, India

Rachna Jain
Bhagwan Parshuram Institute of Technology, India

A volume in the Advances in Educational Technologies and Instructional Design (AETID) Book Series

IGI Global
PUBLISHER of TIMELY KNOWLEDGE

Published in the United States of America by
IGI Global
Information Science Reference (an imprint of IGI Global)
701 E. Chocolate Avenue
Hershey PA, USA 17033
Tel: 717-533-8845
Fax: 717-533-8661
E-mail: cust@igi-global.com
Web site: http://www.igi-global.com

Library of Congress Cataloging-in-Publication Data

Names: Kumar, Ashish (Professor of computer science), editor. | Nayyar, Anand, editor. | Sachan, Rohit Kumar, 1984- editor. | Jain, Rachna (Professor of information technology), editor.
Title: AI-assisted special education for students with exceptional needs / Edited by Ashish Kumar, Anand Nayyar, Rohit Kumar Sachan,and Rachna Jain.
Other titles: Artificial intelligence assisted special education for students with exceptional needs
Description: Hershey, PA : Information Science Reference, [2024] | Includes bibliographical references and index. | Summary: "The book also explores the impact of AI-based special education on both educators and students, providing valuable insights and strategies for stakeholders to adopt and implement these technologies effectively. Legal aspects surrounding the right to education for disabled individuals are discussed, ensuring a comprehensive understanding of the legal framework supporting special education initiatives. Real-world case studies and success stories serve as inspiration, illustrating the transformative potential of AI in special education. Featuring contributions from academicians and professionals from esteemed organizations, this book provides hands-on chapters that cover topics such as research challenges, data analysis, machine learning, intelligent learning environments, IoT wearable devices, comprehensive systems with intelligent teacher assistance, parental and societal roles, and the prospects of AI assisted special education. Whether educator, mentor, training professional, researcher, or student, AI-Assisted Special Education for Students With Exceptional Needs offers a wealth of knowledge and practical insights"-- Provided by publisher.
Identifiers: LCCN 2023027794 (print) | LCCN 2023027795 (ebook) | ISBN 9798369303788 (hardcover) | ISBN 9798369303795 (paperback) | ISBN 9798369303801 (ebook)
Subjects: LCSH: Artificial intelligence--Educational applications. | Artificial intelligence--Educational applications--Research. | Students with disabilities--Education. | Special education--Case studies.
Classification: LCC LB1028.43 .A38 2024 (print) | LCC LB1028.43 (ebook) | DDC 371.9--dc23/eng/20230714
LC record available at https://lccn.loc.gov/2023027794
LC ebook record available at https://lccn.loc.gov/2023027795

This book is published in the IGI Global book series Advances in Educational Technologies and Instructional Design (AETID) (ISSN: 2326-8905; eISSN: 2326-8913)

British Cataloguing in Publication Data
A Cataloguing in Publication record for this book is available from the British Library.

All work contributed to this book is new, previously-unpublished material. The views expressed in this book are those of the authors, but not necessarily of the publisher.

For electronic access to this publication, please contact: eresources@igi-global.com.

Advances in Educational Technologies and Instructional Design (AETID) Book Series

Lawrence A. Tomei
Robert Morris University, USA

ISSN:2326-8905
EISSN:2326-8913

Mission

Education has undergone, and continues to undergo, immense changes in the way it is enacted and distributed to both child and adult learners. In modern education, the traditional classroom learning experience has evolved to include technological resources and to provide online classroom opportunities to students of all ages regardless of their geographical locations. From distance education, Massive-Open-Online-Courses (MOOCs), and electronic tablets in the classroom, technology is now an integral part of learning and is also affecting the way educators communicate information to students.

The **Advances in Educational Technologies & Instructional Design (AETID) Book Series** explores new research and theories for facilitating learning and improving educational performance utilizing technological processes and resources. The series examines technologies that can be integrated into K-12 classrooms to improve skills and learning abilities in all subjects including STEM education and language learning. Additionally, it studies the emergence of fully online classrooms for young and adult learners alike, and the communication and accountability challenges that can arise. Trending topics that are covered include adaptive learning, game-based learning, virtual school environments, and social media effects. School administrators, educators, academicians, researchers, and students will find this series to be an excellent resource for the effective design and implementation of learning technologies in their classes.

Coverage

- Bring-Your-Own-Device
- K-12 Educational Technologies
- Curriculum Development
- Higher Education Technologies
- Virtual School Environments
- Adaptive Learning
- Classroom Response Systems
- Social Media Effects on Education
- E-Learning
- Collaboration Tools

The Advances in Educational Technologies and Instructional Design (AETID) Book Series (ISSN 2326-8905) is published by IGI Global, 701 E. Chocolate Avenue, Hershey, PA 17033-1240, USA, www.igi-global.com. This series is composed of titles available for purchase individually; each title is edited to be contextually exclusive from any other title within the series. For pricing and ordering information please visit http://www.igi-global.com/book-series/advances-educational-technologies-instructional-design/73678. Postmaster: Send all address changes to above address.

Titles in this Series

For a list of additional titles in this series, please visit: www.igi-global.com/book-series

Creative AI Tools and Ethical Implications in Teaching and Learning
Jared Keengwe (University of North Dakota USA)
Information Science Reference • © 2023 • 291pp • H/C (ISBN: 9798369302057) • US $215.00

The Impact of Digitalization in a Changing Educational Environment
Anna A. Arinushkina (Lomonosov Moscow State University, Russia) Alexander V. Morozov (Moscow Social Pedagogical Institute, Russia) and Irena V. Robert (Institute for Strategy of Education Development, Rssia)
Information Science Reference • © 2023 • 336pp • H/C (ISBN: 9798369304334) • US $290.00

New Perspectives in Teaching and Learning With ICTs in Global Higher Education Systems
Madalina Armie (University of Almería, Spain) Germán Asensio (University of Almería, Spain) Maria Enriqueta Cortés de los Ríos (University of Almería, Spain) and Angeles Jordán Soriano (University of Almería, Spain)
Information Science Reference • © 2023 • 314pp • H/C (ISBN: 9781668488614) • US $215.00

Transforming the Language Teaching Experience in the Age of AI
Galip Kartal (Necmettin Erbakan University, Turkey)
Information Science Reference • © 2023 • 328pp • H/C (ISBN: 9781668498934) • US $230.00

Dynamic Curriculum Development and Design Strategies for Effective Online Learning in Higher Education
Kelley Walters (Western Governors University, USA)
Information Science Reference • © 2023 • 320pp • H/C (ISBN: 9781668486467) • US $215.00

Developing Skills and Competencies for Digital and Green Transitions
Patricia Ordóñez de Pablos (The University of Oviedo, Spain) Mohammad Nabil Almunawar (School of Business and Economics, University of Brunei Darussalam, Brunei) and Muhammad Anshari (School of Business and Economics, University of Brunei Darussalam, Brunei)
Business Science Reference • © 2023 • 367pp • H/C (ISBN: 9781668490891) • US $250.00

Artificial Intelligence Applications Using ChatGPT in Education Case Studies and Practices
Muhammad Shahzad Aslam (School of Traditional Chinese Medicine, Xiamen University Malaysia, Malaysia) and Saima Nisar (School of Computing, UUM College of Arts and Sciences, University Utara Malaysia, Sintok, Malaysia)
Information Science Reference • © 2023 • 234pp • H/C (ISBN: 9781668493007) • US $215.00

IGI Global
PUBLISHER of TIMELY KNOWLEDGE

701 East Chocolate Avenue, Hershey, PA 17033, USA
Tel: 717-533-8845 x100 • Fax: 717-533-8661
E-Mail: cust@igi-global.com • www.igi-global.com

Table of Contents

Detailed Table of Contents

Over 30 years the scope of technological support has broadened from overhead projectors, slides, filmstrips, to 21st century technologies such as 3D simulation and VR. Devices from low tech to high tech are commonly used to assist students with a variety of learning challenges. AI animation tools have the potential to be a useful resource for students with disabilities and can help these students achieve their full potential by including accessibility features and making animations that are especially made for students with special needs. Artificial intelligence is being used to individualize instruction, deliver feedback, and monitor student progress. AI-powered tutors, for instance, can help students learn at their own pace, and AI-powered grading software can assist teachers in accurately and quickly grading papers.

Special education recognizes limitations of traditional teaching methods in meeting diverse student needs. It empowers individuals through tailored support, specialized instruction, and assistive technologies, unlocking their full potential. Promoting inclusivity, social, and academic growth, it enables fulfilling lives. Integration of AI technology holds promise for enhancing special education's effectiveness and inclusiveness. This chapter presents a comprehensive methodology and framework for AI-based solutions, offering stakeholders a systematic approach to address specific challenges faced by individuals with special needs. By combining data-driven insights and human expertise, this approach revolutionizes special education delivery, empowering individuals to maximize their potential. However, further research and implementation are necessary to validate its effectiveness and scalability in real-world educational settings.

Artificial intelligence has the ability to radically change how teachers interact with pupils who have special needs. Although the effects of AI and other technologies have been far-reaching in the private and public sectors, they have also had a major impact on the academic world, making learning easier for students with sensory, motor, cognitive, and other forms of impairments. The application of AI in the classroom has encouraged the development of more accessible and inclusive teaching practices for all pupils. This chapter analyzed how AI has influenced special education in the classroom. The study analyzed (a) AI's impact on SEN education and (b) AI's impact on SEN education through its positive effects on SEN educators. This chapter explores how AI has the potential to enhance the lives, careers, and working environments of educators. It also explores how special education supported by AI could personalize lessons for each student and encourage greater involvement on their behalf.

Artificial intelligence and related technological advancements have been a matter of discussion in recent times. There has been regular growth in AI-based methods that have proven useful for various industry verticals. Education is one such critical field where AI can play a monumental role in improving quality and helping individuals strive for better education. Meeting the educational requirements of all children, adolescents, and adults has received more attention in recent years. Recent advancements in technology, such as data analysis and ML, can potentially revolutionize how we approach special education. By using these technologies to personalize learning experiences, track progress, and provide individualized support, educators can improve outcomes for students with special needs. With the right approach, data analysis and ML can be powerful tools for improving special education and supporting students with special needs. The main idea of the study is to outline in detail the various applications of AI-assisted special education and discover the depths of the methods.

Artificial intelligence integration in education is proven to be an easier and convenient way of delivering knowledge to students and hence became the demand of 21st-century classrooms. The findings from the literature review show that implementing artificial intelligence in education by following different pedagogical models of artificial intelligence in education (i.e. the SAMR model, the TPACK model, and the TAM model) can lead to fruitful outcomes in the teaching and learning process, and also this study would help in fulfilling the knowledgeable, contextual, and pedagogical gaps for the integration of artificial intelligence in the era of digitization of education.

AI is transforming the traditional education system globally. The traditional education system based on historical paradigms has a very feeble scope for creating an interactive environment for the specialized students. AI is providing an innovative, diverse, and impactful roadmap in education system to improve the teaching-learning experience not only for teachers but also for students with special needs. AI with its interactive tools has improved the overall educational system by creating enormous opportunities for specialized students. AI-assisted tools such as live chatbots, class dictating software, verbal command-based eBooks, adaptive personalized tutors, image-based learning, and many more have accelerated the teaching-learning experience. Implication of these tools in the education system inculcate critical thinking and improve student engagement in the various teaching activities. The authors have reviewed the impact of AI in transforming the educational system from traditional to AI-assisted modern educational systems.

Special education for students is essential to gain/get/obtain equity and accessibility. AI enables new tools, customized learning, and improved accessibility for students with different learning needs. This chapter examines AI in inclusive education and its benefits for special needs pupils. AI-based adaptive learning, assistive intelligent tutoring, and early intervention data analytics boost inclusive education. AI algorithms customize learning in adaptive learning systems. AI-powered voice recognition and accessibility technologies assist impaired students' study. AI-powered tutoring methods improve student performance. AI-powered data analytics can identify struggling students and give assistance. AI in inclusive education has downsides. The chapter addresses AI bias, fairness, data privacy and security, transparency, explainability, and stakeholder participation. Ethics should govern inclusive education's usage of AI technology. AI should support human judgement and interaction. Responsible AI can improve education for all children, regardless of learning needs.

Dyslexia and dysgraphia are two common learning disabilities that affect children's ability to read, write, and spell accurately. These disabilities can significantly impede a child's academic performance, leading to lack of self-confidence, anxiety, and frustration. Traditional approaches to address these disabilities often involve one-on-one sessions with a tutor or special education teacher, which can be time-consuming and expensive. Artificial intelligence (AI) language learning models have shown tremendous potential in assisting children with dyslexia and dysgraphia. These models can provide real-time feedback and personalized instruction to help children overcome learning difficulties. This chapter highlights the importance of addressing these challenges and proposes a solution that leverages AI language learning models to assist children with dyslexia and dysgraphia. By embracing AI language learning models, educators and parents can empower children with dyslexia and dysgraphia, providing them with the necessary tools and support to overcome their learning challenges.

In recent years, classifiers have been shown to provide highly accurate results in predicting problems; however, the success relies on the classifier as well as the employed dataset. In this study, the success of various classifiers for predicting autism spectrum disorder cases is analysed in terms of different metrics obtained both after testing on the same set and after applying 10-fold cross validation. When the same dataset has been used for the training and testing steps, all the algorithms have shown excellent results. Nevertheless, when 10-fold cross-validation has been applied, sequential minimal optimization has become the most successful classifier in terms of all the performance metrics. Although the results have proven the success of classifiers in predicting problems such as the one addressed in this study, autism spectrum disorder is a complex disorder, and the tools employing classifiers should be used under the supervision of certified professionals or clinicians.

People with visual impairment (PVI) live a dependent life for doing their daily tasks. The most advanced assistive devices for PVIs currently available are either expensive or have poor performance or need extra hardware support. An integrated cognitive assistive tool for PVIs, HearUs, is implemented to handle path obstacle detection, product recognition, weather updates, reading documents or newspapers, automated dialing, and SOS service. It helps and directs the PVIs by giving them pertinent information about their surroundings. Different technologies have been used, like transfer learning, VGGNet 16 model for hurdle detection, barcode scanning for product identification, as well as text recognition and voice assistant capabilities. The Flickr8k dataset and a custom build dataset have been used for training the baseline model on around 8000 images. Furthermore, an experimental result shows that HearUs achieves 82% accuracy as compared to other existing applications.

The chapter aims to demystify AI technologies and their role in enhancing learning experiences and support services for students with disabilities and diverse learning needs. The chapter identifies challenges in implementing AI effectively and advocates for ethical considerations and equitable access to AI-based solutions. It showcases how AI can create personalized learning pathways, adaptive interventions, and data-driven decision-making in special education. The chapter introduces innovative AI applications, including personalized learning platforms and assistive technologies, highlighting the role of data-driven approaches in improving educational outcomes. It emphasizes AI's transformative potential in fostering inclusive and effective special education practices, serving as a valuable resource for educators, administrators, policymakers, and researchers.

Advancements in AI revolutionize learning, automate tasks, and provide insights. During COVID-19, AI connected educators and learners globally, but special education suffered. This chapter aims to define disabilities, explore AI-based diagnosis tools, and envision personalized learning and assistive technology for inclusive education. The lack of affordable and convenient assistive devices and technology combined with taboos stemming from deeply ingrained misconceptions and prejudices, perpetuating stereotypes and marginalizing individuals with disabilities often forces them to live a life devoid of the proper means to engage in schooling for the purpose of attaining an independent lifestyle. The primary objective of the chapter is to define various types of disabilities and consider various AI-based tools for early disability diagnosis, while also looking to the future with personalized learning and AI-based assistive technologies, assisting both learners and educators in achieving the highest level of education.

Preface

As editors, it is with great enthusiasm that we introduce this edited reference book, *AI-Assisted Special Education for Students With Exceptional Needs*. This comprehensive volume is the result of collaborative efforts by a diverse team of experts, each with a deep commitment to improving the educational experience of students with special needs.

Special education has evolved into an innovative and dynamic field dedicated to addressing the unique requirements of individuals with disabilities. It goes beyond traditional classroom approaches, embracing alternative provisions and tailoring instruction to accommodate the individual differences and exceptional needs of students. In this pursuit, our book delves into the profound impact of recent technological advancements, including artificial intelligence (AI), virtual reality (VR), and augmented reality (AR), which have opened up a wealth of creative and innovative resources and services to enhance the learning experiences of students facing various challenges, be they mental, physical, emotional, behavioral, or intellectual.

The chapters within this book are organized into a structured exploration of the critical dimensions surrounding AI-assisted special education. Our journey begins with an in-depth examination of the fundamental concepts, history, realities, and challenges inherent in imparting special education. We scrutinize the contrasting landscapes of special education and traditional education, shedding light on the transformative potential of smart classrooms and cutting-edge technology for disabled students.

The heart of this volume lies in our exploration of AI-assisted tools designed to create interactive and engaging smart classrooms. These tools not only empower students but also support educators in providing adaptive and personalized learning experiences. We delve into the profound impact of AI-based special education on both educators and students, exploring the strategies and planning required for successful adoption by all stakeholders.

Additionally, we address the crucial legal aspects surrounding the right to education for disabled individuals, ensuring that this right is upheld and protected. Throughout the book, you will find illuminating case studies and success stories that exemplify the real-world applications of AI-assisted special education.

A wide array of scholars, educators, mentors, training professionals, researchers, and students will find value in the content presented here. The book not only offers historical perspectives and insights into the organization of special education but also delves into the rapidly evolving field of AI in special education, providing a foundation for understanding the challenges and opportunities it presents.

The chapters contributed by academicians and professionals from reputable organizations provide hands-on knowledge and practical guidance. From data analysis and machine learning for special education to the role of IoT wearable devices and intelligent teacher assistance, this book spans the spectrum of innovative AI-based solutions.

Chapter 1 discusses the evolution of technological support in education over the last thirty years and focuses on the potential of AI to help students with disabilities. From low tech to high tech, devices of various degrees of sophistication have been used to assist students with different challenges. AI animation tools have the potential to be particularly useful for students with special needs by including accessibility features and creating animations specifically tailored to their needs.

Chapter 2 provides a comprehensive methodology and framework for AI-based solutions to address specific challenges faced by individuals with special needs. The chapter emphasizes the importance of combining data-driven insights with human expertise to revolutionize special education delivery and empower individuals to realize their full potential. However, more research and implementation are needed to validate its effectiveness and scalability in real-world educational settings.

Chapter 3 analyzes how AI has influenced special education in the classroom. By personalizing lessons for each student and encouraging greater involvement on their behalf, AI has the potential to enhance the lives, careers, and working environments of educators. The study also explores how AI has impacted SEN education and the benefits of using AI-powered tools to improve the overall educational experience for all pupils.

Chapter 4 examines the potential of data analysis and ML to revolutionize how we approach special education and meet the educational requirements of all children, adolescents, and adults. By using these technologies to personalize learning experiences, track progress, and provide individualized support, educators can improve outcomes for students with special needs.

Chapter 5 shows that implementing artificial intelligence in education through different pedagogical models can lead to fruitful outcomes in the teaching and learning process, fulfilling dig

Chapter 6 discusses how AI-assisted tools such as Live chatbots, image-based learning, verbal command-based eBooks, class dictating software, adaptive personalized tutors, and many more are accelerating the teaching-learning experience and inculcate critical thinking and student engagement by creating enormous opportunities for specialized students.

Chapter 7 addresses AI in inclusive education and its benefits for special needs pupils. AI algorithms customize learning in adaptive learning systems, while also providing assistive, intelligent tutoring and early intervention data analytics for inclusive education. Downside issues and ethics are considered, and the chapter calls for responsible, data-driven, and transparent approaches to the implementation of AI technology.

Chapter 8 highlights how AI language learning models can help children with dyslexia and dysgraphia. These models can provide real-time feedback and personalized instruction, thereby empowering these children to overcome learning difficulties and achieve academically.

Chapter 9 analyzes which classifiers have been most effective in predicting autism spectrum disorder cases. Although the results demonstrate the success of classifiers in predicting problems, autism spectrum disorder is complex, and the tools employing classifiers should be used under the supervision of certified professionals or clinicians.

Chapter 10 introduces HearUs, an integrated cognitive assistive tool that assists visually impaired individuals in their daily tasks by providing pertinent information about their surroundings through transfer learning, VGGNet 16 model for hurdle detection, barcode scanning for product identification, as well as text recognition, and voice assistant capabilities.

Chapter 11 showcases how AI can create personalized learning pathways, adaptive interventions, and data-driven decision-making in special education. The chapter introduces innovative AI applications, including personalized learning platforms and assistive technologies and emphasizes AI's transformative potential in fostering inclusive and effective special education practices.

Chapter 12 defines disabilities, explores AI-based diagnosis tools, and envisions personalized learning and assistive tech for inclusive education. The chapter emphasizes the importance of affordable, convenient assistive devices, and technology and the need for personalized learning and AI-based assistive technologies to assist learners and educators in achieving the highest level of education, highlighting the impact of AI in education during COVID-19.

We also emphasize the critical role of parents and society in developing and supporting special education, recognizing that societal barriers and technological limitations must be addressed to create inclusive and equitable learning environments.

As we gaze into the future, our book explores the prospects and reflections of AI in special education, embracing blended learning as a boon for specialized individuals. Research and evaluation methods are presented to guide educators and researchers in their quest to improve the quality of special education.

We acknowledge the challenges inherent in making special education both successful and innovative, and we confront these issues head-on within these pages. Through a series of enlightening case studies, we showcase the real-world impact of AI on the delivery of special education.

In closing, we extend our gratitude to all the contributors who have shared their expertise and insights. It is our hope that this book will serve as a valuable resource for anyone invested in the advancement of AI-assisted special education, ultimately promoting greater inclusivity and empowering students with exceptional needs to reach their fullest potential.

Sincerely,

Ashish Kumar
Bennett University, India

Anand Nayyar
Duy Tan University, Vietnam

Rohit Kumar Sachan
Bennett University, India

Rachna Jain
Bhagwan Parshuram Institute of Technology, India

Chapter 1
An Overview of the Accessibility and Need of AI Animation Tools for Specially Abled Students

Bhakti Parashar
https://orcid.org/0000-0002-2561-117X
VIT Bhopal University, India

Ravindra Sharma
https://orcid.org/0000-0001-6432-2680
Swami Rama Himalayan University, India

Vaibhav Parashar
Scope Global Skills University, India

Geeta Rana
Swami Rama Himalayan University, India

Anand Nayyar
https://orcid.org/0000-0002-9821-6146
Duy Tan University, Vietnam

V. Harish
PSG Institute of Management, India

ABSTRACT

Over 30 years the scope of technological support has broadened from overhead projectors, slides, film-strips, to 21st century technologies such as 3D simulation and VR. Devices from low tech to high tech are commonly used to assist students with a variety of learning challenges. AI animation tools have the potential to be a useful resource for students with disabilities and can help these students achieve their full potential by including accessibility features and making animations that are especially made for students with special needs. Artificial intelligence is being used to individualize instruction, deliver feedback, and monitor student progress. AI-powered tutors, for instance, can help students learn at their own pace, and AI-powered grading software can assist teachers in accurately and quickly grading papers.

1. INTRODUCTION

The current educational system is complex and constantly changing, with the goal of giving students the knowledge and abilities they need to succeed in life. The system is made up of numerous different elements, such as schools, instructors, curricula, and tests. The goal of the modern education system is to help students learn the skills, knowledge, and values that will help them succeed in life, such as critical thinking, problem solving, communication skills, and teamwork.

DOI: 10.4018/979-8-3693-0378-8.ch001

The way we learn and teach is being revolutionized by artificial intelligence (AI). AI-powered tools and applications make it possible to personalize learning, automate tasks, and provide insights that can help educators improve student outcomes. It is a term that has been used in science fiction for a long time, but it has become more and more popular as it makes its way into more and more areas of our lives. According to Russell and Norvig (2018), AI is rapidly transforming industries such as healthcare, transport, retail, and financial services (Rana et al., 2021).

Another area where AI technology has tremendous potential is education. Personalized learning is one of the most exciting applications of AI in education. With personalized learning, students get personalized learning experiences that are tailored to their unique learning needs.AI-powered systems can analyze student data to identify their strengths and weaknesses. Thus, the achievement gap may be reduced and students may learn more quickly and effectively.

In fact, AI innovations in education have shifted from lab-based paradigms to more challenging real world learning environments. EdTech companies have created ATS, which supports classroom management, grading, assessment, and second language issues, IAS, which supports student enrollment and queries, and ILS, which enables personalized learning. Global investments in AI education totaled USD 1047 billion between 2008 and 2017 (MoU, 2019).

Despite the fact that businesses are making quick progress in AI innovation, there are still problems to be solved in education sector, such as how to connect macro- and micro-institutions with AI-based education systems, what the roles of the various players in the AI education ecosystem are, and whether to build platforms with a business or consumer orientation.

The emergence of new technologies has also transformed the way teaching and learning take place in the education sector (Ravindra et al., 2021). The US education sector's AI market is expected to expand by 48% from 2018 to 2022, according to Business Wire (2018). The application of AI in education has grown dramatically along with the technology itself. It may be used in online, mobile, or blended learning environments to provide dynamic assessments, personalized learning, and meaningful interactions. On the other hand, researchers have proposed the replacement of some teacher roles by robots using AI as a response to the shortage of teachers in the United States (Zhang and Aslan, 2021, Edwards & Cheok, 2018).

However, one of the most effective tools for enhancing learning in numerous ways which is used in modern teaching methodology is animation as well. Animations are employed in education to support students' perceptions, mental models, and comprehension of spatial and temporal changes. The efficacy of animations in teaching, however, has come under scrutiny as a result of three meta analyses that contrast learning from animations to learning from images. When studying the specifics of change, learning from animation is more effective than studying a static image. Animation-based education should not be considered a substitute for conventional teaching strategies. It should be seen as an addition to traditional methods of teaching to make learning more interesting and more effective (Ploetzner et al., 2021).

Animation helps to build mental models of things and promotes better understanding. Computer animation is a powerful way to show processes that are difficult to show in a classroom or even in the lab. In order to develop algorithmic thinking, geometric and algebraic knowledge, and abstract thinking in chemistry, animation-based, technology-based learning environments have been shown to be very effective (Parashar et al., 2023; Ben-Bassat Levy et al., 2003).

AI animation tools can be very effectively used in inclusive education as it has become more prominent in recent years, many countries are moving towards an inclusive education system, where all students (regardless of their disabilities) are educated in the same school. Inclusive education has been proven to benefit students with disabilities as well as their non-disabled peers. It has also gained more prominence in international education policies ever since the Salamanca Declaration, which proclaimed that it must be the "new normal" (UNESCO, 1994). Students with SEN are now able to enroll in mainstream schools and pursue their education alongside other students as a result of this change. In Hungary, regular schools are enrolling an increasing number of students with special needs. In the public schools, 72% of SEN students receive integrated instruction. According to HCSO (2022).

And the quality of the teaching-learning methodology can be improved by combining AI animation tools with the education of students with disabilities. A personalized learning environment that meets the needs of each student can be made using AI animation tools. Students with disabilities may find this particularly helpful as they may have different learning styles and abilities.

Early performance prediction of students enables intervention to enhance learning results. Using academic data, data mining is used to forecast students' performance. An important area of machine learning research is the prediction of student performance using educational data. Accuracy may be hampered by datasets with unequal distributions of classes and the difficulty in creating interpretable models (Sahlaoui et al., 2023).

Learning can be made more interactive and engaging with the aid of AI animation tools, which can keep students' interest and motivation levels high. For students with disabilities who might have trouble focusing, this is particularly crucial.

1.1 Objectives

Special education policies vary greatly from nation to nation. In some nations, there is a strong commitment to inclusive education, which means that all students, regardless of their disabilities, attend the same schools. Segregated education, in which students with disabilities are educated in separate classrooms or schools, is more prevalent in other nations. We must recognize the seriousness of inclusive education's significance and the need for its improvement. In light of this, the following objectives have been set-

1. To determine the status of inclusive education system.
2. To analyse the need, availability and adoption of AI animation tools in education and in inclusive education
3. To explore the problems faced by educators' while dealing with specially abled students and using AI animation tools.
4. To review current AI-powered animation tools and go over how they might help students with disabilities.
5. To give recommendations for future research focuses in the field of AI-powered animation tools for students with special needs.

1.2 Scope of the Study

As technology develops, people are becoming more and more aware of the value of inclusivity and equal opportunities for everyone, including those with disabilities. The use of AI animation tools can be crucial in improving the accessibility of educational materials for students with disabilities. To accommodate various disabilities, these tools can offer alternative formats like text-to-speech functionality, audio descriptions, or sign language interpretation. These tools may undergo further development in the future, improving their accuracy, efficacy, and accessibility.

The present study focuses on the future of accessibility and AI animation tools for specially abled students with possible solution of the problems faced by the education system and educators. With continued advancements in technology and a growing focus on inclusivity, these tools can revolutionize education, providing equal opportunities and empowering specially abled students to reach their full potential.

1.3 Organization of the Study

The present chapter has five major parts. Introduction consist of background of the study along with the evolution and involvement of artificial intelligence, animation in education a with the importance of inclusive education for specially needed students along with objectives and scope of the study. Following that, it was discussed how special education was progressing for these students. The third component, a literature review, assesses the contributions made by earlier researchers and their perspectives on the current study. The analysis of the need, accessibility, and uptake of AI animation tools among both typically developing students and students with disabilities is then included under the analysis section. Next, this chapter looked into a variety of issues teachers may run into when working with students who have special needs and AI animation tools, as well as potential solutions. With references, the study's conclusion is covered in the final section.

2. STATUS OF EDUCATION FOR SPECIALLY ABLED STUDENTS

A disability is a broad term that includes impairments, limitations on activity, and limitations on participation. Another way of describing a disability is that it is a mental or physical condition that limits a person's movement, perception, and ability to do everyday activities. According to India's Census 2011, 2.68 billion people, or 2.21% of the country's population, are physically and mentally challenged (Majumder C, 2019). Disability is essentially a socially created phenomenon. The truth is that a large number of kids and adults had disabilities that prevented them from benefiting from traditional education. Because of social injustice, a lack of a support system at home, inadequate facilities in schools, and a lack of adequate accommodations, disabled people are excluded from the education system. However, education is the most crucial tool for bringing about social, economic, and political change. In societies like India, where social exclusion of physically challenged people (PCP) is very important, socialization of children with disabilities (CWD) through education is not very important. Physically challenged people (PDP) in low developed countries have very low literacy rate. There is no doubt about this fact, although in developed countries there is a lot of emphasis on education of disabled people (Maiumder, C., 2019b).

Students with Exceptional Needs After completing secondary education, students have been successfully admitted to higher education. The local universities and colleges must, however, take special care to meet the needs of students with disabilities. Different disabilities would call for various services. For instance, students with learning disabilities may struggle with managing their information, have low self-efficacy, and have low self-esteem. They must be handled accordingly as a result. A SNS welfare unit that is run by the student affairs office has been established at some higher education institutions. However, this department is also in charge of the welfare of other students.

Due to the significant differences between students with special needs and their peers, it is essential to create a lesson plan that is tailored to the various needs of these students. A disability support office may be beneficial for SNS if they are pursuing higher education, according to Moria et al.(2017) suggestion. According to Baron et al. (1996) and hadjikakou et al. (2010) some institutions used to overlook special needs students.

Each campus must have a disability support office that focuses solely on providing the needs and assistance needed by students with special needs (Yusof et al., 2020). Social and educational inclusion are both fundamental human rights. It is crucial because inclusive education enables marginalized and underprivileged groups to participate in society and open a door to better well-being. The majority of those served by inclusive education are people with disabilities, though it also benefits a number of other underrepresented groups (Vrooman and Coenders2020), and that is the biggest problem with educators to teach in a class where normal students sit along with the disabled one.

3. LITERATURE REVIEW

The world is changing quickly due to artificial intelligence (AI), and education is no exception. AI has the potential to revolutionize education by making it more efficient, interesting, and customized. While most AI research takes place in science, technology, engineering and math (STEM) fields, AIEd's expanding use cases necessitate cross-fertilization ("AIEd": "Artificial Intelligence in Education"; Zawacki Richter, 2019).

Since students are the main focus of the educational system of the twenty-first century, it is essential for contemporary universities to function that education be digitalized and continually improved. Technology is what makes the modern era unique. Every aspect of life is currently connected to technology in the higher education system in some way (Harish et al., 2023). The importance of digital competence in higher education continues to rise, and COVID-19 has increased public awareness of the need for digital skills because college students in the 21st century are the generation who have grown up with the rapid development of computer networks and who have witnessed the unprecedented development of online media represented by the internet, virtual reality, and artificial intelligence (Szyrocka et al., 2023).

The artificial intelligence and machine learning technology can assist in predicting student performance and warning teachers about students who need support (Sahlaoui et al., 2021). In order to build the learning classifier, students' observed records that serve as the training set must be used, along with historical student data that represent features and labels that correspond to actual performance (Almasri et al., 2019).

But, it is challenging to separate almost every aspect of life in the era of the fourth industrial revolution from the use of information technology as an enabler for other processes and services. IT is now a necessary asset that must be owned rather than just a commodity. A high reliance on information technology has resulted from its development, which significantly facilitates human life activities (Rahmatullah et al., 2022). In addition, today's generation is tech-savvy because technology is much more pervasive in the digital age than it was in previous generations. Technology in education has proliferated as a result of recent technological advancements and the rise of literacy.

From young people to Gen-Z; these are the generations who are going to school today. They all have different characteristics that show how old they are. These generations don't like to learn passively and expect to be actively involved in their education. In light of this, technology must be a part of education today, and teachers must incorporate it into their lessons for the students (Haşim, 2018).

In the 1950s, John McCarthy led a two-month seminar at Dartmouth College in New Hampshire, USA, which is when artificial intelligence first emerged. In a proposal for a workshop at Dartmouth in 1956, McCarthy first used the term "artificial intelligence" (Russel et al., 2010). The foundation upon which the study of artificial intelligence will proceed is the notion that "every aspect of learning" or "every characteristic of intelligence" can, theoretically, be described so precisely that a machine can simulate it. The goal will be to discover ways to make it possible for machines to comprehend language, produce abstractions, and comprehend concepts, in order to solve problems currently handled by humans and advance those individuals (Zawacki and Richter 2019).

Recent literature reviews have repeatedly emphasised the dearth of education-related research in AIEd (Chen, Xie, Zou, & Hwang 2020; Hinojo-Lucena et al.,2019; Zawacki, Richter et al., 2019). Concerns about the lack of educationally-related theories and models in the research literature on AI-enabled e-learning over the previous 20 years have also been voiced by Tang, Chang, and Hwang (2021). AI in education also aims to use AI to support the instructional process, which is crucial and where instructors' acceptance of AI is crucial (for example, comprehending and supporting computer-supported collaborative learning through discourse analysis and achieving performance prediction through educational data mining). But because AI is still a relatively new concept to instructors, they frequently have trouble responding quickly and effectively to analytics from AI-enabled applications. As a result, they are less willing to adopt AI and are less open to it. Therefore, it seems crucial to increase instructors' acceptance of AI systems (Chen et al., 2022).

In the last 25 years, artificial intelligence (AI) has become increasingly prevalent in education. Artificial intelligence (AI) has been used extensively in education ever since computers and information processing methods were developed. The use of AI in education creates new opportunities, difficulties, and potentialities for educational practices. By conducting real-world experiments and creating standardized modular prototypes in the areas of statistical reasoning, data visualization, and learning analytics, the project aims to enhance educational practices. Giving each student personalized learning support or guidance based on their learning status, interests, or other characteristics is one of the main aims of AI in Education. (Hwang, G. J. 2014; Hwang et al.,2020).

Since the development of computing and information processing methods, AI has been utilized extensively in education. AI in education brings about new possibilities, difficulties, and opportunities for educational practices (Ouyang & Jiao, 2021). AI for education focuses on using real-world experiments to significantly advance educational techniques creation of common modular prototypes for statistical analysis, data visualization, and analytics in education (Alam, 2021). In the education sector, artificial intelligence (AI) has already had an impact. Its use is an important and strategic component of the advancement of education. AI is also being used more and more as a virtual assistant. AI offers numerous benefits to teachers and students. As an illustration, it gives students access to a variety of learning resources based on their subject matter and learning requirements. AI development does, however, carry some risks, including those related to safety, security, and privacy.

Applications of AI in education offer a wide range of benefits (Owoc et al., 2019). Predictive analytics tools, automated assessments, social media sites, and individualized learning systems are just a few of the AI applications that are increasingly being used in many educational settings and are powered by machine learning systems and algorithms. These AI tools have the potential to help teachers and students in a variety of ways, such as by delivering instruction in mixed-ability classrooms, giving students detailed and timely feedback on their writing, relieving teachers of the burden of knowing everything, allowing them to focus more on supporting their students while they are observing, discussing, gathering information in their cooperative knowledge-building processes, and so on Akgun & Greenhow, 2021; Miao et al., 2021)

The use of digital learning board frameworks is rapidly growing today. Due to the enormous amount of information that is generated, much of which contains hidden patterns and information, many organizations have also switched their educational framework to fully or largely automated frameworks. These frameworks are used to generate important data that will help students get better grades and academic results (Kukkar, A et.al, 2023).

The rapid and widespread adoption of digital learning is largely due to the development of e-learning platforms and virtual education systems that seamlessly integrate with cutting-edge smart devices like smartphones and tablets. The mix also includes specialized learning materials like games, animations, or AI-driven systems created for edutainment. Innovations enabled by technology have made it easier for students of all ages and subject areas to learn. The significance of big data and how it can be used to inform and improve learning outcomes is a crucial but frequently disregarded aspect of educational technologies (Lewis, C et al., 2013). Schools and educational institutions are realizing the value of comprehensive data on student and instructor performance as they expand their use of online exams, e-learning platforms, and virtual classrooms.

To help learners understand complex processes and change, an animated representation can be used (Schnotz & Lowe, 2003). Computer-animated learning, as opposed to traditional learning environments that emphasize word-for-word explanations, improves understanding of complex ideas and systems, according to several studies (Park (1994), Rieber (1991), and Tversky (Bauer-Morrison (2002). For instance, it can be difficult to explain how substances react chemically or how electrons move in an electric system in a traditional classroom setting (Williamson & Abraham, 1995). Today, a variety of instructional materials can be used to support the teaching and learning process and raise student achievement. Modern computer technology has a significant impact on the field of education. To create a multimedia-based simulation, the combination of three elements—text, voice, and visual—is required. (Dubovi, 2019)

Today, a variety of instructional materials can be used to support the teaching and learning process and raise student achievement. Modern computer technology has a significant impact on the field of education. To create a multimedia-based simulation, the combination of three elements—text, voice, and visual—is required Additionally, animation is a crucial tool for engaging students in learning. This is so that the difficult-to-explain lesson content can be explained using the audio that goes along with the mobile's visual presentation. An interactive alphabetical introduction for students was then created in an effort to facilitate the introduction of alphabets Supriyono et al. (2018) and understanding is facilitated by animation, which helps to create mental models of things. Computer animation is a potent tool for demonstrating processes that are challenging to demonstrate in a classroom or lab (Fleming 2000, Hart 2000, Uronen 2003, etc.).

Animation-based, technology-based learning environments are very good for developing algorithmic thinking ((Levy, et al.,2003;Prakash,et al.,2021; Esponda-Argüero, M.2008), geometric and algebraic knowledge (Reed, Suarez et al., 2006), and understanding abstract concepts (Chemistry). In the modern world, using animation computers with the help of AI is advantageous in a variety of fields. The evolution of animations has changed with time and usage context, and they now clarify complex phenomena and ideas. However, animations might not always be helpful, and teachers who use animations need to be aware of its significance (Mansor et al., 2020).

Studies comparing the effectiveness of learning environments based on animation to those that use static images have produced mixed, if not contradictory, results. On the one hand, a number of studies—including those by Betrancourt (2005) and Tversky (2002)—found that learning through animation generally has no advantage over learning through static images. Contrarily, meta-analytic research suggests that dynamic animations have a number of benefits for promoting learning success (Hoeffler & Leutner, 2007).

Although, the uses of computer animation also present a number of difficulties and constraints during the teaching and learning process, necessitating knowledge of animation programs like Flash.As a result, high level skills are required, particularly in the field of education, to integrate such media into one multimedia product. To implement these computer animation programs, teachers are typically required to have at least rudimentary programming knowledge and experience. As a result, not all subject teachers find teaching animation to be simple. Additionally, to improve the effectiveness of teaching and learning, certain factors like graphic design, audio choice, animation presentation, and color choice must be taken into account (Schreglmann & Kazanci, 2018).

In a relatively short amount of time, inclusive education has emerged as a field of educational research, policy, and practice. Simply put, inclusive education is both a methodology and an educational goal. In order for all children to have access to, be present in, and participate in school and achieve the best possible academic and social outcomes, it aims to identify and eliminate barriers to education. With the use of AI animated tools these barriers can be eliminated to some extent. Instead, it requires that mainstream teachers work in partnership with others (such as students, coworkers, other professionals, and parents) to remove obstacles to inclusion and to use data to guide practice improvement (Messiou 2019).

The Education for All (EFA) movement has gradually documented cohorts of excluded students and sparked public support for inclusive education among governments, educational institutions, non-governmental organizations, and civil society (Slee, 2018). One of the more recent developments in psychology and education is special education. This aspect of education has been the subject of scientific research since the turn of the century. Although there have always been children with special needs, special education programs are a more recent development. The ethical and legal implications of this field, as well as its history, are hotly contested (Armstrong, 2003). Additionally, Anastasiou et al. (2020) point out that this definition conveys a "spirit of sameness" that may actually jeopardize all students with disabilities' chances of receiving the quality education to which they are entitled, particularly in regards to students with learning difficulties.

By observing or watching the characters' movements, the setting, their appearances, and the intended message, students will be able to comprehend the information quickly. Animation can benefit classroom instructors in addition to helping students create visually appealing presentations (Bates, 2018). Since they were young children, today's students have been immersed in technology and live in a society where it is a part of daily life (Desai, 2018), especially in the field of inclusive education. A significant issue in the global discussion about education is the education of children with disabilities (Sustainable Development Goal, UN2015a). The EFA declaration that the educational needs of children with disabilities call for special consideration (UNESCO, 2000) shows that education for CwD is not a recent development. The International Disability Organization (IDO), UNICEF, the World Bank, and the Organization for Economic Cooperation and Development (OECD) are all participants in the flagship initiative "The Right to Education for Persons with Disabilities: Towards Inclusion," which is led by UNESCO.

A number of studies incorporating early intervention have been conducted to determine the benefits of early intervention. By identifying difficulties with reading skill acquisition in preschoolers with hearing impairment (HI), (Gowramma et al., 2013) offered a systematic remedial reading programme that improved the fundamental reading skills. One month of planned intensive communication skills training with parents & siblings as partners showed an increase in social participation in the pre-primary CwHI (suresh & gowramma, 2010). A school readiness programme based on strengths & weaknesses identified through pre-test was found to be effective among children with a spectrum disorder (cwASD; Janwadkar 2015).

The preschoolers demonstrated improvement in all of the evaluated domains while maintaining the natural characteristics of the disorder (Mahakud, 2010) suggests that early intervention can serve as a kind of "vaccination" against LD based on the literature review. (Venkatesan,2006) urges professionals to restructure the schedule after discovering that pre-school children with developmental disorders (CwDD) spent a lot of time engaging in sedentary activities. While lamenting the crucial years that were lost because the age of referral was set at 8 to 9 years, (Parasuram,2011) draws attention to neuropsychological studies that encourage early intervention to take advantage of neural plasticity.

Thus, For the education of students with special needs, AI animation tools can be a useful resource. For students with a variety of disabilities, they can assist in enhancing the accessibility, engagement, and effectiveness of learning. A potent tool for the education of students with special needs can be AI animation software. They may contribute to the improvement of learning's effectiveness, accessibility, and personalization.

4. ANALYSIS OF AI ANIMATION TOOLS IN EDUCATION

New standards for the advancement of animation professionals and the innovation of curriculum structures are proposed with the development of the Internet and the advent of the artificial intelligence era. Despite the animation industry, and especially the domestic animation industry, experiencing recent waves of growth and providing a wide range of development opportunities, the lack of highly qualified and experienced animators has gradually grown into a problem that cannot be ignored (Wang, Q, 2022).

4.1. Need

The field of design has many potential uses for artificial intelligence (AI) technology. A trend of high integration between digital technology and design art is demonstrated by the continued adoption of big data technology, 3D printing technology, virtual reality technology, and augmented reality technology (Oliver, 2003; Pushpendu & Ravindra 2021). In order to address the fusion of digital technology and design, some colleges and universities in China offer professional design courses alongside introductory programming courses using tools like Processing and Arduino. The design industry will be forced to make more significant changes in the artistic presentation of design as a result of the widespread use of AI technology.

These changes not only force educators to deal with technological advancements at the level of design education but also force practitioners and students of design to adapt (Tang, T., Li, P., & Tang, Q. 2022). The use of AI system recommendations refers to issues with student behaviour, instructional strategies used by teachers, and difficulties with picking up new digital skills. The effectiveness of technical performance, learning pedagogy, user experience, learning environment, and interactive content, to name a few, are the main problems that need to be solved in the context of AI technology.

AI animation tools can be helpful in many ways in education system given in the figure 1 below: -

Figure 1. Need of AI animation tools in education
Source: Authors own

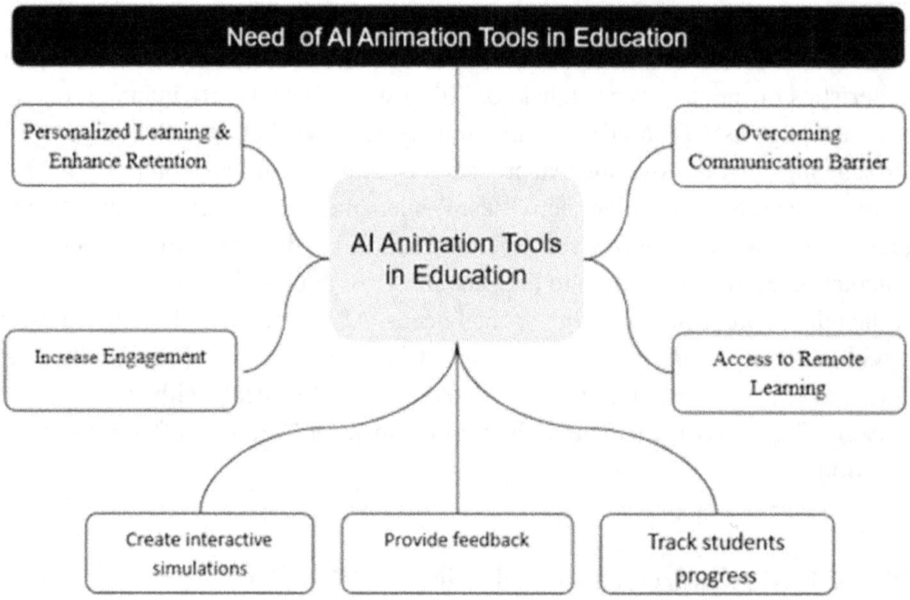

Individualized learning experiences tailored to each student's needs can be created using AI animation tools, which can improve learning, make it more interactive, and maintain students' interest and motivation levels. .AI animation tools can aid students in remembering information by making it more memorable. This is so that animation can take advantage of our innate capacity for memory of visual information. For students with s hesitation who might have trouble speaking or understanding spoken language, AI animation tools can help them get past communication barriers. Online learning materials that students can access from any location can be made using AI animation tools. These tools can be used to monitor students' advancement over time. Students who are having trouble can be identified using this information, and tailored interventions can be given to them.

AI is also used in education to offer insights. Artificial intelligence (AI) systems are capable of analyzing vast amounts of data to find trends and patterns that can help teachers improve student achievement. AI-powered systems can, for example, be used to recognize students who need assistance and then provide it to them.

4.2. Availability

AI animation resources are becoming more widely available in schools. There are many different AI animation tools available today, both free and paid. The most widely used AI animation resources for education are illustrated in Figure 2 and are discussed below:

Figure 2. Available AI animation tools in education
Source: Authors own

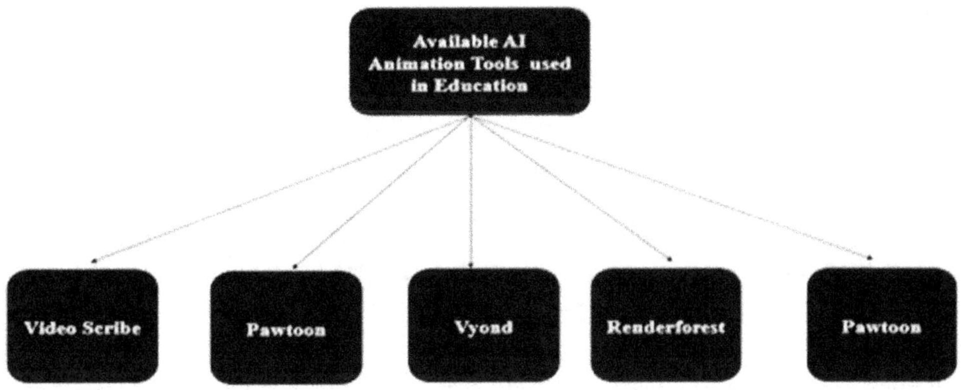

- **PowToon:** PowToon is a user-friendly and reasonably priced cloud-based AI animation tool. It has many features, including a library of pre-made templates, drag-and-drop animation tools, and the capacity to add voiceovers and music, that make it perfect for producing educational animations.
- **Vyond (Previously GoAnimate):** Schools and businesses all over the world use Vyond, another well-liked AI animation tool. It has many features, such as the capacity to design unique characters, backdrops, and accessories, as well as the capacity to export animations in a number of formats. `
- **Moovly:** A cloud-based AI animation tool called Moovly is ideal for producing interactive educational animations. The ability to add quizzes, polls, and other interactive elements is just one of the many features that make it simple to make interesting and interactive animations.
- **VideoScribe:** Create explainer videos and educational animations with ease using VideoScribe, a whiteboard animation programme. It has a variety of features that make it easy to create captivating and aesthetically pleasing animations, like the ability to add voiceovers, music, and images.
- **Renderforest:** Renderforest is a cloud-based AI animation tool that provides a range of features for making animations that look professional, such as the ability to make 2D and 3D animations and the addition of music, voiceovers, and other elements.

These are just a few of the numerous AI animation resources that are accessible to educators. Future developments in technology should result in the availability of even more AI animation tools.

4.3. Adoption

Although the use of AI animation tools in education is still in its early stages, it is obvious that this trend will persist. We can assume that as technology develops, a growing number of AI animation tools will eventually be available. Artificial intelligence is becoming increasingly prevalent in education. A large number of AI-education companies have emerged as a result of the advancement of AI technology, as well as the demand for and popularity of technological innovations (Lin, H. C., Ho, C. F., & Han, Y. 2022).

Through voice interaction, animation capabilities, and movie scenarios using AI, education products with AI are committed to facilitating immersive learning experiences. It is similar to learning in its purest sense. The interface of the electronic screen was significant, according to Liu and Sun's 2011 study on mobile reading services. The interface can influence the user's actual feelings and expectations after initial adoption, in contrast to the conventional paper-based reading method. According to research on the structure of an e-Learning portal by Kolekar et al. (2018), it recognizes the student's preferred method of learning and modifies its content and user interface accordingly.

5. AVAILABILITY AND ACCESSIBILITY OF AI ANIMATION TOOLS FOR SPECIALLY DISABLED STUDENTS

The use of digital learning platforms in educational settings is growing. It may be time to take into account the broader implications of more contemporary digital strategies, even though traditional classroom-based instruction is still a key component of both teaching and learning. While the use of student data in education has always been present, the increasing volumes, diversity, and velocity of data have given rise to a completely new area of study and profession called learning analytics (Long & Siemens, 2011).

Stakeholders (such as students, instructors, administrators, student centres, etc.) may profit from the knowledge provided by student data from digital learning environments as learning becomes more digital and data-driven (Khalil et al., 2018). In other words, it could support the development of courses that are tailored to the needs of each student, promote active learning, identify factors that affect student success, and support the creation and application of better and more effective teaching techniques (Samuelsen et al., 2019; Nguyen, Tuunanen, Gardner, & Sheridan, 2021).

It is morally necessary to recognize this and improve minority students' access to high-quality education, including students with disabilities. Due to data showing that the proportion of disabled students in schools and higher education is increasing (Kourakli et al., 2017; Sale et al., 2015; Moria, 2017), many nations have started to concentrate their efforts on promoting accessibility for people with disabilities by fostering inclusivity and eliminating discrimination. Although these efforts are to be applauded, they should also be continued because not much has changed (UN, 2015; Chen, 2020).

The increasing availability of affordable and easy-to-use AI animation tools. In the past, AI animation tools were expensive and difficult to use. However, the cost of AI animation tools has come down significantly in recent years, and the tools themselves have become much easier to use. This has made AI animation tools more accessible to educators, and has led to a wider adoption of these tools in the classroom.

The potential benefits of AI animation tools for specially abled student learning. AI animation tools can be used to make learning more engaging, interactive, and personalized for students. Additionally, they can be used to simplify complicated ideas for easy comprehension. This has led to a growing interest in AI animation tools among educators who are looking for ways to improve student learning.

For the education of students with special needs, artificial intelligence (AI) animation tools can be very helpful. Several justifications are given below:

- Students who have visual impairments can gain from them. The use of AI animation tools allows blind and visually impaired students to access engaging and interactive animations. This can make it easier for them to learn new ideas and facts in a fun and engaging way.
- AI animation tools can be helpful for students who have hearing impairments. It allow students who are hard of hearing or deaf to access animations that have been narrated or captioned. They might be better able to participate in conversations and understand lessons if they can follow along.
- Students with learning difficulties may benefit from them. For students with learning disabilities, personalized learning experiences can be created using AI animation tools. AI animation tools may enable them to learn at their own rate and in a way that meets their particular requirements.
- These tools can assist students who have physical limitations. Students with physical disabilities that make it challenging for them to use conventional textbooks or materials can access animations made with the help of AI animation tools. They may be able to participate in class and pick up new information as a result without feeling left out.

6. PROBLEMS AND SUGGESTIONS

Teachers in inclusive education have a different role from their traditional roles. It was common practice for teachers to spot students who didn't fit the curriculum as soon as possible with the intention of referring them to an adult outside of school, to specialised classes, or to special education facilities (Du Toit, 1997). According to Forlin (2001), significant changes must be made to the roles and responsibilities of teachers, intervention, and special support services in order to successfully educate students with learning disabilities in a regular classroom.

6.1 Problem Faced by Teachers While Dealing Specially Abled Student

Good thing with teacher handling specially abled student is that these teachers are committed to giving their students a top-notch education. They put a lot of effort into developing individualized learning plans, giving support and encouragement, and forming bonds with their students. They work to make sure their students have access to the resources they need to succeed and serve as their advocates.

Still they have many problems and challenges, some of them are given below: -

- **Lack of Funding:** Special education programs are often underfunded, which can lead to shortages of teachers, materials, and resources. This can make it difficult for teachers to provide the best possible education for their students.
- **High Caseloads:** The education of many students with disabilities falls under the purview of special education teachers, who frequently have heavy caseloads. It may be challenging for teachers to provide each student with the individualized attention they require as a result.

- **Lack of Training:** Many teachers lack sufficient special education training. They may find it difficult to meet the needs of their disabled students as a result.
- **Participation of The Parents:** Parents of children with special needs frequently have high expectations for their kids' education. This can put pressure on educators to deliver a top-notch education even in the face of scarce resources.
- **Behavior Problems**: Some students with disabilities may display problematic behaviors like aggression, self-harm, or disruptive behavior. This can make it challenging for teachers to maintain a secure and structured learning environment.
- **Communication Problems:** Some disabled students might experience communication problems, such as speech problems or autism spectrum disorder. This can make it challenging for educators to interact with students and comprehend their needs.

6.2 Possible Suggestions

Despite these difficulties, special education teachers are committed to giving their students a high-quality education. They put a lot of effort into developing individualized learning plans, giving support and encouragement, and forming bonds with their students. They work to make sure their students have access to the resources they need to succeed and serve as their advocates.

The following some suggestions for educators who work with special needs students:

- **Learn About Your Students:** Spend some time learning about your students' specific needs. This will make it easier for you to design a learning environment that plays to their particular strengths and weaknesses.
- **Be Adaptable:** Be ready to modify your teaching strategies to suit your students' needs. This could entail utilizing different materials, giving each student more one-on-one time, or dividing tasks into manageable chunks.
- **Have Patience:** it might take some time for your students to pick up new ideas or abilities. Encourage them frequently while being patient and understanding.
- **Work with Parents:** Teachers can learn a lot from parents. Develop a plan for their child's education with them, and offer them support.
- **Assist When Required:** Never be embarrassed to seek out assistance from other educators, experts, or administrators. There are lots of tools at your disposal to assist you in teaching special students.

Although it can be difficult, working with special needs students is very rewarding. Successful educators support their pupils in realizing their full potential and leading happy lives.

6.3 Problem Faced by Teachers While Using AI Animation Tools in Teaching

Teachers who are overburdened with duties, particularly school teachers, find it very challenging to adopt technology easily, especially those who are not very computer literate. The use of animation tools powered by artificial intelligence (AI) can be beneficial for educators, but there are drawbacks as well. Here are a few issues educators might run into when utilizing AI animation tools in the classroom:

- **Technical know-how:** Teachers may need to have some technical know-how in order to make the most of the AI animation tools because they can be difficult to use. Teachers who are unfamiliar with technology or do not have the time to learn new skills may find this to be a barrier.
- **Cost:** Since schools often have limited funding, the cost of AI animation tools can be a barrier.
- **Accuracy**: AI animation tools can occasionally produce inaccurate or misleading information, and they are not always accurate. If teachers use the tools to instruct students on scientific or historical subjects, this could be a problem.
- **Bias:** AI animation tools are sometimes biased, and their output occasionally reflects the biases of the people who developed the tool. If teachers use the tools to teach students about delicate subjects, this could be a problem.
- **Privacy:** AI animation tools can gather information about students, and this information may be used to monitor students' progress or to advertise to them. Parents and students may become concerned about their privacy as a result.

Artificial intelligence (AI) animation tools can be a useful addition to the classroom, but they can also be difficult to integrate into current curricula. The use of AI animation tools may require teachers to modify their lesson plans, and they may also need to give students who are unfamiliar with this technology more support. Assessment of student learning presents some difficulties. While AI animation tools can be used to do so, doing so effectively can be difficult. The learning objectives of the lesson plans should be aligned with the AI animation tools that teachers are using, and they should also ensure that they are correctly interpreting the test results.

- Managing student engagement can be difficult because AI animation tools can be both a great learning tool and a distraction. Teachers must make sure they are utilizing AI animation tools in a way that helps students stay focused on the lesson's learning goals.

6.4 Possible Suggestions

Some of the suggestion to improve quality education of teachers by using AI animation tools and make these tools friendly and easily used are given below: -

- **Technical know-how:** The tool's creator, a professional, or a colleague can train teachers on how to use AI animation tools. Teachers can learn how to use these tools from a wealth of online resources as well.
- **Cost:** There are numerous open-source and free AI animation tools available, and some schools may be able to receive grants or donations to help pay for these tools.
- **Accuracy:** Teachers can assess the AI animation tools' accuracy by contrasting them with data from other sources, like textbooks or academic journals. Students may also be asked to comment on how accurate the animations are.
- **Bias:** Teachers can take action to reduce bias by being aware of its potential in AI animation tools. For instance, they can use a variety of AI animation tools to produce a view of a subject that is more impartial. Additionally, they can give students the chance to assess the animations' content in a critical manner.

In addition to these recommendations, teacher should also take initiative like **a** few AI animation tools at once are fine, but not too many. Start with the tool you are most comfortable using and that you believe will be most helpful to your students. Talk to other teachers about your experiences using AI animation tools. By doing this, you can learn from one another and determine how to use these tools most effectively in your classroom. Be ready to change your teaching strategies to make room for the use of AI animation tools. This could entail utilizing different materials, giving each student more one-on-one time, or dividing tasks into manageable chunks.

7. CONCLUSION

This study concludes that how crucial inclusivity and equal access to education are. By offering alternative formats, personalized learning experiences, interactive and immersive learning, collaboration and communication, and opportunities for skill development, AI animation tools have the potential to completely transform the learning experience for students with special needs. With the potential to create a more open and inclusive learning environment for all students as technology develops, the future potential of these tools is encouraging. By embracing these developments, we can make sure that students with special needs have the resources and tools they require to thrive and realize their full potential.

These tools may be a helpful resource for students with special needs. By utilizing these resources, educators can design learning experiences that are tailored to the individual needs of each student. AI animation tools can also be used to create content that is easy for students with disabilities to understand and use. The way AI is developing, applying, and adopting in all fields, AI animation tools will eventually be usable at every level of our educational system. In the future, AI animation tools will be accessible. For students of all ages and skill levels, this will result in even more advantages.

Thus, for inclusive education, AI animation tools can be a useful tool. For students with a variety of disabilities, they can aid in making learning more accessible, interesting, and effective.

REFERENCES

Akgun, S., & Greenhow, C. (2021). Artificial Intelligence in Education: Addressing Ethical Challenges in K-12 Settings. *AI and Ethics*, 1-10.

Alam, A. (2021). Possibilities and Apprehensions in the Landscape of Artificial Intelligence inEducation. In *2021 International Conference on Computational Intelligence andComputing Applications (ICCICA)* (pp. 1-8). IEEE.

Almasri, A., Celebi, E., & Alkhawaldeh, R. S. (2019). EMT: Ensemble Meta-Based Tree Model for Predicting Student Performance. *Scientific Programming*, *2019*, 1–13. doi:10.1155/2019/3610248

Anastasiou, D., Felder, M., Correia, L., Shemanov, A., Zweers, I., & Ahrbeck, B. (2020). The impact of Article 24 of the CRPD on special and inclusive education in Germany, Portugal, the Russian Federation, and Netherlands. *On educational inclusion: Meanings, history, issues and international perspectives*, 236-245.

Armstrong, D. (2003). Experiences of Special Education: Re-evaluating Policy and Practice through. *Life (Chicago, Ill.)*.

Baron, S., Phillips, R., & Stalker, K. (1996). Barriers to training for disabled social work students. *Disability & Society*, *11*(3), 361–378. doi:10.1080/09687599627660

Bates, L. (2018). 5 Real Benefits of Using Animation in the Classroom. *Peninsula Industries*, 1.

Ben-Bassat Levy, R., Ben-Ari, M., & Uronen, P. A. (2003). The Jeliot 2000 programanimation system. *Computers & Education*, *40*, 1–15.

Bergdahl, N., & Nouri, J. (2021). Covid-19 and crisis-prompted distance education in Sweden. Technology. *Knowledge and Learning*, *26*(3), 443–459. doi:10.100710758-020-09470-6

Betrancourt, M. (2005). The animation and interactivity principles in multimedia learning. In R. E. Mayer (Ed.), *The Cambridge handbook of multimedia learning* (pp. 287–296). Cambridge University Press. doi:10.1017/CBO9780511816819.019

Chen, W. (2020). Learning analytics for inclusive higher education. ICCE 2020–28th International Conference on Computers in Education. *Proceedings*, *2*, 113–118.

Chen, X., Xie, H., Zou, D., & Hwang, G.-J. (2020). *Application and theory gaps during the rise of Artificial Intelligence in Education*. Elsevier BV. doi:10.1016/j.caeai.2020.100002

Chen, X., Zou, D., Xie, H., Cheng, G., & Liu, C. (2022). Two Decades of Artificial Intelligence in Education: Contributors, Collaborations, Research Topics, Challenges, and Future Directions. *Journal of Educational Technology & Society*, *25*(1), 28–47.

Desai, A. (2018). *Animation in Education*. Retrieved from CG Pundit: https://www.cgpundit.com/animation-in-education/

Du Toit, L. (1997). Education for all. Pretoria: Unisa. *Educational Research*, *43*, 235–245.

Dubovi, I. (2019). Online Computer-Based Clinical Simulations: The role of Visualizations. *Clinical Simulation in Nursing*, *33*, 35–41. doi:10.1016/j.ecns.2019.04.009

Edwards, B. I., & Cheok, A. D. (2018). Why not robot teachers: Artificial intelligence for addressing teacher shortage. *Applied Artificial Intelligence*, *32*(4), 345–360.

Esponda-Arguero, M. (2008). Algorithmic animation in education—Review of academicexperience. *Journal of Educational Computing Research*, *39*(1), 1–15. doi:10.2190/EC.39.1.a

Fazlinda, A. H., Wan Hanim Nadrah Wan, M., & Saslizawati, I. (2019). The Relationship between Employability Skills and Self-Efficacy of Students With Learning Disabilities In Vocational Stream. *Asian Journal of University Education*, *15*(3), 163–174.

Fleming, S. A., Hart, G. R., & Savage, P. B. (2000). Molecular orbital animations fororganic chemistry. *Journal of Chemical Education*, *77*(6), 790–793.

Forlin, C. (2001). *Inclusion: identifying potential stressors for regular class teachers*. Academic Press.

Gowramma, Nair, & Kumari. (2013). Effectiveness of remedial reading programme for pre-school children with hearing impairment. *Journal of NCED, 5*(1).

Guan, C., Mou, J., & Jiang, Z. (2020). Artificial intelligence innovation in education: A twenty-year data-driven historical analysis. *International Journal of Innovation Studies, 4*(4), 134–147. doi:10.1016/j.ijis.2020.09.001

Hadjikakou, K., Polycarpou, V., & Hadjilia, A. (2010). The Experiences of Students with Mobility Disabilities in Cypriot Higher Education Institutions: Listening to their voices. *International Journal of Disability Development and Education, 57*(4), 403–426. doi:10.1080/1034912X.2010.524445

Harish, V., Sharma, R., Rana, G., Nayyar, A., & Parashar, B. (2023). Expanding the Scope of Learning Analytics in Blended Learning Environments. In N. J. Ahuja, A. Kumar, & A. Nayyar (Eds.), *Sustainable Blended Learning in STEM Education for Students with Additional Needs. Contributions to Environmental Sciences & Innovative Business Technology*. Springer. doi:10.1007/978-981-99-3497-3_14

Hashim, H. (2018). Application of Technology in the Digital Era Education. *International Journal of Research in Counseling and Education, 2*(1), 1–5.

Hinojo-Lucena, F. J., Aznar-Díaz, I., Cáceres-Reche, M. P., & Romero-Rodríguez, J. M. (2019). Artificial intelligence in higher education: A bibliometric study on its impact in the scientific literature. *Education in Science, 9*(1), 51.

Hoeffler, T. N., & Leutner, D. (2007). Instructional animation versus static pictures: A meta-analysis. *Learning and Instruction, 17*(6), 722–738. doi:10.118641239-019-0171-0

Hungarian Central Statistical Office. (2022). *Educational Data*. https://www.ksh.hu/docs/hun/xftp/idoszaki/oktat/oktatas2122e/index.html

Hwang, G. J. (2014). Definition, Framework and Research Issues of Smart Learning Environments - A Context-Aware Ubiquitous Learning Perspective. *Smart Learning Environments, 1*(1), 1-14.

Hwang, G. J., Xie, H., Wah, B. W., & Gašević, D. (2020). Vision, Challenges, Roles andResearch Issues of Artificial Intelligence in Education. *Computers and Education:Artificial Intelligence, 1*, 100001.

Janwadkar, K. (2015). *Effect of school readiness programme on children withautism spectrum disorders* [Unpublished Doctoral dissertation]. Ramakrishna Mission Vivekananda University-FDMSE, Coimbatore.

Khalil, M., Prinsloo, P., & Slade, S. (2018). User consent in MOOCs? Micro, meso, and macro perspectives. *International Review of Research in Open and Distributed Learning, 19*(5).

Kolekar, S.V., & Pai, R.M., & MM, M.P. (2018). Adaptive user interface for Moodle based e-learning system using learning styles. *Procedia Computer Science, 135*, 606–615. doi:10.1016/j.procs.2018.08.226

Kourakli, M., Altanis, I., Retalis, S., Boloudakis, M., Zbainos, D., & Antonopoulou, K. (2017). Towards the improvement of the cognitive, motoric and academic skills of students with special educational needs using Kinect learning games. *International Journal of Child-Computer Interaction, 11*, 28–39. doi:10.1016/j.ijcci.2016.10.009

Kukkar, A., Mohana, R., & Sharma, A. (2023). Prediction of student academic performance based on their emotional wellbeing and interaction on various e-learning platforms. *Education and Information Technologies*, *28*, 9655–9684. doi:10.100710639-022-11573-9

Lewis, C. C., Fretwell, C. E., Ryan, J., & Parham, J. B. (2013). Faculty use of established and emerging technologies in higher education: A unified theory of acceptance and use of technology perspective. *International Journal of Higher Education*, *2*(2), 22–34.

Limna, P., Jakwatanatham, S., Siripipattanakul, S., Kaewpuang, P., & Sriboonruang, P. (2022). A review of artificial intelligence (AI) ineducation during the digital era. *AdvanceKnowledge for Executives*, *1*(1), 1–9.

Lin, H. C., Ho, C. F., & Han, Y. (2022). Understanding adoption of artificial intelligence-enabled language e-learning system: An empirical study of UTAUT model. *International Journal of Mobile Learning and Organisation*, *16*(1), 74. doi:10.1504/ijmlo.2022.119966

Liu, L., & Sun, K. (2011). Theoretical Models and empirical research continued use after the adoption of mobile digital reading service users. *Library and Information Service*, *55*(10), 78–82.

MahaKud, G.C. (2010). Vaccination for the children with learning disabilities: Some psycho-educational instructions for the parents of early learner. Disabilities and Impairments: An Interdisciplinary Research Journal, 24(1), 23–30.

Majumder, C. (2019). Prevalence of Disabled People in India. *International Journal of Trend in Scientific Research and Development*, *3*(2), 846–851.

Majumder, C. (2019b). Educational status of differently abled persons and developed policies in India. *International Journal of Trend in Scientific Research and Development, 3*(3), 341.

Mansor, N. R., Zakaria, R., Rashid, R. A., Arifin, R. M., Rahim, B. H. A., Zakaria, R., & Razak, M. T. A. (2020). A review survey on the use computer animation in education. *IOP Conference Series, 917*(1), 10.1088/1757-899x/917/1/012021

Messiou, K. (2019). The missing voices: Students as a catalyst for promoting inclusive education. *International Journal of Inclusive Education*, *23*(7–8), 768–781. doi:10.1080/13603116.2019.1623326

Miao, F., Holmes, W., Huang, R., & Zhang, H. (2021). *AI and Education: A Guidance for Policymakers*. UNESCO Publishing.

Moriña, A. (2017). Inclusive education in higher education: Challenges and opportunities. *European Journal of Special Needs Education*, *32*(1), 3–17.

Moriña, A., López-Gavira, R., & Morgado, B. (2017). How do Spanish disability support offices contribute to inclusive education in the university? *Disability & Society*, *32*(10), 1608–1626. doi:10.1080/09687599.2017.1361812

Mou, X. (2019). Artificial intelligence: Investment trends and selected industry uses. International Finance Corporation, 8.

Nayyar, A., Żywiołek, J., Rosak Szyrocka, J., & Naved, M. (2023). *Advances in Distance Learning in Times of Pandemic*. Chapman and Hall/CRC.

Nguyen, A., Tuunanen, T., Gardner, L., & Sheridan, D. (2021). Design principles for learning analytics information systems in higher education. *European Journal of Information Systems*, *30*(5), 541–568.

Norvig, P. R., & Intelligence, S. A. (2002). *A modern approach*. Prentice Hall.

Oliver, G. (2003). *Virtual Art: From Fantasy to Immersive Experience*. MIT Press.

Ouyang, F., & Jiao, P. (2021). Artificial Intelligence in Education: The Three Paradigms. *Computers and Education: Artificial Intelligence*, *2*, 100020.

Owoc, M. L., Sawicka, A., & Weichbroth, P. (2019). Artificial Intelligence Technologies in Education: Benefits, Challenges and Strategies of Implementation. *IFIP International Workshop on Artificial Intelligence for Knowledge Management*, 37-58.

Parashar, B., Sharma, R., Rana, G., & Balaji, R. D. (2023). Foundation Concepts for Industry 4.0. In A. Nayyar, M. Naved, & R. Rameshwar (Eds.), *New Horizons for Industry 4.0 in Modern Business. Contributions to Environmental Sciences & Innovative Business Technology*. Springer. doi:10.1007/978-3-031-20443-2_3

Parasuram, K. (2006). Variables that affect teachers' attitudes towards disability and inclusive education in Mumbai, India. Disability and Society, 21(3), 231–242.

Park, O. (1994). Dynamic visual displays in media-based instruction. *Educational Technology*, 21–25.

Ploetzner, R., Berney, S., & Bétrancourt, M. (2021). When learning from animations is more successful than learning from static pictures: Learning the specifics of change. *Instructional Science*, *49*(4), 497–514. doi:10.100711251-021-09541-w

Prakash, C., Saini, R., & Sharma, R. (2021). Role of Internet of Things (IoT) in Sustaining Disruptive Businesses. In R. Sharma, R. Saini, C. Prakash, & V. Prashad (Eds.), *Internet of Things and Businesses in a Disruptive Economy* (1st ed.). Nova Science Publishers.

Pushpendu & Sharma. (2021). A Study to Comprehend Role of Artificial Intelligence in Building Smart Cities. *Engineering and Technology Journal for Research and Innovation, 3*(2).

Rahmatullah, A. S., Mulyasa, E., Syahrani, S., Pongpalilu, F., & Putri, R. E. (2022). Digital Era4.0: The Contribution to Education and Student Psychology. *Linguistics and CultureReview*, *6*, 89–107.

Rana, G., Khang, A., Sharma, R., Goel, A. K., & Dubey, A. K. (Eds.). (2021). *Reinventing Manufacturing and Business Processes Through Artificial Intelligence* (1st ed.). CRC Press. doi:10.1201/9781003145011

Ravindra, Parashar, & Rana. (2021). Chandan Veer .Education: An Enlightened Hope in the Time of Covid-19 Crises. *A Quarterly Refereed Journal of Dialogues on Education, 10*(5), 103-112.

Reed, S. K. (2005). From research to practice and back: The animation tutor project. *Educational Psychology Review*, *17*(1), 55–82.

Rieber, L. P. (1991). *Computer-based microworlds: a bridge between construc-tivism and direct instruction*. Paper presented at the meeting of the Annual Convention of the Association for Educational Communications and Technology.

Roll, I., & Wylie, R. (2016). Evolution and Revolution in Artificial Intelligence in Education. *International Journal of Artificial Intelligence in Education*, *26*(2), 582.

Rubio Garcia, R., Suarez Quiros, J., Gallego Santos, R., & Gonzalez, S. M., & MoránFernanz, S. (2007). Interactive multimedia animation with Macromedia Flashin descriptive geometry teaching. *Computers & Education*, *49*(3), 615–639.

Russell, S. J. (2010). *Artificial intelligence a modern approach*. Pearson Education, Inc.

Sahlaoui, H., Alaoui, E. A., Agoujil, S., & Nayyar, A. (2023). An empirical assessment of smote variants techniques and interpretation methods in improving the accuracy and the interpretability of student performance models. *Education and Information Technologies*. Advance online publication. doi:10.100710639-023-12007-w

Sahlaoui, H., Alaoui, E. A., Nayyar, A., Agoujil, S., & Jaber, M. M. (2021). Predicting and interpreting student performance using ensemble models and shapley additive explanations. *IEEE Access : Practical Innovations, Open Solutions*, *9*, 152688–152703. doi:10.1109/access.2021.3124270

Samuelsen, J., Chen, W., & Wasson, B. (2019). Integrating multiple data sources for learning analytics—Review of literature. *Research and Practice in Technology Enhanced Learning*, *14*(1), 1–20.

Sayghe, A., Hu, Y., Zografopoulos, I., Liu, X., Dutta, R. G., Jin, Y., & Konstantinou, C. (2020). Survey of machine learning methods for detecting false data injection attacks in power systems. *IET Smart Grid*, *3*(5), 581–595. doi:10.1049/iet-stg.2020.0015

Schnotz, W., & Lowe, R. (2003). Introduction. *Learning and Instruction*, *13*(2), 117–124.

Schreglmann, S., & Kazanci, Z. (2018). A Lesson Plan Development Study for Higher Education based on Needs Assessment "Graphics and Animation in Education" course. *International Education Studies*, *11*(7), 155. doi:10.5539/ies.v11n7p155

Seale, J., Georgeson, J., Mamas, C., & Swain, J. (2015). Not the right kind of 'digital capital'? An examination of the complex relationship between disabled students, their technologies and higher education institutions. *Computers & Education*, *82*, 118–128.

Serajul Haq, F. (2007). Educational opportunities for students with disabilities: The experience of auniversity student in Brunei. *Asian Journal of University Education*, *3*(1), 81–91.

Siemens, G., & Long, P. (2011). Penetrating the fog: Analytics in learning and education. Educ. Rev., 46(5).

Slee, R. (2018). *Defining the scope of inclusive education*. http://repositorio.minedu.gob.pe/handle/20.500.12799/5977

Supriyono, S., Siswanto, W. A., Darmawan, A. S., Utomo, W. M., Supriyono, H., Setiawan, W., Solikin, M., Ulinuha, A., Prasetyo, H., & Purnama, H. (2018b). Selected Peer-Reviewed Articles from the International Conference on Engineering Application, Physics and Sciences (ICEAPS2017), Johor Bahru, Malaysia, 26–27 October, 2017. *Advanced Science Letters*. 10.1166/asl.2018.12074

Suresh, C. B., & Gowramma, I. P. (2010). *Promoting Social Integration amongPreschool Children with Hearing Impairment.* Paper presented at the Annual National Conference of National Convention of Educators ofthe Deaf (NCED): Trivandrum, Kerala, India.

Szyrocka, J. R., Żywiołek, J., Nayyar, A., & Naved, M. (Eds.). (2023). *Advances in distance learning in times of pandemic*. CRC Press.

Tang, K. Y., Chang, C. Y., & Hwang, G. J. (2023). Trends in artificial intelligence-supported e-learning: A systematic review and co-citation network analysis (1998–2019). *Interactive Learning Environments, 31*(4), 2134–2152.

Tang, T., Li, P., & Tang, Q. (2022). New Strategies and Practices of Design Education under the background of Artificial Intelligence Technology: Online Animation Design Studio. *Frontiers in Psychology, 13*, 767295. Advance online publication. doi:10.3389/fpsyg.2022.767295 PMID:35651576

Tversky, B., Bauer-Morrison, J., & Betrancourt, M. (2002). Animation: Can it facilitate? *International Journal of Human-Computer Studies, 57*, 247–262.

UNESCO. (1994). *The Salamanca Statement and Framework for action on special needs education: adopted by the World Conference on Special Needs Education; Access and Quality. Schen anca, Spain, 7-10 June 1994*. UNESCO.

UNESCO. (2000). *Education for All: Meeting our collective commitments. The Dakar framework for action*. UNESCO.

United Nations (2015). *Transforming our world: The 2030 agenda for sustainable development*. Author.

United Nations. (2015). *United Nations sustainable development goals*. United Nations. https://sustainabledevelopment.un.org/

Venkatesh, M.N. (2006). *An evaluation of the schemes and programmes of inclusive education of the disabled children in Karnataka and A.P.* Department of Folklore and Tribal Studies, Dravidian University Kuppam, Chittoor.

Wang, Q. (2022). Innovation Strategy of Animation Curriculum Systems Based on Artificial Intelligence. In *Proceedings of the 2022 International Conference on Educational Innovation and Multimedia Technology (EIMT 2022)* (pp. 131–138). Atlantis Press International BV. 10.2991/978-94-6463-012-1_15

Yusof, Y., Chan, C. C., Hillaluddin, A. H., Ahmad Ramli, F. Z., & Mat Saad, Z. (2020). Improving inclusion of students with disabilities in Malaysian higher education. *Disability & Society, 35*(7), 1145–1170. doi:10.1080/09687599.2019.1667304

Zhang, K., & Aslan, A. (2021). AI technologies for education: Recent research & future directions. Computers & Education. *Artificial Intelligence*. Advance online publication. doi:10.1016/j.caeai.2021.100025

Chapter 2
Methodology and Framework for AI-Based Solutions for Special Education

Vishal Ambadas Meshram
https://orcid.org/0000-0001-9950-584X
Vishwakarma Institute of Information Technology, India

Santosh Kumar
Vishwakarma Institute of Information Technology, India

Vidula V. Meshram
Vishwakarma Institute of Information Technology, India

Vivek Patil
Vishwakarma Institute of Information Technology, India

Kailas Patil
Vishwakarma University, India

Laxmi Bewoor
Vishwakarma Institute of Information Technology, India

Pravin Gawande
Vishwakarma Institute of Information Technology, India

ABSTRACT

Special education recognizes limitations of traditional teaching methods in meeting diverse student needs. It empowers individuals through tailored support, specialized instruction, and assistive technologies, unlocking their full potential. Promoting inclusivity, social, and academic growth, it enables fulfilling lives. Integration of AI technology holds promise for enhancing special education's effectiveness and inclusiveness. This chapter presents a comprehensive methodology and framework for AI-based solutions, offering stakeholders a systematic approach to address specific challenges faced by individuals with special needs. By combining data-driven insights and human expertise, this approach revolutionizes special education delivery, empowering individuals to maximize their potential. However, further research and implementation are necessary to validate its effectiveness and scalability in real-world educational settings.

DOI: 10.4018/979-8-3693-0378-8.ch002

INTRODUCTION

The field of special education plays a crucial role in providing tailored support and assistance to individuals with diverse learning needs. Figure 1 describes the Methodology and Framework for AI-based Solution for Special Education in detail. With advancements in technology, there is a growing interest in leveraging artificial intelligence (AI) to develop innovative solutions that can enhance the educational experiences and outcomes for students with special needs (J. Bryant 2020, L. Di Nuovo et al. 2019). This chapter aims to present a comprehensive methodology and framework for the development and implementation of AI-based solutions in the domain of special education.

The chapter begins by highlighting the unique challenges faced by students with special needs and the importance of personalized interventions to meet their specific requirements (Mastropieri, Scruggs, 2020). Traditional approaches to special education often rely on manual assessments and interventions, which can be time-consuming, resource-intensive, and subject to human limitations. However, the integration of AI technologies holds immense potential to address these challenges and revolutionize the field (Fletcher, A. et al., 2019).

The primary focus of this chapter is to provide a systematic methodology for developing AI-based solutions tailored to the needs of students with special education requirements. The proposed framework encompasses various stages, including data collection and preprocessing, feature extraction and representation, model development and training, and system evaluation. Each stage will be discussed in detail, highlighting the key considerations and best practices to ensure the effectiveness and ethical use of AI technologies in special education (Hlosta, M.et al., 2021, Karimi, N. et al., 2020))

Furthermore, the chapter explores the different AI techniques and algorithms commonly employed in special education, such as machine learning, natural language processing, computer vision, and affective computing (Rajkumar, A. et al., 2022, Ven et al., 2020). The discussion encompasses both supervised and unsupervised learning approaches, as well as hybrid models that combine multiple AI techniques to address complex learning challenges (Koedinger, K. et al., 2019))

In addition to the technical aspects, ethical considerations and legal implications associated with AI-based special education solutions will be addressed. Ensuring privacy, data security, and fairness in the use of AI technologies is paramount, and the chapter will provide guidelines and recommendations for responsible development and deployment (Christie, R., and Klinger, T., 2021, Spaulding, J. et al., 2022).

Ultimately, the goal of this chapter is to provide educators, researchers, and practitioners in the field of special education with a comprehensive methodology and framework for leveraging AI technologies effectively. By combining domain expertise with AI capabilities, it is expected that these solutions will enhance the quality and inclusiveness of education for individuals with special needs, fostering their academic, social, and emotional growth (A. Ahmed et al., 2021, I. Giannakos et al., 2020).

In the subsequent sections, we will delve into the specific stages of the proposed methodology and explore various AI techniques and algorithms applicable to special education. The chapter will conclude by discussing the potential future directions and challenges in the field, emphasizing the need for ongoing research, collaboration, and innovation to maximize the benefits of AI-based solutions for special education.

Figure 1. Methodology and framework for AI-based solution for special education

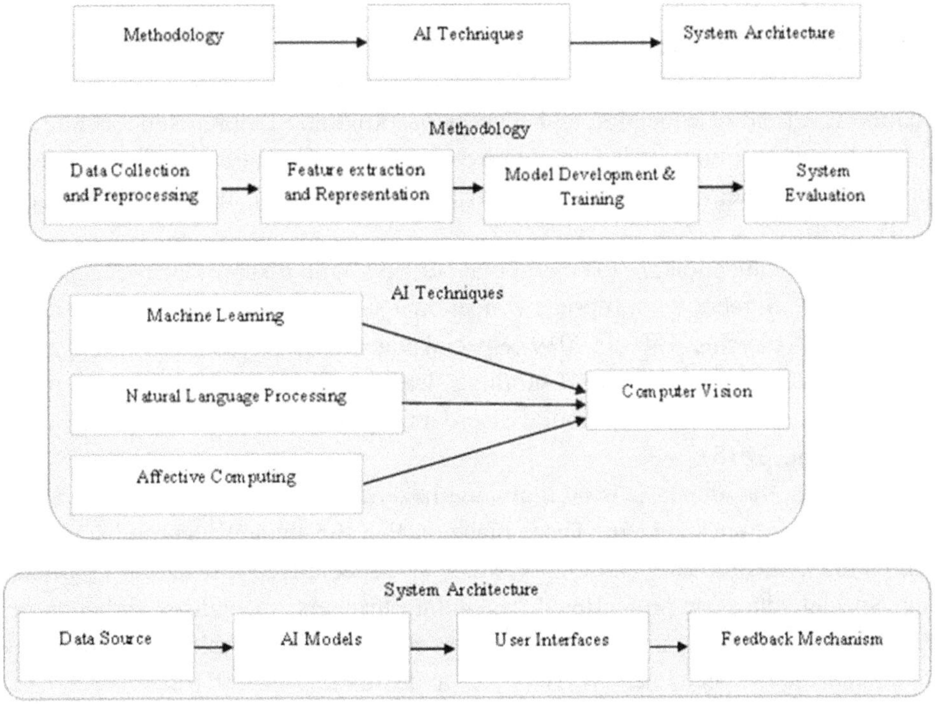

1.1 Objectives

The objectives of the chapter are:

1) Develop a comprehensive methodology and framework for AI-based solutions in special education, including ethical guidelines for responsible development and implementation.
2) Highlight the importance of personalized interventions for students with special needs and explore how AI technologies can revolutionize special education by addressing traditional limitations.
3) Empower educators and practitioners with the knowledge and tools to effectively utilize AI techniques, fostering inclusiveness and growth among individuals with special needs, while also identifying future research directions and challenges.

These objectives aim to provide a comprehensive understanding of the methodology, framework, and potential impact of AI technologies in special education, while also addressing ethical considerations and promoting responsible use.

2. OVERVIEW OF SPECIAL EDUCATION

2.1 Definition and Scope of Special Education

Special education is a field of education that focuses on providing tailored support and assistance to individuals with diverse learning needs. It recognizes that every student is unique and may require personalized interventions to help them overcome barriers and reach their full potential (Mastropieri, M. and Scruggs, T., 2020).

The goals of special education are to ensure that students with disabilities or exceptionalities have equal access to education, receive appropriate educational services, and have opportunities to develop their skills and abilities (Fletcher, T. et al., 2019). Special education addresses a wide range of disabilities and exceptionalities, including intellectual disabilities, learning disabilities, autism spectrum disorders, sensory impairments, emotional or behavioural disorders, and physical disabilities (Hallahan, D. et al., 2017, Turnbull, A. et al., 2015).

In special education, the emphasis is on individualized education plans (IEPs) that are designed to meet the specific needs of each student. These plans outline the student's strengths, weaknesses, and goals, as well as the accommodations, modifications, and specialized instruction required to support their learning. Special education professionals, including teachers, specialists, and support staff, collaborate with parents, caregivers, and other stakeholders to develop and implement effective educational programs for students with special needs (Friend, M. and Bursuck, W., 2018).

The field of special education has evolved significantly over the years, moving away from a segregated approach towards more inclusive practices. Inclusion involves integrating students with disabilities into regular classrooms and providing them with the necessary supports and accommodations to participate in the general education curriculum alongside their peers. This approach promotes social integration, fosters positive relationships, and enhances opportunities for learning and growth (Salend, S. and Duhaney, L., 2017).

Special education encompasses a wide range of instructional strategies and interventions. These may include differentiated instruction, multisensory approaches, assistive technologies, specialized therapies, and individualized supports. The goal is to create a supportive and inclusive learning environment that addresses the unique needs of each student, promotes their independence and self-advocacy skills, and prepares them for success in education and beyond (Westling, D. and Fox, L., 2015).

Collaboration and teamwork are key aspects of special education. Educators, parents, caregivers, and related service providers work together to develop and implement effective educational plans, monitor progress, and make necessary adjustments. Additionally, special education professionals collaborate with general education teachers to ensure that students with special needs can access and participate in the general education curriculum to the fullest extent possible (VanLaarhoven T., and Williams L., 2017).

While special education primarily focuses on students with disabilities or exceptionalities, it also recognizes the importance of addressing the diverse needs of all learners. Differentiated instruction and universal design for learning (UDL) principles are employed to create inclusive classrooms that accommodate a wide range of learning styles, abilities, and strengths (Cook, B. et al., 2014, Schattman et al., 2016, D. J. Sands and S. L. McBride, 2015).

In conclusion, special education is a field dedicated to providing individualized support and educational opportunities for students with diverse learning needs. By embracing inclusivity, collaboration, and personalized approaches, special education aims to empower students with special needs to achieve their full potential and become active participants in society (Sharma, U., and Desai, I., 2002, Turnbull, A. et al., 2017).

2.2 Challenges in Special Education

While the potential for AI-based solutions in special education is promising, it is important to acknowledge and address the challenges that exist within this domain. Special education poses unique complexities that need to be carefully considered when designing AI methodologies and frameworks. The following challenges are commonly encountered in special education:

i) **Diverse and Individualized Needs:** Special education encompasses a wide range of disabilities and learning difficulties, each requiring tailored approaches. Developing AI solutions that can effectively cater to the individual needs of diverse learners is a significant challenge. Customizing algorithms and frameworks to accommodate the specific requirements of each student is essential but can be complex and resource-intensive.

ii) **Data Availability and Quality:** AI models rely heavily on data for training and decision-making. However, special education data is often scarce, fragmented, or of varying quality. The availability of comprehensive and representative data is crucial for developing accurate and reliable AI solutions. Ensuring data privacy and security while collecting and analyzing sensitive student information is also a critical concern.

iii) **Interpretability and Explainability:** Transparency in AI algorithms is essential, especially in the field of special education. Teachers, parents, and administrators need to understand how AI-based solutions arrive at recommendations or decisions. Ensuring that AI models are interpretable and explainable is crucial for building trust and facilitating collaboration between AI systems and human stakeholders.

iv) **Ethical Considerations:** AI applications in special education raise ethical concerns that need to be carefully addressed. Issues such as data privacy, consent, algorithmic bias, and fairness must be taken into account. Ensuring that AI systems are designed and implemented in a way that respects and safeguards the rights and dignity of students with disabilities is of utmost importance.

v) **Teacher Support and Collaboration:** AI should not replace human educators but rather augment their capabilities. Special education teachers play a vital role in providing personalized instruction and support to students. AI-based solutions should be designed to assist and empower teachers, facilitating collaboration and reducing administrative burdens. Ensuring that educators are well-trained and equipped to effectively use AI tools is crucial for their successful integration into the classroom.

vi) **Accessibility and Usability:** It is essential to ensure that AI-based solutions for special education are accessible and usable by all students, including those with disabilities. Considerations should be given to user interfaces, adaptive technologies, and the availability of appropriate assistive devices to accommodate the diverse needs of learners. Furthermore, AI solutions should be inclusive, taking into account factors such as language, cultural background, and socioeconomic status.

vii) **Sustainability and Scalability:** Developing AI-based solutions for special education requires long-term sustainability and scalability. Adequate resources, funding, and technical support are essential for maintaining and upgrading AI systems over time. Ensuring that AI solutions can be implemented across various educational settings and that they remain effective and adaptable in the face of changing requirements is a challenge that needs to be addressed.

By acknowledging and addressing these challenges, researchers, educators, and developers can work together to create AI methodologies and frameworks that have a positive impact on special education. Overcoming these obstacles will contribute to the development of effective, ethical, and inclusive AI solutions that enhance learning opportunities for students with disabilities.

2.3 Role of Technology in Special Education

Technology plays a crucial role in transforming special education by providing innovative solutions and tools that enhance learning experiences and outcomes for students with diverse needs. In recent years, the integration of artificial intelligence (AI) has further revolutionized the field, offering promising opportunities to address individual learning challenges effectively. This section explores the significant role technology plays in special education and highlights the impact of AI-based solutions.

i) **Access to Inclusive Education:** Technology has facilitated greater access to inclusive education for students with disabilities. Assistive technologies such as screen readers, text-to-speech software, and alternative input devices enable students with visual or motor impairments to participate actively in the learning process. According to Smith et al., assistive technology has been shown to improve academic performance and promote independence among students with disabilities (Smith, T. et al., 2020).
ii) **Personalized Learning:** Technology allows for personalized learning experiences tailored to individual students' strengths, weaknesses, and learning styles. Adaptive learning systems, powered by AI algorithms, can analyze student data and provide tailored instruction and support. This individualized approach promotes engagement, self-paced learning, and mastery of skills (Johnson, K. et al., 2018).
iii) **Scaffolding and Support:** Technology provides scaffolding and support to students with special needs. Educational software and applications offer interactive learning experiences, visual aids, and multimedia resources that help break down complex concepts into more manageable components. These tools, as highlighted in (Rodriguez, M. et al., 2019), provide additional support and promote comprehension and retention among students with learning disabilities.
iv) **Data-Driven Decision Making:** Technology enables educators to collect and analyze data on students' progress and performance. AI-based systems can process large volumes of data, identify patterns, and generate actionable insights. This data-driven approach empowers teachers to make informed decisions regarding instructional strategies, interventions, and individualized education plans (IEPs) (Johnson, M. et al., 2021).

v) **Collaborative Learning and Communication:** Technology fosters collaboration and communication among students, teachers, and parents in special education settings. Online platforms, video conferencing tools, and virtual classrooms facilitate real-time interaction, allowing students to connect with peers, engage in group projects, and receive remote support from teachers or specialists (Jones, S., 2022).

vi) **Engagement and Motivation:** Technology offers engaging and interactive learning experiences that can enhance student motivation and participation. Gamification elements, virtual reality simulations, and educational apps create immersive and enjoyable learning environments that capture students' interest and promote active learning (Smith, S. 2019).

In summary, technology, particularly AI-based solutions, plays a vital role in special education by providing access to inclusive education, personalizing learning experiences, offering scaffolding and support, enabling data-driven decision making, fostering collaboration, and enhancing student engagement and motivation. These advancements have the potential to significantly improve educational outcomes and empower students with diverse needs. Figure 2 describes the role of technology in special education.

3. NEEDS ASSESSMENT IN SPECIAL EDUCATION

In order to provide effective and individualized support to students with diverse needs in special education, it is crucial to conduct a comprehensive needs assessment. A needs assessment helps in identifying the specific requirements and challenges faced by students, thereby guiding the development of appropriate interventions and educational plans. This section explores the importance of needs assessment in special education and highlights the key considerations in the assessment process.

i) Understanding Individual Needs: A needs assessment enables educators and specialists to gain a deep understanding of the unique needs of each student. It involves gathering information about the student's strengths, weaknesses, abilities, and areas requiring support (Bailey, D. et al., 2019). By conducting assessments, such as cognitive assessments, behavioral observations, and academic evaluations, professionals can identify the specific areas in which a student may require additional assistance.

ii) Informing Instructional Planning: The data collected through a needs assessment informs the development of individualized instructional plans. By analyzing the assessment results, educators can tailor their teaching strategies, curriculum, and materials to meet the specific needs of each student (Mellard, D., & Johnson, E., 2020). This personalized approach enhances the student's learning experience and increases the chances of academic success.

iii) Identifying Support Services: A needs assessment helps in identifying the appropriate support services and interventions for students with special needs. It provides valuable information about the types of therapies, accommodations, or assistive technologies that may benefit the student (Elliott, S., & Ryan, J., 2021). By matching the identified needs with available resources, educators can ensure that students receive the necessary support to reach their full potential.

iv) Collaborative Decision-Making: The needs assessment process involves collaboration among educators, specialists, parents, and the student (if appropriate). By engaging in collaborative decision-making, all stakeholders contribute their insights and expertise, ensuring that the assessment accurately captures the student's needs (Smith, S., 2019). This collaborative approach fosters a sense of ownership and promotes effective teamwork in supporting the student's development.

v) Monitoring Progress and Adjusting Interventions: A needs assessment is not a one-time event but an ongoing process. Regular assessments allow educators to monitor the student's progress and make adjustments to interventions as needed (Cook, B., & Odom, S., 2021). By continuously evaluating the student's needs, educators can ensure that interventions remain effective and relevant, promoting sustained growth and development.

Figure 2. Role of technology in special education

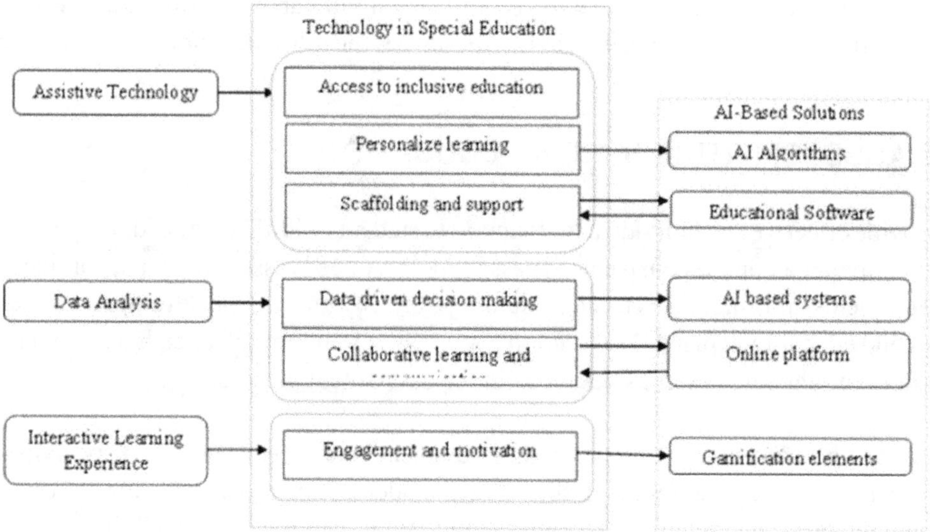

Assessment plays a vital role in special education by providing a comprehensive understanding of students' individual needs. It informs instructional planning, identifies necessary support services, facilitates collaborative decision-making, and enables the monitoring and adjustment of interventions over time. By conducting thorough needs assessments, educators and specialists can ensure that students with diverse needs receive the appropriate support to thrive academically and socially.

3.1 Identifying Learning Needs and Challenges

The first step in needs assessment is to identify the individual learning needs and challenges of students. This involves gathering information about their strengths, weaknesses, abilities, and areas requiring support (Bailey, D. et al., 2019). By conducting assessments such as cognitive assessments, behavioral observations, and academic evaluations, educators and specialists can gain insights into the specific areas in which students may require additional assistance.

3.2 Data Collection and Analysis

Data collection and analysis are crucial components of needs assessment in special education. Educators use various assessment tools and techniques to gather relevant data about students' skills, abilities, and progress student (Mellard, D., & Johnson, E., 2020). This includes formal assessments, informal observations, interviews, and surveys. The collected data is then analyzed to identify patterns, trends, and areas of concern, which helps guide instructional planning and intervention strategies.

3.3 Ethical Considerations in Needs Assessment

Ethical considerations are essential throughout the needs assessment process in special education. Professionals must ensure that assessments are conducted in a fair, unbiased, and culturally sensitive manner (Elliott, S., & Ryan, J., 2021, Cook, B., & Odom, S., 2021). They must also obtain informed consent from parents or legal guardians, protect students' privacy and confidentiality, and adhere to professional ethical guidelines. Additionally, professionals should be aware of any potential conflicts of interest and prioritize the best interests of the students throughout the assessment process.

4. DATA COLLECTION AND PREPROCESSING

Data collection and preprocessing are crucial steps in utilizing AI models for special education. This section explores the types of data commonly used in special education, various data collection methods, and preprocessing techniques for preparing data for AI models.

4.1 Types of Data in Special Education

In special education, various types of data are collected to understand students' needs and improve their learning outcomes. These include:

i) **Demographic Data:** Information such as age, gender, and background helps provide context for understanding students' individual characteristics and needs.
ii) **Assessment Data:** Data obtained from assessments, including cognitive tests, academic evaluations, and behavioral observations, provide insights into students' strengths, weaknesses, and areas requiring support.
iii) **Behavioral Data:** This type of data includes information on students' behavior patterns, social interactions, and emotional well-being, helping identify factors that may impact their learning experience.
iv) **Performance Data:** Data related to students' academic performance, such as grades, test scores, and progress reports, provide valuable information for monitoring their progress and identifying areas for improvement.
v) **Engagement Data:** Information on students' engagement in learning activities, participation rates, and interactions with educational technology tools can help assess their level of involvement and identify strategies to enhance engagement.

Having well-organized and clean datasets is essential for the development of accurate machine learning models (Salvia, J. et al., 2020, Meshram, V., 2021, Meshram, V. et al., 2022, Meshram, V. et al., 2019, Patil, K. et al., 2018, Meshram, V., Patil, K., 2022, Meshram, V. et al., 2022, Meshram V. et al., 2021)). In the context of special education, numerous datasets are readily available for constructing machine learning models tailored to this specific domain (Suryawanshi, Y. et al., 2022, Meshram, V. et al., 2022, Meshram, V., Patil, K., 2022, Pise, R. et al., 2022, Meshram, V. et al., 2023, Meshram, V. et al., 2023, Chumchu, P., Patil, K., 2023).

4.2 Data Collection Methods

Special education utilizes various data collection methods to gather information about students' needs and progress. Common methods include:

i) **Observations:** Observations by educators, specialists, or trained observers help capture students' behaviour, interactions, and learning preferences in natural settings.
ii) **Interviews:** Interviews with students, parents, and teachers provide valuable qualitative data, offering insights into students' experiences, strengths, challenges, and support needs.
iii) **Surveys and Questionnaires:** Surveys and questionnaires allow for systematic collection of data from students, parents, or educators, providing information on various aspects such as learning preferences, attitudes, and perceptions.
iv) **Assessments:** Formal assessments, including standardized tests, cognitive assessments, and specific skill assessments, generate quantitative data that can be used to measure students' abilities, progress, and areas requiring support.

4.3 Preprocessing Techniques for AI Models

Preprocessing techniques are applied to raw data before feeding it into AI models. These techniques help clean, transform, and prepare the data for effective model training. Some common preprocessing techniques include:

i) **Data Cleaning:** Removing duplicate entries, handling missing values, and addressing outliers are essential steps to ensure the quality and integrity of the data.
ii) **Feature Scaling:** Scaling features to a consistent range helps prevent certain features from dominating the model and facilitates more efficient training.
iii) **Feature Encoding:** Converting categorical data into numerical representations, such as one-hot encoding or label encoding, allows AI models to process the data effectively.
iv) **Dimensionality Reduction:** Techniques like Principal Component Analysis (PCA) or feature selection methods can reduce the number of features while preserving the most relevant information, improving model performance and reducing complexity.

Applying appropriate data collection methods and preprocessing techniques is essential to ensure the quality, relevance, and usability of the data for AI models in special education.

5. AI ALGORITHMS AND MODELS FOR SPECIAL EDUCATION

5.1 Introduction to AI in Special Education

In the field of special education, artificial intelligence (AI) algorithms and models play a crucial role in providing personalized and adaptive learning experiences. These models leverage the power of machine learning techniques to analyze data, make predictions, and offer tailored interventions to meet the unique needs of students with diverse learning abilities. Four broad categories can be used to classify machine learning algorithms: Reinforcement learning, semi-supervised learning, unsupervised learning, and supervised learning (Baker, Ryan, 2021).

5.2 Supervised Learning Techniques

Supervised learning techniques are widely employed in special education to develop AI models. These algorithms learn from labelled examples to make predictions or classify new data points. In the context of special education, supervised learning can be applied to various tasks such as predicting student performance, identifying learning disabilities, or recommending appropriate learning materials. Common supervised learning algorithms used in special education include decision trees, random forests, support vector machines, and neural networks (Cho et al., 2022).

5.3 Unsupervised Learning Techniques

Unsupervised learning techniques are particularly valuable in special education for discovering patterns, similarities, and relationships in data without explicit labels or guidance. These algorithms help identify clusters of students with similar learning profiles, uncover hidden patterns in student behavior, or generate personalized recommendations based on individual preferences. Some common unsupervised learning algorithms applied in special education include clustering algorithms like k-means, hierarchical clustering, and dimensionality reduction techniques such as principal component analysis (PCA) and t-SNE (Cho et al., 2022).

5.4 Reinforcement Learning Techniques

Reinforcement learning techniques are gaining traction in special education to create intelligent tutoring systems that can provide adaptive and interactive learning experiences. Reinforcement learning agents learn through trial and error interactions with an environment, receiving rewards or penalties based on their actions. In special education, reinforcement learning can be employed to develop personalized learning environments, adaptive educational games, or virtual agents that provide real-time feedback and support. These systems can adjust the difficulty level, pacing, or content based on individual student progress and performance (Cho et al., 2022).

5.5 Personalization and Adaptation in AI Models

Personalization and adaptation are critical aspects of AI models in special education. These models are designed to adapt to each student's unique learning needs, preferences, and abilities. By leveraging techniques such as collaborative filtering, content-based filtering, and context-aware modeling, AI models can provide personalized recommendations for learning materials, adaptive assessment strategies, or tailored interventions. This level of personalization enables students to engage in learning experiences that align with their strengths, challenges, and individual learning styles, ultimately fostering better learning outcomes (Paweł et al., 2021).

6. COLLABORATIVE APPROACH: INTEGRATING AI AND EDUCATION

Artificial intelligence (AI) has the potential to revolutionize education by enhancing instructional design, providing teacher support, and improving learning outcomes. However, the successful integration of AI into education requires a collaborative approach that involves close collaboration between AI specialists and educators. This section explores various aspects of collaboration in the context of AI and education.

6.1 Collaboration Between AI Specialists and Educators

Collaboration between AI specialists and educators is essential to ensure that AI technologies and solutions are effectively applied in educational settings. AI specialists bring expertise in developing and implementing AI algorithms, while educators provide valuable insights into pedagogy, curriculum, and student needs. By working together, AI specialists and educators can identify opportunities where AI can support and enhance teaching and learning processes (Ishmael et al., 2023).

6.2 Utilizing AI in Instructional Design

AI can play a significant role in instructional design by offering data-driven insights, adaptive learning experiences, and personalized recommendations. AI algorithms can analyze large volumes of educational data to identify patterns and trends, informing the design of effective instructional strategies. By leveraging AI, educators can develop customized learning pathways, adaptive assessments, and intelligent tutoring systems that cater to individual student needs.

6.3 Teacher Support and Professional Development

AI can support teachers by providing real-time data analytics, automating administrative tasks, and offering personalized professional development opportunities. AI-powered tools can analyze student performance data, identify knowledge gaps, and provide targeted recommendations for instructional interventions. Additionally, AI can assist with automating administrative tasks, such as grading assignments, generating progress reports, and managing classroom resources. Furthermore, AI-based platforms can offer personalized professional development resources to support teachers in staying updated with the latest research and pedagogical practices.

6.4 Implementing AI Solutions in Educational Settings

Implementing AI solutions in educational settings requires careful planning, infrastructure considerations, and ongoing evaluation. Collaboration between AI specialists, educators, and school administrators is crucial to ensure the successful integration of AI technologies. It involves determining the appropriate hardware and software infrastructure, addressing privacy and ethical concerns, and providing training and support for all stakeholders involved. Ongoing evaluation and monitoring of AI implementations are necessary to measure their effectiveness, identify areas for improvement, and make necessary adjustments to optimize their impact.

By fostering collaboration between AI specialists and educators, leveraging AI in instructional design, supporting teachers with AI-powered tools, and effectively implementing AI solutions in educational settings, the potential of AI in education can be realized, leading to improved learning outcomes and enhanced educational experiences for students. Figure 3 depicts the various collaborations in the context of AI and education.

Figure 3. Collaboration in the context of AI and education

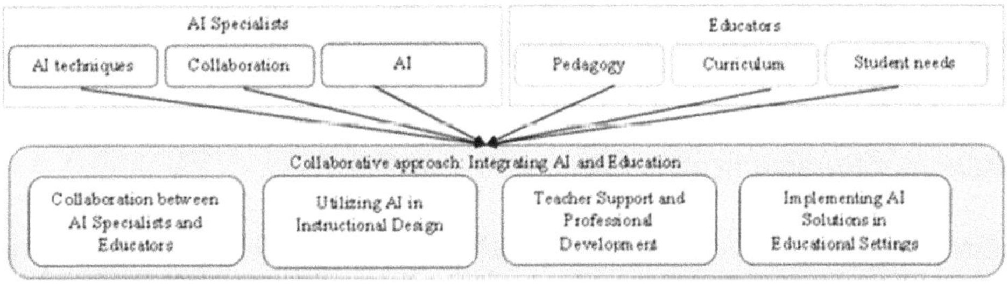

7. MONITORING AND EVALUATION

Monitoring and evaluation are critical aspects of implementing AI-based solutions in special education. Continuous monitoring allows for the assessment of the effectiveness of AI interventions, while evaluation provides valuable insights into the impact and success of these solutions. This section explores the importance of ongoing monitoring, the evaluation of AI-based solutions, and the need for iterative improvements and fine-tuning.

7.1 Importance of Ongoing Monitoring

Ongoing monitoring is essential to track the progress and performance of AI-based solutions in special education. It involves collecting and analyzing data related to student outcomes, engagement levels, and usage patterns. By monitoring these metrics, educators and AI specialists can gain valuable insights into the effectiveness of the implemented AI interventions. Ongoing monitoring helps identify areas of improvement, detect any issues or challenges, and make data-informed decisions to optimize the AI solutions.

7.2 Evaluation of AI-based Solutions

Evaluation plays a crucial role in determining the impact and success of AI-based solutions in special education. It involves conducting rigorous assessments to measure the effectiveness of AI interventions in achieving desired educational outcomes. Evaluation provides valuable insights into the strengths, weaknesses, and overall effectiveness of AI-based solutions, helping inform decision-making and improvement efforts (García-Peñalvo, F. J., et al., 2020).

7.2.1 Evaluation Methods

When evaluating AI-based solutions in special education, a combination of quantitative and qualitative evaluation methods can provide a comprehensive understanding of their impact.

Quantitative evaluation methods involve the use of standardized tests, performance metrics, and data analytics to measure various aspects of student learning and progress. These methods can assess academic achievement, cognitive skills, and behavioral changes resulting from AI interventions. Quantitative measures provide objective data that can be compared across different interventions or student groups.

Qualitative evaluation methods focus on capturing the subjective experiences and perceptions of students, teachers, and other stakeholders. Observations, interviews, surveys, and focus groups can be used to gather qualitative data. These methods allow for a deeper understanding of the contextual factors, student engagement, and the overall effectiveness of the AI solutions in meeting specific educational goals.

7.2.2 Stakeholder Perspectives

The evaluation process should consider multiple stakeholders' perspectives to gather a comprehensive understanding of the impact of AI-based solutions. This includes educators, students, parents, administrators, and other relevant individuals involved in the educational process. Each stakeholder group may provide unique insights regarding the strengths, limitations, and potential improvements of the AI interventions.

Educators can offer valuable perspectives on the alignment of AI solutions with instructional goals, their usability in the classroom, and their potential to enhance teaching and learning practices. Students' experiences and feedback can shed light on the effectiveness of the AI interventions in addressing their specific learning needs and preferences. Parents can provide insights into the impact of AI solutions on their children's educational experiences and overall satisfaction. Administrators' perspectives can help assess the feasibility, scalability, and sustainability of AI implementations within educational settings.

7.2.3 Ethical Considerations

Evaluation of AI-based solutions in special education should also consider ethical considerations. It is essential to ensure that the use of AI aligns with ethical guidelines, privacy regulations, and safeguards student rights and well-being. Ethical considerations may include the transparency of AI algorithms, the protection of sensitive student data, and the prevention of biases or discrimination in decision-making processes.

7.2.4 Continuous Improvement and Adaptation

Evaluation should not be seen as a one-time process but as a continuous cycle that drives improvement and adaptation. The findings and insights gained from the evaluation process should inform the refinement and optimization of AI-based solutions. This includes fine-tuning algorithms, updating content and instructional strategies, addressing usability and accessibility issues, and adapting interventions to better align with students' evolving needs.

By conducting rigorous and comprehensive evaluations of AI-based solutions, educational practitioners and researchers can gain valuable insights into the effectiveness, usability, and ethical implications of these interventions. The evaluation process helps identify areas for improvement, provides evidence for decision-making, and contributes to the ongoing development of AI solutions that better support students with special educational needs.

7.3 Iterative Improvements and Fine-Tuning

Implementing AI-based solutions in special education is an iterative process that requires continuous improvements and fine-tuning (Blikstein, P., 2021). Based on the insights gained from ongoing monitoring and evaluation, adjustments and refinements can be made to optimize the performance and effectiveness of the AI interventions. This may involve fine-tuning the algorithms, updating content and instructional strategies, or addressing usability and accessibility issues. Iterative improvements ensure that AI solutions evolve with changing needs and advancements in the field, resulting in enhanced support for students with special educational needs.

By emphasizing ongoing monitoring, conducting comprehensive evaluations, and embracing iterative improvements, the integration of AI-based solutions in special education can lead to more effective and impactful educational practices. It is through careful monitoring and evaluation that educators and AI specialists can refine and optimize the use of AI, ultimately benefiting students with special educational needs.

8. CASE STUDIES AND SUCCESS STORIES

This section presents case studies and success stories that highlight exemplary applications of AI in special education. These real-world examples provide insights into the effective integration of AI technologies, valuable lessons learned, and best practices in utilizing AI to support students with special educational needs.

8.1 Exemplary Applications of AI in Special Education

In recent years, several exemplary applications of AI in special education have emerged, showcasing the potential of AI technologies to enhance educational outcomes for students with diverse learning needs (Lambert, M. C., et al., 2022). These applications leverage AI techniques such as machine learning, natural language processing, and computer vision to provide personalized, adaptive, and engaging learning experiences.

One notable application is the use of AI-powered virtual tutors that can adapt their instruction to individual student abilities and learning styles (Mueen Uddin, S., et al., 2021). These virtual tutors can provide immediate feedback, offer tailored explanations, and track student progress, helping students develop critical skills in areas such as reading comprehension, mathematics, and language development.

Another exemplary application is the utilization of AI algorithms to analyze large-scale educational datasets and identify patterns and trends related to student performance and interventions (Lee, J., & Heffernan, N., 2018). This data-driven approach allows educators and administrators to make informed decisions, allocate resources effectively, and implement evidence-based practices to support students' unique needs.

8.2 Real-World Case Studies

Real-world case studies provide valuable insights into the practical implementation and impact of AI-based solutions in special education. These case studies demonstrate how AI technologies have been successfully integrated into educational settings, leading to improved student outcomes and enhanced teaching practices (Romero, C., et al., 2019).

For instance, a case study conducted in a special education classroom demonstrated the effectiveness of AI-assisted language instruction for students with language impairments (He, Y., et al., 2021). The AI system used natural language processing to provide real-time feedback and support in language comprehension and production tasks. The study reported significant improvements in students' language skills and increased engagement levels compared to traditional instructional methods.

Another case study explored the use of AI-based virtual reality (VR) applications to create inclusive learning environments for students with autism spectrum disorder (ASD) (DiVittorio, A., et al., 2019). The VR simulations provided interactive and personalized experiences to develop social skills, emotional regulation, and problem-solving abilities. The results indicated improved social interaction and communication skills among students with ASD, along with increased self-confidence and motivation.

8.3 Lessons Learned and Best Practices

Through these case studies and success stories, valuable lessons have been learned, and best practices have emerged in the integration of AI in special education (Li, L., et al., 2018).

One key lesson is the importance of collaboration and co-design between AI specialists, educators, and other stakeholders (Shute, V., et al., 2019). Effective collaboration ensures that AI solutions align with educational goals, are responsive to the unique needs of students, and are implemented in a pedagogically sound manner.

Another best practice is the consideration of ethical and privacy implications throughout the design and implementation of AI-based solutions (Luckin, R., et al., 2016). Safeguarding student data, ensuring transparency in algorithmic decision-making, and addressing biases or discrimination are crucial aspects of responsible AI integration in special education.

Furthermore, continuous monitoring and evaluation are vital for assessing the effectiveness and impact of AI interventions (Wachter-Boettcher, S., 2017). Ongoing evaluation helps identify areas for improvement, adapt interventions to changing needs, and ensure the ethical and equitable use of AI technologies.

By studying these case studies, embracing the lessons learned, and adopting best practices, educators and AI specialists can make informed decisions and maximize the potential of AI to support students with special educational needs.

9. FUTURE DIRECTIONS AND CHALLENGES

This section explores the future directions and challenges in the field of AI for special education. As AI continues to evolve, it opens up new possibilities for supporting students with special educational needs. However, several important considerations need to be addressed to ensure the ethical and responsible use of AI technologies in educational settings.

9.1 Emerging Trends in AI for Special Education

The field of AI for special education is constantly evolving, and several emerging trends show promise for future development. One such trend is the integration of multimodal AI systems that leverage multiple modalities such as speech, gestures, and facial expressions to enhance learning experiences for students with diverse needs. These multimodal systems can provide more personalized and engaging interactions, accommodating different learning styles and preferences (Ifenthaler, D., & Yau, J. Y., 2019).

Another emerging trend is the use of AI-powered adaptive learning platforms that dynamically adjust instructional content and pacing based on individual student progress and needs. These platforms can provide tailored interventions, personalized feedback, and scaffolded support, optimizing learning outcomes for students with special educational needs (Roschelle, J., et al., 2018).

Furthermore, advancements in natural language processing and sentiment analysis offer exciting possibilities for enhancing social and emotional learning support. AI technologies can help identify and analyze students' emotional states, providing timely interventions and strategies to foster emotional well-being and social skills development (Baker, R. S., et al., 2008).

9.2 Ethical and Privacy Concerns

As AI technologies become more prevalent in special education, it is crucial to address ethical and privacy concerns. The collection and analysis of student data raise important considerations regarding data security, privacy protection, and algorithmic bias. Educators, AI specialists, and policymakers must work together to establish clear guidelines and regulations to ensure the responsible and ethical use of student data in AI-driven educational settings (Wachter-Boettcher, S., 2017).

Additionally, transparency and explainability in AI algorithms are essential. Educators and stakeholders should have a clear understanding of how AI models make decisions, ensuring that these models are fair, unbiased, and accountable. Ethical considerations also extend to issues such as informed consent, data ownership, and the responsible use of AI technologies in assessments and decision-making processes (Luckin, R., et al., 2016).

9.3. Recommendations for Future Research

As the field of AI for special education continues to evolve, there are several areas that warrant further research:

1) **Ethical and Privacy Considerations:** Future research should focus on addressing ethical and privacy concerns associated with the use of AI technologies in special education. This includes developing transparent and accountable AI algorithms, ensuring the responsible use of student data, and establishing comprehensive ethical and legal frameworks.
2) **Scalability and Implementation:** The scalability and successful implementation of AI-based solutions in diverse educational settings need further exploration. Research should investigate the infrastructure requirements, technical support, and professional development necessary to integrate AI technologies seamlessly into existing educational systems.
3) **Long-Term Impact and Sustainability:** Future research should aim to examine the long-term impact and sustainability of AI-based solutions in special education. It is important to assess the effectiveness of these interventions over extended periods, considering factors such as student progress, retention of skills, and transfer of knowledge.
4) **Collaborative Partnerships:** Continued collaboration between AI specialists, educators, researchers, policymakers, and stakeholders is crucial. Future research should explore effective models of collaboration, fostering interdisciplinary partnerships that bridge the gap between research and practice.

By addressing these research areas, we can further enhance the development and implementation of AI-based solutions in special education, ultimately improving educational outcomes for students with special needs.

9.4 Challenges

Despite the promising advancements in AI for special education, several challenges need to be addressed:

1. Scalability and Implementation Challenges: Scaling AI-based solutions for special education presents unique challenges. The successful implementation of AI technologies requires considerations such as infrastructure, technical support, and professional development for educators. Collaborative efforts between researchers, educators, and policymakers are needed to create frameworks that support the seamless integration and adoption of AI in diverse educational contexts (Mohammed, M. et al., 2016).
2. Equity and Access: Ensuring equitable access to AI technologies is paramount. Bridging the digital divide and addressing disparities in access to technology and resources is crucial to ensure that all students, including those from marginalized communities, can benefit from AI-powered educational interventions (Han J. et al., 2011).

3. Customization and Adaptability: Developing AI models and algorithms specific to various special educational needs and diverse student populations is an ongoing challenge. Customizing AI solutions to cater to the unique requirements of different disabilities and learning profiles requires interdisciplinary collaboration and a deep understanding of the complex needs of students with special educational needs.
4. Validation and Evaluation: Validating the effectiveness and impact of AI-based solutions in special education poses challenges. Robust evaluation methodologies and frameworks need to be established to assess the efficacy of AI interventions, considering factors such as student outcomes, engagement, and satisfaction.
5. Ethical and Legal Frameworks: Establishing comprehensive ethical and legal frameworks to govern the use of AI technologies in special education is essential. These frameworks should address concerns related to privacy, data protection, algorithmic accountability, and the responsible use of AI in decision-making processes.

10. CONCLUSION

In conclusion, the integration of AI technologies in special education holds great promise for transforming educational practices and improving outcomes for students with diverse learning needs. By leveraging AI algorithms and models, educators and AI specialists can provide personalized and adaptive support, enhancing student engagement, motivation, and overall learning experiences. AI-based solutions offer the opportunity to address individual learning needs, identify disabilities, and deliver tailored interventions. Through collaboration and careful implementation, educators can harness the power of AI to create inclusive and effective educational environments. The successful integration of AI requires careful planning, infrastructure considerations, and ongoing evaluation. By embracing AI in instructional design and supporting teachers with AI-powered tools, educators can optimize their teaching practices and cater to diverse learning profiles.

Ultimately, the integration of AI in special education has the potential to unlock the full potential of students, fostering improved learning outcomes and empowering them to thrive in their educational journey. By embracing this transformative technology, we can create a more inclusive and effective educational landscape for all learners.

REFERENCES

Ahmed, A., Rehman, K., Shahid, M., & Alrajeh, N. A. (2021). Towards effective design of AI-based educational games for children with disabilities. *Computers & Education*, *170*, 104281.

Bailey, D. B., Bruder, M. B., Hebbeler, K., Carta, J., Defosset, M., Greenwood, C., & Schoenbrodt, L. (2019). Recommended outcomes for families of young children with disabilities. *Journal of Early Intervention*, *41*(1), 53–73.

Baker, R. (2021). *Artificial intelligence in education: Bringing it all together.* . doi:10.1787/f54ea644-en

Baker, R. S. (2008). Better to Be Frustrated than Bored: The Incidence, Persistence, and Impact of Learners' Cognitive-Affective States during Interactions with Three Different Computer-Based Learning Environments. *International Journal of Human-Computer Studies, 66*(4).

Blikstein, P. (2021). Artificial Intelligence in Education: Promises and Pitfalls. Technology. *Knowledge and Learning, 26*(1), 1–5.

Bryant, J. (2020). Advancements in artificial intelligence for special education. *Journal of Special Education Technology, 35*(2), 76–82.

Christie, R., & Klinger, T. (2021). Ethics and artificial intelligence in education: Theories and praxis. In *The International Handbook of Educational Technology* (pp. 1–23). Springer.

Chumchu, P., & Patil, K. (2023). Dataset of cannabis seeds for machine learning applications. *Data in Brief, 47*. doi:10.1016/j.dib.2023.108954

Cook, B. G., & Odom, S. L. (2021). Evidence-based practices and implementation science in special education. *Exceptional Children, 87*(1), 7–24.

Cook, B. G., Tankersley, M., Landrum, T. J., & Kauffman, J. M. (2014). *Methods and strategies for teaching students with mild disabilities: A case-based approach*. Cengage Learning.

Di Nuovo, L., Patel, R. S., McNeil, A. R., & Parlanti, G. (2019). Artificial intelligence in education: Current insights and future perspectives. *Frontiers in Psychology, 10*, 2696.

DiVittorio, A. (2019). Evaluating an Adaptive Language Game System for Children with Language Impairments. In *2019 IEEE Conference on Games (CoG)* (pp. 1-8). IEEE.

Elliott, S. N., & Ryan, J. B. (2021). *Educational assessment for diverse learners*. Routledge.

Fletcher, A., Scherer, R., & Wilder, M. S. (2019). *Artificial intelligence and special education. In Handbook of Special Education Technology Research and Practice*. Routledge.

Fletcher, T. V., Wehmeyer, M. L., Smith, S. J., & Palmer, S. B. (2019). *Promoting self-determination in students with developmental disabilities*. Guilford Press.

Friend, M., & Bursuck, W. D. (2018). *Including students with special needs: A practical guide for classroom teachers*. Pearson.

García-Peñalvo, F. J. (2020). Using Artificial Intelligence for Monitoring and Assessing Students' Learning in Formal and Informal Settings. In Artificial Intelligence in Education (pp. 557-560). Springer.

Giangreco, M. F., Dennis, R. E., Cloninger, C. J., Edelman, S. W., & Schattman, R. (2016). *Supporting students with disabilities in inclusive classrooms: Faculty roles and responsibilities*. Routledge.

Giannakos, I., van de Ven, J. P., Sharma, S., & Wu, H. (2020). *Affective and behavioral computing for human factors in education. In Human-Computer Interaction Series*. Springer.

Hallahan, D. P., Kauffman, J. M., & Pullen, P. C. (2017). *Exceptional learners: An introduction to special education*. Pearson.

Han, J., Pei, J., & Kamber, M. (2011). *Data mining: concepts and techniques*. Elsevier.

He, Y. (2021). AI in Education: A Review and Case Studies in K-12 Education. In *2021 IEEE 21st International Conference on Advanced Learning Technologies (ICALT)* (pp. 79-83). IEEE.

Hlosta, M., Zdrahal, M., & Kocvara, V. (2021). Ethical aspects of learning analytics. *Journal of Learning Analytics*, *8*(2), 26–41.

Ifenthaler, D., & Yau, J. Y. (2019). Opportunities and Challenges for Learning Analytics and Educational Data Mining in Computer-Based Learning Environments. *Journal of Educational Technology & Society*, *22*(1), 1–16.

Johnson, K. (2018). Personalized learning and assistive technology: Creating a synergy. *Technology and Innovation in Education*, *1*(1), 43–49.

Johnson, M., & Thompson, L. (2021). Leveraging artificial intelligence to support data-driven decision-making in special education. *Journal of Special Education Technology*, *36*(4), 275–285.

Jones, S. (2022). Enhancing communication and collaboration in special education through technology. *The Journal of Special Education*, *55*(2), 87–95.

Karimi, N., Sundararajan, R., & Kane, R. (2020). Artificial intelligence in healthcare. *AI Matters*, *6*(4), 18–20.

Kim, J., Lee, H., & Cho, Y. (2022). Learning design to support student-AI collaboration: Perspectives of leading teachers for AI in education. *Education and Information Technologies*, *27*(5), 1–36. doi:10.100710639-021-10831-6

Koedinger, K. R., Woolf, B. P., & Schultz, K. R. (2019). Design principles for intelligent tutoring systems. *Psychological Science*, *20*(5), 1–10.

Lambert, M. C. (2022). Enhancing Artificial Intelligence Education Software through Iterative Design and Development. *Journal of Special Education Technology*, *37*(2), 73–82.

Lee, J., & Heffernan, N. (2018). Developing a Virtual Tutor for Fraction Addition and Subtraction: A Reinforcement Learning Approach. In *2018 IEEE International Conference on Data Mining Workshops (ICDMW)* (pp. 453-460). IEEE.

Li, L. (2018). VR Intervention Program for Children with Autism: Case Study. In *2018 10th International Conference on Virtual Worlds and Games for Serious Applications (VS-Games)* (pp. 1-8). IEEE.

Luckin, R. (2016). *Collaboration in the Digital Age: How Technology Enables Individuals, Teams and Businesses*. Springer.

Mastropieri, C. A., & Scruggs, T. E. (2020a). *The inclusive classroom: Strategies for effective instruction*. Pearson.

Mastropieri, M. A., & Scruggs, T. E. (2020b). *The inclusive classroom: Strategies for effective differentiated instruction*. Pearson.

Mellard, D. F., & Johnson, E. (2020). *Response to intervention for all teachers: A practical guide for special and general educators*. Routledge.

Meshram, V., Choudhary, C., Kale, A., Rajput, J., Meshram, V., & Dhumane, A. (2023). Dry fruit image dataset for machine learning applications. *Data in Brief*. doi:10.1016/j.dib.2023.109325

Meshram, V., & Patil, K. (2022). Border-Square net: A robust multi-grade fruit classification in IoT smart agriculture using feature extraction based Deep Maxout network. *Multimedia Tools and Applications*, *81*(28), 40709–40735. doi:10.100711042-022-12855-7

Meshram, V., & Patil, K. (2022). FruitNet: Indian fruits image dataset with quality for machine learning applications. *Data in Brief*, *40*, 107686. doi:10.1016/j.dib.2021.107686 PMID:34917715

Meshram, V., Patil, K., & Chumchu, P. (2022). Dataset of Indian and Thai banknotes with annotations. *Data in Brief*, *41*, 108007. doi:10.1016/j.dib.2022.108007 PMID:35282177

Meshram, V., Patil, K., Meshram, V., Dhumane, A., Thepade, S., & Hanchate, D. (2022). Smart Low Cost Fruit Picker for Indian Farmers. *2022 6th International Conference On Computing, Communication, Control And Automation*, 1-7. doi: 10.1109/ICCUBEA54992.2022.10010984

Meshram, V., Patil, K., Meshram, V., & Hanchate, D. (2021). Machine learning in agriculture domain: A state-of-art survey. *Artificial Intelligence in the Life Sciences, 1*. doi:10.1016/j.ailsci.2021.100010

Meshram, V., Suryawanshi, Y., Meshram, V., & Patil, K. (2023). Addressing misclassification in deep learning: A Merged Net approach. *Software Impacts*. doi:10.1016/j.simpa.2023.100525

Meshram, Thanomliang, Ruangkan, Chumchu, & Patil. (2020). FruitsGB: Top Indian Fruits with quality. *IEEE Dataport*. . doi:10.21227/gzkn-f379

Meshram, V. A., Patil, K., & Ramteke, S. D. (2021). MNet: A framework to reduce fruit image misclassification. *Ingénierie des Systèmes d'Information*, *26*(2), 159–170. doi:10.18280/isi.260203

Meshram, V. V., Patil, K., Meshram, V. A., & Shu, F. C. (2019, October). An Astute Assistive Device for Mobility and Object Recognition for Visually Impaired People. *IEEE Transactions on Human-Machine Systems*, *49*(5), 449–460. doi:10.1109/THMS.2019.2931745

Meshram, V. V., Patil, K. R., Meshram, V. A., & Bhatlawande, S. (2022). SmartMedBox: A smart medicine box for visually impaired people using IoT and computer vision techniques. *Revue d'Intelligence Artificielle*, *36*(5), 681–688. doi:10.18280/ria.360504

Mohammed, M., Khan, M. B., & Bashier Mohammed, B. E. (2016). *Machine learning: algorithms and applications*. CRC Press.

Mueen Uddin, S. (2021). Applications of Artificial Intelligence in Education: A Review. In *2021 4th International Conference on Information Systems and Computer Networks (ISCON)* (pp. 1-6). IEEE.

Owoc, M., Sawicka, A., & Weichbroth, P. (2021). *Artificial Intelligence Technologies in Education: Benefits*. Challenges and Strategies of Implementation. doi:10.1007/978-3-030-85001-2_4

Patil, K., Jawadwala, Q., & Shu, F. C. (2018, April). Design and Construction of Electronic Aid for Visually Impaired People. *IEEE Transactions on Human-Machine Systems*, *48*(2), 172–182. doi:10.1109/THMS.2018.2799588

Rajkumar, A., Gunasekaran, D., & Ponnambalam, P. (2022). Machine learning-based intelligent tutoring systems: A survey. *Artificial Intelligence Review*, *57*(4), 575–628.

Reshma, Patil, Laad, & Pise. (2022). Dataset of vector mosquito images. *Data in Brief*. doi:, doi:10.1016/j.dib.2022.108573

Rodriguez, M. C., Orellana, N., & Villalba, J. (2019). Technology-supported strategies to improve reading skills in students with learning disabilities. *Assistive Technology*, *31*(3), 142–150.

Romero, C. (2019). A Data Mining Approach to Identify Predictive Patterns in Special Education. In *2019 18th IEEE International Conference On Machine Learning And Applications (ICMLA)* (pp. 1377-1380). IEEE.

Roschelle, J. (2018). Beyond Polar Bears and Snakes: Multimodal Learning Analytics at Scale with DataShop. *International Journal of Artificial Intelligence in Education*, *28*(2), 225–253.

Salend, S. J., & Duhaney, L. M. G. (2017). *Creating inclusive classrooms: Effective, differentiated and reflective practices*. Pearson.

Salvia, J., Ysseldyke, J. E., & Bolt, S. (2020). *Assessment: In special and inclusive education*. Nelson Education.

Sands, D. J., & McBride, S. L. (2015). *Inclusive early childhood education: Development, resources, and practice*. Cengage Learning.

Schneider, J., & Vlachos, M. (2021). Personalization of Deep Learning. In P. Haber, T. Lampoltshammer, M. Mayr, & K. Plankensteiner (Eds.), *Data Science – Analytics and Applications*. Springer Vieweg. doi:10.1007/978-3-658-32182-6_14

Sharma, U., & Desai, I. (2002). *Special education in India: A journey of challenges*. SAGE Publications.

Shute, V. (2019). Learning Engineering: A Practical Guide for Effective Learning Design. In *2019 IEEE Conference on Cognitive and Computational Aspects of Situation Management (CogSIMA)* (pp. 1-8). IEEE.

Smith, S. J. (2019). Enhancing engagement and motivation in special education through technology. *Journal of Special Education Technology*, *34*(3), 149–158.

Smith, T., Johnson, M., & Davis, T. (2020). The impact of assistive technology on academic performance for students with disabilities: A systematic review. *Assistive Technology*, *32*(5), 265–275.

Spaulding, J. A., Paulsen, K. L., & Coppess, K. M. (2022). *Ethics and the use of technology in educational settings. In The Wiley Handbook of Educational Supervision*. Wiley.

Suryawanshi, Y., Patil, K., & Chumchu, P. (2022). VegNet: Dataset of vegetable quality images for machine learning applications. *Data in Brief*, *45*, 108657. doi:10.1016/j.dib.2022.108657 PMID:36426086

Turnbull, A., Turnbull, R., Erwin, E. J., & Soodak, L. C. (2015). *Exceptional lives: Special education in today's schools*. Pearson.

Turnbull, A. P., Turnbull, H. R., Wehmeyer, M. L., & Shogren, K. A. (2017). *Exceptional lives: Special education in today's schools*. Pearson.

Van de Walle, K., Haßler, G., & Van de Ven, J. P. H. (2020). Artificial intelligence in education: Promises and pitfalls. *European Journal of Education*, *55*(3), 357–371.

VanLaarhoven, T., & Williams, L. R. (2017). *Collaborating for student success: A guide for school-based occupational therapy*. Slack.

Wachter-Boettcher, S. (2017). *Technically Wrong: Sexist Apps, Biased Algorithms, and Other Threats of Toxic Tech*. W. W. Norton & Company.

Westling, D. L., & Fox, L. (2015). *Teaching students with severe disabilities*. Pearson.

Chapter 3
Impact of AI-Based Special Education on Educators and Students

Swati Sharma
KIET Group of Institutions, Ghaziabad, India

Vivek Tomar
https://orcid.org/0000-0003-4051-6864
Graphic Era University (Deemed), India

Neha Yadav
KIET Group of Institutions, Ghaziabad, India

Mukul Aggarwal
https://orcid.org/0000-0001-8276-313X
KIET Group of Institutions, Ghaziabad, India

ABSTRACT

Artificial intelligence has the ability to radically change how teachers interact with pupils who have special needs. Although the effects of AI and other technologies have been far-reaching in the private and public sectors, they have also had a major impact on the academic world, making learning easier for students with sensory, motor, cognitive, and other forms of impairments. The application of AI in the classroom has encouraged the development of more accessible and inclusive teaching practices for all pupils. This chapter analyzed how AI has influenced special education in the classroom. The study analyzed (a) AI's impact on SEN education and (b) AI's impact on SEN education through its positive effects on SEN educators. This chapter explores how AI has the potential to enhance the lives, careers, and working environments of educators. It also explores how special education supported by AI could personalize lessons for each student and encourage greater involvement on their behalf.

DOI: 10.4018/979-8-3693-0378-8.ch003

1. EVOLUTION OF AI-POWERED LEARNING: A BACKGROUND IN EDUCATIONAL APPLICATIONS

Given that schools have integrated technology into their systems for decades, the concept of utilizing instructional technology is far from new. While AI has already permeated every other aspect of our lives, from commerce to romance, it has only recently begun to show promise in the classroom (AIBuchanan, 2005). The research and creation of intelligent agents that can analyze their surroundings and take appropriate action to maximize their potential (Russell and Stuart, 2003). There is a broad variety of conceivable forms for AI agents because "intellectual" talents can be implemented in both hardware (such as humanoid robots) and software (e.g., a virtual avatar). You may get software powered by AI to assist you learn anything from a new language to general knowledge. Artificial intelligence (AI) is widely recognized as a valuable topic in the academic world. Those in the training and development business who implement AI solutions early will have a leg up on the competition. For children that struggle academically, the use of AI in the classroom can be a real boon. Due to their singular impairment, these youngsters have a very difficult time mastering even the most fundamental academic concepts. Autistic children exist on the spectrum with respect to their impairments and social abilities. These differences highlight the need to provide each student with an individualized learning experience (Athanasios and Rodi-Elein, 2012). The creation of truly intelligent pedagogical materials and innovative digital tutors will likely take some time.

Considering recent technological developments, the following article discusses five ways in which AI is already affecting the special education industry. A few years later, with the advent of new technologies, the concept of Artificial Intelligence in Education (AIE) emerged as its own academic discipline. Artificial intelligence (AI) proponents claim that using AI in the classroom will lead to better teaching methods and more engaging class discussions. Intelligent tutoring, knowledge representation, natural language processing, autonomous agents, and so on are all common applications of AI in the classroom. It has long been suspected that AI has the potential to enhance education. One group studying AI in schools over the past decade, nevertheless, has zeroed in on the areas of overlap between AI and Special Education (Wu et al., 2006). Numerous proposals for defining special education standards have been made over the past few years, but no consensus has yet emerged among experts in the subject. There is some (Fletcher et al., 2004) overlap between the terms 'learning disability' and 'learning difficulty. For our scoping study, we consulted a wide variety of national and international sources, and we divided the ensuing mountain of literature into more digestible sections using the framework provided by the Special Educational Needs (Code of Practice, second edition, 2001). According to the 2001 SEN Code of practice Needs, 2001, areas of need include communication and interaction, cognition and learning, behavior, and emotional and social development, and sensory and/or physical. The Code of Practice also highlights the fact that not all children will grow and mature at the same rate, and that each child has his or her own set of strengths and weaknesses. Next, we need to understand and model learners and the environments in which they are immersed to design and evaluate technology to improve learning across contexts, topics, and periods (Brodin, 2010). Children with exceptional educational difficulties benefit greatly from AI training interventions because they allow for a balance of student independence and more direct control and mentoring (Lanzilotti and Roselli, 2007). A few of the diagnostic and intervention tools that have been created during the past decade are briefly discussed below in fig 1.

Figure 1. Learning disabilities

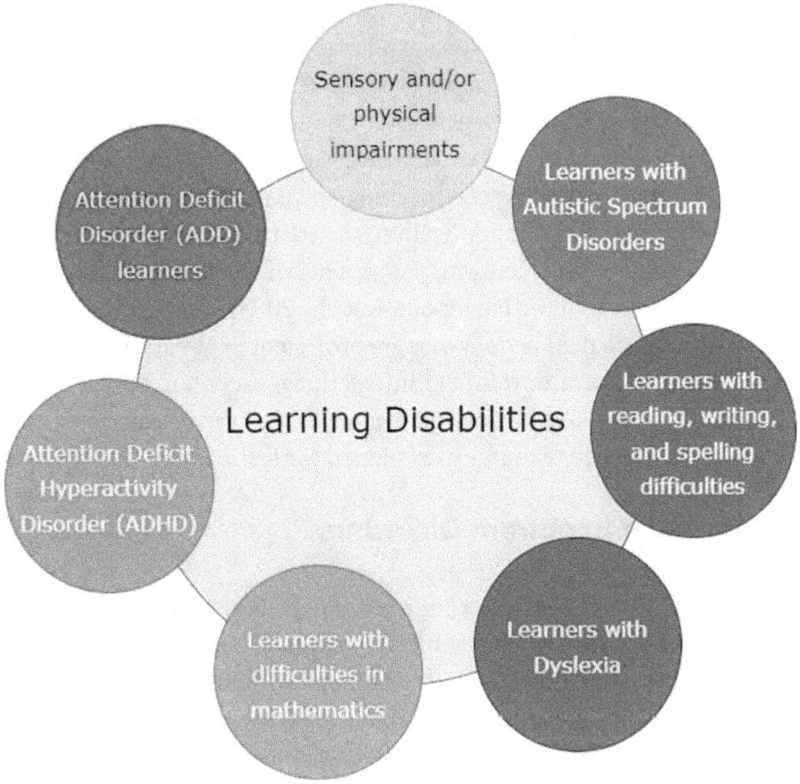

a) Sensory and/or Physical Impairments

To help their students with long-term or more complex physical impairments remain as autonomous and effective as possible, teachers must provide them with the resources they need to do so. Physical and sensory anomalies are typically checked for in newborns by doctors. This is why most AI-based products aimed at parents and teachers tend to concentrate on teaching rather than grading. In 2003, Georgopoulos et al. provided a differential diagnosis of language disability using a fuzzy cognitive map (SLI). Fuzzy cognitive maps are a type of symbolic representation used in soft computing that can be used to describe and simulate complex systems. This tool is meant to assist medical professionals in differentiating SLI from related diseases like dyslexia and autism. The developers of the technology reported successful testing on four clinical cases (Georgopoulos et al., 2003). Students with speech disorders can benefit from the Computer Based Speech Therapy (CBST) system that (Schipor et al., 2003) intended to create using a fuzzy expert system. Using a fuzzy expert system based on forward chaining, we improved upon the original design of the CBST system to create LOGOMON (Logopedics Monitor), whose primary purpose is to recommend the most effective therapeutic interventions for each individual student. The effectiveness of LOGOMON was tested over the course of three months with two groups of children from the Regional Speech Therapy Center in Suceava, Romania. In the first group, the speech therapist utilized LOGOMON without the assistance of the expert system. The second set of patients used an inferentially enhanced version of LOGOMON to assist the speech therapist in making treatment decisions. No statistically significant differences were found in the results between the groups. One of the advantages (Schipor et al., 2010) of using the expert system was that it allowed for more time in therapy, increased predictability, and provided an explanation of the findings. Students' self-evaluation using a neural network model was (Pavlopoulos et al.,2008) implemented and GP-optimized it. The purpose of the procedure is to rate the user's performance on both single- and multiple-choice quizzes administered in a virtual classroom. Grammar/sentence structure; reading/writing; letter recognition and alphabetical order; spelling/vocabulary; and listening/speaking/listening comprehension are the five areas of education that are measured by the application's test data. Accurate evaluation of user responses was achieved through the usage of this platform, and generalizing the evaluation process could lead to the development of an intelligent e-tutor (Pavlopoulos et al., 2008). The 'Dedalos' effort, presented by (Drigas et al.,2008), seeks to teach deaf people who are proficient in Greek sign language to use English as a second language. The process of developing instructional e-content that is suited to the needs of each individual user requires extensive audits and evaluations of the e-learners' language ability. The strategy makes use of an intelligence taxonomy developed for testing and individualizing instruction.

b) Learners With Autistic Spectrum Disorders

ASD is a developmental disability that affects a large percentage of the population, and it is characterized by the 'triad' of impairments. Autistic children exhibit rigid interests and behaviors, and they have trouble interacting with others and understanding language (Rapin and Tuchman, 2008). AI allows professionals to rapidly diagnose a person's autism spectrum disorder severity and start them on the most effective treatment possible. In 2006, Sebe et al. developed an algorithm for automatic emotion recognition based on a combination of visual and aural cues. In addition to the standard six emotions (thrilled, astonished, furious, disgusted, afraid, and sad), this HCI instrument can pick up on more feelings including intrigue, boredom, bewilderment, and aggravation. Although it is beneficial for teaching all children, it has shown exceptional success for dealing with people on the autistic spectrum This technique analyses 38 people's feelings across 11 different states using Bayesian Networks for bimodal fusion. Another indicator that the user is talking is present in a Bayesian Network. Once the model is in place, it can record head motion and detect local deformations of facial features like the eyebrows, eyelids, and mouth. Thirty-eight undergraduates and graduates from various majors were used in the system's initial testing. The results demonstrated that emotion identification accuracy was much improved by combining visual and aural information in categorization (Sebe et al., 2006) (Riedl et al., 2007) built a platform for adolescents with High Functioning Autistic Spectrum Disorders (HFASD) to use in the development and practice of social skills. Students with HFASD are provided with role-playing opportunities in a simulated setting, such as a movie theatre, to hone their social skills. The networks employ AI to make it easier to set up unique social structures for each user. An AI system examines the causal form of the narrative plan automatically, searching for points at which a student's actions can alter the story's progression. The fork in the narrative was designed to accommodate the learner's actions as a contingency. This platform's incorporation of an AI tool eliminates the requirement for human authoring, allowing specialists more time to implement intervention strategies. This social intervention technique is complete and being tested; early results are promising (Riedl et al., 2007). Arthi and Tamilarasi (2008) presented a model that helps in the diagnosis of autism in children using Artificial Neural Networks (ANN) technology. The original autism data is transformed into suitable fuzzy membership values by the model before being fed into the neural network design. In addition, a pseudo method employing the back propagation mechanism for predicting autism is created. The fields of medicine, psychology, and special education stand to gain the most from this approach. The experimental results demonstrated that the method achieved an accuracy of 85% to 90%. The Future use of the k-nearest neighbor technique based on comparative studies to predict autism is possible (Arthi and Tamilarasi, 2008).

c) Learners With Reading, Writing, and Spelling Difficulties

In any given classroom, you will find pupils whose reading, writing, and spelling abilities span a wide spectrum. Each pupil has different strengths and weaknesses, and therefore requires tailored instruction. These problems are usually uncovered throughout a child's school years. Since learning disability specialists are not always on hand, it is ideal for general education instructors to have access to diagnostic and intervention materials. To automatically grade short essays on reading comprehension tests, Srihari et al. developed two computer techniques (2008). The method's stated objective is to assign a score to each essay submission that is generally in line with how a person would rate it. In addition to the difficulties inherent in handwriting recognition, this software must also account for the varying levels of skill among young typists. The results of reading comprehension tests are useful not only for pupils, but also for teachers, parents, and policymakers. There are two sorts of systems discussed in this study. The first makes use of latent semantic analysis (LSA), which is only useful if your handwriting recognition skills are up to par. The second method employed an artificial neural network trained with features taken from the handwritten image (ANN). Both systems were trained and evaluated using essays that students wrote in response to questions on statewide reading comprehension examinations. Mistakes in word recognition were discovered while examining the scoring performance of this platform (Srihari et al., 2008), but it still has potential. In 2009, Jain et al. proposed a model called the Perceptron-based Learning Disability Detector (PLEDDOR). It's an artificial neural network model created to aid in the identification of dyslexia, dysgraphia, and dyscalculia on standardized tests taken by students in need of special education. This computational diagnostic tool consists of an input layer with eleven units (each representing a different portion of a conventional test) and an output layer with one unit (the result of the test). 240 students from Indian schools were used to test the method. Hospitals, with results equivalent to those of current detection methods (Jain et al., 2009), was shown to be simple and reproducible on a wide scale. (Herna'ndez et al., 2009) developed SEDA ('Sistema Experto de Dificultades para el Aprendizaje'; "Expert System for Learning Difficulties" in English) to aid in the diagnosis of Learning Difficulties in young students. This information provides those utilizing the expert system with a better chance of identifying the student's psychological profile. Eighty percent of raters ranked the system as "Efficient" on a scale from "Poor" (0% efficiency) to "Moderately Efficient" (25% efficiency) to "Efficient" (80% efficiency) (Hernandez et al., 2009). In 2010, Baschera and Gross presented an adaptive spelling curriculum. Any student who needs help with spelling can use it. An inference method that can deal with unclassified data with several types of errors as determined by their own faulty rules is the backbone of this system. A Poisson regression-based inference technique uses the student's past error behavior to foresee future difficulties with each individual mal-rule. This knowledge representation has been implemented in a student model for spelling instruction in a variety of methods, including optimized word selection, lessons for individual mal-rules, and pupil-adjusted repetition of incorrectly written words. Two large-scale user evaluations of this system (Baschera and Gross, 2010) indicated that training sessions that could be tailored for individual students considerably improved learning outcomes.

d) Learners With Dyslexia

Because of its prevalence among people of all ages, dyslexia are one of the most researched developmental disorders that impair literacy. Neurodegenerative diseases like this one affect a person for their entire lives (Thomson and Gilchrist, 1997). Diagnosing dyslexia is a complex procedure requiring various forms of evidence. Despite this, the preliminary findings of recent investigations are encouraging and provide new opportunities for diagnosis. It might be a challenging process to identify dyslexia using AI methods. A rule-based classifier was reported in the same year by Palacios et al., who used genetic fuzzy systems to analyses low-quality data from early development. It can be used by both parents and educators to pinpoint concerns that warrant further assessment by a trained professional. Despite working with poor-quality data, the FRBS was able to provide a diagnosis in experiments. However, a sizable fraction of labels was wrong, therefore future research is warranted (Palacios et al., 2009) (Palacios et al., 2010). In 2010, Kohli et al. demonstrated a systematic approach to identifying dyslexia in young children using ANNs (ANN). This technique is one of the earliest applications of ANN to the problems of dyslexia diagnosis. It also differentiates itself from other platforms because it was built using data from tests administered to pupils suspected of having dyslexia between 2003 and 2007. The algorithm takes in students' test data and bases on the results, classifies them as either dyslexic or not. An error back-propagation method is responsible for determining which characteristics are correlated with academic achievement. It appears that this platform can be used to analyses real data as well, as early results on test data were reasonably accurate (Kohli and Prasad, 2010).

e) Learners With Difficulties in Mathematics

Many pupils have difficulty with mathematics despite its importance. Mathematical competency testing and education (Abbott, 2006) are now possible thanks to AI-based technologies and approaches. Active Math, developed by Melis et al., is an online intelligent tutoring system for math (2001). Students have the flexibility to learn at their own pace using Active Math, and ITS (Intelligence Tutoring System). It makes use of several AI methods to facilitate semantic Web–compatible knowledge representation, adaptive course building, student modelling, feedback, and interactive activities. In Active Math, the user generates a unique student model by first taking a self-assessment to determine where they are in terms of subject knowledge, before choosing learning objectives and a scenario, like studying for an exam. Each student's course recommendations and course generation are tailored to their own strengths and weaknesses. On top of that, we make a "poor man's eye-tracker" that can monitor a child's concentration and reading time with great precision. Numerous post-release research articles (citationsMelis et al., 2001) (Melis and Siekmann, 2004). Libbrecht and Melis, 2006 attest to the software's efficacy as an ITS in educational settings. Livne et al. (2007) created an online parser system that automatically evaluates students'-built solutions to mathematical questions by scoring the solutions based on the number and type of errors contained in the solutions. The free math website built on a parser is aimed at helping high school students get ready for college. During training sessions, users are asked to solve mathematical problems and provide their own explanations. Anthony et al. (2008) created an Intelligent Tutoring System to aid students in their understanding of algebraic equation solving (ITS). Algebra is notoriously difficult, and many students struggle to master it. This system's goal is to improve educational outcomes through the widespread adoption of handwriting capable ITSs Expert instructors of the cognitive variety. ITS used in this method gives pupils a taste of the actual world while emphasizing the value of practical application. In Cognitive Tutor Algebra, students work with a tutor to use models, draw functions, and solve equations. More than 40 high school and middle school algebra students were used to train a recognizer for the Freehand Formula Entry System. Results showed an improvement in both usability and understanding. This framework can also be used with a variety of mathematical areas and student skill levels (Anthony et al., 2008). To help teachers provide appropriate feedback to pupils, Gonzalez et al. (2010) created a computerized system to do so. This method is useful for all kids, but it's especially helpful for those who struggle with math fundamentals due to a learning disability or other condition, like Down syndrome. They also developed a methodology that includes a list of student errors with their revised work to facilitate reflective learning. Students with Down syndrome tested the system, and their results confirmed the module's predicted behavior (Gonzalez et al., 2010).

f) Attention Deficit Hyperactivity Disorder (ADHD) and Attention Deficit Disorder (ADD) Learners

Attention deficit hyperactivity disorder (ADHD) or attention deficit disorder (ADD) are conditions that can manifest in a kid throughout their formative years (ADD). Inattention, hyperactivity, and impulsivity are just some of the common behavioral problems they display. Since these problems generally appear in early childhood, it is advised that a diagnosis be made before the age of seven mondiale de la santé, (Organization, et al., 1993)(American Psychiatric Association, Association, et al., 2013). Better diagnostic and intervention tools for a wide range of behavioral disorders have resulted from the use of AI technologies. Performance data and user-generated data from the NeuroSky platform were combined in 2004 by Rebolledo-Mendez and Freitas to create the NeuroSky MindSet (MS) interaction, in order to gauge interest during a test.

NeuroSky uses three electrodes, which are inserted on the scalp, in front of the ears, and in the temples. The amount of attention is determined by the algorithms in NeuroSky, which take the electrical impulses read from specific places as inputs. In addition, a limited-interaction avatar powered by AI was created to pose questions to and get answers from users. It's not required for treatment, it's easy to use, and it doesn't cost much. A favorable association between scientifically measured and subjectively perceived attention was found in subsequent years when this model was applied to first-year college students (Rebolledo-Mendez and De Freitas, 2008). Aguilar et al. (2006) created a fuzzy instructional planner to model the tutoring phase of an ITB (ITS). It is "an interactive teaching style that blends text, graphics, sound, and video into the learning process," as defined by Athanasios S. Drigas and Rodi-Eleni Ioannidou. Both in-person and online students, especially those who struggle with attention, would benefit significantly from this. The fuzzy instructional planner consists of a rule base, inference, fuzzification interface, and defuzzification interface. To achieve its educational goals, this system should mimic the actions of a skilled teacher. An individual human expert supplied the language data used in the input. Several implementations have shown the ITS to be useful, with encouraging outcomes. It's a versatile framework that lets teachers modify expectations in response to individual students' progress. (Anuradha et al., 2010) found a way to diagnose attention deficit hyperactivity disorder better accurately and rapidly. (ADHD). A common AI technique, the SVM algorithm, was used. The authors state that this is the initial use of the SVM algorithm to the ADHD diagnostic process. Support vector machines (SVMs) are useful in both classification and regression problems within the field of supervised learning. To train the SVM component, doctors' questionnaire results and verified medical records were used to create a dataset. After it was finished, we used the SVM module to analyze the dataset. The main advantage of the

SVM method is that it can lessen the likelihood of an unduly convoluted diagnosis. This approach was tested on kids between the ages of 6 and 11, and it was shown to have an 88 percent diagnostic accuracy (Anuradha et al., 2010) (Delavarian et al., 2010) introduced a decision support system to assist medical professionals in distinguishing between ADHD and other related behavioral issues in children, such as depression, anxiety, co-occurring depression and anxiety, and conduct disorder. Distinguishing between the behavioral disorders is both vital and difficult because of the overlap and similarity of symptoms. This tool was created to help psychiatrists, but it can also be used by educators to identify and evaluate potentially troubled children. We looked at RBF and MLP neural networks to see if they would work for the decision support system's construction. The algorithm was trained and verified to aid in the diagnosis of various illnesses. A total of 294 students from 12 different elementary schools participated in the study. When compared to the RBF classifier, whose accuracy reached 96.62 percent, MLP networks' classification accuracy was just 95.50 percent. Specialists make fewer mistakes in diagnosing ADHD when using a system that has been shown to be reliable and valid (Delavarian et al., 2012).

2. NEED OF AI BASED SPECIAL EDUCATION

As technology has progressed, computing power has seeped into ever more areas of contemporary life. There is a growing effort to incorporate technology into the classroom widely accessible. Extensive research is being conducted on the utilization of computers in education, aiming to create learning environments that enhance the learning process across diverse settings (Nanni and Lumini, 2009). Educators have been a focus of study for researchers and computer scientists for numerous years. Technology such as the Internet of Things (IoT), artificial intelligence (AI), machine learning (ML), augmented reality (AR), virtual reality (VR), etc., is changing the nature of employment and making it more difficult for companies to make reasonable accommodations for people with disabilities. In many of the Asia and Pacific region's developing countries, people with disabilities face severe discrimination in all aspects of life, including access to education, employment, and development initiatives. Evidence from the WHO (Laabidi et al., 2013) suggests that more than a billion individuals on the planet are impaired in some way or the other. Low-income individuals often face significant challenges within various societal systems, including the healthcare system, schools, and job markets. These systems often fail to adequately address the needs and provide equal opportunities for individuals with limited financial resources (Garg and Sharma, 2020). As a result, many persons with disabilities are unable to gain the knowledge and skills necessary to live independently and with purpose. According to the World Health Organization (WHO), over a billion individuals worldwide could potentially benefit from utilizing assistive technology. Assistive technology encompasses a wide range of devices, tools, and technologies designed to support and enhance the independence, inclusion, and overall well-being of people with disabilities or functional limitations. The availability of innovative technologies benefits both individuals with and without disabilities. Advancements in technology have allowed companies like Microsoft to develop educational tools that have proven beneficial for children with dyslexia. This progress has further popularized the use of machine learning and artificial intelligence in educational settings. Consequently, the utilization of creative-minded technologies has the potential to enhance learning experiences for diverse populations. Scientists have developed AI technology to perform complex computations with the help of digital devices to make human life easier. Recent developments in AI have the potential to usher in a new era of educational opportunities, which may be especially beneficial to those with disabilities. There is a lot of active research on using AI in the classroom to create learning environments that aid the learning process in different settings (Nanni and Lumini, 2009). Intelligent simulation can significantly enhance the learning outcomes of students requiring extra support in school. Consider adaptive learning systems, which tailor the course's difficulty and content to each student's unique strengths and weaknesses in order to improve their learning experience through the application of artificial intelligence. Improved communication and interaction are just two of the many ways in which AI can be used to benefit students in special education, and two examples are text-to-speech and speech-to-text systems. Data on a child's academic achievement, behaviour, and other aspects can be analysed by AI to determine if he or she would benefit from special education programmes. However, care must be taken when implementing AI in this setting to ensure that individual student requirements and strengths are considered. Also, it's important to remember that AI algorithms are just one of many tools that can be used to identify which children could benefit from supplementary educational services. There are several ways in which artificial intelligence (AI) might help these pupils, including assessment, material descriptions, and online interactions. For instance, we can use state-of-the-art voice synthesis techniques based on machine learning models to better serve students with disabilities who use assistive devices. For pupils that learn better visually, "seeing" AI could read aloud the page's headlines, for instance. This is just one way that AI-based solutions might help students who are visually impaired to interact with course materials. Artificial intelligence (AI) is a method of solving problems that has led to the creation of computational tools for a wide range of applications. When it comes to identifying problems and developing solutions for students with special education needs, AI is one of the most promising tools. Artificial intelligence's primary objective is to improve children's engagement with their surroundings in order to facilitate learning and improve the quality of their daily lives. Microsoft has created a program called AI for Accessibility to help those with disabilities. Knowledge bases, computer vision, expert systems, ML, DL, and natural language are all part of AI. AI eye aid from Google means doctors can check for diabetic retinopathy using a retinal scan and measuring its severity. Robot instructors equipped with artificial intelligence are now commonplace in classrooms. Students benefit greatly from the opportunity to have human-like computing abilities including image recognition, audio perception, decision making, and translation. However, they can supplement classroom instruction by working in tandem with human educators (hybrid approach). This allows for a more personalised and specialised approach to education.

Artificial intelligence methods have been progressively employed to enhance the lives of people with special needs, who face a wide range of challenges related to learning, cognition, communication, behaviour, emotion, sensory, and physical development. The 2001 SEN Code of Practice emphasizes the recognition that children develop at different rates and possess unique capabilities and needs, highlighting the importance of understanding the specific cultural contexts for deploying artificial intelligence (AI) while acknowledging AI's role in fostering collaborative interactive learning environments. Innovations enabled by AI are opening up new doors for people of all linguistic backgrounds and skill levels. Support for young people's mental health is also available through AI-powered text messaging platforms. Artificial intelligence (AI) tools in the classroom help level the playing field for children with learning challenges. Artificial intelligence (AI) provides valuable assistance for e-learning and teaching in many ways, such as student-specific education and adaptive testing. Supporting, assisting, and augmenting the teaching experts is possible with the use of robotics and AI. Students with disabilities can learn to work around their impairments with the help of appropriate assistive technology. The use of this customized technology encourages autonomy and lessens the necessity of supplementary aid. Artificial intelligence aids educators in identifying students who may have learning challenges and providing early intervention.

The ability of AI tools and inventories to integrate the demands of children with special needs makes them an integral element of the educational process. AI is increasingly employed by educators and parents to provide instruction rather than assessment, resulting in a balance between tighter supervision and direction while promoting student autonomy. The objective of this chapter is to examine the impact of AI-based special education on educators and students. The chapter will explore how the integration of artificial intelligence (AI) technologies in special education settings can enhance learning outcomes, improve instructional practices, and support the diverse needs of students with disabilities. Additionally, it will discuss the potential challenges and ethical considerations associated with the use of AI in special education, as well as the role of educators in facilitating its effective implementation.

3. AI TOOLS FOR SPECIAL EDUCATION

Students with Individualized Education Plans (IEPs) benefit from the use of artificial intelligence tools for special education. Over the past few decades, there has been tremendous progress in the study and application of evidence-based techniques in the field of special education. The availability of AI tools to aid the growth of children in special education has been one of the most exciting breakthroughs in recent years. The state of the art in AI tools is improving rapidly. They have several resources available to help those working in special education help their pupils thrive. As a result, educators have more resources at their disposal to innovate their methods of teaching, increase student participation and learning, and make education more accessible to all learners. AI can help special-needs children in many ways educationally. In the classroom, I can imagine it boosting confidence and motivating good behavior. Learners may get the help they need with reading, writing, and speaking thanks to artificial intelligence programs like Readability, Grammarly, and Dragon Naturally Speaking. These resources can help students improve their understanding by correcting their mistakes and offering feedback. In addition, AI systems like Google Classroom can be utilized to tailor instruction to the unique needs of kids in special education settings. This aid will make it easier for students in special education to get into and master the course material. This promotes a setting where all students feel safe and valued. Students' needs can be catered to with these resources. Artificial intelligence can be used to monitor development and help in both academic and social-emotional competencies. Artificial intelligence systems can also help students simplify difficult concepts into more manageable pieces. In addition, AI systems can provide students with immediate feedback while they work to keep them engaged and on task. The most widely used videoconferencing platform for remote postsecondary instruction (Aratani) — Zoom — has just added AI-based live captioning. The same can be said of Microsoft Teams, one of its main rivals. Students with and without disabilities use many of the same apps, however those with disabilities, such as those with vision impairments, have access to specialized AI-based mobile apps (i.e., Seeing AI, Microsoft Lens). Unfortunately, sophisticated virtual assistants—the kind you may find on your phone, tablet, or even a dedicated device—don't seem to be living up to their promise. Accessibility-focused artificial intelligence (AI) is increasingly being built into mainstream technologies, eliminating the need for many costly aids for the disabled. ROYBI Robot is a specialized AI robot that can efficiently aid a youngster who is experiencing a speech delay. Children on the autism spectrum and those with Down syndrome can also benefit from ROYBI's individualized approach to schooling. Autistic children often struggle with both verbal and nonverbal means of expression. This means that AI robots can be created and trained to help autistic children. The key motivation behind assigning AI-based tools to aid in education is to guarantee a hassle-free learning atmosphere. With the use of AI, educators may assess a student's focus, attention span, language and hearing skills and provide instruction accordingly.

The importance of tools for special needs education cannot be overstated. These tools play a crucial role in supporting students with disabilities and learning differences, enabling them to access educational content, participate actively in the learning process, and reach their full potential. Here are a few examples of tools that are used in special needs education, each of which has its own set of traits and features designed to solve difficulties that people with special needs encounter.

1. **Proloquo2Go**: It is an augmentative and alternative communication (AAC) tool made for those who have trouble communicating. It aids people who have speech or language difficulties as well as those who have Down syndrome, autism, or cerebral palsy. Its features include straightforward and customised symbol-based communication that enables users to express themselves through text, photos, and icons. Word prediction, message history, and voice output features are also available in Proloquo2Go.
2. **Read &Write**: It is a literacy support programme that helps people with dyslexia, learning disabilities, and other writing and reading difficulties. It has text-to-speech capabilities that highlight text as it is spoken, improving understanding. Along with these capabilities, Read &Write provides study aids including voice notes and highlighters, a talking dictionary, speech-to-text, and word prediction.
3. **Co-author:** It is a writing aid created for those who have spelling and writing issues, including dyslexia or dysgraphia. It makes use of word prediction technologies to help users create grammatically sound sentences. For more precise and effective written expression, It provides real-time suggestions, vocabulary aid, and speech recognition capabilities.
4. **Mathway**: It is a complete math problem-solving tool appropriate for those who struggle with arithmetic or who need extra assistance in the subject. It offers step-by-step answers to several math issues from a range of subjects, including algebra, calculus, and statistics. Users can enter their maths issues on Mathway and instantly obtain explanations and solutions, which helps them comprehend the process of problem-solving.
5. **Notability**: It is a note-taking app that can be especially helpful for students with attention deficit disorders or organisational issues. It has several features, including the ability to take typed or handwritten notes, record audio, annotate, and sync information between devices. Users of Notability may efficiently organise and search their notes, which facilitates review and study.
6. **Snap &Read:** It is a text-to-speech and reading support programme created to help people who have reading difficulties, such as dyslexia and visual impairments. Its users can have text from a variety of digital sources, such as webpages, documents, and ebooks, read aloud to them. To improve reading comprehension, Snap & Read also has tools like text highlighting, translation, and user-customizable reading preferences.

4. IMPACT OF AI-BASED SPECIAL EDUCATION ON EDUCATORS

One of a teacher's primary responsibilities is to transfer knowledge to students in accordance with predetermined and vetted lesson plans. Teachers use a variety of methods to pass on information. Pedagogical approaches, such as working with students individually, in small groups, or even as a whole class, with or without the use of simple or complicated teaching aids, as appropriate for the material being covered and the students being instructed. A variety of Assistive Technologies (ATs), including AI, have been successfully implemented for children with learning disabilities. Accessible technology (AT) is useful in helping students with disabilities achieve academic and employment independence, engage in classroom debates and discussions, build relationships with peers, role models, and teachers, advocate for themselves, make the most of available educational opportunities, live and learn with minimal assistance, work and perform alongside peers, and succeed in academic and employment settings. Artificial intelligence (AI) aids in the development of high-quality courses, efficient study plans, applicable educational content, and online profiles that may be used to pair students with individual instructors (Burgstahler, 2003). As a result, it can increase efficiency in the classroom and beyond, and most importantly, such portfolios presented classes and courses can be of tremendous use to employers. According to research by Chassignola M. et al.(Chassignol et al., 2018), AI is already being employed in a wide variety of classroom settings, including but not limited to: content creation; teaching approaches; student evaluation; and teacher-student communication (2018). Recent developments in AI and Special Education hold promise for facilitating the development of interactive, collaborative spaces that can enhance the lives of people with and without impairments. In this chapter, we'll look at some of the most compelling real-world applications of AI to date. AI is already being used in some pedagogical materials and standardized testing systems in schools. As AI solutions for education advance, it is hoped that they may eventually aid in reducing the achievement gap by making it possible for students, schools, and educators to accomplish more than ever before. AI has the potential to improve productivity, individualize learning, and streamline administration so that teachers can devote more time to conceptualization and adaptability fail today in its intended purpose. Robots and humans working together to provide the finest education for children is the ideal future for artificial intelligence in education. Teachers must include AI in their lessons because today's students will soon be entering a career that relies heavily on technology.

a) Differentiated and Individualized Learning

Class sizes of 30 students per teacher make it nearly impossible to provide students with individualized instruction, despite widespread recognition of the need to do so. Intelligent instruction design and digital platforms using AI to give learning, testing, and feedback to students from kindergarten through college are currently being developed by several firms, including Content Technologies and Carnegie Learning. Students will be given appropriately difficult tasks, knowledge gaps will be identified, and students will be redirected to other topics as necessary thanks to these tools. Artificial intelligence (AI) is progressing to the point that it may soon be possible for a computer to understand when a student is struggling with a particular idea and alter the lesson accordingly. Although personalizing instruction for each student is not yet feasible, it will be in the future with AI-enabled robots.

b) Universal Access for All Students

With the help of AI, classrooms around the world can be made accessible to students of all linguistic and sensory abilities. Presentation Translator is a free PowerPoint add-on that instantly converts the presenter's voice into subtitles. Those who are ill and unable to attend class or those who need specialized training in a field not taught at their school could also benefit from this. Traditional barriers between grade levels can be eliminated with the use of AI.

c) Automate Admin Tasks

Paper and test grading might consume a significant portion of a teacher's time each week. Artificial intelligence (AI) can step in and speed up these processes while also providing guidance on how to fill in any gaps in knowledge. The potential for machines to analyses essay responses is close at hand, although they can only evaluate right answers on multiple-choice exams now essay purposes. Teachers will have more time for individual students as AI takes over administrative tasks. The use of AI has the potential to significantly improve the enrollment and admissions processes.

d) Tutoring and Support Outside the Classroom

Any parent who has struggled to help their adolescent grasp algebra at home would be overjoyed at the possibility of utilizing AI to guide their child through the process. As AI advances, tutoring and studying programs become more user-friendly and flexible enough to accommodate students with a wide range of needs and preferences. Many more AI applications for education are in the works, including smart materials and virtual international conferences as a form of professional development for instructors.

5. IMPACT OF AI-BASED SPECIAL EDUCATION ON STUDENTS

The Convention on the Protection of the Rights of All Persons Regarding Education and the Economic, Social, and Cultural Rights (1989) and the Convention on the Rights of the Child (1966). However, this right is only guaranteed by the constitutions of a few countries. Therefore, it is evident that disabled people frequently lack the necessary support. The right to an education and the opportunity to learn is sometimes denied to children with disabilities because of a lack of accessible learning resources in traditional classroom settings. Disabled students face many obstacles in their pursuit of an education, including a lack of awareness of their needs, insufficient classroom help, and a paucity of appropriately educated teachers. The first step in ensuring that children with disabilities are supported throughout their educational endeavors is making the system and its regulations accessible to them. Technology has become an intrinsic part of modern society, with its influence permeating nearly every aspect of daily life. Artificial intelligence is one of the most sought-after features of today's technological landscape (AI). Technology and AI advancements have undoubtedly enhanced data availability. The introduction of artificial intelligence. If we can get kids with special needs into a regular classroom, their education will improve. Robots that have been trained in a particular way may be able to teach children with attention deficit hyperactivity disorder (ADHD), speech and hearing impairments, and down syndrome important social and academic skills. According to the CDC, one in every 44 children has been diagnosed with autism, making it an important matter to address the needs of those on the spectrum. The purpose of using technology in the classroom is to facilitate better communication between students and teachers. "An acclaimed approach to education since it allows for customization, specialization, and ongoing development. Those in business that accept the AI challenge early will have an advantage over their academic counterparts "A study is suggested. There is no one correct way to teach or learn. Every child has individual necessities. Let's look at how artificial intelligence can aid kids who use wheelchairs in particular:

a.) **AI can detect early disability:** Recognizing the existence of a problem is the initial step in developing a solution. Smart algorithms can pinpoint students who are having difficulty in the classroom. Young people who are sluggish to grasp concepts or who show little enthusiasm in academics may have a learning disability that teachers miss. Two types of AI, artificial neural networks and cognitive maps have already been used effectively in the diagnosis of autism, apraxia of speech, and dyslexia.

b.) **AI-based tools to aid learning:** Children with special needs should have easy access to cutting-edge educational materials. Incredible progress has been made in this field. Some parents have said that they were able to help their child's speech delay by using the ROYBI Robot. ROYBI's specialized education program is helpful for kids on the autistic spectrum and those with Down syndrome, too. Some children on the autism spectrum have difficulty communicating both verbally and nonverbally. This opens the door to developing and programming AI robots to aid autistic children. Assigning AI-based technologies to aid in education is primarily motivated by a desire to provide a smooth educational experience atmosphere. Artificial intelligence can evaluate a child's concentration, attention span, and language and hearing skills to tailor lessons to everyone's needs.

c.) **AI and adaptive learning:** Students can adjust their study methods to meet the requirements of each course by using AI-based adaptive learning tactics. Adaptive learning uses artificial intelligence to provide training on a wide variety of topics via video conversations with individual mentors and tutors in real-world, online, and hybrid contexts. It can adapt lessons to the strengths and weaknesses of individual students. Assisting teachers in making the necessary but sometimes overlooked adjustments to the curriculum to better accommodate students with impatience and hyperactivity.

d.) **Reliable feedback through AI:** AI-based solutions in education allow students to learn at their own pace while still receiving helpful feedback by delaying progression to the next topic until mastery has been established. The challenge of giving students with disabilities timely feedback in a regular classroom setting is one that can be overcome with the use of artificial intelligence (AI). Personalized learning for each student. First and foremost, thanks to the personalized and engaging nature of AI-powered educational apps, kids can learn at their own pace. Clearly, the tried-and-true, one-size-fits-all approach does not work for students who are part of the special education population. They feel better about themselves because they aren't comparing themselves to their peers on the app. They don't have to adhere to the strict schedules of conventional schools and can instead study whenever it's convenient for them. Enhancing Concentration Time When it comes to artificial intelligence (AI) in the classroom, several studies have shown that children benefit more from technological education than from traditional schooling alone. This is since these apps collect children's focus and maintain it for longer stretches of time. Because their attention span is often only 5-10 minutes, children with specific difficulties benefit most from using AI as a supplement to traditional teaching. Differences in Appearance and Form AI can aid disabled students in reaching their full potential by adapting teachings to each student's individual strengths and shortcomings.

6. CASE STUDY

This case study investigates the effects of AI-based special education on teachers and pupils in a primary school environment in real time. AI technology adoption aims to support individualized learning and advance inclusive learning settings for kids with exceptional needs. The study evaluates the advantages and difficulties that educators and students encounter while utilizing AI-based tools and emphasizes the overall impact on the educational process. Context: The special education program at public school ABC Elementary School now incorporates AI technologies. The school supports a wide range of learners, including those with developmental disorders and a variety of learning difficulties. Adaptive learning platforms, speech recognition software, and customized virtual tutors are some of the AI-based solutions used. These resources seek to cater to individual student needs, increase engagement, and deliver individualized learning experiences. The case study used a mixed-methods approach, combining quantitative data from surveys and academic performance measurements with qualitative data from interviews and observations. Special education instructors, parents, and students with special needs were all there. Six months of data collecting allowed for a thorough evaluation of the effects of special education based on AI.

Findings:

1. Better Individualized training: According to educators, AI-based solutions enable better individualized and customized training to fit each student's particular needs. Effectively addressing individual learning gaps was made possible for instructors by adaptive learning platforms that offered tailored interventions and quick feedback.
2. Increased Student Engagement: When using AI-based technologies, students reported feeling more motivated and involved. The interactive and gamified features of the platforms made learning more fun by promoting sustained attention and active involvement.
3. Support for a Variety of Learning Styles: AI technology provides a variety of material delivery modes, including haptic, aural, and visual components. This made it possible for pupils with various learning preferences and skills to obtain the knowledge in ways that worked best for them.
4. Time Efficiency for Educators: AI tools streamlined administrative tasks, such as progress tracking, assessment, and lesson planning, saving educators valuable time. This allowed them to allocate more time for individualized instruction and fostering positive teacher-student relationships.
5. Increased Collaboration and Communication: AI platforms facilitated seamless communication between educators, parents, and students. Progress reports, personalized recommendations, and real-time updates were easily shared, enhancing collaboration and ensuring that all stakeholders remained informed about students' educational journeys.

7. CRITICAL ANALYSIS

This chapter "Impact of AI-Based Special Education on Educators and Students" navigates the dynamic terrain of AI's influence on special education. It commences by tracing the historical evolution of AI in education, particularly its application for diverse learners. This contextual background prepares the ground for a deeper exploration of the chapter's core aspects.

The imperative for AI-based special education is established, emphasizing the necessity to tailor learning experiences for individual needs. This segues into an exposition of AI tools designed for special education, ranging from adaptive platforms to speech recognition software.

Notably, the chapter dissects the ramifications of AI on educators. It underscores AI's capacity to facilitate personalized learning, universal accessibility, administrative streamlining, and extended tutoring. These insights culminate in a nuanced portrayal of AI's potential to empower educators.

Simultaneously, the chapter investigates AI's impact on students through a case study. By integrating quantitative and qualitative data, it unveils AI's role in fostering engagement and academic progress. The real-world context provided enhances the chapter's authenticity and practical relevance.

Conclusively, the chapter substantiates AI's transformative role in the special education landscape. It adroitly melds historical perspective, theoretical foundation, and empirical case study, accentuating the pivotal role of AI in reshaping special education for educators and students alike.

8. CONCLUSION AND FUTURE DIRECTION

The application of AI to the field of special education has broadened the range of choices available to both parents and teachers. Experts in the field of data science can now look through student records in search of red flags. Several studies on this topic have found promising findings. We can provide these children more freedom to learn at their own pace and in their own way by employing AI-based methods. There are two goals that can be achieved using AI to the subject of special education.

- Artificial intelligence (AI)-driven methods are used to diagnose disabilities.
- Artificial intelligence (AI) based learning tools and methods are being adopted.

This section presents evidence demonstrating the widespread impact of AI technology and its positive effects on children with special needs. In the education sector, there is a growing focus on promoting inclusive education using AI-powered assistive technology, which can replace human labor and reduce prejudice in classrooms.

The chapter advocates for inclusive teaching, where all students have equal opportunities to learn, and suggests developing teaching methods that create comfortable environments for children to think creatively and foster mutual acceptance. In recent years, numerous studies have explored the implementation of AI systems in schools to support individualized education for students with specific needs. These studies address significant challenges in identifying and treating various conditions. The application of AI in special education has had a significant positive impact, helping teachers, parents, and therapists identify and provide proper care for students with special needs. AI computational technology can create more efficient learning environments, save time and money, and enhance the effectiveness of early diagnosis and intervention. Further research is needed to develop diagnostic tools tailored to different learning disorders and streamline the responsibilities of teachers and parents. Nonetheless, AI is recognized as a potentially valuable educational tool for all children, requiring a comprehensive and collaborative approach to service delivery. Considerable investment has been made in developing AI systems to improve accessibility to educational resources, support language development, and enhance assistive technologies. AI-powered innovations in education can also improve accessibility in the workplace, such as job seeking, interviews, and skills upgrading. The education industry in

India has seen substantial growth in AI integration, with a discussion paper published by NITI Aayog in 2018 suggesting that AI could contribute an additional USD 1 trillion to the Indian economy by 2035.

Even with today's advanced technology, we still have a way to go. The silver lining is that this is equally true in reverse. Artificially intelligent specialized apps are transforming education by reimagining how we utilize games in the classroom. They are more pleasurable for kids with special needs, save time and money compared to therapy, and benefit everyone involved. Artificial intelligence (AI) will eventually cause a sea change in Special Education as well. Current AI tool development efforts are largely focused on making educational resources, linguistic development, and assistive technology solutions more accessible. Education innovations powered by AI can help make it easier for people with disabilities to find jobs, prepare for interviews, and learn new skills. Ai has also had a significant role in the expansion of India's education sector. The impact that AI is having on both educators and students with special needs in the classroom is undeniable. Below are some potential future directions that may affect how AI is used in special education. The employment of AI-powered tools in the classroom allows educators to better meet the needs of their students. An AI might potentially determine a student's optimal course load based on how they learn best. Using AI methods, early intervention can be provided to students who could benefit from special education programs. Students may benefit from teachers' abilities to intervene and support them earlier if they do better in school. Communication Enhancement: The usage of artificial intelligence-powered communication tools can be extremely helpful for students with special needs. Artificial intelligence-powered devices can translate a student's spoken words into text or sign language, for example, improving the surrounding community's ability to understand them. Decisions Artificial intelligence can help educators decide which methods and interventions will have the most impact for each kid, based on data. This has the potential to yield better outcomes for disabled children. Children with special needs can benefit greatly from assistive technology, which is created to make it easier for them to carry out tasks that might otherwise be challenging for them. For pupils with visual impairments, AI-powered software may highlight material for easier reading, and for those with motor restrictions, it can provide quick feedback. The application of artificial intelligence (AI) in education technology can help teachers get administrative work done more quickly. The use of artificial intelligence in special education could be beneficial for everyone involved and educators by creating more inclusive school environments and raising students' achievement levels.

REFERENCES

Abbott, R. G. (2006). Automated expert modeling for automated student evaluation. *Intelligent Tutoring Systems: 8th International Conference, ITS 2006, Jhongli, Taiwan, June 26-30, 2006. Proceedings, 8*, 1–10.

American Psychiatric Association. (2013). Diagnostic and statistical manual of mental disorders: Dsm-5 (Vol. 5). American psychiatric association Washington, DC.

Anthony, L., Yang, J., & Koedinger, K. R. (2008). Toward next-generation, intelligent tutors: Adding natural handwriting input. *IEEE MultiMedia, 15*(3), 64–69. doi:10.1109/MMUL.2008.73

Anuradha, J., Ramachandran, V., Arulalan, K., & Tripathy, B. (2010). Diagnosis of adhd using svm algorithm. *Proceedings of the Third Annual ACM Bangalore Conference*, 1–4.

Arthi, K., & Tamilarasi, A. (2008). Prediction of autistic disorder using neuro fuzzy system by applying ann technique. *International Journal of Developmental Neuroscience, 26*(7), 699–704. doi:10.1016/j.ijdevneu.2008.07.013 PMID:18706991

Athanasios, S., & Rodi-Elein, I. (2012). Artificial intelligence in special education: A decade review. *International Journal of Engineering Education, 28*(6), 1366–1372.

Baschera, G.-M., & Gross, M. (2010). Poisson-based inference for perturbation models in adaptive spelling training. *International Journal of Artificial Intelligence in Education*, *20*(4), 333–360.

Brodin, J. (2010). Can ict give children with disabilities equal opportunities in school? *Improving Schools*, *13*(1), 99–112. doi:10.1177/1365480209353483

Buchanan, B. G. (2005). A very brief history of artificial intelligence. *Artificial Intelligence Magazine*, *26*(4), 53–60.

Burgstahler, S. (2003). The role of technology in preparing youth with disabilities for postsecondary education and employment. *Journal of Special Education Technology*, *18*(4), 7–19. doi:10.1177/016264340301800401

Chassignol, M., Khoroshavin, A., Klimova, A., & Bilyatdinova, A. (2018). Artificial intelligence trends in education: A narrative overview. *Procedia Computer Science*, *136*, 16–24. doi:10.1016/j.procs.2018.08.233

Delavarian, M., Towhidkhah, F., Dibajnia, P., & Gharibzadeh, S. (2012). Designing a decision support system for distinguishing adhd from similar children behavioral disorders. *Journal of Medical Systems*, *36*(3), 1335–1343. doi:10.100710916-010-9594-9 PMID:20878211

Drigas, A., Kouremenos, D., & Vrettaros, J. (2008). Teaching of English to hearing impaired individuals whose mother language is the sign language. *Emerging Technologies and Information Systems for the Knowledge Society: First World Summit on the Knowledge Society, WSKS 2008, Athens, Greece, September 24-26, 2008 Proceedings*, *1*, 263–270.

Fletcher, J. M., Coulter, W. A., Reschly, D. J., & Vaughn, S. (2004). Alternative approaches to the definition and identification of learning disabilities: Some questions and answers. *Annals of Dyslexia*, *54*(2), 304–331. doi:10.100711881-004-0015-y PMID:15741940

Garg, S., & Sharma, S. (2020). Impact of artificial intelligence in special need education to promote inclusive pedagogy. *International Journal of Information and Education Technology (IJIET)*, *10*(7), 523–527. doi:10.18178/ijiet.2020.10.7.1418

Georgopoulos, V. C., Malandraki, G. A., & Stylios, C. D. (2003). A fuzzy cognitive map approaches differential diagnosis of specific language impairment. *Artificial Intelligence in Medicine*, *29*(3), 261–278. doi:10.1016/S0933-3657(02)00076-3 PMID:14656490

Gonzalez, C. S., Guerra, D., Sanabria, H., Moreno, L., Noda, M. A., & Bruno, A. (2010). Automatic system for the detection and analysis of errors to support personalized feedback. *Expert Systems with Applications*, *37*(1), 140–148. doi:10.1016/j.eswa.2009.05.027

Hernadez, J., Mousalli, G., & Rivas, F. (2009). Learning difficulties diagnosis for children's basic education using expert systems. *WSEAS Transactions on Information Science and Applications*, *7*(6), 1–25.

Hernandez, J., Mousalli, G., & Rivas, F. (2009). Expert system for the diagnosis of learning difficulties in children's basic education. *WSEAS International Conference. Proceedings. Mathematics and Computers in Science and Engineering*, (8).

Jain, K., Manghirmalani, P., Dongardive, J., & Abraham, S. (2009). Computational diagnosis of learning disability. *International Journal of Recent Trends in Engineering*, *2*(3), 64.

Kohli, M., & Prasad, T. (2010). Identifying dyslexic students by using artificial neural networks. *Proceedings of the World Congress on Engineering, 1* (1), 1–4.

Lanzilotti, R., & Roselli, T. (2007). An experimental evaluation of logiocando, an intelligent tutoring hypermedia system. *International Journal of Artificial Intelligence in Education, 17*(1), 41–56.

Libbrecht, P., & Melis, E. (2006). Methods to access and retrieve mathematical content in activemath. *Mathematical Software-ICMS 2006: Second International Congress on Mathematical Software, Castro Urdiales, Spain, September 1-3, 2006. Proceedings, 2*, 331–342.

Livne, N. L., Livne, O. E., & Wight, C. A. (2007). Can automated scoring surpass hand grading of students' constructed responses and error patterns in mathematics. *Journal of Online Learning and Teaching, 3*(3), 295–306.

Melis, E., Andres, E., Budenbender, J., Frischauf, A., Goduadze, G., Libbrecht, P., Pollet, M., & Ullrich, C. (2001). Activemath: A generic and adaptive web-based learning environment. *International Journal of Artificial Intelligence in Education, 12*, 385–407.

Melis, E., & Siekmann, J. (2004). Activemath: An intelligent tutoring system for mathematics. *Artificial Intelligence and Soft Computing-ICAISC 2004: 7th International Conference,* Zakopane, Poland, June 7-11, 2004. *Proceedings, 7.*

Nanni, L., & Lumini, A. (2009). Ensemble generation and feature selection for the identification of students with learning disabilities. *Expert Systems with Applications, 36*(2), 3896–3900. doi:10.1016/j.eswa.2008.02.065

Needs, S. E. (2001). *Code of practice. London.* Department for Education and Skills.

Palacios, A. M., Sánchez, L., & Couso, I. (2009). Extending a simple genetic cooperative-competitive learning fuzzy classifier to low quality datasets. *Evolutionary Intelligence, 2*(1-2), 73–84. doi:10.100712065-009-0024-1

Palacios, A. M., Sánchez, L., & Couso, I. (2010). Diagnosis of dyslexia with low quality data with genetic fuzzy systems. *International Journal of Approximate Reasoning, 51*(8), 993–1009. doi:10.1016/j.ijar.2010.07.008

Pavlopoulos, J., Vrettaros, J., Vouros, G., & Drigas, A. (2008). The development of a self-assessment system for the learners' answers with the use of gpnn. *WSKS, 1*, 332–340. doi:10.1007/978-3-540-87781-3_37

Rapin, I., & Tuchman, R. F. (2008). Autism: Definition, neurobiology, screening, diagnosis. *Pediatric Clinics of North America, 55*(5), 1129–1146. doi:10.1016/j.pcl.2008.07.005 PMID:18929056

Rebolledo-Mendez, G., & De Freitas, S. (2008). *Attention modeling using inputs from a brain computer interface and user-generated data in second life.* Academic Press.

Riedl, M., Arriaga, R., Boujarwah, F., Hong, H., Isbell, J., & Heflin, L. J. (2007). Graphical social scenarios: Toward intervention and authoring for adolescents with high functioning autism. *Virtual Healthcare Interaction, Papers from the AAAI Fall Symposium.*

Russell, S. J., & Stuart, J. (2003). *Artificial Intelligence: A Modern Approach.* Academic Press.

Schipor, O. A., Pentiuc, S. G., & Schipor, M. D. (2010). Improving computer-based speech therapy using a fuzzy expert system. *Computer Information*, *29*(2), 303–318.

Sebe, N., Cohen, I., Gevers, T., & Huang, T. S. (2006). Emotion recognition based on joint visual and audio cues. *18th international conference on pattern recognition (ICPR'06)*, *1*, 1136–1139.

Srihari, S., Collins, J., Srihari, R., Srinivasan, H., Shetty, S., & Brutt-Griffler, J. (2008). Automatic scoring of short handwritten essays in reading comprehension tests. *Artificial Intelligence*, *172*(2-3), 300–324. doi:10.1016/j.artint.2007.06.005

Thomson, P., & Gilchrist, P. (1997). *Dyslexia: A multidisciplinary approach*. Nelson Thornes.

Wu, T.-K., Meng, Y.-R., & Huang, S.-C. (2006). Application of artificial neural networks to the identification of students with learning disabilities. *IC-AI*, 162–168.

Chapter 4
Data Analysis and Machine Learning in AI-Assisted Special Education for Students With Exceptional Needs

Sakalya Mitra
VIT Bhopal University, India

D. Lakshmi
https://orcid.org/0000-0003-4018-1208
VIT Bhopal University, India

Vishnuvarthanan Govindaraj
VIT Bhopal University, India

ABSTRACT

Artificial intelligence and related technological advancements have been a matter of discussion in recent times. There has been regular growth in AI-based methods that have proven useful for various industry verticals. Education is one such critical field where AI can play a monumental role in improving quality and helping individuals strive for better education. Meeting the educational requirements of all children, adolescents, and adults has received more attention in recent years. Recent advancements in technology, such as data analysis and ML, can potentially revolutionize how we approach special education. By using these technologies to personalize learning experiences, track progress, and provide individualized support, educators can improve outcomes for students with special needs. With the right approach, data analysis and ML can be powerful tools for improving special education and supporting students with special needs. The main idea of the study is to outline in detail the various applications of AI-assisted special education and discover the depths of the methods.

DOI: 10.4018/979-8-3693-0378-8.ch004

1.0 INTRODUCTION

Over the past ten years, technological advancement has fundamentally changed the world and increased computer power in all facets of daily life. Understanding human intelligence in all of its manifestations is one of computing science's most important goals. Over the past 50 years, this quest has inspired numerous researchers to create the science of AI. AI is typically defined as the study and development of intelligent agents that have the ability to perceive their environment and perform actions that maximize their plausibility for success.

The convergence of AI and education is a topic of research in the science of AI. The majority of scientists and academics appear to agree that instruments using AI may successfully support the educational process. The education of all children and meeting the educational requirements of all children, adolescents, and adults have received more attention in recent years. This fact has strengthened the argument for using technology to remove obstacles to learning. The advantages of AI in teaching have long been praised, and the field of special education has long employed AI techniques.

Special education is one of the highly specialized fields within education. that focuses on providing support and assistance to students with special needs. This includes individuals with physical, cognitive, or behavioral disabilities, as well as those with exceptional talents and gifts. While traditional approaches to education have been successful in supporting many students with special needs, there are still many challenges to overcome. One of the most significant challenges is the need to provide individualized support to each student, considering their unique strengths, weaknesses, and learning styles.

Recent advancements in technology, such as data analysis and ML, can potentially revolutionize how we approach special education. By using these technologies to analyze student data, identify patterns, and develop personalized learning plans, educators can provide more effective support for their students. This paper will explore the potential benefits of data analysis and ML in AI-assisted special education.

Special education is a highly complex field that requires a deep understanding of both education and disability. According to the National Center for Education Statistics (2022) under the Individuals with Disabilities Education Act (IDEA), in 2020–21, 7.2 million kids between the ages of 3 and 21 received services with respect to special education. According to the United Nations, Department of Economic and Social Affairs Disability (2015), there are an estimated 1 billion people with disabilities worldwide, or approximately 15% of the populace as a whole, making them the world's biggest minority. Figure 1 from the U.S Department of Education (2021) shows the percentage distribution of IDEA-eligible students aged 3–21 by selected impairment type for the academic year 2020–21. Even with the substantial resources invested in special education, many students with disabilities struggle in conventional classroom environments.

One of the biggest challenges in special education is the need for individualized support. Each student with special needs has unique strengths, weaknesses, and learning styles, thereby making the creation of a universal educational strategy challenging. Hence, this further complicates the fact that many students with special needs may also have co-occurring conditions, such as ADHD or anxiety, that require additional support.

Data analysis and ML are two technologies that have the potential to address the individual needs of students in special education. Data analysis involves using mathematical and statistical techniques to analyze large datasets and identify patterns and insights. A branch of AI known as machine learning (ML) employs statistical modeling and algorithms to learn, comprehend, and perform predictions or decision-making.

Figure 1. Percentage wise distribution of students having ages between three (3) and twenty one (21) who receive IDEA services according to a particular impairment type: The academic year 2020–21

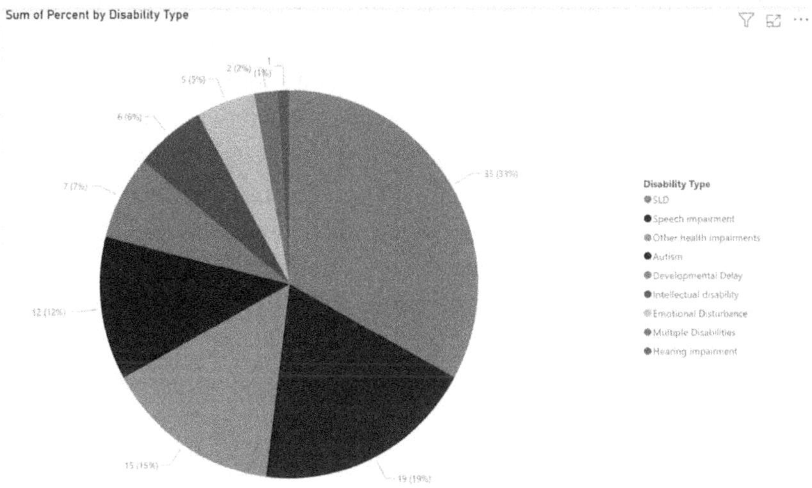

1.1 Objective of the Chapter

The main objectives of the chapter can be described as follows:

- To identify and define the different types of disabilities experienced by individuals and the various AI-based methodologies and diagnostic tools currently available for assisting disabled students in their education
- To explore the current state of Special education by discussing special education awareness, various special education technologies and software, support and career development programs, and the latest advancements in the domain.
- To clarify Data Analysis and Machine Learning's contribution to Special Education by providing an analytical overview of the state of special education at the moment.
- To understand why Data Analysis and Machine Learning are prospective solutions and better analyze and reflect upon the existing AI-assisted solutions through case studies, assisting with the education of students with special needs.

1.2 Organization of the Chapter

The chapter has been divided into nine sections, aimed at helping in the proper presentation of the study. The first section gives the introduction to the chapter with an insight into special education and its importance while exploring the background of the study, highlights the objectives of the chapter, and talks about everything to expect from the chapter. In the second section, the rationale of the chapter focuses on the idea of Data Analysis and Machine Learning in Special education and explores the various plausible convergences of the two domains. The third section deals with the explanation of the various kinds of disabilities and their potential impacts on individual lives. The fourth section reflects on the current state of special education through the lenses of Awareness about Special education, reflecting upon different special education technologies and career development programs, and lastly touching on the latest advancements in AI-assisted special education. In the fifth section, the role of data analysis and machine learning in this sector is examined and views are presented. The sixth section explores the answer to why Data Analysis and ML are prospective solutions for solving problems in Special Education. In the seventh section a comprehensive overview of the existing solutions is presented in the form of case studies citing real-world use cases of AI-Assisted solutions for Special Education. The eighth section reflects on the available pedagogical methodologies and the challenges faced in implementing them in day-to-day lives with touching the general and ethical concerns associated with Data Analysis and ML integration. Finally, the last section concludes by summarizing and reviewing the methodologies discussed so far and also provides insights on the future scope of Data Analysis and ML in the field of Special Education.

2.0 RATIONALE OF THE STUDY

The study's primary goal is to provide a thorough outline relating to the various applications of data analysis and ML in AI-assisted special education and discover the depths of the methods, scrutinizing the benefits and challenges of existing methods and techniques.

Data analysis and ML have numerous applications in education, including identifying at-risk students, tracking student progress, and providing personalized learning experiences. The global market for AI in education is rising exponentially and proves to have huge scope in the future to improve and revolutionize education systems. It has been depicted in Figure 2.

Figure 2. Growth of AI in education market size in the period of 2016-2027

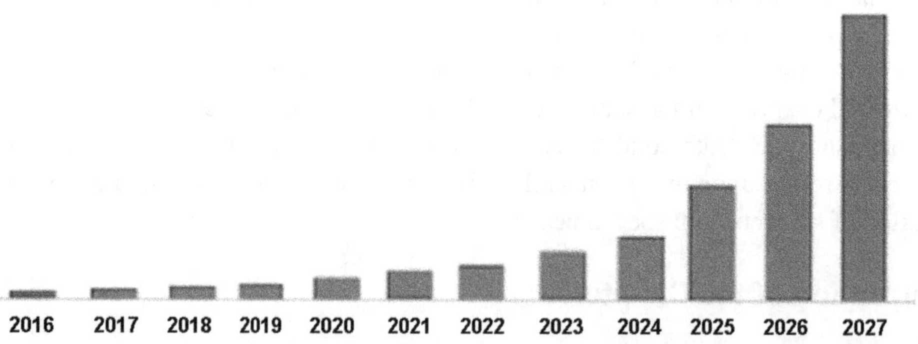

In the context of special education, these technologies can be used to identify specific learning challenges, determine appropriate interventions, and track progress over time. One of the key benefits of data analysis and ML in special education is the ability to impart individualized learning opportunities. ability to provide personalized learning experiences. Educators can create specialized learning plans that cater to each student's needs by analyzing data regarding each student's style of learning, abilities, and weaknesses. This can possibly help improve student engagement, motivation, and overall learning outcomes. Another benefit is the ability to track progress over time. With the help of data analysis and ML, educators can monitor a student's progress and adjust their learning plan as needed. This can help to ensure that students are making consistent progress and achieving their learning goals.

Data analysis and ML can also help increase teacher efficiency. By automating certain tasks, such as grading and data analysis, educators can spend more time working directly with students and providing individualized support. There are several examples of AI-assisted special education initiatives that use data analysis and ML techniques to support students with special needs. The various AI-assisted tools and methods for ASD are shown in Figure 3.

Figure 3. AI-assisted methods for the education of students suffering from ASD

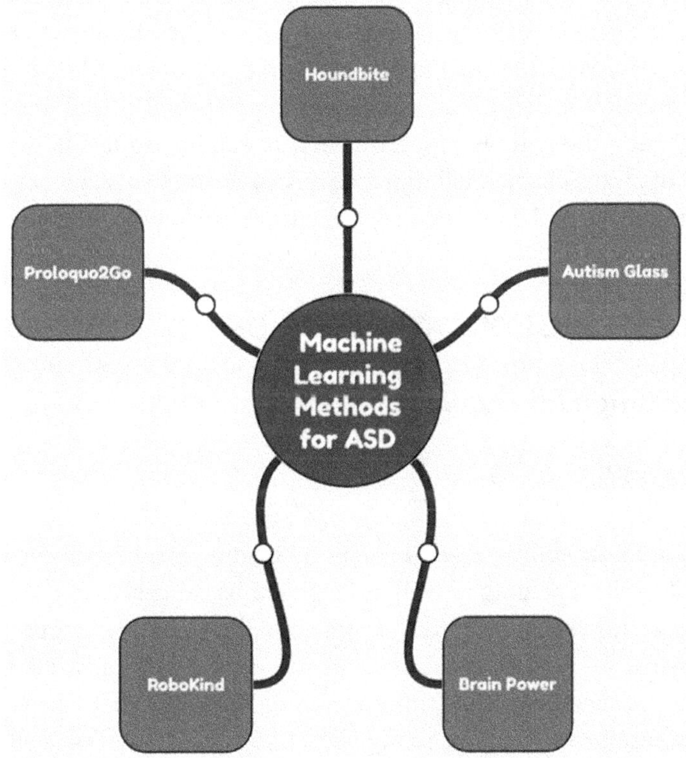

One example is the use of Natural Language Processing technology to help students with reading difficulties. Natural Language Processing can be used to analyze a student's reading abilities and provide personalized feedback on areas that need improvement. For example, a program called Readability uses Natural Language Processing to analyze a student's reading level and provide tailored reading material that is appropriate for their skill level. This can help improve their reading comprehension and overall literacy skills.

Another example is utilizing ML to provide students' support, with autism spectrum disorder (ASD). A program called iSocial uses ML to analyze a student's behavior and provide real-time feedback on social interactions. This can help students with ASD develop social skills and improve their communication with peers.

While there are numerous benefits to using data analysis and ML in AI-assisted special education, there are also several challenges and limitations that must be addressed. One of the biggest challenges is the ethical and legal implications of using these technologies in education. There are concerns about data privacy and security, as well as potential biases in the algorithms used. Another challenge is the need for training and support for educators. Data analysis and ML can be complex and difficult to understand, requiring specialized skills and training. Educators must be provided with the necessary training and support to use these technologies effectively in the classroom.

Data analysis and ML can potentially revolutionize how we approach special education. By using these technologies to personalize learning experiences, track progress, and provide individualized support, educators can improve outcomes for students with special needs. However, addressing the moral and legal ramifications is crucial and providing training and support for educators to use these technologies effectively in the classroom. With the right approach, data analysis and ML can be powerful tools for improving the quality of learning for special students through special education.

Exploring and analyzing the various aspects of ML paradigms to tackle the problems in Special education is the sole aim of this chapter, indulging deeply in the methods and existing technologies and exploring the intricacies of them like advantages, limitations, and obligations in the approaches.

3.0 AI-ASSISTED SPECIAL EDUCATION FOR DIFFERENT SPECIAL NEEDS

3.1 AI-Based Assistance for Dyslexia

3.1.1 What Is Dyslexia?

The most common learning disability, also known as a "reading disability," causes at least 80% of all LDs. Dyslexia primarily affects reading as well as language-based processing skills. It can affect reading, decoding, reading comprehension, recall, writing, spelling, and sometimes speaking, and it can occur with other similar disorders. Dyslexia is sometimes referred to as a learning disability that is language-based, and the severity can vary from person to person. According to one study, problems with phonological processing (that is, processing speech) are at the root of reading disorders. People who have trouble deciphering words into their component sounds or blending various sounds together frequently have trouble reading words quickly and accurately. Muktamath et al. (2021) mentions that reading comprehension problems are frequently a result of the mentioned decoding issues.

Fortunately, technological developments, like those in artificial intelligence, assist dyslexic people in overcoming this significant obstacle. Many studies have shown that those with dyslexia are quick learners who possess strong creative and logical thinking skills.

3.1.2 Existing Solutions

Dystech is an advanced tool developed to detect early dyslexia. Richard (2019) states, the purpose of Dystech is to provide adults and children who are dyslexic with a useful and affordable way to properly diagnose their condition.

Microsoft has made available a free learning resource called Immersive Reader intended to enhance the reading and writing abilities of dyslexic students. By speaking the text aloud and eventually breaking it down into syllables, the full-screen artificial intelligence tool Immersive Reader helps students improve their reading comprehension. This makes it simpler for dyslexics to learn how to read fluently on their own. Additionally improved are Google Docs' artificial intelligence features, such as voice recognition and grammar and spelling checks. Grammarly, on the other hand, is a tool that offers suggestions and corrections, along with error flagging, for more thorough feedback on a student's written work. Grammarly and Google Docs both assist dyslexic students in developing their reading and writing abilities. Richard (2019) additionally mentions, some artificial intelligence programs combine cloud services with smart technology to aid in the early diagnosis of dyslexia in children.

3.2 AI-Based Assistance for Autism Spectrum Disorder (ASD)

Variations in the brain are the cause of Autism Spectrum Disorder, which leads to developmental disabilities. People with ASD frequently struggle with issues such as social communication and interaction, restricted or repetitive behaviors or interests, and more. According to the Centers for Disease Control and Prevention (2023), in addition, individuals with ASD may behave, move, or pay attention differently.

As society does not fully comprehend this condition, children with autism have been stigmatized and shunned. As a result of this progress, more profound understandings of this condition generally and the best ways to interact with autistic children have emerged. When it comes to providing instruction to students with autism, it is anticipated that AI will soon alter the scenario.

AI has a multitude of ways to assist students suffering from ASD. The great advancements in technology lead to the holistic development of the students and provide support in various dimensions to properly assist in the learning process of specially-abled students.

3.2.1 Educational Content Personalization

Personalized content is even more important for autistic children because they struggle to process the world in the same way as typically developing children. Personalizing educational materials for students with autism involves much more than just personal preferences. But it also entails tailoring instruction so that the target student can understand it. To achieve this, special education schools have reduced class attendance, which has raised the need for tuition.

This has left a gap, especially for autistic children from low-income families. In the near future, teachers will be able to provide higher-quality instruction to more students at a lower cost thanks to AI, which aims to close that gap.

With the aid of reasoning systems, students can receive content that is specifically tailored to their learning preferences. Since more students can be enrolled in one class at once, this will help ensure that all children with autism receive an equal and inclusive education.

3.2.2 Meaningful Repetition of Content

Repeating the same thing over and over while teaching kids is part of the process. Dealing with kids who have autism exacerbates. As each student requires individualized attention, it may be difficult to maintain composure while managing an entire class. No matter how much you enjoy your work, it can occasionally be difficult to teach students who have special needs. AI can help with this issue, though it can occasionally have an impact on how effectively students receive instruction. Psychology and science experts for essay writing service reviews claim that the systems utilizing this technology can repeat content continuously without the user becoming impatient. This content is not redundant because of the way it is organized. Contrarily, AI systems reinforce content with students from a variety of backgrounds to make sure they comprehend what is being taught. AI integration can significantly contribute to the transfer of skills and knowledge in the education of autistic children. Additionally, it will eliminate the gap between disadvantaged families raising autistic children.

3.2.3 Performance Monitoring

Sometimes it can be difficult to determine whether an autistic child is understanding what you are teaching because you can't always see inside their head.

Understanding why a student's grades are dropping may be difficult because it can be difficult to read regular facial expressions. You will gain a more profound understanding of what might have gone wrong by closely observing each students' learning process. You can see the student's unique issues when using AI technology. Teachers should consider whether their teaching methods are the most effective for each student if they notice any patterns in the areas where students struggle.

If not, teaching strategies can be modified and adjusted for each student. This provides classes with a comprehensive curriculum that benefits all students. This digital method of monitoring progress has the potential to transform the way children with autism are taught and raise the bar for all students.

3.2.4 Existing Solutions

A piece of equipment called Empower Me was created by a specific business called Brain Power. This solution, which heavily emphasizes helping students recognize their emotions, is very close to being made available to the general public.

When you are aware of and comprehend your students' emotions, you can teach them much more effectively. Empower Me can improve interactions between teachers and students with autism. Children with autism are much better able to comprehend the emotions of their teachers, which helps them feel more at ease when they are aware of those emotions. Students are also able to comprehend their emotional state, including stress, at the same time. AI-driven technology can improve student mindfulness and foster stronger relationships between pupils and teachers. In order to help the wearer better understand the world, it was created as a wearable technology.

Learning social skills for life after school is a part of what students learn in the classroom. As a result, LuxAI created a solution called QTRobot that is specifically made to advance this stage. The robot can be programmed by parents of autistic children to teach the child a particular skill set. According to Gorman (2021), a child can learn a number of pre-programmed skills from this robot. The carer must choose the best program for that child.

Customizing the learning process can help teachers impart knowledge to students more effectively. Tutoring students using this tool might make them feel more at ease since they will be spending a lot of time by themselves without interacting with anyone else. Therefore, this remedy works best for autistic kids who are overly sensitive to people. Perhaps occasionally, even those who are unable to understand nonverbal cues.

3.3 AI-Based Assistance for Auditory Processing Disorder (APD)

APD is a defect in the neural processing of auditory stimuli that is not caused by hearing loss, higher-order language disorders, or cognitive deficits, but is associated with learning disabilities.

The affected child's brain does not "hear" sounds as normally as it would, but it does not affect their meaning-understanding ability. It is a condition that makes it difficult for sound to freely pass through the ear and be processed or interpreted by the brain; it is also known as CAPD. Even when words are loud enough to be heard and have subtle differences in their sounds, people with APD have trouble telling them apart. They might be unable to separate distinct noises, or they might interpret the sequence of sounds incorrectly. Muktamath et al. (2021) articulates that, in APD, the brain processes ear information but then interprets it incorrectly.

3.3.1 Various Assistive Technologies for APD

People who experience these difficulties are not aware of the subtle variations in word sounds. Consequently, they could misunderstand instructions or hear questions incorrectly. Also, background noise may be a distraction for them. Nevertheless, assistive technology (AT) can be very beneficial.

Personal listening devices (PLDs): These devices can improve voice clarity for users. Teachers and managers who are speaking wear a clip-on microphone. The person with the challenges uses an earpiece or personal speaker that receives their voice via the mic. FM listening systems are the name given to some PLDs. This is due to the fact that they utilize the similar FM frequencies, like the broadcasting stations. Some more recent PLDs transmit voice data using Wi-Fi or Bluetooth. Belsky (2019) mentions, there are also apps that enable an iPhone or iPad to function as a PLD.

Sound field technologies: These are special loudspeaker systems for conference rooms, such as classrooms where audio problems are common. It's possible that some places have echoed or muffled sounds. Speakers positioned in specific areas of the room can hear speakers using these systems. This makes it easier for everyone to hear them by dispersing their voice evenly throughout the space. Systems might come with a pass-around microphone that users can use during conversations. Systems for the sound field can be installed permanently. Some can be transported to different rooms and are portable, says Belsky (2019).

Headphones with active noise cancellation: These tools can help reduce background noise for those who are sensitive to sound. Some people might find it helpful to use a white noise app that plays sounds similar to rain or static while they wear headphones. They are utilized by some people when they need to listen to audio (for example, text-to-speech from their device). They can use headphones to listen in order to block out distracting background noises.

Recorders for audio: These enable the recording of discussions or lectures. If they didn't understand or missed something the first time, they can listen again (if they want to) later. To aid in understanding, users can pause the recording or have it play back more slowly. Some note-taking software and hardware enable users to sync their typed or handwritten notes with the recording of the audio. This may make listening to the recording of an audio simpler. To hear what was recorded at the time, the user needs only tap on a note later.

Captioning: People can read text that corresponds to what is being said using this tool. Understanding spoken language may become simpler as a result. The use of closed captioning in films and on television is a prime example. There are numerous platforms and apps that support auto-captioning. It can be activated for PowerPoint slides and Zoom meetings. Additionally, there are YouTube videos associated with it. Just keep in mind that it might not be entirely accurate. That's a result of speech recognition technology.

Text-to-speech (TTS) software: TTS software allows users to simultaneously see and hear text read aloud. An artificial voice created by a computer reads the text. Those who have trouble reading may find this helpful. However, those who struggle with auditory processing may find it difficult to understand some voices. Finding the right voice and reading pace may require some trial and error. Additionally, some of the more recent TTS voices (often referred to as "neural text-to-speech") sound remarkably human. A different choice is audiobooks. The narration is done by people.

Figure 4 shows an illustrative view of the various assistive technologies for dealing with APD.

Figure 4. Various assistive technologies for students with LD

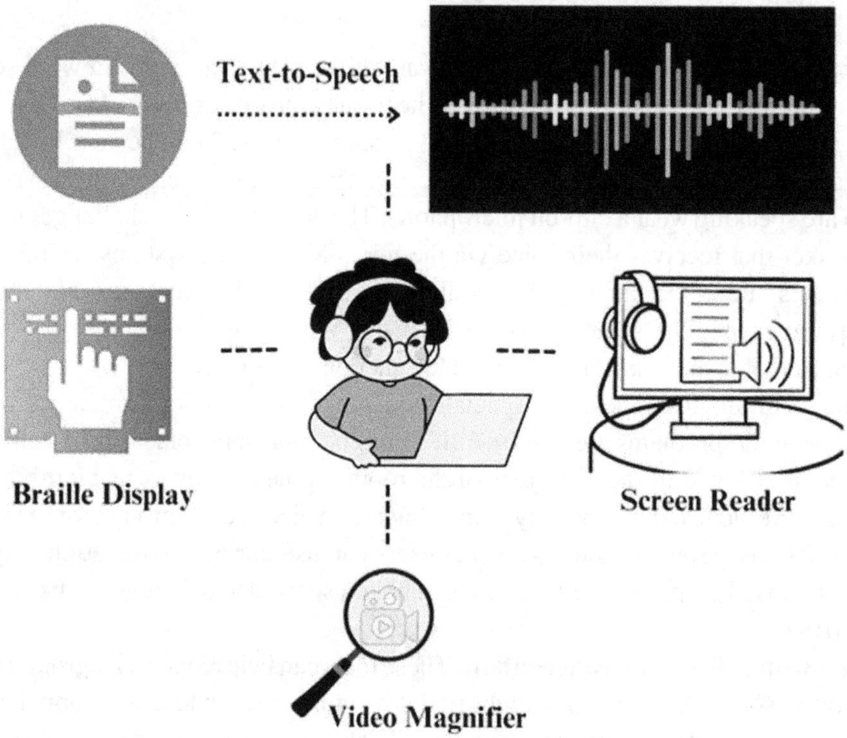

3.3.2 Existing Solutions

Up until now, AI has allowed researchers to make significant advancements in hearing. Some of them are listed below:

- DeLiang Wang, who is a computer science and engineering professor at the Ohio State University, has written in the IEEE Spectrum that the esteemed researchers performing research at the Perception and Neurodynamics Laboratory (PNL) at the Ohio University have worked on training a Deep Neural Network (DNN) that has the capability to differentiate speech that people normally want to hear, from other unwanted noise, such as sounds of humming or background conversations). As per the data submitted by Prof. Wang, when the program was not initiated, people diagnosed with hearing impairments were only able to interpret and make sense of 29% of the words muddled by babble. But after the DNN-based processing, this percentage of correctly interpreted words increased to 84%. Adding to this, Panahi and co-principal investigator Dr. Linda Thibodeau, working at the University of Texas located in Dallas, have utilised AI to develop a smartphone application that has the ability to determine the direction of incoming speech. This app employs models to recognize and minimize background noise so that people can have better hearing. This model was developed utilizing a large library of sounds. Burry (2021) mentions that as per Prof. Panahi, clean and processed speech is transmitted to the hearing devices or earbuds whenever a smartphone having the app installed is placed on a table or in your car's GPS stand.
- The leading and finest hearing aid production companies have recently incorporated AI technology in their higher-end models of hearing aids. For instance, the hearing aid of Widex Moment creates programs for hearing based on the user's typical environment using AI and ML. In addition, Oticon unveiled Oticon MoreTM in January, the brand's newest and first hearing aid with an integrated DNN. Because Oticon More users were trained using more than 12 million actual sounds, they are better able to understand speech and the sounds around them. Consider a crowded airport or hospital emergency room as an example of a complex "sound scene" that the Oticon More's neural network receives as input. The DNN starts by scanning the input and removing fundamental sonic elements and patterns. To comprehend and recognize what is occurring, it combines these elements. In order to ensure that the output is crystal clear and perfectly balanced for the person's particular type of hearing loss, the hearing aids also decide how to balance the sound environment, says Burry (2021).
- According to MedicalXpress (2018), in a recent collaborative study, a machine learning (ML) system that can utilise brain scans to predict a child's ability to speak post cochlear implants procedure, was developed by researchers from Ann & Robert H. Lurie Children's Hospital of Chicago and The Chinese University of Hong Kong. This study's ground-breaking use of artificial intelligence to understand the neural architecture underlying language development will have a significant impact on children who experience developmental difficulties.
- Asokan (2019) researched that, Google's DeepMind has created an AI system that can provide hearing-impaired users with a closed caption by creating lip-reading algorithms. This system was trained using more than 5000 hours of television viewing by DeepMind's algorithms, which were then able to recognize up to 17,500 different words. By correctly interpreting 46.8% of words, the algorithm surpassed expert lip-readers thanks to its extensive training. The Google researchers

are confident that technology will make significant advancements in speech recognition in noisy environments, silent dictation in public spaces, and hearing aids.

- According to Zdravkova et al.(2022), the HearMeOut app combines pictogram-based augmentative and alternative communication with gesture-based text prediction using artificial intelligence (AI). Users with speech impairments can converse using Natural Language Conversation thanks to the program. In addition, it classifies the most likely words from the movements of the visually impaired person as seen by the camera by using a word-level sign language dataset. Gradually, it transforms those words into the most logical and convincing sentences possible using cutting-edge algorithms. Because input and output are continuous processes that do not require storage, reducing the possibility of any information leakage, the app does not save user data due to security concerns.

3.4 AI-Based Assistance for Language Processing Disorder (LPD)

LPD, a subtype of APD, impairs the ability of sufferers to understand the meaning of the sound clusters that make up words, phrases, and narratives. Muktamath et al. (2021) states, while an APD affects how the brain interprets all sounds, a LPD only affects how language is processed.

. This condition arises when a person has specific language comprehension problems that impair both receptive and expressive language. Some of the root causes of these language-related problems include a limited vocabulary, trouble remembering and keeping track of what is said, a concrete way of thinking, or trouble organizing one's thoughts. Children who have a language-based LD, for instance, might have trouble finding the appropriate words and phrases or keeping up with a conversation that moves quickly. According to Muktamath et al. (2021), people with language-based learning disabilities (LDs) may find it difficult to organize ideas or pinpoint a message's main point when they are writing effectively.

One or more of the following characteristics of children who have expressive language difficulties include slow vocabulary growth, pronunciation problems, difficulty in conveying what they are feeling (single words, inadequate or incorrect word retrieval, inadequate narrative and conversational skills, and poor answering), and grammatical problems. Because the appropriate word won't come to them, they frequently use a less appropriate word instead. Table 1 shows some examples of how LPD can be witnessed in a child.

Table 1. Expressive language difficulties in a child with language processing disorder

Difficulty With Word Retrieval	Out of Context Word Usage
5 year old boy Teacher: What do you want, Ram? Ram: (pointing to the apple) "that" Teacher: What is "that" Ram: (still pointing to the apple) That, want that Unable to frame the sentence and get the proper word "**apple**".	**Narrating a story: (Word framing)** They escaped the tiger from getting eaten. **On a hot day: (Wrong word as per context)** I am shivering, put the fan on!

3.4.1 Current Scenario and Future Prospects

As per ongoing research and technological advances, state-of-the-art AI-assisted technology is still not deployed or developed that can handle LPD. Continuous work is being done in the segment to improve the LPD and provide proper education to the children suffering from it. But the future is bright, with great initiatives being taken and grants being given to research institutions to develop state-of-the-art solutions to tackle LPD.

A $20 million grant over the course of 5 years received from the National Science Foundation has led to the establishment of a state-of-the-art institute at the University of Buffalo, that works on developing intriguing AI systems that are capable of recognizing, supporting, and helping young children having difficulties in speech or language processing. Researchers from 9 universities around the world, including Penn State, are an integral part of this established institute. The institute will work to address the speech-language pathologist shortage in the country and make sure that young children who are at risk of experiencing language deficits receive prompt and efficient support. According to the Penn State University (2023), the project aims to create two cutting-edge AI solutions: AI Screener, aimed at detecting potential impairments and disorders in speech or language, and AI Orchestrator, which aims to serve as a virtual teaching assistant and offer students interventions based on their abilities.

The AI Screener will function by listening to and watching students present in the class, and simultaneously gathering their speech, gesture, and body language samples. Then this device will compile the weekly summaries that will enlist each and every child's vocabulary, pronunciation history, different video clips, as well as other skills. The Penn State University (2023) claims that with the aid of these summaries, teachers can keep track of the speech as well as language processing skills of their students, and, in cases of necessity, recommend evaluations with speech-language pathologists.

The AI Orchestrator, according to the researchers, is an app that will help speech-language pathologists, the majority of whom have average caseloads so high that they are forced to provide children with group-based interventions rather than individualized care. The app offers tailored content for students' needs in order to address this. In order to make sure that the interventions are having the desired effect, it keeps track of students' progress and modifies lesson plans, states the Penn State University (2023).

3.5 AI-Based Assistance for Cerebral Palsy

Cerebral palsy is a chronic physical disorder that impairs posture, coordination, and movement. Typically, it is discovered at birth or in the early years of life. Typically, an injury to the brain before, during, or soon after birth—such as a deficiency in oxygen or illness—causes cerebral palsy. The effects of this can range somewhere between mild and severe, depending on the individual. Some people with cerebral palsy will experience physical symptoms that make it more difficult for their muscles to move. Seizures, epilepsy, or issues with speech and language may also affect others. Though cerebral palsy is not a learning disability, some sufferers may be affected.

3.5.1 Current Scenario and AI-Based Solutions

According to research, AI systems support therapy management, selection, and prognosis for children with cerebral palsy. Children with cerebral palsy can benefit from using virtual reality to stay motivated and progress more quickly in their rehabilitation program. Through symptom management tools, AI applications can help children with CP. For instance, navigational aids that help wheelchair users avoid traffic and obstacles are ideal. Using AI and imaging technology together can make it possible to extract large datasets from video content. Additionally, this makes it simpler for medical professionals to inform others of their observations of spontaneous movements linked to CP, aiding in the diagnosis of their patients. These procedures aid in hastening the diagnosis of CP in children. To enable the earliest possible start of treatment, early CP detection is crucial. Therefore, creating AI methods to identify CP could significantly enhance children's lives. These systems provide some reasoning while managing information that is uncertain, lacking, or inconsistent. They arrive at a diagnosis based on knowledge, instinct, and more accurate pattern recognition, states Ojha (2022).

4.0 CURRENT STATE OF SPECIAL EDUCATION

Advanced technological paradigms can only be obtained if the existing paradigms and their criticalities can be scrutinized and future prospects can be clearly visualized. The current state and situation in dealing with and supporting Special Education is an important factor to further understanding the future prospectus and the application of Data Analysis and Machine Learning that can enhance the current state of methods and technologies and lead to a better state of the art in special education measures.

4.1 Special Education Awareness

Over the years, significant progress has been made in special education, including the development of inclusive policies, improved teaching practices, and increased awareness.

According to the United Nations Children's Fund's (UNICEF) report on the Status of Disability in India, established in the year 2000, it is estimated that there are around 30 million present-day children who are suffering from some form of disability. As per the Sixth All-India Education Survey conducted by NCERT in 1998, it was reported that out of the total 200 million children of school-going age (that is, in the age group of 6 to 14 years), 20 million are in need of SNE. According to the 2011 Census of India, it was revealed that around 92 percent of the approximate 25 crore households in the country do not have any disabled person in their family, and more than 2 crore households had one or more people with a disability. A shocking 71 percent of these households are located in rural areas, and the remaining are urban. As mentioned by Habib (2015), the 2011 Census also reveals that among the 5 types of disabilities in India for which data has been collected, the highest is recorded as seeing disability with a whopping 48.5%, followed by disability in movement with 27.9%, Mental with 10.3%, Speech with 7.5%, and disability in hearing with 5.8%.

Throughout this section, we delve into the current state of special education, highlighting the progress in the sector and raising awareness about Special Needs Education (SNE).

4.1.1 Inclusive Education Policies

In recent years, there has been a paradigm shift towards inclusive education policies across the globe. Governments and educational authorities are recognizing the importance of providing an equitable education to all students, regardless of their abilities. Inclusive policies aim to ensure that students with disabilities are educated alongside their peers in regular classrooms, with the necessary support and accommodations.

According to UNICEF (2017), in order to close the achievement gap for children with disabilities, they support government initiatives to promote and monitor inclusive educational systems. They operate in four domains:

Advocacy for special education: UNICEF advocates and voices for the inclusiveness of disabled students in education, in various discussion forums, high-end events, and all other forms of outreach.

Raising awareness: UNICEF works to draw attention to the needs of children with disabilities through research workshops, roundtable meetings, and various other government-partnered events.

Building capacity: UNICEF provided extensive and specialized training to educators, communities, and administrators whilst offering required technical assistance to the government with the aim of increasing the capacity of educational systems in all the partner nations.

Support for implementation: UNICEF also offers monitoring and assistance for evaluation in order to bridge the gap between policy and practise in the partner nations.

4.1.2 Individualized Education Programs (IEPs)

Individualized Education Programs have become a cornerstone of special education. IEPs are individualized education programs that detail precise objectives, accommodations, and assistance services for students with disabilities. To meet the specific needs of each student, these plans are developed in collaboration with parents, teachers, and specialists. IEPs promote individualized learning, ensuring that students receive the necessary resources and support to succeed academically and socially.

The government of India has been proactive in promoting and spreading awareness about special education with specialized and tailored IEPs to help SNE students achieve their full potential.

Inclusive Education for Children with Special Needs (CWSN) is one of the main initiatives of the former Sarva Shiksha Abhiyan (SSA), Right to Education (RTE), and Rashtriya Madhyamik Shiksha Abhiyan (RMSA) programs under the Samagra Siksha campaign.

The component supports a variety of initiatives geared towards students, such as identifying and evaluating CWSN, providing therapeutic services, the development of teaching-learning materials (TLM), the creation of assistive devices and equipment, the development of aids, instruments, appliances, corrective methodologies, Braille books, large print books, and uniforms, as well as environment-building and orientation programs to foster a positive attitude and awareness about the nature and needs of CWSN.

The component also emphasizes how the RTE Act of 2009 is being implemented for children with disabilities in the age group of 6–14 years. To fully accommodate the needs of CWSN inside the school, additional support in the form of resources is made available. In this support, financial assistance is provided for the salaries of special educators.

The Inclusive Education for Disabled at Secondary Stage (IEDSS) program was initiated to meet the educational needs of children with disabilities at the senior secondary and secondary school levels. The scheme provides CWSN having completed eight years of elementary school with the opportunity to complete four years of secondary school inside an inclusive and supportive environment within the general education system for the secondary (class IX–XII).

The current goal of the Samagra Shiksha scheme is to impart services to all CWSNs, starting from class I up to XII. Under the Samagra Shiksha scheme, a budget of Rs. 1023.50 crore was approved for the education and financial support of 21,00,918 CWSN studying in classes I to XII during the 2018-19 academic year. This also includes salaries for the 15,909 special educators in the schools. Along with this, a financial support amounting to Rs. 300 crore was also approved for providing salaries to 11865 resource teachers and persons who are employed by CWSN at BRC, URC, and CRC. As a result of this, 27,774 special educators and other professionals were available to encounter the unique demands and requirements of children with special needs, as claimed by Samagra Shiksha (2020).

4.1.3 Assistive Technology

Advancements in technology have greatly contributed to the field of special education. Assistive technology tools such as speech recognition software, text-to-speech programs, and adaptive learning platforms are increasingly used to support students with disabilities. These technologies enhance accessibility, promote independent learning, and enable students to actively participate in the educational process. In the following section, we will go over the various Special Education technologies in greater detail.

4.1.4 Teacher Training and Professional Development

Educators play a vital role in delivering quality special education. Consequently, there has been an increased emphasis on teacher training and professional development programs. Teachers are equipped with the knowledge and skills necessary to cater to diverse learning needs. This includes training on inclusive teaching strategies, understanding various disabilities, and implementing effective classroom interventions. Professional development programs also encourage collaboration among teachers, fostering an inclusive culture within schools.

To effectively address the learning requirements of CWSN starting from the elementary level up to the secondary level, there has been proper allocation of resources and support in the form of special educators under the Samagra Shiksha Scheme.

Additionally, it also provides funding for pre-existing as well as new special educators honoraria and salaries. This particular allocation for the student-oriented component goes above and beyond the standard of Rs. 3500/-.

4.1.5 Community Involvement and Collaboration

Raising awareness about special education involves engaging the community and fostering collaboration among stakeholders. Community involvement can take various forms, such as workshops, seminars, and awareness campaigns. These initiatives aim to dispel misconceptions, promote understanding, and advocate for the rights of students with disabilities. Building strong partnerships between schools, families, and community organizations helps create a supportive environment that champions inclusive education.

As per the Inclusion BC (2020), the Canadian Institute for Inclusion and Citizenship (CIIC) and Inclusion BC collaborated to create four short documentaries with the goal of educating the public about the exclusion of students with developmental disabilities and providing students, families, and educators with crucial information and potential career paths.

As part of the UNICEF campaign, up to 600 schoolchildren, parents, and teachers attended informational meetings, and more than 280,000 people used social media. By lowering the stigma associated with children who have special educational needs, the goal of the campaign was to continuously and equally provide all children, regardless of their needs, with access to formal and informal education. As stated by Kurtsikidze (2022), the Norwegian government is supporting the initiative.

4.1.6 Parental Empowerment

Empowering parents is crucial for enhancing special education awareness. Parents must be well-informed about their child's rights, available services, and support networks. Schools should actively involve parents in the decision-making process, ensuring their voices are heard and their concerns are addressed. Additionally, providing parents with resources, workshops, and training opportunities equips them to advocate effectively for their child's educational needs.

The ongoing campaigns and awareness programs also involve parents along with children to provide the parents with much-needed knowledge on special education awareness and the steps they can take to ensure the proper growth and support of a special child.

4.1.7 Media and Advocacy

The media significantly shapes and raises public opinion and awareness of special education. By highlighting success stories, challenges, and best practises in special education, the media can promote positive narratives and dispel stereotypes. Advocacy groups and organizations also play a vital role in raising awareness. They work tirelessly to influence policy, provide resources, and support families, further amplifying the importance of special education in society.

Several organizations have been actively involved in promoting and spreading the word about special education, such as UNICEF, the Ministry of Education of India, and several country governments. Such active involvement from the big institutions brings attention to this much-needed topic and spreads awareness about the importance of addressing education for students with special needs.

4.1.8 Inclusion in School Curricula

Integrating special education topics into school curricula fosters awareness from an early age. By teaching students about different disabilities, inclusion, and empathy, we create an accepting and supportive generation. Special education awareness should not be limited to students with disabilities but should extend to their typically developing peers, as they will shape the future of our society. Incorporating special education awareness into school curricula promotes a culture of inclusion, respect, and empathy among students, reducing the stigma associated with disabilities.

The current state of special education reflects significant progress in terms of inclusive policies, individualized support, assistive technology, and teacher training. These advancements have played a crucial role in improving educational outcomes and opportunities for students with disabilities. However, there is still work to be done, particularly in raising special education awareness.

Special education awareness requires collective efforts from communities, the parents, media, advocacy groups, and educational institutions. By involving the community, empowering parents, utilizing media platforms, and integrating special education topics into school curricula, we can create a society that is knowledgeable, accepting, and supportive of individuals with disabilities.

It is essential to continue advocating for inclusive policies and practises, ensuring that students with disabilities have equal access to education, resources, and opportunities. Additionally, ongoing professional development for teachers and collaboration among stakeholders are critical to maintaining high-quality special education services.

4.2 Special Education Technologies

Modern education technologies provide creative answers to assist students with disabilities in their educational journeys. These tools may improve accessibility, enable personalized instruction, and encourage independent participation in the classroom. Let's examine a few of the unique education technologies currently in use:

4.2.1 Virtual and Augmented Reality (AR/VR)

Augmented Reality (AR) and Virtual Reality (VR) technologies have immense potential for transforming the education of students with special needs by providing immersive and interactive learning experiences. These interactive, multisensory experiences that these immersive technologies offer let students explore virtual worlds and interact more deeply with the material, leading to greater engagement and retention of knowledge. Additionally, they can provide a safe space for students to practise skills and make mistakes without fear of real-world consequences.

Sensory Stimulation: AR/VR can simulate different sensory experiences to accommodate the specific needs of students. For example, it can provide visual cues or audio feedback to assist students with visual or hearing impairments. By manipulating sensory inputs, AR/VR can create inclusive learning environments.

Personalized Learning: AR/VR can adapt to individual learning styles and preferences. Through adaptive algorithms, these technologies can customize content, pacing, and difficulty levels based on the student's abilities. This ensures that students with special needs receive personalized instruction, enabling them to learn at their own pace.

Virtual Simulations: AR/VR can create virtual scenarios that simulate real-life situations, allowing students to practise and develop skills in a safe and controlled environment. For instance, students with social communication difficulties can engage in virtual social interactions, improving their social skills and confidence.

Multisensory Engagement: AR/VR can engage multiple senses simultaneously, enhancing the learning experience. By integrating visual, auditory, and tactile elements, students can better comprehend and retain information. This multi-sensory approach is particularly beneficial for students with learning disabilities or cognitive impairments.

Assistive Tools and Accessibility: AR/VR can serve as assistive tools by providing real-time visual aids, closed captions, or translations for students with learning or language barriers. Additionally, AR/VR applications can be designed to be accessible, considering factors such as font size, color contrast, or navigation options for students with visual impairments or motor disabilities.

Virtual Field Trips and Experiences: AR/VR can transport students to virtual worlds, historical sites, or inaccessible locations, providing them with unique learning opportunities. This is especially beneficial for students with mobility limitations, allowing them to explore and experience new environments from the comfort of their classrooms.

Data Collection and Analysis: AR/VR systems can collect data on students' interactions, gaze patterns, or performance. This data can be analyzed using machine learning algorithms to gain insights into students' progress, identify areas for improvement, and personalize instructional strategies further.

AR//VR can be crucial in changing the special education pedagogy and improving upon it to build an advanced system that will be helpful for students with special needs and aid their learning process.

For Physical Disabilities: Children with physical disabilities are taught how to operate and navigate powered wheelchairs using digitally simulated environments. When physical constraints are no longer a barrier, kids can develop into self-sufficient adults. They can experience the benefits of the workplace, just like people without physical disabilities, with the proper education. In addition, this kind of technology can be used to educate non-disabled peers about the obstacles that their disabled peers face in the classroom. This will support the development of an empathetic culture among the kids.

For Sensory Impairment: A child with sensory impairment has difficulties with one or more of their senses—hearing, touch, or vision. Although using technology cannot make these impairments go away, it can greatly aid someone in developing their functional and cognitive abilities. Digitally simulated environments offer effective and individualized instruction.

For Autism: Children with autism have difficulty with the social pragmatics of communication as well as cognitive skills like context-sensing and impulse control. Digitally simulated environments can support these kids' communication skills.. On the other hand, they can create an environment that resonates with their cranial wavelength to help them escape the feeling of social exclusion. According to research, people with autism are able to extend and transfer the skill sets they have learned in virtual worlds to the real world. It promotes learning on multiple levels, such as learning how to control anxicty when entering unfamiliar spaces and honing navigational skills in virtually simulated environments.

For Learning Disabilities: A user-centric digital environment stimulant aids in creating settings that are favorable to the efficient education of kids with learning disabilities.

For ADHD: A person's school and community life are negatively impacted by ADHD. ADHD sufferers often struggle with issues like short attention spans, poor impulse control, and hyperactivity. The child's attention is not diverted by the technological device's closed view frame. They can also be taught to express their reactions appropriately in simulated settings. Such technology can also help with the cognitive impairments brought on by traumatic brain injury and other behavioral disorders.

4.2.2 Devices for Assistive Technology

Designed specifically for people who require assistance, these tools support people with disabilities in their daily lives and in their learning. These gadgets range from straightforward tools to sophisticated electronic hardware and software. Ones that come to mind are adaptive keyboards, switches, and sensory aids, as well as text-to-speech software, speech recognition software, screen readers, alternative and augmentative communication devices, and so forth. Students with physical, sensory, or learning disabilities can communicate, access information, and take an active part in their education thanks to assistive technology.

4.2.2.1 Adaptive Keyboards

An adaptive keyboard is a specialized input device designed to accommodate the unique needs of students with special needs. The various ways adaptive keyboard technology can assist students with needs are

Customizable Key Layout: An adaptive keyboard allows for the customization of key layout and configuration. This feature enables educators and students to design a keyboard layout that suits their specific requirements. Keys can be rearranged, resized, or labeled with symbols or pictures to facilitate easier access and recognition for students with motor impairments or cognitive disabilities.

Assistive Input Options: Adaptive keyboards often include assistive input options such as large keys, raised keys, or keyguards. These adaptations help students with fine motor skill challenges, limited dexterity, or hand-eye coordination difficulties interact with the keyboard more comfortably and accurately.

Switch Access: Many adaptive keyboards support switch access, which allows students to use external switches or alternative input devices to control the keyboard. Switches can be customized to perform different functions, such as keystrokes or mouse movements, based on the student's capabilities. This feature benefits students with limited mobility or motor control.

Accessibility Features: Adaptive keyboards incorporate accessibility features to support students with visual impairments. These features may include high contrast key labels, backlighting, or tactile indicators on specific keys. By enhancing visibility and tactile feedback, students with visual impairments can more easily locate and use the keys.

Programmable Macros: Adaptive keyboards often have programmable macro capabilities, allowing students to assign complex actions or sequences of keystrokes to a single key. This feature streamlines repetitive tasks and reduces the cognitive load for students with learning disabilities or executive functioning challenges.

Integration With Assistive Technology: Adaptive keyboards can be integrated with various assistive technologies, such as speech recognition software or alternative communication devices. Students with speech or language disorders can use the adaptive keyboard as a communication tool or to operate other assistive devices thanks to this integration.

Connectivity and Compatibility: Adaptive keyboards are typically designed to be compatible with various devices, including computers, tablets, and communication devices. They often support different connectivity options, such as USB, Bluetooth, or wireless connections, ensuring seamless integration into the existing technology infrastructure.

By utilizing an adaptive keyboard, students with special needs can overcome physical and cognitive barriers to effectively engage in educational activities involving keyboard input. The customization options, assistive input features, and compatibility with assistive technologies empower these students to access and interact with digital content and educational resources more independently and comfortably.

There are some hardware modifications that completely replace the standard keyboard and mouse for people who cannot use them:

- Expanded keyboards, which feature bigger keys spaced apart, can take the place of standard keyboards for people who struggle with fine motor control.
- Mini-keyboards are an option for people with fine motor skills who lack the range of motion needed to use a standard keyboard.
- For those who must use one hand to operate the computer, there are left-handed and right-handed keyboards available. They provide better key arrangements than standard keyboards designed for two-handed users.
- Trackballs and other specialized input devices can replace a mouse.

4.2.2.2 Text-to-Speech Software (TTS)

TTS software is a program that turns written text into spoken language. enabling specially-abled students to access and comprehend written information. The workflow of how Text to Speech software works for providing help to specially-abled students is:

Text Input: The user provides the TTS software with written text, which can be in various formats such as documents, web pages, or digital books. This text can be typed directly into the software interface or imported from external sources.

Text Analysis: The TTS software analyzes the input text, breaking it down into smaller units, such as sentences, phrases, or individual words. It also considers punctuation, formatting, and other linguistic elements to ensure proper pronunciation and intonation.

Linguistic Processing: The software applies linguistic rules and algorithms to interpret the text structure, grammar, and semantics. This step helps the software determine the appropriate pronunciation, stress patterns, and emphasis for each word and phrase.

Voice Synthesis: Based on the linguistic analysis, the TTS software utilizes a voice synthesis engine to convert the processed text into spoken words. The voice synthesis engine consists of a vast database of recorded or synthesized speech samples.

Naturalness and Intonation: To create a more natural and expressive output, the TTS software incorporates intonation patterns, pauses, and prosody cues. This enhances the clarity and comprehension of the spoken text, making it sound more similar to human speech.

Output Generation: The TTS software generates the synthesized speech output in real-time, which can be played through speakers, headphones, or other audio devices. The user can adjust the playback speed, volume, and other settings to suit their preferences.

Additional Features: Many TTS software applications offer additional features to enhance the user experience. These may include options to highlight the currently spoken words, change the voice characteristics (such as gender or accent), or provide controls for navigation and playback.

By utilizing TTS software, specially abled students, such as those with visual impairments, learning disabilities, or reading difficulties, can access written content more effectively. TTS software enables them to listen to text-based materials, including textbooks, articles, or online resources, allowing for improved comprehension, independent learning, and equal access to information.

Integrating text-to-speech (TTS) technology with existing teaching methods in special education can bring about significant improvements. It can lead to special education becoming more inclusive, accessible, and tailored to the individual needs of students. TTS supports student autonomy, comprehension, and language development, ultimately fostering academic success and positive learning experiences.

Accessibility: TTS technology ensures that written information becomes accessible to students with reading disabilities, visual impairments, or other print-related challenges. By converting text into spoken words, TTS enables students to engage with content that would otherwise be inaccessible to them. This inclusivity promotes equal educational opportunities for all students.

Comprehension and Retention: TTS software aids in improving students' comprehension and retention of information. By listening to the spoken text, students can better understand complex concepts, vocabulary, and sentence structures. TTS can also assist in decoding difficult or unfamiliar words, reinforcing comprehension, and facilitating content retention.

Independent Learning: TTS empowers students with special needs to engage in independent learning. By utilizing TTS, students can access written materials on their own, reducing their dependence on others for reading support Independence fosters these qualities—self-reliance, self-assurance, and ownership of their education.

Differentiated Instruction: TTS integration allows for differentiated instruction in special education. Teachers can use TTS to adapt instructional materials, such as textbooks, worksheets, or handouts, to suit individual student needs. They can customize reading speed, highlight specific words or phrases, and provide additional auditory support as required, ensuring that instruction aligns with each student's unique learning profile.

Multimodal Learning: TTS complements multimodal learning approaches by providing an additional mode of engagement with the content. By combining visual and auditory modalities, TTS enhances students' understanding and information processing. This approach accommodates diverse learning styles and preferences, catering to the specific needs of students with special needs.

Language Development: TTS integration supports language development in students with speech and language impairments. By listening to the spoken text, students can enhance their vocabulary, language fluency, and pronunciation. TTS can also serve as a model for proper intonation, stress, and rhythm, aiding in the development of oral communication skills.

Individualized Support: TTS technology allows for individualized support, enabling students to work at their own pace. Students can repeat or replay sections of the spoken text, review challenging content, and control the speed of the narration. This personalized approach promotes engagement, understanding, and mastery of the material.

4.2.2.3 Speech Recognition Software

The technology that turns spoken language into written text is called speech recognition software. It provides specially-abled students with an alternative means of communication and access to digital content. The workflow of how Speech Recognition works for providing help to specially-abled students:

Audio Input: The user speaks into a microphone or a connected audio input device, providing the speech recognition software with an audio signal containing spoken words and phrases.

Audio Processing: The software processes the audio input, applying techniques such as noise cancellation, audio normalization, and voice activity detection. These steps help enhance the quality and clarity of the audio signal.

Speech Analysis: The speech recognition software analyzes the audio input, breaking it down into smaller units, such as phonemes, words, or phrases. It utilizes linguistic models, acoustic models, and language models to match the audio input with the most likely corresponding text.

Language Processing: The software applies linguistic rules and algorithms to interpret the spoken language. It considers grammar, context, and semantic information to determine the appropriate transcription of the spoken words.

Transcription and Text Generation: Based on speech analysis and language processing, the speech recognition software generates the corresponding written text, representing the spoken words and phrases. This transcription is displayed on a screen or stored as a text file.

Accuracy and Training: Speech recognition software often requires training and adaptation to improve accuracy over time. Users may need to provide feedback, corrections, or additional training data to refine the software's recognition capabilities and optimize accuracy.

Editing and Correction: Once the text is generated, the user can review and edit the transcribed text if needed. The Speech recognition software may provide editing features, such as voice commands for text manipulation or correction suggestions based on context.

Application Integration: The transcribed text can be used within various applications and software. Specially abled students can utilize the transcribed text for writing assignments, composing emails, accessing digital content, or interacting with assistive technologies.

Vocabulary Customization: Some speech recognition software allows for vocabulary customization, enabling users to add or modify words specific to their needs. This feature is particularly useful for students with domain-specific terminology or individuals with unique speech patterns.

By utilizing speech recognition software, specially-abled students, such as those with motor disabilities, learning disabilities, or speech impairments, can overcome communication barriers and access written content more efficiently. Speech recognition technology provides an alternative input method, fostering independence, productivity, and inclusive access to information and educational resources. Integrating speech recognition technology with existing teaching methods in special education can bring about significant improvements. Speech recognition supports communication, writing, independent learning, and multimodal instruction, ultimately promoting academic success, self-confidence, and positive educational experiences.

Communication Support: Speech recognition technology enables students with speech and language impairments to communicate more effectively. Students can use speech recognition software to convert their spoken language into written text, facilitating interactions with teachers, peers, and other educational professionals. This integration enhances their ability to express themselves, participate in discussions, and actively engage in the learning process.

Writing and Composition: Speech recognition integration supports students with writing difficulties or disabilities. They can dictate their ideas and thoughts instead of physically writing them, alleviating the challenges associated with fine motor skills or dysgraphia. Speech recognition software transcribes their spoken words into written text, enabling them to produce written assignments, essays, and other written materials more efficiently.

Accessibility and Inclusion: Speech recognition technology promotes accessibility and inclusion by providing an alternative means of accessing and interacting with digital content. Students with reading difficulties, visual impairments, or other print-related challenges can use speech recognition to convert written materials into spoken words, making them accessible and easier to comprehend. This integration ensures that all students can participate in learning activities regardless of their individual needs.

Independent Learning: Speech recognition integration empowers students to engage in independent learning. They can use speech recognition software to access digital resources, conduct research, and interact with educational materials without relying on their reading abilities. This independence fosters self-reliance, autonomy, and the development of self-advocacy skills.

Multimodal Learning: By combining speech recognition with other modalities, such as text-to-speech or visual aids, special education teachers can implement multimodal learning approaches. This integration accommodates diverse learning styles and preferences, enabling students to engage with content through multiple sensory channels. The combination of speech recognition and other technologies enhances comprehension, retention, and overall learning outcomes.

Personalization and Differentiation: Speech recognition software allows for personalized instruction and differentiated learning experiences. Teachers can customize the software settings, vocabulary, and language models to align with individual student needs. Through personalization, students can work at their own pace, receive individualized support, and interact with material that is appropriate for their skills and interests.

Self-Advocacy and Confidence Building: The integration of speech recognition technology encourages students to advocate for their needs and participate actively in their education. By using speech recognition software, students develop self-confidence, overcome communication barriers, and build essential skills for self-expression and self-advocacy.

4.2.2.4 Screen Reader Software

Screen reader software is a technology designed to assist specially-abled students, particularly those with visual impairments, in accessing digital content. The workflow of how Speech Recognition works for providing help to specially-abled students is:

Text-to-Speech Conversion: Screen reader software utilizes text-to-speech (TTS) technology to convert written text on a computer screen into spoken words. It scans the content displayed on the screen and reads it aloud using synthesized speech.

User Interface Navigation: User interface elements of the operating system, different applications, and websites can all be accessed using the screen reader software. It provides keyboard shortcuts or commands that allow users to move between headings, links, buttons, menus, and other interactive elements.

Structural Analysis: The software analyzes the structure of a document or webpage to provide a meaningful reading experience. It identifies elements such as headings, paragraphs, lists, tables, and images, and announces their presence and context to the user.

Text Rendering: Screen reader software accurately interprets and renders various text formats, including different fonts, font sizes, formatting styles (bold, italic, underline), and text colors. It ensures that the user receives the relevant information regarding text appearance and layout.

Alternative Text for Images: Screen reader software provides alternative text descriptions for images, charts, graphs, and other visual elements that do not have inherent text. It reads these descriptions aloud, enabling visually impaired students to understand the visual content.

Keyboard and Command Feedback: The software gives audio feedback in response to user actions, such as keystrokes or commands. It informs the user of successful interactions, errors, or system notifications, ensuring that the user remains informed and in control of their interactions.

Customization Options: Screen reader software typically offers customization options to suit individual preferences and needs. Users can adjust speech rate, volume, voice characteristics (such as gender or accent), and other settings to optimize their reading experience.

Integration with Assistive Technologies: Screen reader software integrates with other assistive technologies, such as braille displays or refreshable braille devices, to provide tactile feedback in addition to spoken output. This integration allows users to access information through multiple sensory modalities.

Web Accessibility: Screen reader software is designed to support web accessibility standards. It works in conjunction with web browsers to interpret and read the HTML code and other web elements, ensuring that websites are accessible and navigable for visually impaired users.

By utilizing screen reader software, specially-abled students with visual impairments can access and interact with digital content, including documents, websites, emails, and applications. Screen readers provide them with equal access to information, educational resources, and digital platforms, enabling them to participate fully in educational activities and promoting inclusivity in the learning environment.

Integrating screen reader software with existing teaching methods in special education can bring about significant improvements.

Access to Information: Screen reader software ensures that visually impaired students have equal access to information and educational resources. By converting text into spoken words, it enables students to engage with digital content, including textbooks, documents, websites, and online materials. This integration eliminates barriers to accessing information and promotes inclusive learning.

Independent Learning: Screen reader software empowers visually impaired students to engage in independent learning. They can access and navigate digital content on their own, reducing their dependence on others for reading or interpreting information. This independence fosters self-reliance, self-confidence, and a sense of ownership over their education.

Content Comprehension: Screen reader software enhances content comprehension for visually impaired students. By audibly presenting the text, it helps students understand and interpret complex concepts, vocabulary, and sentence structures. The software's ability to navigate headings, lists, and other structural elements also aids in organizing and comprehending content.

Accessible Assessments: Integrating screen reader software enables visually impaired students to access and complete assessments, including quizzes, tests, and assignments. Teachers can ensure that digital assessments are compatible with screen readers, allowing students to independently engage with and respond to the assessment items.

Digital Collaboration: Screen reader software facilitates digital collaboration among students. By giving them access to shared documents and communication tools, it enables visually impaired students to engage in collaborative tasks, group projects, and online discussions. This integration promotes inclusive and collaborative learning experiences.

Adaptation of Materials: Teachers can adapt instructional materials to be compatible with screen reader software. They can ensure that digital resources, documents, and learning materials are properly structured, formatted, and labeled to provide seamless access for visually impaired students. This adaptation supports individualized instruction and ensures equitable access to materials.

Multimodal Learning: By combining screen reader software with other assistive technologies, such as braille displays or magnification tools, teachers can implement multimodal learning approaches. This integration accommodates diverse learning styles and preferences, enabling students to engage with content through multiple sensory modalities.

Inclusive Classroom Environment: The integration of screen reader software fosters an inclusive classroom environment. It promotes awareness and understanding among students and teachers about the needs of visually impaired students. This integration encourages empathy, collaboration, and respect for individual differences.

Screen readers support independent learning, content comprehension, collaboration, and adaptation of materials, ultimately promoting academic success, self-confidence, and positive educational experiences for visually impaired students.

4.2.3 Special Software and Applications

A variety of software and apps for education are available to meet different learning needs. These resources offer adaptive content, interactive, and interesting activities, as well as customized learning opportunities. Several areas, including reading comprehension, math, language development, executive functioning skills, and social and emotional learning, can be supported by educational apps. Some apps also include gamification components, which make learning more entertaining and inspiring for students.

Tools for AAC (Augmentative and Alternative Communication): A key component of education is communication, and for students who struggle with it, assistive and alternative communication methods are priceless. These tools, which include picture-based systems, message boards, speech-generating devices, and mobile applications, facilitate communication in a variety of ways. With the aid of AAC tools, students with speech and language disorders are supported in communicating their ideas, taking part in conversations, and interacting with peers and teachers.

4.2.3.1 Proloquo2Go

For those who have trouble speaking, Proloquo2Go is a robust and sophisticated augmentative and alternative communication (AAC) application. This Augmentative and Alternative Communication (AAC) app for iOS can help people who are unable to speak communicate on a daily basis and improve their language abilities. The app can be fully customized and is made to work with a variety of visual and fine-motor abilities. For non-verbal people with autism, Down syndrome, cerebral palsy, and a variety of other diagnoses or speech impediments like apraxia and dysarthria, the app's adaptability makes it useful. Users can completely tailor their vocabulary with Proloquo2Go for users with a variety of abilities, starting from early symbolic communication to complete literacy. Additional features include advanced word prediction, multiuser support, and two researched-based vocabulary organizations. Additionally, it provides two research-based vocabulary organizations, powerful automatic conjugations, a high-resolution library of over 14,000 symbols, and natural-sounding Text-to-Speech voices.

4.2.3.2 Speech Blubs

Speech Blubs: Language Therapy is a kids' educational app that uses video modeling to encourage kids to make use of new words and thereby increase their vocabulary for language and communication. With the aid of entertaining photo filters, short, highly-engaging videos, and animated content, Speech Blubs is an excellent tool for assisting children who are having difficulty learning to speak. The app is helpful for any child who could use it for speaking practise, but it is especially beneficial for those children. The educational game from Speech Blubs will foster your child's cognitive development, increase their self-assurance, and help them learn useful vocabulary about their favorite season.

4.2.3.3 Talk Tales, Simple Sounds

A speech therapist created Talk Tales, Simple Sounds specifically to help nonverbal or low-verbal kids with childhood apraxia or autism spectrum disorder. An interactive storybook and a movie to watch that includes all the taught sounds enable ongoing repetition.

Talk Tales, Simple Sounds were created based on the motor learning theory to specifically assist kids with childhood apraxia or an autism spectrum disorder, but it will be helpful to all toddlers and kids learning to make their first sounds (animal sounds and exclamations).

Online Learning Platforms and Learning Management Systems (LMS): Due to unforeseen emergence of the pandemic of COVID-19, online learning platforms and LMS have recently gained a lot of attention. A variety of features, including video conferencing, assignment management, content sharing, and collaboration tools, are available on these platforms. Online platforms can offer accessibility features like closed captioning, screen reader compatibility, and scalable fonts to students with disabilities. Individualized instruction, distance learning, and flexible access to educational resources are all made possible by these technologies.

Monitoring student progress, spotting students' areas of strength and weakness, and planning lessons are all made easier by data tracking and assessment tools. These resources can be used to monitor IEP objectives, gauge academic progress, and examine behavior patterns. Teachers can more effectively adapt instruction and interventions to meet the needs of each individual student thanks to data-driven insights.

Social Skills Training Programs: Special education technologies also include social skills training programs that are aimed at helping students with social difficulties or autism spectrum disorder improve their communication and social skills. To teach appropriate social behaviors, perspective-taking, emotion recognition, and problem-solving, these programs make use of video modeling, virtual scenarios, and interactive activities.

4.3 Support and Career Development Initiatives for Specially Abled Students

The already implemented social and support initiatives promoting SNE and the students in need of this are largely responsible for the current state of special education. There has been a uniform growth in awareness and support initiatives for special education students and their needs, as we discussed in the above sections. Advanced technological developments, complemented by developmental plans and acts by governments, non-governmental organizations, and UNICEF, have greatly led to the social and career development of specially-abled students.

The All India Council for Technical Education (AICTE) complying with the Right to Persons with Disabilities Act 2016, has taken steps to ensure accessibility and inclusivity in technical education for specially-abled students. They have made sure that every building on their campuses, both current and future, is accessible to people with disabilities. For the purpose of meeting the specific requirements of those with disabilities, institutions should build specialized facilities, such as ramps, rails, and special restrooms, as well as make other necessary adjustments.

People with different abilities need specialized aids and equipment to function on a daily basis. Through a number of the Ministry of Social Justice and Empowerment's programs, these aids are accessible. To assist students with disabilities enrolled in higher education, the higher education institution may also require the purchase of specialized learning and assessment tools through these programs. Additionally, visually impaired students need readers. It would improve the learning opportunities for people with disabilities if tools like computers equipped with screen reading software, aids for low-vision, scanners, different mobility devices, etc. were accessible in the institutions. Colleges are urged to invest in this technology and provide readers to blind or visually impaired students. All India Council for Technical Education (2017) claimed that this has significantly improved their education and boosted their involvement in extracurricular and social activities.

The special education paradigm has witnessed a lot of initiatives to improve career development initiatives for specially-abled students. Bridges from School to Work, commonly referred to as Bridges, has spent 30 years having an impact in some of the biggest cities in the United States (US). They have leveraged an intensive hands-on approach to assist young adults with disabilities in locating fulfilling employment both during and after high school, additionally linking young people with employers looking for competent entry-level employees and offering them the training, mentoring, and long-term support they require to succeed. According to Bridges from School to Work (2020), nearly 22,000 young adults with disabilities have been placed in jobs with more than 5,300 employers in 12 American cities thanks to their efforts.

Many more initiatives have been ongoing that promote the social and career development of specially-abled students and have been really successful in their own realms. Some of the notable ones include the Asia-Pacific Development Center on Disability (APCD), Enable India (India), National Center for Special Education in Charter Schools (United States), and many more. Looking at the large-scale awareness, societal acceptance, and initiatives for bettering the lives and education perspectives of specially-abled students clearly shows that progress is being made. Following and maintaining the current strategies is good enough for the specially-abled education scenario and development, but it cannot be denied that integration of Data Analysis and ML-based approaches with the current strategies can lead to even greater advancements and improvements in the field. The culmination of state-of-the-art ML techniques can lead to a better understanding and personalized growth of the SNE scenario and a faster convergence of the open problems in this domain.

4.4 Latest Advancements in AI-Assisted Special Education

The field of AI-assisted special education has witnessed several notable advancements in recent years. One key area of progress is the development of advanced natural language processing algorithms that enable more accurate speech recognition and text-to-speech capabilities. These advancements improve the communication experience for students with disabilities, allowing them to express themselves more effectively. Furthermore, ongoing research and development efforts are focused on enhancing the customization and personalization features of AI-assisted tools, enabling educators to tailor interventions and support to the unique requirements of each student. These advancements hold great promise for promoting inclusivity, accessibility, and educational outcomes for individuals with disabilities.

Triboelectric Smart Glove: The already existing solutions for gloves that are used to track dexterous hand movements are far from adequate for meeting the needs of signers' daily communication because they have the capability to only recognize gestures that are discrete and single (that is, numbers, words, or letters) instead of complete functionally used sentences. According to Wen et al. (2021), the researchers here suggest a virtual reality-based interface, deep learning blocks, and sensing gloves for the recognition of sign-language and communication systems powered by AI. The developed model using deep learning, without or with segmentation assistance, can recognize 20 sentences as well as 50 words. The segmentation methodology, which is significant, breaks the complete sentence signal into individual and discrete word units. The deep learning framework then decodes each and every word component, rebuilds sentences backward, and also recognizes them. Wen et al. (2021) also states that, additionally, with an average correct rate of about 86.67%, new/unknown sentences made by recombining the elements of words in a distinct order can also be recognized. The results of the recognition of sign language are then translated into textual and audio formats and projected into virtual space, enabling remote and bi-directional communication between signers and non-signers.

SlAide2Voice: According to a research published by Ciano et al. (2021), the architecture researchers intend to create a tool that can be used in conjunction with any currently available video conferencing tool, which can assist those with visual impairments during online lessons, conferences, and other events, The software's three primary parts are as follows:

- A straightforward client-server interface that enables data sharing between the presenter and the students.
- A plug-in for OpenOffice that must record slide changes and extract their contents (text and images).
- An AI model that can create descriptions and captions for the images on the slide. Both the speaker's computer and the students' computers who are blind must have the software installed.

For the application to pre-process the slides, the presenter must upload them prior to the lesson. The software creates the metadata during this stage, specifically by extracting the text, images, and slide layout using the OpenOffice add-on. The image caption and description will then be generated and extracted using a deep convolutional neural network. Additionally, image borders will be gathered in order to format the images so that they can be displayed on a braille tablet. The software will share an XML file with the students at the start of the lesson that contains all the metadata.

TikTalk: AI can assist children through speech therapy after diagnosing them. Gamifying the process is one of the best methods.

According to Miller (2023), TikTalk is a brand-new AI speech therapy platform, that uses lessons modeled after video games to entice kids to use it more frequently. Speech-language pathologists (SLPs) can use the games on the app to target specific words or speech patterns and customize them to meet the needs of different kids. The AI of the app analyses the outcomes as children play these educational games so that SLPs can make any necessary program adjustments. Children who dislike being away from home or find traditional speech therapy boring may not respond well to it. These gamified, AI-powered apps offer a solution by giving kids interesting options they can use from any location. The speech recognition features provide data on practise frequency, time-span, and correctness/accuracy with quantifiable results. To track practise and make remote adjustments, the SLP uses this platform, which analyses the speech of the children. The only solution that guarantees kids get personalized, accurate feedback while they engage in game-based remote learning is TikTalk, says Martin (2021).

4.5 Overall Analysis

The current state of AI-assisted special education is promising, with a range of solutions and products utilizing AI to support individuals with special needs. These AI-based tools and software programmes could significantly improve the educational experience, communication abilities, and general quality of life for students with disabilities.

The availability of AI-based products such as Dragon NaturallySpeaking, Proloquo2Go, and adaptive learning platforms like TikTalk demonstrates the growing recognition of the unique needs of students with disabilities. These tools leverage AI algorithms, natural language processing, and data analytics to offer individualized learning opportunities, improve accessibility, and sustain the specific requirements of students with diverse learning needs. The latest work and continuous research on products such as SlAide2Voice are also concurrently running to develop and create an industry-ready AI-assisted product to foster the growth of SNE.

AI technologies like speech recognition, text-to-speech, optical character recognition, virtual reality, and learning analytics have been integrated into special education settings, facilitating better communication, information access, and individualized instruction. These advancements empower students with disabilities to proactively engage in the learning procedure, express themselves effectively, and develop critical skills.

Moreover, social initiatives aimed at promoting special education and AI in special education have gained traction. Organizations, advocacy groups, and educational institutions are actively working to raise awareness, support research and development, and ensure the availability of AI-based tools and resources. These programs seek to close the gap between technology and special education, ensuring equal opportunities for individuals with disabilities.

However, despite the progress made, there are still challenges to address. The learning curve associated with AI tools, symbol limitations, contextual understanding constraints, and the need for ongoing customization highlight the importance of adequate training and support for users and educators. Additionally, factors such as cost, availability of technology, and individual variability pose barriers to widespread implementation and access to AI-assisted special education.

To further advance AI-assisted special education, continued research and development are crucial. Further exploration of AI algorithms, natural language processing, and machine learning techniques can enhance the accuracy, adaptability, and personalization of these tools. Additionally, collaborations between researchers, educators, and technology developers can lead to the creation of more comprehensive and inclusive AI solutions.

In conclusion, there have been significant advancements in AI-assisted special education, and we have a better understanding of students with disabilities and their needs in particular. The availability of AI-based tools, ongoing social initiatives, and increasing awareness of the potential of AI in special education indicate a positive trajectory towards providing equitable and effective educational experiences for all learners. Let us look at why ML and related approaches are plausible solutions to be considered. Let's Explore!

5.0 ROLE OF DATA ANALYSIS AND MACHINE LEARNING FOR SPECIAL EDUCATION

Over the years, advancements in technology have opened up new avenues for enhancing educational experiences and outcomes for these students. Among these technological advancements, data analysis, and machine learning have emerged as powerful tools with the potential to revolutionize special education. Here we have scrutinized the role of data analysis and machine learning in special education, highlighting the various ways data analysis and machine learning have carved ways in special education and the potential these advanced techniques bring in.

5.1 Understanding Student Needs Through Data Analysis

Data analysis plays a crucial role in special education by providing insights into individual students' needs and learning patterns. By collecting and analyzing various data points, such as academic performance, behavior records, and assessments, educators can identify patterns and trends that inform personalized instructional strategies.

Assume the educational data as machinery that does the processing of inputs and outputs such as progress, success, and achievement to assist in the operation of the whole process of education. The utilization of data is dependent on some crucial inputs from the parents of students, teachers, the students themselves, as well as the district and the state.

Some particular data outputs comprise of items such as grades, class attendance, scores of various assessments, and graduation rates, while particular data inputs can vary from the effectiveness of teachers to the demographics of students.

Constructive data decipherment allows the identification of individual student requirements and the implementation of strategies for differentiated and converted instructions. Data Scrutiny and analysis facilitate ingrained cultural processes that utilize particular inputs to ensure ideal output, which helps teachers understand the learning ability and the challenges faced by their students.

For example, by examining student performance data, teachers can pinpoint specific difficulties that a student may be having and create interventions that are specifically aimed at resolving those issues.

Furthermore, data analysis enables educators to keep tabs on the progress of their students over time, identify areas for improvement, and make data-informed decisions about individualized educational plans (IEPs). This data-driven approach ensures that interventions are evidence-based, efficient, and effective, ultimately leading to improved outcomes for students in special education.

5.2 Personalized Learning With Machine Learning

Machine learning algorithms have the capability to transform special education by enabling individualized learning opportunities. These algorithms can analyze vast amounts of data, such as student performance data, learning preferences, and individualized goals, to create adaptive and tailored learning pathways for each student.

Machine learning models can identify patterns in student data and make predictions about future learning needs. For example, an algorithm can analyze a student's previous performance and recommend specific instructional strategies or content to address areas of weakness. Through this individualized approach, students can advance at their own pace, and get the support they need, and experience a sense of accomplishment, fostering motivation and engagement.

5.3 Early Intervention and Predictive Analytics

Data analysis and machine learning can also contribute to early intervention in special education. By leveraging predictive analytics, educators can identify students at risk of academic or behavioral challenges before they escalate. Analyzing historical data combined with real-time information, such as attendance records, socio-emotional data, and engagement levels, can provide valuable insights for early identification and intervention.

Early intervention allows educators to implement proactive strategies, such as targeted interventions, counseling, or additional support services, to address potential difficulties. This approach helps prevent the widening of achievement gaps and increases the likelihood of positive educational outcomes for students in special education.

5.4 Individualizing Instructional Approaches

One of the greatest benefits of data analysis and machine learning in special education is the ability to individualize instructional approaches. Each student with special needs requires a customized learning experience tailored to their unique strengths, weaknesses, and learning style. Through the analysis of various data sources, such as behavioral data, academic assessments, and social-emotional records, educators can gain a comprehensive understanding of each student's profile.

Machine learning algorithms can then process this information and generate recommendations for instructional strategies, assistive technologies, or specialized resources that best meet the individual student's needs. This level of personalization ensures that students receive the necessary support and accommodations, leading to increased engagement, improved learning outcomes, and enhanced overall well-being.

6.0 WHY ARE DATA ANALYSIS AND MACHINE LEARNING A PROSPECTIVE SOLUTION IN THIS DOMAIN?

Allam & Martin (2021) mentions that as per a literature survey conducted by the Department of Education, City Division of Ilagan, Philippines, extensive research was conducted on the difficulties and challenges faced by special education (SPED) teachers when instructing students with disabilities.

Allam & Martin (2021) also states that according to this study, the Division of Ilagan's SPED classrooms generally lacks the resources necessary to support students with special needs, lacking resources, a curriculum manual, teaching resources, and classroom facilities as well.

The entire study was divided into five themes on which the teacher's challenges were tested in the implementation of special education. It is displayed in Figure 5.

Figure 5. Themes to challenges of the special education teachers

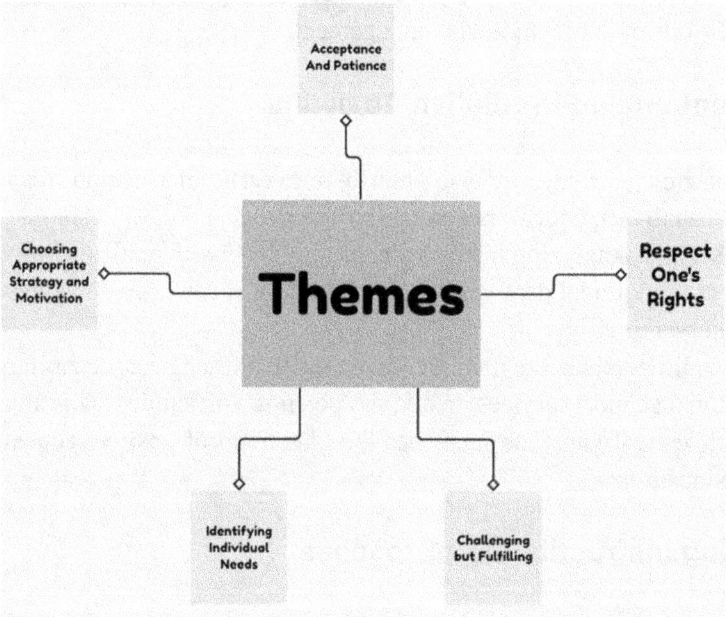

6.1 Choosing an Appropriate Strategy and Motivation

The main challenge that most of the teachers faced in the survey was the inability to devise an appropriate strategy for the students and provide personalized learning tracks for their overall learning. Learners receiving special education have diverse disabilities, and a challenge is to identify a particular category of disability and accordingly choose the strategy to provide the learning.

Machine Learning here can play a pivotal role in analyzing student behaviors, easily categorizing the disability the learner may be suffering from, and providing the learning path along with assistive technology. According to research conducted, Rough Sets and Decision Trees (DT) are two machine learning approaches that can be used to predict Learning Disabilities (LD) in school-aged children, with a focus on data mining applications. Combining these two approaches allows us to quickly and accurately predict the presence of LD in any child, as well as select the best classification strategy. According to David & Balakrishnan (2010) this study, utilises Naive Bayes algorithm and the Johnson's reduction algorithm, respectively, for mining the rules; rough sets attribute reduction, and classification, and the J48 algorithm is utilised for decision tree construction.

Apt disability detection allows teachers to devise a specific and targeted learning plan for the students and reduces the generalization of special education students. It also allows holistic growth for each student by allowing them to learn with peers who have the same disability and in a common environment.

6.2 Acceptance and Patience

The teachers also faced challenges; they have encountered cases where the learner has more than one learning disability, but disclosure of the fact to parents is a difficult task and can lead to their parents being angry or expressing disbelief of the teachers.

Advanced technological developments in the paradigms of Machine Learning can be an aid to such cases. Pre-admission learner checks can be employed by institutions to cross-verify the medical documents submitted by parents and have a second check on them. This not only helps in identifying the true medical condition but also allows for trust-building among parents, teachers, and educational institutions. This prevents later disputes between parents and teachers. In case the parents show less trust in the Machine Learning based medical screening process, a doctor's session can also be booked to gain trust. This can act as a preventive measure to solve the issues. Hence, Machine Learning here enables trust gain, initial screening, and easier acceptance of LD conditions among students.

6.3 Identifying Individual Needs

When teachers get ready to teach, one of the fundamental ideas is to acknowledge the individual differences of the students. Strategic teaching and learning begin with the fundamental premise that the curriculum they choose for the classroom ought to take into account context, instruction, learning, and achievement variables.

Learners receiving special education have diverse disabilities, and a challenge is to identify a particular category of disability and accordingly choose the strategy to provide the learning. It is important to identify the different special needs and develop individual learning patterns and curricula for each of them.

Robots may be able to recognize when an autistic child requires assistance thanks to machine learning algorithms developed by an Israeli research team. Three girls and four boys with autism received a Kiwi robot from the team for a month each. The ages of the children's range from 3 years to 7 years. A green and purple robot named Kiwi with an interactive smile guided the children as they engaged in a math game with a space theme on a tablet. The tablet's camera was mounted there to capture the kids playing. After reviewing the audio, video, and the children's game scores at the end of the month, the researchers trained a machine-learning algorithm to determine when the children were paying attention. They created specialized models for the data from each child as well as broad models using the behaviors of many children. The team kept an eye on whether or not Kiwi's encouragement affected the kids' concentration on the game. According to Dattaro (2020), children paid attention roughly 70% of the time when Kiwi had spoken in the previous minute, as opposed to less than 50% of the time when Kiwi had been silent.

Catering to the learning needs of Autism-based patients, a particular algorithm and method were deployed, leading to a better understanding and handling of the special education needs of the students. Machine Learning and Data Analysis paradigms hence help classify and develop dedicated LD-based routines for the overall holistic development of specially-abled students.

Advanced ML algorithms effectively address the various drawbacks and difficulties that conventional methods are unable to address, assisting the SNE and the students by addressing the root causes of the issues in this paradigm.

7.0 CASE STUDIES

7.1 Case Study 1: Dystech

A screening app for the early detection of learning disorders like dyslexia and dysgraphia is being developed by the Australian startup Dystech, which was co-founded by Richards, Mathieu Serrurier, Jim Radford, and Gilles Richard. Dystech is an advanced tool developed to detect early dyslexia. Richard (2019) states that the purpose of Dystech is to provide adults and children who are dyslexic with a useful and affordable way to properly diagnose their condition.

Users go through a 10-minute screening test with the app, which uses ML and AI and is built on Amazon Web Services (AWS) infrastructure. During the test, participants speak out words aloud that are displayed on the screen while having recordings made on their mobile devices. After that, users are told whether they are likely to have dyslexia. The app trains the AI using datasets of audio recordings from adults and kids who are dyslexic and those who are not.

They discovered that reading reaction time and reading speed are somewhat correlated. It appears that those who are diagnosed with dyslexia take more time to read than those who do not. The reading reaction time measures how long it takes for a word to appear on the screen after someone attempts to read it. According to Richard (2019), Dystech is constantly gathering data to enhance the app's algorithm. However, Dystech faces a problem getting access to the information it requires. It's somewhat private when your child has dyslexia, so it's been difficult for the company to gather information. Even though they follow an ethic of approval, getting it is extremely difficult as expressed by Chanthadavong (2020). Despite these difficulties, Richard (2019) expressed optimism that the Dystech app might eventually replace the current diagnostic procedure and hinted that plans are afoot to integrate Dystech into the Victorian justice system.

7.2 Case Study 2: Dragon Naturally Speaking

7.2.1 About

Dragon Systems of Newton, Massachusetts, created Dragon Naturally Speaking, also known as DNS or Dragon for PC, which Lernout & Hauspie Speech Products, Nuance Communications, and Microsoft later acquired. It can be used on personal computers with Windows. As per Wikipedia of Dragon NaturallySpeaking (2011), Microsoft released Version 15 (Professional Individual and Legal Individual) in August 2016, which supports the 32-bit and 64-bit versions of Windows 7, 8, and 10.

It uses advanced artificial intelligence algorithms to convert spoken language into written text, allowing individuals to interact with computers, applications, and devices through voice commands. Dragon NaturallySpeaking offers a range of features and benefits that enhance productivity, accessibility, and communication for users across various domains. Some of the key features of this software include:

Speech-to-Text Conversion: Dragon NaturallySpeaking accurately transcribes spoken words into written text in real-time. It can capture and interpret natural language, recognizing various accents, dialects, and speech patterns. The software continually adapts and learns from the user's voice to improve accuracy over time.

Voice Commands and Control: Users can navigate and control their computer, applications, and web browsers entirely through voice commands. Dragon NaturallySpeaking supports a wide range of voice-activated tasks, such as opening programs, saving files, sending emails, or browsing the internet.

Customization and Personalization: The software allows users to customize its vocabulary and voice profiles to match their specific needs. Users can create specialized word lists, add industry-specific terminology, and train the software to recognize their unique voice patterns for improved accuracy.

Dictation and Transcription: Dragon NaturallySpeaking excels in dictation capabilities, making it ideal for professionals, writers, and students who need to create written content efficiently. Users can dictate emails, documents, reports, or other textual content, allowing for hands-free and faster composition.

Text-to-Speech PLAYBACK: In addition to speech recognition, Dragon NaturallySpeaking offers text-to-speech functionality, allowing users to have their written content read aloud. This feature can be particularly beneficial for proofreading, editing, or for individuals with visual impairments who rely on auditory feedback.

7.2.2 Use Case

A DSA needs an assessor, for whom Jodie Parkes has experience working with students who have a variety of disabilities, some of which may prevent them from achieving their full capability. He has been offering guidance to various students for a long period of 20 years and has always been amazed by how much Dragon can benefit the pupils he advises.

A major benefit of Dragon, according to Jodie, is how simple it is to use. According to him, for most students, it basically just involves putting on a headset and talking, and things start to happen. According to Nuance Communications (2020), Jodie agrees to the fact that Dragon enables students to quickly enter their thoughts into the computer using dictation to text, which is very advantageous to them. He discussed how dyslexia and other conditions that make it difficult for people to express themselves in writing can be helped by Dragon. Speaking instead of using a keyboard to translate your ideas into words gives you more freedom., and the keyboard is no longer acting as a barrier.

Jodie discussed the help that Dragon can provide for students who are struggling with anxiety-related problems or mental health conditions. Any method that can reduce the amount of effort needed to complete a task is helpful because people often feel overwhelmed by it. Dragon's voice recognition technology quickly converts spoken words into written text, so as published by Nuance Communications (2020), Jodie states, "For the majority of individuals, those disability effects practically vanish.".

If a student has physical difficulties using a keyboard or mouse, Jodie also suggests Dragon. Since there is no physical interface between their thoughts and ideas and the computer, they consider this to be a huge advantage. Students can use Dragon for more than just document creation. Anything can be done more quickly and easily, including sending emails, tweeting, and doing web searches.

7.2.3 Benefits

Dragon Naturally Speaking software is widely used and recommended for students with various disabilities. The wide range of benefits offered by this software makes it a great use case of AI in special education.

Enhancing Productivity: By eliminating the need for manual typing, Dragon NaturallySpeaking greatly increases productivity. Users can create documents, emails, and reports faster, freeing up time for other tasks. The software also offers voice-controlled editing and formatting features, further streamlining the content creation process.

Accessibility and Inclusion: The software greatly enhances accessibility for individuals with physical disabilities or those who have difficulty with traditional keyboard input. Dragon NaturallySpeaking allows them to interact with computers and digital content using only their voice, promoting independence and inclusion.

Language Learning and Pronunciation: Dragon NaturallySpeaking can assist language learners in improving their pronunciation and fluency. By dictating and having their speech converted into text, users can review and correct their spoken language, aiding in language acquisition and proficiency development.

Assistive Technology: The software serves as an assistive technology tool for individuals with conditions such as dyslexia, dysgraphia, or repetitive strain injuries. It allows them to overcome writing challenges by converting spoken words into text, enabling them to participate fully in educational or professional environments.

Hands-Free Computing: Dragon NaturallySpeaking provides hands-free computing, allowing users to control their computers solely through voice commands. This feature is particularly valuable for individuals with mobility impairments or those who need to multitask while using a computer.

7.2.4 Limitations and Considerations

While everything has some advantages, we are also obliged to see through the drawbacks it brings to innovate and look for better approaches building upon the existing architectures. The limitations that Dragon Naturally Speaking comes with are:

Learning Curve: While Dragon NaturallySpeaking offers high accuracy, users may initially require some time to acclimatize to the software. Training the software to understand individual voice patterns and preferences may involve an adjustment period.

Environmental Factors: Background noise or other environmental factors may have an impact on the software's performance. Using Dragon NaturallySpeaking in a quiet and controlled environment can help maximize accuracy.

Hardware Requirements: Dragon NaturallySpeaking is a resource-intensive application that may require a robust computer system to run smoothly. Users should ensure their computer meets the necessary hardware specifications to ensure optimal performance.

Language Support: While Dragon NaturallySpeaking supports multiple languages, the level of accuracy and availability.

7.3 Case Study 3: Proloquo2Go

7.3.1 About

Proloquo2Go is an augmentative and alternative communication (AAC) software application designed to support individuals with communication challenges. People with speech impairments, language disorders, autism spectrum disorder (ASD), cerebral palsy, and other conditions that affect expressive communication frequently use it. Proloquo2Go harnesses the power of AI and natural language processing to facilitate effective communication. Some of the key features of this software include:

Symbol-based Communication: Proloquo2Go uses a symbol-based approach to communication, employing a vast library of symbols, pictures, and icons to represent words, phrases, and concepts. These symbols help users construct sentences and express their thoughts and needs.

Text-to-Speech Functionality: The software incorporates text-to-speech technology, allowing users to generate spoken output based on the text they input. Proloquo2Go leverages AI algorithms to provide high-quality and natural-sounding voices, ensuring that users can communicate with clarity and confidence.

Customization and Personalization: Proloquo2Go offers extensive customization options, enabling users and their support teams to tailor the software to individual needs. It allows for the creation of custom vocabulary, personalized phrases, and unique sentence structures. Users can also choose from a variety of voices, languages, and accents.

Core Word Vocabulary: Proloquo2Go emphasizes the use of core words, which are high-frequency words that form the foundation of communication. The software provides a robust core word vocabulary, empowering users to express a wide range of messages using a relatively small set of core words. This approach promotes efficient and versatile communication.

Quick and Efficient Communication: Proloquo2Go is designed to facilitate rapid communication. It offers features like word prediction and sentence completion, anticipates user input, and provides suggestions to speed up the message formulation process. This functionality especially benefits individuals with motor challenges or limited typing abilities.

Integration with Assistive Technology: Proloquo2Go seamlessly integrates with other assistive technologies, such as switch access, eye-tracking systems, and alternative input devices. This compatibility ensures that individuals with diverse physical abilities can access and use the software effectively.

Data Tracking and Reporting: The software includes built-in data tracking capabilities, allowing support teams to monitor and analyze usage patterns, communication progress, and vocabulary expansion. This information can help inform therapy strategies and track the effectiveness of communication interventions.

7.3.2 Use Case

According to a user, who is a Speech-Language Pathologist, he loves Proloquo2go, and two of his students use it to supplement their communication skills. He has discovered that setting up for a variety of communication opportunities is incredibly simple, and he particularly appreciates the company's video tutorials. When questions arise about its use, it is also discovered that they are promptly addressed on their Facebook page. Although expensive, it's a great substitute for the pricey dedicated communication device, which frequently costs $6000 or more.

His students can "read" adapted books aloud using Proloquo2go, and he has noticed that one student, in particular, has improved verbalizations. In games like "Go Fish" and "Mr. Potato Head," it has also been used to ask for something, to say things like "Good game," and to describe things like "The pumpkin feels smooth and bumpy." The current date and the current weather are also mentioned in it. It has largely been successful for all the language-enrichment activities he designs with these two students, who struggle with oral communication. He occasionally has to program the correct pronunciation of a word, but that is simple to do.

7.3.3 Benefits and Impact

Enhanced Communication: Proloquo2Go empowers individuals with communication challenges to express their thoughts, needs, and emotions more effectively. It provides a voice for individuals who are unable to communicate verbally, fostering greater independence and inclusion in social interactions.

Language Development: Through the use of symbols and core word vocabulary, Proloquo2Go supports language development and expands users' vocabulary and sentence structure. It encourages active participation in conversations, promoting linguistic growth and improved language skills over time.

Educational Support: Proloquo2Go is widely used in educational settings to support students with communication difficulties. The software facilitates participation in classroom activities, promotes academic engagement, and enables students to access the curriculum more effectively.

Social Interaction: By enabling effective communication, Proloquo2Go helps individuals with communication challenges engage in social interactions and build relationships. It enhances their ability to initiate and respond to conversations, fostering social connections and reducing feelings of isolation.

Independence and Empowerment: Proloquo2Go encourages self-expression and autonomy. Users gain greater control over their communication, leading to increased self-confidence, improved self-advocacy, and a sense of empowerment in daily life.

7.3.4 Limitations

While Proloquo2Go is a highly beneficial AAC software application, it does have some limitations. It's important to consider these limitations to ensure the appropriate and effective use of the app:

Steep Learning Curve: Proloquo2Go requires training and familiarization for both users and their support teams. Learning to navigate the app, customize vocabulary, and utilize advanced features can be time-consuming and may require additional support from therapists or educators.

Symbol Limitations: While Proloquo2Go offers a vast library of symbols and pictures, there may be instances where specific symbols are not available or do not accurately represent certain concepts or objects. This can limit the user's ability to express complex or specific ideas.

Limited Contextual Understanding: Proloquo2Go relies on pre-programmed vocabulary and sentence structures, which means it may struggle to comprehend and generate context-specific phrases or idiomatic expressions. Users may need to manually construct more contextually appropriate sentences.

Dependency on Technology: Proloquo2Go is a software application that operates on electronic devices like tablets or smartphones. It is dependent on the availability and functionality of these devices, which can be a limitation in situations where technology is not readily accessible or encounters technical issues.

Motor Limitations: Individuals with severe motor challenges or fine motor control difficulties may find it challenging to navigate the app or accurately select symbols or words on the device's screen. This can impact the speed and accuracy of their communication.

Linguistic Limitations: While Proloquo2Go supports multiple languages and accents, there may still be limitations in terms of language availability or dialect representation. This can affect individuals who primarily communicate in languages or dialects that are not well-supported by the app.

Cost and Availability: Proloquo2Go is a paid app available for iOS devices. The cost of Proloquo2Go is $249.99 for iPhone and iPad, whereas it is $124.99 for Mac on the Educational App Store (2022). The cost of the app and associated devices may pose financial challenges for individuals or organizations with limited resources. Additionally, the app may not be available on all platforms or operating systems.

Individual Variability: Each individual's communication needs and abilities are unique. While Proloquo2Go offers customization options, it may not fully address the specific requirements of every user. Individualized assessment and ongoing adjustments are necessary to optimize the app's effectiveness for each user.

8.0 CHALLENGES AND LIMITATIONS

Challenges and Ethical Considerations

While data analysis and machine learning offer significant potential benefits in special education, they also raise certain challenges and ethical considerations. When it comes to the process of implementation in education, the AI concept must deal with some problems and hassles as an upcoming technology. Before we can implement AI in a particular sector of education, those problems and difficulties should be duly noted. Firstly, it has to be clear which AI tool should be used for which kind of application. It is because factors like geography, politics, societal factors, etc. can influence which of the available AI solutions is the best possible one for the given problem statement. Most of the time, those factors have an impact on the entire educational system.

8.1 General Concerns

a. **Data Privacy:** Proper safeguards must be in place to protect students' sensitive information and ensure compliance with privacy regulations. Data collection, storage, and analysis should prioritize privacy and consent, with a clear understanding of who has access to the data and how it will be used.
b. **Bias and Fairness:** Machine learning models can inadvertently perpetuate biases if not carefully designed and trained. It is essential to consider potential biases within the data and regularly evaluate algorithms to ensure fairness and equity in decision-making processes.

c. **Human Element:** While technology can enhance educational experiences, it is crucial to maintain a balance between automated processes and human expertise. Educators play a vital role in interpreting and contextualizing the insights provided by data analysis and machine learning, and their expertise should guide decision-making.
d. **Resource Availability:** Implementing data analysis and machine learning in special education requires adequate resources, including access to technology, training for educators, and ongoing technical support. Ensuring equitable access to these resources is vital to preventing further marginalization of students with special needs.
e. **Lack of Employment for Teachers in SNE:** With the rise in technological advancements in the Special Education sector, there have been more and more sophisticated machines and assistive technology that have been developed to aid students with disabilities. They are found to be more accurate and adhere to the holistic growth of the children, which might not have been possible with teachers. Advanced disability classification devices and the early interpretation of disability using machine learning have seen a great rise in the past few years. With initiatives like AI Screener and AI orchestrators, the sector is heavily dominated by AI-based methods, says the Penn State University (2023). Hence, the need for teachers in SNE diminishes day by day. But it also cannot be denied that, in spite of the high accuracy of ML and AI systems, the care and attention provided by teachers can never be matched by these advanced systems. This factor can never be achieved, and hence the need for teachers, even if reduced, will still remain for the personal monitoring and care of the students.
f. **Emotional Intelligence Deficit:** Teachers offer more than just information, so technology shouldn't completely replace them. The emotional and personal support that humans and teachers can provide is still untouched by AI. The education sector has a huge dependency on the emotional dependency of students during their learning phase, which is even higher for students with LD. Hence, AI-based systems cannot solely solve this problem. Only recently has AI been used as a tool for interpersonal interaction rather than for direct human-to-human communication. But we are still far from achieving the emotional intelligence that humans currently portray.
g. **Continuous Maintenance and Development:** There are several maintenance-related issues with artificial intelligence in the classroom. For example, the authority should constantly monitor everything AI does because AI has a limited amount of knowledge and can have unintended consequences if it is used beyond its limitations. They might not function well together unless their languages are compatible with those of the other machines, much like how each machine functions differently. This may result in problems like a lack of coordination between two systems, which would prevent them from working when they were most needed.

8.2 Ethical Concerns

Though AI possesses the capability to support both teacher practise and student learning, it is largely inappropriate for use in kindergarten and grades 1 through 12 (K–12) due to its ethical and social flaws. The moral questions that AI in education raises must be acknowledged and brought up with both teachers and students. When anyone constructs and develops an algorithm, they also generate a set of data that portrays the historical biases and systemic prejudice of the society, from which algorithmic bias eventually emerges. In spite of the fact that the bias is implicitly incorporated into the algorithm-based model, we still have the ability to detect various biases in race and gender on various platforms purely based on AI.

One of the most important moral concerns about AI use in in K–12 education is students' and teachers' privacy concerns. The majority of privacy violations occur when users divulge excessive amounts of personal information on digital platforms. Even though sensitive personal data should be protected by existing laws and guidelines, data access and security violations by AI-based tech companies have raised public concerns about privacy. To allay these worries, the AI-based systems ask for the user's permission before they can access the user's personal data. Many individuals provide their consent without even being aware of or considering the extent of information (metadata) they are allowing to be shared with the system, such as the languages they speak, their racial identity, biographical information, and location, in spite of the fact that the request for consent is intended to be protective measures and alleviate worries about privacy. Such kind of uninformed information sharing actually undermines human agency and privacy. Simply put, people's agency is reduced as a result of AI systems that discourage reflection and free thought. As per Akgun & Greenhow (2021), academics have questioned whether it is moral to make parents and kids use these algorithms as part of their education, even if they explicitly agree to giving up privacy, in a related vein. They really have no choice if these systems are required by public schools.

Additional ethical concerns about the application of AI in education of K-12 are brought up by the use of tracking or surveillance systems that gather specific information about the decisions and actions of students and teachers. Algorithms and ML models are used by AI tracking systems to not only track user activity but also forecast their future preferences and actions. AI's predictive systems can incorporate monitoring tools to foresee students' academic progress, areas of weakness, and learning preferences. According to Akgun & Greenhow (2021), researchers have found that teachers using social networking sites (SNSs) for educational purposes may encounter a variety of issues, such as concerns regarding friendship power, privacy limits, responsibility, and accessibility. While monitoring students' online activity may be seen as a teacher's responsibility and a pedagogical tool to handle potentially harmful circumstances (like exposure to sexual content or cyberbullying), such actions can also be seen as intrusive surveillance, which compromises the privacy of students. Monitoring and tracking students' online interactions may restrict their participation in the learning activity, which may prevent them from owning up to their opinions.

9.0 CONCLUSION AND FUTURE SCOPE

Data analysis and machine learning have the capability to transform and revolutionize special education by providing individualized learning experiences, early intervention, and individualized instructional approaches. Through the analysis of student data, educators can gain insights into student needs, track progress, and make data-informed decisions to optimize educational outcomes. These technologies will be employed in more ways to enhance student outcomes as they advance in the future. For instance, using data analysis and machine learning to create new assessment tools that are more precise and effective than current ones. They could also be utilized to develop online tutors who can offer 24/7 individualized training to pupils. The use of machine learning and data analysis in special education has tremendous potential advantages. The way that children with disabilities are taught and supported has the potential to undergo a revolution thanks to these technologies. Endless possibilities are present when Augmented Reality and Virtual Reality is integrated with ML methods to assist student with disabilities through Virtual tutors and AR based study systems that will aid the efficient study of students with disabilities. AI based analysis and student monitoring can lead to personified education curriculum fostering better and holistic growth of students with disabilities. Additional gamification features can further ignite interest among students with disabilities leading to better learning and development through immersive education. Data analysis and machine learning can help to guarantee that all children with disabilities have the chance to thrive by delivering individualized teaching, predicting student success, tracking student progress, and increasing communication between stakeholders.

However, it is crucial to address challenges related to data privacy, bias, and resource availability and ensure that these technologies are used ethically and in conjunction with human expertise. By embracing the power of data analysis and machine learning, special education can evolve to better meet the diverse needs of students and empower them to reach their full potential.

REFERENCES

Akgun, S., & Greenhow, C. (2021, September 22). *Artificial Intelligence in Education: Addressing Ethical Challenges in K-12 Settings*. PubMed Central (PMC).

Allam, F. C., & Martin, M. M. (2021). Issues and challenges in special education: A qualitative analysis from teacher's perspective. *Southeast Asia Early Childhood Journal, 10*(1), 37–49. doi:10.37134aecj.vol10.1.4.2021

Belsky, G. (2019, August 5). Assistive Technology for Auditory Processing Challenges. *Understood.*

Burry, M. (2021, January 25). *Hearing Aids Go High-tech.* Healthy Hearing.

Chanthadavong, A. (2020, September 15). *Dystech Using Artificial Intelligence to Help Speed Screening for Learning Disorders*. ZDNET.

Centers for Disease Control and Prevention. (2023, January 11). *Signs & Symptoms | Autism Spectrum Disorder (ASD).* NCBDDD | CDC.

Dattaro, L. (2020, March 25). *How Autism Researchers Are Applying Machine-learning Techniques.* Academic Press.

David, J. M., & Balakrishnan, K. (2010). Machine learning approach for prediction of learning disabilities in school-age children. *International Journal of Computers and Applications, 9*(11), 7–14. doi:10.5120/1432-1931

Gorman, M. (2021, March 16). *5 Ways AI Will Impact Education for Autistic Children.* Academic Press.

Habib, H. (2015). Awareness about Special Education in Hyderabad. *International Journal of Science and Research.* https://www.ijsr.net/archive/v4i5/SUB154394.pdf

Inclusive Education. (2017) United Nations Children's Fund.

Inclusive Education - Campaigns. (2020). Inclusion BC.

Kurtsikidze, K. (2022, June 14). *See Every Colour Campaign Addressing Stigma Around Children With Special Education Needs Summarizes Results. See Every Colour campaign addressing the stigma around children with special education needs summarizes results.* Government of India.

Martin, D. (2021, January 23). *New AI System Accelerates Speech Therapy*. Unite.AI.

MedicalXpress. (2018, January 15). *Brain imaging predicts language learning in deaf children*. Author.

Muktamath, V. U., Hegde, P. R., & Chand, S. (2021, December 10). *Types of Specific Learning Disability. Types of Specific Learning Disability*. IntechOpen.

National Center for Education Statistics. (2022). *Students With Disabilities. Condition of Education*. U.S. Department of Education, Institute of Education Sciences.

Ojha, S. T. (2022). Artificial Intelligence In Special Education, Id & Cp. *Journal of Positive School Psychology,* 8341-8345.

Penn State University (2023, January 12). *New Institute to Use AI Technology for Children With Speech, Language Disorders*. Author.

Richard, H. R. (2019, June 17). *How Artificial Intelligence Helps Students With Dyslexia*. Academic Press.

United Nations, Department of Economic and Social Affairs Disability. (2015, May 14), *Factsheet on Persons with Disabilities*. U.S. Department of Education, Office of Special Education Programs, Individuals with Disabilities Education Act (IDEA) Database.

Wikipedia. (2011, August 1). *Dragon*. Author.

Zdravkova, K., Krasniqi, V., Dalipi, F., & Ferati, M. (2022). Cutting-edge communication and learning assistive technologies for disabled children: An artificial intelligence perspective. *Frontiers in Artificial Intelligence*, *5*, 970430. doi:10.3389/frai.2022.970430 PMID:36388402

Chapter 5
Integration of Artificial Intelligence in the Modern Classroom:
Prospects for Digitization in Education

Muhammad Mujtaba Asad
Sukkur IBA University, Pakistan

Shahzeen Younas
Sukkur IBA University, Pakistan

Sarfraz Ali
Sukkur IBA University, Pakistan

Prathamesh Padmakar Churi
https://orcid.org/0000-0002-1732-1703
NMIMS University, India

Anand Nayyar
https://orcid.org/0000-0002-9821-6146
School of Computer Science, Duy Tan University, Vietnam

ABSTRACT

Artificial intelligence integration in education is proven to be an easier and convenient way of delivering knowledge to students and hence became the demand of 21st-century classrooms. The findings from the literature review show that implementing artificial intelligence in education by following different pedagogical models of artificial intelligence in education (i.e. the SAMR model, the TPACK model, and the TAM model) can lead to fruitful outcomes in the teaching and learning process, and also this study would help in fulfilling the knowledgeable, contextual, and pedagogical gaps for the integration of artificial intelligence in the era of digitization of education.

DOI: 10.4018/979-8-3693-0378-8.ch005

1. INTRODUCTION

The 21st century has witnessed unprecedented technological advancements, leading to a digitally revolutionized world as depicted in science-fiction movies (Küçük & Gündoğdu, 2020). This transformation has been primarily driven by digitalization, which has permeated virtually every aspect of human life. At the forefront of this digital revolution stands Artificial Intelligence (AI), a technology that is reshaping industries and transforming the way we interact with technology. AI's cognitive abilities, including problem-solving, adaptive learning, and decision-making, are increasingly mirroring human-like intelligence (Zhou, Zhang, & Xu, 2020). One domain where AI has gained substantial ground is education, revolutionizing traditional teaching and learning methods in educational institutions (Kučak et al., 2018). The integration of AI in education has yielded remarkable changes, ranging from enhanced efficiency and global learning opportunities to personalized educational experiences and more intelligent content delivery. By harnessing the potential of AI, educational institutions have witnessed a paradigm shift in teaching practices, administration, and overall effectiveness. Over the past decade, AI has rapidly risen in prominence within the education landscape, fostering innovative approaches to teaching and learning (Sun & Zhang, 2021). Its applications are not limited to specific educational levels or subject areas but encompass various sectors, from primary and secondary education to higher education and professional training. AI's influence in education spans several key areas. Firstly, it streamlines administrative processes, such as enrollment management, student record keeping, scheduling, and resource allocation, enabling educational institutions to operate more efficiently (Kovalchuk, 2021). Secondly, AI-powered tools analyze vast educational data to create personalized curricula and learning materials tailored to individual student needs and learning styles (Zhang et al., 2020). Thirdly, AI facilitates adaptive learning, where learning platforms adjust the pace and content based on individual student progress and performance, ultimately enhancing learning outcomes. Additionally, AI enables the integration of immersive technologies, like augmented reality, virtual reality, and three-dimensional simulations, enriching the learning experience and simplifying complex concepts (Sandhya & Maheshwari, 2021). The success of AI in education is underpinned by various technical advancements, including natural language processing, machine learning algorithms, computer vision, and data analytics (Zhou, Zhang, & Xu, 2020). These technologies empower AI systems to process vast amounts of educational data, understand natural language, and provide personalized learning experiences at an unprecedented scale. Hence, the continuous advancement of AI is expected to further amplify its impact on education, ushering in an era of transformative educational innovation. This chapter explores the diverse applications of AI in education, from administrative tasks to personalized learning experiences, and highlights the technical advancements supporting its success in this domain. By embracing AI's potential, educational institutions can enhance learning outcomes, empower educators, and offer students a more enriching and adaptive educational journey. This research aims to study how using advanced AI in Education 4.0 in digital classrooms affects teaching methods, student involvement, and learning results. We want to understand how AI changes regular classes into exciting, technology-based learning places. One important part of our study is to find and talk about the problems that come up when AI for Education 4.0 is used in digital classrooms. These issues include technical challenges, worries about keeping data private, and how AI should be used in teaching. Apart from finding these problems, we also want to learn about good teaching methods that can overcome the challenges of using AI for Education 4.0 in digital classrooms. Our goal is to find ways for AI tools to work well with human teachers. We want to use these solutions to not only solve the problems but also make learning even better by using AI. By carefully handling the technical, ethical, and teaching parts, our research wants to make the most out of AI for Education 4.0. We hope this will bring better and more effective learning in the digital age.

2. METHODOLOGY

A literature review approach is employed to explore and analyze the existing body of knowledge regarding the integration of artificial intelligence (AI) for personalized learning in the era of digitization, with a specific focus on the global perspective of Education 4.0. A narrative literature review approach is adopted as it allows for the characterization and summary of the available knowledge on integrating AI into personalized learning within the context of digitization in education. This approach facilitates the exploration of academic models and pedagogical frameworks for incorporating AI in education, as well as the investigation of the possibilities and challenges associated with implementing AI in educational settings. To conduct the literature review, electronic databases such as Google Scholar, Scopus, and Web of Science are utilized. A preliminary search of the literature on the integration of AI in education is performed to gain an overview of the existing work in this field. This preliminary search helps identify the various forms of AI integration and the volume of literature available. Based on this initial exploration, a selection of relevant themes and concepts related to AI integration in education is established. Subsequently, a comprehensive literature search is conducted using the identified themes as search terms. The search is conducted in the aforementioned databases, focusing on published, peer-reviewed articles and relevant conference proceedings. The timeframe for the search spans from the advent of Education 4.0 to the present. The inclusion criterion for papers is their relevance to the topic of AI integration in personalized learning within the context of digitization and Education 4.0. Papers that do not provide insights or knowledge about the main study objective or utilize AI concepts as mere synonyms are excluded from consideration. The search process generates a considerable number of records, which are then reduplicated to remove any duplications across databases. After the deduplication process, the unique records are further screened based on their titles and abstracts to determine their eligibility for inclusion in the literature review. Upon assessing the full-text publications that meet the eligibility criteria, a thorough review and analysis of these studies are conducted. Key information, findings, and insights from each study are systematically documented. Common themes, trends, and perspectives across the selected studies are identified and synthesized to provide a comprehensive overview of the integration of AI for personalized learning in the era of digitization from a global perspective in Education 4.0. This methodology ensures a rigorous examination of the available literature, enabling a comprehensive understanding of the integration of AI in personalized learning within the context of digitization. It serves to bridge knowledge gaps, highlight potential challenges, and explore the opportunities associated with implementing AI in education to support Education 4.0 initiatives on a global scale.

2.1 Research Questions

RQ.1 What is the impact of integration of AI for Education 4.0 in digital classroom?
RQ.2 What are the challenges associated with the integration of AI for Education 4.0 in digital classroom?
RQ.3 What are the pedagogical strategies to overcome those challenges in digital classroom?

3. LITERATURE REVIEW

3.1 Digitalization of Education

In the 21st century where innovation is changing at a fast speed. Cell phones, workstations, tablets are not unfamiliar terms any longer. Also, with quick-speed information availability made accessible the nation over, the reception of digitalization has shot to another high. In this day and age, digitalization has been a distinct advantage in one of the main areas of education. In keeping with Machekhina (2017) digitalization in education means conversion of all instruction types (texts, visuals, sounds, video, and other information from different origins) into the digital dialect. Though, the improvement of this present reality with electronic digital gadgets, offices, and frameworks and the foundation of electronic correspondence trade between them prompts the digitalization of education as a segment of the digitalization of society (Matveeva, Akatova, Shcherbakov, & Filinova, 2020).

3.1.1 Digitalization in Education

Digitalization has brought significant changes to the education sector, transforming its dynamics with each passing day. Today's students are incredibly curious and no longer restricted to traditional textbooks found in bookstores or libraries. Their learning methods have evolved rapidly, with many turning to platforms like YouTube, online portals, and applications for knowledge acquisition (Koc & Bakirtas, 2020). This insatiable curiosity cannot be satisfied solely by conventional educational systems, leading to the integration of digitalization to meet the demands of the 21st century (Saad, Hammad, & Barakat, 2021). Across the globe, digitalization has become a necessity in education, making the teaching and learning processes more engaging and accessible. It has simplified knowledge acquisition for both teachers and students, resulting in a wide range of benefits. Therefore, digitalization in education is being implemented across various levels, from administration to teaching-learning, assessment, research, development, and societal support (Marathe, 2018). One of the most noticeable impacts of digitalization in education is the emergence of blended learning and flipped classrooms. This approach combines traditional face-to-face teaching with online resources and activities. In a flipped classroom, students access instructional content online before attending in-person sessions, enabling valuable classroom time to focus on interactive discussions, problem-solving, and collaborative activities. This method has proven effective in engaging students and fostering active learning. Digitalization has also paved the way for personalized learning experiences. With the aid of digital tools, educators can customize instructional content and pace according to individual student needs and learning styles. Adaptive learning platforms analyze student performance data using algorithms to provide personalized recommendations and content, enabling students to progress at their own speed and enhance their understanding of various subjects. Open Educational Resources (OER) have been instrumental in promoting accessibility and affordability in education. OER comprises freely accessible textbooks, multimedia materials, and online courses that can be utilized and modified by educators globally. By leveraging OER, students can access quality educational content without financial burdens, and educators can enhance their teaching resources (Hylén, 2006). The integration of virtual and augmented reality (VR/AR) technologies has introduced immersive learning experiences. Students can now explore complex subjects through interactive simulations and virtual field trips. For instance, medical students can practice surgical procedures in a risk-free virtual environment, while history students can visit historical sites virtually, enriching their learning experiences. Digitalization has also revolutionized assessment methods. Traditional pen-and-paper tests are being replaced by online assessments that offer more dynamic and interactive features. Online assessments provide immediate feedback to students, aiding in their understanding of areas that require improvement. Furthermore, educators can benefit from quicker and more efficient evaluation processes. The power of data analytics has significantly impacted education by enabling the tracking of student progress, identifying learning gaps, and making data-informed decisions to improve teaching methods and curriculum design. Learning analytics provides valuable insights into student behavior and engagement patterns, allowing for early interventions to support struggling students (Sclater, 2018). Massive Open Online Courses (MOOCs) have democratized access to higher education. Learners from around the world can access high-quality courses from prestigious institutions at little to no cost. MOOCs have expanded educational opportunities for millions of learners, fostering a culture of lifelong learning. Digitalization has fostered collaboration among students and educators through various online communication platforms and collaborative tools. Virtual classrooms, online discussion forums, and collaborative document editing tools facilitate seamless communication and teamwork, overcoming geographical barriers and enhancing the learning experience. A notable case study that exemplifies the impact of digitalization in education is Khan Academy. This educational platform offers a vast library of video lessons and interactive exercises on various subjects. Khan Academy's model has transformed education by providing free, high-quality educational content to learners worldwide. Students can learn at their own pace, revisit challenging concepts, and explore a diverse array of subjects beyond their school curriculum. Moreover, the platform's data analytics track student progress and adaptively recommend content, ensuring personalized and effective learning experiences. Digitalization has brought about a paradigm shift in education, making it more accessible, engaging, and personalized. As technology continues to advance, further innovations in digital education are expected to emerge, revolutionizing the way knowledge is acquired and disseminated globally.

3.1.2 Advantages of Digitalization of Education

Advanced education sets out new learning opens doors as understudies participate on the web, intelligent conditions and as personnel shift, the guidance strategies using crossbreed courses, redone educating new models of coordinated effort, and a wide exhibit of imagination connecting with learning methods (Kaçar & Cagiltay, 2021). Likewise, a 21st-century vision of student execution expects understudies to be insightful advanced substance clients, yet in addition useful and cooperative computerized media makers exhibiting abilities and sharing thoughts through imaginative narrating, information representation, and content curation (Maltseva et al., 2020). However, these days, e-learning become more famous than before, particularly in advanced education as utilizations of Information and Communication Technology (ICT) give a wide scope of instructing and learning for both workforce and understudies. Therefore, e-learning is considered as an inventive way to deal with instructive administrations through electronic substance shapes that support students' mindfulness, abilities, and result (Spector et al., 2018).

3.2 Artificial Intelligence in Education 4.0

Artificial Intelligence (AI) has the potential to greatly enhance the field of education in the context of Education 4.0. By integrating AI into the educational system, various tasks and processes can be optimized and improved to provide a more effective learning experience. One operational aspect of AI in

Education 4.0 is personalized learning. Jovanovic and Verbert (2018) found that AI can analyze student data, including performance records and learning preferences, to create personalized learning pathways for each student. Using machine learning algorithms (see Figure 1), AI systems can adapt and recommend tailored educational content and activities to cater to individual student needs. This helps optimize learning outcomes and engagement.

Figure 1. Applications of machine learning

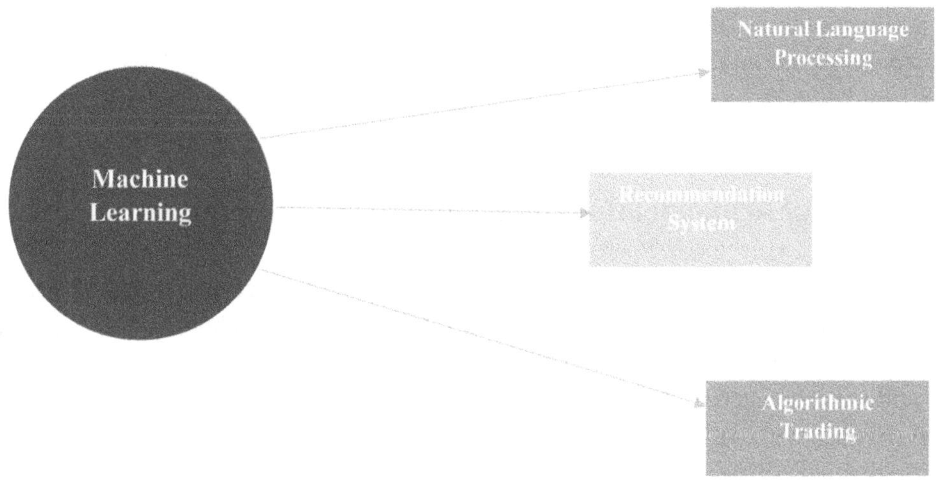

Intelligent tutoring systems powered by AI can provide personalized and adaptive support to students. These systems utilize natural language processing (NLP) algorithms to understand and respond to student queries, offering real-time feedback. They can also track student progress and identify areas where additional support is needed, allowing for targeted intervention (Richter et al., 2019). AI-powered virtual assistants, as highlighted by Kucak et al. (2019), play a significant role in supporting both teachers and students. These virtual assistants can provide information, answer questions, and perform administrative tasks, leveraging NLP algorithms to understand and respond to natural language queries. This improves efficiency and accessibility in the learning process, contributing to a seamless and engaging educational environment. Automated grading and feedback is another important application of AI in Education 4.0 (Joshi & Ungerleider, 2020). AI algorithms can automate the grading process by analyzing student responses and providing immediate feedback. This saves time for teachers and enables students to identify areas for improvement. Moreover, AI can detect patterns in student performance and provide insights to educators for instructional adjustments (Swath, 2018). AI algorithms have the capability to analyze large amounts of educational data, leading to content creation and recommendation. These algorithms can generate educational content such as quizzes, assignments, and lesson plans. Additionally, AI systems can recommend relevant learning resources, including online articles, videos, and interactive simulations, to supplement classroom instruction and enhance student learning experiences (Kucak et al., 2019). Learning analytics powered by AI enable the analysis of student data collected from various sources, such as learning management systems and online platforms. This analysis provides valuable insights into student performance, engagement, and learning patterns (Salloum et al., 2019). Educators can then make data-driven decisions and identify areas for improvement in the curriculum and instructional strategies (Harsimran Singh & Gurpreet Singh Lehal, 2021). Intelligent learning management systems, as highlighted by Swath (2018), can provide a seamless and personalized learning experience by integrating various AI functionalities. These systems can track student progress, provide recommendations for further learning, and facilitate collaboration and communication among students and teachers. The integration of AI in Education 4.0 offers numerous opportunities to optimize and enhance the learning process (Güzeller et al., 2019). By leveraging AI technologies such as machine learning, natural language processing, and data analytics, educational institutions can provide personalized learning experiences, intelligent tutoring, automated grading, and feedback, as well as efficient content creation and recommendation. These operational applications of AI in education have the potential to revolutionize the way students learn and empower educators to make informed decisions for improved educational outcomes (Alenezi & Faisal, 2020).

3.3 Implications of Artificial Intelligence in Education

Due to the development of technology and especially artificial intelligence, there is great change observed in the field of Education. This affiliation of artificial intelligence and technology has flipped the traditional Education system into a modernized Education system where students are introduced to emerging technology and are connected to the world. Also, with this change in education due to technology, the teacher's role has been crucial in the classroom. Instead of transferring knowledge, they are facilitating and involving students in different situations where they can self explore the problems and find appropriate solutions with the help of electronic gadgets (Sharma, Kumar, & Bansal, 2021).

Artificial Intelligence can be integrated into education in two categories. Firstly, it can be integrated for the popularity of any particular institute and management such as for an advertisement, students' assistance, admission purpose, addressing queries of students, etc. Secondly, it is helpful for educators to analyze the collections of information with the help of LMS (Learning Management Systems) and many other academic activities Some other impacts of AI in education.

3.3.1 Intelligence Tutorial System

Most students face many difficulties in learning the material taught by the teacher and they have very limited time to visit the teacher during consulting hours. This leads students to misconceptions and results in limited learning. Undoubtedly, an intelligent tutorial system (ITS) is one of the frequently used applications of Artificial intelligence in education which addresses such issues. ITS is a step-by-step tutoring system that helps students in understanding the entire concept of any particular topic or subject in a well-defined way starting from basic to higher levels (Ali et al., 2021). To teach the students given topic effectively, this system keeps changing, as the students proceed, in the level of difficulty and provide hints to reach a possible answer. Moreover, such systems identify the difficulties of students in the material and generate feedback and work with them directly (Ali & Usman, 2019).

3.3.2 Smart Content

Content has been so crucial for teaching material all the time because it provides teachers an appropriate thought that what to teach and how to teach. By using predictive computing, artificial intelligence creates customizable learning digital interfaces for learners which function according to their needs. Smart Content, also known as dynamic content, is created by analyzing the learner and their needs. Subrahmanyam and Swathi (2018) have mentioned Cram101, a suite of smart content services developed by Content Technologies Inc., which proves teachers step by step guidelines for content that contains flashcard exercises, multiple-choice types of quizzes, and summaries of the chapters of the book.

3.3.3 Virtual Facilitators and Learning Environments

Because of the implementation of technology in the classroom, the role of the teachers has converted into facilitators and motivators instead of a source of knowledge. In this era of the emergence of technology, virtual lectures and learning environment are created to facilitate the process of teaching and learning. Amiri, Mousavi, and Eynollahzadeh (2021) have mentioned the efforts of the University of Southern California (USC) in this regard that uses artificial intelligence based 3-D games and program based animated characters which aim to establish a virtual environment based on virtual characters with the help of augmented and virtual reality to provide a socially interactional environment for learners. Consequently, this environment immerses the learning experience of students and they start exploring things in a virtual environment rather than blindly believing in the knowledge transferred from the teacher.

3.3.4 Digital Assessment Through Artificial Intelligence in Education

Assessment is considered one of the important activities in the instructional process because it measures the learning outcomes of the students. Therefore, teachers spend most of their time creating assessment criteria, tests and assessing those tests. But, due to the spread of artificial intelligence in education, this challenging task has become easy for teachers. Technology allows teachers to utilize such AI-based platforms that measure the learning of students. Additionally, the study of Richter et al. (2019) included the two main steps in the academic measurement and improvement of students through these platforms. They argued that these platforms help teachers in automated grading systems where the result is generated automatically after attempting the test. Light SIDE is software that grades the essays result of postgraduate medical students. Also, while students attempt any quiz this software generates feedback and guides the students to reach the required outcome.

3.4 I.R 4.0 and Its Impact on Education

3.4.1 Impact of IR 4.0

The 4th industrial revolution has introduced surplus opportunities and starts for society. Also, it is advanced from the continuation of plentiful triumphs of the earlier unrests. In a general sense, the 21st century has several complications that will oblige groundbreaking plans to resolve them. The IR 4.0 incorporates distinct rising progress to cybersecurity, internet of things, cloud computing, system integration, simulation, additive manufacturing, autonomous robots, big data, augmented reality (Behzadi, Rao, &

Schellhammer, 2021). The original unrest encloses groundbreaking thoughts, additional openings, new displays, and original creations. Similarly, this original unrest is tight in with breaking limits calls attention to that the new disorder is "termed by a substantially extra omnipresent then portable web, by further modest and all the more striking sensors that have gotten less costly, and through computerized reasoning and Artificial Intelligence." Eventually, Anwar (2021) elaborated that these new improvements have been occurring simultaneously to move the world into another period of development, advancement, and disclosure. The current upheaval is occurring in all fields, areas, and circles of life.

3.4.2 IR 4.0 Implications in Education

Astoundingly, Becker et al. (2018) extrapolated that the site of educational progression has shifted as a result of the fourth Industrial Revolution (IR 4.0). IR 4.0 is compelled by electronic thinking and advanced real-world frameworks that expand the human-machine interface's reach. Education 4.0 is a new type of tutoring that has emerged as a result of the recent uproar. IR 4.0 shifted the place of instruction development. The rapid changes in data have bred a new form of coaching for the future. The fourth IR is notable for its speed, diversity of innovations, breadth, relevance, and return to scale (Kayembe & Nel, 2019). Morally talking, the fourth modern unrest is energized by fake awareness and it changes the workplace after tasks founded properties for the human-centered characteristics (Chen et al., 2021). Without a doubt, Liu, Xu, Zhang, and Gao (2021) expressed that Education 4.0 is an establishment of acceptance that advances astute and brilliant intuition in training. Education 4.0 advances instruction in an unexpected way, principally by devouring innovation-based apparatuses and assets. This implies that understudies will not figure out how to utilize reading material, pens, and article instructors in conventional study halls. All things considered, Education 4.0 permits far-off understudies to get to the Internet and try outflows through an assortment of the open online progress, video visits, and voice calls to study extra powerful measurable about similar understudies. Certainly, Blikstein (2018) extended that Education 4.0 likewise further develops learning as the majority of the instruments and strategies that help Education 4.0 will assist students with learning and successfully than conventional instructing techniques. Generally, learning is customized, so understudies are keen on Education 4.0. As such, there is a characteristic interest in the educational program. Thinking about the exploration, the understudy learning results can improve as training turns out to be more close to home. In Education 4.0, this tweaked study is conceivable. To summarize, modern transformation 4.0 has acquired altogether extraordinary change in the way toward conferring and getting instruction (Fadel, Holmes & Bialik, 2019).

3.5 Artificial Intelligence-Based Digital Classrooms

Without a doubt, Digital Classroom has numerous ideas and definitions. In the innovation see, the keen study hall is a rich blend of savvy gadgets like tablets, TV (Saini & Goel, 2019), VR/AR sensors, and actuators. In the instructive view, the savvy homeroom gives a proper climate and learning devices to improve educating and learning execution. Then again, Chen, Liu, and Liao (2020) communicated his perspectives about digital classrooms based on artificial intelligence that 'Advanced Classroom is perhaps the most possible enterprises in the 21st century. By utilizing extraordinary advances like the Internet of Things, Artificial Intelligence, Cloud Computing, study halls these days can investigate and assess the learning execution constantly'. Digital classroom has multiple features as mentioned in (figure 2),

Figure 2. Features of digital classroom note.
Source: Adopted from Haleem et al. (2022)

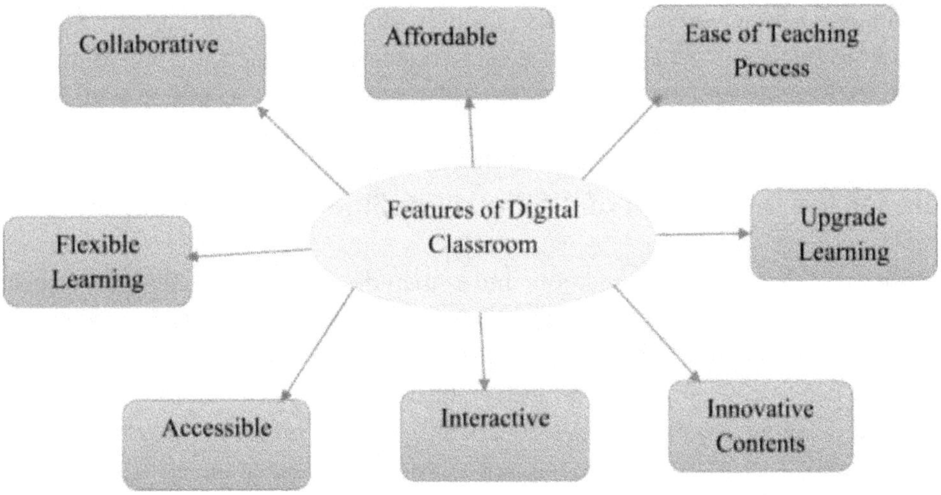

In addition, Darwish and Kamel (2021) examined that the logical leap forward of innovation has contributed tremendously to the considerably more late achievement and headways of schooling. It has made a pathway for students to approach unlimited methods for information and data, it has upgraded learning, and it has changed the substance of schooling forever. During the previous 20 years, advanced innovation has had a colossal effect on the manner that understudies learn. With the continuation of progressions in innovation, the understudies of things to come will be boundless. Innovation's job has been essential in the upgrade of the learning interaction for understudies. In addition to the fact that it enhances learning for understudies, innovation likewise helps educators with having the option to speak with understudies proficiently and simply. PCs and programming programs that are the wellspring of learning materials have permitted innovation to roll out amazing improvements to training (Chia & Yeo, 2020). Similarly, the research has shown that the utilization of innovation can further develop maintenance. Slash and Cheung directed an examination that inspected whether the utilization of webcast, when contrasted with the utilization of a talk, would have an enhancement for the understudy's capacity to hold a greater amount of the exercise. Hence, they presumed that the understudies who utilized the web recording scored fundamentally higher on an ensuing test than the individuals who just educated by a talk (Fardoun, Alghazzawi, & Aldahdouh, 2020).

3.6 Integration of Artificial Intelligence in the Classroom

The utilization of advanced classrooms these days has recently centered on IoT gadgets like lighting frameworks (Montalbo & Enriquez, 2020), participation frameworks (Akbar et al., 2018), and separate artificial intelligence modules like face acknowledgment (Sarkar, Mishra, & Subhramanyam, 2019), feeling identification (Kim, Soyata, & Behnagh, 2018). Also, man-made consciousness in the classroom can undoubtedly follow understudy exercises, smart coaching framework, tutor understudies, long-lasting learning (Chen, Liu, & Liao, 2020). An extraordinary learning experience can be made by instructing in the study hall for various courses by utilizing shrewd artificial intelligence segments. Despite this,

Ghasemi, Ali, and Shirvani (2020)portrayed some brilliant instructive encounters managing understudies finding out about the choice tree parts of artificial intelligence and in any event, having understudies make their chatbots (experiential learning). Increasingly more exploration is additionally showing the practicality and advantages of artificial intelligence frameworks inside the homeroom (Fahimirad & Kotamjani, 2018). Coming up next are some particular ways/projects to utilize artificial intelligence straightforwardly inside a class to improve distinctive instructive cycles.

3.7 Models for the integration of Artificial Intelligence in Education

The transformation of the traditional classroom into a smart digital classroom requires teachers to adopt digital pedagogy to meet the goals of digitalized learning in the 21st century. According to Kukkar et al. (2023) students with different learning styles are engaged in learning through different teaching and learning models. Therefore, these models provide teachers with a systematic way to foster learning and drive professional development among the teachers to make this process of teaching and learning effective. Also, there are several models which can be integrated to make the environment of classroom learner-centered. Castro (2018) has mentioned three important models in his article to integrate artificial intelligence in education. They are the Substitution Augmentation Modification Redefinition (SAMR) model, the Technological Pedagogical Content Knowledge (TPACK), and the Technology Acceptance Model (TAM). These models are briefly discussed below:

3.7.1 The SAMR Model (Substitution, Augmentation, Modification, Redefinition)

The SAMR Model was introduced in 2006 which was part of Dr. Ruben Puentedura's work with the Maine Learning Technologies Initiative (see Figure 3). The SAMR model, introduced by Dr. Ruben Puentedura in 2006, provides a systematic instructional guideline for integrating technology into educational settings (Aldosemani, 2019). The model consists of four classifications - Substitution, Augmentation, Modification, and Redefinition - which represent different levels of technology integration, aiming to enhance instructional activities (Gorman, 2018). These classifications are further divided into two groups: enhancement and transformation (Aldosemani, 2019). At the Substitution stage, technology acts as a direct tool substitute with no functional change in the task. For example, traditional multiple-choice tests that students complete with paper and pencil can be replaced by digital alternatives, such as Google Forms, where students respond using a keyboard and mouse (Chen, Chen, & Lin, 2020; Rahimi et al., 2018). Moving on to Augmentation, technology still acts as a direct substitute tool, but with functional improvement. Students can use word processing software with features like word count, grammar checks, and thesaurus, which go beyond what is possible with traditional pen and paper (Ertmer & Newby, 2018). Additionally, students can share their Google Forms with each other and with teachers, allowing for collaborative assessment and feedback (Olmos-Migueláñez & Pérez-Sanagustín, 2020). Modification allows for significant task redesign through the use of technology. Teachers can design interactive and dynamic tasks, providing alternative approaches to traditional assignments. For instance, instead of delivering presentations in front of the whole class, students can record video presentations using multimedia devices and share them with their peers (Graham, 2021). Finally, at the Redefinition stage, technology enables the creation of new tasks that were previously inconceivable. It involves using technology to foster transformative learning experiences. For example, students can conduct online research using search engines, gather data from various sources, and publish their work online for a broader audience, connecting with their peers and the global community (Graham, 2021; Olmos-Miguelâñez & Pérez-Sanagustín, 2020). In a language arts classroom, teachers can apply the SAMR model by gradually moving from Substitution to Redefinition. Initially, they may replace physical textbooks with digital versions and use interactive tools for reading comprehension at the Augmentation stage. Then, they can redesign assessment methods by introducing collaborative writing platforms and video conferencing at the Modification stage. Finally, they can foster transformative experiences by connecting students with pen pals from other countries, engaging in cross-cultural exchanges, and creating multimedia presentations for a global audience (Graham, 2021; Olmos-Miguelâñez & Pérez-Sanagustín, 2020). By implementing the SAMR model, teachers can effectively integrate technology into the classroom to enhance student engagement, promote 21st-century skills, and ultimately improve learning outcomes (Gorman, 2018). However, it is essential for educators to carefully consider the purpose and pedagogical goals of technology integration to maximize its impact on student learning (Aldosemani, 2019).

Figure 3. The SAMR model note
Source: Adopted from Divakaran (n.d.)

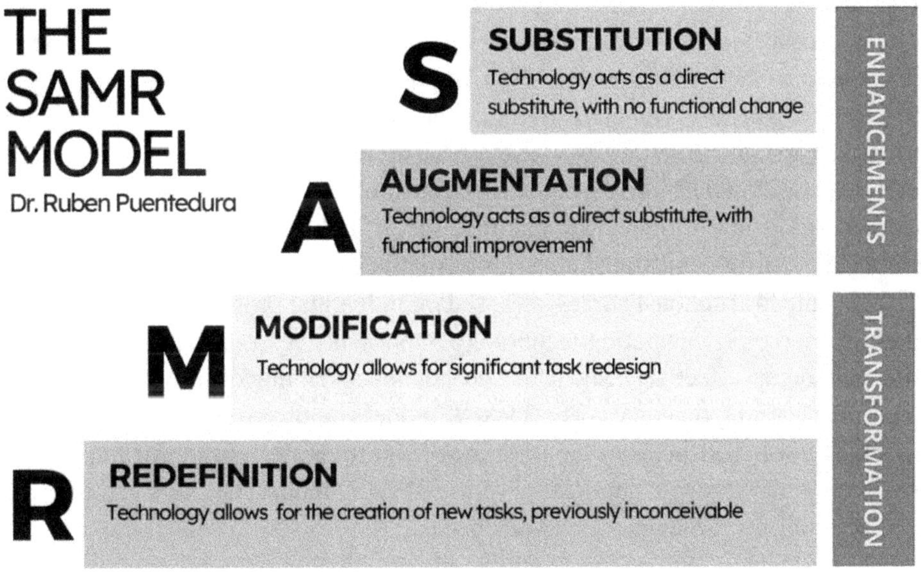

3.7.2 The Technological Pedagogical and Content Knowledge (TPACK) Model

The Technological Pedagogical and Content Knowledge (TPACK) model, derived from Shulman's (1986) Pedagogical Content Knowledge (PCK) model, provides a comprehensive guideline for teachers to effectively integrate technology into their teaching practices and optimize students' learning outcomes (Greiffenhagen & Traxler, 2021). The TPACK model consists of seven components, with three main components - Technology Knowledge (TK), Pedagogical Knowledge (PK), and Content Knowledge (CK) - and the remaining components emerging from the intersection of these three main components (see Figure 4) (Gulati & Arya, 2021). Teachers with a strong understanding of the three main components of the TPACK model possess Technology Knowledge (TK), which refers to their familiarity with various digital technologies that can be integrated into the classroom, such as digital video, interactive projectors, software programs, and the internet. They also have Content Knowledge (CK), which encompasses the mastery of facts and figures related to specific subjects or topics they teach. Additionally, teachers possess Pedagogical Knowledge (PK), which encompasses expertise in various teaching methods, classroom management, lesson planning, assessment, and understanding student learning (Gulati & Arya, 2021). The integration of these three main components leads to the emergence of other critical components in the TPACK model. Technological Content Knowledge (TCK) guides teachers in using technology to support and enhance specific content that allows learners to practice differently and develop a deeper understanding of subject areas. Technological Pedagogical Knowledge (TPK) involves the integration of different technological devices and applications that can alter the teaching style and facilitate instructional processes (Gulati & Arya, 2021). Teachers effectively applying the TPACK model demonstrate Technological Pedagogical Content Knowledge (TPACK), which represents their proficiency in seamlessly blending technology, pedagogy, and content to create transformative learning experiences. This involves using technology to create engaging and interactive lessons that enhance students' understanding and engagement. For instance, teachers may use interactive simulations, virtual field trips, and multimedia presentations to explain complex scientific concepts, fostering a deeper comprehension among students. The TPACK model becomes a valuable framework for teachers' professional development and instructional planning. As educators prepare lessons, they consider how technology can enhance the learning experience and facilitate the instructional process. By integrating technology thoughtfully, teachers can cater to diverse learning needs, promote active student engagement, and provide personalized learning experiences (Hasibuan et al., 2019). In a practical educational scenario, a science teacher applying the TPACK model may use digital labs and data visualization tools to engage students in virtual experiments, allowing them to explore scientific phenomena that are difficult to visualize with traditional methods. The teacher may also utilize educational apps for formative assessments, providing timely feedback to students, and adjusting instructional strategies based on individual progress (Greiffenhagen & Traxler, 2021). Sahlaoui et al. (2023) integrating technology into science lessons, students can develop critical thinking skills, collaborate effectively, and gain a deeper understanding of scientific concepts, ultimately leading to improved learning outcomes. The TPACK model empowers teachers to leverage technology effectively, aligning it with pedagogy and content knowledge to create meaningful and impactful learning experiences. Through the strategic application of the TPACK model, teachers can foster 21st-century skills and enhance students' academic achievements.

3.7.3 Technology Acceptance Model (TAM)

Several studies were conducted in which researchers developed and implemented different models, in different spares of time, to find out the methods for accepting newly introduced technologies. Technology Acceptance Model (TAM) is one of the famous models which sever the same purpose. This model was introduced by Davis in 1989 which is originated from the social psychological theories of reasonable action (TRA) and planned behavior (TPB) (Granić & Marangunić, 2019). Furthermore, the study of Kamal et al. (2020) contained that in the TAM model the motivation of users to accept technology is comprised of three factors: perceived ease of use, perceived usefulness, and attitude towards using (see Figure 5). In the context of education, TAM can be applied to understand students' and teachers' behavior while implementing new technology in the classroom, ultimately impacting learning outcomes. The TAM model comprises three factors that influence users' acceptance of technology: perceived ease of

Figure 4. TPACK model note. Adopted from: Educational Technology. (n.d.). Technological Pedagogical Content Knowledge (TPACK) framework.
Source: Adopted from Educational Technology (n.d.)

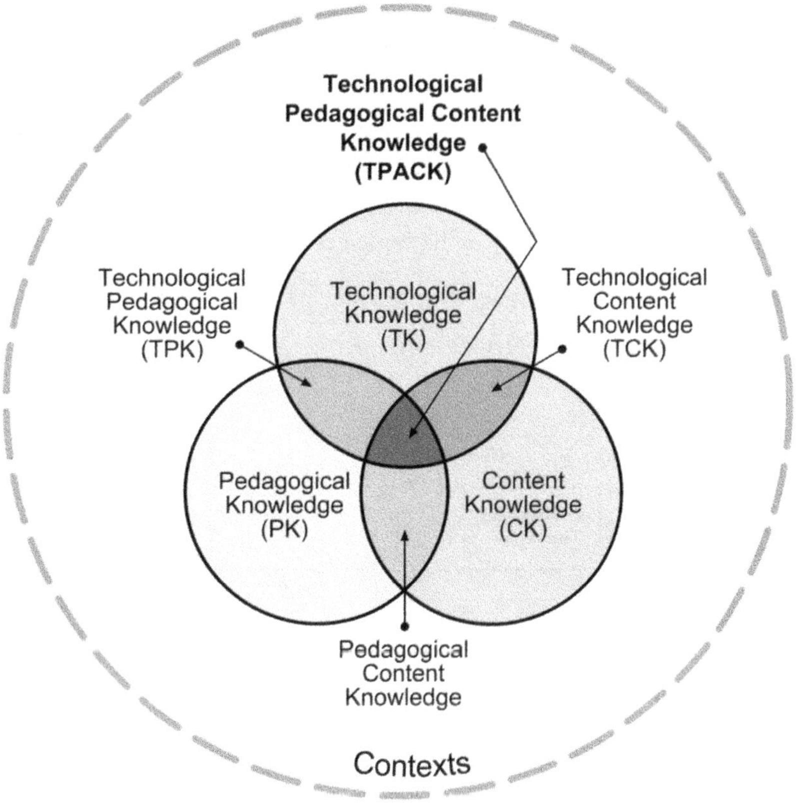

use, perceived usefulness, and attitude towards using the technology (Kamal et al., 2020). As per Kumar et al. (2021), in a blended learning classroom, a math teacher introduces an online learning platform that includes interactive math tutorials, practice exercises, and immediate feedback. To address perceived ease of use, the teacher ensures that the platform is user-friendly, easy to navigate, and accessible on different devices. By providing guidance and support on how to use the platform effectively, students perceive it as easy to use. In terms of perceived usefulness, the math teacher explains the benefits of using the online learning platform. Emphasizing that it provides additional practice opportunities, personalized feedback, and access to resources beyond the traditional classroom setting, the teacher showcases real-life examples of how the platform can improve students' understanding of math concepts and boost their performance in assessments. To influence students' attitudes towards using the technology, the teacher actively encourages them to share their opinions and feedback on the online learning platform. Incorporating surveys and discussions, the teacher aims to gauge students' attitudes and address any concerns they may have. Demonstrating enthusiasm about the platform's potential impact on their learning, the teacher fosters positive attitudes towards its use. Sahlaoui et al. (2021) practical application of the TAM model in the blended learning classroom positively impacts learning outcomes. As students perceive the platform as easy to use and useful for their learning needs, they become more engaged and motivated. They explore its features, actively participate in online activities, and take advantage of its resources.

With a positive attitude towards using the technology, students are more likely to embrace it as a tool to reinforce their understanding of math concepts and improve their problem-solving skills. The immediate feedback provided by the platform allows students to track their own progress, identify areas for improvement, and take ownership of their learning journey. Additionally, the platform promotes collaborative learning, as students engage in virtual discussions, share resources, and collaborate on group projects, fostering a sense of community and peer support. Overall, the Technology Acceptance Model (TAM) has enabled the math teacher to successfully integrate technology into the classroom, creating a positive and effective learning environment. By understanding students' perceptions and attitudes towards using the online learning platform, the teacher has enhanced students' academic achievements and motivation in math, equipping them with the necessary skills for success.

Figure 5. Technology acceptance model (TAM) note
Source: Adopted from Lai (2017)

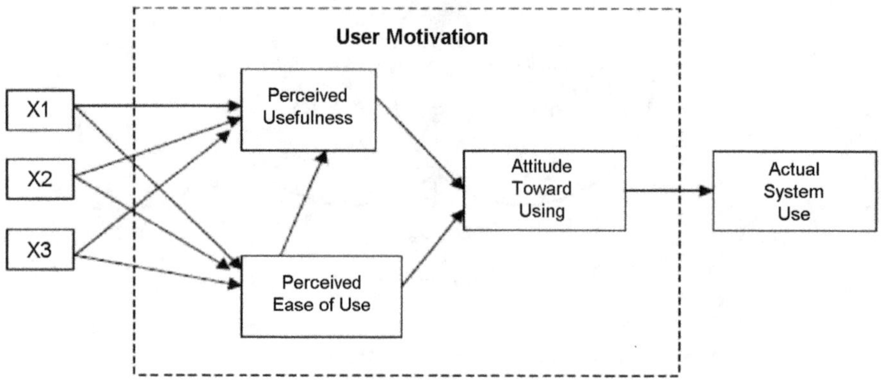

3.8 Challenges in the Integration of Artificial Intelligence in Education

The emergence of artificial intelligence has brought changes in almost all fields of life. The field of education is improved too due to the implications of artificial intelligence and technology, as discussed above (Islam & Lim, 2021). Apart from these changes, artificial intelligence has created challenges as well for educators while integrating artificial intelligence-based technologies in education. So, it is essential to put a deep eye on these challenges and issues to implement artificial intelligence without any interruption. However, some challenges of artificial intelligence are as mentioned below.

3.8.1 Cost of Gadgets and Infrastructure

Schools and Universities attract a large number of students and it is the foremost priority of the institutes to provide their students equivalent support. In order to integrate artificial intelligence in education, modern education requires smart classes where the facility of technological gadgets is available. Also, an IT-based digitalized environment requires a high amount of money to invest which cannot be afforded by underdeveloped countries because many businesses and organizations resist investing in it (Katare, Padihar, & Qureshi, 2018; Verma, Kumar, & Kohli, 2021). Therefore, Subrahmanyam and Swathi (2018) considered financial factors as the restraining factor of the growth of artificial intelligence in the education market. Moreover, the infrastructure of the institute plays a key role to produce maximum outcomes of artificial intelligence. Unlike the traditional classrooms, the infrastructure of artificial intelligence-based classrooms is much more advanced. It includes the availability of internet, electricity and chilled atmosphere of class which again higher the cost of implementation.

3.8.2 Preparing Technological Skilled Teachers

The role of the teacher has been the backbone of the teaching and learning process at all times. Although machines have taken the responsibility of providing content to the students, they cannot replace the role of teachers. The inventions of machines have brought changes in the skills and competencies of the teachers. Artificial intelligence-based education system requires well-trained digitally literate teachers who can beneficiate learning by applying AI-based algorithms to assess, score and provide feedback to their students (Miao, Chen, & Luo, 2021). So, as education keeps developing from time to time, it becomes obligatory for institutes to get education training goals and learning paradigms change by conducting training programs and preparing their teacher's technological development to adapt to emerging teaching environment (Man, 2021).

3.8.3 Software Malfunction

Artificial Intelligence-based algorithms are created by adding a lot of data to teach the machines and these machines learn from the prescribed dataset. It is fact that neither any human nor any machine is perfect humans, sometimes machines made mistakes. Most of the time, these machines find the mistakes but are unable to correct those mistakes (Pedro, Subosa, Rivas, & Valverde, 2019). It is because these machines repeat the actions and it is unable to make changes in the dataset. As a result of this issue, it requires the company to tackle the problem and also it wastes time as well (Mahesh, 2020). Artificial Intelligence-based smart education system requires developing such algorithms which train machines and this training of machine learning algorithms need massive and clean data sets which contain minimum biased (Puteh, Yusoff, Ibrahim, & Alwi, 2020). In addition, due to such challenges occurring from time to time, the motivation level of students as well teachers is lost and a lot of work is left uncompleted (Man, 2021).

3.8.4 Ensuring Digital Equity

A working paper on educational policy by UNESCO (2019) highlights the arising issue of digital equity. Similarly, the report suggests that these issues arise due to the lack of financial support (Pedro etal. 2019). The digital equity has comprised of various compoenets as mentioned in (Figure 6). Likewise, another report of UNESCO (2019) asserted that in most of the under developing countries, 3G network of the internet is available whereas the world has shifted to 5G. Thus, the lack of high-speed internet creates hindrances in promoting participation and communication with another part of the world (Puteh, Yusoff, Ibrahim, & Alwi, 2020). Furthermore, bringing your device is also criticized in the report that all the students cannot afford their device. In addition, such institutes or platforms which implement AI-based environments in teaching and learning, charge higher fesses. Therefore, the poor neither purchase their own devices nor afford fesses and are deprived of such education.

Figure 6. Digital equity note
Source: Adopted from City of Seattle (n.d.)

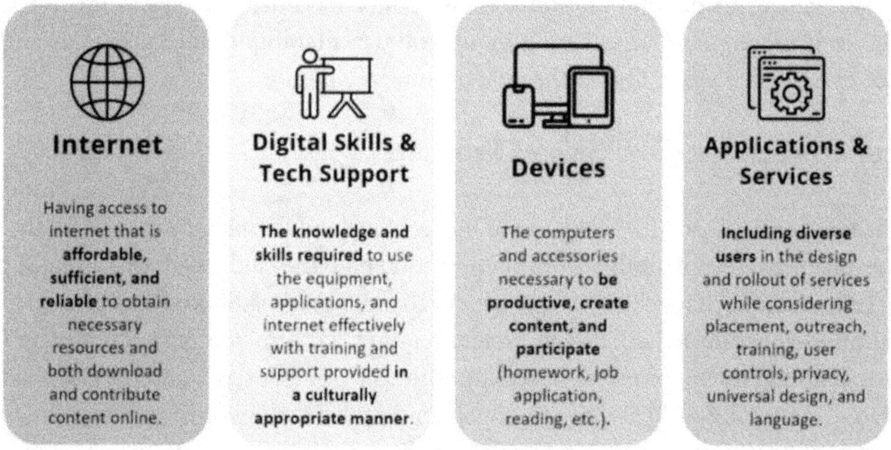

3.8.5 Privacy

The issue of privacy is one of the important concerns that occur while practicing on different artificial intelligence-based platforms. Artificial intelligence software contains a large amount of data of the users (Tiwari, 2019). Therefore, hackers target such type of software to hack the information. This makes users worried about using the technology. In addition to privacy, students with different learning styles require different learning needs and strategies. Most of the time they donot want to show their data to other students because sometimes they are victimized by discrimination based on special learning needs. This makes a sense of insecurity among students. Therefore, they keep their privacy hidden. But when their private data is leaked they feel abashed. Moreover, teachers also keep their important data private. Due to these reasons, data protection must be considered seriously to ensure that the teachers and students have complete ownership and control of their data. Also, to minimize the possibility of data leakage, algorithmic training should be strengthened for the protection of private data (Looi et al., 2019).

3.8.6 Management of a Large Number of Students

Due to the invention of multiple technologies in artificial intelligence, the learning process is not limited to classes. Instead, students can learn the knowledge by sitting at home and from any corner of the world through online learning software (Katare, Padihar & Qureshi, 2018). On such platforms, students can communicate with teachers and can take constructive feedback from the teacher. Ong and Koh (2020) highlighted the issue of massive open online courses (MOOCs) which was implemented in 2008 but the consequences were not as expected. These open courses neither require any fees nor entering was much difficult, anyone from any corner of the world could involve just with the access of the internet (Lin & Huang, 2020). As a result, a big number of students were enrolled. As these students were from different areas of the world, they faced the issue of different time zones. Moreover, another issue was the issue of human capacity. It became challenging for the teachers to engage a big number of diverse students. Due to these reasons the experience to achieve desired outcomes, conduct assessments, and provide constructive personalized feedback remained unsolved issues (Popenic & Kerr, 2017).

3.8.7 Data Governance

One more challenge is data governance, which is identified with the arrangement of information association, assortment, control, stockpiling, utilization, recorded, and obliteration (John & Vijayan, 2021). The way of setting up information administration is driven by a particular program, upheld by specific approaches and methodology, and imparted by authoritative initiative and the executives. By and large, the guidelines should give the entirety of the ability to safeguard the accompanying nonexclusive prerequisites: openness, accessibility, fulfillment, exactness, uprightness, consistency, audit ability, and security (Ahmed, Abdullah, Shah & Rahman, 2021).

4. RECOMMENDATIONS AND RESEARCH AREAS

4.1 Recommendations

To effectively utilize AI in education, several key recommendations can be considered. Firstly, educational institutions should invest in comprehensive professional development programs for educators. These programs should focus on enhancing teachers' digital literacy and AI-related pedagogical skills. By providing educators with the necessary knowledge and training, they can confidently and effectively integrate AI technologies in the classroom, creating engaging and personalized learning experiences for their students. Secondly, ethical considerations should be a top priority in the implementation of AI in education. It is essential to develop clear guidelines and policies that address data privacy, algorithm transparency, and fairness. By prioritizing ethical AI practices, educational institutions can build trust among students, parents, and educators, ensuring a safe and secure learning environment. Additionally, fostering collaboration and knowledge sharing among educators, researchers, and AI developers is crucial. By encouraging partnerships and information exchange, the educational community can benefit from shared best practices and insights, driving innovation in the integration of AI in education. Lastly, adopting a user-centric design approach is vital when developing AI-powered educational tools. Involving stakeholders, including students, teachers, and other end-users, in the design process is essential to ensure that AI solutions are user-friendly and tailored to meet the specific needs and preferences of the users. A user-centric approach will ultimately enhance the usability and impact of AI in the educational setting.

4.2 Research Areas

- AI-Enhanced Assessment: Transforming traditional assessment practices through AI-powered real-time feedback and metacognitive skill analysis tools.
- AI in Special Education: Advancing support for diverse learners with AI-driven assistive technologies and personalized learning plans.
- AI in Social-Emotional Learning (SEL): Promoting students' emotional well-being and social skill development through AI interventions in virtual learning environments.

- Ethical AI in Education: Investigating potential biases in AI algorithms and ensuring fairness and transparency in decision-making processes.
- AI-Driven Personalized Learning: Optimizing individual learning experiences by studying the effectiveness of AI algorithms in tailoring content and learning paths.
- AI and Teacher-Student Interaction: Enhancing teacher-student engagement and support with AI-powered virtual tutors and chatbots.
- AI for Global Collaboration: Fostering cross-cultural exchange and connectivity among students and educators through AI-driven language translation tools and collaborative platforms.

5. CONCLUSION

In this review paper, we have explored the possibilities and potential of integrating artificial intelligence (AI) in education during the era of digitization, with a particular focus on personalized learning. The transformation of traditional classrooms into smart digital classrooms, driven by AI technologies, has revolutionized the teaching and learning process in the 21st century. The digitalization of education extends beyond classroom boundaries, impacting administrative tasks, student information management, progress analysis, and institutional promotion. The integration of AI in education has redefined instructional approaches, allowing teachers to evolve from mere knowledge transmitters to facilitators, guides, and supporters. Digitally literate teachers are leveraging AI technologies to connect real-world scenarios with their teaching practices, resulting in enhanced student engagement and improved learning outcomes. As students actively interact with technological gadgets and independently explore knowledge, they become more motivated and better equipped to excel academically. The success of AI-based learning lies in its effective integration within the education system. By employing AI for administrative purposes and student support, educational institutions can streamline processes and offer personalized assistance to students. Additionally, AI tools such as Learning Management Systems (LMS) empower teachers to analyze data, adapt their teaching styles, and dedicate more time to reflection and improvement. These AI-driven digital classrooms foster inclusive learning environments where students collaboratively co-construct knowledge. To ensure successful implementation, educators can draw on influential models such as the Substitution Augmentation Modification Redefinition (SAMR) model, the Technological Pedagogical Content Knowledge (TPACK) model, and the Technology Acceptance Model (TAM). These frameworks provide valuable guidance for integrating AI and driving professional development among teachers, ultimately enhancing the educational experience. Looking ahead, the future scope of AI in education holds tremendous promise. Advancements in AI technologies will open doors to more sophisticated personalized learning experiences. AI-powered virtual tutors and adaptive learning platforms can offer tailored educational content based on individual learning preferences and progress. Furthermore, AI-driven data analytics will provide valuable insights into student performance, allowing teachers to intervene early and provide targeted support. Beyond the classroom, AI can facilitate administrative tasks, enabling educational institutions to streamline operations and allocate resources efficiently. AI-powered chatbots and virtual assistants can handle student queries, provide guidance, and support administrative staff, freeing up valuable time for educators to focus on teaching and professional development. Additionally, AI holds the potential to foster global collaboration and cross-cultural exchange in education. Virtual classrooms and AI-driven language translation tools can break down language barriers, connecting students and educators from diverse backgrounds. This interconnectedness can foster cultural understanding, promote global citizenship, and enrich the learning experience. However, as we explore the future scope of AI in education, it is essential to maintain a human-centered approach. AI should complement and enhance the role of educators rather than replace them. Teachers will continue to play a central role in guiding and inspiring students, nurturing critical thinking, creativity, and socio-emotional development. As we embark on the future of AI in education, ethical considerations must be paramount. Safeguarding data privacy, ensuring algorithmic transparency, and addressing potential biases in AI systems are vital to fostering a fair and inclusive learning environment. In conclusion, the integration of artificial intelligence for personalized learning in the era of digitization, known as Education 4.0, represents a transformative opportunity for education. It requires educators and institutions to adapt and embrace AI technologies, designing innovative and inclusive courses that prepare students for the challenges of the future. By harnessing the potential of AI while upholding human values, education can enter a new era of innovation and transformation, equipping students with the skills and knowledge they need to thrive in an ever-changing world. The future of AI in education holds tremendous promise, and by embracing its potential, we can create a dynamic and empowering learning ecosystem for the generations to come.

6. FUTURE SCOPE

The future scope of this chapter holds several intriguing directions for further exploration. One avenue is the refinement of pedagogical models that integrate AI, tailoring them to suit diverse learning contexts and subjects. Ethical considerations in AI implementation within education present another crucial area for future study, involving the establishment of robust ethical frameworks and privacy guidelines. The potential of personalized learning through AI calls for deeper investigation into its adaptive capabilities and effectiveness in catering to individual student needs. Long-term impact assessments can provide insights into the sustained benefits of AI integration on learning outcomes. Moreover, research focusing on comprehensive teacher training programs would empower educators to adeptly navigate AI-augmented classrooms. Collaborative AI solutions could be investigated to facilitate enhanced group interactions and project-based learning. Lastly, the creation of AI-generated educational content offers promise in alleviating teaching burdens and expanding resource availability. These future directions collectively contribute to maximizing the transformative potential of AI in education.

REFERENCES

Ahmed, Z., Abdullah, Z., Shah, S., & Rahman, M. A. (2021). Artificial Intelligence in Education: Recent Trends, Challenges, and Future Directions. *SN Computer Science*, *2*(4), 1–17. PMID:34056622

Akbar, M. S., Sarker, P., Mansoor, A. T., Al Ashray, A. M., & Uddin, J. (2018, August). Face recognition and RFID verified attendance system. In *2018 International Conference on Computing, Electronics & Communications Engineering (iCCECE)* (pp. 168-172). IEEE. 10.1109/iCCECOME.2018.8658705

Aldosemani, T. (2019). Inservice Teachers' Perceptions of a Professional Development Plan Based on SAMR Model: A Case Study. *Turkish Online Journal of Educational Technology, 18*(3), 46-53.

Alenezi, H. S., & Faisal, M. H. (2020). Utilizing crowdsourcing and machine learning in education: Literature review. *Education and Information Technologies*, *25*(4), 2971–2986. doi:10.100710639-020-10102-w

Ali, A., Nawaz, A., Noman, M., & Khan, M. S. (2021). Role of Artificial Intelligence in Education 4.0: A Review. In *2021 International Conference on Communication, Computing and Digital systems (C-CODE)* (pp. 327-332). IEEE.

Ali, F., & Usman, M. (2019). Role of Artificial Intelligence in Education 4.0. In *Proceedings of the 1st International Conference on Future of Teaching and Education* (pp. 1-7). ACM.

Amiri, I., Mousavi, S. M., & Eynollahzadeh, M. (2021). Education 4.0 and Artificial Intelligence: An Overview. *Journal of Information Systems and Telecommunication*, *9*(3), 77–86.

Anwar, M. (2021). Prediction of the graduation rate of engineering education students using Artificial Neural Network Algorithms. *International Journal of Research in Counseling and Education*, *5*(1), 15–23. doi:10.24036/00411za0002

Becker, S. A., Brown, M., Dahlstrom, E., Davis, A., DePaul, K., Diaz, V., & Pomerantz, J. (2018). *NMC horizon report: 2018 higher education edition*. Educause.

Behzadi, S., Rao, H. R., & Schellhammer, S. (2021). Artificial Intelligence in Education: Perspectives from Industry 4.0 and Learning Analytics. *Journal of Information Systems Education*, *32*(1), 37–52.

Blikstein, P. (2018). Artificial Intelligence and Machine Learning in Education. In The Cambridge Handbook of Computing Education Research (pp. 617-638). Cambridge University Press.

Castro, S. (2018). Google Forms Quizzes and Substitution, Augmentation, Modification, and Redefinition (SAMR) Model Integration. *Issues and Trends in Educational Technology, 6*(2).

Chen, B., Hu, X., Chen, Y., & Wu, B. (2021). Artificial Intelligence and Education 4.0: Current Trends, Challenges, and Future Directions. *Journal of Educational Technology & Society*, *24*(1), 14–24.

Chen, H., Liu, Y., & Liao, H. (2020). The Impact of Artificial Intelligence on Education: A Review of the Current State and Future Prospects. *Journal of Computers in Education*, *7*(2), 153–170.

Chen, L., Chen, P., & Lin, Z. (2020). Artificial intelligence in education: A review. *IEEE Access : Practical Innovations, Open Solutions*, *8*, 75264–75278. doi:10.1109/ACCESS.2020.2988510

Chia, Y. L., & Yeo, W. (2020). Artificial Intelligence in Education 4.0: Opportunities and Challenges. In *2020 International Conference on Artificial Intelligence in Information and Communication (ICAIIC)* (pp. 1-4). IEEE.

City of Seattle. (n.d.). *Digital Equity*. Seattle Information Technology. Retrieved from https://www.seattle.gov/tech/initiatives/digital-equity

Darwish, A., & Kamel, M. (2021). Artificial Intelligence in Education 4.0: A Systematic Review. *International Journal of Emerging Technologies in Learning*, *16*(3), 148–162.

Dervishi, E., Ergün, E., & Uçak, C. (2019). Artificial Intelligence in Education. In Fourth Industrial Revolution and Its Impact on Education (pp. 41-54). IGI Global.

Divakaran, D. (n.d.). *SAMR model: A practical guide for EdTech integration.* Retrieved from https://www.deepeshdivakaran.com/post/samr-model-a-practical-guide-for-edtech-integration

Educational Technology. (n.d.). *Technological Pedagogical Content Knowledge (TPACK) framework.* Retrieved from https://educationaltechnology.net/technological-pedagogical- content-knowledge-tpack-framework/

Ertmer, P. A., & Newby, T. J. (2018). Artificial Intelligence in Education: Promises and Implications for Teaching and Learning. *International Journal of Artificial Intelligence in Education, 28*(1), 4–17.

Fadel, C., Holmes, W., & Bialik, M. (2019). *Artificial intelligence in education: Promises and implications for teaching and learning*. The Center for Curriculum Redesign.

Fahimirad, M., & Kotamjani, S. S. (2018). A review on application of artificial intelligence in teaching and learning in educational contexts. *International Journal of Learning and Development, 8*(4), 106–118. doi:10.5296/ijld.v8i4.14057

Fardoun, H. M., Alghazzawi, D. M., & Aldahdouh, Z. (2020). Artificial Intelligence in Education: A Comprehensive Review. In *2020 5th MEC International Conference on Big Data and Smart City (ICBDSC)* (pp. 36-41). IEEE.

Ghasemi, A., Ali, S., & Shirvani, F. (2020). The Role of Artificial Intelligence in Education 4.0: Opportunities and Challenges. *International Journal of Advanced Computer Science and Applications, 11*(12), 583–589.

Gorman, M. (2018). *The SAMR model of technology integration article.* Academic Press.

Graham, C. R. (2021). Transforming Higher Education: Leveraging Instructional Technology with the SAMR Model. *EDUCAUSE Review, 56*(1), 41–51.

Granić, A., & Marangunić, N. (2019). Technology acceptance model in educational context: A systematic literature review. *British Journal of Educational Technology, 50*(5), 2572–2593. doi:10.1111/bjet.12864

Greiffenhagen, C., & Traxler, J. (2021). Artificial Intelligence in Education: A Review of AI Education Policy and Implementation. In *2021 IEEE Global Engineering Education Conference (EDUCON)* (pp. 1381-1386). IEEE.

Gulati, S., & Arya, A. (2021). Education 4.0: A Systematic Review of Recent Trends and Future Directions. *Education and Information Technologies, 26*(5), 6977–7003.

Güzeller, C. O., Aksu, G., & Eser, M. T. (2019). Klasik test kuramı ve madde tepki kuramına ilişkin veri analizi yazılımı: Jmetrik [Data on classical test theory and item response theory analysis software: Jmetric]. *Egitimde ve Psikolojide Ölçme ve Degerlendirme Dergisi, 10*(2), 165–178.

Haleem, A., Javaid, M., Qadri, M. A., & Suman, R. (2022). Understanding the role of digital technologies in education: A review. *Sustainable Operations and Computers.*

Hasibuan, M. S., Nugroho, L. E., & Santosa, P. I. (2019). Model Detecting Learning Styles with Artificial Neural Network. *Journal of Technology and Science Education, 9*(1), 85–95. doi:10.3926/jotse.540

Hu, J., Shen, X., Sun, Q., & Wang, T. (2018). Application of Artificial Intelligence in Education: A Review. *Journal of Computers in Education*, *5*(3), 317–347.

Hylén, J. (2006). Open educational resources: Opportunities and challenges. *Proceedings of the 2006 OECD-CERI.*

Islam, M. R., & Lim, Y. (2021). Artificial Intelligence in Education: A Review on its Potential, Challenges, and Future Directions. In *2021 14th International Conference on Electrical and Computer Engineering (ICECE)* (pp. 1-4). IEEE.

John, R. S., & Vijayan, R. (2021). A Comprehensive Study on the Role of Artificial Intelligence in Education 4.0. In *2021 International Conference on Sustainable Engineering and Technology (ICSET)* (pp. 1-5). IEEE.

Joshi, A., & Ungerleider, C. (2020). Artificial Intelligence in Education: *Potential and Possibilities. In International Conference on Artificial Intelligence in Education* (pp. 426-430). Springer.

Jovanovic, V., & Verbert, K. (Eds.). (2018). *Artificial Intelligence Supported Educational Technologies.* Springer International Publishing.

Kaçar, R. N., & Cagiltay, N. E. (2021). A Comprehensive Review of Artificial Intelligence Applications in Education. *Journal of Educational Computing Research*, *59*(4), 1141–1169.

Kamal, S. A., Shafiq, M., & Kakria, P. (2020). Investigating acceptance of telemedicine services through an extended technology acceptance model (TAM). *Technology in Society*, *60*, 101212. doi:10.1016/j.techsoc.2019.101212

Katare, G., Padihar, G., & Qureshi, Z. (2018). Challenges in the integration of artificial intelligence and internet of things. *International Journal of System and Software Engineering*, *6*(2), 10–15.

Kayembe, C., & Nel, D. (2019). Challenges and opportunities for education in the Fourth Industrial Revolution. *African Journal of Public Affairs*, *11*(3), 79–94.

Kim, Y., Soyata, T., & Behnagh, R. F. (2018). Towards emotionally aware AI smart classroom: Current issues and directions for engineering and education. *IEEE Access : Practical Innovations, Open Solutions*, *6*, 5308–5331. doi:10.1109/ACCESS.2018.2791861

Koc, S., & Bakirtas, H. (2020). Artificial Intelligence in Education: A Review of the Literature. *Journal of Computer Assisted Learning*, *36*(6), 713–729.

Kovalchuk, S. (2021). Artificial Intelligence and Machine Learning in Education 4.0: Challenges and Opportunities. In *2021 IEEE 16th International Conference on Advanced Trends in Radioelectronics, Telecommunications and Computer Engineering (TCSET)* (pp. 745- 748). IEEE.

Kučak, D., Juričić, V., & Đambić, G. (2018). Machine learning in education-A survey of current research trends. *Annals of DAAAM & Proceedings, 29.*

Küçük, S., & Gündoğdu, B. A. (2020). The Role of Artificial Intelligence in Education 4.0: A Review Study. *International Journal of Technology in Education and Science*, *4*(2), 138–152.

Kukkar, A., Mohana, R., Sharma, A., & Nayyar, A. (2023). Prediction of student academic performance based on their emotional wellbeing and interaction on various e-learning platforms. *Education and Information Technologies*, *28*(8), 1–30. doi:10.100710639-022-11573-9

Kumar, A., Krishnamurthi, R., Bhatia, S., Kaushik, K., Ahuja, N. J., Nayyar, A., & Masud, M. (2021). Blended learning tools and practices: A comprehensive analysis. *IEEE Access, 9*, 85151-85197.

Lai, P. (2017). *Picture of Original Technology Acceptance Model.* Retrieved from https://www.researchgate.net/figure/Original-Technology-Acceptance-Model-Davis-

Lin, Y. W., & Huang, Y. M. (2020). Artificial Intelligence in Education: Issues and Trends. *International Journal of Distance Education Technologies*, *18*(3), 14–31.

Liu, X., Xu, G., Zhang, X., & Gao, W. (2021). The Fourth Industrial Revolution and Its Impact on Higher Education: A Systematic Literature Review. *Education in Science*, *11*(3), 122.

Looi, C. K., Wong, L. H., So, H. J., Seow, P., Toh, Y., Chen, W., & Norris, C. (2019). Leveraging Artificial Intelligence in Education. In Handbook of Information Technology in Primary and Secondary Education (pp. 369-381). Springer.

Machekhina, O. N. (2017). Digitalization of education as a trend of its modernization and reforming. *Revista Espacios, 38*(40).

Mahesh, B. (2020). Machine learning algorithms-a review. *International Journal of Science and Research, 9*, 381-386.

Maltseva, O. A., Khovanskaya, E. A., Martynova, N. A., & Karpova, I. V. (2020). The Digitalization of Education in Higher Education: Methodological and Practice-Oriented Aspects. *Advances in Social Science, Education and Humanities Research*, *437*, 859.

Man, L. (2021). Research on the Opportunities and Challenges Faced by Educational Leadership Based on Artificial Intelligence in the Education Field. *Journal of Physics: Conference Series*, *1915*(2), 022053. doi:10.1088/1742-6596/1915/2/022053

Marathe, M. S. (2018). Digitalization in education: A transformative tool for the 21st-century learners. *International Journal of Current Research and Modern Education*, *3*(2), 361–365.

Matveeva, S. V., Akatova, N. S., Shcherbakov, Y. I., & Filinova, N. V. (2020). Digitalization of higher education and professional development of educators: Technologies and new opportunities. *Amazonia Investiga*, *9*(29), 77–86. doi:10.34069/AI/2020.29.05.10

Miao, Y., Chen, F., & Luo, X. (2021). AI in Education 4.0: An Overview of the Opportunities and Challenges. *Frontiers in Education*, *6*, 629706.

Mirriahi, N., & Alonzo, D. (2019). Personalizing Learning with Artificial Intelligence. In Transforming Learning with Meaningful Technologies (pp. 163-182). Springer.

Montalbo, F. J., & Enriquez, E. (2020, August). An IoT Smart Lighting System for University Classrooms. In *2020 International Symposium on Educational Technology (ISET)* (pp. 3- 7). IEEE. 10.1109/ISET49818.2020.00011

Olmos-Migueláñez, S., & Pérez-Sanagustín, M. (2020). A Systematic Review of Learning Analytics Applications in Online Learning Environments in Higher Education. *Interactive Learning Environments, 28*(8), 1128–1146.

Ong, C. S., & Koh, J. H. L. (2020). The Role of Artificial Intelligence in Education: A Review. *Educational Technology Research and Development, 68*(4), 1765–1783.

Pedro, F., Subosa, M., Rivas, A., & Valverde, P. (2019). *Artificial intelligence in education: Challenges and opportunities for sustainable development*. Academic Press.

Pence, H. E. (2019). Artificial intelligence in higher education: New wine in old wineskins? *Journal of Educational Technology Systems, 48*(1), 5–13. doi:10.1177/0047239519865577

Popenici, S. A., & Kerr, S. (2017). Exploring the Impact of Artificial Intelligence on Teaching and Learning in Higher Education. *Research and Practice in Technology Enhanced Learning, 12*(1), 22. doi:10.118641039-017-0062-8 PMID:30595727

Puteh, M., Yusoff, R. C., Ibrahim, S., & Alwi, N. H. (2020). Artificial Intelligence in Education 4.0: Opportunities and Challenges. In *2020 IEEE International Conference on Teaching, Assessment, and Learning for Engineering (TALE)* (pp. 1127-1130). IEEE.

Richter, D., Kock, S., Neumann, A., & Wahl, D. (2019). Artificial intelligence in education: Challenges and opportunities for sustainable development. *AI & Society, 34*(4), 749–758.

Saad, A. M., Hammad, R., & Barakat, M. S. (2021). The role of digitalization in modern education: A literature review. *Journal of Educational and Psychological Studies, 15*(2), 189–202.

Saad, N. A., Hammad, D. A., & Barakat, A. (2021). *The Impact of Digitalization on Customers' Satisfaction in Educational Sector: An Empirical Study.* http://www.psychologyandeducation.net/

Sahlaoui, H., Alaoui, E. A. A., Agoujil, S., & Nayyar, A. (2023). An empirical assessment of smote variants techniques and interpretation methods in improving the accuracy and the interpretability of student performance models. *Education and Information Technologies*, 1–37. doi:10.100710639-023-12007-w

Sahlaoui, H., Nayyar, A., Agoujil, S., & Jaber, M. M. (2021). Predicting and interpreting student performance using ensemble models and shapley additive explanations. *IEEE Access, 9*, 152688-152703.

Saini, M. K., & Goel, N. (2019). How smart are smart classrooms? A review of smart classroom technologies. *ACM Computing Surveys, 52*(6), 1–28. doi:10.1145/3365757

Salloum, S. A., Alhamad, A. Q. M., Al-Emran, M., Monem, A. A., & Shaalan, K. (2019). Exploring students' acceptance of e-learning through the development of a comprehensive technology acceptance model. *IEEE Access : Practical Innovations, Open Solutions, 7*, 128445–128462. doi:10.1109/ACCESS.2019.2939467

Sandhya, P. S., & Maheshwari, S. (2021). AI-Driven Smart Learning Systems in Education 4.0: A Review. *International Journal of Intelligent Systems and Applications, 13*(9), 35–42.

Sarkar, P. R., Mishra, D., & Subhramanyam, G. R. (2019). Automatic attendance system using deep learning framework. In *Machine intelligence and signal analysis* (pp. 335–346). Springer. doi:10.1007/978-981-13-0923-6_29

Sclater, N. (2018). *Learning analytics explained.* Routledge.

Shahroom, A. A., & Hussin, N. (2018). Industrial revolution 4.0 and education. *International Journal of Academic Research in Business and Social Sciences, 8*(9), 314–319. doi:10.6007/IJARBSS/v8-i9/4593

Sharma, P. (2019). Digital revolution of education 4.0. *International Journal of Engineering and Advanced Technology, 9*(2), 3558–3564. doi:10.35940/ijeat.A1293.129219

Sharma, P., Kumar, V., & Bansal, R. (2021). Role of Artificial Intelligence in the Fourth Industrial Revolution: Education Perspective. *International Journal of Advanced Research in Computer Science, 12*(5), 204–212.

Singh, H., & Lehal, G. S. (2021). Artificial Intelligence in Education: A Comprehensive Review. *Journal of Educational Technology Systems, 49*(1), 5–33. doi:10.1177/0047239520978500

Spector, J. M., Ifenthaler, D., Sampson, D. G., & Siemens, G. (Eds.). (2018). *Handbook of Research on Educational Communications and Technology* (4th ed.). Springer.

Subrahmanyam, R., & Swath, N. (2018). Artificial intelligence: A paradigm shift in education. *International Journal of Innovative Technology and Exploring Engineering, 7*(5S), 113–117.

Subrahmanyam, V. V., & Swathi, K. (2018, August). Artificial intelligence and its implications in education. In *Int. Conf. Improv. Access to Distance High. Educ. Focus Underserved Communities Uncovered Reg. Kakatiya University* (pp. 1-11). Academic Press.

Sun, L., & Zhang, D. (2021). Artificial intelligence in education: A comprehensive survey. *Computers & Education, 172*, 104213. doi:10.1016/j.compedu.2021.104213

Thappa, S. R., & Baliya, J. N. (2021). Exploring Awareness for Technological Pedagogical and Content Knowledge (TPAC) in Pre-Service Teacher Education Programme. *MIER Journal of Educational Studies Trends and Practices*, 1-14.

Tiwari, P. (2019). Artificial Intelligence in Education: Opportunities and Challenges. *Journal of Emerging Technologies and Innovative Research, 6*(8), 383–387.

UNESCO. (2019). *Artificial Intelligence in Education: Challenges and Opportunities for Sustainable Development.* United Nations Educational, Scientific and Cultural Organization.

Vaidya, S., Ambad, P., & Bhosle, S. (2018). Industry 4.0–a glimpse. *Procedia Manufacturing, 20*, 233–238. doi:10.1016/j.promfg.2018.02.034

Veletsianos, G., & Houlden, S. (2019). A Systematic Analysis and Synthesis of the Empirical MOOC Literature Published in 2013–2015. *The International Review of Research in Open and Distributed Learning, 20*(1), 1–25.

Verma, A., Kumar, Y., & Kohli, R. (2021). Study of AI techniques in quality educations: Challenges and recent progress. *SN Computer Science, 2*(4), 1–7. doi:10.100742979-021-00635-3

Yilmaz, R. M., & Yilmaz, H. B. (2020). Artificial Intelligence in Education: A Bibliometric Analysis. *Journal of Educational Technology & Society*, *23*(1), 185–201.

Yousafzai, S. Y., & Mahmood, N. (2021). Transforming Education 4.0 through Artificial Intelligence and Machine Learning. In *Proceedings of the 2021 2nd International Conference on Big Data, IoT, and Cloud Computing (BIC3)* (pp. 117-121). ACM.

Zawacki-Richter, O., Marín, V. I., Bond, M., & Gouverneur, F. (2019). Systematic review of research on artificial intelligence applications in higher education–where are the educators? *International Journal of Educational Technology in Higher Education*, *16*(1), 1–27. doi:10.118641239-019-0171-0

Zhang, D., Zhao, Z., Zhu, S., Zhang, Y., & Zhang, Y. (2020). Intelligent Education 4.0: Development and Prospects. *IEEE Access : Practical Innovations, Open Solutions*, *8*, 23741–23749.

Zhou, G., Zhang, L., & Xu, X. (2020). The Application of Artificial Intelligence in Education 4.0. In *2020 15th International Conference on Computer Science & Education (ICCSE)* (pp. 380-383). IEEE.

Chapter 6
Improving Learning Abilities Using AI-Based Education Systems

Ashish Kumar
Bennett University, India

Divya Singh
Bennett University, India

Rubeena Vohra
Bharati Vidyapeeth's College of Engineering, India

ABSTRACT

AI is transforming the traditional education system globally. The traditional education system based on historical paradigms has a very feeble scope for creating an interactive environment for the specialized students. AI is providing an innovative, diverse, and impactful roadmap in education system to improve the teaching-learning experience not only for teachers but also for students with special needs. AI with its interactive tools has improved the overall educational system by creating enormous opportunities for specialized students. AI-assisted tools such as live chatbots, class dictating software, verbal command-based eBooks, adaptive personalized tutors, image-based learning, and many more have accelerated the teaching-learning experience. Implication of these tools in the education system inculcate critical thinking and improve student engagement in the various teaching activities. The authors have reviewed the impact of AI in transforming the educational system from traditional to AI-assisted modern educational systems.

DOI: 10.4018/979-8-3693-0378-8.ch006

1. INTRODUCTION

AI (Artificial Intelligence) is a recent and positive technology touching life and providing solutions to many tedious real-time problems such as visual tracking (Kumar et al., 2020), cancerous cell classification (Kumar & Ahluwalia, 2021), tourist recommendation analysis (Kumar & Vohra, 2023), sentiment analysis (Jain et al., 2023) and many more (Kumar, Gupta, Bhasin et al, 2023; Kumar, Mamgai, & Jain, 2023; Kumar, Sareen, & Arora, 2023; Kumar, 2023). Apart from these, AI has extended its support in education by providing innovative tools for improving the teaching-learning experience for specialized students. AI has the potential to access the abilities of specialized students to determine their special educational needs.

Special students' education is impacted as they are suffering from one or more medical disorders such as autism, specific learning disability such as vision, hearing, or verbal impairments, mental disability conditions, a typical health disorder such as asthma, cardiovascular problems, and epilepsy and a pandemic situation like covid-19 (Spencer et al., 2023). These underlying medical, health, and pandemic concerns restrict not only the continuity of attending school but also affect the alertness among the students in understanding the concepts. However, specialized students' requirements and needs are different from the regular students and emphasize the development of a deeper relationship between teacher and students for better upliftment of society (Roorda et al., 2021).

AI aims to provide interactive, innovative, problem-solving tools to facilitate the psychological needs of students with disability (Kumar, Jain, Gupta, & Islam, 2023). In this direction, story-telling tools, chatbots, automated evaluation systems, robots, and prediction systems are employed to enhance the teaching standards and learning capabilities of specialized students (Druga & Ko, 2021; Garg & Sharma, 2020; Hu, 2021; Kim et al., 2021). In Education, AI is impacting various domains that include, teaching, learning, evaluation, curriculum design, and administration. For specialized students, AI aims to provide personalized learning by integrating various other technologies such as augmented reality, and virtual reality (Kumar, Raja, & ljaz, 2023). With the help of these technologies, AI has provided enhanced training to vision and hearing-impaired students so that they can compete with regular students at a faster pace. In addition, AI-based teaching and learning material provide advanced development for assessment of the individual needs by monitoring the assigned independent tasks (Hirankerd & Kittisunthonphisarn, 2020). Figure 2 illustrates the role of AI in the education system.

Recently, with the advancement in AI chatbots and story-telling books, students can communicate with machines about their problems, learning, and thoughts (Kim et al., 2021). AI chatbots enable students to communicate through video, voice, or text. Chatbots are based on natural language processing and hence, provide intelligent answers to students' queries. These applications are quick in providing solutions to the problems anytime, anywhere. Chatbots prove to be efficient learning tools as they provide textual as well as voice-based descriptions (Haristiani, 2019). In addition, chatbots are available in various foreign languages too. The conversation is intelligent and open just like two humans are interacting with each other.

AI has provided a feedback system to ensure effective communication between teachers and students. Students suffering from a certain disorder such as autism demand different teaching strategies in comparison to regular students. There is a requirement for adaptive teaching strategies which can accommodate the needs of special students based on their feedback, responses, and attributes. For this, an AI classifier-based recommendation system is proposed to enable teachers to alter their teaching methodology as per the requirements of students suffering from autism (Lampos et al., 2021).

Figure 1. Role of AI in the educational system

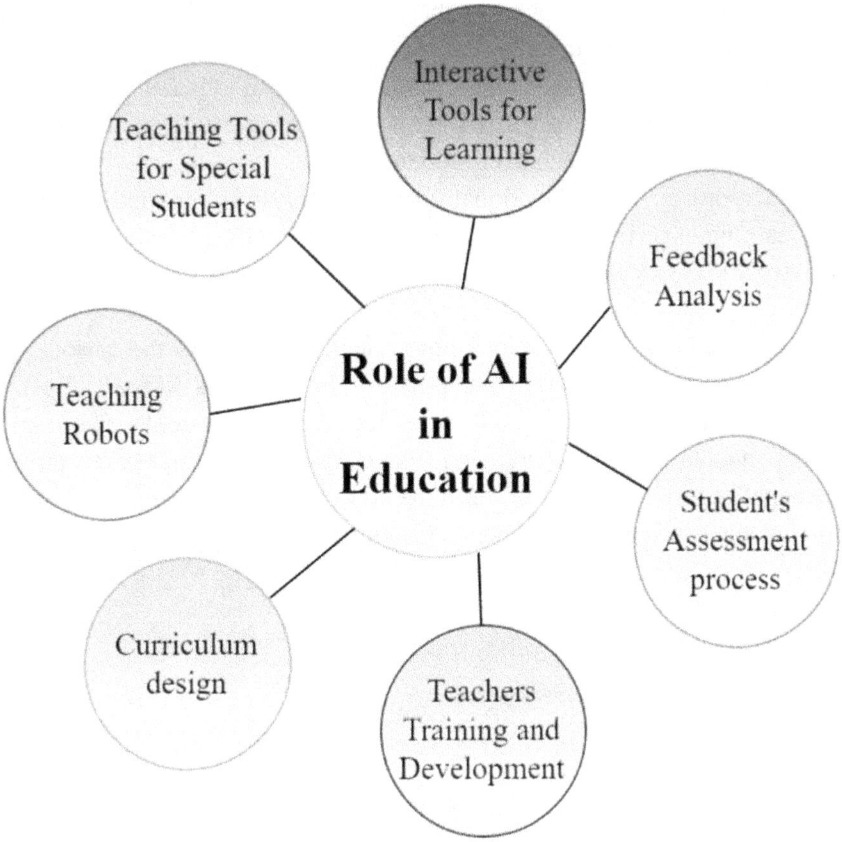

Apart from the teaching and learning strategies, AI has also provided tools for the automatic assessment of students and can be predicting student's performance. AI has provided fast, and accurate grading of the students in various examinations (Alghamdi et al., 2020). The marks can be shared instantly once the students complete the examination. On the other hand, AI-based tools can predict students' performance during online learning. These tools are very helpful during covid-19 pandemic when there was no physical teaching possible (Spencer et al., 2023).

To summarize, AI has provided many tools to make the teaching-learning process easy and interactive not only for students but also for teachers. The human-machine conversational tools simplify the tasks of students in getting a resolution to their queries at any time. Teachers can analyze and provide personalized education to students with special needs. In addition, teachers can adapt their teaching paedology in accordance with the students with impairment or suffering from any disorder. The availability of automatic evaluation tools streamlines the assessment process by providing quick results. The key contributions in the chapter are as follows.

- Educational system is categorized into three levels namely, primary or kindergarten education, secondary or middle education and higher education. The benefits and impact of AI at various educational levels is analysed.

- AI tools for simplifying the teaching-learning process for specialized needs are evaluated. The tools for personalized learning, grading-feedback, conversational chatbots and speech/ visual software are reviewed for the benefits for specialized students.
- Role of robot in modern education is elaborated with the aim to benefits not only to teachers but also to students. Salient features of various types of robots in educational system are explored to determine the future of AI for specialized students.
- Finally, the limitations of AI in educational system is analysed to emphasize that AI can improve the teaching-learning experience to specialized student's but the physical presence of the instructor in the classroom is critically significant.

The layout of the remainder chapter is as follows. Section 2 reviews the various AI tool applications at different educational levels. Section 3 elaborates on the various AI tools imperative to provide personalized teaching environments along with voice/face recognition tools. The roles of teachers to motivate specialized students along with parameters for effective and interactive teaching are highlighted in Section 4. The benefits and limitations of AI in the educational system are highlighted in Section 5. Lastly, Section 6 concludes the chapter with salient findings.

Figure 2. Various educational levels

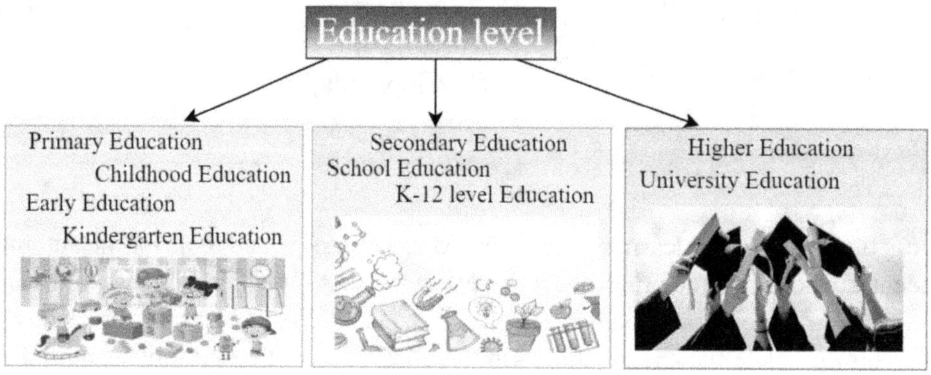

2. LITERATURE REVIEW IN AI-BASED EDUCATION SYSTEM

Educational system can be categorized into three levels namely, primary education, secondary education, and higher education. Primary education includes the first level of education i.e., kindergarten or early childhood education. Secondary education comes after primary education and deals with up to K-12 level students. However, higher education deals with students learning at the university level. Figure 2 illustrates the various educational levels. Table 1 tabulates the salient features along with AI tools at various educational levels. The details about all these educational levels are as follows.

2.1 AI in Primary Education

Primary education is the initial level of education and deals with early childhood learning. AI-assisted teaching and learning tools help in improving the teaching design, pattern, and quality for kindergarten teachers and students. In this direction, authors have analyzed the various AI tools for improving learning in early childhood education (Su & Yang, 2022). Role of robots and robotic toys in early childhood education is also explored to increase children's computational thinking at the preschool level. Robotic toys such as COSMOS, Jibo robots, sponge robot, and many more, as conversational tools such as WeChat and Zhorai are reviewed to determine the impact of AI on teaching methodologies, classroom environment, and student's creativity. Authors have analyzed the competencies of AI in the standardization of curriculum design at the preschool level (Su et al., 2023). AI emphasis to embed computational skills in kindergarten students by including algorithm-based reasoning, problem-solving, and logical reasoning processes. Intelligent agents such as robots are used to provide natural interaction between the students and their queries. Vision and voice-based recognition may be explored for improving the teaching experience for visual and speech-impaired students.

Salas-Pilco (2020) has emphasized the implementation of education robots in primary education for diverse learning and personalized teaching. Robots can improve daily teaching and learning outcomes through effective teaching and constructive learning. On the other hand, Lampos *et al.* (2021) have analyzed the impact of monotonous teaching strategies on the student's progress. AI and machine learning-based techniques are used to predict effective teaching strategies under specific teaching-learning conditions, student attributes, and emotional conditions. Student feedback is analyzed to provide solutions for improving the teacher's contribution to students suffering from autism.

In sum, AI technology is recently explored in education to shed light on improving the teaching-learning aspects at the earliest stages of education i.e. kindergarten or early childhood. AI is quite the latest in the domain and hence, has not been widely explored at its initial stages. At the pre-school level, AI is helpful to provide interactive, and innovative displays of the teaching to attract the students. AR and VR create a virtual environment to gain kids' attention and enhance learning capabilities. Apart from textbooks, AI provides high-quality visuals which are more appealing to the students to embed learning enthusiasm.

2.2 AI in Secondary Education

After the primary education, secondary education is imparted to the students. Secondary education deals from level 6 to level 12 as per the middle education system for the Asia Pacific region. To impart advanced knowledge, AI has attracted many educators and researchers. AI has increased the learning pace by incorporating AI-based concepts, designs, and knowledge into the education system.

In Su et al. (2022), authors have explored the role of AI in curriculum design for K-12 levels. AI-based teaching pedagogies have been incorporated to improve the education standards and course outcomes for effective and inclusive teaching. In secondary education, AI tools and activities have improved the learning progression along with teachers' professional development. Authors have examined the role of machine learning in teaching and training coding students (Druga & Ko, 2021). AI-based smart agents can improve the student's capabilities for taking advantage of agent perspectives. These agents can encourage students and promote perspective learning to help teachers with teaching and assessment processes.

Table 1. Salient features of representative work utilizing AI-tools at various educational levels

Sno	Authors	Year	Educational Level	Application	AI-Tools	Summary
1.	Sweeney (2023)	2023	Higher education	Academic dishonesty	Bard and ChatGPT	AI-based writing tools raise concerns related to ethical issues for students' performance evaluation.
2.	Southworth et al. (2023)	2023	Higher education	Curriculum model	CURE-based AI-focused courses	AI to innovate curriculum in universities with the increase in interdisciplinary involvement for transforming education globally.
3.	Al Kabi (2023)	2023	Higher Education	Improving learning ability	CNN-based model with progressive learning features	Improving the cognitive ability of students by enhancing learning quality and self-esteem.
4.	Su et al. (2023)	2023	Early childhood	AI literacy, Curriculum design, and teaching guidelines	Various teaching, learning, designing, and questionaries tools	Lack of knowledge and training of teachers to utilize the educational upgrade due to AI.
5.	Xia et al. (2022)	2023	Higher, secondary, and early childhood	Learning, teaching, and assessment	-	Reviewed various AI-enabled methods for improving education at various levels for improving cognitive learning.
6.	Gołąb-Andrzejak (2022)	2022	Higher education	Specific AI tools for customer engagement	Sprout Social and Rival IQ	Discuss the role of AI-based tools in enhancing customer engagement in social media for higher education.
7.	Su and Zhong (2022)	2022	Early childhood	Problem-solving learning with future AI	Cognimates, eCraft2Learn, Machine Learning for Kids, Cozmo robot, Calypso for Cozmo, Teachable Machine, QuickDraw, Google's AIY, and TensorFlow Playground	Designing of kindergarten curriculum with the help of AI to standardize it in terms of skills, knowledge, and attitude
8.	Su et al. (2022)	2022	K-12 level	Curriculum design and learning	CUHKiCar, iSTREAM, Educational Broadcasting System, Positive technological development, Scratch, Cozmo, Edomo, and Anki Cozmo	Role of AI tools in improving the curriculum design process and introducing self-learning by implementing AI-based pedagogies for collaborative improvement and advancement.
9.	Laupichler et al. (2022)	2022	Higher and adult education	AI literacy	-	Reviewed the role of AI literacy in improving the current design of teaching, content, and evaluation in various fields.
10.	Su and Yang (2022)	2022	Early childhood/ Kindergarten	Knowledge, and learning	PopBots and Zhorai	Effective teaching and learning from kindergarten to higher education with specialized AI tools for a better understanding of concepts.

continues on following page

Table 1. Continued

Sno	Authors	Year	Educational Level	Application	AI-Tools	Summary
11.	Wang and Wang (2022)	2022	Higher education	Learning		Anxiety scale measurement and validation using AI for motivated learning in students.
12.	Durga and Ko (2021)	2021	Secondary education	Training, learning, and coding	Cognimates AI platform, and perception games	Training AI platforms and robots for measuring students' perception and learning abilities.
13.	Lampos et al. (2021)	2021	Primary education	Teaching and learning	Logistic regression with elastic net regularisation, random forest, and Gaussian process	Analysed long-term effects on students suffering from autism by a specific teaching communication strategy.
14.	Hu (2021)	2021	-	Assessment and evaluation	Weighted naïve Bayes	Machine learning-based evaluation system for teachers to automate and speed up the assessment process.
15.	Kim et al. (2021)	2021	Higher education	Learning and speaking	Chatbot	AI-based chatbots for improving speaking capabilities, response to questions, and response expression.
16.	Hsieh et al. (2020)	2020	Secondary education	Learning, teaching, and interacting	CNN-based face recognition	AI-based teaching robots for improving learning effectiveness by developing motivation and confidence in students.
17.	Salas-Pilco (2020)	2020	Primary education	Learning	WeDo robotic kits	Analyzed the impact of AI and robotics in a balanced and integral way on the learning outcomes.
18.	Garg and Sharma (2020)	2020	Primary and secondary education	Teaching, learning, and training	Learning tools, robots, Equadex, and Microsoft Translator	AI tools for inclusive special education for helping disabled students with learning, teaching, and assessment.

Hsieh *et al.* (2020) have proposed the role of robots as teaching assistants for emphasizing improved learning efficiency and motivation in secondary-level students. Robot-based teaching can answer students' queries effectively and can assess their performance too. Robots can be used as voice assistance and facial recognition system for teaching specialized students. Robots are equipped with an emotion recognition system to observe students' moods and behavior. Also, robots can read students' facial expressions and adjust themselves based on the feedback received. In Garg & Sharma (2020), authors have focussed on the role of AI in training teachers for teaching students with special needs. Students suffering from any kind of disability such as visual, hearing, or physical require special assistance for reading, learning, writing, and understanding. Students with low, blurred or no vision demands either special devices equipped with AR\VR or Braille-based document to provide educational services to those students.

In sum, AI at the secondary education level has provided special teaching and learning aids to teachers for understanding the requirements, and problems of students with special needs. AI can also guide educators to accommodate the changes in teaching style, curriculum design, and learning process as per the skills of disabled students in comparison to regular students. AI focuses on a high teaching style while fulfilling the learning needs of students with disability. AI has ensured that education can be imparted to both regular and disabled students without any discrimination.

2.3 AI in Higher Education

Higher educational institutions deal with imparting education in different fields that include, graduation, engineering, medical and other disciplines. Higher education provides education at the university level for various courses at undergraduate, postgraduate, Ph.D., and other professional levels. AI in higher education is changing the day-to-day learning experience by adapting to students' needs with future-ready tools and activities. In Southworth et al. (2023), authors have emphasized incorporating AI in various curriculum designs to transform the educational system globally. AI can provide quality enhancement tools using highly innovative and interdisciplinary opportunities for students from various courses and programs. The advanced curriculum design focuses to prepare industry-ready students to meet societal needs.

Sweeney (2023) has suggested identifying the cases of academic dishonesty and malpractice in higher education with the help of AI. Students take the help of AI online tools such as ChatGPT to complete their assignments. The usage of tools for completing the assignment is a foremost concern among many teachers. Teachers are not able to provide correct assessments as the source of origin is not clear. However, there are many plagiarism detection software available in the market to overcome assessment challenges. In addition, teachers must be trained adequately to prevent academic misconduct for students' welfare and sound mental health. Laupichler *et al.* (2022) have reviewed the depth of AI literacy in higher and adult education. AI-based teaching content must be added as a part of AI literacy at various education levels to add skills, quality, and knowledge for different populations. AI-based educational programs are paramount to providing clear content and enhanced learning to students. A positive trend can be observed with the incorporation of AI in learning outcome assessments and validations. AI-focused courses such as CURE are proposed to solve real-world questions. These courses inculcate scientific reasoning and critical thinking in the students in higher education.

In Al Ka'bi (2023), authors have investigated methods to ensure fairness and accuracy in AI-based products. AI automates tasks and enhances efficiency in students by incorporating critical thinking and learning. Personalized learning, intelligent tutoring systems, automatic assessments, administrative tasks chatbots, and virtual assistance-based tools are explored to assist students in higher education. Deep learning-based recommendation models are proposed to accelerate quick reading, writing, and cognitive ability in students. The robustness of the system is interpreted by comparing its performance against other state-of-the-art. On the other hand, the author has demonstrated the AI-based tools for supporting customer engagement in social media for presenting a decision support system in higher education (Gołąb-Andrzejak, 2022). AI tools must engage digital platforms such as online advertising, marketing campaigns, chatbots, e-commerce, and voice search optimization system.

In the direction to analyze the anxiety among people due to AI development, authors have proposed the AI anxiety scale (Wang & Wang, 2022). People's mental health is impacted due to irrational fear of its future growth with the practical implications of advanced computer-based technologies. For this, the authors have analyzed a small set of populations. They prepare a questionnaire, gathered respondent characteristics, and determined rotated factor loading to determine the AI anxiety scale. The results provide a generic relationship between AI development and motivated learning behavior. However, Kim *et al.* (2021) have examined AI-based chatbots to improve the chatting and speaking skills of students. AI chatbots allow conversation either in audio or text mode. It has been observed that voice-based chatbots help in improving speaking skills among students. In addition, these chatbots also ensure fluency in foreign languages by understanding the language complexity and incorporating accuracy.

To summarize, there are lots of challenges in high education that includes academic dishonesty, education malpractices, limited interaction between teachers and students, anxiety, and fear due to usage of computer-based tools, and customer engagement in decision systems. AI-based conversation tools such as chatbots are helping to improve communication and speaking skills. There is a requirement for motivational learning and inclusive teaching to impart quality skills to students using AI tools.

3. AI-ASSISTED EDUCATIONAL TOOLS

Broadly, AI has applications in the teaching-learning domain to enhance the skills, capabilities, and quality of education. AI has provided tools for personalized learning, assessment, and teaching. AI has conversational, grading, interactive, adaptive, and feedback tools to make teaching enjoyable, understandable, and innovative not only for students but also for teachers. Facial, emotional, and verbal recognition tools demonstrate the digital environment to facilitate the needs of specialized students. These tools provide a user-friendly system and help teachers in understanding the special requirements of students with disability in a better and more effective way. The aim of the AI tools is not to replace teachers but to help them by reducing the workload on non-essential things such as grading and feedback. The teachers can concentrate more on imparting education so that one-to-one support can be extended to each student.

3.1 Personalized Teaching-Learning Tools

AI has provided tools for personalized teaching-learning tasks based on the capabilities of an individual. In Hirankerd & Kittisunthonphisarn (2020), authors have analyzed AR, VR, and mixed reality for skill training for practical works. E-learning system is also explored for managing learning content and improving learning. However, the author has integrated AI and the Internet of Behavior for addressing the limitations of the traditional education system (Embarak, 2022). Improved personalized content incorporating the needs of individual preferences and requirements for the smart education system are analyzed.

In Kolachalama (2022), authors have evaluated the role of AI and machine learning in imparting pre-medical education and care management. AI in medical has potential applications to ease the workflow of technicians and care providers. The introduction of AI and machine learning in pre-medical education make the healthcare workforce future ready. Munawar *et al.* (2018) have highlighted the requirement of intelligent virtual laboratories for cognitive and personalized education. To provide excellence in laboratory practice and address the limitations of mode-wise education, computer-based E-learning has proved to be effective and efficient. It regulates self-learning among students in a virtual online environment by bridging the gap between practical requirements and available resources.

For personalized learning and tutoring of students, many AI-based tools are available in the market. These tools can adapt to individual needs and capabilities and provide content accordingly. AI-based tools such as Cognii, Queirum, and Carnegie learning platforms are very popular to transform traditional education. These innovative technologies not only reduce the workload of the teacher but also provide individual personalized learning to each student. These tools increase student engagement in personalized lessons by providing step-by-step tutoring assistance. The tools improve quality and speed up the learning process by embedding critical thinking in students. Real-time feedback is also provided to customize the content in accordance with adaptive personalized learning.

3.2 AI-Based Grading and Feedback Tools

For effective assessment of the students, AI has provided many automatic grading and feedback tool such as Gradesope. With the help of this tool, teachers can not only grade students but also can analyze individual performance in comparison to peers. These kinds of tools ensure fairness and accuracy in evaluation and reduce the efforts in terms of time and manpower for compilation and finalization of marks. Smart sparrow is another machine learning based AI-tools. It provides real-time feedback to the students to enhance the quality and pace of their learning.

During covid-era when physical teaching was restricted, online e-learning platforms such as Udemy and Coursera have gained wide popularity as MOOC courses to enable distance learning. These online platforms recommend courses to students to improve their personalized learning experience. Along with learning material from top-rated universities, automatic grading and feedback are also provided to students. Based on their performance, students can understand their potential and weakness in a particular subject. Woot Math is a personalized AI-based tool to improve and evaluate maths skills using personalized learning lessons. This tool also grades students and provides real-time feedback to improve performance.

Eklavvya is an AI-enabled grading and assessment tool. This tool can complete the grading and feedback in a faster way with better accuracy. This tool can be used for grading descriptive answers too. The tool has provided similar evaluation results when the answers are evaluated by the human evaluator. Duolingo is another innovative AI tool to provide real-time feedback, track progress, and make learning easy and enjoyable.

3.3 Speech/Text/Image Recognition Tools

Speech/ Text/ Image based AI-recognition tools help resolve the barriers in the teaching-learning process of specialized students suffering either from visual/voice/hearing impairments or any kind of mental disorder and autism. These recognition tools can be utilized by both teachers and students. AI tools can respond to verbal commands, dictate worksheets, transcribe documents, customize contents, and present assignments with the help of images and videos. Students can upload their work directly and can enjoy faster learning with real-time videos and image examples innovatively.

Speech recognition tools such as Nuance dragon provide accessibility features such as voice-based access and dictation of student's work, assignments, and lesson plans. Intelligent hearing aid is also very popular among hearing-impaired students (Garg & Sharma, 2020). These aids are equipped with many real-time and personalized features such as language translation, scene analysis, and many more. The devices take voice signals as input and produce captions as output for easy understanding of deaf students. For visually impaired students, many tools are available that support Braille to provide access to educational services to these students. Inclusive teaching style should be adopted by teachers to provide quality education to special students.

Smart glasses are recommended for autism students to improve their classroom learning and attention (Vahabzadeh et al., 2018). These devices reduce socio-economic intervention by providing personalized coaching incorporating both AI and AR. With the usage of these devices' improvement in hyperactivity, irritability, chronic behavior, and social withdrawal among students suffering from autism disorder has been observed. Also, google glass-based technology is used to improve the communication skills of autism students. With the utilization of technology and software, the impact of societal barriers on autism students can be minimized.

3.4 Conversational Tools

To bridge the gap between special student requirements and teacher understanding, AI has offered many conversational tools. Visually impaired students can enhance their learning capabilities by accessing AI chatbots and interactive books. Students can ask questions, and develop communication abilities and solutions to tedious problems in a simpler manner. Hearing-impaired students can utilize AR/VR gadgets to improve their skills. These tools are also helpful in enhancing the learning capabilities of students suffering from any other mental disorder.

AI-based chatbots can be useful not only for students but also for teachers and universities. Many universities have deployed real-time chatbots on their websites which can assist students in course selection, admission-related queries, enrolment forms, university fees, location, and many other activities. More detailed information such as scholarships, grants, and education loans can also be extended to the students. This specialized software not only reduces the manual intervention in these preliminary services but also provides smarter and real-time interaction with the users. In addition, the chatbot can provide services and answer user queries anytime, anywhere.

Audio-based AI chatbots can also improve speaking and verbal skills among students (Kim et al., 2021). These tools can assist visually impaired and speech-impaired students. AI chatbots based on text and voice are explored in learning foreign languages too. It has been observed that these chatbots ensure fluency in foreign language learning by providing significant monitoring based on language complexity (Kim, 2017). With the advancement in technology, it is tedious to predict the difference in interaction between the software and human.

To summarize, AI has provided many tools to simplify and accommodate learning requirements based on the personalized needs of special students. AI with AR and VR has improved the teaching-learning experience for visually, hearing, and speech-impaired students. AI has provided many technological tools to eliminate societal fear among autism students. Chatbots, assessment, audio, and video-based AI penetrating the educational system to address its limitations for students with special needs.

4. ROLE OF ROBOTS IN THE MODERN EDUCATION SYSTEM FOR SPECIALIZED STUDENTS

Recently, the role of robots in the modern education system has been explored for addressing the academic difficulties faced by normal as well as specialized students. Robots are like teaching assistants that can answer students' queries, understand their emotions, and adapt the teaching-learning process based on real-time feedback for effective outcomes (Hsieh et al., 2020). Robots are equipped with sign language, suitable for hearing and speech-impaired students. Also, AR and VR are integrated with robots to improve the dynamics of education for teachers and students. Figure 3 illustrates the role of robots in the world of today's digital education.

Figure 3. Role of robots in transforming traditional education

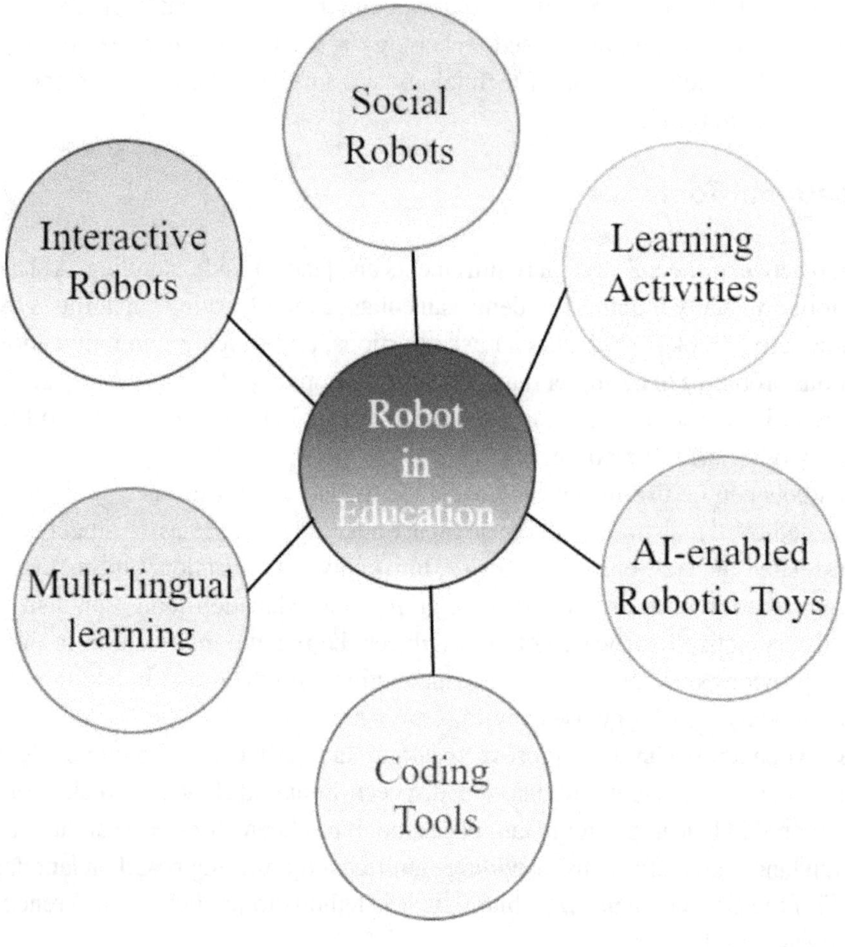

Social robots can provide tutoring assistance to students innovatively and dynamically without any physical restrictions (Belpaeme et al., 2018). The key benefits of social robots in education are reduced manpower cost, instant adaptability in accordance with feedback, more personalized learning, and an understanding of the diverse needs of students in a class. Social robots can understand the physical and economic outcomes of students and teachers by automating various tasks. Social interactive robots such as Tito is humanoid in shape that can move their head and arms (Prentzas, 2013). This tool is helpful for students suffering from autism and has pre-programmed behavior sequences.

Robots are used as teaching assistants to ease the task of teachers and enhance learning activities more interactively and innovatively. Robots can understand the scientific requirements of the subjects and impart education to the students. Teaching robots can act as a helper to the students but cannot substitute them as they lack intelligence. Robots can motivate and encourage students to increase participation in various classroom activities (Druga & Ko, 2021). Intelligent tutoring systems can analyze the learning characteristics of students and customize the content accordingly (Aldeman et al., 2021). Quality content can be selected to provide effective teaching activities.

AI-enabled robotics toys have gained popularity for increasing creativity skills, literacy, and motivation in early childhood education and special education (Su & Yang, 2022). AI tools such as iRobiQ, Kibo, QRIO, Troy, and Trevor for adaptive and intelligent teaching-learning are explored by (Prentzas, 2013). iRobiQ is a robot with arms equipped with voice recognition, face recognition, gesture, and emotion recognition. Another robot that can recognize human gestures is Kibo. The robots have several distributed processing units for instant response to the activities. QRIO is a small robot with audio and visual recognition for several human activities such as jumping, walking, singing, dancing, and many more. Troy and Trevor are humanoid robots developed to address the needs of students suffering from autism. These robots can assist the clinical staff in autism therapy.

AI-enabled robots can teach programming and coding skills to students. Students can be trained, and skills can be developed for designing smart programs (Druga & Ko, 2021). Robots such as ASUS Zenbo and Zenbo scratch can be used for programming interactive animations that can be used by children (Hsieh et al., 2020). Apart from these robots intelligent agents such as Jibo robots and Anki's robot can also be used for teaching coding skills to students (Druga & Ko, 2021).

Multi-lingual robots can be used for teaching and learning foreign languages. It has been observed children can learn the language context easily and improve their attitude toward language complexity. Students can interact with chatbot robots to improve their language skills and update their knowledge (Kim et al., 2021). NAO robot is trained to teach one of the most complex Chinese languages to the students. NAO can demonstrate complex Chinese words in such a way that students can memorize them quickly (Chew & Chua, 2020). Robot provides personalized assistance to the students and engages them in interactive activities as a language tutor.

In education, many interactive robots are used to provide personalized education to students. In the classroom, there are interactive whiteboards that can be used by both teachers and parents to simplify the contents. Entertainment robots like Kibo can also be used to distract the student's attention and normalize their moods during long-duration teachings (Prentzas, 2013). Kibo is a humanoid that can dance and walk. This robot is equipped with a facial expression recognition system that can analyze human expressions and present them.

In sum, robots are very popular at various levels of intelligent educational systems. Robots provide an autonomous intelligent system to enhance the teaching-learning experience for both teachers as well as students. Robots have provided enormous opportunities to teachers by generating the latest tools and gadgets to teach students suffering from visual, hearing, and speech impairments. Educational robots, social robots, and AR-based gaming tools have transformed the traditional education system. With the advancement in technology, personalized assistance can be extended to students to students with disability. Technology encourages and motivates students to learn difficult and tedious concepts quickly.

5. LIMITATIONS OF AI IN MODERN EDUCATION

AI has provided many tools and applications for transforming traditional education (Prentzas, 2013). AI plays a significant role in providing human-machine interactions, adapting to student competence based on feedback, and providing an interactive environment for personalized tutoring (Su & Yang, 2022). However, there are certain limitations that AI has embedded into the system. The details about those technological limitations are as follows:

- AI can assign personalized assignments to each student based on its capabilities. AI systems can develop virtual learning environments with intelligent capabilities to address the needs of specialized students (Garg & Sharma, 2020). But providing dynamic content based on individual competence is a huge challenge. AI is a recent technology and the availability of adequate and sufficient digital content is a big concern for the adaptability of AI in education.
- AI has provided conversational tools such as chatbots, dictating tools, and interactive books to improve the conversational and learning capabilities of students. However, there are no clear guidelines available up to which level the conversational tools are helpful. Chatbots and interactive books are in the experimental phase and their ability to respond to student's queries is not yet fully explored (Kim, 2017). AI tools can improve communication skills in students, but their domain is limited, and accuracy is also not evaluated.
- AI has provided tools that provide real-time feedback to teachers so that they can adapt themselves in accordance with the student's requirements. AI has provided user-friendly tools to monitor the emotions and behavior of disabled students (Lampos et al., 2021). However, the feedback is not dynamically generated and is not able to incorporate diversity of all students in a classroom. The area demands significant work to incorporate the variations in accordance with the personalized need and characteristics of each individual student.
- In covid era, e-learning content has played a significant role in imparting education to students via distance learning (Hirankerd & Kittisunthonphisarn, 2020). A lot of teaching-learning online courses are available to provide automatic feedback and grading of the students. However, evaluating the actual performance along with the overall learning of a student from these courses is the biggest challenge (Kukkar et al., 2023). The authenticity of submitted assignments, benefits and practical testing of the student learning are a few areas that need to manage to enhance the usage of these courses among students.
- Apart from students, AI has provided many tools to help teachers to increase interactivity in the classroom (Roorda et al., 2021). With the progress in technology and the student's special needs, AI has provided support for the professional development of the teacher. AI has provided auto-

matic grading and feedback tools to ease the teacher's burden for unproductive tasks. However, the accuracy of these tools is not yet evaluated, and physical efforts are invested by teachers to verify the results. Also, professional development tools are equipped with limited content and suggestions, which may lack in their applications for experienced teachers.

- AI has provided many grading and assessment tools to reduce the teacher burden and incorporate accuracy and generalizability into the education ecosystem. However, existing tools are monotonous and homogenous. They are domain-specific and are not generic in the application. They lack in incorporating dynamic multiple factors in real-time substantial for a fair evaluation. Many areas demand the physical evaluation of students by experienced teachers. Also, real-time decisions based on the student's progress are missing in these tools.
- Intelligent tutoring is another benefit of AI that is extended into modern education. This concept understands students' emotions and recommends valid content in accordance with students' requirements. This system provides feedback to teachers so that effective communication can take place in the classroom (Lampos et al., 2021). The limitation of these systems is that their impact on student learning and understanding is still not evaluated. The objective and benefits of an intelligent tutoring system in today's educational system are not fully explored which can emphasize the usage of such a system.
- Teachers are benefitted from the recent AI tools and applications. These tools enhance the teaching capabilities and are beneficial for the professional growth of the teachers too. Various classroom tasks such as providing lecture notes to the students, uploading assignments, evaluating assignments, and presenting tedious concepts with the help of audio and video visuals can be simplified by the advent of these tools (Roorda et al., 2021). However, AI tools are very recent and demand proper training for their understanding and usage. Teachers are not that much efficient in operating these tools and require proper guidance for their usage in their day-to-day teaching activities.
- Robots in education are another advancement in the modern education environment. Robots are equipped with emotion and face recognition systems to provide more personalized support to students (Salas-Pilco, 2020). Robots can analyze the facial expressions of students and adapt strategies to deal with them efficiently. But robots lack in understanding of various societal concepts that can only be provided by the physical presence of the teacher in the classroom. Robots can entertain students and improve self-confidence and creativity. Robots lack in integrating the intellectual learning outcomes in students which are necessary for effective learning outcomes.

To summarize, AI has provided many tools to amend the modifications in the traditional education system in accordance with specialized students. With the support of AI, self-confidence, and motivation can be incorporated into students with special needs. Teachers are also equipped with the latest gadgets to improve the classroom activities. Teacher-student relationships can be more interactive and personalized with the help of AI. But AI tools and educational robots cannot replace the physical presence of teachers in the classroom. They can only be utilized by teachers to enhance the intellectual ability of the students by understanding their diverse needs. In addition, AI tools need to be explored along with explainability (Sahlaoui et al., 2021) and blended learning (Kumar et al., 2021) to provide student's with world class learning experience. AI tools are also suffered from bias that also needs to be addressed efficiently before their deployment in real-time (Kumar, Aelgani, Vohra, Gupta, Bhagawati, Paul, Suri, et al., 2023).

6. CONCLUSION

In this chapter, we have explored the benefits of AI-assisted modern resources in transforming the traditional education system and adapting to the needs of specialized students. The computer-based teaching-learning system has improved the teaching pedagogy by incorporating intelligent tutoring systems and adaptive learning strategies. AI-based conversational tools, chatbots, interactive classroom activities, and facial recognition systems are helpful to motivate students which special needs. These tools can enhance the intellectual capabilities of specialized students so that they can compete with regular students. Automatic grading and feedback systems ensure the accuracy, and fairness of the system without any discrimination. Various form of educational robots offers unique advantages to fulfill the needs of students suffering from a disorder such as autism. These robots are equipped with emotional and facial recognition to provide a personal touch and dynamic interaction with the students. In addition, robots are beneficial in understanding the needs of early childhood education limitations and concerns. AI has penetrated deep into the education system, but its overall impact and outcomes are yet to be explored. Also, the technology is evolving and demands further research for its rapid deployment into the educational ecosystem.

In future, blended learning and hybrid learning can be explored with the benefits of AI to full fill the special needs of specialized students. Also, the role of robots in education with improved technology can be another direction of improved in AI-based educational system.

REFERENCES

Al Ka'bi, A. (2023). Proposed artificial intelligence algorithm and deep learning techniques for development of higher education. *International Journal of Intelligent Networks*, *4*, 68–73. doi:10.1016/j.ijin.2023.03.002

Aldeman, N. L. S., de Sá Urtiga Aita, K. M., Machado, V. P., da Mata Sousa, L. C. D., Coelho, A. G. B., da Silva, A. S., da Silva Mendes, A. P., de Oliveira Neres, F. J., & do Monte, S. J. H. (2021). Smartpathk: A platform for teaching glomerulopathies using machine learning. *BMC Medical Education*, *21*(1), 248. doi:10.118612909-021-02680-1 PMID:33926437

Alghamdi, A., Alanezi, M., & Khan, F. (2020). Design and implementation of a computer aided intelligent examination system. *International Journal of Emerging Technologies in Learning*, *15*(1), 30–44. doi:10.3991/ijet.v15i01.11102

Belpaeme, T., Kennedy, J., Ramachandran, A., Scassellati, B., & Tanaka, F. (2018). Social robots for education: A review. *Science Robotics*, *3*(21), eaat5954. doi:10.1126cirobotics.aat5954 PMID:33141719

Chew, E., & Chua, X. N. (2020). Robotic Chinese language tutor: Personalising progress assessment and feedback or taking over your job? *On the Horizon*, *28*(3), 113–124. doi:10.1108/OTH-04-2020-0015

Druga, S., & Ko, A. J. (2021). How do children's perceptions of machine intelligence change when training and coding smart programs? Interaction Design and Children. doi:10.1145/3459990.3460712

Embarak, O. H. (2022). Internet of Behaviour (IoB)-based AI models for personalized smart education systems. *Procedia Computer Science*, *203*, 103–110. doi:10.1016/j.procs.2022.07.015

Garg, S., & Sharma, S. (2020). Impact of artificial intelligence in special need education to promote inclusive pedagogy. *International Journal of Information and Education Technology (IJIET)*, *10*(7), 523–527. doi:10.18178/ijiet.2020.10.7.1418

Gołąb-Andrzejak, E. (2022). Enhancing Customer Engagement in Social Media with AI–a Higher Education case study. *Procedia Computer Science*, *207*, 3028–3037. doi:10.1016/j.procs.2022.09.361

Haristiani, N. (2019). Artificial Intelligence (AI) chatbot as language learning medium: An inquiry. Journal of Physics: Conference Series.

Hirankerd, K., & Kittisunthonphisarn, N. (2020). E-learning management system based on reality technology with AI. *International Journal of Information and Education Technology (IJIET)*, *10*(4), 259–264. doi:10.18178/ijiet.2020.10.4.1373

Hsieh, Y.-Z., Lin, S.-S., Luo, Y.-C., Jeng, Y.-L., Tan, S.-W., Chen, C.-R., & Chiang, P.-Y. (2020). ARCS-assisted teaching robots based on anticipatory computing and emotional big data for improving sustainable learning efficiency and motivation. *Sustainability*, *12*(14), 5605. doi:10.3390u12145605

Hu, J. (2021). Teaching evaluation system by use of machine learning and artificial intelligence methods. *International Journal of Emerging Technologies in Learning*, *16*(5), 87–101. doi:10.3991/ijet.v16i05.20299

Jain, R., Kumar, A., Nayyar, A., Dewan, K., Garg, R., Raman, S., & Ganguly, S. (2023). Explaining sentiment analysis results on social media texts through visualization. *Multimedia Tools and Applications*, *82*(15), 1–17. doi:10.100711042-023-14432-y PMID:36747895

Kim, H.-S., Kim, N. Y., & Cha, Y. (2021). Is It Beneficial to Use AI Chatbots to Improve Learners' Speaking Performance? *Journal of Asia TEFL*, *18*(1), 161–178. doi:10.18823/asiatefl.2021.18.1.10.161

Kim, N.-Y. (2017). Effects of different types of chatbots on EFL learners' speaking competence and learner perception. *Cross-Cultural Studies*, *48*, 223–252. doi:10.21049/ccs.2017.48..223

Kolachalama, V. B. (2022). Machine learning and pre-medical education. *Artificial Intelligence in Medicine*, *129*, 102313. doi:10.1016/j.artmed.2022.102313 PMID:35659392

Kukkar, A., Mohana, R., Sharma, A., & Nayyar, A. (2023). Prediction of student academic performance based on their emotional wellbeing and interaction on various e-learning platforms. *Education and Information Technologies*, *28*(8), 1–30. doi:10.100710639-022-11573-9

Kumar, A. (2023). *Visual Object Tracking Using Deep Learning*. CRC Press.

Kumar, A., Aelgani, V., Vohra, R., Gupta, S. K., Bhagawati, M., Paul, S., ... & Suri, J. S. (2023). Artificial intelligence bias in medical system designs: a systematic review. Multimedia Tools and Applications, 1-53.

Kumar, A., & Ahluwalia, R. (2021). Breast Cancer Detection Using Machine Learning and Its Classification. In Cancer Prediction for Industrial IoT 4.0: A Machine Learning Perspective. Chapman and Hall/CRC. doi:10.1201/9781003185604-4

Kumar, A., Gupta, N., Bhasin, P., Chauhan, S., & Bachri, I. (2023). Security and Privacy Issues in Smart Healthcare Using Machine-Learning Perspectives. In 6G-Enabled IoT and AI for Smart Healthcare. CRC Press. doi:10.1201/9781003321668-3

Kumar, A., Jain, R., Gupta, M., & Islam, S. M. (Eds.). (2023). *6G-Enabled IoT and AI for Smart Healthcare: Challenges, Impact, and Analysis*. CRC Press.

Kumar, A., Krishnamurthi, R., Bhatia, S., Kaushik, K., Ahuja, N. J., Nayyar, A., & Masud, M. (2021). Blended learning tools and practices: A comprehensive analysis. *IEEE Access : Practical Innovations, Open Solutions*, *9*, 85151–85197. doi:10.1109/ACCESS.2021.3085844

Kumar, A., Mamgai, R., & Jain, R. (2023). Application of IoT-Enabled CNN for Natural Language Processing. In IoT-enabled Convolutional Neural Networks: Techniques and Applications. River Publishers. doi:10.1201/9781003393030-6

Kumar, A., Raja, & ljaz, M. F. (2023). Augmented Reality as a Boon to Disability. *Smart Distributed Embedded Systems for Healthcare Applications*, *78*(82), 77–92. doi:10.1201/9781003254119-6

Kumar, A., Sareen, P., & Arora, A. (2023). Healthcare Engineering Using AI and Distributed Technologies. In Smart Distributed Embedded Systems for Healthcare Applications. CRC Press. doi:10.1201/9781003254119-1

Kumar, A., & Vohra, R. (2023). Impact of Deep Learning Models for Technology Sustainability in Tourism Using Big Data Analytics. In Deep Learning Technologies for the Sustainable Development Goals: Issues and Solutions in the Post-COVID Era. Springer. doi:10.1007/978-981-19-5723-9_6

Kumar, A., Walia, G. S., & Sharma, K. (2020). Recent trends in multicue based visual tracking: A review. *Expert Systems with Applications*, *162*, 113711. doi:10.1016/j.eswa.2020.113711

Lampos, Mintz, & Qu. (2021). An artificial intelligence approach for selecting effective teacher communication strategies in autism education. *NPJ Science of Learning*, *6*(1), 25.

Laupichler, M. C., Aster, A., Schirch, J., & Raupach, T. (2022). Artificial intelligence literacy in higher and adult education: A scoping literature review. Computers and Education: Artificial Intelligence, 100101.

Munawar, S., Toor, S. K., Aslam, M., & Hamid, M. (2018). Move to smart learning environment: Exploratory research of challenges in computer laboratory and design intelligent virtual laboratory for eLearning Technology. *Eurasia Journal of Mathematics, Science and Technology Education*, *14*(5), 1645–1662. doi:10.29333/ejmste/85036

Prentzas, J. (2013). Artificial intelligence methods in early childhood education. *Artificial Intelligence, Evolutionary Computing and Metaheuristics: In the Footsteps of Alan Turing*, 169-199.

Roorda, D. L., Zee, M., Bosman, R. J., & Koomen, H. M. (2021). Student–teacher relationships and school engagement: Comparing boys from special education for autism spectrum disorders and regular education. *Journal of Applied Developmental Psychology*, *74*, 101277. doi:10.1016/j.appdev.2021.101277

Sahlaoui, H., Nayyar, A., Agoujil, S., & Jaber, M. M. (2021). Predicting and interpreting student performance using ensemble models and shapley additive explanations. *IEEE Access : Practical Innovations, Open Solutions*, *9*, 152688–152703. doi:10.1109/ACCESS.2021.3124270

Salas-Pilco, S. Z. (2020). The impact of AI and robotics on physical, social-emotional and intellectual learning outcomes: An integrated analytical framework. *British Journal of Educational Technology*, *51*(5), 1808–1825. doi:10.1111/bjet.12984

Southworth, J., Migliaccio, K., Glover, J., Reed, D., McCarty, C., Brendemuhl, J., & Thomas, A. (2023). Developing a model for AI Across the curriculum: Transforming the higher education landscape via innovation in AI literacy. Computers and Education: Artificial Intelligence, 100127.

Spencer, P., Timpe, Z., Verlenden, J., Rasberry, C. N., Moore, S., Yeargin-Allsopp, M., Claussen, A. H., Lee, S., Murray, C., Tripathi, T., Conklin, S., Iachan, R., McConnell, L., Deng, X., & Pampati, S. (2023). Challenges experienced by US K-12 public schools in serving students with special education needs or underlying health conditions during the COVID-19 pandemic and strategies for improved accessibility. *Disability and Health Journal*, *16*(2), 101428. doi:10.1016/j.dhjo.2022.101428 PMID:36610820

Su, J., Ng, D. T. K., & Chu, S. K. W. (2023). Artificial intelligence (AI) literacy in early childhood education: The challenges and opportunities. *Computers and Education: Artificial Intelligence*, *4*, 100124. doi:10.1016/j.caeai.2023.100124

Su, J., & Yang, W. (2022). Artificial intelligence in early childhood education: A scoping review. Computers and Education: Artificial Intelligence, 100049.

Su, J., & Zhong, Y. (2022). Artificial Intelligence (AI) in early childhood education: Curriculum design and future directions. *Computers and Education: Artificial Intelligence*, *3*, 100072. doi:10.1016/j.caeai.2022.100072

Su, J., Zhong, Y., & Ng, D. T. K. (2022). A meta-review of literature on educational approaches for teaching AI at the K-12 levels in the Asia-Pacific region. Computers and Education: Artificial Intelligence, 100065. doi:10.1016/j.caeai.2022.100065

Sweeney, S. (2023). Who wrote this? Essay mills and assessment–Considerations regarding contract cheating and AI in higher education. *International Journal of Management Education*, *21*(2), 100818. doi:10.1016/j.ijme.2023.100818

Vahabzadeh, A., Keshav, N. U., Abdus-Sabur, R., Huey, K., Liu, R., & Sahin, N. T. (2018). Improved socio-emotional and behavioral functioning in students with autism following school-based smartglasses intervention: Multi-stage feasibility and controlled efficacy study. *Behavioral Sciences (Basel, Switzerland)*, *8*(10), 85. doi:10.3390/bs8100085 PMID:30241313

Wang, Y.-Y., & Wang, Y.-S. (2022). Development and validation of an artificial intelligence anxiety scale: An initial application in predicting motivated learning behavior. *Interactive Learning Environments*, *30*(4), 619–634. doi:10.1080/10494820.2019.1674887

Xia, Q., Chiu, T. K., Zhou, X., Chai, C. S., & Cheng, M. (2022). Systematic literature review on opportunities, challenges, and future research recommendations of artificial intelligence in education. Computers and Education: Artificial Intelligence, 100118.

Chapter 7
Inclusion of Children With Special Needs in the Educational System, Artificial Intelligence (AI)

Pradnya Mehta
https://orcid.org/0000-0002-5304-7270
Vishwakarma Institute of Information Technology, India

Geetha R. Chillarge
Marathwada Mitra Mandal's College of Engineering, India

Sarita D. Sapkal
Marathwada Mitra Mandal's College of Engineering, India

Gitanjali R. Shinde
Vishwakarma Institute of Information Technology, India

Pranali S. Kshirsagar
Vishwakarma Institute of Information Technology, India

ABSTRACT

Special education for students is essential to gain/get/obtain equity and accessibility. AI enables new tools, customized learning, and improved accessibility for students with different learning needs. This chapter examines AI in inclusive education and its benefits for special needs pupils. AI-based adaptive learning, assistive intelligent tutoring, and early intervention data analytics boost inclusive education. AI algorithms customize learning in adaptive learning systems. AI-powered voice recognition and accessibility technologies assist impaired students' study. AI-powered tutoring methods improve student performance. AI-powered data analytics can identify struggling students and give assistance. AI in inclusive education has downsides. The chapter addresses AI bias, fairness, data privacy and security, transparency, explainability, and stakeholder participation. Ethics should govern inclusive education's usage of AI technology. AI should support human judgement and interaction. Responsible AI can improve education for all children, regardless of learning needs.

DOI: 10.4018/979-8-3693-0378-8.ch007

1. ORGANIZATION OF THE CHAPTER

Section 1 elaborates about Introduction Inclusion in Education, Section 2 discuss about understanding the needs of inclusive education, The Role of Artificial Intelligence (AI) in Inclusive Education is focused in Section 3, Case Studies and Success Stories of AI implementations in Inclusive Education and future scope is discussed in Section 4.

1.1 Concept of Inclusion in Education

The phrase "inclusion" refers to the practice of ensuring that all students, regardless of their personal backgrounds or other factors, have equivalent opportunities to participate in and benefit from the educational process. It supports the idea that all children should be able to benefit from the resources available in regular classrooms.

An inclusive education is a style of teaching that includes all pupils, regardless of their abilities, demographics, or physical or mental health. It supports the idea that all students should be included in the regular education system and shows appreciation for the fact that students come from a wide variety of backgrounds. That is to say, it recognizes and values the reality that there is not a single optimal method of teaching or learning.

To elaborate, we may state that inclusive education comprises the development of learning environments that can fulfill the needs of all students, the encouragement of a feeling of community, and the respect for the unique strengths and weaknesses of every individual. The goal of an inclusive education is not merely to ensure that all students have physical access to learning environments; rather, it is to ensure that all students are able to participate in and benefit from all learning environments on multiple levels (cognitive, social, and emotional).

Collaborative and customized methods of instruction are emphasized in an inclusive education. Teachers in this model engage with students, parents, and other support staff to develop and implement individualized education programs. It requires adapting pedagogical strategies, course content, and assessments to students with different backgrounds, strengths, and interests.

As part of an inclusive education program, both students with and without impairments are given opportunities to meet and build relationships with one another. It aims to foster an environment where all students feel safe and valued, where differences are celebrated and appreciated, and where everyone may succeed academically.

Inclusion in the classroom has the potential to have numerous beneficial effects. It prepares students for life in a multicultural and diverse society by instilling in them an appreciation for and an openness to difference. This can help pupils of all ability levels succeed in school and feel better about themselves. Furthermore, through breaking down walls, reducing the prevalence of stigma, and promoting equality and social justice, inclusive education aids in the development of an inclusive society.

A commitment to equity and social inclusion, chances for educator professional development, enabling laws and frameworks, and widespread collaboration are all required to successfully implement inclusive education. Constant self-reflection and improvement, along with the participation of all relevant stakeholders, are required to ensure that every child has the opportunity to thrive and realize their full potential within the context of the educational system.

Inclusion is predicated on the idea that people's differences are strengths and that we all benefit from working together and sharing our unique perspectives. It recognizes and appreciates the reality that every student is different in terms of their abilities, challenges, and learning preferences. Inclusion in the classroom refers to the practice of actively involving and supporting students in their intellectual, social, and emotional development. Teachers that use an inclusive pedagogy aim to give every student a sense of belonging and worth while also providing them with the tools they need to develop personally and academically. Through recognizing variety and fostering inclusive behaviors, schools can create an atmosphere where kids are encouraged to actively participate, demonstrate empathy for others, and take responsibility for their actions. The phrase "inclusion" refers to the practice of ensuring that all students, regardless of their personal backgrounds or other factors, have equal opportunities to participate in and benefit from the educational process. It supports the idea that all children should be able to benefit from the resources available in regular classrooms.

An inclusive education is a style of teaching that includes all pupils, regardless of their abilities, demographics, or physical or mental health. It supports the idea that all students should be included in the regular education system and shows appreciation for the fact that students come from a wide variety of backgrounds. That is to say, it recognizes and values the reality that there is not a single optimal method of teaching or learning.

To clarify, it is possible to say that inclusive education entails creating learning environments that can meet the needs of all students, fostering a sense of community, and respecting the individual strengths and weaknesses of each person. The goal of inclusive education is not merely to ensure that all students have physical access to learning environments; rather, it is to ensure that all students can participate in and benefit from all learning environments on multiple levels (cognitive, social, and emotional).

Collaborative and customized methods of instruction are emphasized in inclusive education. Teachers in this model engage with students, parents, and other support staff to develop and implement individualized education programs. It requires adapting pedagogical strategies, course content, and assessments to students with different backgrounds, strengths, and interests.

As part of an inclusive education program, both students with and without impairments are given opportunities to meet and build relationships with one another. It aims to foster an environment where all students feel safe and valued, where differences are celebrated and appreciated, and where everyone may succeed academically.

Inclusion in the classroom has the potential to have numerous beneficial effects. It prepares students for life in a multicultural and diverse society by instilling in them an appreciation for and an openness to difference. This can help pupils of all ability levels succeed in school and feel better about themselves. Furthermore, by breaking down walls, reducing the prevalence of stigma, and promoting equality and social justice, inclusive education aids in the development of an inclusive society.

A commitment to equity and social inclusion, chances for educator professional development, enabling laws and frameworks, and widespread collaboration are all required to successfully implement inclusive education. Constant self-reflection and improvement, along with the participation of all relevant stakeholders, are required to ensure that every child has the opportunity to thrive and realize their full potential within the context of the educational system.

Inclusion is predicated on the idea that people's differences are strengths and that we all benefit from working together and sharing our unique perspectives. It recognizes and appreciates the reality that every student is different in terms of their abilities, challenges, and learning preferences. Inclusion in the classroom refers to the practice of actively involving and supporting students in their intellectual, social, and emotional development. Teachers who use an inclusive pedagogy aim to give every student a sense of belonging and worth while also providing them with the tools they need to develop personally and academically. By recognizing variety and fostering inclusive behaviors, schools can create an atmosphere where kids are encouraged to actively participate, demonstrate empathy for others, and take responsibility for their actions.

1.2 Importance of Inclusive Education

Inclusive education is essential because it helps build a strong, supportive, and equal community of learners. By encouraging students' intellectual, social, and emotional development via an appreciation of and the provision of equitable opportunities for all students, inclusive education prepares them to be active and engaged citizens in a diverse and inclusive environment. Inclusive education is of paramount importance for several reasons:

1. **Equal Opportunities:** Inclusive education promotes access to high-caliber learning opportunities for all students, regardless of their identities, experiences, or circumstances. It encourages fairness and removes obstacles that may prevent some students from fully engaging in the learning process.
2. **Academic and Social Benefits:** There are academic and social benefits to creating inclusive classrooms where students of varying abilities may learn side by side. All pupils will benefit from this since they will be given the opportunity to hear and consider new points of view. Education that takes into account students' individual differences is essential to creating harmonious communities.
3. **Personalized Learning:** Learning that is tailored to each individual student is a hallmark of inclusive education. Teachers can better meet the needs of their students with special education requirements when they implement inclusive practices. This individualized method encourages students' personal growth and academic success.
4. **Improved Academic Outcomes:** Evidence suggests that all students can benefit from inclusive education in terms of their academic performance. Students with a wide range of abilities benefit from inclusion in general education settings because they are more likely to receive high-quality instruction, engage in productive peer interactions, and achieve academic achievement. Student engagement and motivation are both increased in inclusive classroom settings.
5. **Social and Emotional Development:** All pupils' social and emotional growth is supported through an inclusive education model. Students grow in their ability to understand and empathise with others, and they strengthen their ability to connect with their classmates. Students' emotional and physical health benefit from inclusive classrooms because they are able to express themselves freely while receiving positive reinforcement from teachers.
6. **Human Rights and Social Justice:** The values of social justice and respect for human rights form the foundation of inclusive education. It advocates for the premise that all students, regardless of their skills, should have access to the same high-quality learning opportunities. Education that takes into account students of all backgrounds works to create a society free of bias and prejudice. Samim, A. (2023).

1.3 Objectives of Inclusion of Children With Special Need in Education System: AI

The Evaluation for the Efficacy of AI-Based Assistive Technologies are mentioned as below

1. Assess AI-driven assistive tech's uptake, efficacy, and impact on special education, including adaptive learning, communication aids, and sensory gadgets, to promote inclusive education.
2. Designing and Developing AI Algorithms for Personalised Learning
3. Investigating the Potential of Artificial Intelligence in Early Identification and Intervention for Children with exceptional Needs
4. Addressing Bias and Fairness as well as Creating Ethical Principles and Standards for the Application of AI

The topic of inclusion of children who have special needs in the regular classroom setting is a difficult and complicated one. This issue is influenced by a wide variety of factors, some of which are the following:

1. Students that have specific requirements frequently do not have access to the required resources, which is a major barrier to their academic success in school. Assistive technologies, specialized instruction, and various forms of accommodation are all examples of what might fall under this category.
2. Students who have special needs are at risk of not receiving the necessary help from their teachers and classmates because of a possible lack of support from those two groups. Because of this, it may be challenging for them to participate in class and they may not feel like they are included. Isolation from classmates is a common experience for students with special needs who attend regular school. This may be the result of a variety of things, including the individual's impairment, their unique approach to learning, or their deficiency in social skills. The application of artificial intelligence (AI) may provide a solution to at least some of these problems. For instance, AI can be utilized in the following ways:
    - Ø **Individualized instruction:** AI can be used to develop individualized lesson plans for pupils who have specific educational requirements. Students are able to learn at their own pace and concentrate on the subject areas in which they want the most assistance as a result of this.
    - Ø **AI can be used to track student development**: and identify areas of need, which can be accomplished by using the technology. Using this information, one might modify the study schedule so that it better fits their needs.
    - Ø **Create interventions**: Artificial intelligence can be utilized to create interventions that can assist students with special needs in overcoming the difficulties they face. These treatments can be modified to meet the requirements of each individual learner.
    - Ø **Accessibility**: The use of AI allows for the creation of learning environments that are more accessible and inclusive for a wider range of people. This can involve things like making sure the physical setting is accessible, offering closed captioning for videos, and deploying technology that can help those who have disabilities.

However, in order to fully realize the promise that AI has to offer in the field of education for students with special needs, a number of obstacles must first be overcome. These difficulties include the following:

- All students, including those with disabilities, should be able to use the artificial intelligence technologies that are available. This means that the tools need to be developed in a way that is compatible with assistive technology and that they need to be easy to use for students with a variety of abilities. Additionally, the tools need to be accessible to students who are deaf or hard of hearing.
- AI algorithms are educated on data, and if the data is biased in any way, then the algorithms themselves will be biased as a result of the training. It is possible that this will result in tools powered by AI that are biased towards particular groups of students. It is essential to give careful consideration to the data that is utilized in the training of AI algorithms and to take measures to reduce bias.
- It is essential to ensure that the confidentiality of the student information that is gathered by AI-powered technologies, as these tools acquire a great deal of data about students. This implies that the data has to be collected and stored in a secure location, and that students have to be given authority over the data that pertains to them.
- Because of the high cost involved, some schools and families may not be able to afford tools that are powered by artificial intelligence (AI). It is essential to locate methods by which AI-powered products can be made more affordable in order to ensure that they are accessible to all pupils.

In spite of these obstacles, there is great promise for artificial intelligence to assist education for students with special needs. Artificial intelligence has the ability to completely transform the way we educate children with special needs by making the process more individualized, accessible, and successful. We can ensure that artificial intelligence is exploited to its greatest potential to improve the education of all kids if we take steps to address the issues and collaborate with one another.

2. UNDERSTANDING SPECIAL NEEDS

2.1 Overview of Various Special Needs Conditions (e.g., Autism Spectrum Disorder, Attention Deficit Hyperactivity Disorder, Learning Disabilities)

1. Autism Spectrum Disorder (ASD):

Challenges in social contact, difficulty in communication, and limited and repetitive behaviors are hallmarks of Autism Spectrum disease (ASD), a neurodevelopmental disease. Social abilities, verbal and nonverbal communication, and sensory processing may all be impaired to varied degrees in people with ASD. People with ASD can live productive lives with the support of early intervention, specialized education, and therapy.

Ø **Social Interaction:** Children who have ASD could have a hard time interacting with other children their age. It's possible that they didn't comprehend social conventions or know how to play well with others. Because of this, one risks being socially isolated and lonely. Children with ASD may have difficulty processing sensory information. They may be sensitive to noise, touch, or light.

Ø **Repetitive behaviour:** Children with ASD may engage in repetitive behaviors, such as hand flapping or rocking. These behaviors can be disruptive in the classroom and may make it difficult for the child to learn.

If you want to understand the particular needs of children who have autism spectrum disorder (ASD) and are attending an inclusive school, the following are some factors to take into consideration:

Children with ASD may have difficulties communicating either vocally or non-verbally, and this problem may affect both forms of communication. Additionally, it's possible that they have trouble reading social signs and body language. Because of this, it may be challenging for them to take part in classroom discussions, pose questions, or establish friends with other students.

Children who have autism spectrum disorders may have difficulties interacting socially with their peers. It's possible that they don't comprehend social conventions or know how to play well with others. Because of this, one risks being socially isolated and lonely.

Processing of sensory information can be challenging for children who have autism spectrum disorder (ASD). It's possible that they're hypersensitive to sound, touch, or even light. This can make it challenging for them to concentrate during class and take part in activities outside of it.

Children with autism spectrum disorder may engage in repetitive behaviour, such as rocking back and forth or flapping their hands repeatedly. These behaviours can be distracting to the teacher and other students in the classroom, which can make it more challenging for the child to learn.

Children diagnosed with ASD may have trouble paying attention, so keep that in mind. They could quickly become sidetracked and have trouble concentrating on the task at hand. Because of this, it may be challenging for them to learn new information.

It is essential to keep in mind that not every child diagnosed with ASD will experience the same difficulties. There is a possibility that some youngsters will exhibit more severe symptoms than others. It is also essential to keep in mind that children who have ASD are capable of learning and developing. They have the potential to achieve success in inclusive education with the correct help.

The following is a list of particular tactics that can be utilized to support children with autism spectrum disorder (ASD) who are enrolled in inclusive education:

- It is important to provide instructions that are both clear and concise for children who have autism spectrum disorder (ASD). They may also require other forms of support, such as visual aids, in order to be able to comprehend what is expected of them.
- Be patient and compassionate with children who have autism spectrum disorder (ASD), as they may require additional time to comprehend information and finish tasks. It is critical that you treat them with patience and understanding at all times.
- It is important to remember that children with ASD may require breaks at various times throughout the day. Because of this, it will be easier for them to maintain their focus and prevent them from becoming overwhelmed.
- Children who have autism spectrum disorders may require additional encouragement to engage in social engagement with their peers. This can be accomplished by giving them opportunity to play together or by assisting them in joining social groups in the community.
- In order for children with ASD to be able to deal with the difficulties they face, it is important to teach them coping strategies. This can involve instructing them on how to deal with sensory overload, how to manage their emotions, and how to maintain their composure in difficult situations.

Children who have autism spectrum disorder are able to achieve success in inclusive education if they are given the appropriate support. They have the potential to learn and develop just like any other youngster if they receive the appropriate assistance through AI tool.

2. Attention Deficit Hyperactivity Disorder (ADHD):

Disorders of neurodevelopment characterized by inattention, hyperactivity, and impulsivity that can impair everyday functioning and development include attention deficit hyperactivity disorder (ADHD). Children with attention deficit hyperactivity disorder (ADHD) may have trouble concentrating, staying on task, and managing their impulses. ADHD symptoms are often treated with a combination of behavioral therapy, medication, and specialized teaching methods.

If you want to understand the particular demands that children with attention deficit hyperactivity disorder (ADHD) have in inclusive education, the following are some items to take into consideration:

- Ø **Provide clear and concise instructions:**
  - ◦ Children who suffer from ADHD may have trouble paying attention to what's going on around them. They could quickly become sidetracked and have trouble concentrating on the task at hand. Because of this, it may be challenging for them to learn new information.
- Ø **Break down tasks into smaller steps:**
  - ◦ Children who have ADHD may have symptoms including restlessness and fidgeting. They could have trouble sitting still and be a distraction for the other students in the classroom.
  - ◦ Children with ADHD may act without first thinking about the consequences of their actions. They might answer questions aloud in class or disrupt those who are speaking. Because of this, it may be challenging for them to form friendships and get along with their contemporaries.
  - ◦ Children who have attention deficit hyperactivity disorder (ADHD) may have trouble organizing their thoughts and the things they use. Because of this, it may be challenging for children to finish their tasks and keep up with the rest of their schooling.
- Ø **Encourage movement:**
  - ◦ Children who have ADHD may have trouble comprehending social cues and body language, which is a necessary component of social skills. Because of this, it may be challenging for them to form friendships and get along with their contemporaries.
  - ◦ It is essential to keep in mind that not every child diagnosed with ADHD will experience the same difficulties. There is a possibility that some youngsters will exhibit more severe symptoms than others. It is also essential to keep in mind that children who have ADHD are capable of learning and developing. They have the potential to achieve success in inclusive education with the correct help. In inclusive education settings, the following are some specific practices that can be utilized to support children who have ADHD:
  - ◦ Children who have attention deficit hyperactivity disorder (ADHD) may require instructions that are clear and precise. They may also require other forms of support, such as visual aids, in order to be able to comprehend what is expected of them.
- Ø **Provide frequent breaks:**
  - ◦ It may be necessary to break down tasks into smaller parts for children who have attention deficit hyperactivity disorder (ADHD). Because of this, it will be easier for them to maintain their focus and prevent them from becoming overwhelmed.

- Children who have attention deficit hyperactivity disorder (ADHD) may require frequent breaks. This can help children maintain their concentration and prevent them from becoming fidgety.

3. Learning Disabilities:

Conditions affecting the development and use of academic talents fall under the umbrella term "learning disabilities." Reading and language processing difficulties, math difficulties, and writing difficulties are all examples of the more common forms of dyslexia. Specialized education, assistive technology, and classroom adjustments are frequently helpful for students with learning difficulties.

4. Intellectual Disability (ID):

Limitations in intellectual functioning and adaptive behaviour are hallmarks of intellectual impairment (ID). Cognitive ability, social skills, and everyday functioning are all negatively impacted. Reaching one's full potential may include individualized services, individualized schooling programmes, and life skills training for people with ID. Morrison, C., Cutrell, E., & Dhareshwar, A. (2017, October).

5. Speech and Language Disorders:

Conditions affecting verbal expression are included under the umbrella term "speech and language disorders." Problems with speech production, language comprehension, and interpersonal interaction are all possible symptoms of these conditions. Individuals with speech and language impairments might benefit from speech therapy and specialized therapies to enhance their communicative skills.

6. Sensory Processing Disorders (SPD):

Disorders of sensory processing (SPD) manifest themselves in an impaired ability to recognize, organize, and react to information conveyed through the senses of sight, hearing, taste, and smell. People with SPD may experience difficulties in their day-to-day lives and interpersonal relationships due to their hypersensitivity or hyposensitivity to various sensory stimuli. Sensory processing disorders are often treated with occupational therapy and sensory integration strategies.

7. Emotional and Behavioral Disorders:

Disturbances in emotional and behavioral control, behaviour, and interpersonal relationships involve a wide spectrum of problems. Chronic patterns of rebellious or aggressive behaviour characterize conditions like oppositional defiant disorder (ODD) and conduct disorder (CD), whereas the emotional well-being of those affected by mood disorders like sadness and anxiety. Medication, therapy, counseling, or other behavioral treatments may be used to treat the patient.

Keep in mind that these are only broad strokes, and that there is great variation in the intensity and particular features of each ailment. Furthermore, people may suffer from several co-occurring illnesses, necessitating in-depth and individualized care.

3. THE ROLE OF ARTIFICIAL INTELLIGENCE (AI) IN INCLUSIVE EDUCATION

In order to restore the inclusion of children with special needs in the educational system, artificial intelligence (AI) can play a pivotal role.

A student's learning habits, strengths, and weaknesses may be analyzed by AI, and a personalized learning plan can be developed, along with real-time feedback to assist the student focus on the areas in which they need to make improvements. All pupils, regardless of their starting point or aptitude, may benefit from this. Student information such as exam scores, attendance records, and behavior reports can help with this. Students who are having difficulty learning should be identified as soon as possible so that they can receive the aid they need. Find the kids that are having difficulty. Helping children with impairments succeed in school is possible with the aid of artificial intelligence-powered assistive technologies. Software like text-to-speech and voice recognition can aid children who have trouble with reading and writing, respectively. With the use of artificial intelligence, virtual assistants can offer extra help for kids with disabilities outside of the classroom. A virtual assistant may, for instance, aid with schoolwork or remind students of future tasks. Garg, S. (2020, July 7).

AI should not be used in place of human aid for students with disabilities. Artificial intelligence, on the other hand, may be utilized to complement and strengthen the help supplied by human educators and other experts.

3.1 Introduction to Artificial Intelligence and Its Applications in Education

AI is a branch of computer science that focuses on building smart machines capable of performing tasks that require human intelligence. Advances in machine learning and deep learning are creating a paradigm shift in virtually every sector of the tech industry.

AI systems can perform tasks associated with human cognitive functions, such as interpreting speech, playing games and identifying patterns. They typically learn how to do this by processing massive amounts of data and looking for patterns to model in their own decision-making. In some cases, humans will supervise an AI's learning process, reinforcing good decisions and discouraging bad ones. However AI has had a positive impact on education for students with special needs, based on qualitative research conducted with focused interviews.

AI and technology have enabled the educational sector to become more inclusive and accessible for students with visual, hearing, mobility and intellectual disabilities. AI has had a positive impact on students with special needs and educational institutions in creating inclusive pedagogies. Figure 1 illustrates the various problems observed in children.

Figure 1. Problems in children

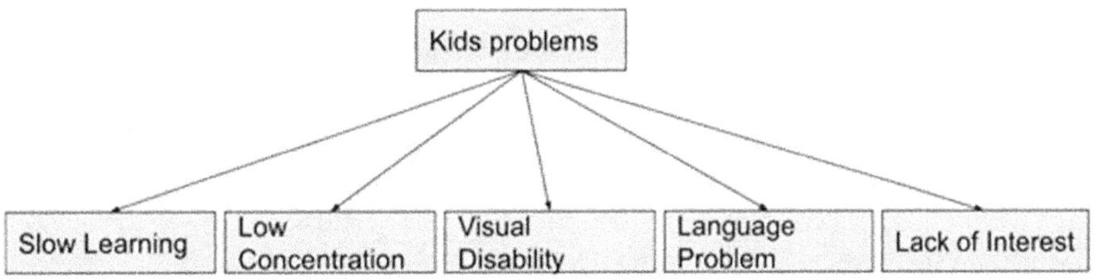

In conventional approaches children find it tough to follow directions, courses, and even their textbooks in traditional classroom settings. To make up for the lack of an inclusive design used in regular classroom instruction, which often stresses such pupils because they cannot take the pressure of competition, they require individualized attention and extra devotion from the instructor. Considering everything, it is clear that children in need of special education cannot use the conventional one-size-fits-all method.

The learning experiences of both students and teachers are impacted by the digital revolution of modern classrooms, which can help them develop more effective and engaging educational processes. However, not every student in a classroom is able to easily blend in with their peers since some may have trouble seeing, hearing, or understanding the teacher's directions or even following what is stated in the textbooks. Students who have been identified as having a physical or mental disability, such as hearing or vision loss

The inclusion of AI (Artificial Intelligence) in accessible education has created new opportunities to improve inclusiveness in the classroom. Numerous research has shown that using AI technologies in teaching and learning may effectively include individuals who have learning problems or impairments. AI-based techniques can be used to provide these pupils greater flexibility because they allow for self-paced learning.

3.2 Artificial Intelligence and Human Relations

AI innovation has also made it feasible to develop products that make it easier for people with hearing loss to live their lives named GnoSys. One of the leading providers of such AI-powered products is "Google Translate for the Deaf and Mute." Using neural networks and computer vision, the AI-based technology instantly transforms hand gestures or sign language into text and speech.

Many officials believe that AI will free up teacher time, but others have predicted that it will eventually render them de facto obsolete. If not, their position will be changed to that of classroom orchestrators or technology facilitators, in charge of overseeing student behaviour and making sure the technology is turned on. The truth is that during the course of its more than 30 years, the majority of AIED research and development has been centered on utilizing AI to directly help learners with the goal of boosting learning. Typically, this has been done by taking over (specifically, replacing) instructor responsibilities, such as through the use of AI-powered adaptive tutoring.

3.3 AI in Education

One of the benefits of AI in education is that it helps to advance individualized instruction and learning. The way that kids learns and how professors educate has both been impacted by AI ; Huang, J., Saleh, S., & Liu, Y. (2021, May). Depending on the demands and learning circumstances of the pupils, it might create a personalised learning plan. One of the benefits of AI in education is that it helps to advance individualized instruction and learning. The way that kids learns and how professors educate has both been impacted by AI. It may create a personalised learning plan based on the requirements and academic circumstances of the pupils.

Based on big data and machine learning, AI can thoroughly assess students' performance on assignments and tests and offer individualized teaching recommendations for students who struggle with certain concepts.

One-on-one personalized instruction between computers and students may be implemented with the use of adaptive learning technologies. With the use of intelligent adaptive learning technology, teachers may mimic one-on-one instruction with students while also enhancing the learning system's capacity for personalized instruction. Another benefit of AI in education is that it may lighten the load on instructors and help them concentrate more on providing humanistic care. Today, homework and test correction takes up a large portion of instructors' time. The time that instructors spend teaching, conducting research, and interacting with students is taken up by these repetitive chores of Smart tutoring systems. Huang, J., Saleh, S., & Liu, Y. (2021, May).

3.4 Potential Benefits of AI in Supporting Children With Special Needs

Artificial intelligence (AI) may provide several advantages for helping youngsters with special needs. Some possible advantages are as follows:

Individualized Instruction: Artificial intelligence has the potential to create individualized instruction plans for each student. Educational platforms powered by AI may help children with special needs learn at their own speed and in a way that suits their learning styles by analyzing data and customizing teaching to give focused information, adaptable activities, and individualized feedback.

Assistive Technologies: Children with special needs can benefit from a wide range of assistive gadgets that are powered by artificial intelligence. People who have trouble communicating because of speech or language impairments can benefit greatly from speech recognition technologies. Artificial intelligence (AI)-powered gadgets and applications can help students with motor impairments control and engage with digital systems.

Enhanced Communication and Social Skills: Artificial intelligence can help youngsters with exceptional difficulties improve their communication and social skills. Training and practicing social skills can benefit from the immersive and interactive settings provided by virtual reality (VR) and augmented reality (AR) applications. Chabot's and other forms of virtual assistance can provide a nurturing environment for people to practice conversational and social skills.

Data-Driven Intervention and Assessment: Educators and therapists can benefit from AI since it can aid in the collection and analysis of massive volumes of data on students' development, behaviour, and interactions. AI can make more precise diagnoses and treatment plans because of the use of machine learning techniques. This data-driven strategy can aid in spotting learning problems early on and directing the creation of effective treatments.

Emotional Support and Well-Being: Children with exceptional needs can benefit from AI-powered systems that offer emotional support and help manage their well-being. Chatbots with NLP skills may have meaningful discussions, give emotional support, and link users to tools for coping with stress and anxiety. Emotional states may be detected by an AI system's analysis of facial expressions and behaviour, allowing for preemptive intervention.

Accessibility and Inclusion: Improvements in Accessibility and Inclusion for Children with Special Needs: Artificial Intelligence Technologies. People who have trouble hearing may benefit from real-time captioning or transcription services made possible by automatic speech recognition. Individuals with visual impairments can get access to and interpret previously inaccessible material

Collaboration and Professional Development: Through the use of AI-powered picture recognition. AI can help teachers, therapists, and parents of children with special needs work together to better serve their children. Platforms driven by AI may facilitate communication, data sharing, and teamwork, all of which are beneficial to the child's development as a whole. AI can help improve the skills of educators and therapists by giving them easier access to online resources and data-driven insights.

Human connection and assistance are still critical in the development and education of children with special needs, despite the impressive capabilities of AI. To fully realize AI's potential in assisting children with special needs, it must be used ethically and in a well-rounded manner that integrates technology advances with human skills.

3.5 Challenges of AI in Education

While AI has many advantages for education, it will also confront some unanticipated difficulties. It will be easier to plan for and enhance future applications of AI in education if people are aware of the potential issues that can arise. These difficulties mostly concern the following areas:

Prior to everything else, fairness must be ensured when using AI in education. Developing nations run the danger of allowing new technologies to exacerbate the gaps in educational attainment as a result of the development of AI. The growing algorithmic divide now threatens to rob many educational possibilities given by AI, much as the digital divide has divided those who can use the Internet from those who cannot. The majority of AI algorithms originate from developed nations, thus they are unable to completely account for the circumstances of developing nations and hence cannot be directly implemented. To provide the necessary circumstances for AI to enhance learning, the education industry must overcome severe challenges such a lack of foundational infrastructure and technology.

Second, we must be aware of the safety and ethical concerns connected to data collection, use, and dissemination. In terms of giving pupils individualized advice, gathering personal data, data privacy, and the ownership of duties and data feed algorithms, AI has created several ethical difficulties . The general public must debate the ethical, responsibility, and safety issues involved in order to strengthen the oversight of AI technology and its products.

Thirdly, it aids educators in becoming ready for AI-assisted instruction. To effectively employ AI to support educational reform, teachers must learn new digital teaching techniques. The creators of AI teaching goods must also comprehend how teachers operate in order to produce a teaching product utilization.

3.6 Student With AI

The information received, processed, and even how it is transmitted can all be negatively impacted by learning disorders, which are neurological illnesses that disrupt the brain's capacity to link communication regions. The neurological condition with the highest prevalence in this diverse population that affects interpersonal communication is dyslexia. In fact, reading problems account for over 80% of instances among these categories of diseases. Yeguas-Bolívar, E., Alcalde-Llergo, J. M., Aparicio-Martínez, et.al (2022, March).

Dyslexic kids have difficulties reading, memorizing information, and understanding concepts, but the severity of these issues can be reduced with therapy and the development of compensatory strategies. Technology has increasingly been used as a therapeutic tool in recent years, particularly when it comes to virtual worlds.

A neurological condition known as a learning impairment (LD) impairs the brain's capacity to receive, analyze, store, and react to information. The difficulty learning fundamental academic abilities that a person with at least average intellect experiences is known as a learning impairment. LD is a spectrum of disorders. It is a name for a collection of illnesses. Therefore, even if a person has average or above-average IQ and no significant sensory issues (such as eyesight or hearing loss), they may still find it difficult to stay up with peers their own age when it comes to learning and day-to-day activities. The subject of LD detection and diagnosis is addressed by the author using (ANN and SVM).

The study recommended a machine learning-based method to assist such students and analyze the intricacies of their learning issues in order to ensure that they benefit from innovative techniques in the post-pandemic age. The suggested method employs a machine learning methodology to diagnose dyslexia, analyzing the primary complications such as word recognition, reading fluency, and writing fluency. This strategy has the potential to revolutionize learning abilities and overcome any learning challenges at various learning and teaching levels. Sharif, M. S., & Elmedany, W. (2022, March).

provides a Web-based application that incorporates machine learning techniques (Decision trees) for determining if children (8-10 years) are at risk of developing Specific Learning impairment by displaying the regions of learning impairment based on clinical data and research. Akhil, R., Soori, A., Shankar, D., Krishnan(2017).

The kid will be in a perpetual state of anguish and mentally fragile if effective detection and support are not provided in the early stages of development. They may lose their self-esteem and blame themselves for their circumstances.

3.7 Assistive Technologies and Ai-Based Tools for Inclusive Education

Text-to-Speech Software?

Text-to-speech software has transformed content consumption. It has made reading more accessible, provided an alternate means for teachers to engage with students when reading via a screen is either hard or inconvenient, and has been a huge help to students and those with learning challenges. In fact, numerous new text-to-speech firms have raised the bar for the whole industry in recent years by allowing users to listen to content on the screen in high-quality, natural-sounding voices.

Effect of Text-to-Speech Software for learners

An electronic gadget that can read written items aloud has a high face value. Reading aloud is, of course, an important component of emerging and early reading and literacy initiatives, but it was also an important component of teaching approaches for struggling readers. For example, identified various reading aloud teaching tactics that might be beneficial to kids who are seriously challenged in reading, such as the neurological impress approach, echo reading, and comprehension for decoding. Students with learning disabilities are commonly provided with instructional help, such as having text materials and tests read aloud to them as part of the requirements of their individualized education programmes.

Murf, Speechify, Speechelo, Google Cloud Text-to-Speech, Amazon Polly, Etc. Are Some Well-Known Text-to-Speech Software

According to Dutoit (1997), the operation of TTS includes two modules: (1) Natural Language Processing (NLP), which is capable of producing voice recordings of articles and combining the tone and rhyme, and (2) Digital Signal Processing (DSP), which is capable of converting the received symbol information into a voice. TTS's four key components were described in depth by Zhu (2005).

1. **Textual Evaluation:** Analyzes the text's syntax and semantics and turns them into language-specific parameters. In other words, the computer can recognize words, phrases, and pronunciations, as well as when and how long to pause.
2. **Sends language characteristic** parameters into the rhythm generator to produce the corresponding rhythm message of each syllable in the text, including the baseband track, volume, and duration, and converts tone, voice, pause mode, and length of pronunciation into rhythmic parameters.
3. **Synthesis Unit Generator:** Generates synthesis units by analyzing monosyllabic phonemes in speech waveform samples stored in the speech database.
4. **Text-to-Speech Synthesizer:** Chooses acoustic characteristics from a sound library to fit the sounds that must be said.

Voice Recognition

Speech recognition is one of the most rapidly evolving technical technologies. It has numerous uses in various fields and offers numerous potential benefits. Many people are unable to converse because of linguistic problems.

The artificial fabrication of human speech is known as speech synthesis. A voice computer, also known as a speech synthesizer, is a computer that is used for this function and can be implemented in software or hardware solutions. A text-to-speech (TTS) system translates text into speech; other systems convert symbolic linguistic representations, such as phonetic transcriptions, into speech.

Concatenating parts of recorded voice kept in a database can be used to create synthesized speech.

The size of the stored speech units varies between systems; a system that stores phones or diphones has the greatest output range but may lack clarity.

A synthesizer can also include a representation of the vocal tract and other human voice features to produce totally synthetic voice output.

TTS (Text to Speech) (Vashisht et al., 2021) is a sort of assistive technology that reads digital text out loud. It is also known as read-aloud technology. TTS may translate words on a computer or other digital device into audio with the click of a button or the touch of a finger. A simple remedy could be to remove this barrier to contact. A simple answer could be to break down this communication barrier with spoken language that a computer can understand.

Optical Character Recognition (OCR)

Those who are visually impaired may now read printed or handwritten text thanks to optical character recognition (OCR) technology. Combining OCR with text-to-speech technology can help pupils better access and comprehend printed materials. Lin, R., He, X., Dong, X. L. (2021, August).

Augmented Reality (AR) and Virtual Reality (VR)

AR and VR technologies provide immersive and interactive learning experiences. They can create simulated environments for students to explore and practice skills, making learning more engaging and accessible to students with various disabilities.

New methods of teaching and learning in blended, face-to-face, and online settings have been prompted by the emergence of immersive technologies. Today, many schools around the country employ electronic tools to make lessons more dynamic, resulting in more effective and interactive learning for students of all ages. Many academic fields and levels are beginning to embrace augmented reality because of its promising educational applications. In real time and with human input, it mixes digital and physical data. his fusion is achieved using many technology platforms, including smartphones and tablets, to produce a new reality infused with elements of both the actual and virtual worlds. Most crucially, this technology "covers a wide range of topics, target groups, academic levels and more. Using a variety of augmented reality technical gadgets, augmented reality enables the actual environment to be fused with digital information. Superimposed onto photographs of the actual environment are pictures of 3D objects, multimedia material, or textual data. These elements increase the possibilities of interaction with the user. Augmented reality is often viewed as a step beyond virtual reality. Badilla-Quintana, M. G., Sepúlveda-Valenzuela(2020). Within the scope of this research; we additionally refine the idea of specific requirements (whether temporary or permanent). Chile's Ministry of Education emphasizes here that the idea of special educational needs entails a shift in how we conceptualize students' learning issues, away from a deficit-focused paradigm and towards a more holistic one.

Intelligent Tutoring Systems (ITS)

ITS stands for intelligent tutoring system and it employs artificial intelligence to tailor lessons to each individual student. Supporting students with a wide range of learning requirements, these systems conduct diagnostic analyzes of students' knowledge and abilities, pinpoint areas of weakness, and provide individualized feedback and instruction. The uses of AI were broken down into the following groups: Student performance; Teaching; Selection and Behaviour; and Other. Zafari, M., Safari Bazargani, J., & Choi, S. M. (2022, January). Predicting who will drop out of school, grading essays, and helping instructors are just some of the many ways AI is being used in education.

Predictive Analytics

These technologies driven by artificial intelligence can sift through mountains of data in search of trends, patterns, and student behaviors. Educators and support staff may use this data to better tailor their lessons, provide necessary modifications, and implement necessary interventions. The results of deep learning are competitive with those of other machine learning methods like k-nearest neighbours, naive Bayes classifiers, and logistic regression. When doing research in the fields of instructional data mining and learning analytics, it is generally accepted that scholars should prioritize explanation over prediction, and the selection of statistical learning approaches should prioritize interpretability. Tenzin Doleck DavidJohn Lemay (2019) . People view attitudes as a multifaceted concept that includes (a) cognitive attitudes, which refer to how users evaluate a technology in terms of its usefulness, (b) emotional attitudes, which refer to how users feel while using the technology, and (c) intentional attitudes, which refer to whether or not users intend to resist or make use of the technology in the future. Each dimension may elicit a unique response; for example, someone may have a very favourable cognitive attitude yet a very negative emotional response. Conflicts between rational and empathetic perspectives may prevent educators from embracing online interventions and increase the prevalence of AR for explanation over prediction. A Technology for Expressive and Functional Purposes: Individuals with speech and language impairments are able to communicate more successfully with the use of AI-based communication devices, such as voice-generating devices or communication applications. These programmes aid in communicating by utilizing natural language processing and predictive text algorithms. Sophisticated statistical and machine learning methods for identifying at-risk children for targeted, cost-saving treatments; "predictive analytics". Confusion matrices are created by adding the True Positive, True Negative, False Positive, and False Negative values across all courses to evaluate OUA's accuracy in making predictions. Accuracy and other performance indicators may be calculated using this matrix. This ensures that higher enrollment courses have a greater effect on overall efficiency indicators. Then, we build measures of precision, recall, F-measure, and accuracy for the courses. The term "precision" refers to the rate at which students "not submit" classifications were spot-on. F-Score is a harmonic mean of Precision and Recall; Accuracy is the ratio of right predictions to the total number of students; and Recall is the fraction of students properly recognizes d as "not submit" of all students who have not submitted an assignment. Students "at risk" ('will-not submit next assignment') are being studied; only those students whose assignments have not been turned in are being predicted for. The next teacher-mark assignment submission outcome is already known (i.e., the student submitted), hence the dashboard does not make any predictions for such learners. TChristothea Herodotou (2019).

Communication and Assistive Devices

Individuals with speech and language impairments are able to communicate more successfully with the use of AI-based communication devices, such as voice-generating devices or communication applications. These gadgets allow those who might otherwise be unable to communicate or participate in class to do so. These programmes aid in communicating by utilizing natural language processing and predictive text algorithms.

Augmentative and Alternative Communication (AAC)

These devices help those who have trouble speaking or who are unable to speak at all. Among these aids are whiteboards, photo-sharing applications, gadgets that convert text to speech, and specialized mobile programmes. Individuals who rely on AAC devices are able to communicate their wants, needs, and ideas via the use of visuals, symbols, and synthetic speech.

Voice Output Communication Aids (VOCAs)

They are gadgets or programmes that can synthesize human speech and output it to the user. They let people who have trouble speaking communicate by typing in or choosing symbols that correspond to words or phrases that the gadget will then read out.

Symbol-Based Systems

Picture Communication Systems (PCS) and Board maker are two examples of symbol-based systems that employ icons to stand in for spoken language. These solutions make it easier for people with language barriers or mental disabilities to communicate and comprehend what they read.

Eye Gaze Technology

Eye gaze technology is a method of controlling electronic equipment by following a person's gaze. It lets people utilize on-screen menus, make selections, and even have conversations by staring intently at individual icons.

Translator Tools

Tools that translate speech into sign language or from sign language into speech are useful for communicating with those who are deaf or hard of hearing. Teachers and translators can use these resources to bridge the gap between people who speak various languages or utilize different forms of communication.

Sensor-Based Technologies

Sensor-based technologies allow people with physical limitations to use digital systems, such as with the use of eye-tracking devices or gesture recognition systems. These aids can facilitate access to educational materials and engagement in related pursuits.

3.8 Ethical and Legal Considerations in AI-Based Inclusion

Privacy and Data Security Concerns in AI for Inclusive Education

When implementing AI for inclusive education, privacy and data security must be top priorities. While there are many advantages to using AI technology, there are also risks associated with collecting, storing, and analyzing private information. Jiageng Chen,Chunhua Hu,ZhengYan (2019). Some issues with privacy and data security are as follows.

1. Data Collection and Storage: The use of AI in inclusive classrooms typically necessitates the capture and storage of sensitive information, such as students' names, email addresses, and academic performance. It is crucial to guarantee that data gathering is legitimate, open, and restricted to what is required for the stated pedagogical goals. It is critical to protect students' personal information by using secure data storage practices including encryption and access limits.
2. Informed Consent: Getting parental permission is a necessary step before collecting and utilizing any student information. Individuals are better able to make educated decisions when they are provided with information about the data gathered, how it will be used, and the protections in place. To guarantee conformity with privacy legislation and policies, transparent consent processes should be created and recorded.

3. Data Security Measures: Strong data security measures are required to prevent data breaches, abuse, and unauthorized access relating to students. This entails things like encrypted data storage, frequent security audits, and stringent access controls for critical information.
4. Anonymization and De-identification: Protecting students' privacy calls for AI systems to use methods of anonymizing and de-identifying student information wherever possible. Reducing the potential for re-identification requires the elimination or encryption of PII from data collections.
5. Third-Party Services and Data Sharing: Collaboration with Third-Party Service Providers and Data Sharing: Efforts to make education more accessible often necessitate sharing student information with non-accredited institutions or using the services of outside consultants. It is vital to develop transparent agreements and rules that guarantee these parties adhere to the same privacy and security standards and offer adequate protections for data protection.
6. Data Retention and Disposal: rules for Data preservation and Disposal establishing data preservation and disposal rules are critical. When it is no longer required, student information should be deleted in a safe manner. As a result, potential threats to data security are reduced and privacy laws are followed.
7. Ethical Use of Data: Artificial intelligence systems should be built and used with morality in mind. Data collected from students should only be used for educational purposes, protecting them from unfair discrimination and unwanted profiling. In order to prevent unjust results or repercussions on vulnerable populations, it is important to constantly assess AI algorithms for bias.

Designing, implementing, and operating AI systems for inclusive education must put privacy and data security at the forefront for educational institutions, policymakers, and AI developers. Stakeholders can guarantee that students' privacy and rights are protected and a trustworthy and secure learning environment is created by addressing these issues.

3.9 Bias and Fairness Issues in AI Algorithms in Education

Equal and inclusive education requires the elimination of bias and unfairness in AI algorithms employed in the classroom. If the data used to train AI algorithms is itself biased or reflects existing inequities, then the algorithms are more likely to reinforce those prejudices in the real world. The algorithm might be biased in its predictions or suggestions, for instance, if discriminatory practices or the presence of underrepresented groups appear in the historical data.

Bias is described as an irrational or unjust tendency in judgment or decision-making. Data gathering, algorithm design, and human interpretation are all potential causes of bias in an AI environment. Machine learning models are a form of artificial intelligence system that may provide biased or unfair results if they internalize and repeat bias patterns seen in their training data. Finding and fixing sources of prejudice in AI is crucial for making the technology truly inclusive and accessible to all people. Ferrara, E. (2023).

Important considerations with respect to bias and fairness in AI systems are as follows:

Data Bias:

Artificial intelligence (AI) algorithms can be biased if the data used to train them is itself biased or reflects preexisting disparities. The algorithm might be biased in its predictions or suggestions, for instance, if discriminatory practices or underrepresented groups are present in the data used to date. This may occur if the data was gathered in a biased manner, if it lacked crucial details, or if it had mistaken.

Algorithmic Bias:

However, algorithmic bias emerges when machine learning models employ algorithms those themselves are subject to biases. This can occur if the underlying assumptions of the algorithm or the decision-making criteria it employs are biased. When humans employing AI systems inadvertently or intentionally inject their own biases or preconceptions into the system, we speak about user bias. This occurs when users' prejudices are reflected in the training data they supply or in the way they engage with the system.

Representation Bias:

When AI algorithms have varying results for various demographics, this is an example of representation bias. This can cause certain pupils to have fewer chances or less successful results in school than others. It is essential to evaluate whether or not the algorithms are successful across diverse student demographics and to rectify any inequities that may emerge.

Cultural Bias:

It is possible for AI systems to display cultural biases if they have been trained on data that is overwhelmingly representative of one culture or setting. This can stymie efforts to create welcoming classroom settings for students of all backgrounds by leading to their exclusion or inaccurate depiction.

Measurement Bias: Some children may be disproportionately affected by measurement bias in inclusive education because of inaccuracies or misconceptions in the assessment and evaluation of their talents, skills, or performance. There are several types of measurement bias, each having potentially serious consequences for pupils with varying academic requirements. Some important considerations about measuring bias in inclusive education are as follows:

Test Bias: When an evaluation tool routinely benefits or disadvantages some students because of their ethnicity, gender, culture, or handicap, we name this phenomenon "test bias." Because of this prejudice, students' talents and capabilities can be misjudged. This would lead to improper evaluation and uneven educational chances.

Access and Accommodations Bias: Allowances for Getting In and Out Discrimination: Some students with impairments need special testing arrangements so that they can take the exams. When people with disabilities aren't given the reasonable adaptations they need to take effective tests, it might induce prejudice. It is crucial to make sure that all students can use the evaluation tools and that they may be modified to meet their individual needs.

Labeling Bias: AI systems rely on labeled data to understand patterns and make predictions, but this might introduce labeling bias. The reliability and fairness of an AI-based evaluation might be compromised if bias or inaccurate assumptions are introduced during the labeling process. Subjective interpretations or social prejudices can lead to biased labeling, which disproportionately affects vulnerable populations.

Ongoing Monitoring and Evaluation: Persistent Assessment and Screening: Monitoring and evaluating AI-based evaluation methods on a regular basis is essential for spotting and reducing bias. The effectiveness of the AI system should be evaluated on a regular basis across a variety of student demographics, biases should be identified, and the system should be adjusted as needed to guarantee fair and accurate measures.

Carefully curating and diversifying training data, prioritizing inclusive labeling procedures, ensuring accessibility for students with impairments, and promoting openness and explainability in AI algorithms are all important ways to reduce measurement bias in AI-based assessments used in inclusive education. Addressing biases and fostering fair and accurate assessment practices in AI-based inclusive education requires continuous review, stakeholder interaction, and effective monitoring.

Fairness in AI for Inclusive Education:

There has been a lot of discussion and controversy in both the academic and professional areas about how to achieve fairness in artificial intelligence. The lack of favoritism or prejudice in an AI system is the essence of fairness. Few are as follows

- Learners with impairments, individuals of various cultural origins, and students with varied learning profiles should all be reflected in the training data utilized by AI systems. To eliminate prejudice and guarantee that the AI system reflects the needs and talents of all students, it is crucial to avoid underrepresentation or unbalanced representation of particular groups.
- Artificial intelligence algorithms should be developed to produce clear and interpretable outcomes. It is crucial that AI systems explain their decision-making processes to stakeholders including teachers, students, and parents. Algorithms that can be examined held accountable and corrected for potential biases or errors are more transparent.
- Predictive and decision-making processes powered by AI shouldn't unfairly benefit or penalize any subset of students. Predictive models and decision-making algorithms should not contribute to discrimination against or disadvantage of students with disabilities or unique learning requirements; hence precautions should be made to prevent such outcomes.
- The requirements, preferences, and feedback of students, teachers, and other stakeholders should be taken into account when AI systems are designed. The AI system may be made more inclusive, accessible, and equitable if people with disabilities and other viewpoints are included in the design process.
- Artificial intelligence (AI) systems should be continuously evaluated and improved to counteract the emergence of new biases, meet the changing demands of users, and conform to the standards of inclusive education. In order to improve AI algorithms and guarantee fairness, it is important to have open lines of communication with students, teachers, and other stakeholders.

4.1 Case Studies and Success Stories AI implementations in Inclusive Education

Intelligent machine learning algorithms are used by adaptive learning systems to tailor instruction to each learner. Data from student performance is analyzed by these systems so that specific lessons, tests, and suggestions may be made for each individual student. Students with impairments or those who choose a different teaching method can all benefit from this method.

Ø **Speech and Language Therapy:** Programmes that use artificial intelligence to help pupils who have trouble communicating are now in development. To aid in the acquisition of a new language, these programmes combine speech recognition and natural language processing to deliver immediate comments, helpful hints, and well-targeted drills.

Case Study 1: Personalized Language Learning Assistant

Use of AI technologies for Speech and Language Therapy in inclusive education:

User: A child of nine who is struggling with an expressive language issue.

Challenge: The child's communication skills and academic performance suffered because they had difficulty in constructing whole phrases and expressing themselves fluently.

AI Solution: The AI is fed digital representations of the recorded voice samples. This requires parsing the speech for elements like pitch, tone, rhythm, and phonetics. The words uttered to the AI are transcribed into text using automatic speech recognition (ASR) technology. Complex models, frequently based on deep learning, are used by ASR algorithms to identify the words being said. With this the introduction of an AI-powered language-study tool each student's linguistic proficiency can be evaluated, and then individualized practice and immediate feedback will be delivered. The AI analyzes the user's voice mistakes and language usage trends through machine learning methods. It pinpoints problematic patterns and reveals where changes are required. The AI learns from the user's past actions and changes its strategy accordingly. As the user improves, the program adapts the workouts to their current skill level and adds more difficult ones if necessary.

Outcome: The students' linguistic competence and fluency increased. The AI system fostered a more welcoming classroom atmosphere by recognizing the value of recognizing and appreciating language variation.

Ø **Auxiliary Methods:** Artificial intelligence is being incorporated into these tools to make them more useful for students with impairments. In the case of pupils with visual impairments or reading challenges, AI-powered text-to-speech and speech recognition systems can be a lifeline. Gesture recognition technologies powered by AI let students with mobility impairments use technology and access online materials.

Natural Language Processing

Students' text data, such as essays and homework assignments, can be analyzed with NLP. Using this information, teachers may pinpoint exactly where their students are struggling and provide them constructive criticism. One use of natural language processing is correcting students' grammar mistakes and offering suggestions for improved writing.

Case Study:

1. Gesture-Based Learning for Motor Impairments:

User: A pupil whose fine motor abilities are impaired due to an intellectual impairment

Challenge: It's difficult for him to take part in digital learning activities that need kids to use conventional input devices like keyboards and mouse.

AI Solution:

At its core, this solution is a gesture recognition system powered by artificial intelligence. The user's hand and gesture movements are recorded by specialized sensors, cameras, or gadgets.

To analyze the data, AI makes use of machine learning algorithms, most frequently those based on deep learning. Based on the patterns they find in the data, these algorithms learn to differentiate between various motions and actions. After an AI has identified a gesture, it assigns that action within the virtual classroom. This may involve making choices, navigating menus, or engaging with instructional materials. As more data is fed into the AI system, its ability to recognize movements improves in precision and speed.

Case Study 2: Real-Time Captioning for Deaf and Hard of Hearing Students

User: A class of students with varying degrees of hearing impairments.

Challenge: It was difficult for deaf and hard of hearing pupils to participate in and understand classroom discussions and lectures delivered orally.

AI Solution:

- Ø Capturing the audio input is the first step in AI-driven real-time captioning, which may be used for anything mentioned in the classroom, from lectures to dialogues.
- Ø Automatic speech recognition (ASR) technology, a cornerstone of AI, is used to process the recorded audio and convert it into text. ASR algorithms transcribe human speech into text.
- Ø The acoustic aspects of the audio, such as pitch, tempo, and speech patterns, are analyzed by AI algorithms. The results of this investigation contribute to better voice recognition.
- Ø The next step in the AI system's language processing is to analyze the newly transcribed text. To guarantee proper grammar, context, and punctuation, it uses language processing techniques.
- Ø Better captions can be generated by AI systems because of their contextual understanding. It's sensitive to subtleties like homophones and can fix typos on the fly.
- Ø The transcribed material is subsequently presented on displays in the classroom in real time for display and visualization purposes. Projectors, screens, and mobile devices are all viable options for this.
- Ø With this kind of "adaptive learning," AI improves with the help of tweaks provided by humans. The algorithm learns to recognize individual speakers' accents, speech patterns, and domain-specific vocabulary as time goes on.
- Ø Captioning driven by AI allows users to select their preferred text size, color, and display style.

Success Story 1: Virtual Reality (VR) for Sensory Exploration

Users: Young people on the autism spectrum who are particularly sensitive to sensory input.

Challenge: Students in conventional classrooms may experience sensory overload, which can lead to anxiety and decreased engagement.

Artificial intelligence (AI) is used to automatically transcribe and caption educational videos and lectures, making them accessible to students who are deaf or hard of hearing and allowing them to participate in real-time or recorded discussions about course content and educational materials.

AI Solution:

Virtual reality simulations are used to produce artificial sensory conditions. Students could work on developing tolerance to new sensory experiences at their own speed.

Success Story 2: Chatbot Assistance for Cognitive Support

Learners: Students that need individualized support due to cognitive impairments.

Challenge: Students' cognitive variances resulted in widely varying rates of learning and degrees of comprehension, necessitating individualized interventions.

AI Solution: To meet the need for instant help, chatbots powered by AI were deployed. Depending on the student's level of understanding, he or she might ask questions, seek clarification, and receive instantaneous answers.

The use of AI's auxiliary approaches has completely changed the landscape of inclusive education by creating a more welcoming and supportive atmosphere for students with a wide range of learning styles and abilities. Through research and examples of success, we have seen how AI-driven solutions may remove obstacles, make accommodations for those with disabilities, and improve educational opportunities. We reaffirm our dedication to offering quality education to all as technological advancements promise more promising auxiliary approaches in inclusive education. Figures 2 depicts the python code snippet for speech to text recognizer.

Figure 2.

```
import pyttsx3
import speech_recognition as sr

def recognize_speech():
    recognizer = sr.Recognizer()
    with sr.Microphone() as source:
        recognizer.adjust_for_ambient_noise(source)
        audio = recognizer.listen(source)

    try:
        # recognize speech using Google Speech Recognition
        transcript = recognizer.recognize_google(audio)
        return transcript
    except:
        return None

def speak(text):
    engine = pyttsx3.init()
    engine.say(text)
    engine.runAndWait()

def main():
    transcript = recognize_speech()
    if transcript is not None:
        speak(transcript)

if __name__ == "__main__":
    main()
```

The software can transcribe spoken words and phrases and play them back to the user. Students who are deaf but are still learning sign language or who are still struggling with lip reading may benefit from this.

Added functionality, such as sign language interpretation of the transcript, can be added by modifying the code. The code can also be used to make games and activities that can teach sign language to the deaf and help them develop their communication abilities.

Data analytics for early intervention makes use of artificial intelligence (AI)-enhanced data analytics and predictive modeling to spot the telltale symptoms and patterns of underperforming pupils. Artificial intelligence algorithms can identify students who may need further help by analyzing data points like academic achievement, attendance, and behaviour, allowing for early intervention and focused interventions. Figure 3 illustrates the python code snippet for data analytics on student's data.

Figure 3.

```
import pandas as pd

# Load the data from a CSV file
data = pd.read_csv("student_data.csv")

# Filter the data for inclusive students
inclusive_students = data[data["inclusive_status"] == "inclusive"]

# Calculate average academic achievement
average_achievement = inclusive_students["academic_achievement"].mean()

# Calculate attendance rate
attendance_rate = (inclusive_students["total_attendance"] / inclusive_studen

# Analyze behavior patterns
behavior_counts = inclusive_students["behavior"].value_counts()

# Print the results
print("Average Academic Achievement: {:.2f}".format(average_achievement))
print("Attendance Rate: {:.2f}%".format(attendance_rate))
print("Behavior Counts:")
```

The code then calculates the average academic achievement by taking the mean of the "academic_achievement" column. It also computes the attendance rate by dividing the "total_attendance" column by the "total_school_days" column and multiplying by 100.

Students who are experiencing emotional or behavioural difficulties are benefiting from the usage of AI in the area of social-emotional assistance. Students may find a safe space to discuss their feelings, get advice and learn coping mechanisms via the use of Chatbots and virtual agents equipped with artificial intelligence. Garg, S., & Sharma, S. (2020).

4.2 Examples and Case Studies of the Use of Artificial Intelligence in Education

1. Brain Power: When it comes to helping those who suffer from autism spectrum disorder (ASD), one business has stepped up to the plate: Brain Power, makers of the "Empower Me" artificial intelligence (AI) wearable device. The technology employs Google Glass and AI algorithms to deliver timely emotional signals, individualized instruction, and collaborative learning. People on the autism spectrum benefit from it because it aids in the development of their interpersonal, affective, and functional abilities.

Several techniques and tools exist for measuring and analyzing the emotional signals sent by the brain. Some frequent methods include the following.

- Ø Electrode placement on the scalp allows for the recording of brain electrical activity during electroencephalography (EEG). Emotional states can be recorded along with the alpha, beta, theta, and gamma brainwave patterns.
- Ø fMRI, or functional magnetic resonance imaging, is a method of gauging mental activity by monitoring variations in blood oxygenation. Emotional processing in the brain can be better understood, and specific patterns linked with various emotions can be uncovered, with the use of functional magnetic resonance imaging.
- Ø Variability in the time between heartbeats is quantified by metric called heart rate variability (HRV). Emotional arousal and control can be reflected in the autonomic nervous system's activity.
- Ø Emotional arousal, stress, and excitement can all be detected by monitoring the skin's electrical conductivity, which is what the Galvanic Skin Response (GSR) does. Emotional responses are identified through changes in sweating.
- Ø Eye-Tracking: This method keeps tabs on your eye movements and how you look around. Emotional processing and attention allocation can be better understood by observing a person's eye movements in response to various emotional stimuli.
- Ø Emotional facial expressions can be detected and analyzed with the use of computer vision algorithms in a field called facial expression analysis. Emotions can be inferred from captured micro expressions and facial muscle movements.

2. Cognoa: Cognoa is an artificial intelligence-powered digital platform designed to aid in the early diagnosis of children's behavioural health and developmental disorders. In order to deliver insights and suggestions for parents, teachers, and healthcare practitioners, their platform utilizes machine learning algorithms, parent-reported data, and digital exams. As a result, children with a wide range of educational requirements might have access to early intervention services.

Case study:

Cognoa was being used by a school system in the United States to help pupils with special needs. There was a student in the school system that was having hard time learning. He was diagnosed with autistic spectrum disorder (ASD), and he was struggling with both reading and mathematics.

Cognoa was utilized by the district's special education staff to develop an individualized curriculum for him. The plan incorporated specific tactics to improve his reading and arithmetic skills and curb his disruptive behaviour. Abbas, H., Garberson et. al(2020).

Cognoa allowed the school to get updates on his performance in real time. The team was able to monitor his development and make any necessary adjustments thanks to the information gathered.

What We Found

His improvement was notable after he used Cognoa for six months. He progressed both academically and behaviorally, making huge strides in reading and mathematics. The results were encouraging for the district's special education staff, so they'll be keeping Cognoa as a resource for students with impairments.

3. Microsoft Learning Tools: Tools like Immersive Reader and Dictation, both driven by artificial intelligence, are now part of Microsoft's array of educational software. For kids who have trouble reading, Immersive Reader offers text-to-speech, customizable font styles, and other features to improve understanding through the use of AI algorithms. Students who have trouble putting their thoughts on paper might benefit from dictation's hands-free writing and note-taking capabilities.

4. **IBM Watson Classroom:** IBM Watson Classroom leverages AI capabilities to assist educators in developing differentiated lessons for their pupils. Teachers can meet the needs of their students in a variety of ways with the help of the platform since it employs AI algorithms to analyze student data, give insights, and provide recommendations for individualized education.

5. **Learning Management Tools:** With the use of artificial intelligence (AI), LMS systems may serve as a single hub where educators and parents can go to view and discuss students' assignments, grades, attendance, and progress. The ensemble model is trained on a dataset of student performance data, and it is used to make predictions about the performance of new students. The Shapley additive explanations are used to provide insights into the factors that contribute to the predictions of the ensemble model. Sahlaoui et. al(2021). Explaining the results of machine learning models is possible with the help of Shapley additive explanations. These clarifications are grounded in the idea of Shapley values, which quantify the importance of each feature in a machine learning model's prediction .Rosak Szyrocka, et. al(2023).On the basis of student performance data, they may provide individualized suggestions or insights, keeping parents abreast of their child's academic progress. Predicting student performance uses an ensemble model of decision trees.

6. Behavior Tracking and Intervention: When it comes to keeping tabs on and intervening with kids' behaviour and general mental health, AI-powered platforms may be a huge help. Artificial intelligence (AI) algorithms may be used to identify trends in student behaviour, flag possible problems, and suggest solutions to educators and parents. Accuracy, Precision, F-measure, and Recall are some of the metrics used to evaluate the Students behaviour and system's efficacy. Various end-to-end deep learning models, such as Artificial Neural Network (ANN), long short-term memory networks (LSTM), recurrent neural network (RNN), Convolutional Neural Network (CNN), and classic machine learning models like Support Vector Machine (SVM), Decision Tree (DT), Naive Bayes (NB), and RF, are compared to the results of the proposed algorithm, which combines LSTM, RF, and GB (referred to as LSTM + RF + B).

These examples illustrate the varied uses of AI in inclusive education, illuminating the ways in which these technologies are being put to work to better serve the educational requirements of children with a wide range of abilities and backgrounds.

CONCLUSION

Promoting inclusive and accessible education requires schools to make accommodations for students with special needs. The proposed word entails providing children with special needs or disabilities with the same access to and experience of educational settings as their typically developing classmates.

There is great potential for artificial intelligence (AI) to contribute to inclusive education by way of new resources, individualized instruction, and simplified access.

Adaptive learning systems, assistive technology, intelligent tutoring systems, and data analytics for early intervention are just some of the ways that AI is making a difference in the realm of inclusive education. By using artificial intelligence (AI) algorithms, adaptive learning systems personalize the learning experience for each learner. Students with impairments are able to overcome obstacles and actively engage in learning with the help of AI-powered assistive technology like speech and language therapy apps and accessibility tools. In order to assist students with a wide range of needs succeed academically, intelligent tutoring systems use AI to give individualized guidance and support. Through data analytics and AI, at-risk pupils may be quickly identified, and then provided with the help they need.

AI can be used to develop adaptive learning platforms that cater to the unique learning styles and needs of students with special needs. These platforms can dynamically adjust content, pace, and difficulty levels to optimize the learning experience for each student. AI can analyze large amounts of data collected from students with special needs, including their performance, behaviors, and progress, to generate insights and inform educational strategies. This data-driven approach can help educators and professionals make informed decisions and implement targeted interventions. AI can facilitate communication and collaboration between teachers, parents, and other stakeholders involved in the education of students with special needs. AI-powered platforms can enable real-time feedback, progress tracking, and effective information sharing, fostering a collaborative and supportive educational ecosystem.

However, there are also serious concerns that must be addressed when introducing AI into inclusive classrooms. Stakeholder involvement in the design and review process, data protection and security, openness and explainability of AI systems, and addressing bias and fairness in AI algorithms are all crucial. Further, ethical norms and policies should be created to control the appropriate use of AI technology in inclusive education, and AI should supplement human interaction and judgment rather than replace it.

In general, AI has the ability to elevate inclusive education by empowering students with special needs through individualized support, expanding access, and lowering barriers to participation. A more just and accessible educational system for all kids is possible if we use AI's powers in a responsible and welcoming way.

In future scope Students with autism spectrum disorder (ASD) are benefiting from the usage of eye-gaze tracking equipment to improve their communication and classroom participation. The student's eye movements are recorded and translated into commands that move the pointer or make selections on the screen. Students who are unable to move their bodies are given a new perspective through the use of virtual reality. Wearing a virtual reality headset allows users to experience computer-generated recreations of real-world settings, which can aid in the development of transferable skills and the mastery of difficult concepts.

REFERENCES

Abbas, H., Garberson, F., Liu-Mayo, S., Glover, E., & Wall, D. P. (2020, March 19). Multi-modular AI Approach to Streamline Autism Diagnosis in Young Children. *Scientific Reports*, *10*(1), 5014. Advance online publication. doi:10.103841598-020-61213-w PMID:32193406

Akhil, R., Soori, A., Shankar, D., Krishnan, M. M., & Poorna, B. R. (2017, March). Detecting specific learning disabilities. In *2017 International Conference on Networks & Advances in Computational Technologies* (pp. 380-385). IEEE. doi: https://webzoom.freewebs.com/sallydoxie/TTS.pdf doi:10.1109/netact.2017.8076796

Badilla-Quintana, M. G., Sepúlveda-Valenzuela, E., & Salazar Arias, M. (2020, December). Augmented reality as a sustainable technology to improve academic achievement in students with and without special educational needs. *Sustainability, 12*(19), 8116. doi:10.3390u12198116

Ferrara, E. (2023). *Fairness And Bias in Artificial Intelligence: A Brief Survey of Sources, Impacts, And Mitigation Strategies*. https://github.com/CuongTrinh3005/Ecommerce-Chatbot

Garg, S., & Sharma, S. (2020, July 7). Impact of Artificial Intelligence in Special Need Education to Promote Inclusive Pedagogy. *International Journal of Information and Education Technology (IJIET), 10*(7), 1418–1425. doi:10.18178/ijiet.2020.10.7.1418

Garg, S., & Sharma, S. (2020). Impact of Artificial Intelligence in Special Need Education to Promote Inclusive Pedagogy. *International Journal of Information and Education Technology (IJIET), 10*(7), 523–527. doi:10.18178/ijiet.2020.10.7.1418

Herodotou, C., Rienties, B., Boroowa, A., Zdrahal, Z., & Hlosta, M. (2019). A large-scale implementation of predictive learning analytics in higher education: The teachers' role and perspective. *Educational Technology Research and Development, 67*(5), 1273–1306. doi:10.100711423-019-09685-0

Holmes, W., Persson, J., Chounta, I.-A., Wasson, B., & Dimitrova, V. (2022). *Artificial intelligence and education: A critical view through the lens of human rights, democracy and the rule of law*. Council of Europe.

Huang, J., Saleh, S., & Liu, Y. (2021, May). A review on artificial intelligence in education. *Academic Journal of Interdisciplinary Studies, 10*(3), 1-16.

Kukkar, A., Mohana, R., Sharma, A., & Nayyar, A. (2023). *Prediction of student academic performance based on their emotional wellbeing and interaction on various e-learning platforms*. Academic Press.

Lin, R., He, X., & Dong, X. L. (2021, August). Personalized learning recommendation with adaptive neural networks. In *Proceedings of the ACM SIGKDD International Conference on Knowledge Discovery and Data Mining* (pp. 1452-1461). ACM. 10.1145/3447548.3467164

Morrison, C., Cutrell, E., & Dhareshwar, A. (2017, October). Imagining AI applications with people with visual disabilities using tactile ideation. In *Proceedings of the 2017 ACM on International Conference on Supporting Personal Capabilities* (pp. 115-124). ACM.

Rosak Szyrocka, J., Żywiołek, J., Nayyar, A., & Naved, M. (Eds.). (2023). *Advances in Distance Learning in Times of Pandemic* (1st ed.). Chapman and Hall/CRC. doi:10.1201/9781003322252

Sahlaoui, H., Alaoui, E. A. A., Nayyar, A., Agoujil, S., & Jaber, M. M. (2021). Predicting and Interpreting Student Performance Using Ensemble Models and Shapley Additive Explanations. *IEEE Access : Practical Innovations, Open Solutions, 9*, 152688–152703. doi:10.1109/ACCESS.2021.3124270

Samim, A. (2023). A New Paradigm of Artificial Intelligence to Disabilities. *International Journal of Science and Research, 12*(1), 1-7.

Sharif, M. S., & Elmedany, W. (2022, March). A proposed machine learning based approach to support students with learning difficulties in the post-pandemic norm. In *2022 IEEE Global Engineering Education Conference EDUCON* (pp. 1988-1993). IEEE. 10.1109/EDUCON52537.2022.9766690

Vashisht, V., Pandey, A. K., & Yadav, S. P. (2021, June). Speech recognition using machine learning. *IEIE Transactions on Smart Processing and Computing, 10*(3), 836–846. doi:10.5573/IEIESPC.2021.10.3.233

Wu, T.-K., Huang, S.-C., & Meng, Y.-R. (2006). Identifying and diagnosing students with learning disabilities using ANN and SVM. In *2006 IEEE International Joint Conference on Neural Network Proceedings* (pp. 2270-2275). IEEE. doi:10.1109/ijcnn.2006.1716707

Yeguas-Bolívar, E., & Alcalde-Llergo, J. M. (2022, March). Determining the difficulties of students with dyslexia via virtual reality and artificial intelligence: An exploratory analysis. In *2022 IEEE International Conference on Metrology for Extended Reality, Artificial Intelligence and Neural Engineering (MetroXRAINE)* (pp. 585-590). IEEE.10.1109/MetroXRAINE54828.2022.9967589

Zafari, M., Safari Bazargani, J., & Choi, S. M. (2022, January). Artificial intelligence applications in K-12 education: A systematic literature review. *IEEE Access : Practical Innovations, Open Solutions, 10*, 3179356. doi:10.1109/ACCESS.2022.3179356

Chapter 8
AI-Assisted Models for Dyslexia and Dysgraphia:
Revolutionizing Language Learning for Children

Lakshmi Shankar Iyer
https://orcid.org/0000-0002-4765-8622
CHRIST University (Deemed), India

K. Nikitha Reddy
CHRIST University (Deemed), India

Tania Chakraborty
https://orcid.org/0009-0008-1868-9420
CHRIST University (Deemed), India

K. Jyothish
https://orcid.org/0009-0003-1375-3407
CHRIST University (Deemed), India

Mallika Krishnaswami
https://orcid.org/0000-0002-7818-0553
CHRIST University (Deemed), India

ABSTRACT

Dyslexia and dysgraphia are two common learning disabilities that affect children's ability to read, write, and spell accurately. These disabilities can significantly impede a child's academic performance, leading to lack of self-confidence, anxiety, and frustration. Traditional approaches to address these disabilities often involve one-on-one sessions with a tutor or special education teacher, which can be time-consuming and expensive. Artificial intelligence (AI) language learning models have shown tremendous potential in assisting children with dyslexia and dysgraphia. These models can provide real-time feedback and personalized instruction to help children overcome learning difficulties. This chapter highlights the importance of addressing these challenges and proposes a solution that leverages AI language learning models to assist children with dyslexia and dysgraphia. By embracing AI language learning models, educators and parents can empower children with dyslexia and dysgraphia, providing them with the necessary tools and support to overcome their learning challenges.

DOI: 10.4018/979-8-3693-0378-8.ch008

BACKGROUND

The use of Artificial Intelligence (AI) in language learning has become increasingly popular in recent years. This is particularly relevant for children with dyslexia and dysgraphia, who face unique challenges when it comes to language acquisition. By leveraging AI technologies, educators and researchers are exploring new ways to support these children and enhance their language skills. In this chapter, we review the current state of research on AI-based language learning for dyslexic and dysgraphia children, with a focus on the benefits and challenges of these technologies. The study conducted by (Gkeka, 2019) discusses the use of techniques supported by AI technologies in the diagnosis and treatment of language disorders, including dyslexia, aphasia, and developmental language disorder. The article emphasizes the importance of early diagnosis and intervention in improving language outcomes for individuals with language disorders. The authors highlight several techniques that can be used in the diagnosis and treatment of language disorders, including computer-based assessments, natural language processing, and AI technologies. The article also discusses the potential of AI-based chatbots and virtual assistants in supporting language learning and communication for individuals with language disorders. The authors conclude that AI techniques have the potential to enhance the accuracy of diagnosis and improve the effectiveness of treatment for individuals with language disorders, and that further research is needed to fully explore the potential benefits of these technologies in language learning and communication (Gkeka, 2019). The work by (Zingoni A, 2021) discusses a proof-of-concept study of a virtual reality (VR) platform that aims to support dyslexic university students. The study investigated the issues and needs of students with dyslexia and how the AI-VR platform can address those needs. The platform includes features such as a text-to-speech system, an AI-powered personalized learning assistant, and a VR environment for immersive learning experiences. The study involved a small group of dyslexic students who used the platform for a period of time and provided feedback on its effectiveness. Preliminary results indicate that the platform has the potential to improve the learning outcomes and confidence of dyslexic students. The authors suggest that further research is needed to refine and improve the platform in order to explore its potential for wider use. Overall, the study highlights the potential of AI and VR technologies to support dyslexic students in higher education settings (Zingoni A, 2021).

In the research article (S. Thelijjagoda, 2019), the authors propose a mobile solution called "The Hope'' which is designed to help individuals with dyslexia overcome their writing, reading, and speaking weaknesses. The solution incorporates several interactive features, such as speech recognition and text-to-speech technology, to assist dyslexic users in their daily activities. Users can dictate texts and have them converted to written words, and vice versa, with the app reading the written texts aloud. Additionally, the app provides personalized feedback on grammar and spelling errors, and includes exercises to improve reading speed and comprehension. The article highlights the potential of such mobile solutions in addressing the challenges faced by dyslexic individuals and the need for further research to evaluate their effectiveness. The Hope offers a promising tool for dyslexic individuals to overcome their communication difficulties and increase their confidence in everyday tasks. A study by (Minoofam, 2022), focuses on the development of an adaptive reinforcement learning framework called RALF to support the teaching of dyslexic students. The article notes that dyslexic students often struggle with language learning, and that traditional teaching methods may not be sufficient to meet their needs. The RALF framework is designed to adapt to the individual learning needs of each dyslexic student, using a reinforcement learning algorithm to adjust the difficulty level of tasks based on the student's performance. The article describes a pilot study in which RALF was used to teach dyslexic students English language skills. The results of the study suggest that RALF can be an effective tool for teaching dyslexic students, with improvements in both accuracy and response times observed over the course of the study. The article concludes that RALF has the potential to be a valuable tool for supporting language learning in dyslexic students, and that further research is needed to fully explore its potential benefits (Minoofam, 2022).

The article (Patra, 2020) explores some possibilities related to the ways AI can be used as a medium or tool to address the discussed challenges for creating a better accessible, inclusive learning environment for all, i.e., Optical character recognition, Speech recognition, Individualization of learning, Language learning, Virtual learning and Universal Design of Learning. The study (Patra, 2020), explores the potential of AI in improving the education of children with disabilities. The authors argue that AI can be used to create personalized learning experiences for children with disabilities, based on their individual strengths and needs. They discuss various AI-based tools and technologies that can be used for this purpose, such as intelligent tutoring systems, adaptive learning algorithms, and virtual assistants. The authors also discuss the potential benefits of AI for teachers, such as automating routine tasks, providing real-time feedback to students, and generating insights into student learning. Finally, the article highlights some of the challenges and limitations of using AI in education, such as the need for adequate training and support for teachers and the potential for biases in AI algorithms. Overall, the article suggests that AI has the potential to transform the education of children with disabilities and improve their learning outcomes (Patra, 2020). The study by (Lakshmanan, 2022), proposes a novel approach for dyslexic reading assistance using language processing algorithms. The authors explain that dyslexia is a learning disability that affects an individual's ability to read and process written language, as the existing reading assistance technologies have limitations in their effectiveness. To address this problem, the authors propose a new algorithmic approach that leverages natural language processing and machine learning techniques to identify and highlight difficult words or phrases for dyslexic readers. The system provides real-time assistance by providing the reader with definitions, synonyms, and pronunciation guides for difficult words. The authors also provide an evaluation of the system's effectiveness in improving reading comprehension for dyslexic readers, and the results show a significant improvement in their reading comprehension scores. The authors conclude that this approach has the potential to improve the reading abilities of dyslexic readers and provide a more accessible and effective reading assistance tool (Lakshmanan, 2022). The study by (Ahmed, n.d.), discusses the use of AI in developing reading and writing skills for kindergarten children with learning disabilities. While the focus of the article is on reading and writing skills development, it does touch on the broader topic of language learning as these skills are essential components of language learning. The authors explain how AI-based tools can be used to provide personalized and engaging learning experiences that improve reading and writing skills, which are essential components of language learning. The article includes a discussion of the potential benefits of AI-based tools in language learning, such as providing individualized support, improving engagement, and increasing motivation. Overall, the article suggests that AI-based tools have the potential to improve language learning outcomes for kindergarten children with learning disabilities (Ahmed, n.d.).

In the research article (Ikermane, 2023), proposes a method for detecting dysgraphia in children using digital handwriting analysis and Artificial Neural Networks (ANNs). The authors explain that dysgraphia is a learning disability that affects handwriting, and early detection is crucial for successful intervention. The article describes a study in which digital handwriting characteristics were analyzed from a group of children, some of whom had been diagnosed with dysgraphia. The authors used ANNs to analyze the data and identify patterns and characteristics that were indicative of dysgraphia. The results of the study showed that ANNs were able to accurately classify children with and without dysgraphia based on their digital handwriting characteristics. The authors suggest that this method has the potential to provide dysgraphia diagnosis by improving the speed and accuracy. The article concludes that digital handwriting analysis using ANNs can be an effective tool for dysgraphia detection, which can lead to early intervention and improved outcomes for children with dysgraphia (Ikermane, 2023). The article (Wang, 2021), discusses how AI based augmentative alternative communication (AAC) can assist dyslexic students in their learning process. Dyslexia is a learning disorder that affects reading, writing, and spelling skills, and can make it difficult for students to communicate effectively. The authors propose a smart AAC system that uses machine learning algorithms to recognize the speech and convert it into text, which can be helpful for dyslexic students. The system also includes a speech synthesizer that can read the text out loud to the students. The article provides a detailed description of the proposed system and how it can be used to improve the communication and learning abilities of dyslexic students. The authors conclude that the smart AAC system can be a valuable tool in assisting dyslexic students in their education and daily life (Wang, 2021). The study by (Lerga, 2021), focuses on assistive technologies that can support language learning in students with dyslexia. The article notes that dyslexic students may struggle with reading, writing, and other language skills, and that assistive technologies can help to mitigate these difficulties. The article reviews a range of assistive technologies, including text-to-speech software, screen readers, speech recognition tools, as well as technologies that use AI and machine learning to personalize learning for dyslexic students. The article also discusses the importance of considering individual needs and preferences when selecting and implementing assistive technologies for dyslexic students. Overall, the article highlights the potential benefits of assistive technologies for supporting language learning in dyslexic students, and suggests that continued research and development in this area is needed to fully realize their potential (Lerga, 2021).

The study by (Maskati, 2021), explores the use of technology to support students with dyslexia and learning disabilities. Data collection involved questionnaires and unstructured interviews with specialists to identify system requirements and user needs. The results revealed that a majority of teachers recognized the effectiveness of using technology in education and identified reading, writing, and mathematics as significant challenges for students with dyslexia. Interviews with specialists highlighted specific difficulties faced by students with dyslexia and autism. To assess the effectiveness of the proposed application, an experiment was conducted with 10 children aged 6-7 years, randomly assigned to two groups. The experiment compared the proposed application (version 1) with traditional learning (version 2) for Arabic language lessons. The findings indicated that students found the app's explanation and demonstration clear, overcame initial difficulties, and enjoyed the experience. They understood the app's icons and displayed positive emotions, focus, and interest. The results underscore the potential of technology-based interventions for students with dyslexia and learning disabilities. The research contributes valuable insights into the preferences and needs of teachers, parents, and specialists, highlighting the importance of innovative approaches to address students' challenges. Further research and development are needed to explore technical details and evaluate the application's effectiveness fully. Overall, this study supports the use of technology in education as a promising tool to enhance learning experiences and support skill development for students with dyslexia and learning disabilities. The study by (Bhatti, 2020), examines the effectiveness of augmented reality (AR) applications in special education, focusing on individuals with special needs. Sixteen single-subject design studies were analyzed to determine the overall effect of AR on social, living, learning, and physical skills acquisition. The findings reveal a large effect of AR across the studies, with the highest impact observed in learning skills, followed by social, physical, and living skills. The results support the potential of AR to support individuals with special needs and provide valuable insights for decision-makers in special education. The use of AR facilitates meaningful interaction, enhances processing skills, and increases learning motivation. AR applications have been successful in promoting social behaviors, improving vocational and daily life skills, and enhancing physical skills through location-based learning. Future research should explore the effectiveness of AR in other skill domains and consider a larger population of individuals with diverse disabilities. This meta-analysis underscores the role of AR in promoting the acquisition of various skills in special education, contributing to the independence and quality of life of individuals with special needs.

Augmented reality (AR) and virtual reality (VR) have shown great importance and potential in supporting individuals with special needs (Papanastasiou, 2019). For individuals with disabilities, AR and VR allow for personalized and individualized learning, accommodating different learning styles and pacing. They offer opportunities for repetition, reinforcement, and scaffolding, facilitating skill acquisition and retention. AR and VR have the potential to improve engagement, motivation, and learning outcomes for individuals with special needs, empowering them to overcome challenges and reach their full potential.

AI has gained popularity in language learning, particularly in supporting children with dyslexia and dysgraphia. Research has been conducted to explore the benefits and challenges of AI-based language learning for dyslexic and dysgraphia children, including the use of computer-based assessments, natural language processing, and AI-based chatbots and virtual assistants (Sharma & Dash, 2023). AI has also been used to develop solutions such as mobile apps and adaptive reinforcement learning frameworks to improve language outcomes for individuals with language disorders. AI has the potential to create personalized learning experiences for children with disabilities, such as dyslexia, by automating routine tasks, providing real-time feedback, and generating insights into student learning. However, there are also challenges and limitations associated with the use of AI in education, including the need for adequate training and support for teachers and the potential for biases in AI algorithms. AI has the potential to transform the education of children with disabilities and improve their learning outcomes.

Incorporating (Shapley Additive Explanations) SHAP values within the student performance prediction framework empowers educators to recognize students at risk and provide timely interventions based on the prediction and explanations generated by the model (Sahlaoui, Alaoui, Nayyar, Agoujil, & Jaber, 2021). This research paper presents an approach that not only improves student performance prediction but also offers explanations for the predicted scores. By combining advanced machine learning techniques, effective class balancing strategies, hyperparameter optimization, and the visualization of influential factors, educators can proactively identify students who require support and provide appropriate guidance in a timely manner.

Artificial Intelligence (AI) has the potential to greatly enhance virtual reality (VR) experiences in several ways (Huang, 2021). Firstly, AI algorithms can enable real-time object recognition and tracking, allowing AR and VR applications adapt to user movements and actions. This enhances the sense of immersion and interactivity within the virtual environment. Secondly, AI-powered computer vision enables image recognition and tracking, enabling VR systems to respond dynamically to the user's real-world surroundings, seamlessly integrating virtual elements. Thirdly, Natural Language Processing (NLP) can be employed to incorporate voice commands in VR environments, simplifying user interactions and enhancing user convenience. Additionally, AI's predictive analytics capabilities can anticipate user behavior, resulting in more personalized and proactive VR experiences. By analyzing usage data and user feedback, businesses can optimize their AR/VR services, leading to improved customer satisfaction. Finally, AI can analyze user behavior and preferences to create personalized experiences in VR, tailoring content and interactions to meet individual needs. This customization enhances user immersion and engagement.

INTRODUCTION

In today's globalized world, language learning has become more pertinent than ever before. Language learning refers to the process of acquiring the ability to communicate in a new language. It involves gaining proficiency in understanding, speaking, reading, and writing in a language other than one's native language. Language learning can take place in a formal setting, such as a classroom or language school, or informally through self-study, immersion, or interaction with native speakers. It requires developing skills in grammar, vocabulary, pronunciation, and cultural understanding, as well as being able to use these skills effectively in real-life situations. With the increasing interconnectedness of the world, the ability to communicate effectively in multiple languages has become a key asset in both personal and professional settings. This has led to the development of language learning models, which are designed to help people learn new languages and improve their skills in existing ones. These models utilize advanced technologies and innovative methodologies to provide effective language learning experiences to learners of all ages and backgrounds. The importance of language learning models in modern communication and education cannot be overstated, as they play a vital role in facilitating cross-cultural communication and fostering understanding between individuals from different linguistic and cultural backgrounds. Language learning models are designed to help people learn new languages or improve their existing language skills. These models can take many forms, such as textbooks, online courses, language exchange programs, or language learning apps. They are based on the principles of language acquisition, which involve exposure to the language, practice, and feedback.

Special learning disorders refer to a broad category of conditions that affect an individual's ability to learn and perform specific tasks. These disorders can manifest in different ways, such as difficulty with reading, writing, speaking, or processing information. Some common examples of special disorders include dyslexia, dysgraphia, attention deficit hyperactivity disorder(ADHD), autism spectrum disorder(ASD), and intellectual disability. Dyslexia and dysgraphia are two common learning disabilities that affect children's ability to read, write, and spell accurately. These disabilities can significantly impede a child's academic performance, leading to a lack of self-confidence, anxiety, and frustration. Traditional approaches to address these disabilities often involve one-on-one sessions with a tutor or special education teacher, which can be time-consuming and expensive. In recent years, AI language learning models have shown tremendous potential in assisting children with dyslexia and dysgraphia. These AI models can provide real-time feedback and personalized instruction to help children overcome learning difficulties. Special disorders can have a significant impact on an individual's ability to learn and function in everyday life. For example, individuals with dyslexia may have trouble decoding and recognizing words, which can make reading and writing challenging. Those with dysgraphia may struggle with the generation of written language, such as forming letters and organizing ideas. ADHD can lead to difficulty with attention and focus, making it hard to concentrate in a classroom or complete tasks. Individuals with ASD may have problems with social communication and interaction, making it challenging to form relationships or navigate social situations. Intellectual disability can result in a range of cognitive deficits, such as difficulty with memory, attention, and problem-solving skills. These challenges can have a significant impact on an individual's educational and career opportunities. There are various types of special disorders that affect individuals in different ways. Below are some common examples and their characteristics (Gururanjan & et.al., 2022):

1. Dyslexia: Dyslexia is a learning disorder that affects reading skills. Individuals with dyslexia may struggle with phonological processing, which means they have difficulty recognizing and decoding words. They may also have difficulty with reading comprehension and spelling. Some common characteristics of dyslexia include difficulty reading aloud, slow reading speed, difficulty with letter and sound recognition, and poor spelling.
2. Dysgraphia: Dysgraphia is a learning disorder that affects writing skills. Individuals with dysgraphia may have difficulty with handwriting, spelling, and organizing their thoughts in writing. They may also struggle with fine motor skills, which can make it hard to form letters and write legibly. Common characteristics of dysgraphia include poor handwriting, difficulty with letter formation, and difficulty with spelling and grammar.
3. Attention-deficit/hyperactivity disorder (ADHD): ADHD is a neurodevelopmental disorder that affects attention and impulse control. Individuals with ADHD may have difficulty with organization, focus, and completing tasks. They may also struggle with hyperactivity or impulsivity, which can make it hard to sit still or control their behavior. Some common characteristics of ADHD include difficulty with attention and focus, forgetfulness, impulsivity, and hyperactivity.
4. Autism spectrum disorder (ASD): ASD is a neurodevelopmental disorder that affects social communication and interaction. Individuals with ASD may have difficulty with social cues and may struggle to form relationships or understand social norms. They may also exhibit repetitive behaviors or have narrow interests. Some common characteristics of ASD include difficulty with social interaction, repetitive behaviors, intense interests in specific topics, and difficulty with verbal and nonverbal communication.
5. Intellectual disability: Intellectual disability is a condition that affects cognitive functioning. Individuals with intellectual disability may have difficulty with memory, problem-solving, and adaptive skills. They may also struggle with language and communication. Common characteristics of intellectual disability include difficulty with learning and problem-solving, delays in language development, and difficulty with self-care and independent living skills.

According to a study published in the Indian Paediatrics journal (Goel, 2021), the incidence of dyslexia among primary school children in India was reported to be 18%, while the incidence of dysgraphia was 14%. Dyslexia and dysgraphia are learning disorders that can make language learning particularly challenging for individuals who experience them. In this chapter, the main focus is on Dyslexia and dysgraphia. Dyslexia affects reading skills, while dysgraphia affects writing skills. For individuals with dyslexia, language learning can be challenging because they may have difficulty decoding and recognizing words. This can make it hard for them to read instructions, vocabulary lists, and other language learning materials. They may also struggle with reading comprehension, making it challenging to understand the meaning of a passage or a sentence. Additionally, individuals with dyslexia may experience difficulty with spelling, which can make it hard for them to write in a new language.

On the other hand, individuals with dysgraphia may find language learning challenging because they may struggle with writing skills. They may have difficulty forming letters, which can make writing in a new language challenging. Dysgraphia can also affect fine motor skills, making it hard to write legibly. This can make it challenging to practice handwriting and develop fluency in a new language. Both dyslexia and dysgraphia can also impact an individual's confidence and self-esteem. Struggling with reading or writing can make individuals feel frustrated and embarrassed, making them avoid language learning activities. This avoidance can further impede their progress in learning a new language. To address these challenges, language learning models should incorporate strategies that support individuals with dyslexia and dysgraphia.

ORGANIZATION OF THE CHAPTER

This chapter is organized to address the challenges faced by children with dyslexia and dysgraphia in traditional language learning approaches. The chapter begins by providing an overview of these challenges, emphasizing the negative impact on academic performance and well-being. It then delves into the potential solution of integrating AI language learning models to assist these children, discussing the benefits and effectiveness of personalized instruction and real-time feedback provided by AI models. The limitations of this solution are also examined, highlighting the need for ongoing research and development to optimize its efficacy. Additionally, the chapter explores the potential impact of integrating technology in special education, showcasing how AI-based interventions can empower educators, parents, and children in overcoming learning difficulties. The chapter concludes by recommending future research directions to advance the field of AI-based interventions, encouraging collaboration and exploration of personalized instruction, multisensory approaches, and long-term outcome evaluation.

MAIN FOCUS

The main focus of the chapter is related to the role of language learning models in helping individuals learn and improve their skills in a new language. It highlights the challenges of individuals with special disorders, such as dyslexia and dysgraphia, which they face in language learning and communication. The chapter emphasizes the need for language learning models to be inclusive and supportive of individuals with special disorders by incorporating strategies that address their specific needs. Dyslexia is a prevalent condition that affects a significant proportion of the population, with estimates ranging from 5 to 10 percent, while some suggest that up to 17 percent of individuals may struggle with reading. Despite the absence of established diagnostic subtypes of dyslexia, past classifications proposed various types based on symptomatology.

Dyslexia is a complex and heterogeneous condition, and individuals with dyslexia may exhibit a combination of symptoms from multiple subtypes. This means that individuals with dyslexia may have unique strengths and challenges that require tailored interventions and accommodations. Dysgraphia is a learning disorder that affects an individual's ability to write or express themselves in written language. People with dysgraphia may struggle with a variety of writing-related tasks, such as spelling, handwriting, organizing their thoughts on paper, and producing written work at an appropriate speed or level of detail.

There is no cure for dysgraphia, but there are several strategies and accommodations that can help individuals with dysgraphia improve their writing skills. These may include the use of assistive technology, such as speech-to-text software or word processing programs with spell-checking and grammar-checking features, as well as specialized writing programs that help individuals with dysgraphia learn to write more efficiently and effectively. Occupational therapy or other specialized interventions may also be helpful in addressing the underlying causes of dysgraphia and improving writing skills. Learning disabilities, such as dyslexia and dysgraphia, can have a significant impact on a person's ability to learn and succeed academically. These conditions can be challenging to address, and traditional teaching methods may not always be effective. However, advances in technology have led to the development of a range of assistive technologies that can help individuals with learning disabilities overcome these challenges. In this chapter, we explore the possibility of combining theoretical models with AI assistive technology which leads to more effective interventions for individuals with learning disabilities.

PROBLEM DEFINITION

Individuals with dyslexia and dysgraphia encounter substantial obstacles when it comes to learning a new language. The inherent difficulties they face in reading, writing, and spelling pose significant challenges. Traditional language learning methods often prove ineffective for these individuals, exacerbating their struggle. Furthermore, there is a notable absence of understanding, support, and accessible materials tailored to their specific needs. Consequently, they frequently experience frustration, discouragement, and a hampered ability to make progress in acquiring a new language.

MOTIVATION

The motivation to address this problem stems from the desire to ensure equal opportunities for individuals with dyslexia and dysgraphia in language learning. Everyone should have the chance to learn and communicate effectively in a foreign language, regardless of their learning differences. By understanding and addressing the specific needs of individuals with dyslexia and dysgraphia, we can create inclusive language learning environments that provide them with the necessary support, resources, and strategies to succeed. This will not only empower individuals with these conditions but also contribute to a more inclusive society that values and accommodates diverse learning styles and abilities.

OBJECTIVES

The objectives of this chapter are:

1. Highlight the challenges faced by children with dyslexia and dysgraphia in traditional language learning approaches, emphasizing the negative impact on academic performance and well-being.
2. Propose the integration of AI language learning models as a solution to assist children with dyslexia and dysgraphia.
3. Emphasize the potential impact of integrating technology in special education.
4. Address the limitations of the proposed solution and emphasize the need for ongoing research.
5. Recommend future research directions to advance the field of AI-based interventions for children with dyslexia and dysgraphia.

ISSUES, PROBLEMS, CHALLENGES

Language learning can be challenging for individuals with dyslexia and dysgraphia, as these disorders can cause difficulties in reading, writing, and spelling. These individuals may experience difficulty in decoding words, recognizing letters and letter patterns, and comprehending text. As a result, they may struggle to learn a new language and communicate effectively in a foreign language. Traditional language learning methods may not be effective for individuals with dyslexia and dysgraphia, as these methods rely heavily on reading and writing activities. These individuals may require alternative methods of learning, such as visual aids, audio materials, and multisensory approaches that cater to their specific needs. However, these alternative methods may not be readily available, making it difficult for them to access quality language learning materials. Another challenge that individuals with dyslexia and dysgraphia face in language learning is the lack of understanding and support from educators and language learning institutions. Many language learning programs do not have adequate provisions in place to support individuals with special needs, and educators may not be trained to identify and address the specific needs of these individuals. This can lead to frustration and discouragement, and may ultimately hinder their progress in language learning. Furthermore, individuals with dyslexia and dysgraphia may face social and emotional challenges in language learning. They may feel embarrassed or ashamed of their difficulties, which can impact their self-esteem and motivation to learn. This can result in a lack of engagement in language learning activities, which may further exacerbate their difficulties in language acquisition. Dyslexia and dysgraphia can cause a range of issues, problems, and challenges for individuals who have these conditions.

Issues related to dyslexia:

- Reading difficulties: Individuals with dyslexia may struggle with reading and have difficulty decoding words. This can make it challenging to read fluently, understand what they read, and keep up with academic demands.
- Writing difficulties: Dyslexia can also affect writing skills, including spelling, grammar, punctuation, and sentence structure. Individuals with dyslexia may struggle to write coherently and may avoid writing tasks due to their difficulties.
- Phonological awareness deficits: Phonological awareness is the ability to identify and manipulate the sounds of language. Dyslexia is often associated with deficits in phonological awareness, which can make it challenging to learn, to read and write.
- Executive functioning difficulties: Executive functioning refers to the cognitive processes involved in planning, organizing, and completing tasks. Individuals with dyslexia may struggle with executive functioning, making it challenging to stay organized and manage academic tasks.
- Social-emotional challenges: Dyslexia can also impact self-esteem and social-emotional well-being. Individuals with dyslexia may feel frustrated, anxious, or ashamed about their difficulties, and may struggle to keep up with their peers academically.

Issues related to dysgraphia:

- Handwriting difficulties: Dysgraphia can cause difficulties with handwriting, including letter formation, spacing, and alignment. This can make it challenging to write legibly and efficiently, and can impact academic performance.

- Spelling and grammar difficulties: Dysgraphia can also affect spelling and grammar, making it challenging to write coherent sentences and convey meaning, effectively.
- Planning and organizing difficulties: Dysgraphia can impact planning and organizing skills, making it challenging to complete writing tasks in a logical and coherent way.
- Fine motor difficulties: Dysgraphia may also be associated with fine motor difficulties, which can impact the ability to manipulate writing tools and form letters and words.
- Social-emotional challenges: Like dyslexia, dysgraphia can impact self-esteem and social-emotional well-being. Individuals with dysgraphia may feel frustrated or ashamed about their difficulties, and may struggle to keep up with academic demands.

Challenges for individuals with dyslexia and dysgraphia:

- Academic challenges: Dyslexia and dysgraphia can make it challenging to keep up with academic demands, including reading, writing, and math. This can impact academic performance and lead to frustration and anxiety.
- Social-emotional challenges: Individuals with dyslexia and dysgraphia may struggle with self-esteem, anxiety, and depression, particularly if their difficulties impact academic performance and social interactions.
- Access to appropriate support: Many individuals with dyslexia and dysgraphia do not receive appropriate support and accommodation, which can impact academic and social-emotional outcomes.
- Stigma and misconceptions: There are still a great deal of stigma and misconceptions surrounding dyslexia and dysgraphia, which can make it challenging for individuals with these conditions to access appropriate support and accommodation.

Individuals with dyslexia and dysgraphia face a range of challenges in language learning. These challenges include difficulties in reading, writing, and spelling, lack of access to alternative learning materials, inadequate support from educators and language learning institutions, and social and emotional challenges. These challenges highlight the need for language learning models to be inclusive and supportive of individuals with special needs, incorporating strategies that address their specific needs and providing the necessary resources and support to ensure their success. AI and technology can play an important role in addressing some of these challenges, by providing assistive technology supports, such as text-to-speech software and speech recognition software, to improve reading and writing skills, and by providing personalized learning tools to support academic progress. However, it is important to recognize that technology alone cannot address all the challenges faced by individuals with dyslexia and dysgraphia, and that appropriate support and accommodation must be provided in a holistic and personalized way.

SOLUTIONS AND RECOMMENDATIONS

One theoretical model that can be used to explain and address the challenges of dyslexia and dysgraphia is the Simple View of Reading (SVR) model. The SVR model is a theoretical model that explains the process of reading comprehension by breaking it down into two main factors: decoding and linguistic comprehension.

1. Decoding: Decoding refers to the ability to accurately recognize words and apply phonics rules. It involves the skills of phonological awareness, phonics, and word recognition. Decoding allows readers to accurately pronounce words and recognize familiar words quickly, freeing up cognitive resources for higher-level comprehension.
2. Linguistic Comprehension: Linguistic comprehension refers to the ability to understand and extract meaning from written texts. It involves the skills of vocabulary knowledge, syntax, and discourse comprehension. Linguistic comprehension allows readers to comprehend the meaning of the text beyond surface-level word recognition.

Figure 1 illustrates the simple view of reading model.

Figure 1. Simple view of reading model
Source: Compiled by authors

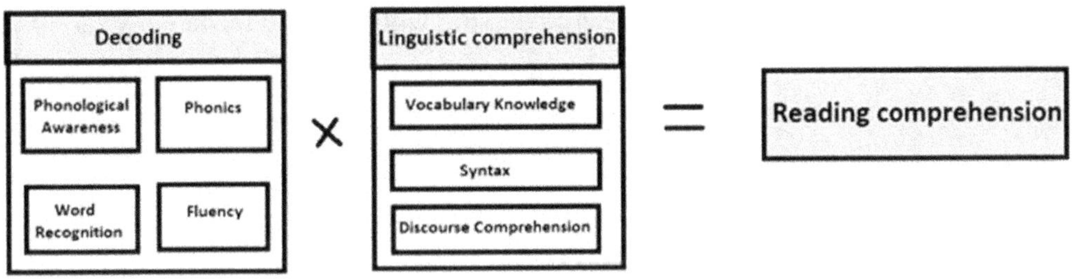

According to the SVR model, reading comprehension is the product of the interaction between decoding and linguistic comprehension. This means that individuals with strong decoding skills but weak linguistic comprehension may struggle with reading comprehension, as will individuals with strong linguistic comprehension but weak decoding skills. Decoding involves several skills that allow readers to accurately recognize and pronounce words:

- Phonological Awareness: The ability to recognize and manipulate the sounds of spoken language, such as identifying rhyming words or breaking words down into syllables.
- Phonics: The ability to understand the relationship between letters and sounds, and to use that knowledge to decode unfamiliar words. Phonics involves knowledge of letter-sound correspondences and the ability to apply that knowledge to read words.
- Word Recognition: The ability to quickly and accurately recognize familiar words by sight, without having to sound them out.
- Fluency: The ability to read with accuracy, speed, and prosody (the rhythm, stress, and intonation of speech).

All of these skills are important for decoding, and they work together to enable readers to accurately recognize and pronounce words, which is a key component of reading comprehension. Linguistic comprehension involves several skills that allow readers to understand and extract meaning from written text:

- Vocabulary Knowledge: The ability to understand the meaning of words. This includes knowledge of both the meanings of individual words and the relationships between words (e.g., synonyms, antonyms, and homophones).
- Syntax: The ability to understand the grammatical structure of sentences and how words relate to each other. This includes knowledge of parts of speech, sentence structure, and sentence-level grammar.
- Discourse Comprehension: The ability to understand how ideas are organized and connected within a larger text. This includes knowledge of text structures (e.g., cause-and-effect, compare-and-contrast) and the ability to make inferences based on information presented in the text.

All of these skills work together to enable readers to understand the meaning of written text beyond surface-level word recognition. Individuals with strong linguistic comprehension are able to extract meaning from the text, understand complex sentences and syntax, and make inferences based on the information presented. Figure 2 illustrates the possible model that integrates the possible model that integrates the theoretical model of phonological processing with assistive technology for dyslexia and dysgraphia is as follows:

Figure 2. The proposed model
Source: Compiled by authors

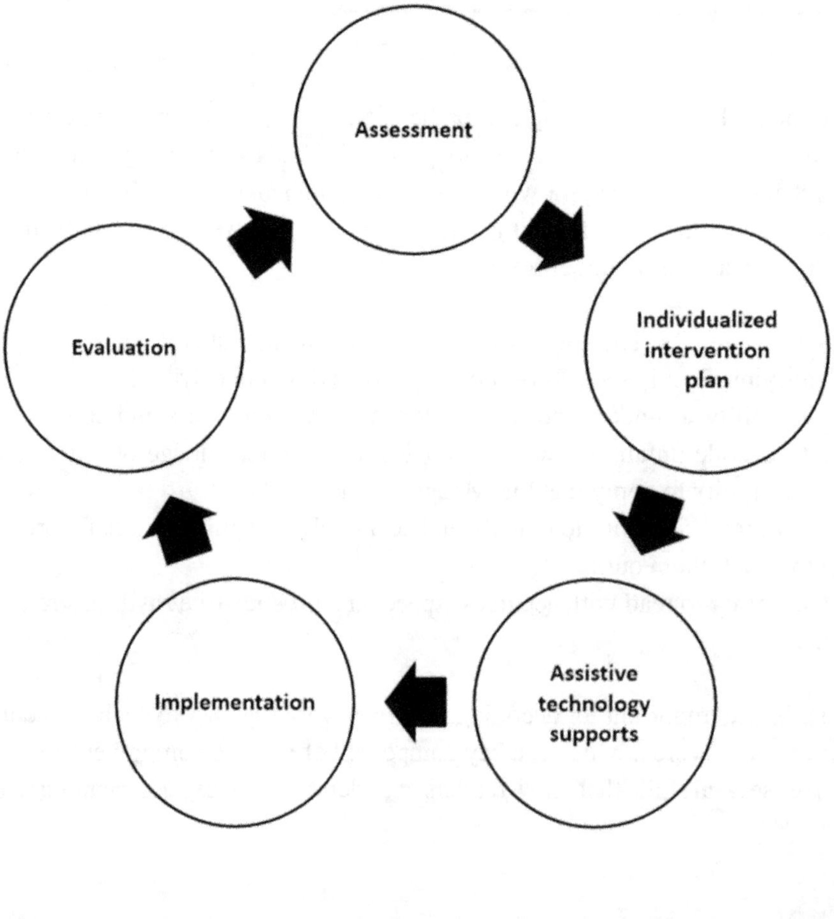

Assessment

Individuals with dyslexia and dysgraphia should undergo a comprehensive assessment to identify their specific strengths and challenges in phonological processing. This assessment should include standardized tests of reading and writing skills, as well as informal measures of phonological awareness, sound-symbol association, and working memory. Assessment for individuals with dyslexia and dysgraphia involves a comprehensive evaluation of their strengths and challenges in phonological processing, reading, and writing skills. The assessment process may include standardized tests, informal measures, and observations of the individual's abilities in different academic tasks.

AI can help with the assessment process by providing computer-based tools that can quickly and accurately measure an individual's reading and writing skills. For example, there are AI-powered apps that can analyze an individual's writing sample to identify patterns of errors that may indicate dysgraphia. Similarly, AI can be used to analyze reading data to identify patterns of errors and areas of weakness that may be indicative of dyslexia. Furthermore, AI can be used to provide personalized feedback and recommendations for intervention plans. AI-powered platforms can analyze an individual's reading and writing data to provide customized suggestions for strategies and assistive technology support that may be most effective for that individual.

Individualized Intervention Plan

Based on the results of the assessment, an individualized intervention plan could be developed that includes specific goals, strategies, and assistive technology supports. The plan should be tailored to the individual's unique needs and should address both reading and writing skills. The individualized intervention plan should outline specific goals and objectives that are measurable and achievable. These goals should be based on the individual's areas of need identified during the assessment, such as improving reading fluency or written expression. The plan should also include specific strategies and interventions that will be implemented to help the individual achieve their goals.

Assistive technology supports should be selected based on the individual's specific challenges and goals. For example, AI-powered speech recognition software can be used to help individuals with dysgraphia improve their writing skills, while AI-powered text-to-speech software can be used to help individuals with dyslexia improve their reading skills. AI can also be used to develop personalized learning plans and provide real-time feedback and support to individuals, which can be especially helpful in remote learning environments. Implementation of the individualized intervention plan should be carried out with regular monitoring and adjustments as needed. AI can help with this by providing real-time data on the individual's progress and identifying areas that require further support or adjustment. Regular evaluation of progress is also important to ensure that the intervention plan is effective and to identify areas for further support or adjustment. AI can help with this by analyzing data on the individual's academic progress and providing insights into areas where the individual may need additional support or intervention.

Assistive Technology Supports

Assistive technology supports the use of technology tools or devices that can help individuals with dyslexia and dysgraphia overcome their challenges in reading and writing. Assistive technology supports should be selected based on the individual's specific challenges and goals. For dyslexia, text-to-speech software can be used to provide auditory feedback and improve phonological awareness, while speech recognition software can be used to support writing skills for dysgraphia. Other supports, such as digital note-taking tools and word prediction software, may also be helpful. Text-to-speech software is a type of assistive technology that can read aloud digital text, helping individuals with dyslexia improve their phonological awareness and comprehension skills. Speech recognition software, on the other hand, can help individuals with dysgraphia by allowing them to dictate their writing instead of physically writing it down. Word prediction software can also be helpful for individuals with dysgraphia as it suggests words or phrases based on what the user has already typed, reducing the need for them to type out each word fully.

AI can play a crucial role in assistive technology by providing personalized and adaptive interventions. For example, AI-powered speech recognition software can learn an individual's unique voice patterns and writing style, allowing for more accurate transcription and dictation. AI algorithms can also analyze data from assessments and monitor progress, allowing for more effective individualized intervention plans. Moreover, AI can be used to develop new assistive technology tools or improve existing ones. For instance, AI algorithms can be used to analyze large datasets of spoken and written language to improve text-to-speech or speech recognition software. AI can also be used to develop natural language processing (NLP) models that can accurately predict what the user intends to say or write, improving the accuracy of word prediction software.

Implementation

Implementation refers to the actual carrying out of the individualized intervention plan that was developed based on the assessment. It involves putting into practice the strategies, goals, and assistive technology supports that were identified as most appropriate for the individual with dyslexia or dysgraphia. The intervention plan should be implemented with regular monitoring and adjustments as needed. Assistive technology supports should be integrated into the individual's daily routine, with training and ongoing support provided as needed. One way that AI can help with implementation is through the use of educational software and digital platforms. AI-powered educational software can provide personalized learning experiences tailored to the individual's unique needs, including specific areas of strength and challenge in phonological processing. This can help to reinforce learning and improve engagement in academic tasks.

AI can also be used to monitor progress and provide ongoing feedback to both the individual and their support team. For example, AI-powered apps can track the individual's progress in real-time, identify areas where they may be struggling, and provide targeted feedback and support. This can help to keep the intervention plan on track and adjust it as needed based on the individual's progress. However, it is also important that AI should be used in conjunction with human support, such as teachers, tutors, and other trained professionals, to ensure the best possible outcomes for the individual.

Evaluation

Evaluation refers to the process of regularly monitoring and measuring the progress of the individual with dyslexia or dysgraphia to determine if the intervention plan and assistive technology supports are effective or if further support or adjustments are needed. It is essential to evaluate progress regularly to ensure that the intervention plan is working as intended and to identify any areas that may require additional support or adjustment. The evaluation should include measures of academic progress, such as reading and writing assessments, to determine if the individual is making progress towards their goals. Additionally, feedback from the individual, their teachers or tutors, and their parents or caregivers should be collected to gain a holistic understanding of the individual's progress and experiences.

AI can be used to support the evaluation process by analyzing and interpreting large amounts of data quickly and accurately. For example, AI-based assessment tools can be used to measure changes in the individual's reading and writing skills over time and provide insights into areas that may require additional support. AI can also be used to analyze feedback from teachers and tutors to identify patterns or trends in the individual's progress or challenges. By leveraging AI, the evaluation process can be more efficient and effective, allowing for timely adjustments to the intervention plan and support for individuals with dyslexia and dysgraphia.

By combining the theoretical model of phonological processing with assistive technology supports, individuals with dyslexia and dysgraphia can receive the targeted interventions they need to overcome their challenges and achieve academic success. The above solution can be combined with some recommendations to enhance the inclusivity and effectiveness of language learning models for individuals with dyslexia and other special disorders like incorporation of multisensory instruction, providing personalization and flexibility, use of visual aids and organizational tools, integration of phonics instruction.

By incorporating multisensory instruction, personalization, visual aids, phonics instruction, and opportunities for practice and feedback, language learning models can provide a supportive and effective learning environment for individuals with dyslexia and other special disorders. In recent years, there has been a growing recognition of the potential of AI in assisting individuals with dyslexia and dysgraphia. A Spanish application that utilizes AI to support individuals with dyslexia has gained recognition, winning the 2019 UNESCO ICT Prize. This application aims to help children overcome dyslexia by providing personalized instruction and feedback using AI language learning models (UNESCO, 2019). Similarly, Richard Branson has launched an AI campaign to assist people with dyslexia, highlighting the significance of AI in addressing learning challenges (Observer, 2023). Research studies have explored the use of AI in various aspects of dyslexia and dysgraphia support. For instance, AI-powered handwriting analysis has been employed to help children improve their handwriting skills. Automated systems for the diagnosis of dysgraphia in children have been developed using machine learning algorithms (Drotár & Dobeš, 2020). AI-enabled personalized assistive tools have been reviewed for their potential to enhance education for children with neurodevelopmental disorders (Laato & et.al., 2023). The integration of large language models and chat-based AI systems have also been investigated for AI-assisted learning in higher education . These diverse studies and initiatives highlight the increasing interest in leveraging AI to support individuals with dyslexia and dysgraphia, providing personalized assistance and improving educational outcomes.

LIMITATIONS

While the proposed solution of integrating the SVR model with assistive technology and AI-powered language learning models offers several advantages, there are also limitations to consider.

- **Individual Variability:** Dyslexia and dysgraphia are complex disorders with significant individual variability. Each person's challenges and strengths may differ, and what works well for one individual may not be as effective for another. The proposed solution provides a general framework, but it may not address all the unique needs of every individual with dyslexia or dysgraphia.
- **Access to Technology:** The effectiveness of AI-powered language learning models and assistive technology relies on access to appropriate devices, software, and internet connectivity. Not all individuals with dyslexia and dysgraphia may have access to these resources, which can limit their ability to benefit from the proposed solution.
- **Generalizability:** The proposed solution assumes that the Simple View of Reading model and the integration of assistive technology supports are universally applicable and effective for individuals with dyslexia and dysgraphia. However, it's important to recognize that research in this field is ongoing, and there may be variations and nuances that need to be considered for different populations, languages, and educational contexts.
- **Training and Support:** While AI-powered language learning models and assistive technology can provide valuable support, they should be used in conjunction with trained professionals such as teachers, tutors, and therapists. Adequate training and ongoing support are necessary to ensure that these tools are utilized effectively and to address any technical or instructional issues that may arise.
- **Overreliance on Technology:** While technology can be beneficial, there is a risk of overreliance on AI-powered language learning models and assistive technology. It's important to strike a balance between utilizing technology as a tool and providing opportunities for human interaction, feedback, and support. Human involvement is crucial for addressing the social and emotional aspects of learning, fostering motivation, and building rapport.
- **Ethical Considerations:** The use of AI in educational settings raises ethical considerations, such as data privacy, security, and algorithmic biases. It is essential to ensure that appropriate measures are in place to protect the privacy and confidentiality of individuals with dyslexia and dysgraphia, and to address any biases or limitations in AI algorithms to prevent further drawback or discrimination.
- **Cost and Sustainability:** Implementing AI-powered language learning models and assistive technology can involve costs related to software licenses, hardware devices, and ongoing technical support. Ensuring the sustainability of these resources and their availability to individuals with dyslexia and dysgraphia over the long term can be a challenge, particularly in resource-constrained settings.

SOME REAL-LIFE EXAMPLES AND USE CASES

AI-Assisted Language Learning models can be incredibly beneficial for children with dyslexia and dysgraphia. These models can offer personalized support and adapt to the specific needs of each child. Here are some use cases of AI-assisted Language Learning models for children with dyslexia and dysgraphia:

- Adaptive Learning: AI models can analyze the learning patterns and progress of children with dyslexia and dysgraphia. Based on this analysis, the system can generate tailored lessons, exercises, and materials that focus on areas where the child needs the most assistance. The adaptive nature of these models ensures that the child receives targeted instruction and reinforcement.
- Multisensory Instruction: AI models can incorporate different sensory modalities to enhance learning for children with dyslexia and dysgraphia. For example, they can provide visual aids, audio prompts, and interactive activities to engage multiple senses, which can help reinforce learning and improve comprehension.
- Speech Recognition and Feedback: AI models can leverage speech recognition technology to assist children with dysgraphia in their writing activities. The models can transcribe spoken words into written text, reducing the frustration and difficulties associated with handwriting. Additionally, the system can provide real-time feedback on pronunciation, intonation, and grammar, helping children improve their language skills.
- Assistive Tools for Reading: AI-Assisted Language Learning models can offer text-to-speech functionality, where written text is converted into spoken words. This feature helps children with dyslexia who struggle with reading, enabling them to follow along and comprehend the text more effectively. The models can also highlight words or phrases as they are spoken, aiding in word recognition and comprehension.

AI-Assisted Language Learning models for children with dyslexia and dysgraphia are absolute game-changcrs. Thcsc modcls arc likc magical unicorns with the power to revolutionize language learning for these kids.

Below are some real-time examples of AI-Assisted Language Learning models that have shown promise in supporting children with dyslexia and dysgraphia:

- Speech Recognition Apps: Several mobile applications utilize AI-powered speech recognition technology to help children with dysgraphia improve their writing skills. These apps transcribe spoken words into written text, enabling children to compose sentences and paragraphs without the physical act of writing. They also provide real-time feedback on grammar, spelling, and punctuation.
- Interactive Reading Platforms: AI-Assisted Language Learning platforms with interactive reading features have proven beneficial for children with dyslexia. These platforms use text-to-speech technology to read aloud text, highlighting words as they are spoken. This synchronized audio-visual experience can enhance reading comprehension and support word recognition.
- Personalized Learning Software: AI algorithms can analyze students' performance data and adapt instructional materials accordingly. Personalized learning software can identify areas of difficulty for children with dyslexia and dysgraphia, providing targeted exercises and interventions. By tailoring the content to each child's needs, these models help promote individualized learning experiences.

Here are some extraordinary examples of AI-Assisted Language Learning models for children with dyslexia and dysgraphia:

- Mind-Reading Tutors: Some AI models are equipped with advanced neural interfaces that can tap into the minds of children. These models can understand their unique cognitive processes and adjust teaching strategies accordingly. It's like having a personal tutor who can read our thoughts and provide tailored instruction without uttering a single word.
- Virtual Reality Language Lessons: Step into the immersive world of virtual reality, where children with dyslexia and dysgraphia can learn languages in extraordinary ways. They can explore ancient civilizations, converse with virtual language mentors, and practice communication skills in simulated real-life scenarios. It is like teleporting to a language-rich utopia.
- Augmented Reality Writing Assistants: With AI-powered augmented reality, children with dysgraphia can bring their written words to life. They can write on a digital surface and see their words transformed into vibrant animations, sparking their creativity and imagination. These virtual assistants provide real-time feedback on handwriting, spelling, and grammar, making writing a captivating adventure.
- Language-Learning Robots: Imagine adorable AI robots designed to engage and support children with dyslexia and dysgraphia in their language learning journey. These robots can interact through speech recognition, guide pronunciation exercises, and offer personalized lessons. With their friendly personalities and unwavering patience, these robotic companions make language learning a joyous experience.

FUTURE SCOPE

The future scope for an article on "AI-Assisted Models for Dyslexia and Dysgraphia: Revolutionizing Language Learning for Children" is vast and holds great potential for advancing our understanding and implementation of AI in supporting children with dyslexia and dysgraphia. Here are some possible directions for further exploration:

- Enhanced Personalization: Investigate how AI models can further personalize language learning experiences for children with dyslexia and dysgraphia. Explore the use of adaptive algorithms to dynamically tailor instructional materials, activities, and interventions based on real-time performance data and individual learning profiles.
- Multimodal Approaches: Explore the integration of various sensory modalities, such as visual, auditory, and kinesthetic cues, in AI-Assisted Language Learning models. Investigate how combining different modalities can optimize learning outcomes and engagement for children with dyslexia and dysgraphia.
- Gamification and Interactive Experiences: Examine the effectiveness of incorporating gamification elements, virtual reality, and augmented reality in AI-Assisted Language Learning for children with dyslexia and dysgraphia. Investigate how these interactive and immersive experiences can enhance motivation, attention, and language skill development.
- Long-Term Effectiveness: Assess the long-term impact of AI-Assisted Language Learning models on children with dyslexia and dysgraphia. Conduct longitudinal studies to measure the sustained benefits of AI interventions on language proficiency, reading comprehension, writing skills, and overall academic achievement.

- Ethical Considerations: Explore the ethical implications of AI-Assisted Language Learning models in terms of data privacy, algorithmic biases, and informed consent. Investigate how to address these concerns and ensure responsible and equitable use of AI technologies in educational settings.
- User Experience and User-Centered Design: Investigate the user experience of children with dyslexia and dysgraphia interacting with AI-Assisted Language Learning models. Explore the role of user-centered design principles in creating intuitive, accessible, and inclusive interfaces that cater to the specific needs and preferences of these learners.
- Teacher Collaboration and Support: Explore how AI-Assisted Language Learning models can facilitate collaboration between educators, speech therapists, and parents in supporting children with dyslexia and dysgraphia. Investigate the role of AI as a tool for data-driven decision-making, progress monitoring, and generating personalized recommendations for intervention strategies.
- Neural Network Telepathy: Delve into the theoretical realm of AI models that can establish telepathic connections with children with dyslexia and dysgraphia. Explore how these models tap into neural networks, bypassing conventional communication channels to directly transmit language skills and knowledge. It is like uploading language proficiency directly to the brain.
- Holographic Language Teachers: Imagine a future where holographic language teachers materialize in classrooms or homes, guiding children with dyslexia and dysgraphia through immersive language learning experiences. Investigate how these 3D virtual instructors can dynamically adapt their teaching methods and styles based on real-time learner feedback, creating a personalized learning extravaganza.
- Quantum Language Algorithms: Dive into the quantum realm and explore the potential of quantum computing to revolution.

These are just a few potential avenues to explore in a research paper on AI-Assisted Models for Dyslexia and dysgraphia. The field is rapidly evolving, and new developments in AI, neuroscience, and educational technology continue to shape the possibilities for revolutionizing language learning for children with these learning differences.

CONCLUSION

In conclusion, there is no doubt that dyslexia and dysgraphia can significantly hinder an individual's ability to learn and communicate in a new language. However, with the advent of advanced AI-powered language learning models, these individuals can now overcome their challenges and achieve proficiency in new languages. The language learning models can provide personalized and adaptive learning experiences that cater to the specific needs of individuals with special disorders, such as dyslexia and dysgraphia. By using techniques such as repetition, multisensory learning, and interactive engagement, these models can help individuals build a strong foundation in the language and improve their language skills. Moreover, these models can offer a supportive and inclusive learning environment that fosters positive learning experiences for individuals with special disorders. By incorporating strategies such as font and color customization, dyslexic-friendly formatting, and speech-to-text and text-to-speech features, these models can create an environment that accommodates the diverse learning needs of all individuals. AI-powered language learning models have immense potential to revolutionize the way individuals with dyslexia and dysgraphia learn and communicate in new languages. They offer a promising solution to bridge the learning gap and enable these individuals to unlock their full potential in language learning.

REFERENCES

Ahmed, W. A. (n.d.). *Reading and Writing Skills Development for Kindergarten Children with Learning Disabilities Using Artificial Intelligence Applications*. Retrieved from ekb: https://jchild.journals.ekb.eg/article_183573_c1f4fba55ce150d8fc8d98815c707284.pdf

Bhatti, Z. B. (2020). Augmented Reality based Multimedia Learning for Dyslexic Children. *2020 3rd International Conference on Computing, Mathematics and Engineering Technologies (iCoMET)*. 10.1109/iCoMET48670.2020.9073879

Drotár, P., & Dobeš, M. (2020). Dysgraphia detection through machine learning. *Scientific Reports*, (10). Retrieved from https://www.nature.com/articles/s41598-020-78633-1

Gkeka, E. A. (2019). Artificial Techniques for Language Disorders. *International Journal of Recent Contributions from Engineering, Science & IT (iJES)*. doi:10.3991/ijes.v7i4.11845

Goel, U. (2021). Prevalence of selected learning disabilities among primary schoolchildren through primary school teachers: A descriptive survey. *Indian Journal of Psychiatric Nursing*, *18*(1), 23–28. doi:10.4103/iopn.iopn_51_20

Gururangan. (2022). *Artificial Intelligence Enabled Personalised Assistive Tools to Enhance Education of Children with Neurodevelopmental Disorders—A Review*. Retrieved from https://www.researchgate.net/publication/358016972_Artificial_Intelligence_Enabled_Personalised_Assistive_Tools_to_Enhance_Education_of_Children_with_Neurodevelopmental_Disorders-A_Review

Huang, X., Zou, D., Cheng, G., & Xie, H. (2021). A systematic review of AR and VR enhanced language learning. *Sustainability*, *13*(9), 4639. doi:10.3390u13094639

Ikermane, M. (2023). Digital handwriting characteristics for dysgraphia detection using artificial neural network. *Bulletin of Electrical Engineering and Informatics*. https://beei.org/index.php/EEI/article/download/4571/3239

Kunhoth. (2022). *Automated Systems for Diagnosis of Dysgraphia in Children: A Survey and Novel Framework*. Retrieved from https://www.researchgate.net/publication/361581698_Automated_Systems_For_Diagnosis_of_Dysgraphia_in_Children_A_Survey_and_Novel_Framework

Laato. (2023). *AI-assisted Learning with ChatGPT and Large Language Models: Implications for Higher Education*. Retrieved from https://www.researchgate.net/publication/370535123_AI-assisted_Learning_with_ChatGPT_and_Large_Language_Models_Implications_for_Higher_Education

Lakshmanan, S. (2022). *Dyslexic Reading Assistance with Language Processing Algorithms*. Retrieved from SSRN: https://papers.ssrn.com/sol3/papers.cfm?abstract_id=4264858

Lerga, R. C. (2021). *A Review on Assistive Technologies for Students with Dyslexia.* Retrieved from CSEDU: https://pdfs.semanticscholar.org/ff92/837cfdf462adc914cf6fc0fd9e7388fd7152.pdf

Maskati, E. A. (2021). Using Virtual Reality (VR) in Teaching Students with Dyslexia. *International Journal of Emerging Technologies in Learning (iJET).* https://online-journals.org/index.php/i-jet/article/view/19653

Minoofam, S. B. (2022). *RALF: an adaptive reinforcement learning framework for teaching dyslexic students.* SpringerLink. doi:10.100711042-021-11806-y

Observer. (2023). *Richard Branson Launches A.I. Campaign to Help People with Dyslexia.* Retrieved from https://observer.com/2023/04/richard-branson-launches-a-i-campaign-to-help-people-with-dyslexia/

Papanastasiou, G., Drigas, A., Skianis, C., Lytras, M., & Papanastasiou, E. (2019). Virtual and augmented reality effects on K-12, higher and tertiary education students' twenty-first century skills. *Virtual Reality (Waltham Cross), 23*(4), 425–436. doi:10.100710055-018-0363-2

Patra, G. (2020). *Education of Children with Disabilities: Exploring Possibilities with Artificial Intelligence.* http://pedagogyoflearning.com/wp-content/uploads/4-Ganesh-Patra-Education-of-Children-with-Disabilities-Exploring-Possibilities-with-Artificial-Intelligence.pdf

Sahlaoui, H., Nayyar, A., Agoujil, S., & Jaber, M. M. (2021). Predicting and interpreting student performance using ensemble models and shapley additive explanations. *IEEE Access : Practical Innovations, Open Solutions, 9*, 152688–152703. doi:10.1109/ACCESS.2021.3124270

Sharma, P., & Dash, B. (2023). AI and VR Enabled Modern LMS for Students with Special Needs. *Journal of Foreign Language Education and Technology, 8*, 1.

Szyrocka, J. R., Żywiolek, J., Nayyar, A., & Naved, M. (Eds.). (2023). *Advances in distance learning in times of pandemic.* CRC Press.

Thelijjagoda, S. M. C. (2019). The Hope: An Interactive Mobile Solution to Overcome the Writing, Reading and Speaking Weaknesses of Dyslexia. *International Conference on Computer Science & Education (ICCSE).* https://ieeexplore.ieee.org/abstract/document/8845396

UNESCO. (2019). *Spanish Application Using AI to Help Overcome Dyslexia Wins 2019 UNESCO ICT Prize.* Retrieved from https://www.unesco.org/en/articles/spanish-application-using-ai-help-overcome-dyslexia-wins-2019-unesco-ict-prize

Wang, M. M. (2021). Smart assistance to dyslexia students using artificial intelligence based augmentative alternative communication. *International Journal of Speech Technology.* https://idp.springer.com/authorize/casa?redirect_uri=https://link.springer.com/article/10.1007/s10772-021-09921-0&casa_token=xTNoUYMrz_sAAAAA:XmBs-O1BmI9kGjCkVrp5JDBMzzjVv2O_WkaxPIG5aKbmxfh-9w4imEDsqrBKWLMDWh0rqfaJftDViwivO43E

Zingoni, T. J.-M. (2021). Investigating Issues and Needs of Dyslexic Students at University: Proof of Concept of an Artificial Intelligence and Virtual Reality-Based Supporting Platform and Preliminary Results. *Appl. Sci.* doi:10.3390/app11104624

Chapter 9
Diagnosing Autism Spectrum Disorder in Children:
Appropriateness of Classifiers

Ebru Efeoğlu
Kütahya Dumlupınar University, Turkey

Ayşe Tuna
Trakya University, Turkey

ABSTRACT

In recent years, classifiers have been shown to provide highly accurate results in predicting problems; however, the success relies on the classifier as well as the employed dataset. In this study, the success of various classifiers for predicting autism spectrum disorder cases is analysed in terms of different metrics obtained both after testing on the same set and after applying 10-fold cross validation. When the same dataset has been used for the training and testing steps, all the algorithms have shown excellent results. Nevertheless, when 10-fold cross-validation has been applied, sequential minimal optimization has become the most successful classifier in terms of all the performance metrics. Although the results have proven the success of classifiers in predicting problems such as the one addressed in this study, autism spectrum disorder is a complex disorder, and the tools employing classifiers should be used under the supervision of certified professionals or clinicians.

INTRODUCTION

Autism spectrum disorder (ASD) is a complex developmental disability with two main characteristics: (i) difficulty with social interactions and communication and (ii) repetitive behaviours, interests, and activities (American Psychiatric Association, 2013). As well as adults and adolescents with ASD, children suffering from this disorder also exhibit restricted and repetitive patterns of behaviours, interests, or activities and experience significant difficulties in social communication and interaction. In boys, indications are typically recognised around one to two years of age (McPartland & Volkmar, 2012). Late

DOI: 10.4018/979-8-3693-0378-8.ch009

diagnosis and over-diagnosis are common problems particularly among girls; many children with ASD are not finally diagnosed until they are older. Sometimes girls with ASD are not diagnosed until late in their development (Gould & Ashton-Smith, 2011). Early diagnosis allows early intervention and thereby provides better outcomes (Crais & Watson, 2014). On the other hand, sometimes indications similar to the ones found in ASD can occur to a moderate degree when children are stressed, depressed and anxious due to some reasons (White et al., 2009). For instance, children may exhibit restricted interests and social avoidance when they have dyslexia, speech and language disorders, and intellectual disabilities. There is diversity in the type and severity of ASD indications (American Psychiatric Association, 2013). Therefore, while some individuals in the severe range may need substantial support in their daily lives, some in the mild range may live independently. Although treatment efforts are generally individualised and can involve behavioural therapy and teaching of coping skills, psychotropic medications are widely utilised in alleviating associated behavioural and emotional indications (Accordino et al., 2016).

The Autism Diagnostic Interview-Revised (ADI-R) (Lord et al., 1994), consisting of 93 questions, is the most established and one of the most widely used autism-specific diagnostic interviews (Pasco, 2010). In this interview, an overall diagnostic algorithm collects scores from items in a number of domains relating to communication, social interaction, repetitive, restricted and stereotyped behaviours and the age of onset, and generates outcomes relating to The Diagnostic and Statistical Manual of Mental Disorders (DSM) and The International Classification of Diseases (ICD) definitions of core autism only (Lord et al., 1994). Autism Diagnostic Observation Schedule (ADOS) (Lord et al., 2000), a semi-structured interactive assessment conducted by a certified professional, is the best validated and most widely used diagnostic assessment. It consists of four modules and in accordance with the age and expressive language level of the case being assessed, the appropriate module is selected. Module 1 of ADOS is suitable for young nonverbal children. Module 4 is suitable for verbally fluent adolescents and adults. Modules 2 and 3 are suitable for the remaining groups (Pasco, 2010). Cut-off scores obtained when the appropriate module has been applied are the indicator of whether outcomes fulfil criteria for ASD (Lord et al., 2000). Nevertheless, the diagnostic algorithm of ADOS does not take scores of items relating to restricted, repetitive and stereotyped behaviours into consideration. Consequently, information from other sources is required for a full clinical diagnosis.

In this study, it is aimed to analyse the success of various classifiers for predicting ASD cases in terms of different metrics. It is known that when the same dataset is used for training and testing steps, unrealistic results may be obtained (Varoquaux & Cheplygina, 2022). However, applying cross validation generally leads to more realistic results that can be generalised (Korjus et al., 2016). Therefore, both approaches are to be used in order to make a fair comparison between the classifiers.

The chapter is organised is as follows. A focused literature review is presented in the related work section. In the methodology section, the methodology of this study is presented along with the questionnaire used to prepare the dataset. In the data analysis and performance metrics section, performance metrics used in this study are reviewed. The results of this study are presented and discussed in the results and discussion sections, respectively. Finally, this chapter is concluded in the conclusion section.

RELATED WORK

The standard approaches for diagnosing ASD evaluate several behaviours, take a few hours to complete, and are not available everywhere. However, machine learning techniques can offer alternative methods for ASD diagnosis, as well as accelerating it. Considering the worldwide acceptance and use of ADI-R and ADOS, Wall et al. (2012a) and Wall et al. (2012b) applied machine learning algorithms in datasets obtained using them. In (Wall et al., 2012b) 93 items of the ADI-R dataset were summarised as 7 items by Alternating Decision Tree (ADTree) algorithm was applied. In their research, Wall et al. (2012b) made a distinction between Autism and Non-Autism by executing a total of 1000 training steps. Similarly, in (Wall et al., 2012a), 29 items of module 1 of the ADOS dataset were summarised as by ADTree algorithm was applied. Again, by executing a total of 1000 training steps, a distinction between Autism and Non-Autism was made. Different from (Wall et al., 2012a) and (Wall et al., 2012b), Duda et al. (2014) also predicted the subgroup of Pervasive Developmental Disorder-Not Otherwise Specified (PDD-NOS) in the DSM-IV-TR (American Psychiatric Association, 2013) diagnostic system by applying Observation-Based Classifier algorithm.

Choi et al. (2020) used a dataset obtained from the Bundang Seoul National University Hospital to predict ASD and PDD-NOS. The dataset consisted of a total of 1269 individuals with ASD and their unaffected siblings, and 127 of them were used to verify the model. Choi et al. (2020) achieved positive prediction rate of 98.5% and negative prediction rate of 94.9% using multiclass decision forest with 1 tree and positive prediction rate of 97.0% and negative prediction rate of 97.4% using multiclass decision forest with four trees. On the other hand, they achieved positive prediction rate of 71.4% when the total number of decision trees was two and the positive prediction rate of 81.0% when the total number of decision trees was four. In their experiments, after macro averaging, the average accuracy was 0.963, precision was 0.927, and finally, recall was 0.918.

Support Vector Machine (SVM) is widely used in different classification applications; however, its accuracy is usually low when a single SVM is used as classifier. Bi et al. (2018) used multiple SVMs to classify individuals with ASD and non-ASD control group. Functional magnetic resonance imaging (fMRI) data of 45 individuals with ASD and 39 non-ASD individuals from the control group were used in the classification using a random SVM cluster. Classification accuracy rate of 96.15% was achieved at the end of the experiment.

Convolutional neural networks (CNN) have been successfully used for image classification, speech recognition and in neural science. Sherkatghanad et al. (2020) focused on identifying ASD cases using CNN with fMRI data obtained from the Autism Brain Imaging Exchange. In the experiment they obtained an accuracy rate of 70.22% even if their CNN model used fewer parameters compared to the literature. ASD is typically characterised by stereotypical motor movements (SMM). Therefore, CNN was used to track and identify SMMs. Sadouk, Gadi, & Essoufi (2018) proposed a CNN model for SMM detection and the parameters of the model were set in accordance with the analysis of SMM signals. After training a time-domain CNN on SMMs for each atypical subject, they obtained an overall F-measure of 0.8459. On the other hand, after training a frequency-domain CNN on SMMs for each atypical subject, they obtained an overall F-measure of 0.9345.

Tariq et al. (2018) proposed to use machine learning based analysis on home videos to accelerate the diagnosis of ASD. For this, they first designed a web page for video raters to assess 30 behavioural features that are employed by eight different machine learning models to identify ASD. Then, they collected 116 short home videos of children with ASD and 46 videos of typically developing children (TDC). After these steps were completed, three raters blind to the diagnosis independently measured each of the 30 features from the eight machine learning models in around four minutes. Among the employed models, a sparse 5-feature Logistic Regression (LR) classifier yielded an Area under the Receiver Operating Characteristic (ROC) (AUC) curve of 0.92; thereby achieved the highest accuracy. Later, an independent set of 33 short home videos of children with ASD and 33 videos of TDC was collected, and three independent rater measurements were used to validate the research outcome. In this case, an AUC of 0.89 was achieved.

As discussed in this section, in parallel with the increasing interest in machine learning techniques, various classifiers have been tested in ASD diagnosis. However most of the researches have focused on the use of a single classifier. On the other hand, in this study the use of well-known classifiers in ASD diagnosis are evaluated in terms of different performance metrics.

METHODOLOGY

In this study, WEKA (Frank, Hall, & Witten, 2016) and a dataset used in (Thabtah, 2019) has been preferred. The dataset involves a total of 292 records consisting of behavioural based attributes for each child, i.e. replies given to questions in Table 1 by each participant's parents/supervisors, and it has been used to train K-Nearest Neighbours (K-NN), K-Star (K*), SVM, Naïve Bayes (NB) and Sequential Minimal Optimization (SMO) algorithms. K-NN tries to classify an unknown instance based on the known classification of its neighbours. It is one of the most commonly used classifiers due to its simple structure and ease-of-use (Mucherino et al., 2009). K* is an instance-based classifier with an entropy-based distance function (Cleary & Trigg, 1995). SVM is a supervised machine learning model for binary classification problems. After sets of labelled training data for each class are given, SVM can categorise new data points (Cortes & Vapnik, 1995). Its principle lies on separating data points using a hyperplane with the largest amount of margin (Cortes & Vapnik, 1995). NB relies on based on Bayes' Theorem with an independence assumption among predictors. An NB classifier relies on assuming that the presence of a particular feature in a class is unrelated to the presence of any other features. SMO is an optimisation algorithm for training an SVM classifier (Platt, 1998). It is more efficient than the standard quadratic problem solvers (Platt, 1998).

Although the original dataset consisted of all attributes listed in Table 1, in this study, only the first 10 attributes have been used. Because, in the trials conducted before the classifications, the attributes between 12-17 did not affect the overall results and did not prove to be reliable. Therefore, they were excluded from the study.

DATA ANALYSIS AND PERFORMANCE METRICS

Accuracy, recall, precision, Kappa statistic, F-measure, ROC curve, Matthews Correlation Coefficient (MCC) and Root Mean Square Error (RMSE) are among the most popular performance metrics. Accuracy summarises the performance of a classification model as the number of correct predictions divided by the total number of predictions (1).

$$\text{Accuracy} = \frac{TP+TN}{TP+TN+FP+FN} \tag{1}$$

Table 1. Questions in the questionnaire

No	Question
1	Does the child frequently notice sounds or audio that others do not?
2	Rather than small details, does the child tend to focus more on the whole picture?
3	In a social group, can the child easily keep track of different peoples' conversations?
4	Can the child easily shift his/her attention from one task to another?
5	Does the child know how to start and continue a conversation with his/her peers?
6	Is the child good at social chats?
7	When a story is told, can the child easily work out the characters' feelings and/or intentions?
8	Does the child enjoy playing games involving pretending with other children?
9	Can the child easily understandf what someone is feeling or thinking just by looking at their faces?
10	Is the child able to easily make new friends?
11	The type of screening method chosen based on age category
12	How old is the child?
13	Is the child male or female?
14	What is the child's ethnicity?
15	Was the child born with neonatal jaundice?
16	Is any immediate family member with ASD?
17	What is the child's country of residence?

where TP (True Positives) represents instances that the classification algorithm has correctly classified as positives, TN (True Negatives) represents instances that the classification algorithm has correctly classified as negatives, FP (False Positives) represents instances that the classification algorithm has incorrectly classified as positives, and finally, FN (False Negatives) represents instances that the classification algorithm has incorrectly classified as negatives. In this study, TP refers to children with ASD and TN refers to non-ASD cases, i.e. TDC.

Precision represents the fraction of relevant instances among the retrieved instances and is calculated using (2). Recall represents the fraction of relevant instances that has been retrieved, and is calculated using (3). On the other hand, F measure combines precision and recall and it is more suitable for imbalanced classification problems. It is calculated using (4). Other performance metrics employed in this study are Kappa statistic and RMSE. While Kappa statistic is a measure of inter-rater and intra-rater reliability for qualitative items (McHugh, 2012), RMSE is the standard deviation of prediction errors. MCC is used as a measure of the quality of binary classifications (Matthews, 1975) and compared to the other metrics, it is more suitable for imbalanced data sets. It is calculated using (5)

$$\text{Precision} = \frac{TP}{TP + FP} \tag{2}$$

$$\text{Recall} = \frac{TP}{TP + FN} \tag{3}$$

$$\text{F} - \text{measure} = 2 \times \frac{\text{Precision} \times \text{Recall}}{\text{Precision} + \text{Recall}} \quad (4)$$

$$\text{MCC} = \frac{TP{*}TN - FP{*}FN}{\sqrt{(TP+FP)*(TP+FN)*(TN+FP)*(TN+FN)}} \quad (5)$$

ROC curve is a graph showing the performance of a classifier at different thresholds, and uses True Positive Rate (TPR) and False Positive Rate (FPR) values. TPR is another name for Recall, which is calculated using (3). On the other hand, FPR is calculated using (6). In a ROC curve, the vertical axis represents TPR and the horizontal axis represents FPR. If AUC has a value of 1, it means that the classification has been perfect. On the other hand, if AUC has a value of 0.5 or less, it is an indication of a low-performance classifier and also the indication of the fact that the classification has been randomly made.

$$\text{FPR} = \frac{FP}{FP+TN} \quad (6)$$

Cross validation reveals how accurately a predictive model will do in practice (Arlot & Celisse, 2010). In each round of cross validation, training and testing steps of traditional classification process are repeated with different partitions, and then the results of the validation step are averaged over the rounds to reduce variability (Arlot & Celisse, 2010).

RESULTS

After testing on the same data set and applying 10-fold cross validation, as listed in Table 2 and Table 3, two sets of performance metrics have been obtained for both ASD and non-ASD cases in order to evaluate the performance of different classifiers. While the performance metrics of all the algorithms have been 1 without cross validation, after cross validation they have been fewer. After cross validation, KNN algorithm has had the highest performance decrease. This means that when an instance that is not included in the training data set is given, KNN algorithm will have a higher possibility in failing to classify it correctly, compared to the others. The higher recall value of K* algorithm for the ASD class compared to the Non-ASD class indicates that the algorithm is more successful in detecting individuals belonging to the ASD class. The opposite is true for SVM and NB algorithms. For all the algorithms, MCC and AUC values have been the same for both of the classes.

Kappa, RMSE and accuracy values of the algorithms are shown in Figure 1. As revealed in the results, when the same dataset has been used for the training and testing steps, all the algorithms have shown excellent results in terms of all the performance metrics listed in Table 2 and Table 3 and shown in Figure 1. However, after 10-fold cross validation has been applied, SMO has been the most successful classifier in terms of all the performance metrics.

Table 2. Performance metrics after testing on the same test that the classifier has been trained on

Metric	Class	K-NN	K*	SVM	NB	SMO
Precision	Non-ASD	1	1	1	1	1
	ASD	1	1	1	1	1
Recall	Non-ASD	1	1	1	1	1
	ASD	1	1	1	1	1
F-Measure	Non-ASD	1	1	1	1	1
	ASD	1	1	1	1	1
MCC	Non-ASD	1	1	1	1	1
	ASD	1	1	1	1	1
AUC	Non-ASD	1	1	1	1	1
	ASD	1	1	1	1	1

Table 3. Performance metrics after 10-fold cross validation has been applied

Metric	Class	K-NN	K*	SVM	NB	SMO
Precision	Non-ASD	0.91	0.97	1	0.99	1
	ASD	0.85	0.94	0.99	0.98	1
Recall	Non-ASD	0.85	0.94	0.99	0.98	1
	ASD	0.91	0.97	1	0.99	1
F-Measure	Non-ASD	0.88	0.96	0.99	0.99	1
	ASD	0.88	0.96	0.99	0.98	1
MCC	Non-ASD	0.76	0.92	0.99	0.97	1
	ASD	0.76	0.92	0.99	0.97	1
AUC	Non-ASD	0.89	0.98	0.99	1	1
	ASD	0.89	0.98	0.99	1	1

Table 4 lists the confusion matrices of all the algorithms. In the confusion matrices, both the number of correctly classified individuals by the algorithms and the number of incorrectly classified individuals by the algorithms are shown. For example, when the results achieved by K* algorithm have been cross-validated, it has correctly predicted 138 of 141 children with ASD, but it has not been able to detect three individuals with ASD and predicted them as Non-ASD. Total number of ASD cases correctly classified by the K* algorithm has been 281, and the number of cases classified incorrectly has been 11. The results prove that classifiers are successful at identifying ASD cases when a reliable dataset is provided. The results obtained in this study are in parallel with the results reported in (Grønborg et al., 2013) and in (Wu et al., 2016).

As it can be seen in Table 3, without cross validation, all the algorithms correctly classified all of the instances. On the other hand, as it is given in Figure 2, when cross validation was applied, except for SMO, all of the classifiers incorrectly classified some of the instances.

Figure 1. Performance metrics: Kappa, RMSE, and accuracy

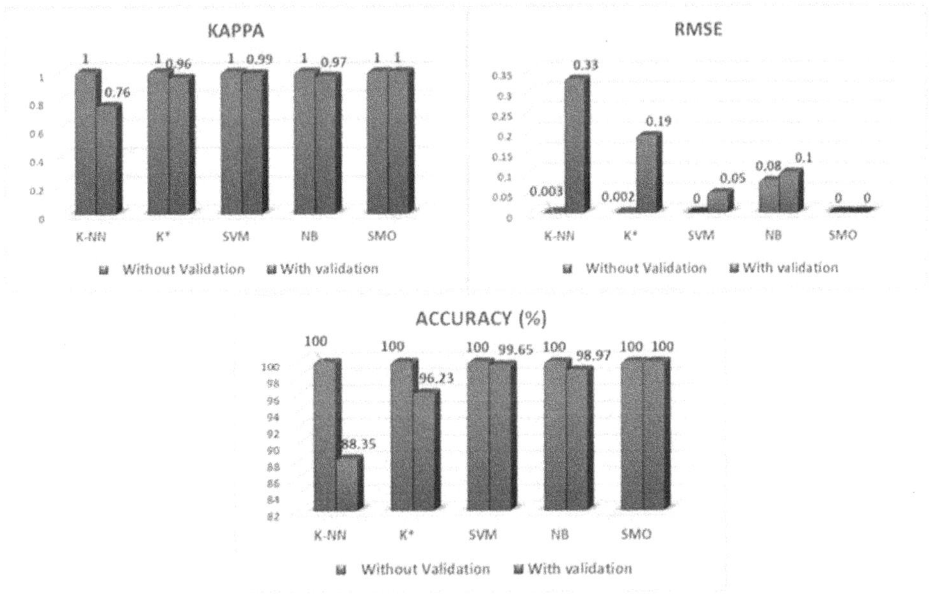

Table 4. Confusion matrices of the classifiers

KNN Predicted								
Actual	**Without cross validation**		TP	TN	**With cross validation**		TP	TN
		TP	141	0		TP	129	12
		TN	0	151		TN	22	129
K* Predicted								
Actual	**Without cross validation**		TP	TN	**With cross validation**		TP	TN
		TP	141	0		TP	138	3
		TN	0	151		TN	8	143
SVM Predicted								
Actual	**Without cross validation**		TP	TN	**With cross validation**		TP	TN
		TP	141	0		TP	141	0
		TN	0	151		TN	1	150
NB Predicted								
Actual	**Without cross validation**		TP	TN	**With cross validation**		TP	TN
		TP	141	0		TP	140	1
		TN	0	151		TN	2	149
SMO Predicted								
Actual	**Without cross validation**		TP	TN	**With cross validation**		TP	TN
		TP	141	0		TP	141	0
		TN	0	151		TN	0	151

Figure 2. Percentages of correctly and incorrectly classified instances by the classifiers after cross validation: KNN, K, SVM, NB, and SMO*

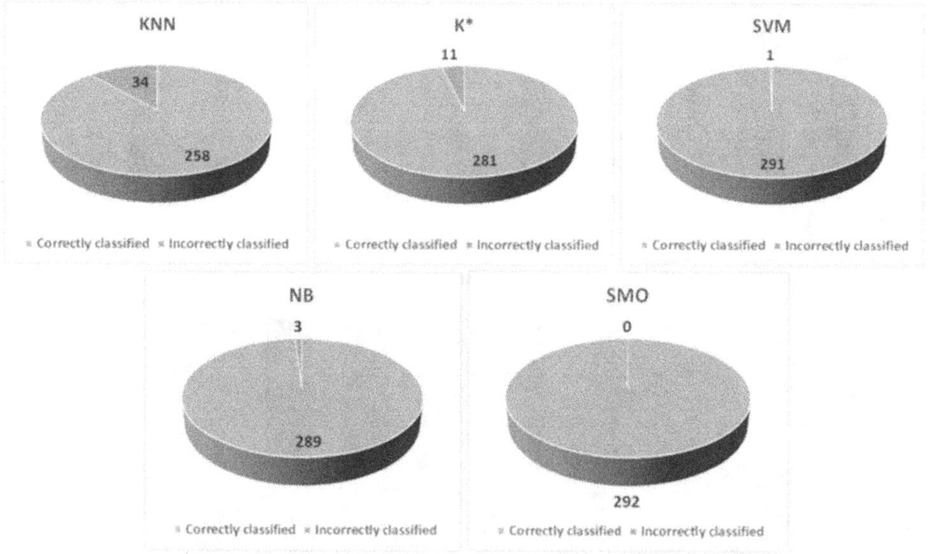

Although the results provided by classifers are quite promising, software-based approaches cannot replace the role of clinicians in the final diagnosis of ASD but can help the professionals working in this field to accelerate or enhance the diagnostic processes. Because as well as undesired results that can be experienced by the child and his/her family in case of misdiagnosis, in the use of machine learning models for identifying ASD cases suffering from several issues related to conceptualisation, implementation and data, including the type of feature selection methodology employed, the way diagnostic codes used, the evaluation metrics chosen, training set imbalances and processing of noise should be taken into consideration (Thabtah, 2019).

DISCUSSION

It has been shown that human-robot interaction and technological-based tools are suitable for automated behaviour assessment and the early detection of ASD is possible through naturalistic behavioural observation and classifiers (Ramírez-Duque et al., 2019). When being integrated into a robot-assisted system proposed for ASD diagnosis, computer vision can be used to analyse the child's behaviours and with the help of automated video coding process it can summarise and deliver the responses to clinicians (Ramírez-Duque et al., 2019).

There are alternative methods for ASD diagnosis and these can be useful to address the difficulties in working with young children. For instance, eye tracking has a potential for the early detection of ASD. Wan et al. (2019) investigated the fixation times of a total of 74 children, 37 children with ASD and 37 TDC, ages between four to six while the children were watching a short video clip, 10-sec video of a female speaking. It was shown that the children with ASD exhibited considerable reductions in fixation time. At the end of their research, Wan and colleagues discriminated the children with ASD from the

TDC with an accuracy of 85.1%, a sensitivity of 86.5%, and a specificity of 83.8%. Another alternative method for ASD diagnosis is based on taking into consideration distinctive, atypical acoustic patterns of speech of individuals with ASD (Fusaroli et al., 2017). Children with ASD often exhibit abnormal voice quality and speech prosody if they can speak. Although the underlying mechanisms of those abnormalities have not been known yet, Bonneh et al. (2011) recorded speech samples of 83 children, 41 of them with ASD and 42 of them are TDC, and quantified speech abnormalities of them in terms of the properties of the long-term average spectrum and pitch variability. The children with ASD had a considerably larger pitch range and variability across time and the average spectra of the children with ASD was shallower and with less harmonic structure (Bonneh et al., 2011). This variability allowed classifying ASD with an accuracy of 86%, a sensitivity of 80%, and a specificity of 90%. However, such novel software/hardware-based tools relying on classifiers should be used under the supervision of a certified professional or clinicians due to the complexity and heterogeneity of the disorder.

Robles et al. (2022) proposed a virtual reality social interaction based ASD screening system with an embodied agent. The system was named "shopping experience" and during it, behavioural responses were tracked and recorded. Then, this behaviour was analysed with machine learning approaches to identify participants with ASD. It was shown that the proposed system was able to detect individual with ASD with high accuracy. It has been shown that platforms and equipment based on virtual reality technology offer many advantages in training of social communication and interaction skills (Zhang et al., 2022). Incorporating virtual reality into training programs or therapy sessions is effective in improving the social aspects of performances among individuals with ASD. Because virtual reality based intervention can lead to considerable improvement in emotion recognition, social functioning, and speech and language (Zhang et al., 2022).

Considering the variability in the indications of ASD and the need for quickly administered diagnosis methods in a clinical setting, Bosl et al. (2018) proposed the use of Electroencephalogram (EEG), an easy-to-use brain measurement tool for monitoring atypical brain development. They obtained EEG measurements from 99 infants with an older sibling diagnosed with ASD and 89 infants in low risk category, and computed nonlinear features from the EEG measurements. The measurements were obtained beginning at the children's three months of age and continuing until three years of age. At the end of the prediction, positive predictive values, sensitivity and specificity exceeded 95% at some ages.

Although ASD cases could be identified using classifiers, there are still open research issues. First of all, for almost all of the countries, there is a need for nation-wide surveys on prevalence using the same scales for screening and diagnosis. Second, both screening and diagnostic scales must be developed, evaluated and implemented for children with different ages. Finally, multidisciplinary diagnostic and treatment groups that include child psychiatrist, pediatrician and neurologist, if needed, speech and language pathologist and occupational therapist as well, must be organised.

CONCLUSION

When children with ASD are diagnosed at early ages and appropriate interventions are immediately applied, they will possibly have the chance of reaching their full potential. Machine learning techniques can provide accurate and reliable results for a wide range of problems if they employ reliable datasets with abundant features, and suitable classifiers. By considering the focus of this study, the suitability and success of various classifiers for detecting ASD cases have been analysed using a set of performance metrics.

As revealed in the results, when the same dataset has been used for the training and testing steps, all the algorithms have shown excellent results in terms of all the performance metrics. However, after 10-fold cross validation, SMO has reached the best results in terms of all the performance metrics. As the results show, ASD cases can be quickly and accurately detected using classifiers. But, because of the complexity and heterogeneity of ASD cases, final diagnosis should be made by child psychiatrists or certified professionals. The limitation of this study lies in the fact that the dataset used in this study consists of data obtained using a questionnaire. In addition, there is a limited number of instances in the dataset. The development of an application to be deployed on a humanoid robot, called NAO, to detect ASD cases is going on as our future work.

REFERENCES

Abbas, H., Garberson, F., Glover, E., & Wall, D. P. (2018). Machine learning approach for early detection of autism by combining questionnaire and home video screening. *Journal of the American Medical Informatics Association, 25*(8), 1000–1007. doi:10.1093/jamia/ocy039 PMID:29741630

Accordino, R. E., Kidd, C., Politte, L. C., Henry, C. A., & McDougle, C. J. (2016). Psychopharmacological interventions in autism spectrum disorder. *Expert Opinion on Pharmacotherapy, 17*(7), 937–952. doi:10.1517/14656566.2016.1154536 PMID:26891879

American Psychiatric Association, DSM-5 Task Force. (2013). *Diagnostic and statistical manual of mental disorders: DSM-5* (5th ed.). American Psychiatric Publishing, Inc. doi:10.1176/appi.books.9780890425596

Arlot, S., & Celisse, A. (2010). A survey of cross-validation procedures for model selection. *Statistics Surveys, 4*(none), 40–79. doi:10.1214/09-SS054

Bi, X. A., Wang, Y., Shu, Q., Sun, Q., & Xu, Q. (2018). Classification of Autism Spectrum Disorder Using Random Support Vector Machine Cluster. *Frontiers in Genetics, 9*, 18. Advance online publication. doi:10.3389/fgene.2018.00018 PMID:29467790

Bonneh, Y. S., Levanon, Y., Dean-Pardo, O., Lossos, L., & Adini, Y. (2011). Abnormal speech spectrum and increased pitch variability in young autistic children. *Frontiers in Human Neuroscience, 4*, 237. doi:10.3389/fnhum.2010.00237 PMID:21267429

Bosl, W. J., Tager-Flusberg, H., & Nelson, C. A. (2018). EEG Analytics for Early Detection of Autism Spectrum Disorder: A data-driven approach. *Scientific Reports, 8*(1), 6828. Advance online publication. doi:10.103841598-018-24318-x PMID:29717196

Cleary, J. G., & Trigg, L. E. (1995). K*: An Instance-based Learner Using and Entropic Distance Measure. *International Conference on Machine Learning*. 10.1016/B978-1-55860-377-6.50022-0

Cortes, C., & Vapnik, V. (1995). Support-vector networks. *Machine Learning, 20*(3), 273–297. doi:10.1007/BF00994018

Crais, E. R., & Watson, L. R. (2014). Challenges and opportunities in early identification and intervention for children at-risk for autism spectrum disorders. *International Journal of Speech-Language Pathology, 16*(1), 23–29. doi:10.3109/17549507.2013.862860 PMID:24328367

Duda, M., Kosmicki, J. A., & Wall, D. P. (2014). Testing the accuracy of an observation-based classifier for rapid detection of autism risk. *Translational Psychiatry*, *4*(8), e424. doi:10.1038/tp.2014.65 PMID:25116834

Frank, E., Hall, M. A., & Witten, I. H. (2016). *The WEKA Workbench. Online Appendix for "Data Mining: Practical Machine Learning Tools and Techniques"*. Morgan Kaufmann.

Fusaroli, R., Lambrechts, A., Bang, D., Bowler, D. M., & Gaigg, S. B. (2017). Is voice a marker for Autism spectrum disorder? A systematic review and meta-analysis. *Autism Research*, *10*(3), 384–407. doi:10.1002/aur.1678 PMID:27501063

Gould, J., & Ashton-Smith, J. (2011). Missed diagnosis or misdiagnosis? Girls and women on the autism spectrum. *Good Autism Practice*, *12*(1), 34–41.

Grønborg, T. K., Schendel, D. E., & Parner, E. T. (2013). Recurrence of autism spectrum disorders in full- and half-siblings and trends over time: A population-based cohort study. *JAMA Pediatrics*, *167*(10), 947–953. doi:10.1001/jamapediatrics.2013.2259 PMID:23959427

Korjus, K., Hebart, M. N., & Vicente, R. (2016). An Efficient Data Partitioning to Improve Classification Performance While Keeping Parameters Interpretable. *PLoS One*, *11*(8), e0161788. doi:10.1371/journal.pone.0161788 PMID:27564393

Lord, C., Risi, S., Lambrecht, L., Cook, E. H. Jr, Leventhal, B. L., DiLavore, P. C., Pickles, A., & Rutter, M. (2000). The autism diagnostic observation schedule-generic: A standard measure of social and communication deficits associated with the spectrum of autism. *Journal of Autism and Developmental Disorders*, *30*(3), 205–223. doi:10.1023/A:1005592401947 PMID:11055457

Lord, C., Rutter, M., & Le Couteur, A. (1994). Autism Diagnostic Interview-Revised: A revised version of a diagnostic interview for caregivers of individuals with possible pervasive developmental disorders. *Journal of Autism and Developmental Disorders*, *24*(5), 659–685. doi:10.1007/BF02172145 PMID:7814313

Matthews, B. W. (1975). Comparison of the predicted and observed secondary structure of T4 phage lysozyme. *Biochimica et Biophysica Acta (BBA)- Protein Structure*, *405*(2), 442–451. doi:10.1016/0005-2795(75)90109-9 PMID:1180967

McHugh, M. L. (2012). Interrater reliability: The kappa statistic. *Biochemia Medica*, *22*(3), 276–282. doi:10.11613/BM.2012.031 PMID:23092060

McPartland, J., & Volkmar, F. R. (2012). Autism and related disorders. *Handbook of Clinical Neurology*, *106*, 407–418. doi:10.1016/B978-0-444-52002-9.00023-1 PMID:22608634

Mucherino, A., Papajorgji, P. J., & Pardalos, P. M. (2009). k-Nearest Neighbor Classification. In Data Mining in Agriculture. Springer Optimization and Its Applications (vol. 34). Springer. doi:10.1007/978-0-387-88615-2_4

Pasco, G. (2010). Identification and diagnosis of autism spectrum disorders: An update. *Pediatric Health*, *4*(1), 107–114. doi:10.2217/phe.09.64

Platt, J. (1998). *Sequential Minimal Optimization: A Fast Algorithm for Training Support Vector Machines*. Microsoft Research, Technical Report msr-tr-98-14.

Ramírez-Duque, A. A., Frizera-Neto, A., & Bastos, T. F. (2019). Robot-Assisted Autism Spectrum Disorder Diagnostic Based on Artificial Reasoning. *Journal of Intelligent & Robotic Systems*, *96*(2), 267–281. doi:10.100710846-018-00975-y

Robles, M., Namdarian, N., Otto, J., Wassiljew, E., Navab, N., Falter-Wagner, C., & Roth, D. (2022). A Virtual Reality Based System for the Screening and Classification of Autism. *IEEE Transactions on Visualization and Computer Graphics*, *28*(5), 2168–2178. doi:10.1109/TVCG.2022.3150489 PMID:35171773

Sadouk, L., Gadi, T., & Essoufi, E. H. (2018). A Novel Deep Learning Approach for Recognizing Stereotypical Motor Movements within and across Subjects on the Autism Spectrum Disorder. *Computational Intelligence and Neuroscience*, *2018*, 7186762. Advance online publication. doi:10.1155/2018/7186762 PMID:30111994

Sherkatghanad, Z., Akhondzadeh, M., Salari, S., Zomorodi-Moghadam, M., Abdar, M., Acharya, U. R., Khosrowabadi, R., & Salari, V. (2020). Automated Detection of Autism Spectrum Disorder Using a Convolutional Neural Network. *Frontiers in Neuroscience*, *13*, 1325. Advance online publication. doi:10.3389/fnins.2019.01325 PMID:32009868

Tariq, Q., Daniels, J., Schwartz, J. N., Washington, P., Kalantarian, H., & Wall, D. P. (2018). Mobile detection of autism through machine learning on home video: A development and prospective validation study. *PLoS Medicine*, *15*(11), e1002705. doi:10.1371/journal.pmed.1002705 PMID:30481180

Thabtah, F. (2019). Machine learning in autistic spectrum disorder behavioral research: A review and ways forward. *Informatics for Health & Social Care*, *44*(3), 278–297. doi:10.1080/17538157.2017.1399132 PMID:29436887

Varoquaux, G., & Cheplygina, V. (2022). Machine learning for medical imaging: Methodological failures and recommendations for the future. *NPJ Digital Medicine*, *5*(1), 48. doi:10.103841746-022-00592-y PMID:35413988

Wall, D. P., Dally, R., Luyster, R., Jung, J. Y., & DeLuca, T. F. (2012). Use of Artificial Intelligence to Shorten the Behavioral Diagnosis of Autism. *PLoS One*, *7*(8), e43855. doi:10.1371/journal.pone.0043855 PMID:22952789

Wall, D. P., Kosmicki, J. A., DeLuca, T., Harstad, E. B., & Fusaro, V. A. (2012). Use of Machine Learning to Shorten Observation-based Screening and Diagnosis of Autism. *Translational Psychiatry*, *2*(4), e100. doi:10.1038/tp.2012.10 PMID:22832900

Wan, G., Kong, X., Sun, B., Yu, S., Tu, Y., Park, J., Lang, C., Koh, M., Wei, Z., Feng, Z., Lin, Y., & Kong, J. (2019). Applying Eye Tracking to Identify Autism Spectrum Disorder in Children. *Journal of Autism and Developmental Disorders*, *49*(1), 209–215. doi:10.100710803-018-3690-y PMID:30097760

White, S. W., Oswald, D., Ollendick, T., & Scahill, L. (2009). Anxiety in children and adolescents with autism spectrum disorders. *Clinical Psychology Review*, *29*(3), 216–229. doi:10.1016/j.cpr.2009.01.003 PMID:19223098

Wu, Y. W., Kuzniewicz, M. W., Croen, L., Walsh, E. M., McCulloch, C. E., & Newman, T. B. (2016). Risk of Autism Associated with Hyperbilirubinemia and Phototherapy. *Pediatrics, 138*(4), e20161813. doi:10.1542/peds.2016-1813 PMID:27669736

Zhang, M., Ding, H., Naumceska, M., & Zhang, Y. (2022). Virtual Reality Technology as an Educational and Intervention Tool for Children with Autism Spectrum Disorder: Current Perspectives and Future Directions. *Behavioral Sciences (Basel, Switzerland), 12*(5), 138. doi:10.3390/bs12050138 PMID:35621435

ADDITIONAL READING

Aggarwal, C. C. (2015). *Data classification: algorithms and applications.* CRC Press.

Géron, A. (2023). *Hands-on machine learning with scikit-learn keras and tensorflow: concepts tools and techniques to build intelligent systems (Third).* O'Reilly.

Price, D. (2022). *Unmasking Autism: Discovering the New Faces of Neurodiversity.* Harmony Books.

Rothman, D. (2020). *Artificial intelligence by example; acquire advanced ai machine learning and deep learning design skills (Second).* PACKT Publishing.

Zhou, Z.-H. (2021). *Machine learning.* Springer. doi:10.1007/978-981-15-1967-3

KEY TERMS AND DEFINITIONS

Autism Spectrum Disorder: It is a neurological and developmental disorder that affects how people interact with others, communicate, learn, and behave.

Classification Algorithms: They are used to categorise data into a class or category.

Performance Metrics: They are used to evaluate machine learning models and measure their effectiveness. They help to determine whether the machine learning model is making accurate predictions, and how well it is generalising to new data.

SMO: It is an algorithm used to solve the quadratic programming problem that arises during the training of support vector machines.

Virtual Reality: It is the use of computer modeling and simulation that enables an individual to interact with an artificial three-dimensional visual or other sensory environment.

Chapter 10
HearUs:
A Cognitive Assistive Tool for People With Visual Impairment

Shweta Taneja
Department of Computer Science and Engineering, Bhagwan Parshuram Institute of Technology, Delhi, India

Mohini Vaish
Department of Computer Science and Engineering, Bhagwan Parshuram Institute of Technology, Delhi, India

Bhawna Suri
Department of Computer Science and Engineering, Bhagwan Parshuram Institute of Technology, Delhi, India

Rahul Jain
Department of Computer Science and Engineering, Bhagwan Parshuram Institute of Technology, Delhi, India

Narina Thakur
Department of Computer Science and Engineering, Bhagwan Parshuram Institute of Technology, Delhi, India

Akshat Bisht
Department of Computer Science and Engineering, Bhagwan Parshuram Institute of Technology, Delhi, India

ABSTRACT

People with visual impairment (PVI) live a dependent life for doing their daily tasks. The most advanced assistive devices for PVIs currently available are either expensive or have poor performance or need extra hardware support. An integrated cognitive assistive tool for PVIs, HearUs, is implemented to handle path obstacle detection, product recognition, weather updates, reading documents or newspapers, automated dialing, and SOS service. It helps and directs the PVIs by giving them pertinent information about their surroundings. Different technologies have been used, like transfer learning, VGGNet 16 model for hurdle detection, barcode scanning for product identification, as well as text recognition and voice assistant capabilities. The Flickr8k dataset and a custom build dataset have been used for training the baseline model on around 8000 images. Furthermore, an experimental result shows that HearUs achieves 82% accuracy as compared to other existing applications.

DOI: 10.4018/979-8-3693-0378-8.ch010

1. INTRODUCTION

According to the world health organization, around 40 million people in the world are blind, while another 250 million have some form of visual impairment. The age-related disorders like glaucoma and diabetes are rising in the elderly population (Proulx, 2021). In India with a population of 1.38 billion, there are 120 million people who are physically disabled. Among this set of people with different physical disabilities, 10.32% of people are PVIs (R. S. Krishnan et al., 2021) as identified facts from the statistics represented in Figure 1.

Figure 1. Indian statistics of people with physical disabilities
Source: R. S. Krishnan et al. (2021)

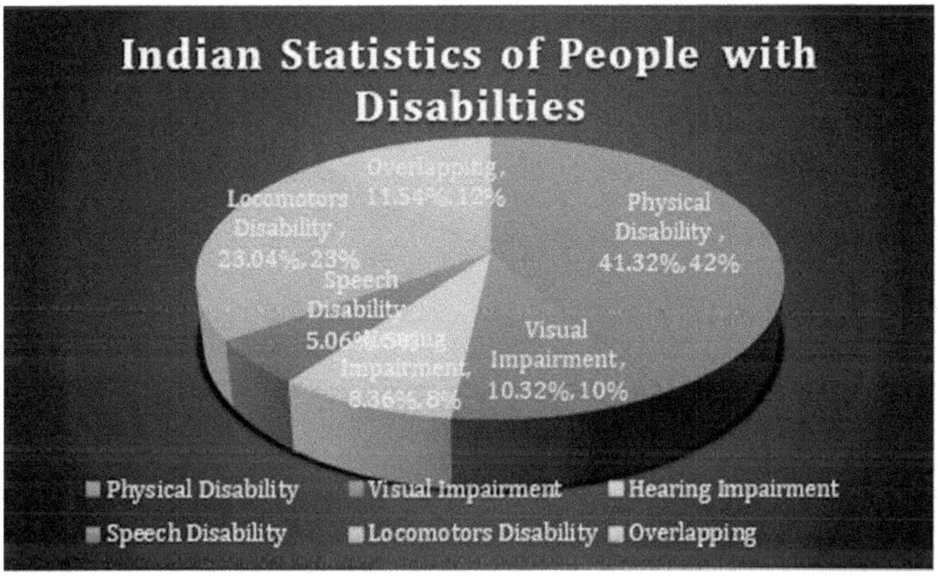

All five senses of human body - see, hear, touch, smell and taste play a very important role in his day-to-day activities. Unfortunately, not everyone is blessed with all these senses. Sight and vision play a vital role in a person's life to connect and access their surroundings. There are many people who either by birth or by some mis-happenings may lose these senses. Although the Indian government has launched numerous programs to assist PVIs, by distributing walker, walking stick, and personal assistance free or a nominal cost. Nowadays, due to factors such as portability, pocket-friendly, and advancement in technology, mobile phones have grown in popularity to become the most common gadget for consumers. Thus, the technology can be exploited as a solution for beating the challenges faced by PVIs, like reading and writing documents/newspapers/books, identifying surroundings, visiting places on their own like for their daily needs. The aim of this work is to propose an android-based voice automated assistive tool for PVIs. It provides the cognitive ability through voice commands. HearUs is an Android 5.0 application with minimum SDK version 21.

1.2 Problem Statement

There are many assisting tools available for PVIs but none of them caters all the daily needs under one umbrella. We have built the HearUs - Android Application as an assistive tool handling:

1. Hurdle Detection through voice
2. Shopping at the stores using the Barcode feature of the app
3. Reading documents, newspapers etc
4. Weather updates
5. SOS Services

1.3 Chapter Organization

This research work is divided into various sections as follows: Section 2 presents the literature review of assistive tools for PVIs. Section 3 shows the material and methods elaborating data collection, model formulation and proposed methodology. Section 4 discusses and analyzes the experimental results. Finally, the work is concluded in Section 5 with its future scope.

1.4 Objective

The objective of our work is to assist PVIs for their independent survival by

- Going out independently, where the hurdle can be detected and conveyed to the person through voice.
- Can do shopping through barcode detection helping the PVI to identify the price and other details of the product
- Reading documents or newspapers through text to speech
- Weather updates
- SOS services

2. LITERATURE REVIEW

The work done by different authors for the PVIs to live their life independently is discussed below:

Senjam, S. (2019) and Manjari, K. etal. (2020) discussed about the different assistive tools of PVIs. In the field of the latest technology of computer vision, automated caption generation has received increasing interest, because of recent research advancements in natural language processing (NLP) (Makav and Kılıc, 2019) and artificial intelligence (AI). However, the main problem with the most fundamental kind of communication that the majority of people can understand continues to exist in the technologies that we employ. Doshi et al., 2018 have worked on image analysis using Google Cloud Vision API for the detection of individual objects within images, recognize and read text contained within images. The Cloud Vision API was used for noise filtering. Staniūtė et al., in 2019 have presented an extensive systematic literature review and summaries the findings of advancements made in image captioning (Staniūtė and Šešok, 2019). Convolutional neural networks are efficient for tasks involving visual recognition. Among the well-known networks are ResNet, AlexNet, VGG, Inception, and others. After VGG, the notion of blocks and modules proliferated throughout the networks. Three fully linked comprises of various after the VGG convolutional layers. Such deep networks can be trained using residual networks, which generate the network from modules described as residual models (Koustubh, 2018).

The image content description (Kinghorn et al., 2018) and the caption generation of an image is a challenging task. Deep learning has evolved and with the advancement in the region-based deep learning architecture image descriptions can be generated more accurately. It uses a regional object detector, recurrent neural network (RNN) based attribute prediction, and an encoder-decoder language generator integrated with two RNNs. An image captioning algorithm based on deep learning was proposed to label an individual image as well as images in the image stream (Fan., C., & Crandall., D.J. (2016)). (Makav et al., 2019) used Long Short-Term Memory (LSTM) model to generate a caption of the images which were trained using deep learning architecture VGG16. This VGG16 is used to extract the attributes which are visible in the image and their inference is then fed into LSTM model for generating captions. This feature is then embedded in their Android application.

Another challenge for these people is to do daily household shopping independently. Different researchers have done work in this direction. Foo, 2009 has used computer vision for locating products and guiding the PVI's to the product location. Also, special hand gloves were designed for tracking the Products. Another work done in this area is assisting PVI's to locate the shelf of the product which they are looking for and also helping to identify the correct product among similar shaped products, labels etc. (Sarit Szpiro et al., 2016). A wearable device called ShopTalk developed by (John Nicholson et al. 2009). can do barcode scanning for product identification using verbal directions. Another work done for assisting PVI's in shopping is through speech, non-speech, and a combination of speech, non-speech and haptic vibrations (Sooyeon Lee et al., 2017). P. A. Zientara, 2017 have designed a shopping assistant tool using hardware devices, wearable cameras and algorithms.

Roger Boldu et al., 2018 designed a device – Finger Reader 2.0, which is a camera based ring worn on the index finger of PVI's thereby assisting them in shopping. Further, (Roger Boldu et al., 2020) extended his work by inventing a bone conduction headset, a cognitive assistive device that assists the blind people for doing grocery shopping. The device consists of a camera, processing unit and transducers. They have also devised a Bluetooth enabled ring which triggers the headset after identifying the product. The prototype developed was tested on blind people and has achieved a significant performance. In (Kuriakose, B etal 2022), different navigation systems were investigated but many of them were not successful in terms of comfort, user interface etc.

The research gap identified in the existing research work is that many assisting tools are available for PVIs but none is catering to all these tasks as a one product or in one umbrella. The Android Application has been proposed and implemented in this work as an assistive tool for the PVIs. Also Android phones are mostly affordable and all the features of our proposed model will make the PVI's independent to do their daily tasks by leveraging the technologies.

3. MATERIALS AND METHODS

This section materializes the data set used, its pre-processing, architecture and the detailed description of the features.

3.1 Materials

This section discusses the dataset used and its preprocessing.

3.1.1 Dataset

The dataset like Flickr8k and a custom dataset is created from our local area is used for training the baseline model on around 8000 images. The dataset contains multiple images of different objects like planters, cars, bikes, chairs with different sample captions for model training.

3.1.2 Data Preprocessing

The model eliminates unnecessary punctuations from the given caption and maps each word to an image after recognizing the suitable pattern. These words are then indexed and stored in a dictionary with their frequency. Then the caption is generated based on the frequency of the words used in context with a particular image. This caption is further then communicated to the person through voice by using the text-to-speech option of the tool.

3.2 Methods

The underlying methods to support different features of HearUs are as follows. Image detection feature is implemented using android (Kotlin), flask framework, and VGGNet-16 computer vision model.

4. PROPOSED METHODOLOGY

4.1 System Model

The tool has three-tier architecture – Presentation layer, Application layer & Data layer. The presentation layer is the topmost layer of the architecture implemented using Android and its other utilities for handling voice input & response. The application layer helps in fetching the information from the data layer (bottom most layer) and forwarding it to the presentation layer. The Convolution Neural Network Model (CNN) -VGGNet 16 is used for path hurdle detection, deployed on Flask, are well trained for reading the images to predict its caption in textual form. Also, database services employed at bottom-most layer are used in storing the product details, their detection and retrieving the product details when the product is scanned by the user's mobile phone through this application. The proposed architecture is showing the complete features are shown in Figure 2.

Figure 2. HearUs architecture

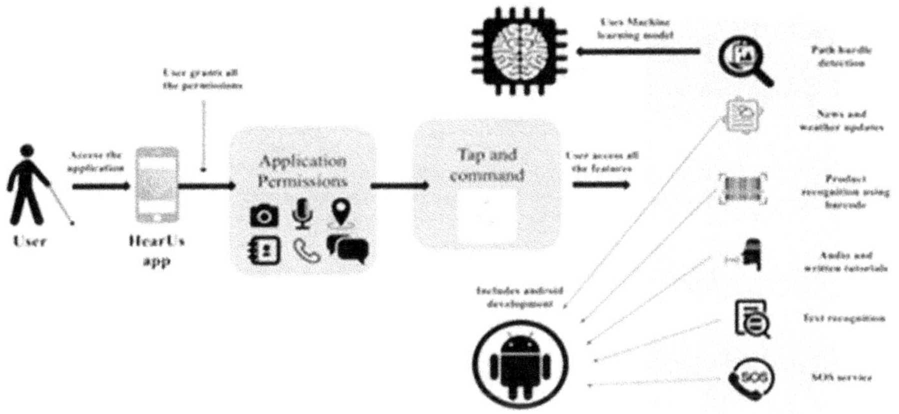

4.2 Working

The different features of HearUs are explored in the following subsections.

4.2.1 Image Detection Feature

Using this feature, the assistance is provided to warn the blind person about any hurdle in his/her path. Predictive model to is used identify objects. The PVI's android phone camera captures the object at an approximate distance of 150cm, the VGG16 model then takes 8 -10 sec in detecting the image. The caption for that hurdle will then be generated and warning message will be prompted to the person through voice. The different cases that may arise

- The object may have just crossed at 150cm but captured in the camera, the message prompted to the person through voice is -"Be Careful" and not a risky affair.
- The object captured earlier at the distance of 150 cm is approaching near and at the approximate distance of 70cm the person is warned that the hurdle is nearby.

The working of image detection is shown in Figure 3.

VGG model contains 16 layers which is a combination of convolutional layer, fully connected layer, and max pool layers. This model takes an image as an input that has dimensions (224, 224, 3) and gives an output as a vector of 1000 values which is (1,1,1000). There are total of 64 channels of size 3*3 which have the same padding. After that, there are max pool layers of stride (2, 2) and convolutional layers containing 256 filters with filter size (3, 3).

After that, there is a max pool layer of dimension (2, 2) which is the same as the previous layer. As we move forward there are two convolution layers that have 256 filters and filter size (3, 3). Lastly, there are two sets that contain three convolution layers and one max pool layer. Each has the same adding with size (3, 3) and the number of filters as 512. The model works as discussed in Table1.

Figure 3. Image detection using CNN

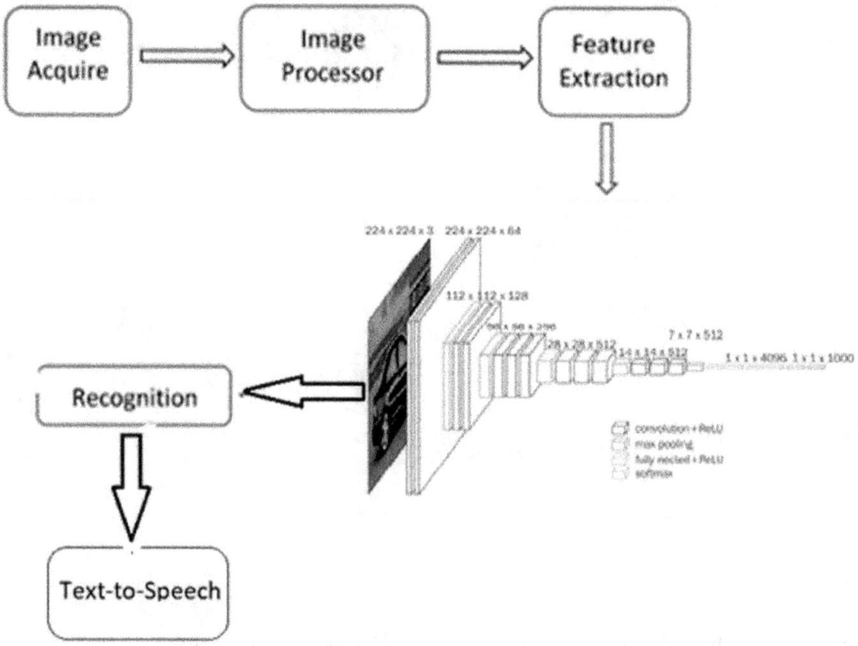

Table 1. Hyper parameters used for the baseline model's training

Number of CNN Layers	13 (Including 64, 128, 216, and 512 Channels of 3x3 Kernel and Same Padding)
Number of Maxpool Layers	5 (each of 2x2 pool size and stride 2x2)
Number of fully connected layers	3 layers
Number of Softmax layer	1 Layer
Drop Out	0.5
Learning Rate	0.001
Batch Size	256
Epochs	25

The model tries to identify patterns in the detected image and provide a suitable caption for it. Firstly, the image is clicked and stored in the database. From there it is loaded into PIL format using the PIL library. This PIL image is converted into a 3-D array in RGB format. Another dimension is added to it to convert it into a 4-D array. This array is provided as an input to the model. The image array goes through feature extraction. Here the algorithm tries to find patterns in the array and generates a suitable caption for the provided image. The model is trained and assigns the correct caption to the image.

4.2.2 Barcode Detection Feature

One of the main dependencies which the PVIs feel is that he/she is not able to identify stuff in a mart or a shop. They require some assistance that will help them shop easily. For example, the PVI goes to a shopping place to buy some items like groceries, clothes, etc. The person needs assistance from the entrance of the shopping mart to reach out to that section from where he/she wants to buy things. The person can now pick up any item from the shelf but cannot identify what it is and its price. Then he/she can rely on the barcode scanning feature of the HearUs application. The person must rotate the product in such a way that the barcode should come in front of his mobile camera scanner. The barcode will then be scanned, and the product details mentioned on the barcode are told to the person through voice.

The technology stacks used for achieving this feature are the NoSQL MongoDB database, a third-party barcode scanner view, JavaScript language coded Node.js API, and Kotlin language coded front-end application. The API acts as an HTTP handshake for the backend database and the frontend Android

4.2.3 Text Recognition Feature

The daily life struggle of the PVIs also includes reading newspapers, books, documents, and more. Not everything in our country is available in the form of Braille, a system that blind people use to read and write. To read any document the proposed application helps to recognize digital text written in English language through Text-to-Speech service. Also, any document can be read, by scanning the text and then the Text-to-Speech makes it loud. The combination of these two allows impaired people to scan any text and make the assistant read it for them. For Text recognition feature, the orientation of the phone as well as text matters. The phone should be in the portrait mode, i.e, the phone must be kept straight. An inverted or upside-down text will not provide the desired result for the PVI, so the camera of the phone can be adjusted in alignment of the text to get accurate results. Open-source Google Mobile Vision API, and standard Java and Android libraries are used to read the scanned text out loud.

4.2.4 Live Weather and News Updates Feature

Many people have encountered a situation where they step out for some errands and due to sudden rainfall, storm, or drastic weather conditions that you are unaware of might have returned home without completing their work. By every morning almost everyone wants to know what is happening around the city, country, or beyond. Knowing the weather condition would help by informing them when not to step out. This can be achieved through reading newspapers or watching shows that provide news. Keeping such problems in mind, the proposed system offers a live news and weather updates feature. The news headlines feature provides the top news headlines from the world. Also, the current weather details of the current or some other location can be done through voice support.

4.2.5 SOS Services

SOS - A call for help. The feature holds huge importance in the daily life of a PVI. In a state where PVI wants assistance from the ones known to them, this feature can be a go-to. The feature includes sending SMS, calling, and also notifying a list of persons when required. This list must be added by the user so that, at times of emergency, each added person is notified immediately. A brief explanation of the feature is given below:

- Phone Dialing: This App will facilitate the user making phone calls. Instead of scrolling your contact list to find the person and then making a call to him/her, you just require the name of your saved contact and all you have to do is to say 'CALL <contact_name>'.
- SMS: Using this application, the user can send SMS to any of his saved contacts by just saying 'SMS' provided by the contact's name and a message added for that specific person.
- Emergency Alert: Using this feature, a user can send their live location to the emergency contacts saved initially by them in the app. This will help in alerting people nearby in case of any emergency. The keyword 'EMERGENCY' can be used to activate the alert button

5. EXPERIMENTAL RESULTS

This section demonstrates the proposed system and its working. For this purpose, screen layouts of the different features are given below.

Figure 4. Main screen of HearUs

The user has to install the 'HearUs' application first, to use it daily. To use this application, the user can communicate through voice command to his mobile phone. The different features can be explored by double-tapping at any part of the screen and speak the already defined keyword for each feature as shown in Figure 4. For example, if the user wishes to detect products in a mart, then he/she can double-tap the main screen and speak 'product' out loud. Thus, in the same way, all other features can be accessed.

The features work one at a time based on the keyword. For example - using keyword read would open the camera and start reading text, while using the keyword detect would open the camera and start captioning the image it captures (the captions are generated based on dataset training). The user can speak 'help' if he/she is unsure of different keywords. These keywords are told to the PVI through a demo which automatically runs after installation. The main screen also has a menu consisting of useful features for the ones who are not completely visually impaired.

5.1 Image Detection

Image Detection is used for Path Hurdle detection. As and when the PVI wishes to navigate, this feature can be used by the voice command 'detect'. If any hurdle/object is found on his way, this feature identifies the object and generates the caption of that object which is then told to the person through voice so that he can be made alert regarding this as shown in Figure 5.

Figure 5. Scanning image for path hurdle detection

The response time is approximately 3-5 seconds. This working of this feature is shown below in Figure 5. This feature is implemented using VGG 16 model.

5.2 Barcode Scanning

This feature can be explored by double-tap at any part of the screen in the application and speak the keyword "PRODUCT". On conveniently doing so, a barcode scanner view pops up and on every successful scan, the details of the product are verbally conveyed to the user as shown in Figure 6. If the product details are not available in the database, then a not-found message is also conveyed. The placement of the mobile phone should be in front of the barcode and PVI needs assistance to reach to that shelf or place to buy a particular product which he wants to purchase.

Figure 6. Scanning barcode and product details screen

5.3 Text Recognition

The user can double-tap at any part of the screen in the application and speak the keyword "READ". On conveniently doing so, the camera screen pops up, which on a single tap can read any text subjected to the camera. The text recognition feature is shown in Figure 7.

Figure 7. Scanner view and recognized text screen

5.4 News and Weather Updates

The weather information and news updates can be explored through "weather" and "news" feature. The current weather conditions can be retrieved by the current latitudinal and longitudinal location of the user through the open weather API. With just a double-tap and the corresponding keyword, the application assistant read the top news headlines to the user as shown in Figure 8.

5.5 SOS Services

Keeping safety measures in mind, this feature includes sending SMS, calling saved contacts, and also notifying the persons in their emergency contacts. These emergency contacts are added by some other person. The user, after opening the proposed system, can double-tap and speak voice commands for either "call <contact_name>" or "SMS <message> to <contact_name>" or "emergency".

Figure 9 shows the call feature which is activated when the blind user double taps the main screen and say 'call <person_name>'. While the second screenshot, Figure 10 shows an emergency note with the current location which is sent to the predefined persons when the user speaks 'emergency'. Android Studio and some basic Java and Kotlin libraries are used for implementation.

Figure 8. Live news and weather updates screen

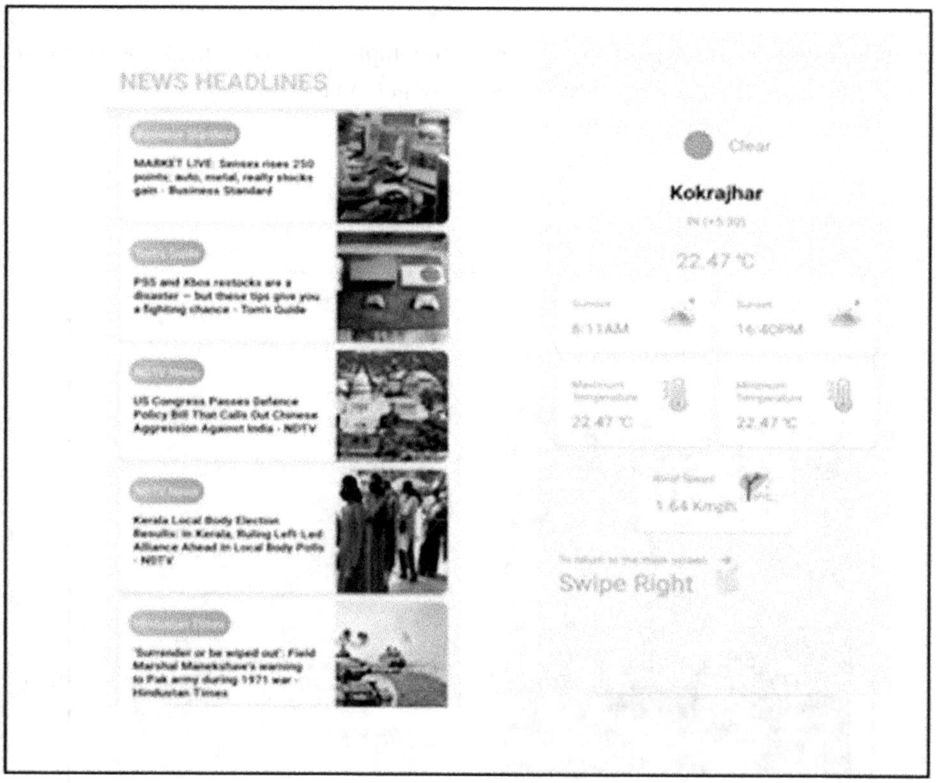

6. PERFORMANCE ANALYSIS

The proposed tool-"HearUs" successfully and effectively performs the feature-based tasks. The tool features Image Captioning, Text Recognition, Barcode Detection, News and Weather Updates, SOS services Modules which are performing well in the application in comparison to other applications being developed or deployed. Features like speech or voice commands, touch, and performing different gestures, make the tool more interactive and user-friendly.

The comparison of our tool with other existing tools based on different features is shown in Figure 11 and Figure 12. After thorough analysis, it was observed that our application has successfully managed to target different varieties of features while many systems were just based on singular functionality.

The technology stacks used for achieving this feature are python programming language, android (kotlin), flask framework, and VGGNet-16 prediction model. VGG16; a computer vision model is one of the best models for detecting objects. As the name suggests, this model contains 16 layers which is a combination of convolutional layer, fully connected layer, and max pool layers. This model is trained on the input images having dimensions (224, 224, 3) and gives an output of (1,1,1000).

We used VGG-16 in the experiment. The default image size was 224x224, which was the same size as the size of the image in the dataset to train and test. Table 2 shows the VGG-16 model summary.

Figure 13 illustrate the VGG-16 model achieved a diagnostic efficiency accuracy of 85.5% on the Flickr8k dataset images. Figure 14 illustrates the evaluation of the loss function for the VGG16 model.

Figure 9. Calling feature

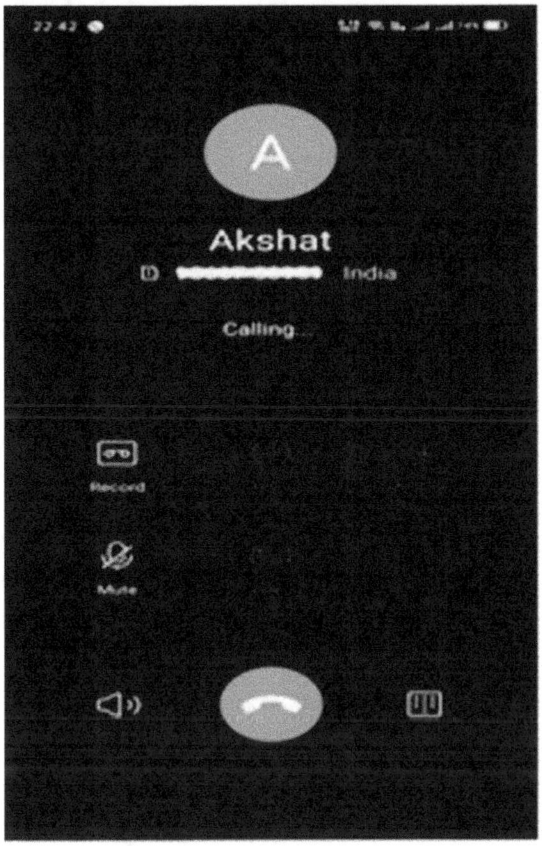

Figure 10. Alert message in emergency

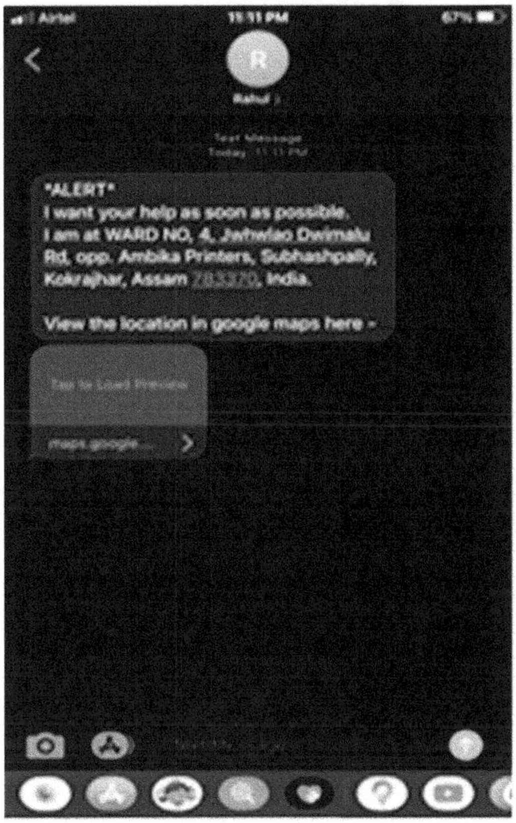

Figure 11. Performance comparison chart

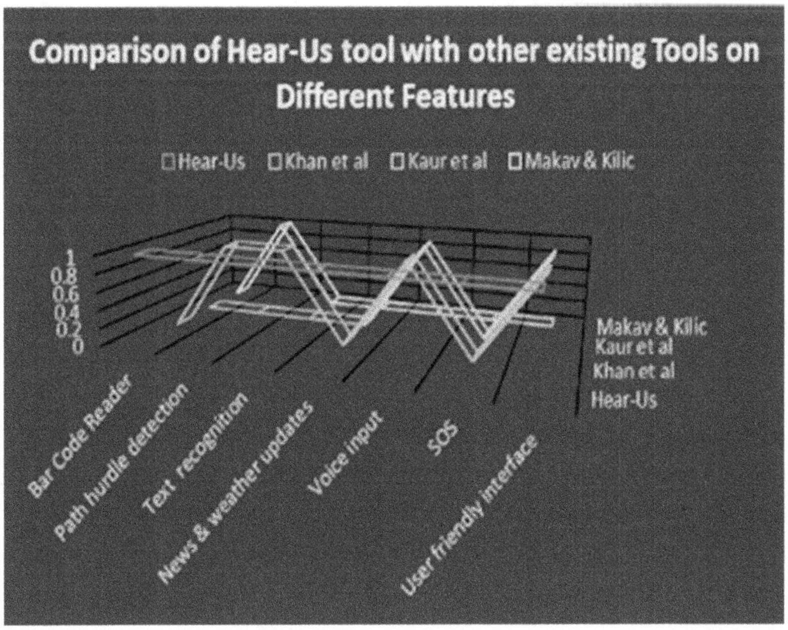

Figure 12. Performance comparison chart

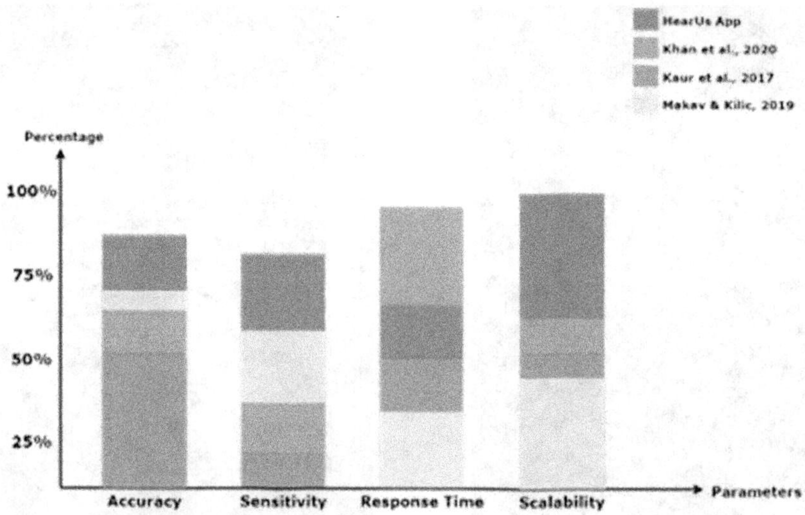

Table 2. Model summary

Layer		Feature Map	Size	Kernel Size	Stride	Activation
Input	Image	1	224 x 224 x 3	-	-	-
1	2 X Convolution	64	224 x 224 x 64	3x3	1	relu
	Max Pooling	64	112 x 112 x 64	3x3	2	relu
3	2 X Convolution	128	112 x 112 x 128	3x3	1	relu
	Max Pooling	128	56 x 56 x 128	3x3	2	relu
5	2 X Convolution	256	56 x 56 x 256	3x3	1	relu
	Max Pooling	256	28 x 28 x 256	3x3	2	relu
7	3 X Convolution	512	28 x 28 x 512	3x3	1	relu
	Max Pooling	512	14 x 14 x 512	3x3	2	relu
10	3 X Convolution	512	14 x 14 x 512	3x3	1	relu
	Max Pooling	512	7 x 7 x 512	3x3	2	relu
13	FC	-	25088	-	-	relu
14	FC	-	4096	-	-	relu
15	FC	-	4096	-	-	relu
Output	FC	-	1000	-	-	Softmax

We have compared our HearUs tool with some of the existing works in this field of research and have presented some observations and stats based on the factors like accuracy, scalability, sensitivity, and response time, using a performance bar chart. One of the main parameters includes accuracy. It measures the correctness of a system. This means how well the features of the application work and provide the expected outcomes. The proposed system is expected to be correct and must deliver the solutions in the most efficient way possible. Our system successfully manages to provide the best accuracy (>=82%) amongst all. As shown in Figure 14, it was observed that the system under Kaur et al., 2017 was not able to provide a better accuracy comparatively (<60%).

Figure 13. Diagnostic efficiency accuracy plot for VGG16

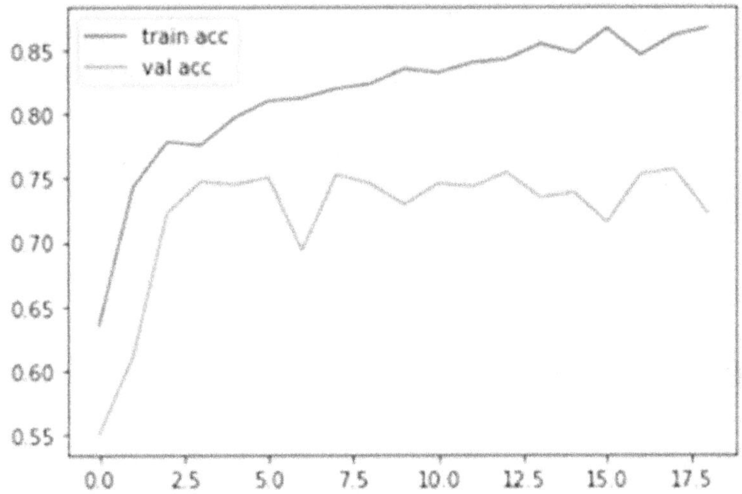

Figure 14. Evaluation of loss function for the VGG16

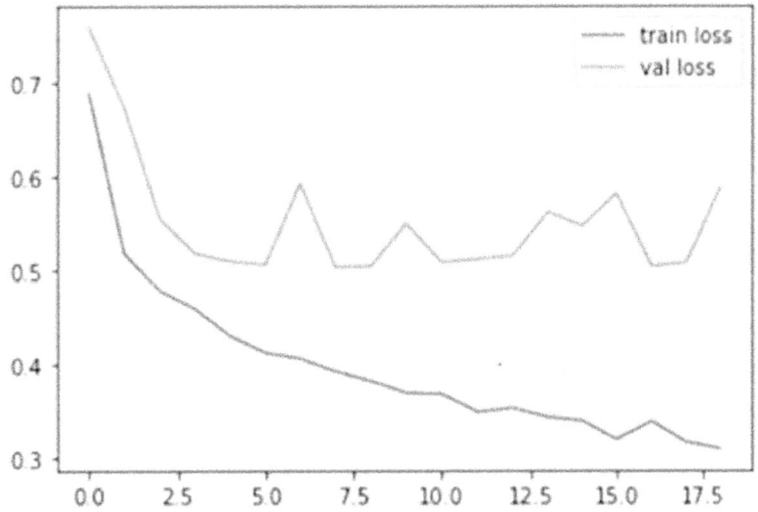

Sensitivity is another important parameter of comparison that marks the responsiveness of a system related to screening touch, swipe, and other gestures, so as to make a system respond to certain stimuli. Our HearUs application achieves the highest sensitivity (>=75%) of all, leading Makav and Kilic, 2019 with (50%) sensitivity and Kaur et al., 2017 has the lowest sensitivity as compared to other applications. The performance comparison chart is shown below in Figure 14. Response Time is one of the main parameters as it is the measure of the time taken by the Application Server to return the results of a request to the user i.e. how quickly you are getting your results or outputs in an application. Considering the response time, the best response timing results were provided by the application having Khan et al., 2017 but this includes the cost of some good hardware equipment involved. As our application is deployed on a server and network calls require a few seconds to provide fair and good results. It is observed that HearUs has the response time as (<=75%) which can be optimized further based on system model training. Then comes scalability which deals with the potential of an application to grow in time and handle more and more requests per minute (RPM) efficiently. Hence, Scalability becomes yet another important parameter for comparing different applications. As per analysis, it was observed that the proposed application has the highest scalability (>90%), leading to all the other applications in the chart above. The stats and parameter percentages presented above for our proposed work can be increased further by applying cost-effective integrations.

7. CONCLUSION AND FUTURE WORK

According to the studies, there are more than 200 million disabled people in the world, and the number is growing by the day. Currently there are many assistive tools are available to aid PVI's but no tool present is with a complete solution for all concerns. In this work we have done an extensive literature review to identify the proposed features. This work proposes "HearUs" an android-based assistive tool incorporating features such as hurdle detection, image detection/ object detection, caption generation, product recognition with description using a bar code scanner, news and weather updates, SOS call, and voice messages/call features. It help PVI's to independently do almost all the basic daily activities and needs, right from the start of day like reading the newspaper, going for a walk, and doing daily shopping for daily household items from even the mart to the extent of handling any emergency, hence making a PVI's life easier, comfortable and safe. The VGGNet-16 prediction model demonstrated a great promise in detecting objects in the environment with high accuracy of 85.5%. HearUs can even send an emergency alert by using reverse Geocoding to provide the exact location of the user to any saved emergency contact, allowing them to receive immediate assistance. Furthermore, all the HearUs' features are successfully developed and tested. The accuracy, scalability, sensitivity, and response time of the HearUs app has been compared to other state-of-the-art tools. In the future, the image detection system can be improved with bilingual or multi-lingual features to attract more PVI customers. Also, to increase its scalability, the system can be deployed using hardware or IoT based solutions. The features like focusing on entertainment functionality can be added considered in future research.

REFERENCES

Azmi, N., Maryono, D., & Yuana, R. (2017, June). Development of an Android-based Learning Media Application for Visually Impaired Students. *Indonesian Journal of Informatics Education, 1*(1), 61–68. doi:10.20961/ijie.v1i1.11796

Boldu, R., Dancu, A., Matthies, D. J. C., Buddhika, T., Siriwardhana, S., & Nanayakkara, S. Finger-Reader2.0: Designing and Evaluating a Wearable Finger-Worn Camera to Assist People with Visual Impairments while Shopping. In *Proc. of IMWUT'18*. ACM. 10.1145/3264904

Boldu, R., Matthies, D. J. C., Zhang, H., & Nanayakkara, S. 2020. AiSee: An Assistive Wearable Device to Support Visually Impaired Grocery Shoppers. *Proc. ACM Interact. Mob. Wearable Ubiquitous Technol.* 10.1145/3432196

Doshi, P., Shirke, Y., Hegde, T., & Dhanvij, P. (2018). Text Reader for Visually Impaired Using Google Cloud Vision API. *International Journal Of Innovative Research In Technology*, *4*(12), 863–873.

Fan, C., & Crandall, D. J. (2016). DeepDiary: Automatic caption generation for lifelogging image streams. *European Conference on Computer Vision*, 459–473.

Foo. (2009). *Grocery Shopping Assistant for the Blind / Visually Impaired.* http://grozi.calit2.net/files/TIESGroZiSu09.pdf

Hill, D. R., & Grieb, C. (1988, March-April). Substitution for a restricted visual channel in multimodal computer-human dialogue. *IEEE Transactions on Systems, Man, and Cybernetics*, *18*(2), 285–304. doi:10.1109/21.3467

Kaur, P., Ganore, M., Doiphode, R., Garud, A., & Ghuge, T. (2017). *Be My Eyes: Android App for visually impaired people.* Research Gate. doi:10.13140/RG.2.2.12307.48164

Khan, M. A., Paul, P., Rashid, M., Hossain, M., & Ahad, M. A. R. (2020). An AI-Based Visual Aid With Integrated Reading Assistant for the Completely Blind. *IEEE Transactions on Human-Machine Systems*, *50*(6), 507–517. doi:10.1109/THMS.2020.3027534

Kinghorn, P., Zhang, L., & Shao, L. (2018). A region-based image caption generator with refined descriptions. *Neurocomputing*, *272*, 416–424. doi:10.1016/j.neucom.2017.07.014

Koustubh. (2018). *ResNet, AlexNet, VGGNet, Inception: Understanding Various Architectures of Convolutional Networks.* Retrieved from https://cv-tricks.com/cnn/understand-resnet-alexnet-vgginception/

Krishnan, R. S., Narayanan, K. L., Murali, S. M., Sangeetha, A., Sankar Ram, C. R., & Robinson, Y. H. (2021). IoT based Blind People Monitoring System for Visually Impaired Care Homes. *2021 5th International Conference on Trends in Electronics and Informatics (ICOEI)*, 505-509. 10.1109/ICOEI51242.2021.9452924

Kumar, A., Krishnamurthi, R., Bhatia, S., Kaushik, K., Ahuja, N. J., Nayyar, A., & Masud, M. (2021). Blended learning tools and practices: A comprehensive analysis. *IEEE Access : Practical Innovations, Open Solutions*, *9*, 85151–85197. doi:10.1109/ACCESS.2021.3085844

Kuriakose, B., Shrestha, R., & Sandnes, F. E. (2022). Tools and technologies for blind and visually impaired navigation support: A review. *IETE Technical Review*, *39*(1), 3–18. doi:10.1080/02564602.2020.1819893

Lee, S., Chien, W. Y., Hanrahan, B. V., Rosson, M. B., & Carroll, J. M. (2017). Reaching Out: Investigating Different Modalities to Help People with Visual Impairments Acquire Items. In *Proceedings of the 19th International ACM SIGACCESS Conference on Computers and Accessibility - ASSETS '17*. ACM Press. 10.1145/3132525.3134817

Makav, B., & Kılıc, V. (2019). Smartphone-based Image Captioning for Visually and Hearing Impaired. *11th International Conference on Electrical and Electronics Engineering*, 950-953, 10.23919/ELECO47770.2019.8990395

Manjari, K., Verma, M., & Singal, G. (2020). A survey on assistive technology for visually impaired. *Internet of Things*, *11*, 100188. doi:10.1016/j.iot.2020.100188

Muhammad, U., Wang, W., Chattha, S. P., & Ali, S. (2018). Pre-trained VGGNet Architecture for Remote-Sensing Image Scene Classification. *2018 24th International Conference on Pattern Recognition (ICPR)*, 1622-1627. 10.1109/ICPR.2018.8545591

Nicholson, J., Kulyukin, V., & Coster, D. (2009). ShopTalk: Independent blind shopping through verbal route directions and barcode scans. *The Open Rehabilitation Journal*, *2*(1), 11–23. doi:10.2174/1874943700902010011

Norhashimah., M., S. (2013). Barcode Recognition System. *International Journal of Emerging Trends & Technology in Computer Science, 2*, 1-6.

Proulx, M. (n.d.). *University of Bath: How Blind People See The World*. Retrieved from https://www.bath.ac.uk/case-studies/how-blind-people-see-the-world/

Saha, S. S., Hagawane, D. S., Kulkarni, P. C., Dhamane, S. R., & Agrawal, S. A. (2013). Mobile Based Text Detection and Extraction from an Image. *International Journal of Emerging Technology and Advanced Engineering, 3*(11), 79-82.

Senjam, S. (2019). Assistive Technology for People with Visual Loss. *Delhi Journal of Ophthalmology, 30*(2).

Staniūtė, R., & Šešok, D. (2019). A Systematic Literature Review on Image Captioning. *Applied Sciences (Basel, Switzerland)*, *9*(10), 2024. doi:10.3390/app9102024

Szpiro, S., Zhao, Y., & Azenkot, S. (2016). Finding a store, searching for a product: a study of daily challenges of low vision people. In *Proceedings of the 2016 ACM International Joint Conference on Pervasive and Ubiquitous Computing*. ACM. 10.1145/2971648.2971723

Tatiraju, R. (2020). *Speech-to-text and Text-to-speech with Android*. Retrieved from https://medium.com/@rtficial/speech-to-text-and-text-to-speech-with-android-85758ff0f6d3

Vanderheiden, G. C. (1996). Use of audio-haptic interface techniques to allow nonvisual access to touchscreen appliances. *Human Factors and Ergonomics Society Annual Meeting, 40*(24), 1266–1266. 10.1177/154193129604002430

Zientara, Lee, Smith, Brenner, Itti, Rosson, Carroll, Irick, & Narayanan. (2017). *Third Eye: A Shopping Assistant for the Visually Impaired*. doi:10.1109/MC.2017.36

Chapter 11
Concept and Administration for Developing Special Education Using AI

Santosh Kumar
Vishwakarma Institute of Information Technology, India

Vivek D. Patil
Vishwakarma Institute of Information Technology, India

Parikshit N. Mahalle
Vishwakarma Institute of Information Technology, India

Vishal Meshram
https://orcid.org/0000-0001-9950-584X
Vishwakarma Institute of Information Technology, India

ABSTRACT

The chapter aims to demystify AI technologies and their role in enhancing learning experiences and support services for students with disabilities and diverse learning needs. The chapter identifies challenges in implementing AI effectively and advocates for ethical considerations and equitable access to AI-based solutions. It showcases how AI can create personalized learning pathways, adaptive interventions, and data-driven decision-making in special education. The chapter introduces innovative AI applications, including personalized learning platforms and assistive technologies, highlighting the role of data-driven approaches in improving educational outcomes. It emphasizes AI's transformative potential in fostering inclusive and effective special education practices, serving as a valuable resource for educators, administrators, policymakers, and researchers.

DOI: 10.4018/979-8-3693-0378-8.ch011

INTRODUCTION

Overview of the Chapter

The field of special education has long been dedicated to providing tailored support and services to students with diverse learning needs, ensuring they have equal opportunities to thrive academically and personally. As technology continues to advance, one of the most promising and transformative developments in the educational landscape is the integration of artificial intelligence (AI) in special education.

AI has the potential to revolutionize how educators, administrators, and policymakers approach special education by offering personalized, data-driven, and inclusive educational practices. By harnessing AI technologies, educators can gain valuable insights into students' learning patterns, preferences, and challenges, enabling them to create tailored interventions and support systems. Furthermore, AI can facilitate early detection of learning difficulties, allowing educators to intervene proactively and enhance students' academic outcomes.

Special education is a field that focuses on providing education and support to students with special needs. These students may have disabilities such as autism, dyslexia, or ADHD, which can make it challenging for them to learn in a traditional classroom setting. The use of artificial intelligence (AI) technologies in special education has the potential to transform the way educators support these students. This book chapter will explore the concept and administration for developing special education using AI.

The concept of developing special education using AI involves using AI technologies to support students with special needs. This can include adaptive learning software, speech recognition, natural language processing, and personalized learning programs. AI-based solutions can help identify the unique needs of each student, define goals and objectives, choose the right AI tools, and provide ongoing support to teachers and support staff.

The administration of developing special education using AI involves several key steps. The first step is to develop a plan for implementing the AI-based solution. This may involve identifying the roles and responsibilities of teachers and support staff, establishing protocols for data collection and analysis, and developing a timeline for implementation. The second step is to implement the AI-based solution. This may involve training teachers and support staff on how to use the AI tools, integrating the AI solution with existing systems, and collecting data on student performance. The third step is to monitor and evaluate the effectiveness of the AI-based solution. This may involve analyzing data to identify trends and patterns in student performance, conducting surveys to gather feedback from teachers and support staff, and making adjustments to the AI solution as needed.

The purpose of this book chapter is to provide an overview of the concept and administration for developing special education using AI. The chapter will begin by defining AI and exploring the different AI-based solutions that can be used in special education. The benefits of using AI in special education will also be discussed. The administration for developing special education using AI will be explored in detail, including identifying the unique needs of each student, defining goals and objectives, choosing the right AI tools, and providing professional development to educators. The methodology and framework for developing AI-based solutions for special education will also be discussed, including identifying the problem, collecting relevant data, algorithm development, integration with existing systems, and pilot testing. Case studies on successful implementation of AI in special education will be presented, along with ethical considerations in developing special education using AI. Finally, the chapter will conclude by summarizing the key points and discussing future directions for AI-based solutions in special education and their implications for policy and practice.

Background and Related Work

Sahlaoui, H., Nayyar, A., Agoujil, S., & Jaber, M. M. (2021) propose an AI-based approach to predict students' academic performance and gain insights into the factors contributing to their achievements.

The study explores how ensemble models, a combination of multiple machine learning algorithms, can be used to predict student performance accurately. It highlights the importance of leveraging AI technologies to analyze various academic data, such as grades, attendance, and engagement, to predict future outcomes and identify students at risk of falling behind.

Additionally, the edited volume might include research and case studies on the successful implementation of AI in distance learning (Szyrocka et al., 2023), including its impact on educational outcomes, student engagement, and personalized support. It could also delve into the administrative aspects of integrating AI in distance learning environments for special education, such as the professional development of educators, planning and implementation of AI-based solutions, and monitoring of their effectiveness.

Kukkar et al. (2023) likely presents a study that examines the relationship between emotional wellbeing, engagement, and academic performance. It explores how AI algorithms can process data related to students' emotional responses, such as sentiment analysis of their interactions and activities on e-learning platforms. The findings may highlight correlations between emotional states, learning engagement, and academic outcomes.

In a series of research papers exploring the integration of artificial intelligence (AI) in special education, several authors highlight its potential to revolutionize the field. Hlavacs and Savina (2021) emphasize the need for collaboration between researchers and practitioners to fully harness AI's potential. They discuss AI-based interventions like adaptive learning platforms and data-driven decision-making, offering promising avenues for personalized support to students with diverse learning needs.

Bonvicini and Qi (2020) delve into the current applications and future role of AI in special education. They recognize the importance of AI technologies, such as natural language processing and machine learning, in facilitating communication support and early detection of learning difficulties, fostering inclusive learning environments.

Ferdig and Archambault (2018) discuss the opportunities and challenges associated with integrating AI in special education. They identify personalized learning pathways and data analytics as promising opportunities, while addressing ethical considerations and the need for teacher professional development as essential challenges.

Choi and Kim (2021) conduct a comprehensive literature review on the integration of technology and AI in special education. They find that AI has the potential to promote personalized learning, enhance student engagement, and support data-driven decision-making, resulting in improved educational outcomes.

McNamara (2019) focuses on machine learning applications in special education, particularly in intelligent tutoring systems. The paper reveals opportunities for AI to provide tailored interventions based on individual student needs, while also highlighting potential challenges related to data privacy.

Loukina and Flor (2019) explore the opportunities and challenges of leveraging AI to enhance special education services. They emphasize AI's role in creating inclusive and personalized learning environments, while also emphasizing the importance of addressing ethical considerations, data security, and AI literacy among educators.

Reich (2020) investigates the various applications of AI in special education and its potential to support diverse learners. The paper highlights opportunities for AI to enhance teacher expertise and student engagement while acknowledging and addressing challenges related to data privacy and algorithmic bias.

Together, these research papers contribute to the growing understanding of AI's transformative potential in special education. They shed light on opportunities for personalized support, data-driven decision-making, and inclusive learning environments while acknowledging the need to navigate ethical and practical challenges. As the field continues to evolve, these studies provide valuable insights for educators, administrators, and policymakers in leveraging AI to benefit students with diverse learning needs.

Importance of Developing Special Education Using AI

The importance of developing special education using AI lies in its potential to improve the quality of education and support provided to students with special needs. AI-based solutions can provide personalized and targeted support to each student, helping them to achieve their full potential and promoting inclusivity and equity in education. The use of AI can also help to address the shortage of trained educators and support staff in the special education field, reduce the workload and stress of educators and support staff, and increase the engagement and motivation of students with special needs. Overall, the development of special education using AI has the potential to revolutionize the way we support and educate students with special needs, leading to better outcomes and a more inclusive and equitable society.

The development of special education using AI is of great importance for several reasons. First, it has the potential to improve the learning outcomes and academic performance of students with special needs. AI-based solutions can help teachers and support staff to better understand the unique needs of each student and provide personalized support and learning experiences.

Second, AI-based solutions can help to address the shortage of trained educators and support staff in the special education field. With the help of AI tools, teachers and support staff can be more effective and efficient in their work, providing high-quality education and support to a greater number of students.

Third, the use of AI in special education can help to reduce the workload and stress of educators and support staff. With AI tools handling routine tasks such as grading, data analysis, and feedback, teachers and support staff can focus on more creative and engaging activities, improving the overall quality of education.

Fourth, the development of special education using AI can help to promote inclusivity and equity in education. AI-based solutions can help to identify and address biases in teaching and learning, ensuring that all students have equal access to high-quality education and support. Figure 1 illustrates the integration of AI into the domain of special education.

Figure 1. Integrating artificial intelligence (AI) into the domain of special education

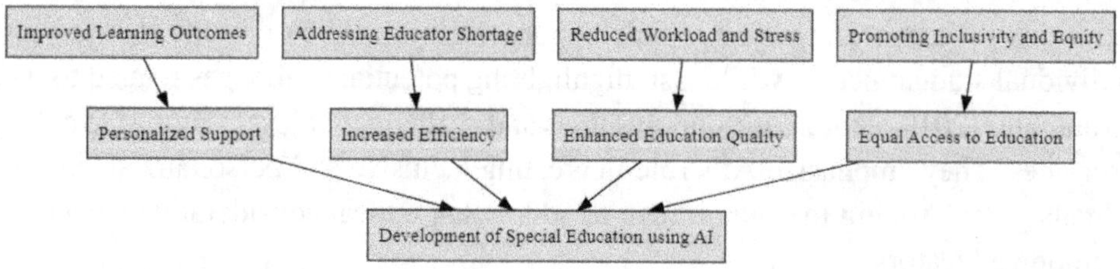

The flowchart presented above serves to underscore the significance of integrating artificial intelligence (AI) into the domain of special education, elucidating the manifold advantages it offers to both students with special needs and educators. Let's delve into each component of the diagram:

Improved Learning Outcomes: The flowchart aptly highlights that by embracing AI-based solutions in special education, a marked enhancement in learning outcomes for students with special needs can be achieved. These AI-driven solutions proffer personalized support and tailored learning experiences, catering to the distinctive requirements of each student. The adaptability of AI to individual learning styles and paces fosters heightened student engagement and motivation, culminating in superior academic performance and learning achievements.

Addressing Educator Shortage: Within the realm of special education, the scarcity of trained educators and support staff poses a challenge. The flowchart cogently posits that AI-based solutions can effectively address this issue by rendering teachers and support staff more proficient and productive in their roles. By leveraging AI tools, educators can streamline routine tasks like grading and data analysis, enabling them to devote more time to providing high-quality education and support to a larger cohort of students.

Reduced Workload and Stress: The integration of AI in special education promises to significantly alleviate the workload and stress endured by educators and support staff. The automation capabilities of AI-driven tools expedite time-consuming tasks, empowering teachers to devote greater attention to crafting creative and captivating activities that enrich the learning experience. Consequently, educators can cultivate a positive and supportive learning environment for students with special needs, fostering an overall elevation in the quality of education.

Promoting Inclusivity and Equity: The flowchart astutely underscores the potential of AI-based solutions to promote inclusivity and equity in education. Through the utilization of AI, educators can identify and rectify biases in teaching and learning methodologies, ensuring that all students, irrespective of their backgrounds or abilities, gain equitable access to high-quality education and support. This fosters an all-embracing educational milieu wherein every student is empowered to flourish.

In conclusion, the flowchart compellingly accentuates the transformative impact of AI on special education. With its capacity to provide personalized support, address educator shortages, reduce workload, and champion inclusivity, AI-based solutions herald a promising paradigm shift in how we nurture and educate students with special needs. This, in turn, bears the potential to yield superior learning outcomes and foster greater equity in education for all students. The visual representation of the diagram effectively communicates the core imperatives for developing special education using AI and vividly illustrates the potential benefits that can be harnessed through its successful implementation.

Overall, the development of special education using AI has the potential to revolutionize the way we support and educate students with special needs, leading to better outcomes and greater equity in education.

Objectives of the Chapter

The primary objective of the book chapter "Concept and Administration for Developing Special Education using AI" is to offer a comprehensive exploration of the integration of artificial intelligence (AI) in special education. The chapter aims to achieve the following objectives:

Establishing a Clear Understanding of AI in Special Education: The chapter seeks to provide readers with a solid grasp of AI's theoretical foundations and its potential applications in special education. It aims to demystify AI technologies and their role in enhancing learning experiences and support services for students with disabilities and diverse learning needs.

Identifying Challenges and Ensuring Effective Implementation: Through insightful analysis, the chapter addresses the challenges in effectively implementing AI in special education. It examines potential hurdles and offers strategies to overcome them, allowing educators, administrators, and policymakers to make informed decisions.

Emphasizing Ethical Considerations and Equitable Access: The chapter highlights the significance of ethical considerations in AI-assisted special education. It advocates for equitable access to AI-based solutions for all students, ensuring that technology-driven practices promote inclusivity and diversity.

Strategically Creating Personalized Learning Pathways: One of the central objectives is to showcase how AI can strategically create personalized learning pathways for students with diverse needs. The chapter explores adaptive interventions and demonstrates how AI can tailor education to individual strengths and weaknesses.

Utilizing Data-Driven Decision-Making: The chapter underscores the role of data-driven approaches in special education. It presents how AI can harness data to inform decision-making processes, enabling educators and administrators to make evidence-based choices that optimize educational outcomes.

Exploring Innovative AI Applications: Through case studies and examples, the chapter introduces innovative AI applications in special education. It presents personalized learning platforms and assistive technologies that empower students and educators in the learning process.

Enabling Inclusive and Effective Special Education Practices: The chapter highlights AI's transformative potential in fostering inclusive and effective special education practices. By showcasing AI's capabilities, it empowers stakeholders to utilize technology for the benefit of students with diverse learning needs.

Overall, the chapter aims to provide a comprehensive and informed perspective on AI's integration in special education. It serves as a valuable resource for educators, administrators, policymakers, and researchers, inspiring them to embrace AI's potential in creating a more personalized, inclusive, and data-driven educational environment for all students.

Organization of the Chapter

In this chapter, the concept of developing special education using AI is explored in depth. The section begins by delving into the definition and capabilities of AI, setting the foundation for its application in special education. Various AI applications in this context, such as adaptive learning platforms, natural language processing for communication support, and emotional well-being tools, are discussed, emphasizing the benefits they bring, including personalized learning experiences and early detection of learning difficulties.

Moving on to the administration aspect, the chapter highlights the significance of a robust administrative framework for effectively implementing AI in special education. Key steps are outlined, starting with the identification of unique student needs and defining clear goals and objectives. The selection of suitable AI tools and providing professional development to educators are addressed to ensure successful integration. Moreover, the planning and seamless implementation of AI-based solutions, alongside the essential monitoring and evaluation of their effectiveness, are crucial considerations for administrators.

The methodology and framework for AI-based solutions are presented as building blocks upon the administrative foundation. The process of identifying problems, collecting relevant data, and developing algorithms for AI analysis is thoroughly explored. Integration with existing systems is discussed, and the importance of pilot testing to refine AI solutions before full-scale implementation is highlighted.

To illustrate the real-world impact of AI in special education, case studies of successful AI implementations are presented. These examples showcase how AI positively influences student learning outcomes and supports the academic journey of students with diverse learning needs. Challenges and limitations faced during the implementation of AI-based solutions are candidly addressed, offering insights for future developments.

The ethical considerations of AI in special education are emphasized in a dedicated section. Privacy and security concerns related to data collection and usage are discussed, and strategies to address potential biases in AI algorithms are explored. The aim is to ensure equitable access to AI-based solutions and uphold ethical practices.

The chapter concludes by recapping the key points discussed throughout. The significance of developing special education using AI to enhance learning outcomes and provide personalized support is underscored. Future directions for AI-based solutions in special education are outlined, along with their potential implications for policy and practice. The chapter calls for continued research, collaboration, and ethical considerations to harness AI's transformative potential positively in the field of special education.

CONCEPT OF DEVELOPING SPECIAL EDUCATION USING AI

Definition of AI

AI stands for Artificial Intelligence, which is a branch of computer science that focuses on developing intelligent machines that can perform tasks that typically require human intelligence. AI involves developing algorithms and computer programs that can analyze data, learn from experience, and make decisions and predictions based on that learning. The goal of AI is to create machines that can reason, perceive, understand natural language, and make decisions that are typically associated with human intelligence. Examples of AI include chatbots, autonomous vehicles, facial recognition technology, and predictive analytics.

AI-Based Solutions for Special Education

AI-based solutions for special education are designed to provide personalized and targeted support to students with special needs. Here are some examples of AI-based solutions for special education:

- Adaptive learning platforms: These platforms use AI algorithms to analyze student performance data and adapt the learning experience to meet the individual needs of each student. Adaptive learning platforms can adjust the difficulty level of assignments and assessments, provide personalized feedback, and offer additional resources and support as needed.
- Speech recognition and natural language processing tools: These tools can help students with communication disorders to improve their speech and language skills. Speech recognition tools can transcribe speech into text, provide real-time feedback on pronunciation, and generate speech for non-verbal students. Natural language processing tools can help students to improve their grammar, syntax, and vocabulary skills.

- Assistive technology: AI-powered assistive technology can help students with special needs to access educational materials and tools. For example, screen readers and text-to-speech tools can help students with visual impairments to read text, while augmented and virtual reality tools can provide interactive and engaging learning experiences.
- Data analysis and prediction tools: AI-based data analysis and prediction tools can help teachers and support staff to identify students who may need additional support, track progress, and make data-driven decisions about instructional strategies. These tools can also help to identify patterns and trends in student data, enabling educators to make informed decisions about resource allocation and program development.

Overall, AI-based solutions for special education have the potential to improve learning outcomes, increase engagement and motivation, and promote inclusivity and equity in education for students with special needs.

Benefits of Using AI in Special Education

In recent years, artificial intelligence (AI) has been increasingly used in various fields, including education. AI-based solutions have the potential to transform traditional teaching methods, and can provide significant benefits to students with special needs. In the field of special education, the use of AI-based solutions has been gaining momentum, as it can provide personalized and targeted support to students with unique learning requirements.

The benefits of using AI in special education are numerous and significant. AI-based solutions can provide personalized learning experiences, improve communication, make learning more accessible, support data-driven decision making, and increase efficiency for educators and support staff.

In this section, we will explore the benefits of using AI in special education in greater detail, highlighting the potential impact of AI-based solutions on learning outcomes and student engagement. We will examine the different types of AI-based solutions that are currently available for special education, and discuss how these solutions can be implemented in the classroom to support students with special needs and the same is depicted in Figure 2.

The presented flow chart demonstrates the myriad benefits of incorporating artificial intelligence (AI) in special education. By delineating various AI-based solutions, it highlights the advantages they offer in supporting students with diverse learning needs. Firstly, "Personalized Learning" using AI allows for tailored experiences, accommodating individual learning styles, pacing, and abilities, thereby leading to "Better Learning Outcomes." AI's "Improved Communication" capabilities empower students with communication disorders to enhance their language skills through real-time feedback on pronunciation, grammar, and syntax. Additionally, AI enables "Support for Non-Verbal Students" by generating speech, facilitating effective communication and social skills development.

In the realm of "Accessible Learning," AI-driven assistive technology, like "Screen Readers and Text-to-Speech," enables visually impaired students to access educational materials effectively. Moreover, "Augmented and Virtual Reality Tools" based on AI create interactive and immersive learning experiences, enhancing engagement and accessibility for students with special needs. AI's potential in "Data-driven Decision Making" is evident as it aids in "Identifying Students Needing Support" by analyzing data, allowing educators to provide timely interventions and personalized assistance. "Progress Tracking" empowers educators to monitor academic performance effectively, aiding informed decision-making for addressing individual learning needs.

Figure 2. Benefits of incorporating artificial intelligence (AI) in special education

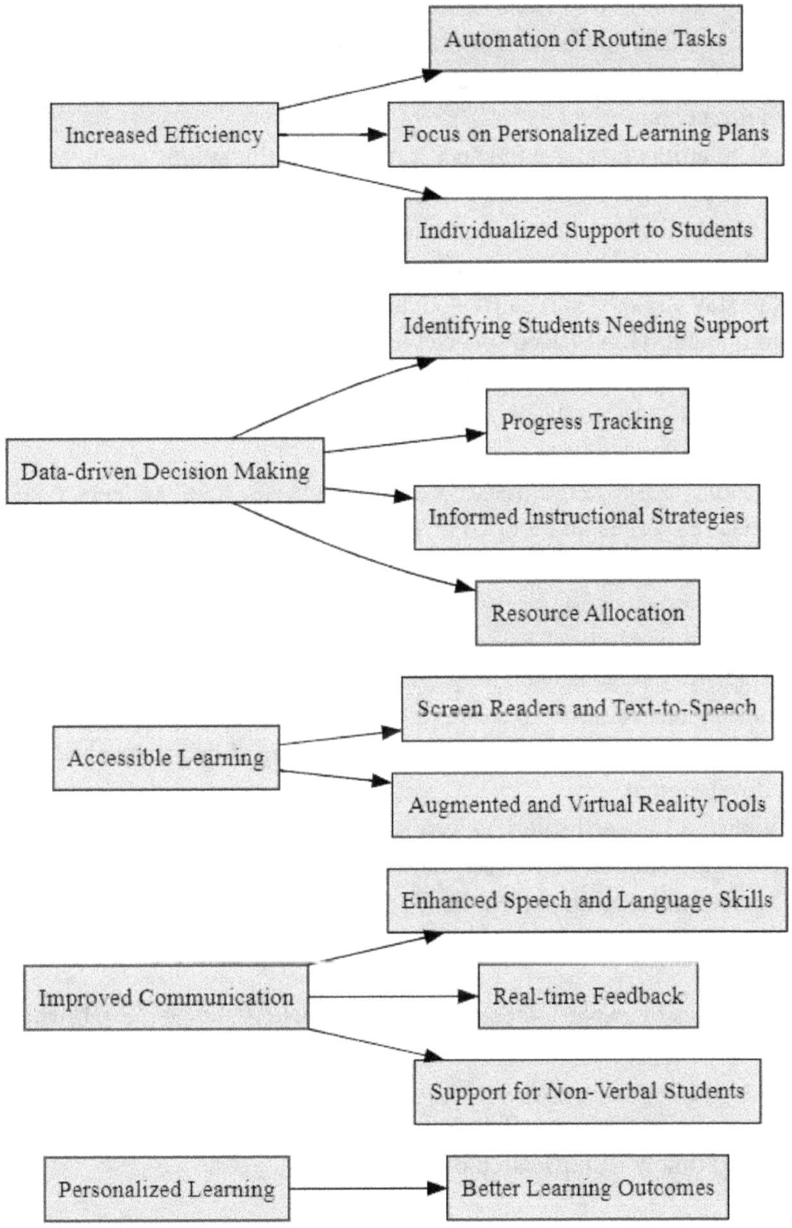

Through "Informed Instructional Strategies," AI-generated data insights inform educators about the most effective teaching methods, further optimizing learning outcomes. AI also assists in "Resource Allocation," identifying patterns and trends in student data, leading to more efficient allocation of resources tailored to meet specific needs. The flow chart illustrates AI's "Increased Efficiency" through "Automation of Routine Tasks," freeing up time for educators to focus on "Personalized Learning Plans" for each student, ensuring individualized attention. Lastly, AI's efficiency enables educators to provide "Individualized Support to Students," fostering a supportive educational environment for students with diverse needs.

The flow chart demonstrates that AI-based solutions in special education bring numerous benefits, including personalized learning experiences, improved communication skills, accessibility to learning materials, data-driven decision-making, and increased efficiency for educators. These advantages collectively contribute to creating an inclusive and supportive educational ecosystem for students with unique learning requirements.

There are several benefits of using AI in special education, including:

- Personalized learning: AI-based solutions can adapt to each student's unique learning style, pace, and level of ability, providing customized support and feedback. This personalized approach can help students to stay engaged and motivated, and can lead to better learning outcomes.
- Improved communication: AI-based speech recognition and natural language processing tools can help students with communication disorders to improve their speech and language skills. These tools can provide real-time feedback on pronunciation, grammar, and syntax, and can even generate speech for non-verbal students.
- Accessible learning: AI-powered assistive technology can help students with special needs to access educational materials and tools. For example, screen readers and text-to-speech tools can help students with visual impairments to read text, while augmented and virtual reality tools can provide interactive and engaging learning experiences.
- Data-driven decision making: AI-based data analysis and prediction tools can help teachers and support staff to identify students who may need additional support, track progress, and make data-driven decisions about instructional strategies. These tools can also help to identify patterns and trends in student data, enabling educators to make informed decisions about resource allocation and program development.
- Increased efficiency: AI-based solutions can help to automate routine tasks and reduce the workload of educators and support staff. This can free up time and resources to focus on more meaningful tasks, such as developing personalized learning plans and providing individualized support to students.

The section commences by exploring the meaning and potential of AI, establishing its relevance in the realm of special education. It examines diverse AI applications tailored to this field, including adaptive learning systems, communication aid through natural language processing, and tools for emotional well-being. The discussion underscores the advantages of these applications, including personalized learning encounters and timely identification of learning challenges.

ADMINISTRATION FOR DEVELOPING SPECIAL EDUCATION USING AI

The administration of special education programs is a critical component of ensuring that students with special needs receive the appropriate support and resources to achieve their full potential. In recent years, the use of AI-based solutions has emerged as a promising approach for improving the administration of special education programs. In this section, we will provide an overview of the key considerations and strategies for developing and implementing AI-based solutions for special education administration.

Identifying the Unique Needs of Each Student

The figures 3 and 4 represent a high-level overview of the system architecture for a special education system that utilizes AI-based solutions for identifying student needs and adapting learning experiences. The system includes several main components, including Data Storage, Security, User Interfaces, and AI, which are integrated together to create a cohesive system.

The Data Storage component includes a Database that stores student data and learning progress, as well as Cloud Storage that provides scalability and backups for student data. The Security component includes measures such as Authentication, Encryption, and Logging to protect student data from unauthorized access.

The User Interfaces component includes several subcomponents, including Dashboard, Reporting, and Communication, which enable educators and support staff to access and interact with the system.

Finally, the main Special Education System component brings together all of the subcomponents and interactions between them, allowing for AI-based solutions to access and store student data, while also protecting that data using the Security measures in place.

Defining Goals and Objectives

The goal of developing a special education system using AI is to provide personalized and effective learning experiences to students with special needs. The system should be designed to identify each student's unique learning style and adapt the learning experience accordingly. The objective of the system is to improve the student's academic performance and overall well-being by providing a customized and inclusive learning environment.

Figure 3. Identification process of unique needs of students

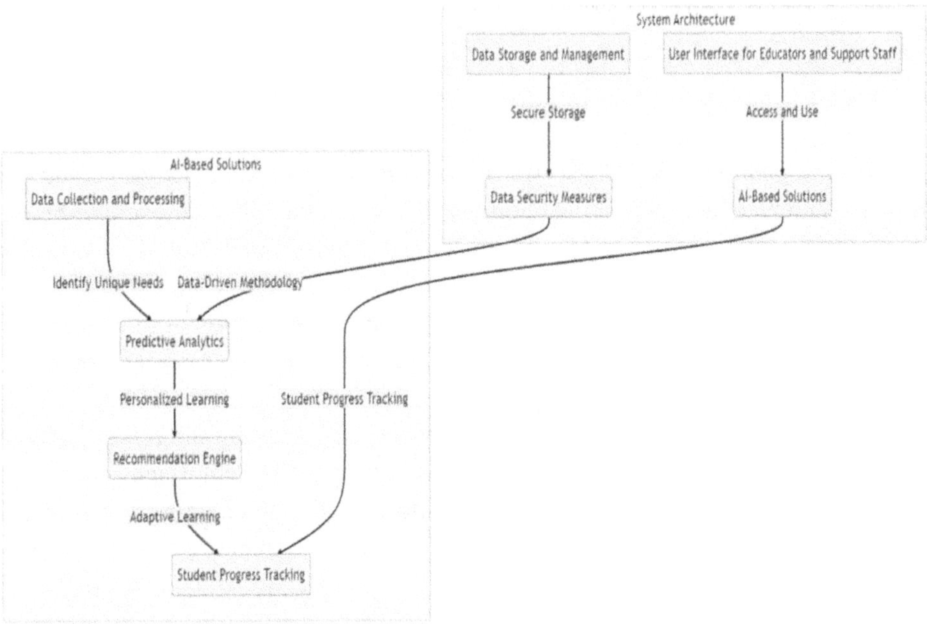

Figure 4. AI-based solutions

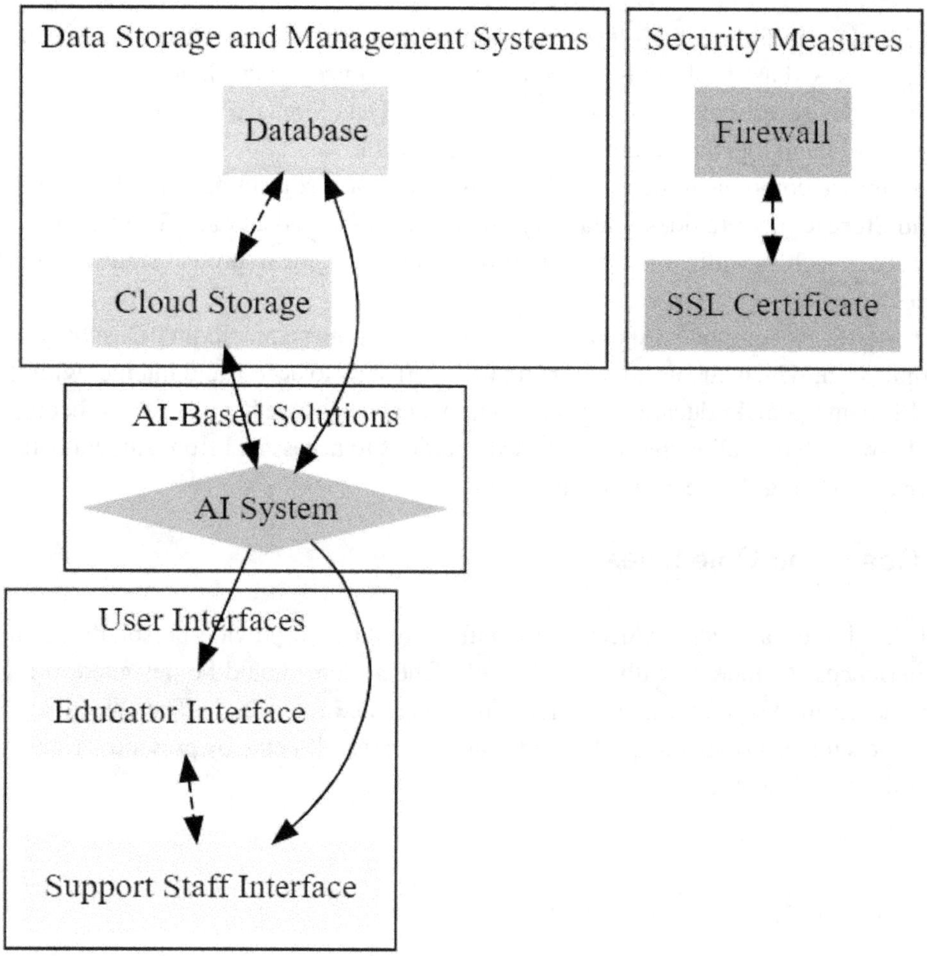

To achieve this goal, the system architecture must be designed with the following objectives in mind:

- *Data storage and management*: The system should have a robust data storage and management system that securely stores student data and learning progress. This data should be easily accessible to educators and support staff to monitor student progress and adapt the learning experience as needed.
- *Security measures*: The system should have strong security measures in place to protect student data from unauthorized access or breaches. This includes measures such as user authentication, encryption of sensitive data, and logging of system activity.
- *User interfaces:* The system should have intuitive and user-friendly interfaces for educators and support staff to access student data and AI-based solutions. The interfaces should provide relevant information to enable educators to make informed decisions about the student's learning experience.

- *AI-based solutions:* The system should integrate AI-based solutions to identify student needs and adapt the learning experience accordingly. The AI should be able to analyze student data and provide personalized recommendations to educators and support staff.

By achieving these objectives, the special education system using AI can create a positive learning experience for students with special needs, improving their academic performance and overall well-being.

Choosing the Right AI Tools

Choosing the right AI tools is crucial for the success of any special education system that relies on AI technologies. Here are some reasons why it is important to select the appropriate AI tools:

- Efficiency and Effectiveness: The right AI tools can significantly improve the efficiency and effectiveness of special education systems. AI tools can automate tedious and repetitive tasks, allowing educators and support staff to focus on more important tasks such as developing personalized learning plans for students with special needs.
- Customization: Special education systems need to be customizable to meet the unique needs of each student. The right AI tools can be customized to adapt to different learning styles and disabilities, allowing for a more personalized learning experience.
- Accuracy and Reliability: AI tools that are accurate and reliable can provide educators and support staff with valuable insights into student progress and learning needs. This can help identify areas where students need additional support, and improve the overall quality of education.
- Data Security: Special education systems often deal with sensitive student data that needs to be protected. The right AI tools can ensure that student data is secure by implementing measures such as encryption and secure access controls.
- Cost-Effective: Choosing the right AI tools can be cost-effective in the long run. By selecting tools that are compatible with existing technology infrastructure and scalable, special education systems can avoid expensive overhauls and upgrades.

Effective administration of special education programs is vital for providing optimal support to students with special needs. The integration of AI-based solutions has emerged as a promising avenue to enhance these administrative processes. This section has explored the essential aspects and tactics involved in creating and deploying AI-driven solutions for managing special education programs, contributing to better outcomes for students in need of individualized support.

Overall, selecting the appropriate AI tools is critical for developing effective and efficient special education systems that can improve the quality of education for students with special needs.

Providing Professional Development to Educators

The section on providing professional development to educators focuses on the importance of equipping teachers with the necessary skills and knowledge to effectively integrate AI tools and technologies into special education settings. It highlights the need for ongoing training and support to ensure that educators have the confidence and competence to use these tools to enhance teaching and learning outcomes for students with disabilities.

It explores different approaches to providing professional development, including in-person workshops, online courses, and mentoring programs. It also discusses the benefits of collaborative professional development, where educators have opportunities to learn from and with each other and to engage in ongoing reflection and evaluation of their practice.

Emphasizes the importance of tailoring professional development to the unique needs of educators and students in special education settings. This includes considering factors such as different learning styles, diverse student populations, and varying levels of technological proficiency among educators.

Providing professional development to educators is essential to ensure that they have the necessary knowledge and skills to effectively teach students, especially those with special needs. Here are some steps that can be taken to provide effective professional development to educators:

Assess the needs of educators: Before providing professional development, it's important to assess the specific needs of educators. This can be done through surveys, interviews, and observations to determine what areas of knowledge and skills they need to improve upon.

Develop a plan: Based on the needs assessment, a plan for professional development can be developed. This plan should be tailored to meet the specific needs of educators and include clear objectives, timelines, and methods of evaluation.

Provide training: The training provided should be interactive, engaging, and hands-on. It can include workshops, seminars, online courses, and coaching. The training should be designed to enhance the knowledge and skills of educators and provide practical strategies that can be implemented in the classroom.

Follow-up and support: After the training, it's important to provide follow-up support to educators. This can include mentoring, coaching, and feedback. It's also important to provide ongoing support and resources to help educators implement the strategies they learned during the training.

Evaluate the effectiveness: It's important to evaluate the effectiveness of the professional development provided to educators. This can be done through surveys, focus groups, and classroom observations. The evaluation should be used to determine the impact of the training on educators and their students and to make any necessary adjustments to the training plan.

Overall, the section stresses the importance of investing in ongoing professional development for educators to ensure that they have the skills and knowledge needed to effectively integrate AI tools and technologies into special education settings and to promote positive outcomes for students disabilities.

Planning and Implementing the AI-Based Solution

The section on planning and implementing the AI-based solution in the context of special education focuses on the various stages involved in developing and deploying an AI system for special education. This section covers topics such as defining the problem, designing the system, selecting appropriate AI tools, developing a data strategy, and ensuring data privacy and security. It also delves into the importance of involving stakeholders in the design process and the need for continuous monitoring and evaluation to ensure the effectiveness of the AI system. Finally, the section discusses the importance of professional development for educators in effectively using and integrating the AI-based solution into their teaching practices.

Planning and implementing an AI-based solution involves several steps that need to be carefully executed to ensure the success of the project. Here are some key considerations for planning and implementing an AI-based solution:

- Define the problem: The first step is to define the problem you want to solve using AI. This involves understanding the specific challenges faced by the target audience and identifying the type of AI solution that would be most effective.
- Gather and preprocess data: To create an effective AI solution, you need to collect and preprocess the relevant data. This involves identifying the sources of data and ensuring that it is clean, accurate, and relevant to the problem you want to solve.
- Select the AI tools: Once you have the data, the next step is to select the AI tools that will be used to create the solution. This involves evaluating the different AI tools available and choosing the ones that are best suited for the specific problem you are trying to solve.
- Develop the AI solution: With the data and AI tools in hand, the next step is to develop the AI solution. This involves designing the AI model, training it on the data, and testing it to ensure that it is accurate and effective.
- Deploy and integrate the solution: Once the AI solution has been developed and tested, it is time to deploy it and integrate it into the existing systems and processes. This involves ensuring that the solution is compatible with the existing infrastructure and that it can be easily accessed and used by the target audience.
- Monitor and evaluate the solution: After the AI solution has been deployed, it is important to monitor and evaluate its performance. This involves tracking key metrics and user feedback to identify areas for improvement and ensure that the solution is meeting the needs of the target audience.

By following these steps and carefully planning and implementing the AI-based solution, you can create an effective and impactful solution that can improve the lives of the target audient.

Monitoring and Evaluating the Effectiveness of the AI Solution

Monitoring and evaluating the effectiveness of the AI solution is an essential step in ensuring that the system is meeting the needs of the students and the educators. This section of the book chapter will cover the key considerations for monitoring and evaluating the effectiveness of the AI solution, including setting clear objectives and performance indicators, collecting and analyzing data, and making necessary adjustments to the system based on the results. The section will also discuss the importance of involving stakeholders in the monitoring and evaluation process to ensure their feedback is incorporated into the decision-making process.

Monitoring and evaluating the effectiveness of the AI solution is a critical step in the implementation process. It allows educators to assess whether the AI-based solution is achieving its intended goals and making a positive impact on student learning outcomes. Here are some key considerations when monitoring and evaluating the effectiveness of the AI solution:

1. Define clear objectives and goals: Before implementing the AI-based solution, it's important to define clear objectives and goals that align with the needs of the students and educators. This will help guide the monitoring and evaluation process and ensure that the AI solution is making a positive impact on student learning outcomes.

2. Collect and analyze data: To monitor the effectiveness of the AI solution, educators need to collect and analyze relevant data. This may include data on student performance, engagement, and behavior. It's important to use a variety of data sources, such as pre- and post-assessments, observations, and surveys, to get a comprehensive understanding of the impact of the AI solution.
3. Use data visualization tools: Data visualization tools, such as graphs and charts, can help educators analyze and interpret data more effectively. They can help identify trends and patterns in the data, making it easier to make data-driven decisions and adjust the AI solution accordingly.
4. Monitor regularly: Monitoring the effectiveness of the AI solution should be an ongoing process. Regular monitoring can help educators identify any issues or challenges early on, allowing them to make timely adjustments to the AI solution.
5. Evaluate and adjust: Once data has been collected and analyzed, it's important to evaluate the effectiveness of the AI solution and make any necessary adjustments. This may involve modifying the AI algorithm or changing the instructional approach.
6. Share results: Sharing the results of the monitoring and evaluation process with all stakeholders, including students, parents, and administrators, can help build support for the AI solution and ensure its continued success.

The section on educator professional development emphasizes the significance of empowering teachers with essential competencies to seamlessly incorporate AI tools into special education contexts.

METHODOLOGY AND FRAMEWORK FOR AI-BASED SOLUTIONS FOR SPECIAL EDUCATION

The chapter section on Methodology and Framework for AI-based Solutions for Special Education aims to provide an overview of the key methodologies and frameworks that can be used for the development of AI-based solutions in the field of special education. The section starts by introducing the concept of special education and the various challenges that exist in this field. It then goes on to discuss the importance of AI-based solutions in addressing these challenges and improving the learning outcomes of students with special needs.

The section then provides an overview of the various methodologies and frameworks that can be used for the development of AI-based solutions, such as machine learning, deep learning, and natural language processing. It discusses the strengths and limitations of each of these approaches and highlights their applications in the field of special education.

Identifying the Problem

Identifying the problem is the first step in developing any AI-based solution for special education. It involves recognizing the areas of special education where AI can be applied to improve the learning outcomes of students. The problem identification process should be conducted in collaboration with special education teachers, parents, and students. The goal is to identify the most pressing needs and challenges facing the special education community that can be addressed through the development and implementation of AI-based solutions.

Once the problem has been identified, it is essential to gather and analyze data to gain a deeper understanding of the issue. This may involve collecting data on student performance, teacher practices, and other relevant factors that impact the learning outcomes of students with special needs. The data should be used to inform the development of the AI-based solution, ensuring that it is tailored to address the specific needs of the special education community.

Overall, identifying the problem is a critical first step in developing an effective AI-based solution for special education. It sets the foundation for the rest of the development process, ensuring that the solution is focused on addressing the most pressing needs of students with special needs and their educators.

Collecting Relevant Data

Collecting relevant data is a crucial step in developing an AI-based solution for special education. The data collected should be relevant to the problem identified in the previous step.

The type of data collected will depend on the specific problem being addressed. For example, if the problem is related to identifying students with learning disabilities, then data may be collected on student performance, behavior, and any other relevant information that could help identify the issue.

Data can be collected from a variety of sources, including student records, teacher observations, surveys, and assessments. It is important to ensure that the data collected is accurate and reliable to ensure that the AI-based solution is effective.

In addition, it is important to consider ethical considerations when collecting data. This includes obtaining informed consent from participants, protecting the privacy of sensitive information, and ensuring that the data is used only for its intended purpose.

Overall, collecting relevant data is an essential step in developing an effective AI-based solution for special education.

Algorithm Development

Algorithm development is the process of creating a set of instructions or rules that a computer program follows to perform a specific task. In the context of AI-based solutions for special education, algorithm development refers to the creation of a set of instructions that will enable the system to identify and analyze relevant data and provide meaningful insights to educators and students. This involves designing algorithms that can process data from various sources, such as student assessments, performance data, and other relevant information, and use this information to make recommendations for teaching and learning strategies. The development of algorithms requires a deep understanding of the problem domain and a thorough analysis of the available data, as well as expertise in machine learning and other AI technologies.

Integration With Existing Systems

Integration with existing systems is an important consideration when implementing an AI-based solution for special education. It involves ensuring that the new system can work seamlessly with the existing infrastructure, such as student information systems, learning management systems, and other educational technologies.

One of the key challenges in integration is the need to maintain data consistency and accuracy between the new AI system and the existing systems. This can be achieved through the development of appropriate data integration protocols and the use of data validation and cleaning tools.

Another important consideration is the compatibility of the AI-based solution with the existing hardware and software infrastructure. This may require upgrades or modifications to the existing infrastructure, such as increasing the storage capacity or processing power of servers and workstations.

In addition, it is important to ensure that the new system is compatible with the existing workflows and processes in the educational setting. This may require modifications to existing procedures and protocols to accommodate the new system.

Overall, effective integration of the AI-based solution with the existing systems is critical to ensure its successful implementation and adoption in the special education context.

Pilot Testing

Pilot testing is a crucial step in the development and implementation of any new AI-based solution. This step involves testing the solution on a smaller scale, often with a limited number of users or in a controlled environment, to identify any potential issues or areas for improvement before the solution is fully rolled out.

During the pilot testing phase, it is important to collect feedback from users and stakeholders, including educators, students, and administrators, to ensure that the solution is meeting their needs and effectively addressing the identified problem. Any issues or areas for improvement identified during the pilot testing phase can then be addressed before the solution is fully implemented.

Pilot testing can also help to build buy-in and support for the solution among stakeholders, as they can see firsthand how the solution works and its potential benefits. This can be particularly important in the context of special education, where there may be concerns about the use of AI and its potential impact on students.

Overall, pilot testing is an important step in the development and implementation of any AI-based solution for special education, as it can help to ensure that the solution is effective, user-friendly, and well-suited to the needs of students and educators.

CASE STUDIES ON AI-BASED SOLUTIONS FOR SPECIAL EDUCATION

In this section of the chapter, the focus will be on presenting case studies that demonstrate the successful implementation of AI-based solutions for special education. The case studies will highlight the key features of the solutions, their effectiveness in addressing the identified problems, and the lessons learned from their implementation. The case studies will cover a range of special education needs, including learning disabilities, autism, and emotional and behavioral disorders. The section will also discuss the ethical considerations and potential challenges associated with implementing AI-based solutions in special education settings.

Examples of Successful Implementation of AI in Special Education

There are several examples of successful implementation of AI in special education, some of which are:

1. Reading comprehension: AI-based solutions can help students with reading comprehension difficulties by analyzing texts and providing them with personalized feedback.
2. Speech recognition: AI-based solutions can be used to improve speech recognition in students with speech disorders. For example, some solutions use speech recognition to help students with dysarthria to speak more clearly.
3. Personalized learning: AI-based solutions can help create personalized learning experiences for students with disabilities. By analyzing their learning styles, strengths and weaknesses, the solution can adapt the content and pace of the learning material to suit their individual needs.
4. Augmentative and alternative communication (AAC): AI-based AAC devices can help students with communication difficulties to communicate effectively. These devices use natural language processing and machine learning to understand the student's intentions and generate appropriate responses.
5. Assistive technology: AI-based assistive technology can help students with disabilities to access technology and educational content. For example, some solutions use eye-tracking technology to help students with mobility impairments to navigate a computer interface.

Overall, AI-based solutions have the potential to revolutionize special education by providing personalized, adaptive and accessible learning experiences for students with disabilities.

Impact on Student Learning Outcomes

The impact of AI-based solutions on student learning outcomes in special education can vary depending on various factors such as the specific solution implemented, the student population, and the quality of implementation. However, some studies have shown positive results in student learning outcomes when using AI-based solutions in special education.

For example, a study conducted by researchers at the University of South Florida found that using a personalized learning system that incorporated AI algorithms improved the reading and math performance of students with learning disabilities compared to a control group who received traditional instruction (Baker et al., 2015).

Another study conducted by researchers at Carnegie Mellon University found that using a speech recognition tool helped students with autism spectrum disorder improve their speech articulation and fluency (Gorman et al., 2016).

These and other studies suggest that AI-based solutions can have a positive impact on student learning outcomes in special education when implemented effectively. However, it is important to note that AI-based solutions should not replace human teachers or interventions, but rather be used as a tool to support and enhance instruction.

Challenges and Limitations

In this subsection, we will discuss the various challenges and limitations that can arise in the implementation of AI-based solutions for special education. These challenges can include technical limitations such as the availability and quality of data, the difficulty of developing effective algorithms, and the potential for bias in the AI system. Other challenges may include ethical considerations, such as ensuring student privacy and maintaining transparency in the use of AI.

Additionally, we will discuss the limitations of AI-based solutions, such as the potential for the system to be overly reliant on technology and the need for human intervention in the learning process. Finally, we will explore the financial and resource constraints that can limit the widespread implementation of AI in special education. By acknowledging and addressing these challenges and limitations, we can work towards developing more effective and equitable AI-based solutions for special education.

Implementing AI-based solutions in special education can be a challenging process, and some of the key challenges include:

- Access to relevant data: AI algorithms require large amounts of data to learn and improve their accuracy. However, in special education, there may be limited data available, and it may not be in a suitable format for use with AI algorithms.
- Lack of technical expertise: Implementing AI-based solutions requires technical expertise in areas such as machine learning, data analysis, and software development. Many schools and educational organizations may not have staff with these skills.
- Cost: Developing and implementing AI-based solutions can be expensive, especially for smaller schools and educational organizations with limited budgets.
- Privacy and ethical concerns: AI-based solutions may collect and process sensitive data about students, which raises privacy and ethical concerns. It is important to ensure that these solutions comply with relevant privacy laws and ethical guidelines.
- Resistance to change: Implementing AI-based solutions requires changes in the way that educators and administrators work. Some may be resistant to these changes, which can make implementation more challenging.
- Lack of customization: AI-based solutions are often designed to work in a generic way for a large number of students, which can make it difficult to tailor the solution to the specific needs of individual students.
- Reliability and accuracy: AI-based solutions rely on algorithms, and there may be errors or biases in the data that can affect the reliability and accuracy of the results. It is important to ensure that these solutions are thoroughly tested and validated before being implemented.

There are several limitations to the implementation of AI-based solutions in special education. Some of the key limitations include:

- Access to technology: Not all schools and students have access to the necessary technology to implement AI-based solutions. This can create a digital divide where some students are at a disadvantage.
- Cost: Implementing AI-based solutions can be expensive, especially for schools with limited budgets. This can limit the ability of schools to invest in AI-based solutions.

- Data privacy concerns: Collecting and storing student data can raise concerns about data privacy and security. Schools need to ensure that they have appropriate measures in place to protect student data.
- Technical expertise: Implementing AI-based solutions requires technical expertise, which may not be available in all schools. Schools need to invest in training and development to ensure that they have the necessary technical expertise.
- Ethical considerations: There are ethical considerations around the use of AI-based solutions in special education. For example, there are concerns about the potential for AI to perpetuate biases and discrimination.
- Cultural differences: AI-based solutions may not be effective in all cultural contexts. Schools need to ensure that the solutions they implement are culturally appropriate and sensitive to the needs of their students.
- Human element: AI-based solutions cannot replace the human element in special education. Teachers and other professionals play a critical role in supporting the learning and development of students with special needs.

The challenges and limitations in implementing AI-based solutions in special education focuses on the potential obstacles and drawbacks that must be considered when implementing such solutions. The challenges discussed include the need for a strong technical infrastructure, the cost and complexity of AI development, the need for appropriate training for educators and support staff, the potential for bias and ethical concerns in AI systems, and the challenge of ensuring data privacy and security. The limitations of AI-based solutions in special education include their inability to replace human interaction and support, the potential for technical errors or failures, and the need for ongoing evaluation and adaptation of the technology.

ETHICAL CONSIDERATIONS IN DEVELOPING SPECIAL EDUCATION USING AI

In this chapter section, we will explore the ethical considerations that need to be taken into account when developing AI-based solutions for special education. The integration of AI in the education sector has raised several ethical questions related to privacy, security, and bias. It is crucial to address these concerns to ensure that AI is used ethically and responsibly in the field of special education. We will discuss the ethical considerations and guidelines that should be followed when developing AI-based solutions for special education, and the impact of ethical violations on students and the wider community.

Privacy and Security Concerns

One of the key ethical considerations in developing special education using AI is privacy and security concerns. These include concerns around the collection and use of sensitive student data, such as their learning disabilities or behavioral issues. It is important to ensure that the data is stored securely and that only authorized personnel have access to it. Additionally, there is a need for transparency around the collection and use of data, including obtaining informed consent from students and their families. Any potential risks to privacy and security should be identified and addressed through appropriate safeguards and protocols.

Privacy and security concerns are critical in the development of special education using AI. Special education data can be sensitive and personal, and it must be kept confidential to protect the privacy of students, their families, and educators. Additionally, data breaches and cyber-attacks can cause significant harm, and precautions must be taken to ensure the security of data. Therefore, it is important to ensure that privacy and security concerns are addressed in the development of AI-based solutions for special education to maintain the trust of stakeholders and safeguard their rights.

Bias in AI Algorithms

Bias in AI algorithms is a critical ethical consideration in developing special education using AI. AI algorithms are designed to make decisions based on patterns and data, but if the data used to train the algorithm is biased, it can result in biased decisions. This can lead to unfair treatment of certain students and perpetuate existing societal inequalities. It is important for developers of AI-based solutions for special education to be aware of the potential for bias in their algorithms and to take steps to mitigate it, such as using diverse training data and regular audits of the algorithm's decisions.

Bias in AI algorithms refers to the systematic errors or inaccuracies in the results produced by AI systems, which can result in unfair treatment or discrimination against certain individuals or groups. Bias can arise due to various reasons such as inadequate or biased data sets, inaccurate or incomplete algorithms, and insufficient or biased training data.

In the context of special education, bias in AI algorithms can have serious consequences as it can result in incorrect diagnosis or inappropriate treatment of students with special needs. For instance, a bias in the algorithm that is used to diagnose a learning disability may lead to misdiagnosis, resulting in the student not receiving the appropriate support and accommodations they need to succeed in their education.

It is, therefore, essential to ensure that AI algorithms used in special education are designed and developed with careful consideration of potential biases and with a commitment to fairness and equity. This requires a comprehensive approach that includes identifying and addressing biases in data collection and training, using transparent and explainable algorithms, and regularly monitoring and evaluating the performance of the AI systems to ensure they are meeting the needs of all students fairly and equitably.

Some examples of bias in AI algorithms are:

- Facial Recognition Technology: Studies have shown that facial recognition algorithms are less accurate for people with darker skin tones, leading to bias against people of color.
- Job Advertisements: Some algorithms used by companies to sort job applications have been found to favor male applicants over female applicants.
- Criminal Sentencing: AI algorithms used in criminal sentencing have been found to disproportionately sentence people of color to longer prison terms than white defendants.
- Healthcare: AI algorithms used in healthcare have been found to have biases against certain racial and ethnic groups, leading to disparities in treatment and outcomes.
- Online Advertising: AI algorithms used in online advertising have been found to target certain groups based on factors such as age, gender, and race, leading to potential discrimination.

It is important to note that bias in AI algorithms can occur in any application where algorithms are used to make decisions that impact people.

We have discussed the issue of bias in AI algorithms. Bias can be introduced at various stages of the development process and can have negative consequences, particularly in special education where students with diverse backgrounds and abilities are involved. We have explored some of the examples of bias in AI algorithms and their impact on special education. It is crucial to address this issue and ensure that AI algorithms are developed and deployed in an ethical and equitable manner to ensure fair treatment for all students.

Ensuring Equitable Access to AI-Based Solutions

Ensuring equitable access to AI-based solutions is an important consideration when developing and implementing AI in special education. This subsection discusses the potential for AI to perpetuate inequalities if not implemented carefully, and the importance of addressing these concerns to ensure that all students have equal opportunities to benefit from AI-based solutions. It also explores strategies for promoting equitable access, such as involving stakeholders from diverse backgrounds in the design process, addressing barriers to access such as cost or language barriers, and providing training and support for educators to ensure that they are able to use the technology effectively.

The use of AI in special education should not widen the digital divide or create further disparities in access to education. One way to ensure equitable access is to consider the availability and accessibility of technology and internet access for all students. This means that schools and educators need to provide necessary technology and infrastructure to ensure that all students can access AI-based solutions. Additionally, it is important to ensure that AI-based solutions are culturally responsive and sensitive to the diverse needs and backgrounds of students. This involves considering the diversity of the student population, including cultural and linguistic diversity, and designing AI-based solutions that are inclusive and accessible to all students. Furthermore, it is important to involve families and caregivers in the implementation and use of AI-based solutions to ensure that they are aware of the technology and can support their child's learning at home.

Finally, the section outlines a framework for the development of AI-based solutions for special education. This framework includes various stages, such as problem identification, data collection and preparation, algorithm selection and development, model training and testing, and deployment and evaluation. The section also discusses the ethical considerations that need to be taken into account while developing AI-based solutions for special education.

CONCLUSION

The chapter "Concept and Administration for Developing Special Education using AI" underscores the transformative potential of AI-based solutions in special education. AI technologies offer a promising way to address challenges in traditional special education, such as limited resources and teacher expertise. The integration of AI presents a multitude of benefits, including personalized learning experiences, improved communication skills, enhanced accessibility to learning materials, data-driven decision-making, and increased efficiency for educators.

Nevertheless, it is imperative to address ethical considerations related to AI implementation, including privacy, security, and algorithmic bias. Ensuring equitable access to AI-based solutions is of utmost importance to ensure that all students, regardless of their backgrounds, can benefit from these advancements. As the field of AI continues to evolve, it is essential for educators, administrators, and policymakers to stay informed and engaged to maximize the potential benefits while proactively addressing any potential risks and challenges.

Looking ahead, several promising directions for AI-based solutions in special education emerge. Enhancing personalization can lead to tailored learning plans for each student based on their unique strengths and weaknesses. Integrating AI with other technologies, such as virtual and augmented reality, can create more immersive and engaging learning experiences. Real-time feedback and sophisticated assistive technology for students with disabilities offer opportunities for growth.

Policy implications should focus on equitable access, privacy, and security concerns. Continuous professional development for educators is pivotal to ensure effective implementation and monitoring of AI-based solutions. Addressing potential bias in AI algorithms is crucial to promote fairness and inclusivity.

In practice, ongoing research is imperative to assess the effectiveness of AI-based solutions on student learning outcomes both in the short and long term. Practitioners must be mindful of AI's limitations, ensuring that human interaction and personalized instruction remain integral to the learning process.

AI-based solutions present a significant opportunity to revolutionize special education, fostering inclusivity, enhancing learning experiences, and supporting data-driven decision-making to improve educational outcomes for students with disabilities. However, responsible development, vigilant attention to ethical concerns, and thoughtful policy implementation are paramount to ensure that AI integration in special education remains effective, equitable, and inclusive.

Future Scope

The future of AI-based solutions in special education holds several promising directions. Personalization through AI can tailor learning plans to students' strengths and weaknesses. Integration with technologies like virtual reality can enhance engagement. AI-enabled collaboration can improve student-teacher teamwork. Real-time feedback aids adaptive learning. Advanced assistive technology for disabilities is possible. Ethical concerns, including privacy and bias, must be addressed. The potential to enhance outcomes for students with disabilities is high. Continued refinement and development are crucial for equitable and effective integration of these technologies in the special education landscape.

Overall, the chapter has highlighted the potential of AI-based solutions in special education. It has also discussed the challenges and ethical considerations associated with AI integration, and the implications for policy and practice. The chapter concludes by calling for careful consideration of these issues in order to ensure that AI-based solutions are used effectively and equitably to improve the educational outcomes of students with special needs.

REFERENCES:

Baker, R. (2021). *Artificial intelligence in education: Bringing it all together.* . doi:10.1787/f54ea644-en

Bonvicini & Qi. (2020). The Current and Future Role of Artificial Intelligence in Special Education. *Journal of Special Education Technology.*

Choi & Kim. (2021). Integrating Technology and Artificial Intelligence in Special Education: A Systematic Literature Review. *International Journal of Educational Research.*

Ferdig & Archambault. (2018). Artificial Intelligence and Special Education: Opportunities and Challenges. *Journal of Special Education Technology.*

Hlavacs & Savina. (2021). Artificial Intelligence in Special Education: Bridging the Gap between Research and Practice. *Frontiers in Education.*

Kukkar, A., Mohana, R., Sharma, A., & Nayyar, A. (2023). Prediction of student academic performance based on their emotional wellbeing and interaction on various e-learning platforms. *Education and Information Technologies, 28*(8), 1–30. doi:10.100710639-022-11573-9

Loukina & Flor. (2019). Using Artificial Intelligence to Improve Special Education Services: Opportunities and Challenges. *International Journal of Artificial Intelligence in Education.*

McNamara. (2019). Machine Learning in Special Education: Applications, Opportunities, and Challenges. *Journal of Special Education Technology.*

Reich, J. (2020). Artificial Intelligence and Special Education: Applications, Opportunities, and Challenges. *Journal of Special Education Technology.*

Sahlaoui, H., Nayyar, A., Agoujil, S., & Jaber, M. M. (2021). Predicting and interpreting student performance using ensemble models and shapley additive explanations. *IEEE Access : Practical Innovations, Open Solutions, 9*, 152688–152703. doi:10.1109/ACCESS.2021.3124270

Szyrocka, J. R., Zywiolek, J., Nayyar, A., & Naved, M. (Eds.). (2023). *Advances in distance learning in times of pandemic*. CRC Press.

ADDITIONAL READING

Alemi, M., Meghdari, A., & Moghimi, A. (2019). Artificial intelligence for special education: Opportunities, challenges, and recommendations. *Education and Information Technologies, 24*(2), 1207–1232.

Bashir, M., & Khair, M. U. (2019). Artificial intelligence in special education: Opportunities and challenges. *International Journal of Computer Science and Mobile Computing, 8*(7), 174–180.

Deng, L., Wang, S., Huang, J., Hu, J., & Peng, Y. (2021). Review on the application of artificial intelligence in special education. *Journal of Intelligent & Fuzzy Systems, 40*(1), 25–41.

Huang, R., He, Y., Wu, X., & Chen, L. (2019). An application of artificial intelligence in special education. *Journal of Physics: Conference Series, 1280*(3), 032077. doi:10.1088/1742-6596/1187/3/032077

Huang, R., Wu, X., He, Y., & Chen, L. (2020). Artificial intelligence for special education: A survey. *Journal of Physics: Conference Series, 1642*(1), 012041. PMID:34191934

Liu, X., Zou, X., & Xie, Q. (2019). Application of artificial intelligence in special education. *Journal of Physics: Conference Series*, *1303*(1), 012015.

Vahdat, S., Darabi, S., & Ghasemi, S. R. (2021). Artificial intelligence in special education: A systematic review of the literature. *Journal of Computers in Education*, *8*(1), 109–128.

Zhang, C., Xiang, Q., & Zhang, X. (2021). The application of artificial intelligence in special education. *Journal of Physics: Conference Series*, *1736*(1), 012023.

Chapter 12
Looking Into the Future With AI for Special Education:
Prospects and Reflections

Arjama Pal
School of Computing Science and Engineering, VIT Bhopal University, Madhya, India

D. Lakshmi
https://orcid.org/0000-0003-4018-1208
School of Computing Science and Engineering, VIT Bhopal University, Madhya, India

Vishnuvarthanan Govindaraj
School of Computing Science and Engineering, VIT Bhopal University, Madhya, India

ABSTRACT

Advancements in AI revolutionize learning, automate tasks, and provide insights. During COVID-19, AI connected educators and learners globally, but special education suffered. This chapter aims to define disabilities, explore AI-based diagnosis tools, and envision personalized learning and assistive technology for inclusive education. The lack of affordable and convenient assistive devices and technology combined with taboos stemming from deeply ingrained misconceptions and prejudices, perpetuating stereotypes and marginalizing individuals with disabilities often forces them to live a life devoid of the proper means to engage in schooling for the purpose of attaining an independent lifestyle. The primary objective of the chapter is to define various types of disabilities and consider various AI-based tools for early disability diagnosis, while also looking to the future with personalized learning and AI-based assistive technologies, assisting both learners and educators in achieving the highest level of education.

DOI: 10.4018/979-8-3693-0378-8.ch012

1.0 INTRODUCTION

In the past decade, technology infused with AI has significantly left its imprint on our day-to-day lives, transforming various industries, and the education sector is no exception. Especially after the COVID-19 outbreak, AI-powered educational tools have been successfully proving their potential to revolutionize ways of learning by personalizing the learning experience, automating administrative tasks, and providing data-driven insights. With the implementation of distance learning solutions, on the one hand, AI-based tools helped connect millions of educators as well as learners worldwide, but, on the other hand, it proved to be a challenging situation for users with any kind of disability who relied on special education.

Special education refers to the guidance of youngsters who deviate from what is considered typical in terms of their social, cognitive, or physical development to the extent that they need modifications to customary educational practices. It serves all children, including those with psychological, cognitive, or behavioural impairments, learning disabilities, visual, hearing, or speech impairments, emotional or cognitive impairments, gifted students with exceptional academic abilities, and those with orthopaedic or neurological disorders as defined by Encyclopedia Britannica (2023). According to the National Center for Education Statistics (2022), under the Individuals with Disabilities Education Act (IDEA), In 2020–21, 7.2 million kids between the ages of 3 and 21 got special education assistance. According to the United Nations, Department of Economic and Social Affairs Disability (2023), it is estimated that there are 1 billion people with disabilities worldwide, or around 15% of the total population, forming the largest minority in the world. The percentage breakdown of IDEA-eligible students aged between 3 and 21 by selected disability type for the academic year 2020–21 has been represented in Figure 1, as represented by the U.S. Department of Education (2021).

Figure 1. Percentage distribution of students aged 3 to 21 who receive IDEA services according to a particular impairment type: The academic year 2020–21

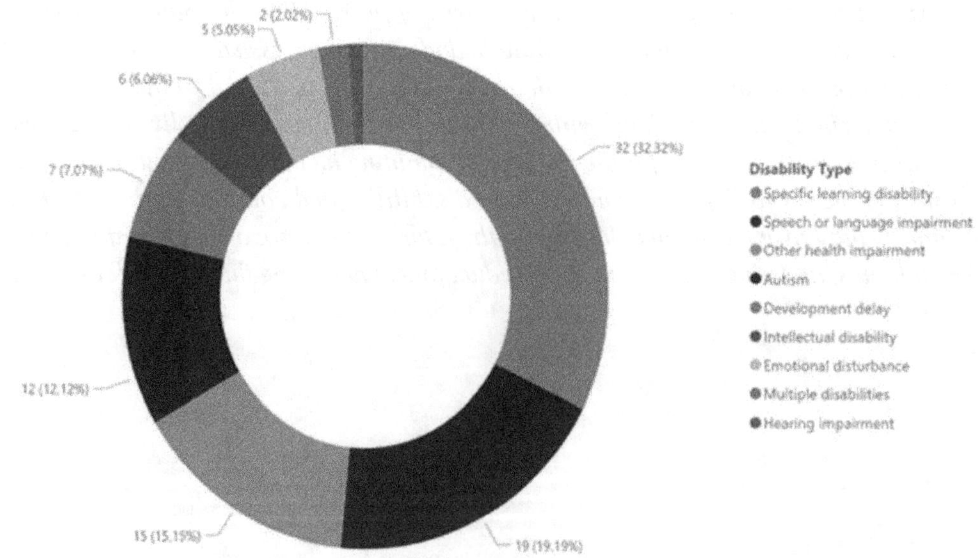

Additionally, according to the Department of Economic and Social Affairs Disability (2023) of United Nations Educational, Scientific, and Cultural Organization - UNESCO, in impoverished countries, 90% of handicapped children seldom go to school. While technology continues to make learning solutions and the workplace more adoptable and thereby accessible, and multiple research projects are going on to make education more inclusive and accessible to everyone, irrespective of their disabilities, the barrier to education is even more challenging to navigate for differently abled individuals in developing countries. The lack of affordable and convenient assistive tools and technology combined with taboos stemming from deeply ingrained misconceptions and prejudices, perpetuating stereotypes, and marginalizing individuals with disabilities often forces them to live a life devoid of the proper means to engage in schooling for the purpose of attaining an independent lifestyle. Moreover, similar struggles are also encountered by the family members of a differently-abled individual, and it is important to address their issues as well to better understand the ways of helping them with the help of AI.

Although AI can never be the replacement for human beings, the integration of AI-based instructional methods with pupils with unique necessities has ushered in new periods and styles that call for the use of specialised tools and novel approaches to enhance children's lives in both the home and the classroom. In the past decade, a significant amount of research has focused on the practical application of AI computing tools to enhance the educational experience of students who struggle with learning. In this chapter, we'll focus on the presently available methods and tools aiding in special education and the challenges they offer, along with the future prospects of AI in this particular field.

1.1 Objective of the Chapter

The main objectives of the chapter can be described as follows:

- To identify and define the different types of disabilities experienced by individuals
- To discuss the various methodologies and diagnostic tools currently available for early disability diagnosis
- To explore the availability of AI-based tools to aid the education of specially-abled students
- To analyse the challenges and advantages of the available pedagogical tools
- To look towards the future with personalized AI-based assistive technologies that will help both students and educators

1.2 Organization of the Chapter

The chapter has been divided into the following six sections, aimed at providing a proper presentation of the study:

Section One: The first section gives the introduction to the chapter with an insight into special education and its importance. It also explores the background of the study, highlights the objectives of the chapter, and talks about everything to expect from the chapter.

Section Two: In the second section, the rationale of the chapter emphasises the definition of disabilities and their modification over time, as well as why AI-based educational tools are needed more than ever.

Section Three: The third section deals with the explanation of the various kinds of disabilities and their potential impacts on individual lives. It also focuses on the exploration, discussion, and analysis of various case studies and AI-based tools available for diagnosis and assisting students with special needs.

Section Four: The fourth section reflects on the available pedagogical methodologies and the challenges faced in implementing them throughout the course of our daily lives. It also explores the landscape of special education in the post-pandemic world.

Section Five: In the fifth section, several future prospects and further research recommendations in this field are examined.

Section Six: Finally, the sixth section concludes by summarizing and reviewing the methodologies discussed so far.

2.0 RATIONALE OF THE STUDY

The chapter's main objective is to determine different types of disabilities and reflect on different AI-based tools available for the early diagnosis of disabilities, looking into the future with personalized learning and AI-based assistive technologies, helping both the learner and the educator attain the highest level of education.

2.1 Disabilities

According to World Health Organization (WHO), disability is humane. Currently, it is estimated that 1.3 billion people, or 16% of the world's population, are substantially impaired. For children aged 3-9, the IDEA Amendments of (1997), which is the most recent statute rendered by Knoblauch & Sorenson (1998), permits educational institutions in states and localities to use the term "developmental delay". This concept is used to apply to kids between the ages of 3 and 5. The term "child with a disability" for kids ages 3 to 9 may, at the state's and the local education agency's discretion, encompass kids who have developmental difficulties in the following categories, if not all: physical impairments (visual, hearing and/or speech), cognitive impairments, communication, social or emotional skills, or adaptive abilities. The different disabilities can be loosely categorised into the following groups, as represented in Figure 2.

The definition of disability has recently undergone a radical change, reflecting a more accepting and empowering viewpoint. Disability is now viewed as a crucial aspect of the human experience, inspiring efforts to build a more just and inclusive society. The term "special need" is now frequently used because disability is recognized as a characteristic structure of society, which is influenced by attitudes, legislation, and infrastructure. To cater to these needs, early recognition of disabilities is extremely crucial, and AI-catered tools aid in helping them adapt to the requirements. In the post-COVID-19 world, these tools have become increasingly integrated into the day-to-day lives of people and, in turn, have assisted differently-abled individuals with innovations. For instance, voice-enabled assistants like Google Alexa and Siri have enabled them to access important functions without clicking on them. But at the same time, they can prove challenging for users with speech impairments. This chapter aims to investigate the AI-based methodologies available to cater to the needs of individuals with special needs.

3.0 MATERIALS AND METHODS

It can be challenging for specially-abled children to get along with their peers, but it is not impossible. In order for such kids to feel involved in the classroom, they need a different set of educational aids.

Figure 2. Disabilities and their categories

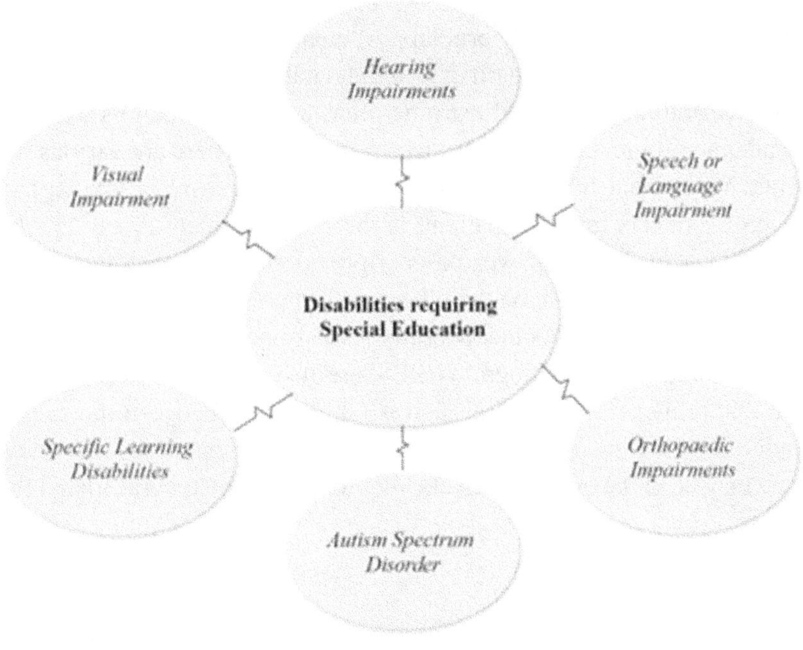

3.1 Visual Impairments

3.1.1 Impact

Sight plays a pivotal role in our ability to perceive and comprehend the world. It allows us to see colours, shapes, and depth, providing a multi-dimensional experience of our surroundings. A person who is unable to see well and whose eyesight cannot be restored to a "normal" level is said to have vision impairment or vision loss. Objects are no longer seen by the eye as clearly as they once were due to loss of visual acuity or loss of visual field, where the eyes cannot perceive wide vision, resulting in vision impairment. Globally, there are at least 2.2 billion in the human population with near- or distant vision problems. A minimum of 1 billion of these instances had avoidable or untreated visual loss mentions the WHO (2022).

The two groups of people with visual impairment—the blind and those who have poor eyesight —each have unique needs and features. Even after the optical correction, people with low vision still have impaired vision and struggle to use their vision for daily tasks. Students with low vision who have residual vision can read written materials with the use of instructional materials and specialised technology in the educational setting, whereas blind students need to rely on other means to have access to education, as informed by Resnikoff et al. (2004). Young children with significant visual impairment that develops early can have long-term effects on their motor, cognitive, linguistic, social, and emotional development. Additionally, school-aged children with vision problems show lower levels of academic accomplishment states the WHO (2022).

3.1.2 Diagnosis

Early detection of impairment is extremely crucial as it enables timely intervention and aid, leading to better denouements and an improved standard of living. It enables educators to implement tailored strategies, accommodations, and individualized learning plans to meet the child's particular requirements, promoting their academic progress and overall success in school. There are various tests that check for an individual's visual impairment. Snellen's chart, containing progressively smaller letters and numbers placed at a distance of 6 meters from the patient, is the most prevalent test to test for any issue with vision. The visual field test evaluates the wearer's peripheral vision by placing a device over their eyes while flashing a light. A tonometry test, on the other hand, checks for the fluid pressure inside the eyes to diagnose glaucoma. Other tests like Ocular Motility Assessment, Electro-oculogram (EOG), Visually Evoked Potential (VEP), and Electroretinogram (ERG) are also prescribed to check for other issues with vision or to ensure that proper signal transmission is taking place between the eyes and the brain, as suggested by Mandal (2012). If the examination reveals no visual conditions that could account for the symptoms, the issue may lie in the brain, which can require a test for Cerebral Visual Impairment (CVI).

3.1.3 Assistive Technology

Braille has been the primary writing system for visually impaired individuals or people with low vision. For visually challenged pupils, hearing the teacher's voice might not be sufficient, especially when teaching remotely, where the audio quality may suffer from poor connections or sound overlapping. There are certain tools that are already available, to help students with visual impairments. These can be listed as follows:

1. **Text-to-Speech Software:** Text-to-Speech (TTS) software, also known as 'Read Aloud' software, is an assistive technology used to convert digital text into an audio format to help people listen to the text displayed on the screen. The speed and volume of this computer-generated audio can be controlled as per the individual's needs.
2. **Screen Reader:** An application's or website's menus, buttons, and other general navigational aids can all be described to the user using a screen reader's speech synthesiser. For example, VoiceOver, a built-in gesture-based screen-reading feature on iOS devices, allows users to use iPhones even when the viewer can't exclusively see the screen. It gives audible descriptions of everything present on the screen and is accessible in over 30 languages. It also lets users control and modify the speaking rate and pitch according to their preferences.
3. **Refreshable Braille Display:** It can be used to view text output by visually impaired computer users who are unable to use a regular computer monitor.
4. **SceneEye 500:** It is a mobile desktop camera with a very simple user interface that was created primarily for use with touchscreen tablets. A visually impaired student can easily see the whiteboard or any other classroom presentation with the help of this simple-to-connect device, which amplifies the image by up to 50X. The image can be made easier to read by adjusting the contrast function. The visuals can also be recorded for visually impaired students to watch later in class or at home, providing them with a permanent study tool for the material being covered in class.

5. **Braille Compass:** Howe Press's Braille Compass enables blind students to complete math assignments independently. These compasses have point ends that work similar to a regular compass, but they enable students to trace the tracing wheels with their fingers and adjust accordingly.
6. **Video Magnifier:** A video magnifier with a tilt screen and a variety of magnification options allows for the best viewing.
7. **Braille Note Apex:** A blind or visually challenged student can type notes in Braille using the Braille Note Apex note taker, which they can then convert to audio or print off.
8. **ViewPlus Max Embosser:** The quickest and most functional braille printer in the Desktop series is the ViewPlus Max Embosser. It enables the user to print anything that has been converted into Braille from their personal computer.
9. **Aira:** It is a wearable device that gives consumers a means to converse with human agents who act as blind people's visual interpreters. Microsoft's free Seeing AI programme makes it easier for those with vision impairments to discriminate between items, decipher handwriting, identify money, and recognise faces.

Figure 3 illustrates the different available means of assistive technology that make the lives of visually challenged students easier.

Figure 3. Assistive technology for visually-impaired students

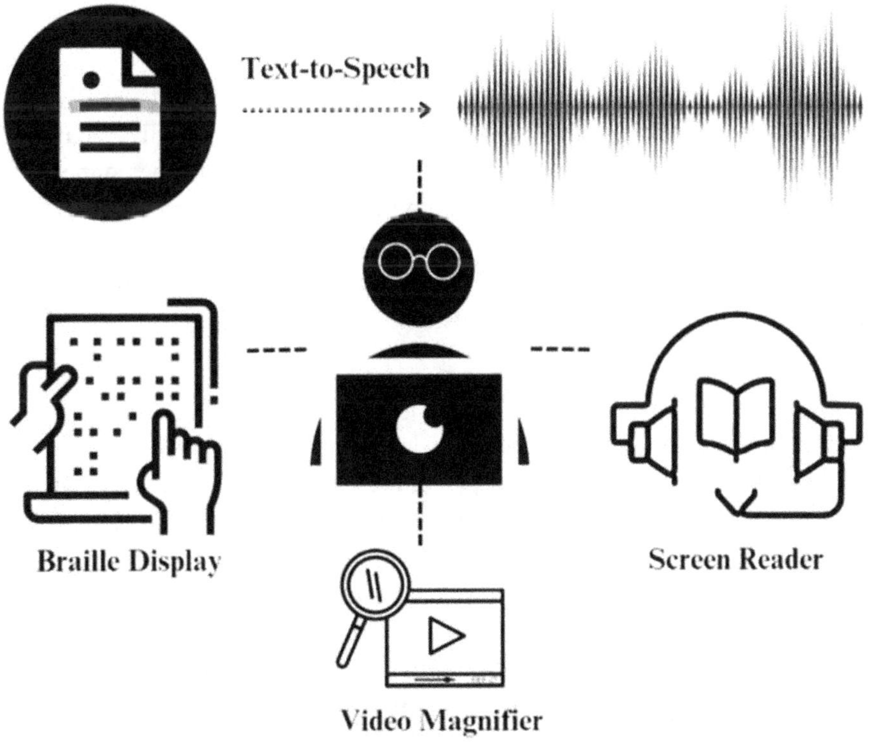

Along with the available assistive technologies, continuous and ongoing research is being conducted to make education more accessible. Some prominent studies are as follows:

- To help visually-impaired students access laboratory workspaces, a study by Jacob & Cary (2021) recently developed a new artificial tool named MSU Denver Virtual Lab Assistant (VLA) with the help of the Amazon Alexa Kit, Amazon Web Services (AWS), and a microcontroller (Raspberry Pi). With the help of voice control, the VLA enables students with visual impairments to complete practical laboratory work independently.
- In another study made by Giovanna et al. (2021), the researchers aimed to develop a tool named SlAide2Voice, based on three basic components: a client-server architecture, an OpenOffice add-on, and an artificial intelligence module that can assist visually impaired students not just during online lectures but also during independent study.
- Another research study accomplished by Daniela et al. (2021) focused on making block-based programming, where visual signals are crucial, accessible to visually-impaired students with assistance from the newest keyboard navigation from Google and auditory cues combined with custom TTS software.

3.1.4 Case Study: Be My Eyes

Be My Eyes is free smartphone software with the sole objective of providing accessibility for individuals suffering from blindness or those who struggle with low vision. The application connects blind and low-vision individuals with sighted people and organisations throughout the world via a live video call.

3.1.4.1 About

Be My Eyes was founded by Hans Jørgen Wiberg (Be My Eyes, 2015), a visually impaired Danish craftsman, with the aim of making the world more accessible to visually impaired personnel. Volunteers from Be My Eyes lend their eyesight to those who have limited vision every day so that they may conquer hurdles and resolve problems together. In 2018, The Be My Eyes partnered with Microsoft to launch a new feature called Specialized Help. Users of Specialized Help can communicate with authorised company personnel for accessible and effective customer help.

3.1.4.2 Benefits

The software provides a free service to the blind or low-vision community. Their detail-oriented and passionate workforce not only works for blind personnel but also with the active involvement of the low-vision community. They also offer multiple corporate solutions like Be My Eyes Work, Be My Eyes Experiences, Be My Eyes Careers, and so on. They are trusted partners of various noteworthy organizations like Microsoft, Google, Salesforce, Genesys, and more. They operate in over hundred and fifty countries and speak more than hundred and eighty languages. They provide visually impaired individuals with a sense of independence. They allow the users to stay 100% anonymous, are available 24x7, and simplify daily tasks like reading small texts, giving a summary, or distinguishing patterns or colours.

3.1.4.3 Latest Advancements

Recently, Be My Eyes launched the Virtual Volunteer Tool as a partner of OpenAI's new GPT-4 model. The new GPT-4 language model from OpenAI, which includes a dynamic new image-to-text generator, will power the new feature when it is integrated into the current app. Users can use the app to transmit photographs to an AI-driven Virtual Volunteer, who can instantly provide visual assistance for a range of activities and answer any questions about the image. The context provided by the Virtual Volunteer tool, along with a level of knowledge and conversational skills not yet seen in the world of digital assistants, sets it apart from other image-to-text solutions currently on the market. This feature is still in development and is being tested by a small subset of users in its closed beta version.

3.2 Hearing Impairment

Spoken communication is exclusive to human beings. People with hearing loss are unable to perceive the noises made by other people and the natural world if their hearing is impaired or nonexistent. Hearing thresholds of 20 dB or better in both ears are considered normal hearing, and a person is considered to have hearing damage if their hearing abilities fall below that range. One or both ears may be affected, and it may be mild, moderate, moderately severe, severe, or profound. Hearing loss affects more than 1.5 billion people worldwide, i.e., 20% of the global population, 430 millions of whom are completely disabled. Over 700 million individuals may suffer from severe hearing loss by the year 2050. 34 million children worldwide suffer from hearing loss or deafness, and 60% of those cases can be avoided, as voiced by WHO (2023).

3.2.1 Impact

The effects of hearing loss involve a decreased ability to interact socially and slower language development in children. These effects can give rise to societal isolation, solitariness, and resentment in youngsters. Individuals may face negative effects on scholastic success and career prospects due to a lack of adequate hearing adaptations. Deaf children in impoverished nations hardly ever attend school. The total yearly cost of untreated hearing loss worldwide is approximately $980 billion, as publicized by WHO (2023). Hearing loss or hearing loss reduction impairs children's ability to hear speech and, as a result, absorb the subtleties of the spoken language in their environment. If they are born to hearing parents, hearing loss affects their capacity to produce, monitor, and understand the conventions of how speech sounds, also referred to as phonemes, are used in their native tongue. Vowel and consonant articulation issues, insufficient vowel distinction, and the inability to discriminate between voiceless and voiced consonant sounds, such as "t" and "d," are all examples of speech sound production issues. Children with hearing loss experience these issues together with a noticeably slower pace of general speech sound comprehension (phonological development). They may also have limited vocabulary understanding or vocabulary that is age-appropriate. In particular, the use of abstract or nonliteral words could be deficient. Grammatical knowledge is likewise diminished along with the expansion of vocabulary, as mentioned by Dobie and Hemel (2004).

3.2.2 Diagnosis

If suitable advanced detection is unavailable in no more than the earliest six to twelve months, even mild hearing impairment can have a devastating impact on the growth of verbal interaction with peers and family members who are able to hear normally, the building of complex vocabulary, and many other features of academic growth as discovered by Dobie and Hemal (2004). Hearing impairments can be of two types: sensorineural hearing loss, caused by a damaged cochlea or the auditory nerve, and conductive impairment, when sound can't travel through the ear because of a foreign blockage, built-up fluid, or a punctured eardrum. The kind and severity of the hearing loss will be determined by an audiometry examination, which measures the capacity to distinguish between sounds based on intensity and tone. This test is used by audiologists to identify hearing loss brought on by noise. For the detection of hearing loss induced by noise, there are three essential requirements. Hearing loss tested by high-frequency is the first. The second is being subjected to noise levels that could be dangerous, and the third is an audible high-frequency notch. To check whether the eardrum can vibrate freely, the doctor may use an otoscope to inspect the ear. Additionally, the physician can request a tympanogram, a test designed to identify issues with the middle ear. If a tumour or fracture is suspected, a CT or MRI scan can be recommended. Alternatively, a recent study made by Shew et al. (2019) suggested a technique to apply ML to predict sensorineural hearing loss. The study proposed that ML can be used to build disease-specific algorithms using expression profiles of micro Ribonucleic Acid (miRNA). Establishing a connection between perilymph miRNA expression patterns and clinically accessible metrics is the first step in the development of miRNAs as biomarkers for inner ear disorders. This approach may provide a way to diagnose individuals with acute inner ear conditions in addition to providing the chance to discover the issue at the atomic level.

3.2.3 Assistive Technology

In a recent article, Chazen (2019) elaborates that the National Institute on Deafness and Other Communication Disorders (NIDCD) says, alternative and augmentative communication devices, assistive listening devices, and alerting devices are the three categories of technology that can benefit children with impaired hearing in the classroom.

1. **Assistive Listening Devices:** Chazen (2019) says that according to the NIDCD, "Assistive learning tools aid in amplifying the sounds one would like to hear, particularly in environments where there is a lot of background auditory disruption". The American Speech-Language-Hearing Association (ASHA) says, it is possible for institutions to use a wire that spans the room to directly link a student's hearing aid to the professor's microphone. Even in a huge or noisy class, the lecture is audible to the student as an electric current travels through the wire while the lecturer speaks. Similar to this, frequency-modulated (FM) systems can send audio from a lecturer's microphone using radio waves.
2. **Augmentative and Alternative Communicative Devices:** Students with hearing impairments can speak more effectively and understand others thanks to assistive technology. Chazen (2019) also explains that in order to increase communication, NIDCD recommends using touchscreens and keyboards and a "display panel facing outward so that both individuals can communicate information while addressing each other." Campuses can employ these technologies in offices that

offer student services as well as in lectures to improve communication. Professors can interact with students better and more effectively by enhancing their explanations with simple text and visuals.

3. **Alerting Devices:** Alerting systems for various types of communication are used to modify sound. For instance, Chazen (2019) mentions a fire siren on campus might flutter frantically and brightly in red to draw the attention of pupils who are unable to hear.
4. **Automatic Speech Recognition:** Automatic Speech Recognition, or ASR software, frequently aids the distinction of separate voices in the setting of a classroom. Students may use the text transcription to ascertain who said what. When students talk before their turn or during class participation, this technology is used.
5. Real-time closed captioning as well as transcription technologies help students understand course materials with visual aids, making the process easier, faster, and more cost-effective.
6. Academic transcription software also helps students who struggle to take notes in class as the materials are taught simultaneously or require access to lecture materials later.
7. Speech-to-Text devices, also known as speech synthesis, often help translate human speech into text.

The main means of interaction between hearing-impaired persons and other communities is Sign Language (SL), which is represented through both manual (gestures and body movements) and non-manual (facet reactions) elements. These characteristics combine to create expressions, which are used to communicate the meaning of words or phrases. The Deaf community must be able to recognise and comprehend the relationship between pronouncements and words. Sign language technologies include a wide spectrum, from the capture of signs to their accurate depiction, in order to facilitate communication in the deaf community as well as between hearing-impaired and speaking people. In more detail, capturing sign language entails employing the appropriate detection tools to extract mouth, hand, and bodily expressions. Figure 4 demonstrates the processing of algorithms that emphasise sign language recognition.

Figure 4. Sign language recognition algorithm

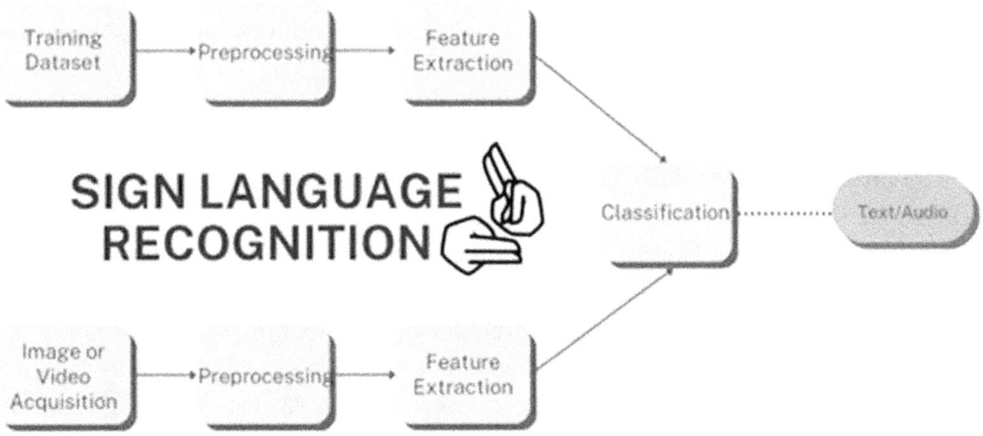

A recent study performed by Papastratis et al. (2021) summarizes the technologies required to combine AI with SL to improve communication. Sign language capturing, recognition, translation, and representation are the necessary steps to be implemented via AI to facilitate the use of the language in daily life. classifying signed videos into complete sentences.

- **Sign Language Capturing:** Different kinds of sensors, like Kinect Sensors proposed by Zhang (2012), Leap Motion Sensors by Mittal et al. (2019), and different wearable devices using electromyography (EMG) by Galea and Smeaton (2019), are used for sign language capturing.
- **Sign Language Recognition:** Continuous sign language recognition is the process of classifying signed videos into complete sentences. Isolated sign language identification refers to the task of precisely detecting single sign motions from videos when it comes to other kinds of video interpretation and categorization assignments, such as action and gesture recognition. This problem is typically approached by extracting and discovering extremely discriminating traits.
- **Sign Language Translation:** The process of converting sign language movies into spoken language, known as SL Translation, requires simulating the target language's syntax and vocabulary in addition to its glosses.
- **Sign Language Representation:** The usage of three-dimensional avatars, which can accurately and realistically imitate countenance and gestures in a form that represents symbols comprehensible by the deaf community, is a prevalent method of representing sign language. A noteworthy contribution in this field is the research work done by Das Chakladar et al. (2021) on producing SL from Indian speech or text. Here, using Natural Language Processing (NLP) principles and techniques, the input was first translated into English before being converted to the equivalent Indian sign language. A preset sign vocabulary and Blender were used to create the final avatar movements.
- **Sign Language Production:** By using methods of sign language production, it is possible to replace the avatar's stiff body language with the physical characteristics of a genuine person. These techniques frequently use a model of a human and sign language glosses to accomplish this, and they then produce a video using sign language in which the human performs more lifelike and pragmatic signs.

Along with the available tools to aid students with hearing disabilities, continuous research is being conducted to further advance this field:

- In a recent collaborative study published by MedicalXpress (2018), an ML algorithm that examines brain imaging to forecast language capacity in deaf kids after receiving cochlear implants was developed by researchers from the Ann & Robert H. Lurie Children's Hospital of Chicago and The Chinese University of Hong Kong. The groundbreaking application of artificial intelligence in this study to comprehend the brain architecture behind language development has far-reaching consequences for kids who struggle with developmental issues.
- DeepMind by Google has created an AI algorithm to provide closed captioning for its deaf customers by creating lip-reading algorithms, as researched by Asokan (2019). DeepMind's algorithms watched more than 5000 hours of television to train the system, and they were able to recognise up to 17,500 different words. This extensive training enabled the algorithm to surpass professional lip-readers by accurately interpreting 46.8% of words. The Google researchers are

optimistic that technology will significantly advance hearing aids, silent dictation in public places, and noisy-environment speech recognition.

- The HearMeOut app by Zdravkova et al. (2022) uses AI to combine pictogram-based augmentative and alternative communication with gesture-based text prediction. The programme makes use of Natural Language Conversation to allow users who are speech-impaired to converse. Additionally, it classifies the most likely words from the camera-captured movements of the visually impaired individual using a word-level sign language dataset. Then, it uses cutting-edge algorithms to turn those words into the most logical and plausible sentences. The app does not save user data due to security concerns because input and output are continuous processes that do not require storage, which reduces the possibility of any information leakage.

3.2.4 Case Study: Circa AI

Circa AI is an advanced hearing aid by Nuear - The Hearing Solution Group (Malaysia Hearing Solution, 2021). Circa AI's robust artificial intelligence gives it an advantage over competing hearing aids in every device. With their ground-breaking audio technology, even the most challenging listening conditions are simple to hear. As part of this, voice sounds are amplified to make it easier to hear people wearing face masks. It promises to have exceptional sound quality and the capacity to function as a personal tracking device that can monitor bodily functions and mental well-being.

3.2.4.1 About

Hearing Reality Pro, a built-in sound categorization system, is included with Circa AI hearing aids. This cutting-edge system works in spite of the noisiest circumstances, filtering out undesirable noise and boosting desired sounds, making the users feel at ease in both loud and quiet environments, and granting them access to exceptional improved speech clarity. The ear delivers much more accurate data than the wrist, which is usually where fitness tracking gadgets collect their data. Circa AI is the pioneering device to do this. They not only improve the hearing of their users but also promise to act as an assistant and a lifestyle device.

3.2.4.2 Benefits

The AI-based sophisticated sound processing technology in the Circa AI hearing aids improves voice audibility in difficult listening situations. Edge Mode offers comfortable, feedback-free listening by optimising for masks, social distance, and background noise. Users of the Thrive assistance app may easily alter their hearing while on the go and personalise it with geotagged memories. Up to 24 hours of better hearing can be experienced with rechargeable hearing aids, and the Thrive app offers customised control in various listening situations. Additionally, the Thrive app provides a brand-new, high-quality way to listen to music. Users can hear noises in their weaker-hearing ear via their good ear thanks to the CROS technology, which enables streaming between hearing aids. They have Surface NanoShield and Advanced Multiflex Tinnitus Technology, which make them trustworthy and robust. The users can also stream calls and messages straight to the hearing aids from their mobile devices.

3.2.4.3 Latest Advancements

Circa Edge AI is an improved version of the existing Circa AI that does more than just promises superior-quality sounds. Circa Edge AI offers a built-in Body Tracking feature that tracks everyday motion and activity. This feature motivates users to communicate with others more, which improves their cognitive function. The hearing aid also serves as an individualised assistant, assisting users with note-taking, language translation, and scheduling management. The robust "Thrive Assistant" function of the Circa Edge AI hearing aids also enables users to adjust hearing aid volume, recall memories, inquire about issues, and troubleshoot accessories. For older people, falls pose a serious health concern, and even slight hearing loss makes falls more likely. The risk doubles by 1.4 for each additional 10 dB of hearing loss. If a fall occurs, the hearing aids will send up to three people—including caregivers—a text message, prompting them to immediately check on the individual for any sign of injury. This is a life-saving feature, especially for those staying alone.

3.3 Learning Disabilities

Learning Disability (LD) is a neurodevelopmental disorder impacting the mind's capacity to efficiently and accurately detect and/or take into account both non-verbal and verbal cues. It results from the combination of genetic, epigenetic, and environmental factors based on biological aspects. The traditional notions of learning disabilities as being reading or letter problems are not accurate and fail to capture the complexity of the disorder. They differ greatly in terms of the interpretations they affect as well as the rigour of their influence.

Specific Learning Disabilities, or SLD, do not always include all of the learning challenges that the educational system has established. IDEA defines a specific learning disability as a condition that affects one or more of the basic psychological functions required to understand or utilise language, whether it is spoken or written, and that shows up as a lack of ability to communicate, listen, think, read, write, spell, or execute mathematical operations, as researched by Muktamath et al. (2022). LDs are detected from both a medical and pedagogical standpoint. It demonstrates unequivocally that specific learning problems are not largely brought on by impairments of the eyesight, ears, or muscles, emotional instability, mental illness, or cultural or socio-economic disadvantage.

3.3.1 Types of Learning Disabilities

In any categorization, whether governmental or not, LD is rarely thought of as a single impairment; instead, it is described as a wide spectrum consisting of challenges in single or multiple scholastic areas. According to Muktamath et al. (2022), seven domains are listed in the federal definition from 1968: speaking, hearing, basic reading (word recognition and decoding), reading comprehension, written expression, arithmetic operations, and mathematical reasoning. Figure 5 demonstrates the encompassing nature of the distinct learning disabilities.

Many mental health professionals see the seven disorders listed below as distinct learning disabilities, including the Learning Impairments Association of America. They categorise Attention Deficit Hyperactivity Disorder (ADHD) and Autism Spectrum Disorder (ASD) as related but different learning disorders that have an impact on learning.

Figure 5. Learning disabilities and their types

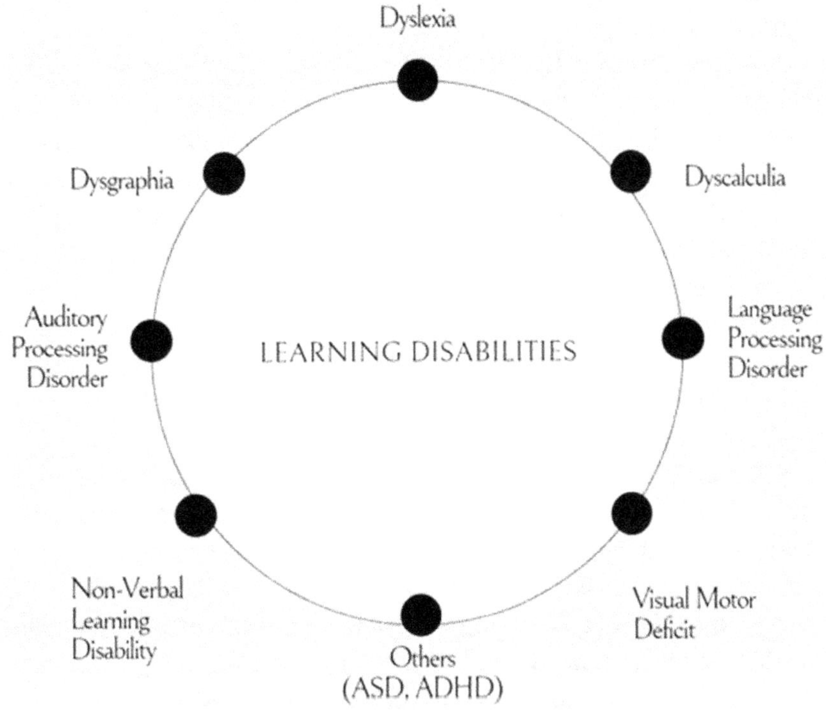

- **Dyslexia:** The most common learning impairment, dyslexia (sometimes called a reading disability), affects reading and other language-based cognitive functions and contributes to a minimum of 80% of all LDs. Greek in origin, dyslexia means "impaired" in English. It may occur alongside other related issues and affect speaking sometimes, as well as proficiency in reading, comprehension, decoding, recollection, typing, and spelling. While dyslexia are occasionally described as a language-based learning problem, every individual's degree of severity might differ.
- **Dysgraphia:** Dysgraphia is a learning disorder that impairs a person's fine motor skills and writing. It is characterised by insufficient skills that are below a child's schooling level, age, and IQ which have an impact on their academic advancement and other key areas. Spelling dyslexia or spelling disorders are other terms by which dysgraphia is sometimes referred to. Indecipherable handwriting, erratic intervals, subpar paper design, incorrect spelling, and syntax and punctuation errors are all problems. The kids have trouble writing and thinking simultaneously.
- **Dyscalculia:** A learning condition called dyscalculia makes it difficult to understand arithmetic facts, ideas, and numbers. It may lead to problems with remembering, planning, keeping track of time, and counting. Early problems could start, while later grades might struggle with reasoning. Children who have dyscalculia may also have difficulty choosing the appropriate computing strategy, selecting important data, and assessing the appropriateness of their results.
- **Auditory Processing Disorder (APD):** APD, often referred to as Central Auditory Processing Disorder (CAPD), is a disorder in which a child's brain has difficulty processing sounds normally. This disorder impairs the auditory system's capacity to absorb and interpret sounds, making it

challenging to distinguish minute changes, filter out background noises, and comprehend the order of sounds, even when they are distinguishably audible. After digesting auditory information, the brain interprets it erroneously.

- **Language Processing Disorder (LPD):** LPD is a variant of APD that influences both expressive and receptive speech in terms of language interpretation. In contrast to APD, which is affected by all sounds, LPD impacts how the brain processes sound patterns in words, phrases, and narratives. Finding the right terms and expressions or keeping up with a fast-paced discussion may be exacting for kids with LDs based on languages, which can also make it challenging for the students to write effectively since it may be challenging to organise thoughts or discern the primary point of a written communication.
- **Nonverbal Learning Disabilities (NLD or NVLD):** A large disparity in verbal and motor skills, which affect social ability, characterises NLD. In spite of struggling with abstract concepts and nonverbal clues in social circumstances, children suffering from NVLD frequently have outstanding speech and writing abilities.
- **Visual Perceptual or Visual Motor Deficit:** People with visual perceptual/visual motor impairments have poor hand-eye coordination, frequently lose their place when reading, and have trouble with fine motor skills such as using pencils, crayons, scissors, and other tools. Additionally, individuals could have trouble navigating their environment, mistake letters that appear alike when reading or performing tasks or exhibit unusual eye movement. It makes it difficult for someone to comprehend what they see, create, duplicate, or comprehend knowledge acquired through the use of images. The sensory information a person receives from visual cues may be impacted by flaws in the way their eyes move. Due to their visual impairments, these kids have trouble drawing or copying information, have short attention spans, and have limited reading comprehension skills.

Apart from the seven described disabilities, ASD and ADHD also hamper the students' learning capabilities.

- **Attention Deficit Hyperactivity Disorder (ADHD):** ADHD is a condition that makes it difficult to pay attention and stay focused, as well as manage behaviour and hyperactivity. Although ADHD is not a learning impairment, a research by Learning Disabilities Association of America (2020) indicates that anywhere from 30 to 50 percent of children having ADHD also have a specific learning limitation and that the two conditions can interact to make learning extremely challenging. Impetuousness, hyperactivity, and inattention are the three hallmarks of ADHD. There are three subtypes of ADHD: the predominantly inattentive type (which does not exhibit notable hyperactive-impulsive behaviour), the predominantly hyperactive/impulsive type (also known as ADD), and the combined type (which displays a combination of distracted and hyperactive-impulsive symptoms).
- **Autism Spectrum Disorder (ASD):** ASD is a developmental disability that results from abnormalities in the brain. It affects restricted behaviours, repeated interests, social involvement, and communication. Learning, mobility, and attention problems can manifest themselves in different ways for different people as found and revealed by Centers for Disease Control and Prevention (CDC, 2023).

3.3.2 Diagnosis

Learning difficulties cannot be largely attributable to mental disorders, emotional instability, cultural variation, or disadvantage, as said by Lyon (1996). This is a crucial aspect of what defines LD. The concept of a disparity between an individual's educational achievement and their apparent ability to learn is therefore at the centre of the LD concept.

Dyslexia is diagnosed in early graders who have difficulty remembering sequences, perceiving correspondences and contrasts between letters and words, correctly spelling words, hearing that one is "not performing well in school," being unable to read words with one syllable, connecting sounds and letters, sequencing numbers and letters, and writing backwards. According to Muktamath et al. (2022), senior graders have difficulty writing backwards, acquiring prefixes and suffixes, and it is tedious for them to read isolated words and related text. Useful reading subtests like the Woodcock-Johnson Psycho-Educational Battery-Revised, the Test of Word Reading Efficiency (TOWRE), and the Peabody Individual Achievement Test-Revised help in assessing the severity of the disorder as specified by Muktamath et al. (2022), while assessments that are standardised to evaluate writing, including the Wechsler Individual Achievement Test (WIAT-II), the Test of Written Spelling (TOWS), the Test of Early Written Language (TEWL), and the Test of Written Expression (TOWE) help in assessing symptoms of dysgraphic individuals like illegible handwriting, inconsistent and disorganized written work, a cramped odd grip of the writing instrument, and so on.

Similarly, the tools used to assess dyscalculia, such as the Keymath Diagnostic Arithmetic Test, Woodcock-Johnson Achievement Battery-III, Test of Early Mathematical Abilities, Teacher Academic Attainment Scale (TAAS), Child Self-Reported Math Anxiety Scales, and Mathematics Anxiety Scale for Children. Muktamath et al. (2022) mentions that they assess mathematical content, function, and calculation.

A set of sophisticated listening tests where the youngster listens to various sounds and responds to them can help an audiologist identify APD. The listening assessment may not yield valid results in younger children, so children are typically not evaluated for APD until they are 7 years old.

Clinicians search for the following four categories of persistent, limiting patterns of behaviour, interests, or activities: stereotypes, repetitive motions with the body, the use of things or words, similarity insistence, common interests, and sensory sensitivity to diagnose autism or ADHD. Autism cannot be diagnosed with a single test at any age. However, as researched by Benjamin (2021), there are gold standard diagnostic and screening methods that professionals use to assess individuals for autism: Comprehensive developmental histories, the Adaptive Behaviour Assessment, the Autism Diagnostic Observation Schedule-2 (ADOS), and other autism screening tools.

Along with the clinically approved learning disabilities, eminent scientist Baum (1990) has defined gifted students with LD as individuals displaying extraordinary abilities or aptitude in certain fields and crippling deficiency in others. Methods like scatter analysis, theories of LD that account for ability-achievement discrepancies, profile analysis, and broadly construed notions of intellectual ability and giftedness help in diagnosing gifted kids with learning disabilities.

Another study by Anuradha et al. (2010) created a system to diagnose ADHD more quickly and accurately. The authors claim that this is the first attempt to diagnose ADHD using Support Vector Machines (SVMs), a group of supervised learning procedures appropriate for regression and classification. The SVM module received a data set that had been corroborated by a physician and contained the answers to a set of questions used by physicians to identify the disease. The data set was then introduced before returning to the SVM module, which is ultimately what gives us the diagnostic. The ability to manage the complexity of the diagnostic procedure is the SVM algorithm's most significant benefit.

3.3.3 Assistive Technology

Recently, new approaches to addressing ever-more complicated difficulties have emerged as a result of the rapid growth of AI, such as assisting those who have complex communication demands in overcoming barriers. AI's potent tools have the power to revolutionise Augmented and Alternative Communication (AAC) systems, including low-tech ones that use sentences and glyphs and advanced digital ones with outputs of human voice as suggested by Delipetrev et al. (2020).

- The OTTAA project sanctioned by the UNICEF Innovation Fund (2021) is the first AAC platform utilising a coalition of potent AI algorithms (NLP and ML) and communication codes based on pictograms to generate words and effective communication. It was developed as part of UNICEF's Innovation Fund Investments in Skills and Connectivity. With just three taps, the portal of OTTAA enables people with speech impairments to interact and give voice to themselves. Children with impairments will have the chance to communicate more effectively and quickly by using suitable pictogram-based communication and AI algorithms.
- The GoVisual app developed by Attainment Company (2022) is a programme that transforms images and videos into chances for communication and literacy. This ground-breaking method integrates computer vision employing innovation in image recognition (gathering photos and videos), NLP tools to aid in the production of stories, and finally ML to aid in object and form identification for simplified programming. Combining these three strategies gives disabled children the chance to become independent and self-reliant in their educational setting.
- An AI-enhanced writing tool called "Fluent" put forth by Ghai and Mueller (2021) helps people who stammer recognise phrases that they would have trouble enunciating and provides a list of substitutes that have alike implications but are simpler to say. This app uses NLP-based software systems, which make up the majority of the state of writing tools powered by AI, but it also uses a subdivision of ML called active learning (AL) to see if it can aid in the learning of particular phonetic patterns that a person might have difficulty pronouncing. The stuttering problem is disguised by the app rather than being improved.
- In a recent study performed by Valliappan et al. (2020), machine learning was used to provide precise hardware-free gaze monitoring via smartphone. The study's findings, which support earlier oculomotor task research, emphasize the usefulness of smartphones for gaze tracking for identifying challenges in comprehending reading materials. Another research work has been conducted by Deepika and Murugesan (2015) to improve eye-tracking technology-based communication between computers and individuals with special needs. Under favourable lighting conditions, the proposed system's performance accuracy was 97%.
- Empower Me is software that is compatible with any kind of smart glasses. The glasses are used in conjunction with a digital coach who helps the wearer identify emotions and gives feedback to encourage involvement. By supporting them in analysing social situations, this device helps people with ASD who have trouble recognising social signs learn and communicate with others.
- In a recent study done by Dutt et al. (2022), software called the Intelligent Tutoring System (ITS) was created to use learner preferences in adaptive tutoring applications. In order to create learner-

specific content, and ITS is developed using AI approaches and psychosomatic considerations. In this situation, ITS, as opposed to humans and other instructional techniques, can efficiently complete the necessary action without wasting time or resources. For adopting the involvement of the learners, ITS can also observe the results and comments of the learners. Without the assistance of a human teacher, ITS applications enable students to study and perform to the best of their abilities, available time, and interests with the help of four modules - the learner model, the pedagogical model, the domain model, and the user interface.

- In the Virtual Learning Environment (VLE), there has been an increase in the appeal of deciphering students' feelings from their expressions. It is crucial to decipher students' intentions from their facial expressions in the VLE in order to provide them with the right kind of feedback. In addition, various studies have found that taking children with LDs' effects into account is a crucial area of research. It is possible to determine a learner's level of knowledge and pleasure with the learning activities by monitoring their emotional state while they interact in a VLE. The findings of a new study by Ouherrou et al. (2019) provide credence to the notion that children experience a wide range of emotions, and that using ICT may enable them to interact with virtual learning environments (VLEs) with fewer negative emotions expressed. ICT is particularly beneficial for supporting kids with LDs in a variety of ways, including (1) reaching high levels of individual learning; (2) increasing independence in tasks related to school and work; (3) taking part in classroom discussions; (4) engaging with teachers and peers; (5) being privy to all available educational options; (6) collaborating with classmates; and (7) completing challenging academic assignments.

3.3.4 Case Study: QTrobot

A humanoid social robot called QTrobot was developed by a company named LuxAI (2022) to help ASD kids learn social skills.

3.3.4.1 About

Individuals with ASD frequently worry about being too sensitive while dealing with a human therapist. A robot can accelerate direct communication and guide directions without needing to consider societal prompts. As a result, children with ASD can focus on learning new abilities rather than trying to interpret social cues. By means of straightforward language and visual aids, QTrobot creates interesting education via interactive games, role-playing, and social narratives. As kids advance, it teaches them complicated relationships while also teaching them social, communicative, and emotional skills.

3.3.4.2 Benefits

QTrobot is an engaging and motivating autism robot that helps children learn easily through its clear expressions and behaviors. It is consistent, predictable, and tireless, ensuring children's comfort and preventing distractions. QTrobot's non-judgmental approach allows children to practise skills multiple times without feeling overwhelmed or distracted. This non-judgmental approach ensures a positive and consistent learning environment for children with autism. They follow a scientifically curated, evidence-based curriculum proven to help children with ASD. They also allow the users to curate individual plans and programs, suited to each child's unique needs. They have been reviewed and trusted by parents and teachers worldwide, who deal with children with ASD.

3.3.4.3 Latest Advancements

QTrobot Studio allows individuals from a non-technical background, like psychologists, researchers, and more, to program, and modify the robot's settings as easily as a person from a technical background. The QTrobot Software Development Kit (SDK) provides excellent software for developing QTrobot applications, including Respeaker for sound detection and picture recognition, Acapela for speech recognition technology, Nuitrack for skeletal tracking, and Nuitrack for gesture recognition. The Wizard of Oz conversation, robot voice, facial expressions, gestures, interactive tablet applications, automatic session reports, and progress evaluations may all be programmed using QTrobot Studio. Additionally, the platform offers session reports, automatic chats, and interactive programmes. Additionally, QTrobots by LuxAI (2023) are being used to develop certain projects at École Polytechnique Fédérale de Lausanne (EPFL), like the CoWriter Project to help children with autism attain handwriting and the JUSThink project to promote calculative and the computational skills through reasoning exercises in children with ASD.

4.0 REFLECTIONS ON THE AVAILABLE TECHNOLOGIES: ADVANTAGES AND CHALLENGES

As observed, AI-enabled technologies have the potential to greatly support children with disabilities by providing personalized and inclusive learning experiences. Here are some examples of AI-enabled goals that can benefit children with disabilities:

- **Personalized Learning:** AI may modify instructional materials to accommodate each child's unique demands. By inspecting their learning styles, strengths, and weaknesses, AI algorithms can generate tailored educational materials, exercises, and assessments. This personalization helps children access information in a way that suits their specific learning abilities, making learning more engaging and effective.
- **Assistive Communication:** AI-powered systems can assist children with communication disabilities by providing alternative means of communication. NLP algorithms can interpret and generate text or speech, allowing children with speech impairments or non-verbal disabilities to express themselves using AAC devices. These AI-based communication tools can enhance social interactions and foster independence.
- **Emotional Support:** AI can assist children with disabilities in recognizing and managing their emotions. Facial recognition algorithms can interpret facial expressions and provide feedback to help children understand and express their emotions. AI chatbots can offer emotional support, provide coping strategies, and offer guidance during stressful situations. These AI tools can create a safe and supportive environment, helping children develop emotional intelligence and resilience.
- **Sensory Support:** Many children with disabilities, such as autism spectrum disorders, have sensory sensitivities. AI can help create sensory-friendly environments by monitoring and adjusting lighting, sound levels, and other environmental factors in real time. AI-enabled wearable devices can also assist children in managing sensory overload by providing calming stimuli or alerting them to potential triggers.

- **Adaptive Learning Games:** AI has the ability to enhance perceptive games and activities to serve children with disabilities AI algorithms may dynamically change the games' content, tempo, and difficulty levels by looking at the child's performance and progress. This adaptive approach ensures that children remain engaged and challenged at an appropriate level while accommodating their specific learning requirements.
- **Early Detection and Intervention:** AI can aid in the early detection of developmental delays or disabilities in children. By analyzing data from various sources, such as medical records, assessments, and behavioural observations, AI algorithms can identify patterns and indicators of potential disabilities. Early identification enables prompt assistance and treatments, which improve results for children with disabilities.
- **Remote Learning and Teletherapy:** AI-powered platforms and tools enable remote learning and teletherapy for children with disabilities, particularly those who may face challenges attending physical classrooms or therapy sessions. AI can facilitate virtual classrooms, interactive lessons, and teletherapy sessions, providing access to specialized educators and therapists from anywhere. These AI-enabled solutions confirm that children having disabilities can obtain the support they require, regardless of their geographical location.

It is crucial to remember that while AI can provide valuable support, it should always be used in conjunction with human expertise and guidance. Human supervision is crucial to face and tackle challenges discussed further to ensure ethical considerations, safeguard privacy, and maintain a child-centred approach to supporting children with disabilities. Moreover, the future of AI in special education looks promising, as systems that enable communication by using steady-state visuals and stimulate brain electrical activity, regardless of eye movements, are already available for people with vision impairments. A few individuals with degenerative retinal disorders have previously had their vision restored by electronic retinal implants. People who are hard of hearing or even deaf are successfully given a sensation of sound thanks to cochlear implants. With the use of new brain implants, people may create simple sentences and words that assist communication. These accomplishments felt like science fiction a few years ago. Soon, brain implants that enhance human senses will become commonplace, thanks to the present pace of technological advancement, enabling the greater inclusion of people with impairments. The benefits of AI-based assistive education methods are illustrated in Figure 6.

4.1 Challenges in Implementing AI-Based Technologies for Special Education

There are currently two main obstacles that restrict the usage of AI in clinical decision-making: the limited availability of labelled information for algorithm training and the black-box nature of deep neural network models, as found and mentioned by Zdravkova et al. (2022). Other primary fields of concern include:

- The use of high-tech communication devices is undoubtedly extremely expensive to implement, and this prevents a whole community from adapting to these devices. Selective use of assistive technology will increase economic inequality, or the disparity between the affluent and the poor. The gender and racial disparities may also widen in certain wealthy societies, harming minorities, and young women. In order to use AI in the classroom, a lot of educational institutions lack the budget to purchase and maintain the necessary technology. As a result, they might need to search for outside financing or partner with other organisations.

Figure 6. Benefits of AI in special education

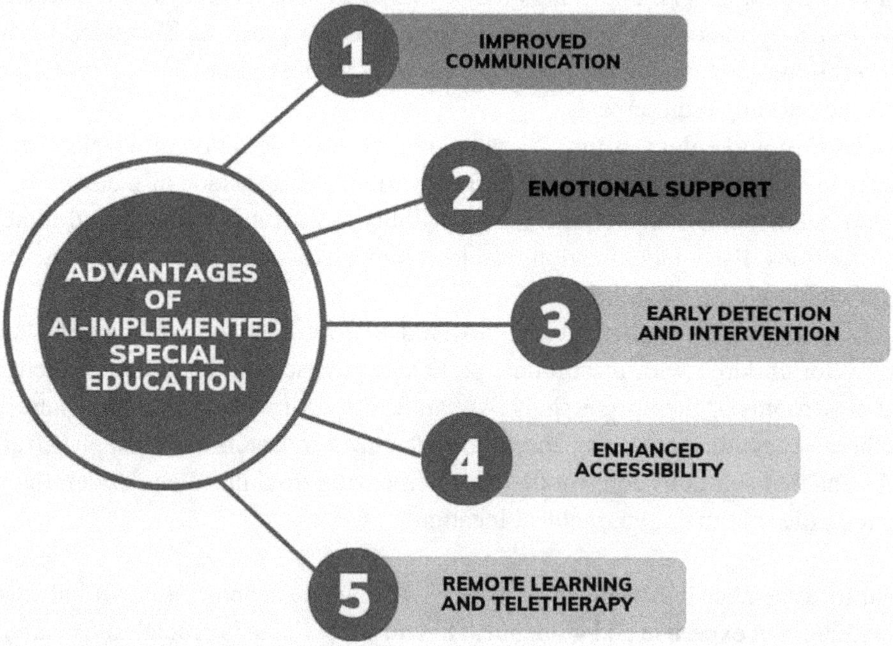

- The second question of liability arises from the effects of available technologies and devices on the physical and emotional health of patients. Shanmugam and Marimuthu (2021) mentions that still-untested communication technologies could aggravate the condition of already fragile sight and hearing sensory organs, increasing the risk of permanent deafness or blindness.
- The next hurdle is privacy. In order to conduct research studies or monitor patient health, several pieces of communication equipment are wirelessly linked to medical facilities. During the COVID epidemic, the rising trend of cyber-security threats had an impact on healthcare institutions all over the world. In order to develop related learning plans for children with special needs, the application of AI must be integrated with big data support, grasp all relevant information about youngsters with special needs, and import it into the learning system. Special children's private information, such as physical characteristics, personality features, level of IQ, and degree of impairment, will be involved in this procedure.
- The demand for technological expertise is another primary obstacle. Teachers who are not familiar with AI may find it difficult to integrate cutting-edge technology that is based on AI into their teaching methods, and they may need help and training to get started. Artificial intelligence has largely taken over the repetitive and mechanistic instructional tasks that teachers once performed. While AI has somewhat liberated the teaching workforce, it ultimately cannot take the place of the teacher in developing moral cognition, moral judgement, and appropriate behaviour in particular teaching situations. In the teaching process, the teacher's role has been modified to that of an advisor and facilitator of students' learning. Inappropriate usage of instructional technology can even alienate teachers and pupils, which causes ethical issues in the classroom.

- The final difficulty is related to how society perceives new technologies as pointed by Koelle et al. (2018). Innovative technology and apps might lead to novel risks, worries, and disputes between users and non-users. Many societies are technophobic, and when new technologies are introduced, they are met with utter opposition. A significant number of handicapped individuals will be worried about their aftermath creating a heinous cycle if it is formally accepted, because that might make the situation worse rather than better.

4.2 Challenges of a Differently-Abled Student: An Interview

Linda Corcoran, a member of an online platform named 'Disabled in Higher Ed' aimed to help and celebrate differently, abled students pursuing higher education have commented on the challenges faced by her and her peers in a recent interview by eLife (2021). She conveyed that although the quantity of support available differs between institutions, most universities have a variety of procedures in place to assist people, particularly students, in getting the essential support they need. However, in order to receive that assistance or accommodations, one must essentially provide proof of their handicap, which calls for maintaining accurate medical records and completing all required tests. This can be a significant obstacle for anyone attempting to gain a diagnosis, and it frequently means that kids and staff don't get the care they need while they delay being diagnosed. It's also essential to remember that impairment is fluid and that a person's support requirements may alter over time. She further elaborated that during university, she faced challenges and harsh attitudes, including ableism in teaching techniques. She had to argue with lecturers to publish slides online, and she even needed an attendance waiver due to medication. However, she also had supportive lecturers who encouraged and empowered her. She also comments that it is critical to acknowledge disabled individuals in academia because they may experience stigma or exclusion owing to inaccessibility. It's crucial to address disability as a diversity issue and make sure accessibility is taken into account right away. The use of Universal Design in all facets of higher education, including teaching methods, can be beneficial. It is crucial to make sure that physical locations, tools, and activities assist both staff and students with disabilities.

4.3 Case Study: Special Education in the Post-Pandemic World

The post-COVID-19 world has seen an exponential increase in the rise of e-learning, or web-based learning. Teaching and learning have taken a drastic turn as the spread of the fatal virus drove both educators and learners out of the classroom environment and remote education took over on online platforms. E-learning includes interactive, digital, online learning supported by computers. In this system, the learner learns anytime, anyplace, simultaneously, and autonomously, thus gaining self-direction. Though the most significant disadvantage of e-learning is that it only allows for the theoretical acquisition of knowledge without providing sufficient opportunities or resources to put that knowledge into practice and hone practical application skills. For both instructors and students, the abrupt shift to online instruction has presented several difficulties. Faculty members might need more time to carefully plan online courses that fully exploit the advantages of the online format. Some professors might have had a deeper learning curve because they had never taught online prior to the current scenario. But online learning's main advantage is its capacity to upend and change the traditional idea of a genuine school into a new, more individualised, student-centred one.

Due to their special demands and methods of absorbing concepts, kids in special education require stronger supervision. By addressing the key shortcomings of conventional traditional schools, the distinctive environment established by cyber charter schools may enhance outcomes for special education kids. In the post-pandemic world, special education faculties kept carrying the continuous burden of providing high-quality education to learners despite the challenges. An analysis of responses conducted by a recent qualitative report of Cousik (2022) revealed that teachers struggled with a number of issues, including student engagement, motivation, and concentration; little to no district support, insufficient family engagement, new and unclear state and district mandates; and the demand for additional instructors in general education to participate in special education. Online education poses several difficulties to learners requiring special education, like decreased attention span, self-consciousness due to the intrusion of family and parents hindering the method of independent education, difficulty understanding the complexity of rapidly advancing technologies, and so on. Students exhibit signs of over-responsiveness and irritability as they adapt to this new mode of learning. The absence of human presence in the online form is also a significant negative. The educators concentrated on how the absence of face-to-face interaction with their pupils was impeding teaching and learning. They even mentioned how the lack of physical and eye contact harmed the bond they felt with the children. Some of these responders went so far as to describe how their pupils' lack of peer contact lowered their interest and reduced their participation in class. Recently, a study was conducted that included the special educators from reputed organizations in Kolkata, India, who had prior experience teaching in offline mode and are highly qualified and experienced in their field of work. Figure 7 explains the problems faced by these educators in the era of e-learning.

Figure 7. Problems faced by special educators in online mode

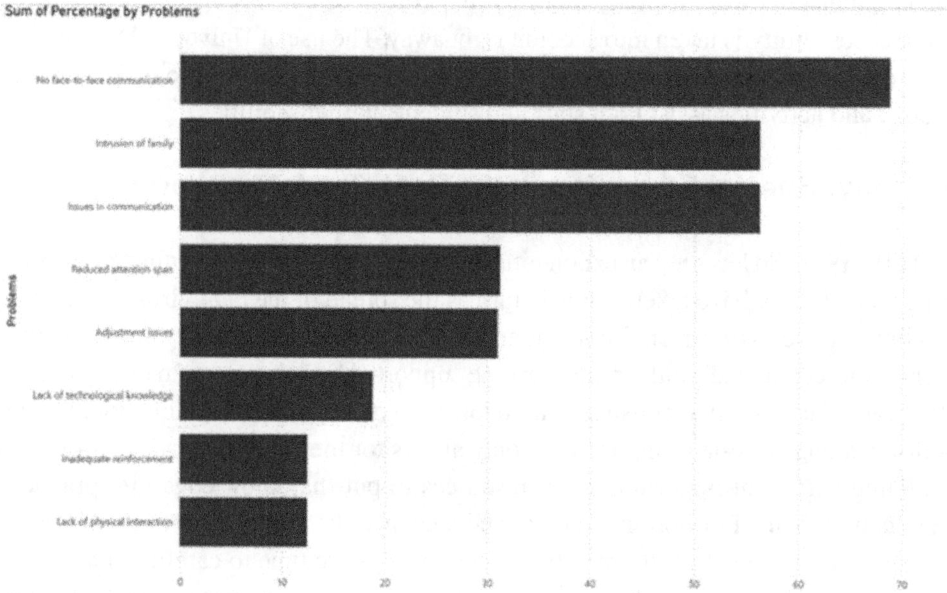

In these times, special educators often took the help of online interfaces like Google Meet, Zoom, Microsoft Teams, etc. to connect with their students, and several applications like Whiteboard, Canva, Powerpoint, and Google Bolo helped them bring the course materials to life. They also wished for the availability of an application or software that enabled the students to connect with each other as well as with the faculties in a blended mode of both offline and online interfaces.

5.0 FUTURE PROSPECTS AND FURTHER RESEARCH RECOMMENDATIONS

Experts in the domains of education, technology, and disability studies must continue to conduct research, develop new ideas, and work together if AI in special education is to have a bright future. Designing AI systems that are inclusive, approachable, and continuously improved based on user feedback and changing best practices is vital.

5.1 Future Prospects of Special Education using AI

AI-based tools will improve and revolutionize the future of special education with the help of the following tools:

- **Personalized Learning Assistants:** The implementation of AI-based tools providing personalized learning assistants for students with special needs in their daily lives can improve with more technological advancements, be more adaptive to each student's unique learning style, and provide customized learning materials, interactive activities, and real-time feedback. For example, an AI tool can analyze a student's strengths and weaknesses and dynamically generate lessons and exercises that cater to their individual needs.
- **Speech and Language Therapy:** Implementation of AI-based assistive tools can analyze a student's speech patterns, identify areas for improvement, and provide targeted exercises and feedback to help them develop their communication skills. In the future, more use of these tools will provide more data to train the algorithms and thereby help in building better assistive tools. Virtual speech therapists can also engage in interactive conversations with students, simulating real-life scenarios to practice their language skills.
- **Intelligent Assistive Technologies:** Advanced computer vision algorithms can enable individuals with mobility impairments to control their devices using gestures or eye movements. These tools can track and interpret the user's movements, allowing them to navigate computer interfaces, interact with educational software, and communicate effectively. With more improvements, they can be a part of the daily lives of students with special needs.
- **Emotional Support Systems:** With the rise in understanding the importance of mental health and taking care of it, tools to provide emotional aid to specially-abled individuals will be the need of the hour. AI algorithms can be utilized to detect and respond to students' emotional states, providing valuable support for those with emotional and behavioral disorders. These systems can analyze facial expressions, tone of voice, and other physiological cues to identify signs of distress or frustration. Based on this analysis, the AI tool can offer appropriate interventions, such as suggesting calming techniques or notifying a teacher or counselor for further assistance.

- **Adaptive Assessments:** AI-powered assessments adapting to the individualized requirements and abilities of students with special needs are extremely required to allow these students to showcase their full potential. These assessments can dynamically modify the questions' level of difficulty depending on a learner's academic performance, ensuring a fair evaluation. Furthermore, the AI tool can analyze patterns in the student's responses and provide actionable insights to educators, helping them understand the student's progress and tailor their instruction accordingly. Along with this, it is also needed to help more educators be specially trained to help such students exactly the way they need it.
- **Augmented Reality for Sensory Learning:** Augmented reality (AR) technology combined with AI can create immersive learning experiences for students with sensory impairments. AR applications can provide visual and auditory cues, enhancing the learning environment and facilitating a better understanding of abstract concepts. For example, a visually impaired student can use AR glasses to explore a three-dimensional representation of a historical artefact or experience a virtual science experiment. These adaptive devices are to be popularized and made available to commoners so they can take advantage of them for their own betterment.
- **Data-Driven Intervention Planning**: AI tools can examine and interpret enormous student records, including academic performance, behavior patterns, and personal preferences, to inform intervention planning. By identifying trends and correlations in the data, AI can assist educators in developing Individualized Education Plans (IEPs) that address the specific needs of each student. This data-driven approach can enhance the effectiveness of interventions and optimize educational outcomes.

5.2 Further Research Recommendations

To combat the challenges faced by both faculties and students requiring special education, further research is needed. Research innovations need to be extremely responsible if we want to avoid all of the issues that were raised above. Every possible moral and legal dilemma must be foreseen in advance, and new, cutting-edge assistive technology should be carefully designed to address them.

- To start with the issue of limited availability of labelled data, significant dense representation from small data pieces has recently been developed using self-supervised representation learning. Furthermore, by utilising an exploration-exploitation framework, reinforcement learning approaches can be used to optimise given environment.
- By producing information that explains a decision's rationale and process and suggests the variables that most strongly influenced the outcome, explainable AI technologies can be utilised to increase accountability for decisions, thereby increasing confidence and transparency. As AI algorithms take care of data gathering and analysis, researchers will be able to focus on precision in studies of intervention and customised therapy models. Strong legal privacy frameworks should be established to prevent data leaks and greatly improve the degree of data protection in the public health sector.
- In the case of hard-of-hearing individuals, the higher-level auditory skills of children with similar audiograms are frequently substantially different, such as spoken word recognition. Even less obviously, there are connections between the degree of hearing damage and prospective results such as academic success, employment position, and general psychosocial development. It's critical

to pinpoint additional causes of these consequences in people who were born deaf or with damaged hearing. It's crucial to understand how these elements affect the long run, in particular: the complexity of lingual conditions in the spheres of the classroom and the home, such as polyglot settings and verbal and signed modes of directions; and the complexity of institutional and scholastic enforcement, along with the different kinds of mediation, the time at which it begins and how long it lasts, the type of educational environment (mainstream, self-contained, at home), and the education of intervention professionals. There is a significant lack of research in this field that can potentially lead to better innovations and, subsequently, better standards of living.

- There is also a clear need for newborns and young children to have standardised speech perception tests that account for their developmental stage and level of hearing loss. Such examinations ought to be created in both English and other languages. In order to replicate real-life scenarios, such as classrooms, such assessments should include an examination of comprehension and reception both in silence and with pertinent contradictory sounds.
- The relationship between listening and seeing in the growth of conveying abilities is poorly understood. When auditory information is insufficient, there may be significant individual variances in the reliance on visual information. There aren't any measurements for the visual, auditory, or mixed perception of speech at the moment. The creation of normative clinical measures that take into account auditory and visual evaluations is highly necessary. Further research is required to determine the exact condition or type of malady in such kids' communication development, academic performance, and social adjustment, particularly in educational settings, as well as the potential for intervention that might help to lessen such disturbances.
- Moreover, in most cases, different types of LD affect an individual together. So a student might need more assistance for more than one type of disability. There needs to be more investigation to focus more on combating the joint effects of multiple disabilities.

6.0 CONCLUSION

In conclusion, the prospect of AI in the near future in special education promises immense potential for transforming the lives of children with disabilities. AI-enabled technologies have the potential to create inclusive and personalized learning environments, enhance communication capabilities, provide emotional support, adapt to individual needs, and enable early detection and intervention. These advancements can break down barriers, empower children with disabilities, and promote their educational and social development.

Nevertheless, it is crucial to approach the integration of AI in special education with caution and a human-centred mindset. Ethical considerations, privacy protection, and the need for human supervision should always be at the forefront. AI should be viewed as a complementary tool that works in collaboration with educators, therapists, and caregivers, rather than a replacement for human support.

Overall, we have seen that AI-powered initiatives to help kids with impairments encompass a range of applications. These goals include personalized learning experiences tailored to individual needs, adaptive communication tools to assist those with speech impairments, emotional support systems to help children manage their emotions, and sensory support technologies that create inclusive environments. AI can also enhance educational games by adapting difficulty levels, offering early detection and intervention for developmental delays, and facilitating remote learning and teletherapy sessions. But simultaneously, we have observed that high-tech communication devices are expensive and can lead to economic inequality, gender and racial disparities, and challenges in adapting to AI in the classroom. Liability concerns include the potential for physical and emotional health issues, privacy concerns, and the need for technical skills to integrate AI into teaching practises. Teachers may need assistance and training to integrate AI-based technology into their teaching practises, as AI cannot replace teachers in developing moral cognition, judgement, and appropriate behavior. Additionally, the acceptance of new technologies by society can create risks, raise questions, and create debates between supporters and non-supporters. Many disabled individuals may be concerned about the impact of AI on their lives, creating a vicious circle that may worsen the situation rather than improve it. The future of AI in special education also requires ongoing research, development, and collaboration between experts in the fields of education, technology, and disability studies. It is crucial to design AI systems that are inclusive, accessible, and continually refined based on user feedback and evolving best practises.

Ultimately, with responsible implementation, AI has the potential to revolutionize special education by providing tailored support, promoting inclusion, and empowering children with disabilities to reach their full potential. By harnessing the power of AI, we can create a more equitable and inclusive education system, ensuring that every child, regardless of their abilities, has equal opportunities to learn, grow, and thrive.

REFERENCES

ADHD – Learning Disabilities Association of America. (n.d.). Retrieved June 10, 2023, from https://ldaamerica.org/disabilities/adhd/#:~:text=A%20disorder%20that%20includes%20difficulty,difficulty%20controlling%20behavior%20and%20hyperactivity

Anuradha, J., Tisha, Ramachandran, V., Arulalan, K.V., & Tripathy, B.K. (2010). Diagnosis of ADHD using SVM algorithm. In *Proceedings of the Third Annual ACM Bangalore Conference (COMPUTE '10).* Association for Computing Machinery. 10.1145/1754288.1754317

Asokan, A. (2019, February 13). 5 Ways in Which AI Is Improving Accessibility for the Hearing Impaired. *Analytics India Magazine.* Retrieved June 9, 2023, from https://analyticsindiamag.com/5-ways-in-which-ai-is-improving-accessibility-for-the-hearing-impaired/

Attainment Company. (2022). *GoVisual™*.Retrieved June 11, 2023, from https://www.attainmentcompany.com/govisual

Baum, S. (1990). *Gifted but learning disabled: A puzzling paradox.* Retrieved on June 16, 2004, from http://www.hoagiesgifted .org/eric/e479.html

Be My Eyes. (2015). Be My Eyes - See the world together. https://www.bemyeyes.com/

Benjamin, E. (2021, June 16). *ADHD and Adult Autism: Symptoms, Diagnosis & Interventions for Both.* ADDitude. Retrieved June 11, 2023, from https://www.additudemag.com/adult-autism-symptoms-adhd/

CDC. (2023, January 11). *Signs & Symptoms | Autism Spectrum Disorder (ASD) | NCBDDD | CDC.* Centers for Disease Control and Prevention. Retrieved June 10, 2023, from https://www.cdc.gov/ncbddd/autism/signs.html

Chazen, D. (2019). *Assistive Technology for Deaf and Hard of Hearing Students | Verbit*. Verbit. Retrieved June 9, 2023, from https://verbit.ai/assistive-technology-for-deaf-and-hard-of-hearing-students/

Cousik, R. (2022). COVID-19 Pandemic and Special Education Teacher Voices. *Qualitative Report, 27*(11), 2486–2500. doi:10.46743/2160-3715/2022.5553

Daniela, Mahender, & Ayanna. (2021). *Universal Access in HumanComputer Interaction*. Academic Press.

Das Chakladar, D., Kumar, P., Mandal, S., Roy, P. P., Iwamura, M., & Kim, B. (2021). 3D Avatar Approach for Continuous Sign Movement Using Speech/Text. *Applied Sciences (Basel, Switzerland), 11*(8), 3439. doi:10.3390/app11083439

Deepika, S. S., & Murugesan, G. (2015). A novel approach for Human-Computer Interface based on eye movements for disabled people. *2015 IEEE International Conference on Electrical, Computer and Communication Technologies*, 1–3. 10.1109/ICECCT.2015.7226124

Delipetrev, B., Tsinaraki, C., & Kostic, U. (2020, November 20). *Historical Evolution of Artificial Intelligence*. JRC Publications Repository. Retrieved June 11, 2023, from https://publications.jrc.ec.europa.eu/repository/handle/JRC120469

Dobie, R. A., & Hemel, S. V. (2004, January 1). *Hearing Loss in Children - Hearing Loss - NCBI Bookshelf*. Hearing Loss in Children - Hearing Loss - NCBI Bookshelf.

Dutt, S., Ahuja, N. J., & Kumar, M. (2022). An intelligent tutoring system architecture based on fuzzy neural network (FNN) for special education of learning disabled learners. *Education and Information Technologies, 27*(2), 2613–2633. doi:10.100710639-021-10713-x

eLife. (2021, May 5). Equity, Diversity and Inclusion: Disabled in Higher Ed.

Encyclopedia Britannica. (2023, February 23).. . *Special Education*.

Galea, L. C., & Smeaton, A. F. (2019). Recognising Irish sign language using electromyography. *Proceedings of the IEEE 2019 International Conference on Content-Based Multimedia Indexing (CBMI)*, 1–4.

Ghai, B., & Mueller, K. (2021). Fluent: An AI Augmented Writing Tool for People who Stutter. *23rd International ACM SIGACCESS Conference On Computers And Accessibility*. 10.1145/3441852.3471211

GiovannaAlbertoGiorgiaSimonePaoloElisa. (2021). *In teleXbe*.

Jacob & Cary. (2021). *Journal of Science Education for Students with Disabilities 24*.

Knoblauch, B., & Sorenson, B. (1998, April). ERIC EC Digest #E560.

Koelle, M., Boll, S., Olsson, T., Williamson, J., Profita, H., Kane, S., & Mitchell, R. (2018). (Un acceptable!?! re-thinking the social acceptability of emerging technologies. *Extended Abstracts of the 2018 CHI Conference on Human Factors in Computing Systems*, 1–8.

LuxAI S.A. (2022, September 21). How one year with an in-home robot helps children with autism.

LuxAI S.A.(2023, April 21). QTrobot - expressive humanoid social robot for research and teaching.

Lyon, G. R. (1996). Learning Disabilities. *The Future of Children*, *6*(1), 54. doi:10.2307/1602494 PMID:8689262

Malaysia Hearing Solution. (2021, March 11). Circa AI - The World's First Healthable Hearing Aids with AI | Malaysia Hearing Solution.

Mandal, A. (2012, June 27). News-Medical.net.

Medical Xpress (2018, January 15). *Brain Imaging Predicts Language Learning in Deaf Children.* Retrieved June 9, 2023, from https://medicalxpress.com/news/2018-01-brain-imaging-language-deaf-children.html

Mittal, A., Kumar, P., Roy, P. P., Balasubramanian, R., & Chaudhuri, B. B. (2019). A modified LSTM model for continuous sign language recognition using leap motion. *IEEE Sensors Journal*, *19*(16), 7056–7063. doi:10.1109/JSEN.2019.2909837

Muktamath, V. U., Hegde, P. R., & Chand, S. (2022). *Types of Specific Learning Disability.* IntechOpen. doi:10.5772/intechopen.100809

National Center for Education Statistics. (2022). Students With Disabilities. In *Condition of Education.* U.S. Department of Education, Institute of Education Sciences. Retrieved 11.05.2023, from https://nces.ed.gov/programs/coe/indicator/cgg

OTTAA Project: Accessible Communication for Children With Disabilities | UNICEF Innovation Fund. (2021, October 26). Retrieved June 11, 2023, from https://www.unicefinnovationfund.org/broadcast/updates/ottaa-project-accessible-communication-children-disabilities

Ouherrou, N., Elhammoumi, O., Benmarrakchi, F., & El Kafi, J. (2019). Comparative study on emotions analysis from facial expressions in children with and without learning disabilities in virtual learning environment. *Education and Information Technologies*, *24*(2), 1777–1792. doi:10.100710639-018-09852-5

Papastratis, I., Chatzikonstantinou, C., Konstantinidis, D., Dimitropoulos, K., & Daras, P. (2021). Artificial Intelligence Technologies for Sign Language. *Sensors (Basel)*, *21*(17), 5843. doi:10.339021175843 PMID:34502733

Resnikoff, S., Pascolini, D., Etya'Ale, D., Kocur, I., Pararajasegaram, R., Pokharel, G. P., & Mariotti, S. P. (2004). Global data on visual impairment in the year 2002. *Bulletin of the World Health Organization*, *82*(11), 844–851. PMID:15640920

Shanmugam, A. K., & Marimuthu, R. (2021). A critical analysis and review of assistive technology: Advancements, laws, and impact on improving the rehabilitation of dysarthric patients. *Handb. Dec. Supp. Syst. Neurol. Disorders*, *15*, 263–281. doi:10.1016/B978-0-12-822271-3.00001-3

Shew, M., New, J., Wichova, H., Koestler, D. C., & Staecker, H. (2019). Using Machine Learning to Predict Sensorineural Hearing Loss Based on Perilymph Micro RNA Expression Profile. *Scientific Reports*, *9*(1), 3393. doi:10.103841598-019-40192-7 PMID:30833669

United Nations, Department of Economic and Social Affairs Disability. (n.d.). Factsheet on Persons with Disabilities. https://www.un.org/development/desa/disabilities/resources/factsheet-on-persons-with-disabilities.html

U.S. Department of Education. Office of Special Education Programs, Individuals with Disabilities Education Act (IDEA) database. (n.d.). Retrieved February 25, 2022, from https://data.ed.gov/dataset/idea-section-618-data-products

Valliappan, N., Dai, N., Steinberg, E., He, J., Rogers, K., Ramachandran, V., & Navalpakkam, V. (2020). Accelerating eye movement research via accurate and affordable smartphone eye tracking. *Nature Communications*, *11*(1), 1–12. doi:10.103841467-020-18360-5 PMID:32917902

World Health Organisation (2022, October 13). Blindness and vision impairment.

World Health Organisation (2023, March 3). Hearing loss.

Zdravkova, K., Krasniqi, V., Dalipi, F., & Ferati, M. (2022). Cutting-edge communication and learning assistive technologies for disabled children: An artificial intelligence perspective. *Frontiers in Artificial Intelligence*, *5*, 970430. doi:10.3389/frai.2022.970430 PMID:36388402

Zhang, Z. (2012). Microsoft Kinect sensor and its effect. *IEEE MultiMedia*, *19*(2), 4–10. doi:10.1109/MMUL.2012.24

Compilation of References

Abbas, H., Garberson, F., Glover, E., & Wall, D. P. (2018). Machine learning approach for early detection of autism by combining questionnaire and home video screening. *Journal of the American Medical Informatics Association, 25*(8), 1000–1007. doi:10.1093/jamia/ocy039 PMID:29741630

Abbas, H., Garberson, F., Liu-Mayo, S., Glover, E., & Wall, D. P. (2020, March 19). Multi-modular AI Approach to Streamline Autism Diagnosis in Young Children. *Scientific Reports, 10*(1), 5014. Advance online publication. doi:10.103841598-020-61213-w PMID:32193406

Abbott, R. G. (2006). Automated expert modeling for automated student evaluation. *Intelligent Tutoring Systems: 8th International Conference, ITS 2006, Jhongli, Taiwan, June 26-30, 2006. Proceedings, 8*, 1–10.

Accordino, R. E., Kidd, C., Politte, L. C., Henry, C. A., & McDougle, C. J. (2016). Psychopharmacological interventions in autism spectrum disorder. *Expert Opinion on Pharmacotherapy, 17*(7), 937–952. doi:10.1517/14656566.2016.1154536 PMID:26891879

ADHD – Learning Disabilities Association of America. (n.d.). Retrieved June 10, 2023, from https://ldaamerica.org/disabilities/adhd/#:~:text=A%20disorder%20that%20includes%20difficulty,difficulty%20controlling%20behavior%20and%20hyperactivity

Ahmed, W. A. (n.d.). *Reading and Writing Skills Development for Kindergarten Children with Learning Disabilities Using Artificial Intelligence Applications.* Retrieved from ekb: https://jchild.journals.ekb.eg/article_183573_c1f4fba55ce150d8fc8d98815c707284.pdf

Ahmed, A., Rehman, K., Shahid, M., & Alrajeh, N. A. (2021). Towards effective design of AI-based educational games for children with disabilities. *Computers & Education, 170*, 104281.

Ahmed, Z., Abdullah, Z., Shah, S., & Rahman, M. A. (2021). Artificial Intelligence in Education: Recent Trends, Challenges, and Future Directions. *SN Computer Science, 2*(4), 1–17. PMID:34056622

Akbar, M. S., Sarker, P., Mansoor, A. T., Al Ashray, A. M., & Uddin, J. (2018, August). Face recognition and RFID verified attendance system. In *2018 International Conference on Computing, Electronics & Communications Engineering (iCCECE)* (pp. 168-172). IEEE. 10.1109/iCCECOME.2018.8658705

Akgun, S., & Greenhow, C. (2021). Artificial Intelligence in Education: Addressing Ethical Challenges in K-12 Settings. *AI and Ethics*, 1-10.

Akgun, S., & Greenhow, C. (2021, September 22). *Artificial Intelligence in Education: Addressing Ethical Challenges in K-12 Settings*. PubMed Central (PMC).

Akhil, R., Soori, A., Shankar, D., Krishnan, M. M., & Poorna, B. R. (2017, March). Detecting specific learning disabilities. In *2017 International Conference on Networks & Advances in Computational Technologies* (pp. 380-385). IEEE. doi: https://webzoom.freewebs.com/sallydoxie/TTS.pdf doi:10.1109/netact.2017.8076796

Al Ka'bi, A. (2023). Proposed artificial intelligence algorithm and deep learning techniques for development of higher education. *International Journal of Intelligent Networks*, *4*, 68–73. doi:10.1016/j.ijin.2023.03.002

Alam, A. (2021). Possibilities and Apprehensions in the Landscape of Artificial Intelligence inEducation. In *2021 International Conference on Computational Intelligence andComputing Applications (ICCICA)* (pp. 1-8). IEEE.

Aldeman, N. L. S., de Sá Urtiga Aita, K. M., Machado, V. P., da Mata Sousa, L. C. D., Coelho, A. G. B., da Silva, A. S., da Silva Mendes, A. P., de Oliveira Neres, F. J., & do Monte, S. J. H. (2021). Smartpathk: A platform for teaching glomerulopathies using machine learning. *BMC Medical Education*, *21*(1), 248. doi:10.118612909-021-02680-1 PMID:33926437

Aldosemani, T. (2019). Inservice Teachers' Perceptions of a Professional Development Plan Based on SAMR Model: A Case Study. *Turkish Online Journal of Educational Technology, 18*(3), 46-53.

Alenezi, H. S., & Faisal, M. H. (2020). Utilizing crowdsourcing and machine learning in education: Literature review. *Education and Information Technologies*, *25*(4), 2971–2986. doi:10.100710639-020-10102-w

Alghamdi, A., Alanezi, M., & Khan, F. (2020). Design and implementation of a computer aided intelligent examination system. *International Journal of Emerging Technologies in Learning*, *15*(1), 30–44. doi:10.3991/ijet.v15i01.11102

Ali, A., Nawaz, A., Noman, M., & Khan, M. S. (2021). Role of Artificial Intelligence in Education 4.0: A Review. In *2021 International Conference on Communication, Computing and Digital systems (C-CODE)* (pp. 327-332). IEEE.

Ali, F., & Usman, M. (2019). Role of Artificial Intelligence in Education 4.0. In *Proceedings of the 1st International Conference on Future of Teaching and Education* (pp. 1-7). ACM.

Allam, F. C., & Martin, M. M. (2021). Issues and challenges in special education: A qualitative analysis from teacher's perspective. *Southeast Asia Early Childhood Journal*, *10*(1), 37–49. doi:10.37134aecj.vol10.1.4.2021

Almasri, A., Celebi, E., & Alkhawaldeh, R. S. (2019). EMT: Ensemble Meta-Based Tree Model for Predicting Student Performance. *Scientific Programming*, *2019*, 1–13. doi:10.1155/2019/3610248

American Psychiatric Association, DSM-5 Task Force. (2013). *Diagnostic and statistical manual of mental disorders: DSM-5* (5th ed.). American Psychiatric Publishing, Inc. doi:10.1176/appi.books.9780890425596

American Psychiatric Association. (2013). Diagnostic and statistical manual of mental disorders: Dsm-5 (Vol. 5). American psychiatric association Washington, DC.

Amiri, I., Mousavi, S. M., & Eynollahzadeh, M. (2021). Education 4.0 and Artificial Intelligence: An Overview. *Journal of Information Systems and Telecommunication*, *9*(3), 77–86.

Anastasiou, D., Felder, M., Correia, L., Shemanov, A., Zweers, I., & Ahrbeck, B. (2020). The impact of Article 24 of the CRPD on special and inclusive education in Germany, Portugal, the Russian Federation, and Netherlands. *On educational inclusion: Meanings, history, issues and international perspectives*, 236-245.

Anthony, L., Yang, J., & Koedinger, K. R. (2008). Toward next-generation, intelligent tutors: Adding natural handwriting input. *IEEE MultiMedia*, *15*(3), 64–69. doi:10.1109/MMUL.2008.73

Anuradha, J., Tisha, Ramachandran, V., Arulalan, K.V., & Tripathy, B.K. (2010). Diagnosis of ADHD using SVM algorithm. In *Proceedings of the Third Annual ACM Bangalore Conference (COMPUTE '10).* Association for Computing Machinery. 10.1145/1754288.1754317

Anuradha, J., Ramachandran, V., Arulalan, K., & Tripathy, B. (2010). Diagnosis of adhd using svm algorithm. *Proceedings of the Third Annual ACM Bangalore Conference*, 1–4.

Anwar, M. (2021). Prediction of the graduation rate of engineering education students using Artificial Neural Network Algorithms. *International Journal of Research in Counseling and Education*, *5*(1), 15–23. doi:10.24036/00411za0002

Arlot, S., & Celisse, A. (2010). A survey of cross-validation procedures for model selection. *Statistics Surveys*, *4*(none), 40–79. doi:10.1214/09-SS054

Armstrong, D. (2003). Experiences of Special Education: Re-evaluating Policy and Practice through. *Life (Chicago, Ill.)*.

Arthi, K., & Tamilarasi, A. (2008). Prediction of autistic disorder using neuro fuzzy system by applying ann technique. *International Journal of Developmental Neuroscience*, *26*(7), 699–704. doi:10.1016/j.ijdevneu.2008.07.013 PMID:18706991

Asokan, A. (2019, February 13). 5 Ways in Which AI Is Improving Accessibility for the Hearing Impaired. *Analytics India Magazine*. Retrieved June 9, 2023, from https://analyticsindiamag.com/5-ways-in-which-ai-is-improving-accessibility-for-the-hearing-impaired/

Athanasios, S., & Rodi-Elein, I. (2012). Artificial intelligence in special education: A decade review. *International Journal of Engineering Education*, *28*(6), 1366–1372.

Attainment Company. (2022). *GoVisual™*.Retrieved June 11, 2023, from https://www.attainmentcompany.com/govisual

Azmi, N., Maryono, D., & Yuana, R. (2017, June). Development of an Android-based Learning Media Application for Visually Impaired Students. *Indonesian Journal of Informatics Education*, *1*(1), 61–68. doi:10.20961/ijie.v1i1.11796

Badilla-Quintana, M. G., Sepúlveda-Valenzuela, E., & Salazar Arias, M. (2020, December). Augmented reality as a sustainable technology to improve academic achievement in students with and without special educational needs. *Sustainability*, *12*(19), 8116. doi:10.3390u12198116

Bailey, D. B., Bruder, M. B., Hebbeler, K., Carta, J., Defosset, M., Greenwood, C., & Schoenbrodt, L. (2019). Recommended outcomes for families of young children with disabilities. *Journal of Early Intervention*, *41*(1), 53–73.

Baker, R. (2021). *Artificial intelligence in education: Bringing it all together*. . doi:10.1787/f54ea644-en

Baker, R. S. (2008). Better to Be Frustrated than Bored: The Incidence, Persistence, and Impact of Learners' Cognitive-Affective States during Interactions with Three Different Computer-Based Learning Environments. *International Journal of Human-Computer Studies*, *66*(4).

Baron, S., Phillips, R., & Stalker, K. (1996). Barriers to training for disabled social work students. *Disability & Society*, *11*(3), 361–378. doi:10.1080/09687599627660

Baschera, G.-M., & Gross, M. (2010). Poisson-based inference for perturbation models in adaptive spelling training. *International Journal of Artificial Intelligence in Education*, *20*(4), 333–360.

Bates, L. (2018). 5 Real Benefits of Using Animation in the Classroom. *Peninsula Industries*, 1.

Baum, S. (1990). *Gifted but learning disabled: A puzzling paradox*. Retrieved on June 16, 2004, from http://www.hoagiesgifted .org/eric/e479.html

Be My Eyes. (2015). Be My Eyes - See the world together. https://www.bemyeyes.com/

Becker, S. A., Brown, M., Dahlstrom, E., Davis, A., DePaul, K., Diaz, V., & Pomerantz, J. (2018). *NMC horizon report: 2018 higher education edition*. Educause.

Behzadi, S., Rao, H. R., & Schellhammer, S. (2021). Artificial Intelligence in Education: Perspectives from Industry 4.0 and Learning Analytics. *Journal of Information Systems Education*, *32*(1), 37–52.

Belpaeme, T., Kennedy, J., Ramachandran, A., Scassellati, B., & Tanaka, F. (2018). Social robots for education: A review. *Science Robotics*, *3*(21), eaat5954. doi:10.1126cirobotics.aat5954 PMID:33141719

Belsky, G. (2019, August 5). Assistive Technology for Auditory Processing Challenges. *Understood.*

Ben-Bassat Levy, R., Ben-Ari, M., & Uronen, P. A. (2003). The Jeliot 2000 programanimation system. *Computers & Education*, *40*, 1–15.

Benjamin, E. (2021, June 16). *ADHD and Adult Autism: Symptoms, Diagnosis & Interventions for Both.* ADDitude. Retrieved June 11, 2023, from https://www.additudemag.com/adult-autism-symptoms-adhd/

Bergdahl, N., & Nouri, J. (2021). Covid-19 and crisis-prompted distance education in Sweden. Technology. *Knowledge and Learning*, *26*(3), 443–459. doi:10.100710758-020-09470-6

Betrancourt, M. (2005). The animation and interactivity principles in multimedia learning. In R. E. Mayer (Ed.), *The Cambridge handbook of multimedia learning* (pp. 287–296). Cambridge University Press. doi:10.1017/CBO9780511816819.019

Bhatti, Z. B. (2020). Augmented Reality based Multimedia Learning for Dyslexic Children. *2020 3rd International Conference on Computing, Mathematics and Engineering Technologies (iCoMET).* 10.1109/iCoMET48670.2020.9073879

Bi, X. A., Wang, Y., Shu, Q., Sun, Q., & Xu, Q. (2018). Classification of Autism Spectrum Disorder Using Random Support Vector Machine Cluster. *Frontiers in Genetics*, *9*, 18. Advance online publication. doi:10.3389/fgene.2018.00018 PMID:29467790

Blikstein, P. (2018). Artificial Intelligence and Machine Learning in Education. In The Cambridge Handbook of Computing Education Research (pp. 617-638). Cambridge University Press.

Blikstein, P. (2021). Artificial Intelligence in Education: Promises and Pitfalls. Technology. *Knowledge and Learning*, *26*(1), 1–5.

Boldu, R., Matthies, D. J. C., Zhang, H., & Nanayakkara, S. 2020. AiSee: An Assistive Wearable Device to Support Visually Impaired Grocery Shoppers. *Proc. ACM Interact. Mob. Wearable Ubiquitous Technol.* 10.1145/3432196

Boldu, R., Dancu, A., Matthies, D. J. C., Buddhika, T., Siriwardhana, S., & Nanayakkara, S. FingerReader2.0: Designing and Evaluating a Wearable Finger-Worn Camera to Assist People with Visual Impairments while Shopping. In *Proc. of IMWUT'18*. ACM. 10.1145/3264904

Bonneh, Y. S., Levanon, Y., Dean-Pardo, O., Lossos, L., & Adini, Y. (2011). Abnormal speech spectrum and increased pitch variability in young autistic children. *Frontiers in Human Neuroscience*, *4*, 237. doi:10.3389/fnhum.2010.00237 PMID:21267429

Bonvicini & Qi. (2020). The Current and Future Role of Artificial Intelligence in Special Education. *Journal of Special Education Technology.*

Bosl, W. J., Tager-Flusberg, H., & Nelson, C. A. (2018). EEG Analytics for Early Detection of Autism Spectrum Disorder: A data-driven approach. *Scientific Reports*, *8*(1), 6828. Advance online publication. doi:10.103841598-018-24318-x PMID:29717196

Brodin, J. (2010). Can ict give children with disabilities equal opportunities in school? *Improving Schools*, *13*(1), 99–112. doi:10.1177/1365480209353483

Bryant, J. (2020). Advancements in artificial intelligence for special education. *Journal of Special Education Technology*, *35*(2), 76–82.

Buchanan, B. G. (2005). A very brief history of artificial intelligence. *Artificial Intelligence Magazine*, *26*(4), 53–60.

Burgstahler, S. (2003). The role of technology in preparing youth with disabilities for postsecondary education and employment. *Journal of Special Education Technology, 18*(4), 7–19. doi:10.1177/016264340301800401

Burry, M. (2021, January 25). *Hearing Aids Go High-tech.* Healthy Hearing.

Castro, S. (2018). Google Forms Quizzes and Substitution, Augmentation, Modification, and Redefinition (SAMR) Model Integration. *Issues and Trends in Educational Technology, 6*(2).

CDC. (2023, January 11). *Signs & Symptoms | Autism Spectrum Disorder (ASD) | NCBDDD | CDC.* Centers for Disease Control and Prevention. Retrieved June 10, 2023, from https://www.cdc.gov/ncbddd/autism/signs.html

Centers for Disease Control and Prevention. (2023, January 11). *Signs & Symptoms | Autism Spectrum Disorder (ASD).* NCBDDD | CDC.

Chanthadavong, A. (2020, September 15). *Dystech Using Artificial Intelligence to Help Speed Screening for Learning Disorders.* ZDNET.

Chassignol, M., Khoroshavin, A., Klimova, A., & Bilyatdinova, A. (2018). Artificial intelligence trends in education: A narrative overview. *Procedia Computer Science, 136*, 16–24. doi:10.1016/j.procs.2018.08.233

Chazen, D. (2019). *Assistive Technology for Deaf and Hard of Hearing Students | Verbit.* Verbit. Retrieved June 9, 2023, from https://verbit.ai/assistive-technology-for-deaf-and-hard-of-hearing-students/

Chen, B., Hu, X., Chen, Y., & Wu, B. (2021). Artificial Intelligence and Education 4.0: Current Trends, Challenges, and Future Directions. *Journal of Educational Technology & Society, 24*(1), 14–24.

Chen, H., Liu, Y., & Liao, H. (2020). The Impact of Artificial Intelligence on Education: A Review of the Current State and Future Prospects. *Journal of Computers in Education, 7*(2), 153–170.

Chen, L., Chen, P., & Lin, Z. (2020). Artificial intelligence in education: A review. *IEEE Access : Practical Innovations, Open Solutions, 8*, 75264–75278. doi:10.1109/ACCESS.2020.2988510

Chen, W. (2020). Learning analytics for inclusive higher education. ICCE 2020–28th International Conference on Computers in Education. *Proceedings, 2*, 113–118.

Chen, X., Xie, H., Zou, D., & Hwang, G.-J. (2020). *Application and theory gaps during the rise of Artificial Intelligence in Education.* Elsevier BV. doi:10.1016/j.caeai.2020.100002

Chen, X., Zou, D., Xie, H., Cheng, G., & Liu, C. (2022). Two Decades of Artificial Intelligence in Education: Contributors, Collaborations, Research Topics, Challenges, and Future Directions. *Journal of Educational Technology & Society, 25*(1), 28–47.

Chew, E., & Chua, X. N. (2020). Robotic Chinese language tutor: Personalising progress assessment and feedback or taking over your job? *On the Horizon, 28*(3), 113–124. doi:10.1108/OTH-04-2020-0015

Chia, Y. L., & Yeo, W. (2020). Artificial Intelligence in Education 4.0: Opportunities and Challenges. In *2020 International Conference on Artificial Intelligence in Information and Communication (ICAIIC)* (pp. 1-4). IEEE.

Choi & Kim. (2021). Integrating Technology and Artificial Intelligence in Special Education: A Systematic Literature Review. *International Journal of Educational Research.*

Christie, R., & Klinger, T. (2021). Ethics and artificial intelligence in education: Theories and praxis. In *The International Handbook of Educational Technology* (pp. 1–23). Springer.

Chumchu, P., & Patil, K. (2023). Dataset of cannabis seeds for machine learning applications. *Data in Brief, 47*. doi:10.1016/j.dib.2023.108954

City of Seattle. (n.d.). *Digital Equity*. Seattle Information Technology. Retrieved from https://www.seattle.gov/tech/initiatives/digital-equity

Cleary, J. G., & Trigg, L. E. (1995). K*: An Instance-based Learner Using and Entropic Distance Measure. *International Conference on Machine Learning*. 10.1016/B978-1-55860-377-6.50022-0

Cook, B. G., & Odom, S. L. (2021). Evidence-based practices and implementation science in special education. *Exceptional Children, 87*(1), 7–24.

Cook, B. G., Tankersley, M., Landrum, T. J., & Kauffman, J. M. (2014). *Methods and strategies for teaching students with mild disabilities: A case-based approach*. Cengage Learning.

Cortes, C., & Vapnik, V. (1995). Support-vector networks. *Machine Learning, 20*(3), 273–297. doi:10.1007/BF00994018

Cousik, R. (2022). COVID-19 Pandemic and Special Education Teacher Voices. *Qualitative Report, 27*(11), 2486–2500. doi:10.46743/2160-3715/2022.5553

Crais, E. R., & Watson, L. R. (2014). Challenges and opportunities in early identification and intervention for children at-risk for autism spectrum disorders. *International Journal of Speech-Language Pathology, 16*(1), 23–29. doi:10.3109/17549507.2013.862860 PMID:24328367

Daniela, Mahender, & Ayanna. (2021). *Universal Access in HumanComputer Interaction*. Academic Press.

Darwish, A., & Kamel, M. (2021). Artificial Intelligence in Education 4.0: A Systematic Review. *International Journal of Emerging Technologies in Learning, 16*(3), 148–162.

Das Chakladar, D., Kumar, P., Mandal, S., Roy, P. P., Iwamura, M., & Kim, B. (2021). 3D Avatar Approach for Continuous Sign Movement Using Speech/Text. *Applied Sciences (Basel, Switzerland), 11*(8), 3439. doi:10.3390/app11083439

Dattaro, L. (2020, March 25). *How Autism Researchers Are Applying Machine-learning Techniques*. Academic Press.

David, J. M., & Balakrishnan, K. (2010). Machine learning approach for prediction of learning disabilities in school-age children. *International Journal of Computers and Applications, 9*(11), 7–14. doi:10.5120/1432-1931

Deepika, S. S., & Murugesan, G. (2015). A novel approach for Human-Computer Interface based on eye movements for disabled people. *2015 IEEE International Conference on Electrical, Computer and Communication Technologies*, 1–3. 10.1109/ICECCT.2015.7226124

Delavarian, M., Towhidkhah, F., Dibajnia, P., & Gharibzadeh, S. (2012). Designing a decision support system for distinguishing adhd from similar children behavioral disorders. *Journal of Medical Systems, 36*(3), 1335–1343. doi:10.100710916-010-9594-9 PMID:20878211

Delipetrev, B., Tsinaraki, C., & Kostic, U. (2020, November 20). *Historical Evolution of Artificial Intelligence*. JRC Publications Repository. Retrieved June 11, 2023, from https://publications.jrc.ec.europa.eu/repository/handle/JRC120469

Dervishi, E., Ergün, E., & Uçak, C. (2019). Artificial Intelligence in Education. In Fourth Industrial Revolution and Its Impact on Education (pp. 41-54). IGI Global.

Desai, A. (2018). *Animation in Education*. Retrieved from CG Pundit: https://www.cgpundit.com/animation-in-education/

Di Nuovo, L., Patel, R. S., McNeil, A. R., & Parlanti, G. (2019). Artificial intelligence in education: Current insights and future perspectives. *Frontiers in Psychology, 10*, 2696.

Divakaran, D. (n.d.). *SAMR model: A practical guide for EdTech integration*. Retrieved from https://www.deepeshdivakaran.com/post/samr-model-a-practical-guide-for-edtech-integration

DiVittorio, A. (2019). Evaluating an Adaptive Language Game System for Children with Language Impairments. In *2019 IEEE Conference on Games (CoG)* (pp. 1-8). IEEE.

Dobie, R. A., & Hemel, S. V. (2004, January 1). *Hearing Loss in Children - Hearing Loss - NCBI Bookshelf*. Hearing Loss in Children - Hearing Loss - NCBI Bookshelf.

Doshi, P., Shirke, Y., Hegde, T., & Dhanvij, P. (2018). Text Reader for Visually Impaired Using Google Cloud Vision API. *International Journal Of Innovative Research In Technology*, *4*(12), 863–873.

Drigas, A., Kouremenos, D., & Vrettaros, J. (2008). Teaching of English to hearing impaired individuals whose mother language is the sign language. *Emerging Technologies and Information Systems for the Knowledge Society: First World Summit on the Knowledge Society, WSKS 2008, Athens, Greece, September 24-26, 2008 Proceedings*, *1*, 263–270.

Drotár, P., & Dobeš, M. (2020). Dysgraphia detection through machine learning. *Scientific Reports*, (10). Retrieved from https://www.nature.com/articles/s41598-020-78633-1

Druga, S., & Ko, A. J. (2021). How do children's perceptions of machine intelligence change when training and coding smart programs? Interaction Design and Children. doi:10.1145/3459990.3460712

Du Toit, L. (1997). Education for all. Pretoria: Unisa. *Educational Research*, *43*, 235–245.

Dubovi, I. (2019). Online Computer-Based Clinical Simulations: The role of Visualizations. *Clinical Simulation in Nursing*, *33*, 35–41. doi:10.1016/j.ecns.2019.04.009

Duda, M., Kosmicki, J. A., & Wall, D. P. (2014). Testing the accuracy of an observation-based classifier for rapid detection of autism risk. *Translational Psychiatry*, *4*(8), e424. doi:10.1038/tp.2014.65 PMID:25116834

Dutt, S., Ahuja, N. J., & Kumar, M. (2022). An intelligent tutoring system architecture based on fuzzy neural network (FNN) for special education of learning disabled learners. *Education and Information Technologies*, *27*(2), 2613–2633. doi:10.100710639-021-10713-x

Educational Technology. (n.d.). *Technological Pedagogical Content Knowledge (TPACK) framework*. Retrieved from https://educationaltechnology.net/technological-pedagogical- content-knowledge-tpack-framework/

Edwards, B. I., & Cheok, A. D. (2018). Why not robot teachers: Artificial intelligence for addressing teacher shortage. *Applied Artificial Intelligence*, *32*(4), 345–360.

eLife. (2021, May 5). Equity, Diversity and Inclusion: Disabled in Higher Ed.

Elliott, S. N., & Ryan, J. B. (2021). *Educational assessment for diverse learners*. Routledge.

Embarak, O. H. (2022). Internet of Behaviour (IoB)-based AI models for personalized smart education systems. *Procedia Computer Science*, *203*, 103–110. doi:10.1016/j.procs.2022.07.015

Encyclopedia Britannica. (2023, February 23).. . *Special Education*.

Ertmer, P. A., & Newby, T. J. (2018). Artificial Intelligence in Education: Promises and Implications for Teaching and Learning. *International Journal of Artificial Intelligence in Education*, *28*(1), 4–17.

Esponda-Arguero, M. (2008). Algorithmic animation in education—Review of academicexperience. *Journal of Educational Computing Research*, *39*(1), 1–15. doi:10.2190/EC.39.1.a

Fadel, C., Holmes, W., & Bialik, M. (2019). *Artificial intelligence in education: Promises and implications for teaching and learning*. The Center for Curriculum Redesign.

Fahimirad, M., & Kotamjani, S. S. (2018). A review on application of artificial intelligence in teaching and learning in educational contexts. *International Journal of Learning and Development*, *8*(4), 106–118. doi:10.5296/ijld.v8i4.14057

Fan, C., & Crandall, D. J. (2016). DeepDiary: Automatic caption generation for lifelogging image streams. *European Conference on Computer Vision*, 459–473.

Fardoun, H. M., Alghazzawi, D. M., & Aldahdouh, Z. (2020). Artificial Intelligence in Education: A Comprehensive Review. In *2020 5th MEC International Conference on Big Data and Smart City (ICBDSC)* (pp. 36-41). IEEE.

Fazlinda, A. H., Wan Hanim Nadrah Wan, M., & Saslizawati, I. (2019). The Relationship between Employability Skills and Self-Efficacy of Students With Learning Disabilities In Vocational Stream. *Asian Journal of University Education*, *15*(3), 163–174.

Ferdig & Archambault. (2018). Artificial Intelligence and Special Education: Opportunities and Challenges. *Journal of Special Education Technology*.

Ferrara, E. (2023). *Fairness And Bias in Artificial Intelligence: A Brief Survey of Sources, Impacts, And Mitigation Strategies*. https://github.com/CuongTrinh3005/Ecommerce-Chatbot

Fleming, S. A., Hart, G. R., & Savage, P. B. (2000). Molecular orbital animations fororganic chemistry. *Journal of Chemical Education*, *77*(6), 790–793.

Fletcher, A., Scherer, R., & Wilder, M. S. (2019). *Artificial intelligence and special education. In Handbook of Special Education Technology Research and Practice*. Routledge.

Fletcher, J. M., Coulter, W. A., Reschly, D. J., & Vaughn, S. (2004). Alternative approaches to the definition and identification of learning disabilities: Some questions and answers. *Annals of Dyslexia*, *54*(2), 304–331. doi:10.100711881-004-0015-y PMID:15741940

Fletcher, T. V., Wehmeyer, M. L., Smith, S. J., & Palmer, S. B. (2019). *Promoting self-determination in students with developmental disabilities*. Guilford Press.

Foo. (2009). *Grocery Shopping Assistant for the Blind/Visually Impaired*. http://grozi.calit2.net/files/TIESGroZiSu09.pdf

Forlin, C. (2001). *Inclusion: identifying potential stressors for regular class teachers*. Academic Press.

Frank, E., Hall, M. A., & Witten, I. H. (2016). *The WEKA Workbench. Online Appendix for "Data Mining: Practical Machine Learning Tools and Techniques"*. Morgan Kaufmann.

Friend, M., & Bursuck, W. D. (2018). *Including students with special needs: A practical guide for classroom teachers*. Pearson.

Fusaroli, R., Lambrechts, A., Bang, D., Bowler, D. M., & Gaigg, S. B. (2017). Is voice a marker for Autism spectrum disorder? A systematic review and meta-analysis. *Autism Research*, *10*(3), 384–407. doi:10.1002/aur.1678 PMID:27501063

Galea, L. C., & Smeaton, A. F. (2019). Recognising Irish sign language using electromyography. *Proceedings of the IEEE 2019 International Conference on Content-Based Multimedia Indexing (CBMI)*, 1–4.

García-Peñalvo, F. J. (2020). Using Artificial Intelligence for Monitoring and Assessing Students' Learning in Formal and Informal Settings. In Artificial Intelligence in Education (pp. 557-560). Springer.

Garg, S., & Sharma, S. (2020). Impact of artificial intelligence in special need education to promote inclusive pedagogy. *International Journal of Information and Education Technology (IJIET), 10*(7), 523–527. doi:10.18178/ijiet.2020.10.7.1418

Georgopoulos, V. C., Malandraki, G. A., & Stylios, C. D. (2003). A fuzzy cognitive map approaches differential diagnosis of specific language impairment. *Artificial Intelligence in Medicine, 29*(3), 261–278. doi:10.1016/S0933-3657(02)00076-3 PMID:14656490

Ghai, B., & Mueller, K. (2021). Fluent: An AI Augmented Writing Tool for People who Stutter. *23rd International ACM SIGACCESS Conference On Computers And Accessibility*. 10.1145/3441852.3471211

Ghasemi, A., Ali, S., & Shirvani, F. (2020). The Role of Artificial Intelligence in Education 4.0: Opportunities and Challenges. *International Journal of Advanced Computer Science and Applications, 11*(12), 583–589.

Giangreco, M. F., Dennis, R. E., Cloninger, C. J., Edelman, S. W., & Schattman, R. (2016). *Supporting students with disabilities in inclusive classrooms: Faculty roles and responsibilities*. Routledge.

Giannakos, I., van de Ven, J. P., Sharma, S., & Wu, H. (2020). *Affective and behavioral computing for human factors in education. In Human-Computer Interaction Series*. Springer.

GiovannaAlbertoGiorgiaSimonePaoloElisa. (2021). *In teleXbe*.

Gkeka, E. A. (2019). Artificial Techniques for Language Disorders. *International Journal of Recent Contributions from Engineering, Science & IT (iJES)*. doi:10.3991/ijes.v7i4.11845

Goel, U. (2021). Prevalence of selected learning disabilities among primary schoolchildren through primary school teachers: A descriptive survey. *Indian Journal of Psychiatric Nursing, 18*(1), 23–28. doi:10.4103/iopn.iopn_51_20

Gołąb-Andrzejak, E. (2022). Enhancing Customer Engagement in Social Media with AI–a Higher Education case study. *Procedia Computer Science, 207*, 3028–3037. doi:10.1016/j.procs.2022.09.361

Gonzalez, C. S., Guerra, D., Sanabria, H., Moreno, L., Noda, M. A., & Bruno, A. (2010). Automatic system for the detection and analysis of errors to support personalized feedback. *Expert Systems with Applications, 37*(1), 140–148. doi:10.1016/j.eswa.2009.05.027

Gorman, M. (2018). *The SAMR model of technology integration article*. Academic Press.

Gorman, M. (2021, March 16). *5 Ways AI Will Impact Education for Autistic Children*. Academic Press.

Gould, J., & Ashton-Smith, J. (2011). Missed diagnosis or misdiagnosis? Girls and women on the autism spectrum. *Good Autism Practice, 12*(1), 34–41.

Gowramma, Nair, & Kumari. (2013). Effectiveness of remedial reading programme for pre-school children with hearing impairment. *Journal of NCED, 5*(1).

Graham, C. R. (2021). Transforming Higher Education: Leveraging Instructional Technology with the SAMR Model. *EDUCAUSE Review, 56*(1), 41–51.

Granić, A., & Marangunić, N. (2019). Technology acceptance model in educational context: A systematic literature review. *British Journal of Educational Technology, 50*(5), 2572–2593. doi:10.1111/bjet.12864

Greiffenhagen, C., & Traxler, J. (2021). Artificial Intelligence in Education: A Review of AI Education Policy and Implementation. In *2021 IEEE Global Engineering Education Conference (EDUCON)* (pp. 1381-1386). IEEE.

Grønborg, T. K., Schendel, D. E., & Parner, E. T. (2013). Recurrence of autism spectrum disorders in full- and half-siblings and trends over time: A population-based cohort study. *JAMA Pediatrics*, *167*(10), 947–953. doi:10.1001/jamapediatrics.2013.2259 PMID:23959427

Guan, C., Mou, J., & Jiang, Z. (2020). Artificial intelligence innovation in education: A twenty-year data-driven historical analysis. *International Journal of Innovation Studies*, *4*(4), 134–147. doi:10.1016/j.ijis.2020.09.001

Gulati, S., & Arya, A. (2021). Education 4.0: A Systematic Review of Recent Trends and Future Directions. *Education and Information Technologies*, *26*(5), 6977–7003.

Gururangan. (2022). *Artificial Intelligence Enabled Personalised Assistive Tools to Enhance Education of Children with Neurodevelopmental Disorders—A Review*. Retrieved from https://www.researchgate.net/publication/358016972_Artificial_Intelligence_Enabled_Personalised_Assistive_Tools_to_Enhance_Education_of_Children_with_Neurodevelopmental_Disorders-A_Review

Güzeller, C. O., Aksu, G., & Eser, M. T. (2019). Klasik test kuramı ve madde tepki kuramına ilişkin veri analizi yazılımı: Jmetrik [Data on classical test theory and item response theory analysis software: Jmetric]. *Egitimde ve Psikolojide Ölçme ve Degerlendirme Dergisi*, *10*(2), 165–178.

Habib, H. (2015). Awareness about Special Education in Hyderabad. *International Journal of Science and Research.* https://www.ijsr.net/archive/v4i5/SUB154394.pdf

Hadjikakou, K., Polycarpou, V., & Hadjilia, A. (2010). The Experiences of Students with Mobility Disabilities in Cypriot Higher Education Institutions: Listening to their voices. *International Journal of Disability Development and Education*, *57*(4), 403–426. doi:10.1080/1034912X.2010.524445

Haleem, A., Javaid, M., Qadri, M. A., & Suman, R. (2022). Understanding the role of digital technologies in education: A review. *Sustainable Operations and Computers*.

Hallahan, D. P., Kauffman, J. M., & Pullen, P. C. (2017). *Exceptional learners: An introduction to special education.* Pearson.

Han, J., Pei, J., & Kamber, M. (2011). *Data mining: concepts and techniques.* Elsevier.

Harish, V., Sharma, R., Rana, G., Nayyar, A., & Parashar, B. (2023). Expanding the Scope of Learning Analytics in Blended Learning Environments. In N. J. Ahuja, A. Kumar, & A. Nayyar (Eds.), *Sustainable Blended Learning in STEM Education for Students with Additional Needs. Contributions to Environmental Sciences & Innovative Business Technology*. Springer. doi:10.1007/978-981-99-3497-3_14

Haristiani, N. (2019). Artificial Intelligence (AI) chatbot as language learning medium: An inquiry. Journal of Physics: Conference Series.

Hashim, H. (2018). Application of Technology in the Digital Era Education. *International Journal of Research in Counseling and Education*, *2*(1), 1–5.

Hasibuan, M. S., Nugroho, L. E., & Santosa, P. I. (2019). Model Detecting Learning Styles with Artificial Neural Network. *Journal of Technology and Science Education*, *9*(1), 85–95. doi:10.3926/jotse.540

He, Y. (2021). AI in Education: A Review and Case Studies in K-12 Education. In *2021 IEEE 21st International Conference on Advanced Learning Technologies (ICALT)* (pp. 79-83). IEEE.

Hernadez, J., Mousalli, G., & Rivas, F. (2009). Learning difficulties diagnosis for children's basic education using expert systems. *WSEAS Transactions on Information Science and Applications*, *7*(6), 1–25.

Hernandez, J., Mousalli, G., & Rivas, F. (2009). Expert system for the diagnosis of learning difficulties in children's basic education. *WSEAS International Conference. Proceedings. Mathematics and Computers in Science and Engineering*, (8).

Herodotou, C., Rienties, B., Boroowa, A., Zdrahal, Z., & Hlosta, M. (2019). A large-scale implementation of predictive learning analytics in higher education: The teachers' role and perspective. *Educational Technology Research and Development*, *67*(5), 1273–1306. doi:10.100711423-019-09685-0

Hill, D. R., & Grieb, C. (1988, March-April). Substitution for a restricted visual channel in multimodal computer-human dialogue. *IEEE Transactions on Systems, Man, and Cybernetics*, *18*(2), 285–304. doi:10.1109/21.3467

Hinojo-Lucena, F. J., Aznar-Díaz, I., Cáceres-Reche, M. P., & Romero-Rodríguez, J. M. (2019). Artificial intelligence in higher education: A bibliometric study on its impact in the scientific literature. *Education in Science*, *9*(1), 51.

Hirankerd, K., & Kittisunthonphisarn, N. (2020). E-learning management system based on reality technology with AI. *International Journal of Information and Education Technology (IJIET)*, *10*(4), 259–264. doi:10.18178/ijiet.2020.10.4.1373

Hlavacs & Savina. (2021). Artificial Intelligence in Special Education: Bridging the Gap between Research and Practice. *Frontiers in Education.*

Hlosta, M., Zdrahal, M., & Kocvara, V. (2021). Ethical aspects of learning analytics. *Journal of Learning Analytics*, *8*(2), 26–41.

Hoeffler, T. N., & Leutner, D. (2007). Instructional animation versus static pictures: A meta-analysis. *Learning and Instruction*, *17*(6), 722–738. doi:10.118641239-019-0171-0

Holmes, W., Persson, J., Chounta, I.-A., Wasson, B., & Dimitrova, V. (2022). *Artificial intelligence and education: A critical view through the lens of human rights, democracy and the rule of law*. Council of Europe.

Hsieh, Y.-Z., Lin, S.-S., Luo, Y.-C., Jeng, Y.-L., Tan, S.-W., Chen, C.-R., & Chiang, P.-Y. (2020). ARCS-assisted teaching robots based on anticipatory computing and emotional big data for improving sustainable learning efficiency and motivation. *Sustainability*, *12*(14), 5605. doi:10.3390u12145605

Huang, J., Saleh, S., & Liu, Y. (2021, May). A review on artificial intelligence in education. *Academic Journal of Interdisciplinary Studies, 10*(3), 1-16.

Huang, X., Zou, D., Cheng, G., & Xie, H. (2021). A systematic review of AR and VR enhanced language learning. *Sustainability*, *13*(9), 4639. doi:10.3390u13094639

Hu, J. (2021). Teaching evaluation system by use of machine learning and artificial intelligence methods. *International Journal of Emerging Technologies in Learning*, *16*(5), 87–101. doi:10.3991/ijet.v16i05.20299

Hu, J., Shen, X., Sun, Q., & Wang, T. (2018). Application of Artificial Intelligence in Education: A Review. *Journal of Computers in Education*, *5*(3), 317–347.

Hungarian Central Statistical Office. (2022). *Educational Data*. https://www.ksh.hu/docs/hun/xftp/idoszaki/oktat/oktatas2122e/index.html

Hwang, G. J. (2014). Definition, Framework and Research Issues of Smart Learning Environments - A Context-Aware Ubiquitous Learning Perspective. *Smart Learning Environments, 1*(1), 1-14.

Hwang, G. J., Xie, H., Wah, B. W., & Gašević, D. (2020). Vision, Challenges, Roles andResearch Issues of Artificial Intelligence in Education. *Computers and Education:Artificial Intelligence*, *1*, 100001.

Hylén, J. (2006). Open educational resources: Opportunities and challenges. *Proceedings of the 2006 OECD-CERI.*

Ifenthaler, D., & Yau, J. Y. (2019). Opportunities and Challenges for Learning Analytics and Educational Data Mining in Computer-Based Learning Environments. *Journal of Educational Technology & Society*, *22*(1), 1–16.

Ikermane, M. (2023). Digital handwriting characteristics for dysgraphia detection using artificial neural network. *Bulletin of Electrical Engineering and Informatics*. https://beei.org/index.php/EEI/article/download/4571/3239

Inclusive Education - Campaigns. (2020). Inclusion BC.

Inclusive Education. (2017) United Nations Children's Fund.

Islam, M. R., & Lim, Y. (2021). Artificial Intelligence in Education: A Review on its Potential, Challenges, and Future Directions. In *2021 14th International Conference on Electrical and Computer Engineering (ICECE)* (pp. 1-4). IEEE.

Jacob & Cary. (2021). *Journal of Science Education for Students with Disabilities 24*.

Jain, K., Manghirmalani, P., Dongardive, J., & Abraham, S. (2009). Computational diagnosis of learning disability. *International Journal of Recent Trends in Engineering*, *2*(3), 64.

Jain, R., Kumar, A., Nayyar, A., Dewan, K., Garg, R., Raman, S., & Ganguly, S. (2023). Explaining sentiment analysis results on social media texts through visualization. *Multimedia Tools and Applications*, *82*(15), 1–17. doi:10.100711042-023-14432-y PMID:36747895

Janwadkar, K. (2015). *Effect of school readiness programme on children withautism spectrum disorders* [Unpublished Doctoral dissertation]. Ramakrishna Mission Vivekananda University-FDMSE, Coimbatore.

John, R. S., & Vijayan, R. (2021). A Comprehensive Study on the Role of Artificial Intelligence in Education 4.0. In *2021 International Conference on Sustainable Engineering and Technology (ICSET)* (pp. 1-5). IEEE.

Johnson, K. (2018). Personalized learning and assistive technology: Creating a synergy. *Technology and Innovation in Education*, *1*(1), 43–49.

Johnson, M., & Thompson, L. (2021). Leveraging artificial intelligence to support data-driven decision-making in special education. *Journal of Special Education Technology*, *36*(4), 275–285.

Jones, S. (2022). Enhancing communication and collaboration in special education through technology. *The Journal of Special Education*, *55*(2), 87–95.

Joshi, A., & Ungerleider, C. (2020). Artificial Intelligence in Education: *Potential and Possibilities. In International Conference on Artificial Intelligence in Education* (pp. 426-430). Springer.

Jovanovic, V., & Verbert, K. (Eds.). (2018). *Artificial Intelligence Supported Educational Technologies*. Springer International Publishing.

Kaçar, R. N., & Cagiltay, N. E. (2021). A Comprehensive Review of Artificial Intelligence Applications in Education. *Journal of Educational Computing Research*, *59*(4), 1141–1169.

Kamal, S. A., Shafiq, M., & Kakria, P. (2020). Investigating acceptance of telemedicine services through an extended technology acceptance model (TAM). *Technology in Society*, *60*, 101212. doi:10.1016/j.techsoc.2019.101212

Karimi, N., Sundararajan, R., & Kane, R. (2020). Artificial intelligence in healthcare. *AI Matters*, *6*(4), 18–20.

Katare, G., Padihar, G., & Qureshi, Z. (2018). Challenges in the integration of artificial intelligence and internet of things. *International Journal of System and Software Engineering*, *6*(2), 10–15.

Kaur, P., Ganore, M., Doiphode, R., Garud, A., & Ghuge, T. (2017). *Be My Eyes: Android App for visually impaired people*. Research Gate. doi:10.13140/RG.2.2.12307.48164

Kayembe, C., & Nel, D. (2019). Challenges and opportunities for education in the Fourth Industrial Revolution. *African Journal of Public Affairs, 11*(3), 79–94.

Khalil, M., Prinsloo, P., & Slade, S. (2018). User consent in MOOCs? Micro, meso, and macro perspectives. *International Review of Research in Open and Distributed Learning, 19*(5).

Khan, M. A., Paul, P., Rashid, M., Hossain, M., & Ahad, M. A. R. (2020). An AI-Based Visual Aid With Integrated Reading Assistant for the Completely Blind. *IEEE Transactions on Human-Machine Systems, 50*(6), 507–517. doi:10.1109/THMS.2020.3027534

Kim, H.-S., Kim, N. Y., & Cha, Y. (2021). Is It Beneficial to Use AI Chatbots to Improve Learners' Speaking Performance? *Journal of Asia TEFL, 18*(1), 161–178. doi:10.18823/asiatefl.2021.18.1.10.161

Kim, J., Lee, H., & Cho, Y. (2022). Learning design to support student-AI collaboration: Perspectives of leading teachers for AI in education. *Education and Information Technologies, 27*(5), 1–36. doi:10.100710639-021-10831-6

Kim, N.-Y. (2017). Effects of different types of chatbots on EFL learners' speaking competence and learner perception. *Cross-Cultural Studies, 48*, 223–252. doi:10.21049/ccs.2017.48..223

Kim, Y., Soyata, T., & Behnagh, R. F. (2018). Towards emotionally aware AI smart classroom: Current issues and directions for engineering and education. *IEEE Access : Practical Innovations, Open Solutions, 6*, 5308–5331. doi:10.1109/ACCESS.2018.2791861

Kinghorn, P., Zhang, L., & Shao, L. (2018). A region-based image caption generator with refined descriptions. *Neurocomputing, 272*, 416–424. doi:10.1016/j.neucom.2017.07.014

Knoblauch, B., & Sorenson, B. (1998, April). ERIC EC Digest #E560.

Koc, S., & Bakirtas, H. (2020). Artificial Intelligence in Education: A Review of the Literature. *Journal of Computer Assisted Learning, 36*(6), 713–729.

Koedinger, K. R., Woolf, B. P., & Schultz, K. R. (2019). Design principles for intelligent tutoring systems. *Psychological Science, 20*(5), 1–10.

Koelle, M., Boll, S., Olsson, T., Williamson, J., Profita, H., Kane, S., & Mitchell, R. (2018). (Un acceptable!?! re-thinking the social acceptability of emerging technologies. *Extended Abstracts of the 2018 CHI Conference on Human Factors in Computing Systems*, 1–8.

Kohli, M., & Prasad, T. (2010). Identifying dyslexic students by using artificial neural networks. *Proceedings of the World Congress on Engineering, 1* (1), 1–4.

Kolachalama, V. B. (2022). Machine learning and pre-medical education. *Artificial Intelligence in Medicine, 129*, 102313. doi:10.1016/j.artmed.2022.102313 PMID:35659392

Kolekar, S.V., & Pai, R.M., & MM, M.P. (2018). Adaptive user interface for Moodle based e-learning system using learning styles. *Procedia Computer Science, 135*, 606–615. doi:10.1016/j.procs.2018.08.226

Korjus, K., Hebart, M. N., & Vicente, R. (2016). An Efficient Data Partitioning to Improve Classification Performance While Keeping Parameters Interpretable. *PLoS One, 11*(8), e0161788. doi:10.1371/journal.pone.0161788 PMID:27564393

Kourakli, M., Altanis, I., Retalis, S., Boloudakis, M., Zbainos, D., & Antonopoulou, K. (2017). Towards the improvement of the cognitive, motoric and academic skills of students with special educational needs using Kinect learning games. *International Journal of Child-Computer Interaction, 11*, 28–39. doi:10.1016/j.ijcci.2016.10.009

Koustubh. (2018). *ResNet, AlexNet, VGGNet, Inception: Understanding Various Architectures of Convolutional Networks*. Retrieved from https://cv-tricks.com/cnn/understand-resnet-alexnet-vgginception/

Kovalchuk, S. (2021). Artificial Intelligence and Machine Learning in Education 4.0: Challenges and Opportunities. In *2021 IEEE 16th International Conference on Advanced Trends in Radioelectronics, Telecommunications and Computer Engineering (TCSET)* (pp. 745- 748). IEEE.

Krishnan, R. S., Narayanan, K. L., Murali, S. M., Sangeetha, A., Sankar Ram, C. R., & Robinson, Y. H. (2021). IoT based Blind People Monitoring System for Visually Impaired Care Homes. *2021 5th International Conference on Trends in Electronics and Informatics (ICOEI)*, 505-509. 10.1109/ICOEI51242.2021.9452924

Kučak, D., Juričić, V., & Đambić, G. (2018). Machine learning in education-A survey of current research trends. *Annals of DAAAM & Proceedings, 29*.

Küçük, S., & Gündoğdu, B. A. (2020). The Role of Artificial Intelligence in Education 4.0: A Review Study. *International Journal of Technology in Education and Science*, *4*(2), 138–152.

Kukkar, A., Mohana, R., Sharma, A., & Nayyar, A. (2023). *Prediction of student academic performance based on their emotional wellbeing and interaction on various e-learning platforms*. Academic Press.

Kukkar, A., Mohana, R., & Sharma, A. (2023). Prediction of student academic performance based on their emotional wellbeing and interaction on various e-learning platforms. *Education and Information Technologies*, *28*, 9655–9684. doi:10.100710639-022-11573-9

Kumar, A., & Ahluwalia, R. (2021). Breast Cancer Detection Using Machine Learning and Its Classification. In Cancer Prediction for Industrial IoT 4.0: A Machine Learning Perspective. Chapman and Hall/CRC. doi:10.1201/9781003185604-4

Kumar, A., & Vohra, R. (2023). Impact of Deep Learning Models for Technology Sustainability in Tourism Using Big Data Analytics. In Deep Learning Technologies for the Sustainable Development Goals: Issues and Solutions in the Post-COVID Era. Springer. doi:10.1007/978-981-19-5723-9_6

Kumar, A., Aelgani, V., Vohra, R., Gupta, S. K., Bhagawati, M., Paul, S., ... & Suri, J. S. (2023). Artificial intelligence bias in medical system designs: a systematic review. Multimedia Tools and Applications, 1-53.

Kumar, A., Gupta, N., Bhasin, P., Chauhan, S., & Bachri, I. (2023). Security and Privacy Issues in Smart Healthcare Using Machine-Learning Perspectives. In 6G-Enabled IoT and AI for Smart Healthcare. CRC Press. doi:10.1201/9781003321668-3

Kumar, A., Krishnamurthi, R., Bhatia, S., Kaushik, K., Ahuja, N. J., Nayyar, A., & Masud, M. (2021). Blended learning tools and practices: A comprehensive analysis. *IEEE Access, 9*, 85151-85197.

Kumar, A., Mamgai, R., & Jain, R. (2023). Application of IoT-Enabled CNN for Natural Language Processing. In IoT-enabled Convolutional Neural Networks: Techniques and Applications. River Publishers. doi:10.1201/9781003393030-6

Kumar, A., Sareen, P., & Arora, A. (2023). Healthcare Engineering Using AI and Distributed Technologies. In Smart Distributed Embedded Systems for Healthcare Applications. CRC Press. doi:10.1201/9781003254119-1

Kumar, A. (2023). *Visual Object Tracking Using Deep Learning*. CRC Press.

Kumar, A., Jain, R., Gupta, M., & Islam, S. M. (Eds.). (2023). *6G-Enabled IoT and AI for Smart Healthcare: Challenges, Impact, and Analysis*. CRC Press.

Kumar, A., Krishnamurthi, R., Bhatia, S., Kaushik, K., Ahuja, N. J., Nayyar, A., & Masud, M. (2021). Blended learning tools and practices: A comprehensive analysis. *IEEE Access : Practical Innovations, Open Solutions*, *9*, 85151–85197. doi:10.1109/ACCESS.2021.3085844

Kumar, A., Raja, & ljaz, M. F. (2023). Augmented Reality as a Boon to Disability. *Smart Distributed Embedded Systems for Healthcare Applications*, *78*(82), 77–92. doi:10.1201/9781003254119-6

Kumar, A., Walia, G. S., & Sharma, K. (2020). Recent trends in multicue based visual tracking: A review. *Expert Systems with Applications*, *162*, 113711. doi:10.1016/j.eswa.2020.113711

Kunhoth. (2022). *Automated Systems for Diagnosis of Dysgraphia in Children: A Survey and Novel Framework.* Retrieved from https://www.researchgate.net/publication/361581698_Automated_Systems_For_Diagnosis_of_Dysgraphia_in_Children_A_Survey_and_Novel_Framework

Kuriakose, B., Shrestha, R., & Sandnes, F. E. (2022). Tools and technologies for blind and visually impaired navigation support: A review. *IETE Technical Review*, *39*(1), 3–18. doi:10.1080/02564602.2020.1819893

Kurtsikidze, K. (2022, June 14). *See Every Colour Campaign Addressing Stigma Around Children With Special Education Needs Summarizes Results. See Every Colour campaign addressing the stigma around children with special education needs summarizes results.* Government of India.

Laato. (2023). *AI-assisted Learning with ChatGPT and Large Language Models: Implications for Higher Education.* Retrieved from https://www.researchgate.net/publication/370535123_AI-assisted_Learning_with_ChatGPT_and_Large_Language_Models_Implications_for_Higher_Education

Lai, P. (2017). *Picture of Original Technology Acceptance Model.* Retrieved from https://www.researchgate.net/figure/Original-Technology-Acceptance-Model-Davis-

Lakshmanan, S. (2022). *Dyslexic Reading Assistance with Language Processing Algorithms.* Retrieved from SSRN: https://papers.ssrn.com/sol3/papers.cfm?abstract_id=4264858

Lambert, M. C. (2022). Enhancing Artificial Intelligence Education Software through Iterative Design and Development. *Journal of Special Education Technology*, *37*(2), 73–82.

Lampos, Mintz, & Qu. (2021). An artificial intelligence approach for selecting effective teacher communication strategies in autism education. *NPJ Science of Learning*, *6*(1), 25.

Lanzilotti, R., & Roselli, T. (2007). An experimental evaluation of logiocando, an intelligent tutoring hypermedia system. *International Journal of Artificial Intelligence in Education*, *17*(1), 41–56.

Laupichler, M. C., Aster, A., Schirch, J., & Raupach, T. (2022). Artificial intelligence literacy in higher and adult education: A scoping literature review. Computers and Education: Artificial Intelligence, 100101.

Lee, S., Chien, W. Y., Hanrahan, B. V., Rosson, M. B., & Carroll, J. M. (2017). Reaching Out: Investigating Different Modalities to Help People with Visual Impairments Acquire Items. In *Proceedings of the 19th International ACM SIGACCESS Conference on Computers and Accessibility - ASSETS '17.* ACM Press. 10.1145/3132525.3134817

Lee, J., & Heffernan, N. (2018). Developing a Virtual Tutor for Fraction Addition and Subtraction: A Reinforcement Learning Approach. In *2018 IEEE International Conference on Data Mining Workshops (ICDMW)* (pp. 453-460). IEEE.

Lerga, R. C. (2021). *A Review on Assistive Technologies for Students with Dyslexia.* Retrieved from CSEDU: https://pdfs.semanticscholar.org/ff92/837cfdf462adc914cf6fc0fd9e7388fd7152.pdf

Lewis, C. C., Fretwell, C. E., Ryan, J., & Parham, J. B. (2013). Faculty use of established and emerging technologies in higher education: A unified theory of acceptance and use of technology perspective. *International Journal of Higher Education*, *2*(2), 22–34.

Li, L. (2018). VR Intervention Program for Children with Autism: Case Study. In *2018 10th International Conference on Virtual Worlds and Games for Serious Applications (VS-Games)* (pp. 1-8). IEEE.

Libbrecht, P., & Melis, E. (2006). Methods to access and retrieve mathematical content in activemath. *Mathematical Software-ICMS 2006: Second International Congress on Mathematical Software, Castro Urdiales, Spain, September 1-3, 2006. Proceedings*, *2*, 331–342.

Limna, P., Jakwatanatham, S., Siripipattanakul, S., Kaewpuang, P., & Sriboonruang, P. (2022). A review of artificial intelligence (AI) ineducation during the digital era. *AdvanceKnowledge for Executives*, *1*(1), 1–9.

Lin, H. C., Ho, C. F., & Han, Y. (2022). Understanding adoption of artificial intelligence-enabled language e-learning system: An empirical study of UTAUT model. *International Journal of Mobile Learning and Organisation*, *16*(1), 74. doi:10.1504/ijmlo.2022.119966

Lin, R., He, X., & Dong, X. L. (2021, August). Personalized learning recommendation with adaptive neural networks. In *Proceedings of the ACM SIGKDD International Conference on Knowledge Discovery and Data Mining* (pp. 1452-1461). ACM. 10.1145/3447548.3467164

Lin, Y. W., & Huang, Y. M. (2020). Artificial Intelligence in Education: Issues and Trends. *International Journal of Distance Education Technologies*, *18*(3), 14–31.

Liu, L., & Sun, K. (2011). Theoretical Models and empirical research continued use after the adoption of mobile digital reading service users. *Library and Information Service*, *55*(10), 78–82.

Liu, X., Xu, G., Zhang, X., & Gao, W. (2021). The Fourth Industrial Revolution and Its Impact on Higher Education: A Systematic Literature Review. *Education in Science*, *11*(3), 122.

Livne, N. L., Livne, O. E., & Wight, C. A. (2007). Can automated scoring surpass hand grading of students' constructed responses and error patterns in mathematics. *Journal of Online Learning and Teaching*, *3*(3), 295–306.

Looi, C. K., Wong, L. H., So, H. J., Seow, P., Toh, Y., Chen, W., & Norris, C. (2019). Leveraging Artificial Intelligence in Education. In Handbook of Information Technology in Primary and Secondary Education (pp. 369-381). Springer.

Lord, C., Risi, S., Lambrecht, L., Cook, E. H. Jr, Leventhal, B. L., DiLavore, P. C., Pickles, A., & Rutter, M. (2000). The autism diagnostic observation schedule-generic: A standard measure of social and communication deficits associated with the spectrum of autism. *Journal of Autism and Developmental Disorders*, *30*(3), 205–223. doi:10.1023/A:1005592401947 PMID:11055457

Lord, C., Rutter, M., & Le Couteur, A. (1994). Autism Diagnostic Interview-Revised: A revised version of a diagnostic interview for caregivers of individuals with possible pervasive developmental disorders. *Journal of Autism and Developmental Disorders*, *24*(5), 659–685. doi:10.1007/BF02172145 PMID:7814313

Loukina & Flor. (2019). Using Artificial Intelligence to Improve Special Education Services: Opportunities and Challenges. *International Journal of Artificial Intelligence in Education.*

Luckin, R. (2016). *Collaboration in the Digital Age: How Technology Enables Individuals, Teams and Businesses*. Springer.

LuxAI S.A. (2022, September 21). How one year with an in-home robot helps children with autism.

LuxAI S.A.(2023, April 21). QTrobot - expressive humanoid social robot for research and teaching.

Lyon, G. R. (1996). Learning Disabilities. *The Future of Children*, *6*(1), 54. doi:10.2307/1602494 PMID:8689262

Machekhina, O. N. (2017). Digitalization of education as a trend of its modernization and reforming. *Revista Espacios, 38*(40).

MahaKud, G.C. (2010). Vaccination for the children with learning disabilities: Some psycho-educational instructions for the parents of early learner. Disabilities and Impairments: An Interdisciplinary Research Journal, 24(1), 23–30.

Mahesh, B. (2020). Machine learning algorithms-a review. *International Journal of Science and Research, 9*, 381-386.

Majumder, C. (2019b). Educational status of differently abled persons and developed policies in India. *International Journal of Trend in Scientific Research and Development, 3*(3), 341.

Majumder, C. (2019). Prevalence of Disabled People in India. *International Journal of Trend in Scientific Research and Development*, *3*(2), 846–851.

Makav, B., & Kılıc, V. (2019). Smartphone-based Image Captioning for Visually and Hearing Impaired. *11th International Conference on Electrical and Electronics Engineering*, 950-953, 10.23919/ELECO47770.2019.8990395

Malaysia Hearing Solution. (2021, March 11). Circa AI - The World's First Healthable Hearing Aids with AI | Malaysia Hearing Solution.

Maltseva, O. A., Khovanskaya, E. A., Martynova, N. A., & Karpova, I. V. (2020). The Digitalization of Education in Higher Education: Methodological and Practice-Oriented Aspects. *Advances in Social Science, Education and Humanities Research*, *437*, 859.

Mandal, A. (2012, June 27). News-Medical.net.

Manjari, K., Verma, M., & Singal, G. (2020). A survey on assistive technology for visually impaired. *Internet of Things*, *11*, 100188. doi:10.1016/j.iot.2020.100188

Man, L. (2021). Research on the Opportunities and Challenges Faced by Educational Leadership Based on Artificial Intelligence in the Education Field. *Journal of Physics: Conference Series*, *1915*(2), 022053. doi:10.1088/1742-6596/1915/2/022053

Mansor, N. R., Zakaria, R., Rashid, R. A., Arifin, R. M., Rahim, B. H. A., Zakaria, R., & Razak, M. T. A. (2020). A review survey on the use computer animation in education. *IOP Conference Series, 917*(1), 10.1088/1757-899x/917/1/012021

Marathe, M. S. (2018). Digitalization in education: A transformative tool for the 21st-century learners. *International Journal of Current Research and Modern Education, 3*(2), 361–365.

Martin, D. (2021, January 23). *New AI System Accelerates Speech Therapy*. Unite.AI.

Maskati, E. A. (2021). Using Virtual Reality (VR) in Teaching Students with Dyslexia. *International Journal of Emerging Technologies in Learning (iJET)*. https://online-journals.org/index.php/i-jet/article/view/19653

Mastropieri, C. A., & Scruggs, T. E. (2020a). *The inclusive classroom: Strategies for effective instruction*. Pearson.

Mastropieri, M. A., & Scruggs, T. E. (2020b). *The inclusive classroom: Strategies for effective differentiated instruction*. Pearson.

Matthews, B. W. (1975). Comparison of the predicted and observed secondary structure of T4 phage lysozyme. *Biochimica et Biophysica Acta (BBA)- Protein Structure*, *405*(2), 442–451. doi:10.1016/0005-2795(75)90109-9 PMID:1180967

Matveeva, S. V., Akatova, N. S., Shcherbakov, Y. I., & Filinova, N. V. (2020). Digitalization of higher education and professional development of educators: Technologies and new opportunities. *Amazonia Investiga*, *9*(29), 77–86. doi:10.34069/AI/2020.29.05.10

McHugh, M. L. (2012). Interrater reliability: The kappa statistic. *Biochemia Medica*, *22*(3), 276–282. doi:10.11613/BM.2012.031 PMID:23092060

McNamara. (2019). Machine Learning in Special Education: Applications, Opportunities, and Challenges. *Journal of Special Education Technology.*

McPartland, J., & Volkmar, F. R. (2012). Autism and related disorders. *Handbook of Clinical Neurology, 106*, 407–418. doi:10.1016/B978-0-444-52002-9.00023-1 PMID:22608634

Medical Xpress (2018, January 15). *Brain Imaging Predicts Language Learning in Deaf Children.* Retrieved June 9, 2023, from https://medicalxpress.com/news/2018-01-brain-imaging-language-deaf-children.html

MedicalXpress. (2018, January 15). *Brain imaging predicts language learning in deaf children.* Author.

Melis, E., Andres, E., Budenbender, J., Frischauf, A., Goduadze, G., Libbrecht, P., Pollet, M., & Ullrich, C. (2001). Activemath: A generic and adaptive web-based learning environment. *International Journal of Artificial Intelligence in Education, 12*, 385–407.

Melis, E., & Siekmann, J. (2004). Activemath: An intelligent tutoring system for mathematics. *Artificial Intelligence and Soft Computing-ICAISC 2004: 7th International Conference,* Zakopane, Poland, June 7-11, 2004. *Proceedings, 7.*

Mellard, D. F., & Johnson, E. (2020). *Response to intervention for all teachers: A practical guide for special and general educators.* Routledge.

Meshram, Thanomliang, Ruangkan, Chumchu, & Patil. (2020). FruitsGB: Top Indian Fruits with quality. *IEEE Dataport.* . doi:10.21227/gzkn-f379

Meshram, V., Choudhary, C., Kale, A., Rajput, J., Meshram, V., & Dhumane, A. (2023). Dry fruit image dataset for machine learning applications. *Data in Brief.* doi:10.1016/j.dib.2023.109325

Meshram, V., Patil, K., Meshram, V., & Hanchate, D. (2021). Machine learning in agriculture domain: A state-of-art survey. *Artificial Intelligence in the Life Sciences, 1.* doi:10.1016/j.ailsci.2021.100010

Meshram, V., Patil, K., Meshram, V., Dhumane, A., Thepade, S., & Hanchate, D. (2022). Smart Low Cost Fruit Picker for Indian Farmers. *2022 6th International Conference On Computing, Communication, Control And Automation*, 1-7. doi: 10.1109/ICCUBEA54992.2022.10010984

Meshram, V., Suryawanshi, Y., Meshram, V., & Patil, K. (2023). Addressing misclassification in deep learning: A Merged Net approach. *Software Impacts.* doi:10.1016/j.simpa.2023.100525

Meshram, V. A., Patil, K., & Ramteke, S. D. (2021). MNet: A framework to reduce fruit image misclassification. *Ingénierie des Systèmes d'Information, 26*(2), 159–170. doi:10.18280/isi.260203

Meshram, V. V., Patil, K. R., Meshram, V. A., & Bhatlawande, S. (2022). SmartMedBox: A smart medicine box for visually impaired people using IoT and computer vision techniques. *Revue d'Intelligence Artificielle, 36*(5), 681–688. doi:10.18280/ria.360504

Meshram, V. V., Patil, K., Meshram, V. A., & Shu, F. C. (2019, October). An Astute Assistive Device for Mobility and Object Recognition for Visually Impaired People. *IEEE Transactions on Human-Machine Systems, 49*(5), 449–460. doi:10.1109/THMS.2019.2931745

Meshram, V., & Patil, K. (2022). Border-Square net: A robust multi-grade fruit classification in IoT smart agriculture using feature extraction based Deep Maxout network. *Multimedia Tools and Applications, 81*(28), 40709–40735. doi:10.100711042-022-12855-7

Meshram, V., & Patil, K. (2022). FruitNet: Indian fruits image dataset with quality for machine learning applications. *Data in Brief, 40*, 107686. doi:10.1016/j.dib.2021.107686 PMID:34917715

Meshram, V., Patil, K., & Chumchu, P. (2022). Dataset of Indian and Thai banknotes with annotations. *Data in Brief, 41*, 108007. doi:10.1016/j.dib.2022.108007 PMID:35282177

Messiou, K. (2019). The missing voices: Students as a catalyst for promoting inclusive education. *International Journal of Inclusive Education, 23*(7–8), 768–781. doi:10.1080/13603116.2019.1623326

Miao, F., Holmes, W., Huang, R., & Zhang, H. (2021). *AI and Education: A Guidance for Policymakers*. UNESCO Publishing.

Miao, Y., Chen, F., & Luo, X. (2021). AI in Education 4.0: An Overview of the Opportunities and Challenges. *Frontiers in Education, 6*, 629706.

Minoofam, S. B. (2022). *RALF: an adaptive reinforcement learning framework for teaching dyslexic students*. SpringerLink. doi:10.100711042-021-11806-y

Mirriahi, N., & Alonzo, D. (2019). Personalizing Learning with Artificial Intelligence. In Transforming Learning with Meaningful Technologies (pp. 163-182). Springer.

Mittal, A., Kumar, P., Roy, P. P., Balasubramanian, R., & Chaudhuri, B. B. (2019). A modified LSTM model for continuous sign language recognition using leap motion. *IEEE Sensors Journal, 19*(16), 7056–7063. doi:10.1109/JSEN.2019.2909837

Mohammed, M., Khan, M. B., & Bashier Mohammed, B. E. (2016). *Machine learning: algorithms and applications*. CRC Press.

Montalbo, F. J., & Enriquez, E. (2020, August). An IoT Smart Lighting System for University Classrooms. In *2020 International Symposium on Educational Technology (ISET)* (pp. 3- 7). IEEE. 10.1109/ISET49818.2020.00011

Moriña, A. (2017). Inclusive education in higher education: Challenges and opportunities. *European Journal of Special Needs Education, 32*(1), 3–17.

Moriña, A., López-Gavira, R., & Morgado, B. (2017). How do Spanish disability support offices contribute to inclusive education in the university? *Disability & Society, 32*(10), 1608–1626. doi:10.1080/09687599.2017.1361812

Morrison, C., Cutrell, E., & Dhareshwar, A. (2017, October). Imagining AI applications with people with visual disabilities using tactile ideation. In *Proceedings of the 2017 ACM on International Conference on Supporting Personal Capabilities* (pp. 115-124). ACM.

Mou, X. (2019). Artificial intelligence: Investment trends and selected industry uses. International Finance Corporation, 8.

Mucherino, A., Papajorgji, P. J., & Pardalos, P. M. (2009). k-Nearest Neighbor Classification. In Data Mining in Agriculture. Springer Optimization and Its Applications (vol. 34). Springer. doi:10.1007/978-0-387-88615-2_4

Mueen Uddin, S. (2021). Applications of Artificial Intelligence in Education: A Review. In *2021 4th International Conference on Information Systems and Computer Networks (ISCON)* (pp. 1-6). IEEE.

Muhammad, U., Wang, W., Chattha, S. P., & Ali, S. (2018). Pre-trained VGGNet Architecture for Remote-Sensing Image Scene Classification. *2018 24th International Conference on Pattern Recognition (ICPR)*, 1622-1627. 10.1109/ICPR.2018.8545591

Muktamath, V. U., Hegde, P. R., & Chand, S. (2021, December 10). *Types of Specific Learning Disability. Types of Specific Learning Disability*. IntechOpen.

Muktamath, V. U., Hegde, P. R., & Chand, S. (2022). *Types of Specific Learning Disability*. IntechOpen. doi:10.5772/intechopen.100809

Munawar, S., Toor, S. K., Aslam, M., & Hamid, M. (2018). Move to smart learning environment: Exploratory research of challenges in computer laboratory and design intelligent virtual laboratory for eLearning Technology. *Eurasia Journal of Mathematics, Science and Technology Education, 14*(5), 1645–1662. doi:10.29333/ejmste/85036

Nanni, L., & Lumini, A. (2009). Ensemble generation and feature selection for the identification of students with learning disabilities. *Expert Systems with Applications, 36*(2), 3896–3900. doi:10.1016/j.eswa.2008.02.065

National Center for Education Statistics. (2022). *Students With Disabilities. Condition of Education.* U.S. Department of Education, Institute of Education Sciences.

National Center for Education Statistics. (2022). Students With Disabilities. In *Condition of Education.* U.S. Department of Education, Institute of Education Sciences. Retrieved 11.05.2023, from https://nces.ed.gov/programs/coe/indicator/cgg

Nayyar, A., Żywiołek, J., Rosak Szyrocka, J., & Naved, M. (2023). *Advances in Distance Learning in Times of Pandemic.* Chapman and Hall/CRC.

Needs, S. E. (2001). *Code of practice. London.* Department for Education and Skills.

Nguyen, A., Tuunanen, T., Gardner, L., & Sheridan, D. (2021). Design principles for learning analytics information systems in higher education. *European Journal of Information Systems, 30*(5), 541–568.

Nicholson, J., Kulyukin, V., & Coster, D. (2009). ShopTalk: Independent blind shopping through verbal route directions and barcode scans. *The Open Rehabilitation Journal, 2*(1), 11–23. doi:10.2174/1874943700902010011

Norhashimah., M., S. (2013). Barcode Recognition System. *International Journal of Emerging Trends & Technology in Computer Science, 2,* 1-6.

Norvig, P. R., & Intelligence, S. A. (2002). *A modern approach.* Prentice Hall.

Observer. (2023). *Richard Branson Launches A.I. Campaign to Help People with Dyslexia.* Retrieved from https://observer.com/2023/04/richard-branson-launches-a-i-campaign-to-help-people-with-dyslexia/

Ojha, S. T. (2022). Artificial Intelligence In Special Education, Id & Cp. *Journal of Positive School Psychology,* 8341-8345.

Oliver, G. (2003). *Virtual Art: From Fantasy to Immersive Experience.* MIT Press.

Olmos-Migueláñez, S., & Pérez-Sanagustín, M. (2020). A Systematic Review of Learning Analytics Applications in Online Learning Environments in Higher Education. *Interactive Learning Environments, 28*(8), 1128–1146.

Ong, C. S., & Koh, J. H. L. (2020). The Role of Artificial Intelligence in Education: A Review. *Educational Technology Research and Development, 68*(4), 1765–1783.

OTTAA Project: Accessible Communication for Children With Disabilities | UNICEF Innovation Fund. (2021, October 26). Retrieved June 11, 2023, from https://www.unicefinnovationfund.org/broadcast/updates/ottaa-project-accessible-communication-children-disabilities

Ouherrou, N., Elhammoumi, O., Benmarrakchi, F., & El Kafi, J. (2019). Comparative study on emotions analysis from facial expressions in children with and without learning disabilities in virtual learning environment. *Education and Information Technologies, 24*(2), 1777–1792. doi:10.100710639-018-09852-5

Ouyang, F., & Jiao, P. (2021). Artificial Intelligence in Education: The Three Paradigms. *Computers and Education: Artificial Intelligence, 2,* 100020.

Owoc, M. L., Sawicka, A., & Weichbroth, P. (2019). Artificial Intelligence Technologies in Education: Benefits, Challenges and Strategies of Implementation. *IFIP International Workshop on Artificial Intelligence for Knowledge Management*, 37-58.

Owoc, M., Sawicka, A., & Weichbroth, P. (2021). *Artificial Intelligence Technologies in Education: Benefits*. Challenges and Strategies of Implementation. doi:10.1007/978-3-030-85001-2_4

Palacios, A. M., Sánchez, L., & Couso, I. (2009). Extending a simple genetic cooperative-competitive learning fuzzy classifier to low quality datasets. *Evolutionary Intelligence*, *2*(1-2), 73–84. doi:10.100712065-009-0024-1

Palacios, A. M., Sánchez, L., & Couso, I. (2010). Diagnosis of dyslexia with low quality data with genetic fuzzy systems. *International Journal of Approximate Reasoning*, *51*(8), 993–1009. doi:10.1016/j.ijar.2010.07.008

Papanastasiou, G., Drigas, A., Skianis, C., Lytras, M., & Papanastasiou, E. (2019). Virtual and augmented reality effects on K-12, higher and tertiary education students' twenty-first century skills. *Virtual Reality (Waltham Cross)*, *23*(4), 425–436. doi:10.100710055-018-0363-2

Papastratis, I., Chatzikonstantinou, C., Konstantinidis, D., Dimitropoulos, K., & Daras, P. (2021). Artificial Intelligence Technologies for Sign Language. *Sensors (Basel)*, *21*(17), 5843. doi:10.339021175843 PMID:34502733

Parashar, B., Sharma, R., Rana, G., & Balaji, R. D. (2023). Foundation Concepts for Industry 4.0. In A. Nayyar, M. Naved, & R. Rameshwar (Eds.), *New Horizons for Industry 4.0 in Modern Business. Contributions to Environmental Sciences & Innovative Business Technology*. Springer. doi:10.1007/978-3-031-20443-2_3

Parasuram, K. (2006). Variables that affect teachers' attitudes towards disability and inclusive education in Mumbai, India. Disability and Society, 21(3), 231–242.

Park, O. (1994). Dynamic visual displays in media-based instruction. *Educational Technology*, 21–25.

Pasco, G. (2010). Identification and diagnosis of autism spectrum disorders: An update. *Pediatric Health*, *4*(1), 107–114. doi:10.2217/phe.09.64

Patil, K., Jawadwala, Q., & Shu, F. C. (2018, April). Design and Construction of Electronic Aid for Visually Impaired People. *IEEE Transactions on Human-Machine Systems*, *48*(2), 172–182. doi:10.1109/THMS.2018.2799588

Patra, G. (2020). *Education of Children with Disabilities: Exploring Possibilities with Artificial Intelligence*. http://pedagogyoflearning.com/wp-content/uploads/4-Ganesh-Patra-Education-of-Children-with-Disabilities-Exploring-Possibilities-with-Artificial-Intelligence.pdf

Pavlopoulos, J., Vrettaros, J., Vouros, G., & Drigas, A. (2008). The development of a self-assessment system for the learners' answers with the use of gpnn. *WSKS*, *1*, 332–340. doi:10.1007/978-3-540-87781-3_37

Pedro, F., Subosa, M., Rivas, A., & Valverde, P. (2019). *Artificial intelligence in education: Challenges and opportunities for sustainable development*. Academic Press.

Pence, H. E. (2019). Artificial intelligence in higher education: New wine in old wineskins? *Journal of Educational Technology Systems*, *48*(1), 5–13. doi:10.1177/0047239519865577

Penn State University (2023, January 12). *New Institute to Use AI Technology for Children With Speech, Language Disorders*. Author.

Platt, J. (1998). *Sequential Minimal Optimization: A Fast Algorithm for Training Support Vector Machines*. Microsoft Research, Technical Report msr-tr-98-14.

Ploetzner, R., Berney, S., & Bétrancourt, M. (2021). When learning from animations is more successful than learning from static pictures: Learning the specifics of change. *Instructional Science*, *49*(4), 497–514. doi:10.100711251-021-09541-w

Popenici, S. A., & Kerr, S. (2017). Exploring the Impact of Artificial Intelligence on Teaching and Learning in Higher Education. *Research and Practice in Technology Enhanced Learning*, *12*(1), 22. doi:10.118641039-017-0062-8 PMID:30595727

Prakash, C., Saini, R., & Sharma, R. (2021). Role of Internet of Things (IoT) in Sustaining Disruptive Businesses. In R. Sharma, R. Saini, C. Prakash, & V. Prashad (Eds.), *Internet of Things and Businesses in a Disruptive Economy* (1st ed.). Nova Science Publishers.

Prentzas, J. (2013). Artificial intelligence methods in early childhood education. *Artificial Intelligence, Evolutionary Computing and Metaheuristics: In the Footsteps of Alan Turing*, 169-199.

Proulx, M. (n.d.). *University of Bath: How Blind People See The World.* Retrieved from https://www.bath.ac.uk/case-studies/how-blind-people-see-the-world/

Pushpendu & Sharma. (2021). A Study to Comprehend Role of Artificial Intelligence in Building Smart Cities. *Engineering and Technology Journal for Research and Innovation, 3*(2).

Puteh, M., Yusoff, R. C., Ibrahim, S., & Alwi, N. H. (2020). Artificial Intelligence in Education 4.0: Opportunities and Challenges. In *2020 IEEE International Conference on Teaching, Assessment, and Learning for Engineering (TALE)* (pp. 1127-1130). IEEE.

Rahmatullah, A. S., Mulyasa, E., Syahrani, S., Pongpalilu, F., & Putri, R. E. (2022). Digital Era4.0: The Contribution to Education and Student Psychology. *Linguistics and CultureReview*, *6*, 89–107.

Rajkumar, A., Gunasekaran, D., & Ponnambalam, P. (2022). Machine learning-based intelligent tutoring systems: A survey. *Artificial Intelligence Review*, *57*(4), 575–628.

Ramírez-Duque, A. A., Frizera-Neto, A., & Bastos, T. F. (2019). Robot-Assisted Autism Spectrum Disorder Diagnostic Based on Artificial Reasoning. *Journal of Intelligent & Robotic Systems*, *96*(2), 267–281. doi:10.100710846-018-00975-y

Rana, G., Khang, A., Sharma, R., Goel, A. K., & Dubey, A. K. (Eds.). (2021). *Reinventing Manufacturing and Business Processes Through Artificial Intelligence* (1st ed.). CRC Press. doi:10.1201/9781003145011

Rapin, I., & Tuchman, R. F. (2008). Autism: Definition, neurobiology, screening, diagnosis. *Pediatric Clinics of North America*, *55*(5), 1129–1146. doi:10.1016/j.pcl.2008.07.005 PMID:18929056

Ravindra, Parashar, & Rana. (2021). Chandan Veer .Education: An Enlightened Hope in the Time of Covid-19 Crises. *A Quarterly Refereed Journal of Dialogues on Education, 10*(5), 103-112.

Rebolledo-Mendez, G., & De Freitas, S. (2008). *Attention modeling using inputs from a brain computer interface and user-generated data in second life*. Academic Press.

Reed, S. K. (2005). From research to practice and back: The animation tutor project. *Educational Psychology Review*, *17*(1), 55–82.

Reich, J. (2020). Artificial Intelligence and Special Education: Applications, Opportunities, and Challenges. *Journal of Special Education Technology.*

Reshma, Patil, Laad, & Pise. (2022). Dataset of vector mosquito images. *Data in Brief.* doi:, doi:10.1016/j.dib.2022.108573

Resnikoff, S., Pascolini, D., Etya'Ale, D., Kocur, I., Pararajasegaram, R., Pokharel, G. P., & Mariotti, S. P. (2004). Global data on visual impairment in the year 2002. *Bulletin of the World Health Organization*, *82*(11), 844–851. PMID:15640920

Richard, H. R. (2019, June 17). *How Artificial Intelligence Helps Students With Dyslexia*. Academic Press.

Richter, D., Kock, S., Neumann, A., & Wahl, D. (2019). Artificial intelligence in education: Challenges and opportunities for sustainable development. *AI & Society*, *34*(4), 749–758.

Rieber, L. P. (1991). *Computer-based microworlds: a bridge between construc-tivism and direct instruction*. Paper presented at the meeting of the Annual Convention of the Association for Educational Communications and Technology.

Riedl, M., Arriaga, R., Boujarwah, F., Hong, H., Isbell, J., & Heflin, L. J. (2007). Graphical social scenarios: Toward intervention and authoring for adolescents with high functioning autism. *Virtual Healthcare Interaction, Papers from the AAAI Fall Symposium*.

Robles, M., Namdarian, N., Otto, J., Wassiljew, E., Navab, N., Falter-Wagner, C., & Roth, D. (2022). A Virtual Reality Based System for the Screening and Classification of Autism. *IEEE Transactions on Visualization and Computer Graphics*, *28*(5), 2168–2178. doi:10.1109/TVCG.2022.3150489 PMID:35171773

Rodriguez, M. C., Orellana, N., & Villalba, J. (2019). Technology-supported strategies to improve reading skills in students with learning disabilities. *Assistive Technology*, *31*(3), 142–150.

Roll, I., & Wylie, R. (2016). Evolution and Revolution in Artificial Intelligence in Education. *International Journal of Artificial Intelligence in Education*, *26*(2), 582.

Romero, C. (2019). A Data Mining Approach to Identify Predictive Patterns in Special Education. In *2019 18th IEEE International Conference On Machine Learning And Applications (ICMLA)* (pp. 1377-1380). IEEE.

Roorda, D. L., Zee, M., Bosman, R. J., & Koomen, H. M. (2021). Student–teacher relationships and school engagement: Comparing boys from special education for autism spectrum disorders and regular education. *Journal of Applied Developmental Psychology*, *74*, 101277. doi:10.1016/j.appdev.2021.101277

Roschelle, J. (2018). Beyond Polar Bears and Snakes: Multimodal Learning Analytics at Scale with DataShop. *International Journal of Artificial Intelligence in Education*, *28*(2), 225–253.

Rubio Garcia, R., Suarez Quiros, J., Gallego Santos, R., & Gonzalez, S. M., & MoránFernanz, S. (2007). Interactive multimedia animation with Macromedia Flashin descriptive geometry teaching. *Computers & Education*, *49*(3), 615–639.

Russell, S. J. (2010). *Artificial intelligence a modern approach*. Pearson Education, Inc.

Russell, S. J., & Stuart, J. (2003). *Artificial Intelligence: A Modern Approach*. Academic Press.

Saad, N. A., Hammad, D. A., & Barakat, A. (2021). *The Impact of Digitalization on Customers' Satisfaction in Educational Sector: An Empirical Study*. http://www.psychologyandeducation.net/

Saad, A. M., Hammad, R., & Barakat, M. S. (2021). The role of digitalization in modern education: A literature review. *Journal of Educational and Psychological Studies*, *15*(2), 189–202.

Sadouk, L., Gadi, T., & Essoufi, E. H. (2018). A Novel Deep Learning Approach for Recognizing Stereotypical Motor Movements within and across Subjects on the Autism Spectrum Disorder. *Computational Intelligence and Neuroscience*, *2018*, 7186762. Advance online publication. doi:10.1155/2018/7186762 PMID:30111994

Saha, S. S., Hagawane, D. S., Kulkarni, P. C., Dhamane, S. R., & Agrawal, S. A. (2013). Mobile Based Text Detection and Extraction from an Image. *International Journal of Emerging Technology and Advanced Engineering, 3*(11), 79-82.

Sahlaoui, H., Nayyar, A., Agoujil, S., & Jaber, M. M. (2021). Predicting and interpreting student performance using ensemble models and shapley additive explanations. *IEEE Access, 9*, 152688-152703.

Sahlaoui, H., Alaoui, E. A. A., Nayyar, A., Agoujil, S., & Jaber, M. M. (2021). Predicting and Interpreting Student Performance Using Ensemble Models and Shapley Additive Explanations. *IEEE Access : Practical Innovations, Open Solutions*, *9*, 152688–152703. doi:10.1109/ACCESS.2021.3124270

Sahlaoui, H., Alaoui, E. A., Agoujil, S., & Nayyar, A. (2023). An empirical assessment of smote variants techniques and interpretation methods in improving the accuracy and the interpretability of student performance models. *Education and Information Technologies*. Advance online publication. doi:10.100710639-023-12007-w

Sahlaoui, H., Alaoui, E. A., Nayyar, A., Agoujil, S., & Jaber, M. M. (2021). Predicting and interpreting student performance using ensemble models and shapley additive explanations. *IEEE Access : Practical Innovations, Open Solutions*, *9*, 152688–152703. doi:10.1109/access.2021.3124270

Saini, M. K., & Goel, N. (2019). How smart are smart classrooms? A review of smart classroom technologies. *ACM Computing Surveys*, *52*(6), 1–28. doi:10.1145/3365757

Salas-Pilco, S. Z. (2020). The impact of AI and robotics on physical, social-emotional and intellectual learning outcomes: An integrated analytical framework. *British Journal of Educational Technology*, *51*(5), 1808–1825. doi:10.1111/bjet.12984

Salend, S. J., & Duhaney, L. M. G. (2017). *Creating inclusive classrooms: Effective, differentiated and reflective practices*. Pearson.

Salloum, S. A., Alhamad, A. Q. M., Al-Emran, M., Monem, A. A., & Shaalan, K. (2019). Exploring students' acceptance of e-learning through the development of a comprehensive technology acceptance model. *IEEE Access : Practical Innovations, Open Solutions*, *7*, 128445–128462. doi:10.1109/ACCESS.2019.2939467

Salvia, J., Ysseldyke, J. E., & Bolt, S. (2020). *Assessment: In special and inclusive education*. Nelson Education.

Samim, A. (2023). A New Paradigm of Artificial Intelligence to Disabilities. *International Journal of Science and Research, 12*(1), 1-7.

Samuelsen, J., Chen, W., & Wasson, B. (2019). Integrating multiple data sources for learning analytics—Review of literature. *Research and Practice in Technology Enhanced Learning*, *14*(1), 1–20.

Sandhya, P. S., & Maheshwari, S. (2021). AI-Driven Smart Learning Systems in Education 4.0: A Review. *International Journal of Intelligent Systems and Applications*, *13*(9), 35–42.

Sands, D. J., & McBride, S. L. (2015). *Inclusive early childhood education: Development, resources, and practice*. Cengage Learning.

Sarkar, P. R., Mishra, D., & Subhramanyam, G. R. (2019). Automatic attendance system using deep learning framework. In *Machine intelligence and signal analysis* (pp. 335–346). Springer. doi:10.1007/978-981-13-0923-6_29

Sayghe, A., Hu, Y., Zografopoulos, I., Liu, X., Dutta, R. G., Jin, Y., & Konstantinou, C. (2020). Survey of machine learning methods for detecting false data injection attacks in power systems. *IET Smart Grid*, *3*(5), 581–595. doi:10.1049/iet-stg.2020.0015

Schipor, O. A., Pentiuc, S. G., & Schipor, M. D. (2010). Improving computer-based speech therapy using a fuzzy expert system. *Computer Information*, *29*(2), 303–318.

Schneider, J., & Vlachos, M. (2021). Personalization of Deep Learning. In P. Haber, T. Lampoltshammer, M. Mayr, & K. Plankensteiner (Eds.), *Data Science – Analytics and Applications*. Springer Vieweg. doi:10.1007/978-3-658-32182-6_14

Schnotz, W., & Lowe, R. (2003). Introduction. *Learning and Instruction*, *13*(2), 117–124.

Schreglmann, S., & Kazanci, Z. (2018). A Lesson Plan Development Study for Higher Education based on Needs Assessment "Graphics and Animation in Education" course. *International Education Studies, 11*(7), 155. doi:10.5539/ies.v11n7p155

Sclater, N. (2018). *Learning analytics explained.* Routledge.

Seale, J., Georgeson, J., Mamas, C., & Swain, J. (2015). Not the right kind of 'digital capital'? An examination of the complex relationship between disabled students, their technologies and higher education institutions. *Computers & Education, 82*, 118–128.

Sebe, N., Cohen, I., Gevers, T., & Huang, T. S. (2006). Emotion recognition based on joint visual and audio cues. *18th international conference on pattern recognition (ICPR'06), 1*, 1136–1139.

Senjam, S. (2019). Assistive Technology for People with Visual Loss. *Delhi Journal of Ophthalmology, 30*(2).

Serajul Haq, F. (2007). Educational opportunities for students with disabilities: The experience of auniversity student in Brunei. *Asian Journal of University Education, 3*(1), 81–91.

Shahroom, A. A., & Hussin, N. (2018). Industrial revolution 4.0 and education. *International Journal of Academic Research in Business and Social Sciences, 8*(9), 314–319. doi:10.6007/IJARBSS/v8-i9/4593

Shanmugam, A. K., & Marimuthu, R. (2021). A critical analysis and review of assistive technology: Advancements, laws, and impact on improving the rehabilitation of dysarthric patients. *Handb. Dec. Supp. Syst. Neurol. Disorders, 15*, 263–281. doi:10.1016/B978-0-12-822271-3.00001-3

Sharif, M. S., & Elmedany, W. (2022, March). A proposed machine learning based approach to support students with learning difficulties in the post-pandemic norm. In *2022 IEEE Global Engineering Education Conference EDUCON* (pp. 1988-1993). IEEE. 10.1109/EDUCON52537.2022.9766690

Sharma, P. (2019). Digital revolution of education 4.0. *International Journal of Engineering and Advanced Technology, 9*(2), 3558–3564. doi:10.35940/ijeat.A1293.129219

Sharma, P., & Dash, B. (2023). AI and VR Enabled Modern LMS for Students with Special Needs. *Journal of Foreign Language Education and Technology, 8*, 1.

Sharma, P., Kumar, V., & Bansal, R. (2021). Role of Artificial Intelligence in the Fourth Industrial Revolution: Education Perspective. *International Journal of Advanced Research in Computer Science, 12*(5), 204–212.

Sharma, U., & Desai, I. (2002). *Special education in India: A journey of challenges.* SAGE Publications.

Sherkatghanad, Z., Akhondzadeh, M., Salari, S., Zomorodi-Moghadam, M., Abdar, M., Acharya, U. R., Khosrowabadi, R., & Salari, V. (2020). Automated Detection of Autism Spectrum Disorder Using a Convolutional Neural Network. *Frontiers in Neuroscience, 13*, 1325. Advance online publication. doi:10.3389/fnins.2019.01325 PMID:32009868

Shew, M., New, J., Wichova, H., Koestler, D. C., & Staecker, H. (2019). Using Machine Learning to Predict Sensorineural Hearing Loss Based on Perilymph Micro RNA Expression Profile. *Scientific Reports, 9*(1), 3393. doi:10.103841598-019-40192-7 PMID:30833669

Shute, V. (2019). Learning Engineering: A Practical Guide for Effective Learning Design. In *2019 IEEE Conference on Cognitive and Computational Aspects of Situation Management (CogSIMA)* (pp. 1-8). IEEE.

Siemens, G., & Long, P. (2011). Penetrating the fog: Analytics in learning and education. Educ. Rev., 46(5).

Singh, H., & Lehal, G. S. (2021). Artificial Intelligence in Education: A Comprehensive Review. *Journal of Educational Technology Systems, 49*(1), 5–33. doi:10.1177/0047239520978500

Slee, R. (2018). *Defining the scope of inclusive education.* http://repositorio.minedu.gob.pe/handle/20.500.12799/5977

Smith, S. J. (2019). Enhancing engagement and motivation in special education through technology. *Journal of Special Education Technology, 34*(3), 149–158.

Smith, T., Johnson, M., & Davis, T. (2020). The impact of assistive technology on academic performance for students with disabilities: A systematic review. *Assistive Technology, 32*(5), 265–275.

Southworth, J., Migliaccio, K., Glover, J., Reed, D., McCarty, C., Brendemuhl, J., & Thomas, A. (2023). Developing a model for AI Across the curriculum: Transforming the higher education landscape via innovation in AI literacy. Computers and Education: Artificial Intelligence, 100127.

Spaulding, J. A., Paulsen, K. L., & Coppess, K. M. (2022). *Ethics and the use of technology in educational settings. In The Wiley Handbook of Educational Supervision.* Wiley.

Spector, J. M., Ifenthaler, D., Sampson, D. G., & Siemens, G. (Eds.). (2018). *Handbook of Research on Educational Communications and Technology* (4th ed.). Springer.

Spencer, P., Timpe, Z., Verlenden, J., Rasberry, C. N., Moore, S., Yeargin-Allsopp, M., Claussen, A. H., Lee, S., Murray, C., Tripathi, T., Conklin, S., Iachan, R., McConnell, L., Deng, X., & Pampati, S. (2023). Challenges experienced by US K-12 public schools in serving students with special education needs or underlying health conditions during the COVID-19 pandemic and strategies for improved accessibility. *Disability and Health Journal, 16*(2), 101428. doi:10.1016/j.dhjo.2022.101428 PMID:36610820

Srihari, S., Collins, J., Srihari, R., Srinivasan, H., Shetty, S., & Brutt-Griffler, J. (2008). Automatic scoring of short handwritten essays in reading comprehension tests. *Artificial Intelligence, 172*(2-3), 300–324. doi:10.1016/j.artint.2007.06.005

Staniūtė, R., & Šešok, D. (2019). A Systematic Literature Review on Image Captioning. *Applied Sciences (Basel, Switzerland), 9*(10), 2024. doi:10.3390/app9102024

Su, J., & Yang, W. (2022). Artificial intelligence in early childhood education: A scoping review. Computers and Education: Artificial Intelligence, 100049.

Su, J., Zhong, Y., & Ng, D. T. K. (2022). A meta-review of literature on educational approaches for teaching AI at the K-12 levels in the Asia-Pacific region. Computers and Education: Artificial Intelligence, 100065. doi:10.1016/j.caeai.2022.100065

Subrahmanyam, V. V., & Swathi, K. (2018, August). Artificial intelligence and its implications in education. In *Int. Conf. Improv. Access to Distance High. Educ. Focus Underserved Communities Uncovered Reg. Kakatiya University* (pp. 1-11). Academic Press.

Subrahmanyam, R., & Swath, N. (2018). Artificial intelligence: A paradigm shift in education. *International Journal of Innovative Technology and Exploring Engineering*, 7(5S), 113–117.

Su, J., Ng, D. T. K., & Chu, S. K. W. (2023). Artificial intelligence (AI) literacy in early childhood education: The challenges and opportunities. *Computers and Education: Artificial Intelligence, 4*, 100124. doi:10.1016/j.caeai.2023.100124

Su, J., & Zhong, Y. (2022). Artificial Intelligence (AI) in early childhood education: Curriculum design and future directions. *Computers and Education: Artificial Intelligence, 3*, 100072. doi:10.1016/j.caeai.2022.100072

Sun, L., & Zhang, D. (2021). Artificial intelligence in education: A comprehensive survey. *Computers & Education, 172*, 104213. doi:10.1016/j.compedu.2021.104213

Supriyono, S., Siswanto, W. A., Darmawan, A. S., Utomo, W. M., Supriyono, H., Setiawan, W., Solikin, M., Ulinuha, A., Prasetyo, H., & Purnama, H. (2018b). Selected Peer-Reviewed Articles from the International Conference on Engineering Application, Physics and Sciences (ICEAPS2017), Johor Bahru, Malaysia, 26–27 October, 2017. *Advanced Science Letters*. 10.1166/asl.2018.12074

Suresh, C. B., & Gowramma, I. P. (2010). *Promoting Social Integration amongPreschool Children with Hearing Impairment.* Paper presented at the Annual National Conference of National Convention of Educators ofthe Deaf (NCED): Trivandrum, Kerala, India.

Suryawanshi, Y., Patil, K., & Chumchu, P. (2022). VegNet: Dataset of vegetable quality images for machine learning applications. *Data in Brief*, *45*, 108657. doi:10.1016/j.dib.2022.108657 PMID:36426086

Sweeney, S. (2023). Who wrote this? Essay mills and assessment–Considerations regarding contract cheating and AI in higher education. *International Journal of Management Education*, *21*(2), 100818. doi:10.1016/j.ijme.2023.100818

Szpiro, S., Zhao, Y., & Azenkot, S. (2016). Finding a store, searching for a product: a study of daily challenges of low vision people. In *Proceedings of the 2016 ACM International Joint Conference on Pervasive and Ubiquitous Computing*. ACM. 10.1145/2971648.2971723

Szyrocka, J. R., Żywiołek, J., Nayyar, A., & Naved, M. (Eds.). (2023). *Advances in distance learning in times of pandemic*. CRC Press.

Tang, K. Y., Chang, C. Y., & Hwang, G. J. (2023). Trends in artificial intelligence-supported e-learning: A systematic review and co-citation network analysis (1998–2019). *Interactive Learning Environments*, *31*(4), 2134–2152.

Tang, T., Li, P., & Tang, Q. (2022). New Strategies and Practices of Design Education under the background of Artificial Intelligence Technology: Online Animation Design Studio. *Frontiers in Psychology*, *13*, 767295. Advance online publication. doi:10.3389/fpsyg.2022.767295 PMID:35651576

Tariq, Q., Daniels, J., Schwartz, J. N., Washington, P., Kalantarian, H., & Wall, D. P. (2018). Mobile detection of autism through machine learning on home video: A development and prospective validation study. *PLoS Medicine*, *15*(11), e1002705. doi:10.1371/journal.pmed.1002705 PMID:30481180

Tatiraju, R. (2020). *Speech-to-text and Text-to-speech with Android.* Retrieved from https://medium.com/@rtficial/speech-to-text-and-text-to-speech-with-android-85758ff0f6d3

Thabtah, F. (2019). Machine learning in autistic spectrum disorder behavioral research: A review and ways forward. *Informatics for Health & Social Care*, *44*(3), 278–297. doi:10.1080/17538157.2017.1399132 PMID:29436887

Thappa, S. R., & Baliya, J. N. (2021). Exploring Awareness for Technological Pedagogical and Content Knowledge (TPAC) in Pre-Service Teacher Education Programme. *MIER Journal of Educational Studies Trends and Practices*, 1-14.

Thelijjagoda, S. M. C. (2019). The Hope: An Interactive Mobile Solution to Overcome the Writing, Reading and Speaking Weaknesses of Dyslexia. *International Conference on Computer Science & Education (ICCSE)*. https://ieeexplore.ieee.org/abstract/document/8845396

Thomson, P., & Gilchrist, P. (1997). *Dyslexia: A multidisciplinary approach*. Nelson Thornes.

Tiwari, P. (2019). Artificial Intelligence in Education: Opportunities and Challenges. *Journal of Emerging Technologies and Innovative Research*, *6*(8), 383–387.

Turnbull, A., Turnbull, R., Erwin, E. J., & Soodak, L. C. (2015). *Exceptional lives: Special education in today's schools*. Pearson.

Tversky, B., Bauer-Morrison, J., & Betrancourt, M. (2002). Animation: Can it facilitate? *International Journal of Human-Computer Studies*, *57*, 247–262.

U.S. Department of Education. Office of Special Education Programs, Individuals with Disabilities Education Act (IDEA) database. (n.d.). Retrieved February 25, 2022, from https://data.ed.gov/dataset/idea-section-618-data-products

UNESCO. (1994). *The Salamanca Statement and Framework for action on special needs education: adopted by the World Conference on Special Needs Education; Access and Quality. Schen anca, Spain, 7-10 June 1994*. UNESCO.

UNESCO. (2000). *Education for All: Meeting our collective commitments. The Dakar framework for action*. UNESCO.

UNESCO. (2019). *Artificial Intelligence in Education: Challenges and Opportunities for Sustainable Development*. United Nations Educational, Scientific and Cultural Organization.

UNESCO. (2019). *Spanish Application Using AI to Help Overcome Dyslexia Wins 2019 UNESCO ICT Prize*. Retrieved from https://www.unesco.org/en/articles/spanish-application-using-ai-help-overcome-dyslexia-wins-2019-unesco-ict-prize

United Nations (2015). *Transforming our world: The 2030 agenda for sustainable development*. Author.

United Nations, Department of Economic and Social Affairs Disability. (2015, May 14), *Factsheet on Persons with Disabilities*. U.S. Department of Education, Office of Special Education Programs, Individuals with Disabilities Education Act (IDEA) Database.

United Nations, Department of Economic and Social Affairs Disability. (n.d.). Factsheet on Persons with Disabilities. https://www.un.org/development/desa/disabilities/resources/factsheet-on-persons-with-disabilities.html

United Nations. (2015). *United Nations sustainable development goals*. United Nations. https://sustainabledevelopment.un.org/

Vahabzadeh, A., Keshav, N. U., Abdus-Sabur, R., Huey, K., Liu, R., & Sahin, N. T. (2018). Improved socio-emotional and behavioral functioning in students with autism following school-based smartglasses intervention: Multi-stage feasibility and controlled efficacy study. *Behavioral Sciences (Basel, Switzerland)*, *8*(10), 85. doi:10.3390/bs8100085 PMID:30241313

Vaidya, S., Ambad, P., & Bhosle, S. (2018). Industry 4.0–a glimpse. *Procedia Manufacturing*, *20*, 233–238. doi:10.1016/j.promfg.2018.02.034

Valliappan, N., Dai, N., Steinberg, E., He, J., Rogers, K., Ramachandran, V., & Navalpakkam, V. (2020). Accelerating eye movement research via accurate and affordable smartphone eye tracking. *Nature Communications*, *11*(1), 1–12. doi:10.103841467-020-18360-5 PMID:32917902

Van de Walle, K., Haßler, G., & Van de Ven, J. P. H. (2020). Artificial intelligence in education: Promises and pitfalls. *European Journal of Education*, *55*(3), 357–371.

Vanderheiden, G. C. (1996). Use of audio-haptic interface techniques to allow nonvisual access to touchscreen appliances. *Human Factors and Ergonomics Society Annual Meeting*, *40*(24), 1266–1266. 10.1177/154193129604002430

VanLaarhoven, T., & Williams, L. R. (2017). *Collaborating for student success: A guide for school-based occupational therapy*. Slack.

Varoquaux, G., & Cheplygina, V. (2022). Machine learning for medical imaging: Methodological failures and recommendations for the future. *NPJ Digital Medicine*, *5*(1), 48. doi:10.103841746-022-00592-y PMID:35413988

Vashisht, V., Pandey, A. K., & Yadav, S. P. (2021, June). Speech recognition using machine learning. *IEIE Transactions on Smart Processing and Computing*, *10*(3), 836–846. doi:10.5573/IEIESPC.2021.10.3.233

Veletsianos, G., & Houlden, S. (2019). A Systematic Analysis and Synthesis of the Empirical MOOC Literature Published in 2013–2015. *The International Review of Research in Open and Distributed Learning*, *20*(1), 1–25.

Venkatesh, M.N. (2006). *An evaluation of the schemes and programmes of inclusive education of the disabled children in Karnataka and A.P.* Department of Folklore and Tribal Studies, Dravidian University Kuppam, Chittoor.

Verma, A., Kumar, Y., & Kohli, R. (2021). Study of AI techniques in quality educations: Challenges and recent progress. *SN Computer Science*, *2*(4), 1–7. doi:10.100742979-021-00635-3

Wachter-Boettcher, S. (2017). *Technically Wrong: Sexist Apps, Biased Algorithms, and Other Threats of Toxic Tech*. W. W. Norton & Company.

Wall, D. P., Dally, R., Luyster, R., Jung, J. Y., & DeLuca, T. F. (2012). Use of Artificial Intelligence to Shorten the Behavioral Diagnosis of Autism. *PLoS One*, *7*(8), e43855. doi:10.1371/journal.pone.0043855 PMID:22952789

Wall, D. P., Kosmicki, J. A., DeLuca, T., Harstad, E. B., & Fusaro, V. A. (2012). Use of Machine Learning to Shorten Observation-based Screening and Diagnosis of Autism. *Translational Psychiatry*, *2*(4), e100. doi:10.1038/tp.2012.10 PMID:22832900

Wang, M. M. (2021). Smart assistance to dyslexia students using artificial intelligence based augmentative alternative communication. *International Journal of Speech Technology*. https://idp.springer.com/authorize/casa?redirect_uri=https://link.springer.com/article/10.1007/s10772-021-09921-0&casa_token=xTNoUYMrz_sAAAAA:XmBs-O1BmI9kGjCk-Vrp5JDBMzzjVv2O_WkaxPIG5aKbmxfh9w4imEDsqrBKWLMDWh0rqfaJftDViwivO43E

Wang, Q. (2022). Innovation Strategy of Animation Curriculum Systems Based on Artificial Intelligence. In *Proceedings of the 2022 International Conference on Educational Innovation and Multimedia Technology (EIMT 2022)* (pp. 131–138). Atlantis Press International BV. 10.2991/978-94-6463-012-1_15

Wan, G., Kong, X., Sun, B., Yu, S., Tu, Y., Park, J., Lang, C., Koh, M., Wei, Z., Feng, Z., Lin, Y., & Kong, J. (2019). Applying Eye Tracking to Identify Autism Spectrum Disorder in Children. *Journal of Autism and Developmental Disorders*, *49*(1), 209–215. doi:10.100710803-018-3690-y PMID:30097760

Wang, Y.-Y., & Wang, Y.-S. (2022). Development and validation of an artificial intelligence anxiety scale: An initial application in predicting motivated learning behavior. *Interactive Learning Environments*, *30*(4), 619–634. doi:10.1080/10494820.2019.1674887

Westling, D. L., & Fox, L. (2015). *Teaching students with severe disabilities*. Pearson.

White, S. W., Oswald, D., Ollendick, T., & Scahill, L. (2009). Anxiety in children and adolescents with autism spectrum disorders. *Clinical Psychology Review*, *29*(3), 216–229. doi:10.1016/j.cpr.2009.01.003 PMID:19223098

Wikipedia. (2011, August 1). *Dragon*. Author.

World Health Organisation (2022, October 13). Blindness and vision impairment.

World Health Organisation (2023, March 3). Hearing loss.

Wu, T.-K., Meng, Y.-R., & Huang, S.-C. (2006). Application of artificial neural networks to the identification of students with learning disabilities. *IC-AI*, 162–168.

Wu, T.-K., Huang, S.-C., & Meng, Y.-R. (2006). Identifying and diagnosing students with learning disabilities using ANN and SVM. In *2006 IEEE International Joint Conference on Neural Network Proceedings* (pp. 2270-2275). IEEE. doi:10.1109/ijcnn.2006.1716707

Wu, Y. W., Kuzniewicz, M. W., Croen, L., Walsh, E. M., McCulloch, C. E., & Newman, T. B. (2016). Risk of Autism Associated with Hyperbilirubinemia and Phototherapy. *Pediatrics, 138*(4), e20161813. doi:10.1542/peds.2016-1813 PMID:27669736

Xia, Q., Chiu, T. K., Zhou, X., Chai, C. S., & Cheng, M. (2022). Systematic literature review on opportunities, challenges, and future research recommendations of artificial intelligence in education. Computers and Education: Artificial Intelligence, 100118.

Yeguas-Bolívar, E., & Alcalde-Llergo, J. M. (2022, March). Determining the difficulties of students with dyslexia via virtual reality and artificial intelligence: An exploratory analysis. In *2022 IEEE International Conference on Metrology for Extended Reality, Artificial Intelligence and Neural Engineering (MetroXRAINE)* (pp. 585-590). IEEE.10.1109/MetroXRAINE54828.2022.9967589

Yilmaz, R. M., & Yilmaz, H. B. (2020). Artificial Intelligence in Education: A Bibliometric Analysis. *Journal of Educational Technology & Society, 23*(1), 185–201.

Yousafzai, S. Y., & Mahmood, N. (2021). Transforming Education 4.0 through Artificial Intelligence and Machine Learning. In *Proceedings of the 2021 2nd International Conference on Big Data, IoT, and Cloud Computing (BIC3)* (pp. 117-121). ACM.

Yusof, Y., Chan, C. C., Hillaluddin, A. H., Ahmad Ramli, F. Z., & Mat Saad, Z. (2020). Improving inclusion of students with disabilities in Malaysian higher education. *Disability & Society, 35*(7), 1145–1170. doi:10.1080/09687599.2019.1667304

Zafari, M., Safari Bazargani, J., & Choi, S. M. (2022, January). Artificial intelligence applications in K-12 education: A systematic literature review. *IEEE Access : Practical Innovations, Open Solutions, 10*, 3179356. doi:10.1109/ACCESS.2022.3179356

Zdravkova, K., Krasniqi, V., Dalipi, F., & Ferati, M. (2022). Cutting-edge communication and learning assistive technologies for disabled children: An artificial intelligence perspective. *Frontiers in Artificial Intelligence, 5*, 970430. doi:10.3389/frai.2022.970430 PMID:36388402

Zhang, D., Zhao, Z., Zhu, S., Zhang, Y., & Zhang, Y. (2020). Intelligent Education 4.0: Development and Prospects. *IEEE Access : Practical Innovations, Open Solutions, 8*, 23741–23749.

Zhang, K., & Aslan, A. (2021). AI technologies for education: Recent research & future directions. Computers & Education. *Artificial Intelligence.* Advance online publication. doi:10.1016/j.caeai.2021.100025

Zhang, M., Ding, H., Naumceska, M., & Zhang, Y. (2022). Virtual Reality Technology as an Educational and Intervention Tool for Children with Autism Spectrum Disorder: Current Perspectives and Future Directions. *Behavioral Sciences (Basel, Switzerland), 12*(5), 138. doi:10.3390/bs12050138 PMID:35621435

Zhang, Z. (2012). Microsoft Kinect sensor and its effect. *IEEE MultiMedia, 19*(2), 4–10. doi:10.1109/MMUL.2012.24

Zhou, G., Zhang, L., & Xu, X. (2020). The Application of Artificial Intelligence in Education 4.0. In *2020 15th International Conference on Computer Science & Education (ICCSE)* (pp. 380-383). IEEE.

Zientara, Lee, Smith, Brenner, Itti, Rosson, Carroll, Irick, & Narayanan. (2017). *Third Eye: A Shopping Assistant for the Visually Impaired.* doi:10.1109/MC.2017.36

Zingoni, T. J.-M. (2021). Investigating Issues and Needs of Dyslexic Students at University: Proof of Concept of an Artificial Intelligence and Virtual Reality-Based Supporting Platform and Preliminary Results. *Appl. Sci.* doi:10.3390/app11104624

About the Contributors

Ashish Kumar, Ph.D., is working as an assistant professor with Bennett University, Greater Noida, U.P., India. He has completed his Ph.D. in Computer Science and Engineering from Delhi Technological University (formerly DCE), New Delhi, India in 2020. He has received best researcher award from the Delhi Technological University for his contribution in the computer vision domain. He has completed M.Tech with distinction in computer Science and Engineering from GGS Inderpratha University, New Delhi. He has published more than 25 research papers in various reputed national and international journals and conferences. He has published 15+ book chapters in various Scopus indexed books. He has authored/edited many books in AI and computer vision domain. He is an active member in various international societies and clubs. He is reviewer with many reputed journals and in technical program committee of various national/ international conferences. Dr. Kumar also served as a session chair in many international and national conferences. His current research interests include object tracking, image processing, artificial intelligence, and medical imaging analysis.

Anand Nayyar received Ph.D (Computer Science) from Desh Bhagat University, India. He is currently working as Assistant Professor, Scientist, Vice-Chairman (Research) and Director (IoT and Intelligent Systems Lab) in School of Computer Science, Duy Tan University, Da Nang, Viet Nam.

* * *

Mukul Aggarwal is currently associated with KIET Group of Institutions, Ghaziabad, India in the capacity of Assistant Professor in Information Technology Department.

Tania Chakraborty is a researcher with a keen interest in the field of computer vision revolving around leveraging advanced algorithms and techniques to enhance the understanding, analysis, and interpretation of visual data. She is passionate about the following areas: 3D Reconstruction, Deep Learning for Computer Vision, Visual Understanding and Interpretation. By pursuing research in these areas, she aims to contribute to the advancement of computer vision, enabling applications in fields such as robotics, autonomous systems, healthcare, surveillance, and human-computer interaction.

Prathamesh Churi is PhD research Scholar in Computer Science and Information Technology Symbiosis International (Deemed University), Pune, India. He is also Assistant Professor of Computer Engineering Department from SVKM's NMIMS Mukesh Patel School of Technology Management and Engineering, Mumbai, India. He is Associate Editor of International Journal of Advances in Intelligent

Informatics (Indexed by Scopus), Indonesia. He has published more than 35 research papers in various international journals and conferences. He has been Co-Convener, Keynote Speaker, Session Chair and TPC Member of many reputed conferences at international level. His area of expertise includes Security and Privacy, Education Technology, Internet of Things.

Lakshmi D. is presently designated as a Senior Associate Professor in the School of Computing Science and Engineering (SCSE) & Assistant Director, at the Centre for Innovation in Teaching & Learning (CITL) at VIT Bhopal. She has 17 international conference presentations, and 21 international journal papers inclusive of SCOPUS & SCI (cumulative impact factor 31). 3 SCOPUS inee book chapters. A total of 24 patents are in various states and 18 patents have been granted at both national and international levels. One Edited book with Taylor & Francis (SCOPUS Indexed). She has won two Best Paper awards at international conferences, one at the IEEE conference and another one at EAMMIS 2021. She received two awards in the year 2022. She received two awards in the year 2022. She has addressed innumerable guest lectures, acted as a session chair, and was invited as a keynote speaker at several international conferences. She has conducted FDPs that cover approximately ~80,000 plus faculty members including JNTU, TEQIP, SERB, SWAYAM, DST, AICTE, MHRD, ATAL, ISTE, Madhya Pradesh Government-sponsored, and self-financed workshops across India on various titles.

Ebru Efeoğlu is currently an Assistant Professor at Kutahya Dumlupinar University Software Department. She received her B.S. degree in Geophysics Engineering from Kocaeli University and Management Information Systems from Anadolu University, Turkey. She received her Ph.D. degree in Computer Engineering from Trakya University, Turkey in 2021. She has authored several papers in international conference proceedings and SCI-Expanded journals. Her research interests include machine learning and data mining, and their applications in various research domains.

Vishnuvarthanan Govindaraj, born in 1986, is an Associate Professor at VIT-Bhopal University, Bhopal, Madhya Pradesh, in the Division of Data Science of the School of Computing Science and Education. He earned a PhD in Electronics and Communication Engineering for his thesis "Tumor Detection and Tissue Segmentation in Multimodal MR Brain Images Using Fuzzy and Optimization Techniques" in 2015. He taught at three of Tamil Nadu's top engineering schools for fourteen years. He has published more than 100 journal papers in 31 international journals included in the Science Citation Index Database, with the greatest impact factor being 17.560 and the average being 4.923. His publications in IEEE Transactions on Fuzzy Systems (12.253), Industrial Informatics (11.648), and Information Fusion (Elsevier) are notable. He has written or co-written more than 70 SCOPUS-indexed conference papers. He has two Scopus-indexed book chapters and has reviewed fourteen journals, including IEEE Transactions on Fuzzy Systems, Neural Networks and Learning Systems, Current Medical Imaging and Reviews, and Neural Processing Letters. Three journals—Computers in Biology and Medicine, Applied Soft Computing, and OPTIK—have accredited him as a reviewer. Medical Image Processing, AI, Machine Learning, and Pattern Recognition are his specialties.

Mallika Krishnaswami is an academic, researcher and translator. Her areas of interest include Comparative literature, Culture Studies, Language Learning, Translation and Higher Education. With a teaching career spanning over several decades, Dr Krishnaswami is quite well versed with the different strategies in teaching and uses them extensively to ensure that learning objectives are met through active classroom engagement and participation. Excited about the advances made by technology through AI assisted tools and Machine Learning in overcoming the challenges faced by children with language learning problems, she tries to keep abreast with them, confident that they may offer the much needed support for these children.

Parikshit Mahalle is a senior member IEEE and is Professor, Dean Research and Development and Head - Department of Artificial Intelligence and Data Science at Vishwakarma Institute of Information Technology, Pune, India. He completed his Ph. D from Aalborg University, Denmark and continued as Post Doc Researcher at CMI, Copenhagen, Denmark. He has 23 + years of teaching and research experience. He is an ex-member of the Board of Studies in Computer Engineering, Ex-Chairman Information Technology, Savitribai Phule Pune University and various Universities and autonomous colleges across India. He has 15 patents, 200+ research publications (Google Scholar citations-2870 plus, H index-25 and Scopus Citations are 1400 plus with H index -18, Web of Science citations are 438 with H index - 10) and authored/edited 54 books with Springer, CRC Press, Cambridge University Press, etc. He is editor in chief for IGI Global –International Journal of Rough Sets and Data Analysis, Inter-science International Journal of Grid and Utility Computing, member-Editorial Review Board for IGI Global – International Journal of Ambient Computing and Intelligence and reviewer for various journals and conferences.

Vishal Meshram is a highly accomplished researcher and educator, having completed his Ph.D. in the application of machine learning in agriculture from Vishwakarma University in October 2022. With over 18 years of teaching experience, he possesses a strong command of machine learning, cloud computing, and DevOps. Driven by a passion for advancing agricultural practices, his research focuses on leveraging machine learning techniques for fast & accurate fruit classification. He has actively collaborated with industry experts and government organizations, and his work has been published in reputable journals and presented at national and international conferences. With a commitment to bridging the gap between academia and practical implementation.

Sakalya Mitra is currently a pre-final year student at VIT Bhopal University, pursuing Integrated M.Tech in Computer Science with specialization in Artificial Intelligence and Machine Learning. He is an AI and ML enthusiast who wishes to pursue his career in the field of Data Science and Machine Learning. He has achieved the 2nd Position in BPlan Competition at IIT Kharagpur among 10K+ Teams and have also won 2nd prize at the WCE Hackathon. He aims to bring a revolutionary impact by harnessing the true power of AI based methodologies and contributing to the convergence of AI in different domains, shaping the future of automation.

Arjama Pal is currently a final year student at VIT Bhopal University, pursuing B.Tech in Computer Science with specialization in Artificial Intelligence and Machine Learning. She is an UI/UX enthusiast who aims to pursue her career in the filed of Human Computer Interaction (HCI) and bring a positive impact on lives along with contributing towards innovative experiences to shape the future of digital interaction.

K. Nikitha Reddy is an upcoming author with a passion for research. She is pursuing an MBA in Business Analytics at Christ University, Bangalore, set to graduate this year. With a past degree in Electronics and Communication Engineering from Dayananda Sagar College of Engineering, Bangalore.

Nikitha has a diverse academic background. She has actively participated in research projects focusing on data analysis, machine learning, and business intelligence. Nikitha's research interests include data analytics, artificial intelligence, and business strategy. Her goal is to contribute to the advancement of knowledge in these areas. Alongside her studies, she has gained practical experience through associations with various organizations, broadening her industry insights. With her strong research acumen and interdisciplinary background, Nikitha is poised to make a significant impact as an author and researcher in the field of Business analytics.

Ravindra Sharma is an Assistant Professor in Himalayan School of Management studies at Swami Rama Himalayan University, Dehradun India. He has more than 14 years of corporate and academic experience. He holds degrees of MBA and MCA. He also qualified UGC-NET in Management. He has credit over six papers published in refereed indexed journals of Emerald, Sage, Springer, and IGI Global. He also presented several research papers in national and international conferences. Mr. Sharma has contributed chapters in four different books published by Springer IGI Global, Tailor & Frances and Palgrave Macmillan. He has co- authored a book titled "Hands on approach on Applications of Internet of Things in various Domain of Engineering published by International Research Publication House. He has honored as a Session Chair in four international conferences in various universities. He has attended various workshops, FDPs and MDPs. His areas of research interest are Employer Branding, Employee Engagement & Commitment and Talent Management.

Swati Sharma is currently associated with KIET Group of Institutions, Ghaziabad, India in the capacity of Assistant Professor in Computer Science & Engineering Department.

Divya Singh is currently working as an assistant professor in the School of computer science and Engineering, at Bennett University, Greater Noida. She holds the degree of B.tech in information technology and an M.tech, Ph.D. degree in computer science engineering and technology. She has 2 years of teaching experience. She has published various research publications in reputed international journals and conferences. Her research interests include the areas of Image and Video Processing, Computer Vision, Artificial Intelligence (AI), Machine Learning and Deep learning.

Vivek Tomar is currently associated with Graphic Era (Deemed to be University), Dehradun, India in the capacity of Assistant Professor in Computer Science & Engineering Department.

Ayşe Tuna is a lecturer at Trakya University, Turkey since 2005. She has authored papers in international conference proceedings, and has been actively serving as a reviewer for international conferences and journals. Her research interests are support services for the elderly and disabled, education of autistic and related communication handicapped children, human-robot interaction, human-computer interaction, and data management methodologies.

Rubeena Vohra was born in Ludhiana, India, in 1981. She received B.Tech. degree in Electronics and Communication Engineering (ECE) from Punjab Technical University, Jalandhar, India, in 2003, M.Tech degree in ECE from Guru Gobind Singh Indraprastha University(GGSIPU), New Delhi, in 2011, and Ph.D. degree in Civil Engineering from Delhi Technological University (DTU), New Delhi, India, in 2020, respectively. In 2009, she joined the Department of Electronics and Communication Engineering in BharatiVidyapeeth's College of Engg.(BVCOE), as a Lecturer, and thereafter became Assistant Prof. Since August 2009, she has been with the Department of ECE, BVCOE, New Delhi. Her current research interests include digital image processing, remote sensing in satellite imageries and geo-informatics. She was awarded the topper certificate in B.Tech in ECE, LLRIET, PTU, in year 2003. She received Gold Medal in 2011 from GGSIPU, New Delhi for being the topper in M.Tech. She has published research papers in referred SCIE, SCI, ESCI, SCOPUS international and national journals/conferences. She has also published book chapters in SCOPUS indexed books and has authored 01 book in remote sensing.

Neha Yadav is currently associated with KIET Group of Institutions, Ghaziabad, India in the capacity of Assistant Professor in Computer Science & Engineering Department.

Index

E

F

H

I

K

L

M

N

O

P

R

S

T

V

www.ingramcontent.com/pod-product-compliance
Lightning Source LLC
LaVergne TN
LVHW062139300926
849161LV00010B/2571